T0135190

Lecture Notes in Electrical Engineering

Volume 393

About this Series

"Lecture Notes in Electrical Engineering (LNEE)" is a book series which reports the latest research and developments in Electrical Engineering, namely:

- Communication, Networks, and Information Theory
- Computer Engineering
- Signal, Image, Speech and Information Processing
- Circuits and Systems
- Bioengineering

LNEE publishes authored monographs and contributed volumes which present cutting edge research information as well as new perspectives on classical fields, while maintaining Springer's high standards of academic excellence. Also considered for publication are lecture materials, proceedings, and other related materials of exceptionally high quality and interest. The subject matter should be original and timely, reporting the latest research and developments in all areas of electrical engineering.

The audience for the books in LNEE consists of advanced level students, researchers, and industry professionals working at the forefront of their fields. Much like Springer's other Lecture Notes series, LNEE will be distributed through Springer's print and electronic publishing channels.

More information about this series at http://www.springer.com/series/7818

James J. (Jong Hyuk) Park
Hai Jin · Young-Sik Jeong
Muhammad Khurram Khan
Editors

Advanced Multimedia and Ubiquitous Engineering

FutureTech & MUE

 Springer

Editors
James J. (Jong Hyuk) Park
Department of Computer Science
  and Engineering
Seoul National University of Science
  and Technology
Seoul
Korea (Republic of)

Hai Jin
School of Computer Science
  and Technology
Huazhong University of Science
  and Technology
Wuhan
China

Young-Sik Jeong
Department of Multimedia Engineering
Dongguk University
Seoul
Korea (Republic of)

Muhammad Khurram Khan
College of Computer and Information
  Sciences
King Saud University
Riyadh
Saudi Arabia

ISSN 1876-1100   ISSN 1876-1119   (electronic)
Lecture Notes in Electrical Engineering
ISBN 978-981-10-9379-1   ISBN 978-981-10-1536-6   (eBook)
DOI 10.1007/978-981-10-1536-6

Printed on acid-free paper

This Springer imprint is published by Springer Nature
The registered company is Springer Science+Business Media Singapore Pte Ltd.

Message from the FutureTech2016 General Chairs

FutureTech2016 is the 11th event of the series of international scientific conference. This conference takes place on April 20–22, 2016, in Beijing, China. The aim of the FutureTech2016 is to provide an international forum for scientific research in the technologies and application of information technology. FutureTech 2016 is the next edition of FutureTech2015 (Hanoi, Vietnam), FutureTech2014 (Zhangjiajie, China), FutureTech2013 (Gwangju, Korea), FutureTech2012 (Vancouver, Canada), FutureTech2011 (Loutraki, Greece), and FutureTech2010 (Busan, Korea, May 2010) which was the next event in a series of highly successful the International Symposium on Ubiquitous Applications & Security Services (UASS-09, USA, Jan. 2009), previously held as UASS-08 (Okinawa, Japan, March 2008), UASS-07 (Kuala Lumpur, Malaysia, August, 2007), and UASS-06 (Glasgow, Scotland, UK, May, 2006).

The conference papers included in the proceedings cover the following topics: Hybrid Information Technology, High Performance Computing, Cloud and Cluster Computing, Ubiquitous Networks and Wireless Communications, Digital Convergence, Multimedia Convergence, Intelligent and Pervasive Applications, Security and Trust Computing, IT Management and Service, Bioinformatics and Bio-Inspired Computing, Database and Data Mining, Knowledge System and Intelligent Agent, Game and Graphics, and Human-centric Computing and Social Networks. Accepted and presented papers highlight the new trends and challenges of future information technologies. We hope readers will find these results useful and inspiring for their future research.

We would like to express our sincere thanks to program chairs: Gangman Yi (Gangneung-Wonju National University, Korea), Zhangdui Zhong (Beijing Jiaotong University, China), Yu Chen (State University of New York, USA), Mingquan Zhou (Beijing Normal University, China), Kwang-il Hwang (Incheon National University, Korea), Ka Lok Man (Xi'an Jiaotong-Liverpool University, China), Neil Yen (University of Aizu, Japan), and Ying Zhao (Beijing University of Chemical Technology, China), all program committee members, and all reviewers for their valuable efforts in the review process that helped us to guarantee the highest quality of the selected papers for the conference.

We cordially thank all the authors for their valuable contributions and the other participants of this conference. The conference would not have been possible without their support. Thanks are also due to the many experts who contributed to making the event a success.

FutureTech2016 General Chairs
Jia Weijia, Shanghai Jiaotong University, China
Wanlei Zhou, Deakin University, Australia
Young-Sik Jeong, Dongguk University, Korea
Qun Jin, Waseda University, Japan
Hong Shen, University of Adelaide, Australia
Muhammad Khurram Khan, King Saud University, Saudi

Message from the FutureTech2016 Program Chairs

Welcome to the 11th International Conference on Future Information Technology (FutureTech 2016), which will be held in Beijing, China, on April 20–22, 2016. FutureTech2016 will the most comprehensive conference focused on the various aspects of information technologies. It will provide an opportunity for academic and industry professionals to discuss recent progress in the area of future information technologies. In addition, the conference will publish high-quality papers which are closely related to the various theories and practical applications in multimedia and ubiquitous engineering. Furthermore, we expect that the conference and its publications will be a trigger for further related research and technology improvements in these important subjects.

For FutureTech2016, we received many paper submissions, and after a rigorous peer-review process, we accepted only articles with high quality for the FutureTech2016 proceedings, published by the Springer. All submitted papers have undergone blind reviews by at least two reviewers from the technical program committee, which consists of leading researchers around the globe. Without their hard work, achieving such a high-quality proceeding would not have been possible. We take this opportunity to thank them for their great support and cooperation. We would like to sincerely thank the following invited speakers who kindly accepted our invitations and, in this way, helped to meet the objectives of the conference: Prof. Yi Pan, Regents' Professor of Computer Science, Interim Associate Dean and Chair of Biology, Georgia State University, USA. Finally, we would like to thank all of you for your participation in our conference, and also thank all the authors, reviewers, and organizing committee members. Thank you and enjoy the conference!

FutureTech2016 Program Chairs
Gangman Yi, Gangneung-Wonju National University, Korea
Zhangdui Zhong, Beijing Jiaotong University, China
Yu Chen, State University of New York, USA
Mingquan Zhou, Beijing Normal University, China
Kwang-il Hwang, Incheon National University, Korea
Ka Lok Man, Xi'an Jiaotong-Liverpool University, China
Neil Yen, University of Aizu, Japan
Ying Zhao, Beijing University of Chemical Technology, China

Organization

General Chairs

Jia Weijia, Shanghai Jiaotong University, China
Wanlei Zhou, Deakin University, Australia
Young-Sik Jeong, Dongguk University, Korea
Qun Jin, Waseda University, Japan
Hong Shen, University of Adelaide, Australia
Muhammad Khurram Khan, King Saud University, Saudi Arabia

Program Chairs

Gangman Yi, Gangneung-Wonju National University, Korea
Zhangdui Zhong, Beijing Jiaotong University, China
Yu Chen, State University of New York, USA
Mingquan Zhou, Beijing Normal University, China
Kwang-il Hwang, Incheon national University, Korea
Ka Lok Man, Xi'an Jiaotong-Liverpool University, China
Neil Yen, University of Aizu, Japan
Ying Zhao, Beijing University of Chemical Technology, China

Workshop Chairs

Jungho Kang, Sungsil University, Korea
Jian Chen, Taiyuan University of Technology, China

International Advisory Committee

James J. (Jong Hyuk) Park, SeoulTech, Korea (Steering Chair)
Doo-soon Park, SoonChunHyang University, Korea
Laurence T. Yang, St. Francis Xavier University, Canada
Jason C. Hung, Oversea Chinese University, Taiwan
Jianhua Ma, Hosei University, Japan
C.S. Raghavendra, University of Southern California, USA
Philip S. Yu, University of Illinois at Chicago, USA
Hai Jin, Huazhong University of Science and Technology, China
Yi Pan, Georgia State University, USA
Shu-Ching Chen, Florida International University, USA
Victor Leung, University of British Columbia, Canada
Vincenzo Loia, University of Salerno, Italy
Hsiao-Hwa Chen, National Cheng Kung University, Taiwan

Publicity Chairs

Kevin Cheng, Tatung University, Taiwan
Eunyoung Lee, Dongduk Women's University, Korea
Yishui Zhu, Chang'an University, China
Byung-Gyu Kim, Sunmoon University, Korea
Weimin Li, Shanghai University, China
Yishui Zhu, Chang'an University, China

Program Committee

Abdelbadeeh Salem, Ain Shams University, Egypt
Amagasa Toshiyuki, University of Tsukuba, Japan
Bhattacharya Maumita, Charles Sturt University, Australia
Caldelli Roberto, Universita degli Studi di Firenze
Chi-Fu Huang, National Chung Cheng University, Taiwan
Chien Been-Chian, National University of Tainan, Taiwan
Epaminondas Kapetanios, University of Westminster, UK
Fu Song, University of North Texas, USA
Gasteratos Antonis, Democritus University of Thrace, Greece
Guillermo Diaz Diaz-Delgado, Universidad Autonoma da guadalajara, Mexico
Homenda Wadysaw, Instytut Badan Systemowych Polskiej Akademii Nauk, Poland
Hongmei Chi, Florida Agricultural and Mechanical University, USA

Message from the MUE2016 General Chairs

MUE2016 is the 10th event of the series of international scientific conference. This conference takes place on April 20–22, 2016, in Beijing, China. The aim of the MUE2016 is to provide an international forum for scientific research in the technologies and application of multimedia and ubiquitous engineering. Ever since its inception, International Conference on Multimedia and Ubiquitous Engineering has been successfully held as MUE-15 (Hanoi, Vietnam, May 2015), MUE-14 (Zhangjiajie, China, May 2014), MUE-13 (Seoul, Korea, May 2013), MUE-12 (Madrid, Spain, July 2012), MUE-11 (Loutraki, Greece, June 2011), MUE-10 (Cebu, Philippines, August 2010), MUE-09 (Qingdao, China, June 2009), MUE-08 (Busan, Korea, April 2008), and MUE-07 (Seoul, Korea, April 2007).

The conference papers included in the proceedings cover the following topics: Multimedia Modeling and Processing, Multimedia and Digital Convergence, Ubiquitous and Pervasive Computing, Ubiquitous Networks and Mobile Communications, Ubiquitous Networks and Mobile Communications, Intelligent Computing, Multimedia and Ubiquitous Computing Security, Multimedia and Ubiquitous Services, and Multimedia Entertainment. Accepted and presented papers highlight the new trends and challenges of multimedia and ubiquitous engineering. We hope readers will find these results useful and inspiring for their future research.

We would like to express our sincere thanks to steering chair: James J. (Jong Hyuk) Park (SeoulTech, Korea). Our special thanks go to the program chairs: Yunsick Sung (Keimyung University, Korea), Wei Song (North China University of Technology, China), Chengcui Zhang (The University of Alabama at Birmingham, USA), Ching-Hsien (Robert) Hsu (Chung Hua University, Taiwan), and Lei Wang (Dalian University of Technology, China), all program committee members, and all reviewers for their valuable efforts in the review process that helped us to guarantee the highest quality of the selected papers for the conference.

MUE2016 General Chairs
Albert Zomaya, University of Sydney, Australia
Hai Jin, Huazhong University of Science and Technology, China
Gangman Yi, Gangneung-Wonju National University, Korea
Laurence T. Yang, St. Francis Xavier University, Canada
Cho-Li Wang, The University of Hong Kong, Hong Kong
Jianhua Ma, Hosei University

Message from the MUE2016 Program Chairs

Welcome to the 10th International Conference on Multimedia and Ubiquitous Engineering (MUE2016), which will be held in Beijing, China, on April 20–22, 2016. MUE2016 will the most comprehensive conference focused on the various aspects of multimedia and ubiquitous engineering. It will provide an opportunity for academic and industry professionals to discuss recent progress in the area of multimedia and ubiquitous environment. In addition, the conference will publish high-quality papers which are closely related to the various theories and practical applications in multimedia and ubiquitous engineering. Furthermore, we expect that the conference and its publications will be a trigger for further related research and technology improvements in these important subjects.

For MUE2016, we received many paper submissions, and after a rigorous peer-review process, we accepted only articles with high quality for the MUE2016 proceedings, published by the Springer. All submitted papers have undergone blind reviews by at least two reviewers from the technical program committee, which consists of leading researchers around the globe. Without their hard work, achieving such a high-quality proceeding would not have been possible. We take this opportunity to thank them for their great support and cooperation. Finally, we would like to thank all of you for your participation in our conference and also thank all the authors, reviewers, and organizing committee members. Thank you and enjoy the conference!

MUE2016 Program Chairs
Yunsick Sung, Keimyung University, Korea
Wei Song, North China University of Technology, China
Chengcui Zhang, The University of Alabama at Birmingham, USA
Ching-Hsien (Robert) Hsu, Chung Hua University, Taiwan
Lei Wang, Dalian University of Technology, China

Organization

Steering Chair

James J. (Jong Hyuk) Park, SeoulTech, Korea

General Chairs

Albert Zomaya, University of Sydney, Australia
Hai Jin, Huazhong University of Science and Technology, China
Gangman Yi, Gangneung-Wonju National University, Korea
Laurence T. Yang, St. Francis Xavier University, Canada
Cho-Li Wang, The University of Hong Kong, Hong Kong
Jianhua Ma, Hosei University, Japan

Program Chairs

Yunsick Sung, Keimyung University, Korea
Wei Song, North China University of Technology, China
Chengcui Zhang, The University of Alabama at Birmingham, USA
Ching-Hsien (Robert) Hsu, Chung Hua University, Taiwan
Lei Wang, Dalian University of Technology, China

Workshop Chairs

Jungho Kang, Sungsil University, Korea
Xu Shuo, ISTIC, China
Yizhi Ren, Hangzhou Dianzi University, China
Shangguang Wang, Beijing University of Posts and Telecommunications, China

International Advisory Committee

Doo-soon Park, SoonChunHyang University, Korea
Shu-Ching Chen, Florida International University, USA
Young-Sik Jeong, Dongguk University, Korea
Han-Chieh, Chao National Ilan University, Taiwan
Weijia Jia, Shanghai Jiaotong University, China
Hwa-Young Jeong, Kyung Hee University, Korea
Borko Furht, Florida Atlantic University, USA
Thomas Plagemann, University of Oslo, Norway
Roger Zimmermann, National University of Singapore, Singapore
Stephan Olariu, Old Dominion University, USA
Yi Pan, Georgia State University, USA
Koji Nakano, University of Hiroshima, Japan

Publicity Chairs

Wei-Bang Chen, VSU, USA
Kehua Guo, Central South University, China
Zhi Li, Guizhou University, China
Ruisheng Shi, Beijing University of Posts and Telecommunications, China
Sung-Ki Kim, Sunmoon University, Korea
Kuan-Ching Li, Providence University, Taiwan
Namje Park, Jeju National University, Korea

Program Committee

Afrand Agah, West Chester University of Pennsylvania, USA
Akihiro Sugimoto, National Institute of Informatics, Japan
Angel D. Sappa, Universitat Autonoma de Barcelona, Spain
Bin Lu, West Chester University, USA

Ch. Z. Patrikakis, Technological Education Institute of Pir, Greece
Chao-Tung Yang, Tunghai University, Taiwan
Dalton Lin, National Taipei University, Taiwan
Dongkyun Kim, KISTI, Korea
Hai Jin, Huazhong University of Science and Technology, China
Hari Om, Indian School of Mines University, India
HeonChang Yu, Korea University, Korea
Jinye Peng, Northwest University, China
Joyce El Haddad, Universite Paris-Dauphine, France
Jun-Won Ho, Seoul Women's University, Korea
Kilhung Lee, Seoul National University of Science and Technology, Korea
Marco Cremonini, University of Milan, Italy
Maytham Safar, Kuwait University, Kuwait
Mi-hye Kim, Catholic University of Daegu, Korea
Muhammad, Younas Oxford Brookes University, UK
Muneesawang, Naresuan University, Thailand
Pascal Lorenz, University of Haute Alsace, France
Qinghua Lu, China University of Petroleum, China
Quanqing Xu, Data Storage Institute, A*STAR, Singapore
Rachid Anane, Coventry University, UK
Reinhard Klette, The University of Auckland, New Zealand
Sagarmay Deb, University of Southern Queensland, Australia
Seunghae Kim, KISTI, Korea
Shingo Ichii, University of Tokyo, Japan
Sokratis Katsikas, University of Piraeus, Greece
Wei Wang, Dongguan Branch of Institute of Computing Technology,
Chinese Academy of Sciences, China
Wei Wei, Xi'an University of Technology, China
Yang Yang, National University of Singapore, Singapore
Yong-Yoon Cho, Sunchon University, Korea
Young-Gab Kim, Sejong University, Korea
Yunhee Kang, Baekseok University, Korea
Zhenquan Qin, Dalian University of Technology, China
Zheng-Jun Zha, National University of Singapore, Singapore

Contents

Network Traffic Classification Model Based on MDL Criterion

Ying Zhao, Junjun Chen, Guohua You and Jian Teng

Abstract Network traffic classification is elementary to network security and management. Recent research tends to apply machine learning techniques to flow statistical feature based classification methods. The Gaussian Mixture Model (GMM) based on the correlation of flows has exhibited superior classification performance. It also has several important advantages, such as robust to distributional assumptions and adaption to any cluster shape. However, the performance of GMM can be severely affected by the number of clusters. In this paper, we propose the minimum description length (MDL) criterion which can balance the accuracy and complexity of the classification model effectively by evaluating the optimal number of clusters. We establish a new classification model and analyze its performance. A large number of experiments are carried out on two real-world traffic data sets to validate the proposed approach. The results demonstrate the efficiency of our approach.

Keywords Traffic classification · MDL criterion · Gaussian mixture model

Y. Zhao · J. Chen (✉) · G. You · J. Teng
College of Information Science and Technology, Beijing University
of Chemical Technology, Beijing, People's Republic of China
e-mail: chenjj@mail.buct.edu.cn

Y. Zhao
e-mail: zhaoy@mail.buct.edu.cn

G. You
e-mail: yough@mail.buct.edu.cn

J. Teng
e-mail: tengj@mail.buct.edu.cn

© Springer Science+Business Media Singapore 2016   1
J.J. (Jong Hyuk) Park et al. (eds.), *Advanced Multimedia and Ubiquitous
Engineering*, Lecture Notes in Electrical Engineering 393,
DOI 10.1007/978-981-10-1536-6_1

1   Introduction

In recent years, as the Internet continues to expand its scale, network traffic classification plays an increasingly important role in network security and management, such as quality of service (QoS) control, intrusion detection, network planning and usage reporting [1]. Traditional network traffic classification methods include port-based prediction method, deep packet inspection (DPI) method and Machine learning method [2]. The port-based prediction method and DPI method are widely deployed in industry, but their drawbacks are obvious. The port-mapping strategy can no longer ensure accuracy as some non-standard ports and dynamic ports are used by some applications, and DPI fails by design in the case of encryption, protocol obfuscation or encapsulation. Recently, some researchers have begun to use the machine learning methods to solve network traffic classification problems [3]. Machine learning methods can classify the network traffic accurately and quickly, but its classification performance depends on the choice of the training sets. The supervised machine learning methods often require sufficient labeled training samples. The unsupervised methods (or clustering) use labeled traffic data and assign test samples to the application-based class of its nearest cluster. Wang et al. [4] proposed to use a Gaussian Mixture Model (GMM) with set-based equivalence constraint to classify the network traffic and proposed a constrained Expectation Maximization algorithm for clustering. The Gaussian Mixture Model is one of the most statistically mature classical methods for clustering. The standard approach used to fit the Gaussian Mixture Model to sample data is the expectation-maximization (EM) algorithm [5], which can converge to a maximum likelihood (ML) estimate of the Gaussian Mixture Model parameters. Unfortunately, the ML estimate of model parameters is not well defined because the likelihood may always be made better by choosing a larger number of clusters. Intuitively, the value of likelihood may always be increased by growing number of clusters because more clusters can be used to more accurately fit the data. However, the model will become more complex with the increase of the clusters.

In order to balance the complexity and accuracy of classification model, a minimum description length (MDL) criterion is proposed to estimate the optimal number of clusters in this paper. In order to further improve the classification performance, the correlation of flows [6] will be used in the cluster process.

The remainder of the paper is organized as follows: the proposed network traffic classification model is presented in the next section. In Sect. 3, we present the MDL value and accuracy corresponding to different number of clusters, and give experiments results compared other three classification methods. Finally, the conclusion are given in Sect. 4.

2 Network Traffic Classification Model

2.1 MDL for the Gaussian Mixture Model

Clustering algorithm based on mixture model is flexible and efficient, suitable for multidimensional data. The Gaussian Mixture Model (GMM) is one of the most statistically mature classical methods for clustering. In this paper, a MDL-GMM algorithm is proposed. In the algorithm, a GMM with set-based equivalence constraint is used to identify the network traffic applications, and the MDL criterion is used to balance the complexity and accuracy of the classification model.

Through the analysis of the TCP/IP network model and the observation of the communications in client/server mode, Zhang et al. [7] considered that flows (a set of sequenced packets transmitted through two terminal applications with the same {srcIP, dstIP, srcPort, dstPort, protoType}) are not isolated from each other and the flows sharing the same three-tuple {dstIP, dstPort, protoType} are normally generated by the same application.

Definition 1 Gaussian Mixture Model is described by:

$$p(x|\theta) = \sum_{i=1}^{K} a_i p_i(x|\theta_i) \tag{1}$$

where a_i is the mixing proportion of each component, K is the number of components; $p_i(x|\theta_i)$ is the respective Gaussian density function with the corresponding parameter vector $\theta_i = (\mu_i, \Sigma_i)$; μ_i denotes the means and Σ_i denotes covariances matrix.

Based on [8], the correlation of flows is presented by the constraint set adopt in the clustering procedure. In other words, flows with 3-tuple {dstIP, dstPort, protoType} are in the same constraint set.

Let $X = \{x_1, \ldots, x_N\}$ denote N observed flows. After the introduction of constraint sets, $X = \{X_1, \ldots, X_M\}$ denotes M constraint sets, where each set X_S consists of N_S flows $\{x_1^S, \ldots, x_{N_S}^S\}$. Let $Y = \{y_1, \ldots, y_N\}$ denote the assignments of the respective flows, (i.e. $y_i \in \{1, \ldots, K\}$). Let Y_S denote the assignment of constraint set X_S. With the correlation of flows, the space of values is:

$$\Omega = \{Y|(y_1^s = \cdots = y_{N_s}^s), s = 1, \ldots, M\} \tag{2}$$

Definition 2 Minimum Description Length is defined as:

$$MDL(K, \theta) = -\log p(X, Y|Y \in \Omega, \theta) + \frac{1}{2} T \log MD \tag{3}$$

where $\log p(X, Y|Y \in \Omega, \theta)$ is the log-likelihood of the mixture model, where D denotes vector dimension, and T is:

$$T = K\left[1 + D + \frac{D(D+1)}{2}\right] - 1 \tag{4}$$

In order to formally derive the EM algorithm update equations, a penalty term, second term in Eq. (5) is introduced and the ML function is defined as follows:

$$Q^C(\theta, \theta^g, K) = E[\log p(X, Y|Y \in \Omega, \theta)|X, Y \in \Omega, \theta^g] - \frac{1}{2}T \log MD$$

$$= \sum_{y \in \Omega} \log p(X, y|y \in \Omega, \theta)P(y|X, y \in \Omega, \theta^g) - \frac{1}{2}T \log MD \tag{5}$$

In order to maximize the likelihood function, iteration update of model parameters is required, and the formula is as follows:

$$\mu_i = \frac{\sum_{S=1}^{M} p(i|X_S, y \in \Omega, \theta^g) \sum_{n=1}^{Ns} x_n^S}{\sum_{S=1}^{M} p(i|X_S, y \in \Omega, \theta^g) N_S} \tag{6}$$

$$\Sigma_i = \frac{\sum_{S=1}^{M} p(i|X_S, y \in \Omega, \theta^g) \sum_{n=1}^{Ns} (x_n^S - \mu_i)(x_n^S - \mu_i)^T}{\sum_{S=1}^{M} p(i|X_S, y \in \Omega, \theta^g) N_S} \tag{7}$$

$$a_i = \frac{1}{M} \sum_{S=1}^{M} p(i|X_S, y \in \Omega, \theta^g) \tag{8}$$

2.2   Algorithm Steps

The MDL-GMM algorithm is described as follows:

1. Set the maximum number of clusters K_{max} and minimum number of clusters K_{min} in initialization stage.
2. Construct constraint sets based on the correlation of flows.
3. Perform the EM algorithm by iteratively applying the E-step and M-step until convergence is achieved.
4. Record the ML function value and parameters of models.
5. Merged the two most similar clusters. Specifically, the two clusters and are specified as a single cluster with mixing proportions, mean and covariance as given by [8].

6. If the number of cluster is equal to the minimum number,determine the optimal number of clusters K^* and the parameter vector θ^* based on Eq. (9), or go back to step 3.

$$\{K^*, \theta^*\} = \arg\min\{MDL(K, \theta), K_{\min} \leq K \leq K_{\max}\} \qquad (9)$$

3 Experiments and Results

3.1 Data Sets

In order to evaluate the proposed algorithm, we adopt two real-world network traffic data sets: the BUCT set and the CHI set. Table 1 shows the details of these data sets.

The BUCT set is captured at an Ethernet link in Beijing University of Chemical Technology. This data set contains full flow payload. The CHI set is collected by the CAIDA [8], which provided public traffic data to researchers. This data set is backbone traffic and has been anonymized.

In order to evaluate the performance of the proposed algorithms, the ground truth has been established by port-based tool (CoralReef [9]) and deep packet inspection tools (NetTraMark [10], l7-filter) that match signatures against packet payload. For the encrypted traffic, we classify them according to the standard server port number assignment (e.g., the flow with 443 port is HTTPS). We identify 9 application classes in the BUCT set: Web, DNS, SSH, FTP, Games, Mail, NetOP, P2P, SSL, and there are other 2 application classes (Chat, Stream) in the CHI set.

The training sets are extracted from the data sets using the following approach. For each data set, we randomly sample 200 flows for each application. We get rid of the unknown flows which can't be labeled by DPI and manual methods make the result more credible. After the above steps, the BUCT training set consists 1800 flows that belong to 9 applications, and the CHI training set consists 2200 flows that belong to 11 applications. Furthermore, we randomly extract 1000 flows for each application of each data sets as the test sets from BUCT and CHI data sets.

Table 1 Traffic information

Trace	Date	Duration (h)	Type	Packets (million)	Size (G)	Payload
BUCT	2015-1-29	1	Edge	328	240.5	Full
CHI	2014-3-20	1	Backbone	1050	63.7	40 bytes

3.2 *Results*

From the Fig. 1a, when the number of cluster is 112, the MDL takes the minimum value, and the accuracy is 92.2 % which is the second highest accuracy. The highest accuracy is 92.5 % when the number of clusters is 135. The two accuracy is very close. However, more clusters will cost more computational resource. The number of clusters estimated by MDL criterion balances the complexity and accuracy of the classification model. From (b), when the number of cluster is 103, the MDL takes the minimum value, and the accuracy is 93.17 % which is the highest accuracy.

In order to evaluate the proposed model, the MDL-GMM model is compared to three classified network traffic classification methods, KNN [11], C4.5 [12] and K-means. Figure 2 illustrates the overall-accuracy results of different algorithms. For the BUCT test data set, the overall-accuracy is 92.21, 85.6, 82.1 and 71.1 % for

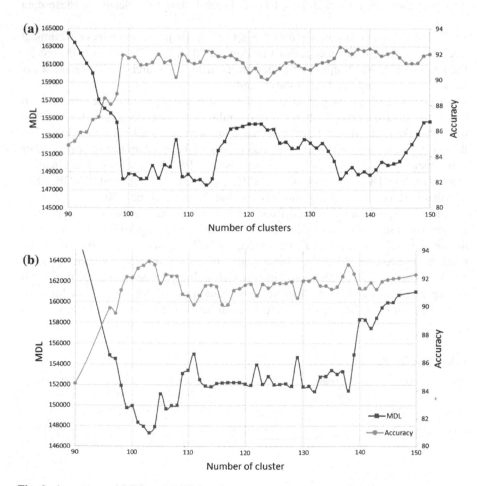

Fig. 1 Accuracy and MDL. **a** BUCT, **b** CHI

Fig. 2 Overall accuracy

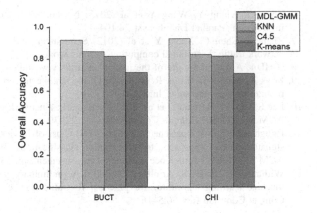

MDL-GMM, KNN, C4.5 and K-means respectively. For the CHI test data set, the overall-accuracy is 92.5, 85.1, 83.2 and 72.3 % for MDL-GMM, KNN, C4.5 and K-means respectively. In summary, the proposed algorithm can achieves the desired results in the term of overall-accuracy.

4 Conclusion

This paper proposes an improved network traffic classification model based on GMM, which has significantly improved in the term of the overall-accuracy compared to the k-NN, C4.5 and K-means algorithms. In the modeling process, the MDL criterion is used to estimate the optimal number of clusters. Due to the self-similarity of network traffic, the number of clusters only need to be estimated once in the modeling process. As we can see from experiment results the MDL criterion can give the optimal numbers of clusters to balance the complexity and accuracy of the classification model well.

References

1. Valenti S, Rossi D, Dainotti A et al (2013) Reviewing traffic classification. Data Traffic Monit Anal 123–147
2. Dainotti A, Pescape A, Claffy KC (2012) Issues and future directions in traffic classification. Network 35–40
3. Nguyen TTT, Grenville A (2008) A survey of techniques for internet traffic classification using machine learning. Commun Surv Tutorials 56–76
4. Wang Y, Xiang Y, Zhang J et al (2014) Internet traffic clustering with side information. J Comput Syst Sci 80:1021–1036
5. Celeux G, Chrétien S, Forbes F et al (2001) A component-wise EM algorithm for mixtures. J Comput Graph Stat 10

6. Zhang J, Xiang Y, Wang Y et al (2013) Network traffic classification using correlation information. Parallel Distrib Syst 24:104–117
7. Zhang J, Chen C, Xiang Y et al (2012) Semi-supervised and compound classification of network traffic. Distributed computing systems workshops (ICDCSW), pp 617–621
8. CAIDA. A day in the life of the internet. http://www.caida.org/projects/ditl/
9. Keys K, Moore D, Koga R et al (2001) The architecture of CoralReef: an internet traffic monitoring software suite. In: PAM
10. Lee S, Kim H, Barman D et al (2011) Netramark: a network traffic classification benchmark. ACM SIGCOMM Comput Commun Rev 41:22–30
11. Roughan M, Sen S, Spatscheck O et al (2004) Class-of-service mapping for QoS: a statistical signature-based approach to IP traffic classification. In: Proceedings of the 4th ACM SIGCOMM conference on internet measurement, pp 135–148
12. Williams N, Zander S, Armitage G (2006) A preliminary performance comparison of five machine learning algorithms for practical IP traffic flow classification. ACM SIGCOMM Comput Commun Rev 36:5–16

What Motivates Users to Play Mobile Phone Games More?

Wonjin Jung and Taehwan Kim

Abstract The literature review suggests that a high quality of system and service, which mobile phone games should provide, appear to be a critical determinant of not only user satisfaction but also the motivation to spend more time and play more games. However, not many past studies in IS have shown much interest in the issues about the effects of the quality of system and service that mobile phone games provide for user satisfaction. Furthermore, there is little research about the relationship between user satisfaction and the motivation to play in the context of mobile phone games. Therefore, this study aims to examine: (1) the effects of the system quality or the service quality of mobile phone games on user satisfaction, (2) the relationship between user satisfaction and motivation to play more games. Structural Equation Modeling (SEM) was employed to analyze data collected through a survey. The results showed that the system quality and the service quality of mobiles games both have a positive impact on user satisfaction. A strong causal relationship between user satisfaction and motivation was also found.

Keywords Smartphone · Application · Information · Usability · Loyalty

1 Introduction

With the advent of the smartphones, mobile phone games have gained popularity. The ownership of a smartphone boosted the possibility that users will play mobile games. According to Crosett [1], in 2011 over 90 % of smartphone owners played a mobile game at least once a week. Another industry report by a game industry expert showed that there was a tremendous growth in the mobile gaming world in

W. Jung · T. Kim (✉)
The School of Business and Economics, Dankook University,
152, Jook-Jun-Ro, Soo-Ji-Goo, Gyeonggi-do Yongin-si 448-701, Korea
e-mail: thkim@dankook.ac.kr

W. Jung
e-mail: jungw@dankook.ac.kr

© Springer Science+Business Media Singapore 2016
J.J. (Jong Hyuk) Park et al. (eds.), *Advanced Multimedia and Ubiquitous Engineering*, Lecture Notes in Electrical Engineering 393,
DOI 10.1007/978-981-10-1536-6_2

2015; and furthermore the mobile games industry is projected to gross over $40 billion by 2017 [2].

As a number of technical innovations and advances were made in smartphones, their capabilities also significantly improved. At the same time, in general, mobile phone games also became increasingly complicated because the technical innovations and advances allow game developers deploy a wide variety of sophisticated functionalities in their games. Accordingly, some are neither easy to play, nor even to understand. Another potential problem is that there can be a decline in the quality of system and service that mobile games offer, which is an expected result of this technical trend. If too many features and functions are deployed in a game, then, in general the likelihood of malfunctioning also increases. If that happens, then it may have a negative impact on user satisfaction and their motivation to play mobile games.

A literature review found that system and service qualities are strongly related to the issues of user satisfaction [3–5]. This can be also applicable to mobile games. If mobile games do not provide adequate quality for their system and service, then users will not be satisfied, or consider playing the games. If the game users do not even consider playing them, then it may be difficult for developers to secure a user base, as well as to make a profit off of the games. In fact, maintaining a higher level of system and service quality is a precondition for surviving in a highly competitive game industry. Thus, it is not too much to say that providing the users of mobile phone games with a high-quality system and service is more imperative than ever before.

In brief summary, the literature review and the discussion above suggest that a high quality of system and service, which mobile phone games should provide, appear to be a critical determinant of not only user satisfaction but also the motivation to spend more time and play more games. However, a review of the relevant literature in IS found that not many past studies have shown much interest in the issues about the effects of the quality of system and service that mobile phone games provide for user satisfaction. Furthermore, there is little research about the relationship between user satisfaction and the motivation to play in the context of mobile phone games. Therefore, the hypotheses below are proposed to test those relationships in a mobile phone game context.

H1   The quality of a system that mobile phone games offer positively affects user satisfaction with the games.
H2   The quality of service that mobile phone games offer positively affects user satisfaction with the games.
H3   The user satisfaction of mobile phone games positively affects the motivation to play more mobile phone games more.

2 Research Methodology, Data Analysis, and Results

The goals of this study are not only to explore the factors that have an impact on user satisfaction but also to examine the relationship between user satisfaction and motivation in the mobile phone game context. This study gathered data by a survey, with a convenient sampling method being used for the survey. A total of 219 college students took part in the survey. They were recruited from various academic programs at two major universities in South Korea, including economics, business, and the humanities. Although a convenient sample of college students was used, efforts were made to gather diverse data in terms of gender, age, and games. The main reasons for using students are not only that they are frequent online-game players but they also play many kinds of games. Thus, the surveyed group of students was considered suitable subjects for this study.

This study employed Structural Equation Modeling (SEM) to analyze the proposed research model and used SPSS statistics and AMOS ver. 18 as the statistical software. First, the measurement model of this study was tested by examining the reliability of all observable variables in the model. The loadings of the variables on their respective constructs are required a minimum of 0.6 to meet the reliability standard [6, 7]. The results of this study showed that all of the loadings were 0.7 or higher, indicating that the reliability is appropriate (see Table 1).

Next, this study tested the convergent validity of the model by examining the composite reliability (CR) and the average variance extracted (AVE) of the latent variables in the model. These values are calculated manually because AMOS does not have the functions to calculate the values of CR and AVE. The formulas suggested by Fornell and Larcker [8] and Hair et al. [9] were used for the calculations. The results of the calculations showed that the values of CR for all latent

Table 1 Standardized regression weights of observable variables, composite reliability (CR), and average variance extracted (AVE)

Latent variables		Estimates	Composite reliability	AVE
System quality	Sys1	0.835	0.879	0.669
	Sys2	0.850		
	Sys3	0.767		
Service quality	Srv1	0.822	0.896	0.687
	Srv2	0.852		
	Srv3	0.811		
Satisfaction	Stf1	0.733	0.897	0.637
	Stf2	0.793		
	Stf3	0.864		
Motivation	Mtv1	0.703	0.864	0.671
	Mtv2	0.971		
	Mtv3	0.759		

variables in the model were of 0.8 or higher, well above the recommended tolerance of 0.7 (see Table 1). Moreover, the values of AVE for all the variables in the model also had values for AVE higher than the recommended cutoff of 0.5 (see Table 1). Thereby, the measurement model of this study demonstrated a satisfactory convergent validity.

$$CR = \left(\sum \text{Standardized Regression Weights}\right)^2 / \left(\left(\sum \text{Standardized Regression Weights}\right)^2\right) \quad [6]$$
$$+ \left(\sum \text{Variance}\right)\right)$$
$$AVE = \left(\sum \text{Standardized Regression Weights}^2\right)/N \quad [7]$$

Then, this study examined the discriminant validity of the measurement model. To do so, this study compared the square root of the AVE for all latent variables with the correlations among the variables. To satisfy the requirements of the discriminant validity, all latent variables should have the square root of their AVEs be greater than the correlations with other variables [7]. The results of analyses showed that this study is the case (see Table 2). Therefore, the discriminant validity of the measurement model was also confirmed.

Finally, the structural model of the proposed model was tested. First, the goodness of fit was examined by the indices including x^2/df, GFI, AGFI, NFI, TLI, and CFI. The results were as follows: $x^2/df = 2.925$, GFI = 0.905, AGFI = 0.854, NFI = 0.900, TLI = 0.910, and CFI = 0.931. Based upon the results of the goodness of fit, the structural model of the proposed research model turned out to have a fairly good fit.

Then, the significance of the relationships between the variables was examined to test the structural model. As expected, system quality had a significant influence on user satisfaction ($\beta = 0.242$, p = 0.000). Service quality also had a positive

Table 2 Correlation coefficient value between constructs and AVE

Constructs	AVE	$\emptyset^2$	$\emptyset^2$	$\emptyset^2$	$\emptyset^2$
System quality	0.669	0.002	0.281	0.282	1.000
Service quality	0.687	0.039	0.422	1.000	
Satisfaction	0.637	0.071	1.000		
Motivation	0.671	1.000			

Table 3 Hypothesis test

	Paths	Coeff.	Stand. coeff.	P	Results
H1	System quality → satisfaction	0.242	0.303	0.0001	Accept
H2	Service quality → satisfaction	0.481	0.556	0.0001	Accept
H3	Satisfaction → motivation	0.297	0.256	0.0001	Accept

Fig. 1 Structural model results

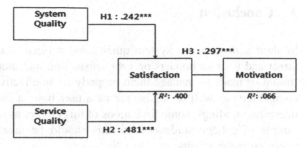

Chi-square=149.168 (df=51) p=.000

impact on user satisfaction (β = 0.481, p = 0.000). In addition, user satisfaction also had a positive impact on motivation (β = 0.297, p = 0.000). Therefore, all hypotheses were supported. Table 3 shows the results of the test in detail. Figure 1 also presents the results with R^2 values representing the amount of variance.

3 Discussion

This study empirically examined whether the system quality or the service quality of mobile games have an impact on user satisfaction. Furthermore, there was an examination of the relationship between user satisfaction and motivation to play mobile games. The results of the analyses revealed that the system quality and the service quality of mobiles games both have a positive impact on user satisfaction. A strong causal relationship between user satisfaction and motivation was also found. These results mean that when the system quality and the service quality of games reach a certain level that the users expect, then the users are generally satisfied with the games. Moreover, when they are satisfied, they are more motivated to play the games.

Mobile game developers may use these findings to have users spend more time with their games. In particular, the attributes of system quality and service quality in the survey questionnaire can be used to check whether the system quality and the service quality of their games meet the users' expectations, which in turn lead to user satisfaction. Based on this kind of evaluation, the developers may formulate a strategy to enhance the system and service qualities of their games that satisfies the users' standards. Once the system quality and the service quality of games are improved from the aspects of the attributes in the survey, then the users would not only be satisfied, but also motivated to play more games. Thus, developers who have considered system and service quality attributes when developing their mobile games can improve the competitiveness of their games, as well as secure large numbers of users who want to play the games. That is, the economic value that they can possibly achieve is significant.

4   Conclusion

In short summary, the system quality and service quality in mobile games have direct and indirect impacts on user satisfaction and motivation; therefore an effort should be made to manage them properly as an effective strategy to compete with competitors, as well as to also secure a user base at the same time. Despite some interesting findings, some limitations of this empirical study include a convenience sample of college students, thus this should be taken into consideration when interpreting the results.

References

1. Crosett K (2011) Mobile game marketing to increase. http://wayback.archive.org/web/20120321162003/http://www.marketingforecast.com/archives/10608. Accessed 18 Mar 2011
2. Meunier N (2015) 6 Trends shaping the games industry in 2015. http://vungle.com/blog/2015/03/12/6-trends-shaping-the-games-industry-in-2015/. Accessed Sept 2015
3. Bove LL, Johnson LW (2001) Customer relationships with service personnel: do we measure closeness, quality of strength? J Bus Res 54(3):189–197
4. Cronin JJ, Brady MK, Hult GTM (2000) Assessing the effects of quality, value, and customer satisfaction on consumer behavioral intentions in service environments. J Retail 76(2):193–218
5. Lai F, Griffin M, Babin BJ (2009) How quality, value, image, and satisfaction create loyalty at a chinese telecom. J Bus Res 62(10):980–986
6. Barclay D, Higgins C, Thompson R (1995) The partial least squares (PLS) approach to causal modeling: personal computer adoption and use as an illustration. Technol Stud 2:285–324
7. Chin WW (1998) The partial least squares approach for structural equation modeling. In: Marcoulides GA (ed) Modern methods for business research. Lawrence Erlbaum, Mahwah, pp 295–336
8. Fornell C, Larcker DF (1981) Evaluating structural equation models with unobservable variables and measurement error. J Mark Res 18:39–50
9. Hair JF, Black B, Babin B, Andersong RE, Tatham RL (2006) Multivariate data analysis, 6th edn. Pearson Prentice Hall, Upper Saddle River

A Certain Theory Based Trust and Reputation Model in VANETs

Na Fan, Zongtao Duan, Chao Wang and Qinglong Wang

Abstract Vehicle ad hoc networks (VANETs) are prone to security risk, especially node misbehavior arising from attacks. In this paper, a certain theory model based model is proposed. We define reputation of a node in VANETs that consist of direct reputation and indirectly reputation. s, direct reputation can be calculated base on certain-factor model according to the records of history communication behaviors. And indirect reputation of a node can be computed based on fuzzy C-means algorithm. The simulation experiment results show that, compared with the baseline method, the proposed methods has better false alarm rate and misdetection rate.

Keywords Combined reputation · Vanets · C-F model · Fuzzy C-means

1 Introduction

VANETs are composed of vehicular nodes equipped with wireless sensors and roadside infrastructure and are designed to provide safe and comfortable driving experience for people. VANETs is a kind of ephemeral networks, so it is prone to security risk. Researchers have discussed various security issues, especially the problem of trustworthiness [1–6]. How to identify whether a vehicle node is trustworthy or not is a challenging problem. In this paper, we will construct a new reputation model to evaluate the level of trustworthy of a node In VANETs.

The rest of this paper is organized as follows. Related work is discussed in Sect. 2. Section 3 construct a reputation model to calculate a node's reputation. Simulation experiment and results are described in Sect. 4. We conclude in the last section and discuss the future work.

N. Fan (✉) · Z. Duan · C. Wang · Q. Wang
Information Engineering Institute, Chang'an University, Xi'an, China
e-mail: fnsea@chd.edu.cn

© Springer Science+Business Media Singapore 2016
J.J. (Jong Hyuk) Park et al. (eds.), *Advanced Multimedia and Ubiquitous Engineering*, Lecture Notes in Electrical Engineering 393,
DOI 10.1007/978-981-10-1536-6_3

2   Related Work

A lot of research work have been done. Some main works will be listed. Auxeeliya et al. [7] propose a payment punishment scheme which encourages nodes to tell truth, and regarded nodes working together as team as a cluster. Dhurandher et al. [8] proposed a event-based approach that uses a reputation system. The proposed algorithm has accomplished of trust levels for nodes by plausibility check and reputation, so it can detect malicious nodes in VANETs. Rawat et al. [9] present a combined method to secure VANETs. The probabilistic approach is used to calculate the trust level of vehicular node and the deterministic approach is adopted to compute the trust level of received messages. Lipinski et al. [10] propose a comprehensive security framework for safety of VANETs. This frame includes PKI system centralized CA which is used to enhance safety of exchanging messages, and also includes trust managements system. Compared with the above work, we propose a combined method to construct a model to calculate reputation of a node in VANETs and can alleviate the effect resulted from malicious and selfish nodes.

3   Trust and Reputation Model

In this section, the proposed model will be described. Certain theory is used to calculate reputation of nodes in VANETs and clustering algorithm can be used to detect the truth of messages.

3.1   Direct Reputation

Certain theory always adopts the level of trust to estimate uncertainties. Generally, C-F model includes many knowledge rules which are used to describe conclusions under various uncertain premises. One piece of rule can be described as follows: If E Then H. Where E denotes preconditions and H means a piece of conclusion. CF (H, E) denotes credibility of this rule and the value of it covers $[-1,1]$. CF(H) and CF(E) separately denote the credibility H and E. The relationship of CF(H) and CF (E) can be described as follows:

$$CF(H) = CF(H, E) \times \{0, CF(E)\} \tag{1}$$

Reputation of a vehicular node is divided into two parts: direct reputation and indirect reputation. Direct reputation is calculated by the communication experiences between sender node and destination node. And indirect reputation is calculated according to the reputation recommend by the neighbor nodes. Then certain theory is used to get a combined reputation.

In this paper, we make some changes for C-F model. $n_{i,j}$ denotes the total number of communication between sender node i and destination node j in a short period of time T, and $a_{i,j}$ denotes the total number of cooperative communication. $CF(H_{i,j})$ denotes a conclusion that node j is a normal node.

If node i directly observes the behavior of node j Then node j is a normal node.

$$CF(H, E_{i,j}) = \frac{a_{i,j} - (n_{i,j} - a_{i,j})}{n_{i,j}} \qquad (2)$$

where $E_{i,j}$ denotes that node i directly observed the behavior of node j, so $E_{i,j}$ is the first-hand information and it can be trustworthy. That means $CF(E_{i,j})$ equals to 1. According to (1), $DB_{i,j}$ which denotes direct reputation of node j can be calculated as follows.

$$DB_{i,j} = CF(H_{i,j}, E_{i,j}) \times \max\{0, CF(E_{i,j})\} = \frac{a_{i,j} - (n_{i,j} - a_{i,j})}{n_{i,j}} \qquad (3)$$

When node i has never communication experience with node j, $DB_{i,j}$ equals to 0. In order to reflect the changing behavior of destination of node j with time and get more accurate value of $DB_{i,j}$, $DB_{i,j}$ will be updated after every time η. Meanwhile avoiding the malicious nodes quickly increase reputation by spoofing, we proposed a weight coefficient to address this issue. When $T = t + \tau$, the total number of cooperative behavior in the period of η is $a_{i,j}$ and the total number of uncooperative behavior is $b_{i,j}$. Weight coefficient is defined as follows:

$$w = \begin{cases} 0 & \left| \frac{a_{i,j}^{\tau}}{a_{i,j}^{\tau} + b_{i,j}^{\tau}} - \frac{a_{i,j}^{t} - (n - a_{i,j}^{t})}{n} \right| < \theta \\ \frac{a_{i,j}^{\tau} - b_{i,j}^{\tau}}{a_{i,j}^{\tau} + b_{i,j}^{t}} & \left| \frac{a_{i,j}^{\tau}}{a_{i,j}^{\tau} + b_{i,j}^{\tau}} - \frac{a_{i,j}^{t} - (n - a_{i,j}^{t})}{n} \right| \geq \theta \end{cases} \qquad (4)$$

θ represents a threshold. When the changing behavior of is not sharp, w equals to 0. On the contrary, if the changing of behavior is obvious, weight coefficient will neutralize the effect from violent changes. So, $DB_{i,j}$ can be updated and represented as follows:

$$DB_{i,j}^{t+\tau} = \frac{a_{i,j}^{t} - \left(n - a_{i,j}^{t}\right) + (a_{i,j}^{\tau} - b_{i,j}^{\tau}) \times (1 + w)}{n + a_{i,j}^{\tau} - b_{i,j}^{\tau}} \qquad (5)$$

3.2 Indirect Reputation

Node i sends request messages which ask for reputation of node j assigned by nodes that are in node i' neighborhood. If a neighbor node has direct communication with node j, it will send back a reply message which include reputation of node j assigned by itself to the node i, otherwise it does not send reply message. When node i receives its neighbors' feedback messages, it will calculate indirect reputation of node j. But in the real VANETs, some selfish nodes or malicious nodes may send false or forge reputation message to node i because of their own benefit or selfish reason. In order to deal with these problem, we propose fuzzy C-means clustering algorithm. Because false or forge reputation messages are in a tiny minority in all feedback messages real reputation messages always have similarities each other, According to this method, real reputation messages can be clustered and the effect from false or forge reputation message can be alleviated. The algorithm is described as follows:

Algorithm 1 This algorithm calculates indirect reputation of node j, based upon messages from sender node i's neighbor nodes.

---

1 node i send request message to it's neighbor nodes
2 For any neighbor node k check its reputation table
3   If it has communication with node j
4   send a reply message which include rk,j to node i
5   else it does not send any reply message to node i.
6   end if
7 all reply messages received by node i are input into Data set 1
8 set threshold Y
9 For Rk(k from 1 to n) n = total number of neighbor nodes
10   If Rk >Y
11   put rk,j in Data set 2
12   else discard rk,j
13 end if
14using fuzzy C-Means clustering algorithm on Data set 2
15 output Data set 3

Where Rk represents the reputation of node k, and rk,j denotes the reputation of node j assigned by node k.

3.3 Combined Reputation

In Sect. 3.2, we get Data set 3. And indirect reputation can be calculated based on this Data set by using C-F model.

$$IB_{i,j} = \frac{p - q}{p + q} \times \frac{\sum_{k=1}^{n} r_{k,j}}{n} \tag{6}$$

where p represents the total number of nodes which of value reputation is bigger than 0, and q denotes the total number of nodes which of value reputation equals to or is smaller than 0. Then we use C-F model to calculate the combined reputation of node j.

$$R_{i,j} = DB_{i,j} \times \alpha + IB_{i,j} \times \beta \qquad (7)$$

Set $\alpha + \beta = 1$, And these two parameters α and β are used to adjust the proportion of direct reputation and indirect reputation in calculation process.

This combined reputation can be use in choosing a suitable forwarding node in order to improve the success rate of forwarding in VANETs. It can also be used to help a node to analyzing truth in received messages, and the details will be described in Sect. 3.2.

4 Experiment and Results

4.1 Simulating Experiment

In order to evaluate the performance of the method proposed in this paper, we product simulation experiments on NS2. The simulation parameters setup in experiments are showed in Table 1.

In these experiments, the ratio of selfish and malicious nodes varies from 10 to 40 % of all nodes. The experiments repeated 100 times with different seed numbers setup in VANETs, and the final result data were average over all of those runs.

4.2 Experiment Results

Figure 1 shows that with changing percentage of malicious and selfish nodes, throughput of VANETs converges by using our solution. Because the method proposed can efficiently relieve the effect resulted from the bad nodes, changing of throughput is steady.

Figure 2 shows that using the combine reputation method, the messages of forwarding is better than other methods when the percentage of malicious and selfish nodes is 45 %. In Fig. 2, C-R represents combined reputation method. D-R and I-R separately represent direct reputation and indirect methods. The method proposed can calculate the combined reputation and make a decision of choosing a

Table 1 Simulation parameters	Parameters	Describe ion
	Area	2500 m × 2000 m
	Transmission range	180 m
	Speed of vehicles	30–65 mile/h
	The total number of vehicles	280
	Simulation	300 min

good forwarder. When a sender want to send a message, it can use the combined reputation to choose a more trustworthy node so forwarding based on this method is more reliable.

We regard S-R method [4] and RFSN method [7] as baseline approaches. False alarm rate and missed detection rate are used as index signs to evaluate these methods. Figures 3 and 4 show that compared with other two methods, our method has better performance in identifying trustworthy nodes.

Fig. 1 Throughput of VANETs with different percentage of malicious and selfish nodes

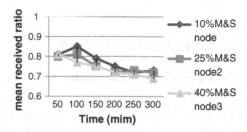

Fig. 2 Comparison of forwarding of VANETs

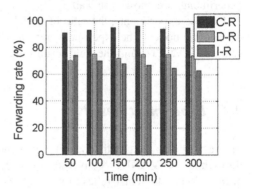

Fig. 3 FRT of comparison

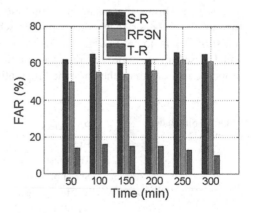

Fig. 4 MDR of comparison

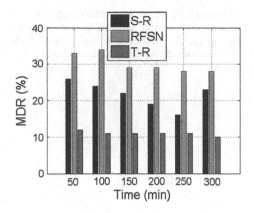

5 Conclusion

In this paper, we have presented a reputation model for VANETs. C-F model is used to get direct reputation of a node and a method based on fuzzy C-means algorithm is used to achieve indirect reputation of the node. A combined reputation of the node is calculated based on direct reputation and indirect reputation. The approaches proposed in this paper can reduce effect from selfish and malicious nodes on calculating reputation and improves the accuracy of identify trustworthy nodes.

References

1. Zhang J (2011) A survey on trust management for vanets. In: 2011 IEEE international conference on advanced information networking and applications (AINA), IEEE, pp 105–112
2. Raya M, Hubaux J-P (2007) Securing vehicular ad hoc networks. J Comput Secur 15(1):39–68
3. Wex P, Breuer J, Held A, Leinmuller T, Delgrossi L (2008) Trust issues for vehicular ad hoc networks. In: Vehicular technology conference, 2008. VTC Spring 2008. IEEE, pp 2800–2804
4. Kamat P, Baliga A, Trappe W (2006) An identity-based security framework for VANETs. In: Proceedings of the 3rd international workshop on vehicular ad hoc networks. ACM
5. Wagan AA, Mughal BM, Hasbullah H (2010) VANET security framework for trusted grouping using TPM hardware. In: Second international conference on communication software and networks, 2010. ICCSN'10. IEEE, pp 309–312
6. Wang Z, Chigan C (2007) Countermeasure uncooperative behaviors with dynamic trust-token in VANETs. In: IEEE international conference on communications, 2007. ICC'07, IEEE, pp 3959–3964
7. Jesudoss A, Kasmir Raja SV, Sulaiman A (2015) Stimulating truth-telling and cooperation among nodes in VANETs through payment and punishment scheme. Ad Hoc Netw 24: 250–263
8. Dhurandher SK, Obaidat MS, Jaiswal A, Tiwari A, Tyagi A (2014) Vehicular security through reputation and plausibility checks. Syst J 8(2):384–394

9. Rawat DB, Yan G, Bista BB, Weigle MC (2015) Trust on the security of wireless vehicular ad-hoc networking. Ad Hoc Sens Wireless Netw 24(3–4):283–305
10. Lipinski B, Mazurczyk W, Szczypiorski K, Smietanka P (2015) Towards effective security framework for vehicular ad-hoc networks. J Adv Comput Netw 3(2):134–140

A Weakly-Secure and Reliable Network Coding Scheme

Hao Wu, Hui Li and Mengjing Song

Abstract It has been shown that network coding can effectively improve the throughput of multicast communication sessions in directed acyclic graphs, achieving their cut-set capacity bounds. However, network coding is highly susceptible to eavesdropping and pollution attacks in which malicious nodes attacks cannot be prevented. In this paper, we propose several ways to enhance the security and reliability of random networking coding transmission. Schemes which encrypt the random coefficients and the coding payload could ensure the information has a relatively low probability to be cracked. We also implement the reliable transmission by forward error-correction. It has been shown that random network coding with encryption and forward error-correction can help achieve provably good overall security and reliability performance.

Keywords Network coding · Security · Reliability · Error-correction

1 Introduction

The peer-to-peer communication paradigm has been successfully in live multimedia streaming applications over Internet. The essential advantage of live peer-to-peer streaming is to dramatically increase the number of peers a streaming session may sustain with several dedicated streaming servers.

Sponsors: National Basic Research Program of China (973 program No. 2012CB315904); National Natural Science Foundation of China (No. NSFC 61179028); Basic Research of Shenzhen (NJCYJ20130331144502026); Natural Science Foundation of Guangdong Province (S2013020012822).

H. Wu · H. Li (✉) · M. Song
ECE, Peking University, Beijing, China
e-mail: lih64@pkusz.edu.cn

H. Wu
e-mail: wuhao@sz.pku.edu.cn

© Springer Science+Business Media Singapore 2016   23
J.J. (Jong Hyuk) Park et al. (eds.), *Advanced Multimedia and Ubiquitous Engineering*, Lecture Notes in Electrical Engineering 393,
DOI 10.1007/978-981-10-1536-6_4

However, while random network coding can increase throughput, it suffers from a serious weakness: its susceptibility to wiretap in which malicious irrelevant users may spy and collect information the source node don't want others know [1]. Meanwhile, the targets couldn't reconstruct the information if a malicious node inject into the network invalid packets.

In this paper, we propose two schemes to resolve such problems. To prevent wiretap, encryption is required, both the coefficient encryption and encoded result encryption are effective. After the encryption, even if the eavesdropper have access to the information, it cannot reconstruct the original file sent by the source from the packet they received. A core technique we must develop for the above encryption is encoding over integers rather than over a field [2]. As for the pollution, what needed is a way for intermediate nodes to be able to verify the validity of incoming vectors [3]. Cyclic redundancy check (CRC) is used in this paper to verify the validity of the packet. If the packet is not valid, which means it may have lost some data (or have been maliciously modified) on the peer Internet, we employ forward error correction to generate the correct packet. Therefore, with the combination of encryption scheme and CRC FEC algorithms, we present a relative secure and reliable transmission mechanism based on random network coding.

In order to reduce the computation amount, cooperative security is required, users not only cooperate to distribute content, but also cooperate to protect themselves against malicious users by alerting affected nodes when a malicious block is found [4].

The remainder of this paper is organized as follows. Sections 2 and 3 elaborate the details of our secure and reliable transmission scheme which based on network coding. Section 4 illustrates the evaluation result based on simulations. Section 5 concludes this paper.

2 Payload Encryption with Cooperative Security

Encoding the coefficients could guarantee the security of information transferred via the random network coding system. However, we noticed that, when the total amount of coefficients in each block is bigger and bigger, the complexity of encryption is increasing at the same time. Is there any effective means for solving the problem?

We found that encoding the result could rapidly reduce the encryption complexity. We need four steps to complete the whole encryption.

Step 1: the source node p chooses a specific segment to be send, and cut it into n slices [b1, b2,...,bn]

Step 2: node p randomly generates k coefficients [c1, c2,...,ck], then multiply the mth block with the mth coefficient (m < k)

Step 3: sum up all the products, then we got the computation payload

Step 4: encrypt the payload, RSA is one of the algorithms could be implemented to encode the payload (Fig. 1)

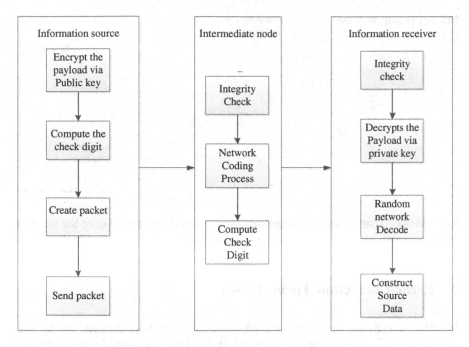

Fig. 1 Basic flow diagram of payload encryption

After the encryption, we send all those coefficients payload and check digit to downstream nodes. Once downstream nodes received the packet sent from source node p, the following three steps should be executed to reconstruct the segment.

Step 1: check the integrity using the check digit, if the packet has been modified or destroyed, throw the packet without noticing the source node p;

Step 2: decode the payload with specific decode algorithm, like what has mentioned above, malicious node couldn't decode the payload as the decode algorithm is unknown to it

Step 3: for each newly received coded block, Gauss-Jordan elimination is applied to the coding coefficient matrix. Once the last block is received, the segment is recovered with a final iteration

We compute the check digit according to $M = \sum_{m=1}^{n} (x_{im})^{m+1}$, i = 1,2...k at first. Meanwhile recover the check digit from the packet received. Then compare the two check digits, if they are the same, prove that the packet is not damaged, otherwise, throw the packet without noticing the source node p (Fig. 2).

Both encrypt a serial of coefficients and encrypt the payload could guarantee the security from eavesdropping. Obviously, the amount of coefficients is much larger than the payload which is a single number, that's to say, the second method has a smaller encryption complexity than the first one. If there are k coefficients are multiplied in the encoding process, then k coefficients are to be encrypted. However, no matter how many coefficients exist, the second method encrypts only

Fig. 2 Comparison of the
two encryption complexity

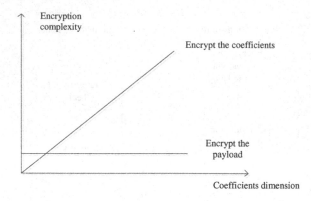

one number. Apart from the encryption, other parts of the process are the same in both methods. So they have the same level of security.

3 Error-Correction Turbo Codes

In order to improve the error-correcting ability of our transmission mechanism, Turbo coding is implemented to our mechanism. Turbo codes are error-correcting codes that are able to perform in conditions close to the theoretical limits predicted by C.E. Shannon, while other code could not reach so close [5].

Turbo-codes results from concatenation of two recursive systematic convolutional codes, in Fig. 3, an example of a rate R = 1/3 Turbo-encoder is shown. Two RSC elementary encoders C1 and C2 with the same constraint length are used. Both C1 and C2 receive the same data. However, due to the presence of interleaver I1 and delay line L1, the data is arranged into different sequences.

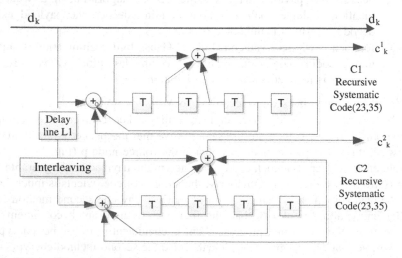

Fig. 3 Turbo-codes encoding process

The decoding of a traditional encoded sequence is very sensitive to errors arriving in packets. Encoding the sequence twice, in different orders, before and after permutation, makes less likely the simultaneous appearance of clustered errors at the decoder inputs of C1 and C2, and vice versa. Thus, the bidimensional encoding, formed by either a parallel or a serial concatenation, markedly reduces the vulnerability of convolutional encoding toward packets of errors [6]. But which decoder should one rely on to take the final decision? No criterion allows us to trust either one or other. The answer is supplied by the Turbo algorithm, which spares us from having to make a choice [7]. This algorithm works out exchanges of probabilistic information between both decoders and forces them to converge towards the same decision, as these exchanges take place.

The Turbo-decoder consists P pipelined identical modules shown in Fig. 4, as we could see the structure of turbo-decoder is modular. The pth module input at time k is made up of demodulator outputs $(X_k)_{p-1}$ and $(Y_k)_{p-1}$ through a delay line and of extrinsic information $(Z_k)_{p-1}$ provided by the $(p-1)$th module. Extrinsic information $(Z_k)_{p-1}$ is new information concerning bit d_k but affected by a noise weakly correlated with the noise that perturbs the observations $(X_k)_{p-1}$ and $(Y_k)_{p-1}$. The extrinsic information acts as a diversity affect and can therefore improve the decoder performance [8].

As Turbo-codes process an error capability unmatched at present time, we designed a system that makes payload encryption merged with Turbo-codes. This system not only guaranteed the security of the source information with a very low computation complexity, but also joined the advantage of error-correction.

The system frame diagram is depicted in Fig. 5. From the discussion above we have acquired that this system need at least two encode phases, the first phase emphasis on the security, and the second phase emphasis on the error-correction. Here we proposed two methods to guarantee the security of information, the first

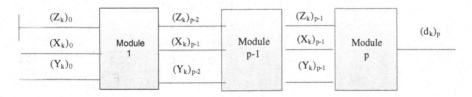

Fig. 4 Turbo-codes decoding process

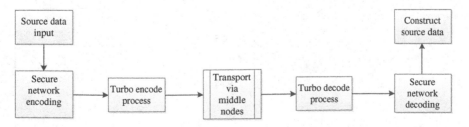

Fig. 5 Basic transmission mechanism diagram

one is to encrypt coefficients of random network coding, and second method is to encrypt the payload of random network coding. The latter one has a prominent less computation complexity compared to the former one. We implement Turbo-codes to ensure the error-correction of this system.

Our system is suitable for situations that have the characteristic of power limited, band abundance, data security is needed such as satellite communication and mobile communication in remote areas.

4 Simulation and Discussion

Simulations are conducted based on ns-2 simulator and MATLAB to evaluate the effectiveness of the two proposed algorithm. All the instances used in the simulation were generated randomly, multicast system has 1 source and 4 sink nodes. The network is defined by three parameters, the number of intermediate nodes N, the probability of malicious nodes in intermediate node p and the successful rate of transmission r.

In Fig. 6, we set N = 50 an as we could see, the r decreases and falling rapidly while p increases in the range of [0.01–0.4]. In Fig. 6, we set p = 0.2 and vary N from 50 to 100, with the increase of N, the r is relatively stable. As illustrated in Fig. 7 the scheme proposed in this paper is applicable to the larger network environment.

Fig. 6 Successful rate r versus p

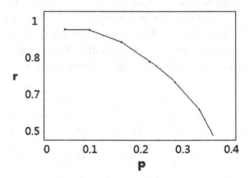

Fig. 7 Successful rate r versus N

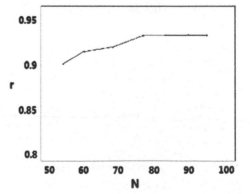

5   Conclusion

This paper presents two methods to strengthen the security of random network coding. The first one is based on encrypting the coefficients of random network coding, the second method is based on encrypting the payload of random network coding. The encryption complexity of the former method is related to dimensionality of the coefficients, while the complexity of the latter one is fixed equals to the length of the payload. Then we introduce a system that could provide a secure transmission mechanism with error-correction. The error-correction is enabled due to the implementation of Turbo-codes. Our system is suitable for satellite communication and mobile communication in remote areas.

References

1. Grnnaro R, Katz J, Krawczyk H, Rabin T (2010) Secure network coding over the integers. Lect Notes Comput Sci 6056:142–160
2. Ahlswede R, Cai N, Li SR, YeungRW (2000) Network information flow. IEEE Trans Inf Theory
3. Gkantsidis C, Rodriguez P (2006) Cooperative security for network coding file distribution. IEEE Inforcom Barcelona, April, pp 13–26
4. Goff S, Glavieux A, Berrou C (1994) Turbo-codes and high spectral efficiency modulation. IEEE international conference on communications, 1994. ICC'94, SUPERCOMM/ICC'94, Conference Record, Serving humanity through communications. IEEE, pp 645–649
5. Jin Hui, Mceliece RJ (2002) Coding theorems for turbo code ensembles. IEEE Trans Inf Theory 48(6):1451–1461
6. Divsalar D, Jin H, Mceliece RJ (1998) Coding theorems for "Turbo-Like" codes. In: Proceedings of annual Allerton conference on communication, control, and computing
7. Goff S, Glavieux A, Berrou C (1994) Turbo-codes and high spectral efficiency modulation Communications, 1994. In: IEEE international conference on ICC'94, SUPERCOMM/ ICC'94, conference record, serving humanity through communications. IEEE, pp 645–649
8. Divsalar D, Pollara F (1995) On the design of turbo codes. In: The telecommunications and data acquisition progress report 42-123, pp 99–120
9. Wang M, Li B (2007) R2: random push with ramdom network coding in live peer-to-peer streaming. IEEE J Sel Areas Commun 25(9), 1655–1666
10. Cai N, Marh FF, Yeung RW (2002) Proceedings of secure network coding, information theory
11. Wang M, Li B (2007) Network coding in live peer-to-peer streaming. IEEE Trans Multimedia 9(8)
12. Bhattad K, Nayayanan KR (2005) Weakly secure network coding. In: Proceedings of Winmee Rawnet & Netcod workshops Riva Del Garda, pp 281–285

Elderly People and Their Attitude Towards Mobile Phones and Their Applications—A Review Study

Blanka Klimova and Petra Maresova

Abstract At present elderly people seem to be one of the rapidly growing population groups in the developed countries. This trend of aging population causes additional problems such as increased costs on the treatment and care about this elderly people. Therefore there is ongoing effort to extend the active age of this group of people in order to enable them to stay economically and socially independent. And current technological devices and services can assist them in this process. The purpose of this article is to discuss an attitude of elderly people towards mobile technological devices and benefits and limitations of mobile applications for this group of people. The author used a method of literature review of available sources exploring research studies focused on mobile devices and applications for elderly people in the acknowledged databases and a method of comparison and evaluation of their findings.

Keywords Elderly people · Mobile phones · Mobile applications · Benefits

1 Introduction

At present elderly people seem to be one of the rapidly growing population groups in the developed countries. In fact, by 2020 the percentage of people older than 60 years should reach 30 % out of the total number of inhabitants living in the developed European countries [1]. The same increase is more or less similar in the developed economies all over the world [2]. This trend of aging population causes

B. Klimova (✉) · P. Maresova
Department of Applied Linguistics, Faculty of Informatics and Management,
University of Hradec Kralove, Hradec Kralove, Czech Republic
e-mail: blanka.klimova@uhk.cz

P. Maresova
e-mail: petra.maresova@uhk.cz

© Springer Science+Business Media Singapore 2016   31
J.J. (Jong Hyuk) Park et al. (eds.), *Advanced Multimedia and Ubiquitous Engineering*, Lecture Notes in Electrical Engineering 393,
DOI 10.1007/978-981-10-1536-6_5

additional problems such as increased costs on the treatment and care about this elderly people [3, 4]. Therefore there is ongoing effort to extend the active age of this group of people in order to enable them to stay economically and socially independent. And current technological devices and services can assist them in this process.

2   Methods

The author used a method of literature review of available sources exploring research studies focused on mobile phones and their applications for elderly people in the acknowledged databases and a method of comparison and evaluation of their findings. This review was done by searching databases such as Web of Science, ProQuest, Elsevier, Science Direct, and Springer in the period from 1990 to 2015 for the following key words: *elderly people* and *mobile applications, elderly people* and *mobile devices, elderly people* and *mobile phones, elderly people* and *portable computers, or elderly people* and *tablets.* In addition, other relevant studies were reviewed on the basis of the reference lists of the research articles from the searched databases. The search showed that there were not many research articles exploring the issue of elderly people and mobile technologies in general, but there is a growing number of articles describing the role of mobile technologies in monitoring their health and treatment. Furthermore, these articles date back mainly to the year of 2005.

3   Elderly and Their Attitude to Mobile Phones and Applications

Recent research studies [5–7] have also proved that older generation of people, aged 58–77, are nowadays much more digitally aware than they used to be ten years ago. This is caused not only by acquiring more experience through different kinds of community and nationwide projects aimed at older people [8, 9], but also their desire to communicate with their family, e.g. grandchildren, or to find the information they need if they it.

In addition, out of mobile devices such as a portable computer, a mobile phone or a tablet, most of elderly people now prefer to use a mobile phone. For example, in the USA it is 74 % of people aged 65+ [10], the same number is true for the UK [11], while in the Czech Republic 84 % of elderly people aged 65+ own a mobile phone [12]. Interestingly, some of elderly people even use a smartphone. For example, in the UK 20 % of elderly people use a smartphone to go online [11]. In the Czech

Republic 31 % of seniors have a smartphone and 14 % of them actively use the Internet in their mobile phone [13, 14]. However, the number is still low. The reason of such a low number of elderly users is that a construction of these smartphones does not meet the specific needs of elderly people who require the mobile phone that is easy to use, provides safety and security, and is relatively cheap [15–17]. Elderly people value services which can maintain their quality of life.

Recently, the producers of mobile phones have realized this fact and they try to develop special mobile phones for elderly people. These mobile phones have sufficiently big keys and the charger connector. Moreover, these phones dispose other features such as DUAL SIM or touch screen. All phone settings are simple, the main menu has only several functions and they are clearly structures. The most popular functions include: calling, phonebook, clock, emergency service, alarm, camera, calculator and text messages [18, 19]. One of the specific functions of the mobile phones for elderly people is SOS Locator service which after pressing SOS key enables to send the localization of the phone via text message. This is particularly suitable for ill seniors who need a tool for fast localization and the subsequent medical aid [20].

Nevertheless, there are elderly people, usually younger seniors, who prefer to use a smartphone and its applications which are supported by its operation system. However, mobile applications are not always adjusted to the special abilities and skills of elderly people [21]. Therefore, the producers of smartphones should address specific needs of this group, which are as follows [18, 22–24]:

- *Healthcare and monitoring the state of health needs*: At present, there is an increasing number of elderly people who exploit the so-called mobile health-care, i.e. remote care service, due to the limitation of aged care resources. This remote care service might include, for example, obtaining information on their health, receiving reminders for scheduled visits, medication instructions, or consulting a doctor at a distance [25].
- *Social Needs*: Most elderly people live on their own and want to be in contact with their loved ones and friends. They also want to use the technologies their children like using.
- *Leisure and sales needs*: Personal leisure (entertainment or self-education) is important for senior citizens in what constitutes their free time occupation. They can also do shopping via mobile phones, order meals or play computer games in order to maintain quality of their life in case they are not able to go out regularly.
- *Safety and privacy needs*: This is considered as the most critical aspect for senior citizens. The user's activity must be monitored by using presence sensors and be analyzed with consideration to different scenarios.

On the basis of these needs, the producers have developed the following mobile applications:

- *Applications which convert the smartphone into a simpler and safer senior's mobile phone.* Elderly people follow rooted stereotypes and archetypes, which are reflected in the use of mobile phones as well. They want their new, modern smartphones to possess the designs of old-fashioned land lines, with similar keypad and features in order to conduct all their daily tasks. In addition, they want to feel safe when they are home alone. Such an application which can meet these requirements is, for example, Koala Phone Launcher [26].

- *Application and use of mobiles for healthcare or monitoring the state of health.* Elderly people use mobile applications for monitoring their state of health or obtaining information about healthcare. This is especially true for people suffering from dementia or diabetes [27–29].
- *Applications focused on entertainment* [30], *education and improvement of cognitive functions.* Playing games help elderly people to spend their time in an entertaining way. In addition, it develops their memory, socializing and it has a positive impact on their psyche and overall state of health [31]. Some research studies [32] also prove that playing games can assist in the delay of Alzheimer disease symptoms and other dementias.

4 Discussion

It seems that elderly people, particularly those aged 58–77 or younger, are now more digitally aware than they used to be ten years ago [6, 8]. They do not seem to be submissive users of cell phones any more as the findings by Kurniawan [33] indicate although they still prefer simpler versions of mobile phones containing the features that require less mental effort to perform [18].

Moreover, since there is a growing number of elderly people in the developed countries, governments develop strategic plans on how to deal with additional issues connected with this demographic trend such as increasing costs on quality care or prolonging an active life of elderly people [3, 4]. As the findings of this review study show, the use of mobile technologies, particularly mobile phones and their applications, can be one of the solutions. Society, however, should raise awareness among elderly people about the benefits of these technologies. Table 1 outlines the key benefits and limitations of mobile applications for elderly people.

Table 1 Outline of the key benefits and limitations of mobile applications for elderly people

Benefits	Limitations
• Providing safety and security, healthcare, socializing, and entertainment • Overall improvement of quality of life of elderly people • Cutting potential costs on care and treatment of elderly people	• Mobile applications are not always adopted to the special needs of elderly people • Elderly people prefer simpler features • Low awareness of the benefits of using mobile applications • A limited offer of mobile applications for elderly people on the market

5 Conclusion

It seems that the importance of mobile technologies and especially of mobile phones thanks to their beneficial aspects such as monitoring of healthcare or socializing will dramatically expand in future due to the growth of older generation. Companies trading with mobile devices have already seized this opportunity and try to develop the mobile devices that would satisfy specific needs of this group of people [20], which could improve quality of their life since the predicted demographic trends appear to be quite threatening.

Acknowledgments This review study is supported by the SPEV project 2016, Faculty of Informatics and Management, University of Hradec Kralove, Czech Republic.

References

1. Benacova H, Valenta M (2009) Moznosti informaticke vyuky senioru v CR a EU, [Possibilities of Computer Science Teaching of Older People in the Czech Republic and EU]. Systemova Integrace 4:77–86
2. As Europe Ages, Its Economies Look Vulnerable (2011) Retrieved 22 Oct 2015, from http://www.npr.org/2011/09/24/140736119/as-europe-ages-its-economies-look-vulnerable
3. Maresova P, Klimova B, Kuca K (2015) Alzheimer's disease: cost cuts call for novel drugs development and national strategy. Ceska Slov Farm 64:25–30
4. Maresova P, Mohelska H, Valis M, Kuca K (2015) Alzheimer disease and its treatment costs, case study in the Czech. Neuropsychiatric Dis Treat 11:2349–2354
5. Hanson VL (2009) Age and web access: the next generation. In: Proceedings of the 2010 W4A—technical, Madrid, pp 7–15
6. Hernandez-Encuentra E, Pousada M, Gomez-Zuniga B (2009) ICT and older people: beyond usability. Educ Gerontol 35:226–245
7. Sayago S, Sloan D, Blat J (2011) Everyday use of computer-mediated communication tolls and its evolution over time: an ethnographical study with older people. Interact Comput 23:543–554
8. Bishop J (2009) Increasing participation in online communities: a framework for human computer interaction. Comput Hum Behav 23:1881–1893
9. Godfrey M, Johnson O (2009) Digital circles of support: meeting the information needs of older people. Comput Hum Behav 25:633–642
10. Older Adults and Technology Use (2014) Retrieved 22 Oct 2015, from http://www.pewinternet.org/2014/04/03/older-adults-and-technology-use/
11. Adults' Media Use and Attitudes Report 2014 (2014) Retrieved 22 Oct 2015, from http://stakeholders.ofcom.org.uk/market-data-research/other/research-publications/adults/adults-media-lit-14/
12. Czech Statistical Office (2014) Temer tri ctvrtiny Cechu jsou online. [Almost three forths of the Czechs are online] Retrieved 22 Oct 2015, from http://www.czso.cz/csu/tz.nsf/i/temer_tri_ctvrtiny_cechu_jsou_online_20141202
13. Herma J (2014) Tretina senior vlastni chytry telefon, mobilni internet je vsak zatim neoslovil [One third of seniors own a smartphone, however, the mobile Internet has not addressed them yet]. Retrieved 22 Oct 2015, from http://smartmania.cz/bleskovky/tretina-senioru-vlastni-chytry-telefon-mobilni-internet-je-vsak-zatim-nenadchl-8710

14. Kubec P (2014) Cesti seniori ovladli mobilni technologie, Telefonuji vice nez mladi [Czech seniors have dominated mobile technologies, They phone more than young people]. Retrieved 22 Oct 2015, from http://zpravy.tiscali.cz/cesti-seniori-ovladli-mobilni-technologie-telefonuji-vice-nez-mladi-243395
15. Gilly M, Zeithmal V (1987) The elderly consumer and adoption of technologies. J Consum Res 12:353–357
16. Glasscock NF, Ogalter MS (2006) Evaluating preferences for mobile phone features. In: Proceedings of the human factors and ergonomics society 50th annual meeting. USA, San Francisco, pp 1259–1263
17. Mallenius S, Rossi M, Tuunainen VK (2010) Factors affecting the adoption and use of mobile devices and services by elderly people—results from a pilot study. Retrieved 22 Oct 2015, from http://citeseerx.ist.psu.edu/viewdoc/download?doi=10.1.1.130.2463&rep=rep1&type=pdf
18. Chen K, Chan AHS (2014) Cell phone features preferences among older adults: a paired comparison study. Gerontechnology 13:184
19. Chen K, Chan AHS, Tsang SNH (2014) Older people's preferences for mobile phone features. In: Ao SI, Chan AHS, Kagiri H, Xu L (eds) IAENG transactions on engineering sciences. London, UK, pp 287–293
20. Simple Phone for Elderly, Retrieved 22 Oct 2015, from https://www.google.cz/search?q= mobile+phone+for+elderly+people&biw=1280&bih=642&source=lnms&tbm=isch&sa= X&ved=0CAYQ_AUoAWoVChMIgaKk8d_VyAIVjA8sCh0iTgu_#imgrc= xKh7roNuCSI0SM%3A
21. Garcia-Penalvo FJ, Conde MA, Matellan-Olivera V (2014) Mobile apps for older users—the development of a mobile apps repository for older people. Learning and collaboration technologies, technology-rich environments for learning and collaboration, lecture notes in computer science, vol 8524, pp 117–126
22. Gao J, Koronios A (2010) Mobile application development for senior citizens. Retrieved 22 Oct 2015, from http://www.pacis-net.org/file/2010/S05-03.pdf
23. Hameed K (2003) The application of mobile computing and technology to health care services. Telematics Inform 20:99–106
24. Lapinsky SE (2007) Mobile computing in critical care. J Crit Care 22:41–44
25. Bujnowska-Fedak MM, Pirogowicz I (2014) Support for E-health services among elderly primary care patients. Telemedicine J E-Health 20:696–704
26. Lipertova M (2014) Koala phone launcher: promente smartphone na mobil pro seniory, [Koala Phone Launcher: convert the smartphone into a mobile phone for elderly people]. Retrieved 22 Oct 2015, from http://svetaplikaci.tyden.cz/koala-phone-launcher-promente-smartphone-na-mobil-pro-seniory/
27. Amstrong N, Nugent C, Moore G, Finlay D (2010) Using smartphones to address the needs of persons with Alzheimer's disease. Ann Telecommun 65:485–495
28. Chomutare T, Fernandez-Luque L, Arsand E, Hartvigsen G (2011) Features of mobile diabetes applications: review of the literature and analysis of current applications compared against evidence-based guidelines. J Med Internet Res 13:e65
29. Liang X, Wang Q, Yang X, Cao J, Chen J, Mo X et al (2011) Effect of mobile phone intervention for diabetes on glycaemic control: a meta-analysis. Diabet Med 28:455–463
30. Vanden Abeele VA, Van Rompaey V (2006) Introducing human-centered research to game design: designing game concepts for and with senior citizens. In: Proceedings of CHI 06 extended abstracts on human factors in computing systems. ACM, New York, pp 1469–1474
31. Gerling KM, Schulte FP, Masuch M (2011) Designing and evaluating digital games for frail elderly persons. Retrieved 22 Oct 2015, from http://dl.acm.org/citation.cfm?id=2071501
32. Heart T, Kalderon E (2013) Older adults: are they ready to adopt health-related ICT? Int J Med Inf 82:e209–e231
33. Kurniawan SH (2008) Older people and mobile phone: a multi-method investigation. Int J Human Comput Stud [Special Issue on Mobility, Oulasvirta A, Brewster S (eds)] 66:889–901

AI Meets Geography: A Heuristic Geographic Routing Algorithm for Wireless Networks

Shijie LV, Jinchen AN and Hui LI

Abstract Geographic routing (GR) is designed for forwarding packets within a specific geographic region, and it enjoys the advantages of its scalability and simplicity. GR can provide a promising solution for packet delivering in next generation wireless network, and has gained much research attention in the areas of Wireless Sensor Networks (WSNs), Vehicular Ad Hoc Networks (VANETs) and Mobile Ad hoc Networks (MANETs). However, it suffers from communication holes or voids in the network areas due to network dynamics or random deployments. Most of current void handling schemes use local or whole topology information. In this paper, we propose a heuristic geographic routing (HGR) to avoid holes over a few iterations by using only local geographic information. Through simulation and analysis, we find that HGR has an outstanding performance in the respect of void bypassing. In addition, this algorithm keeps simplicity and has low communication overhead.

Keywords Wireless communication · Geographic routing · Heuristic search · Void handling

1 Introduction

With the increasing popularity of position systems, such as Global Positioning System (GPS) and Beidou Satellite System (BSS), a lot of new applications and services have emerged, like location-based services (LBSs) on smartphones. Geographic information has great commercial prospects and important academic value. This paper focuses on geographic routing (GR), which means that the determination of next hop is decided on the local location information rather than the topological connectivity. As a result, there is no need for the network to maintain the complete routes, or each node to store routing table. In general, GR

S. LV · J. AN · H. LI (✉)
PKU Shenzhen Graduate School, Shenzhen, China
e-mail: huilihuge@163.com

© Springer Science+Business Media Singapore 2016   37
J.J. (Jong Hyuk) Park et al. (eds.), *Advanced Multimedia and Ubiquitous Engineering*, Lecture Notes in Electrical Engineering 393,
DOI 10.1007/978-981-10-1536-6_6

algorithm is characterized by these features: (1) localized operation, making it simple and scalable; (2) directional forwarding, avoiding the routing loop and reducing flooding overhead; (3) a geographic service in itself, providing location information when a packet is delivered. Unlike non-GR protocols, GR has to handle the communication hole or void, which may be caused by node failing, random deployment or node mobility.

There are two main kinds of GR algorithms: directional region flooding and greedy forwarding. The former, like LAR [1], picks out a region in the direction from the source node to the destination node as the flooding region (FR), and allows nodes only in this region to participate in the packet forwarding. However, such simple flooding method has problem with the appropriate definition of FR if there is a hole in the FR. The latter, like GPSR [2], forwards the packet to the most promising neighbor to make a gradual progress recursively until the destination node is reached. The key of this design is the promising metric selection, like distance to destination, deviating angle, etc. Unfortunately, it has a local optimum problem when facing a communication hole. GPSR [2] adopts a classical right/left hand rule to bypass the void after planarizing the topology. It is simple, but may lose some useable links during planarization and cannot be applied to 3D scenario [3]. Zhang et al. [4–6] propose to detect the void first and then bypass it. However, the detecting method is too complex for a single node to carry out. Some other algorithms [7–9] have in common with constructing the cost function of path, and the neighbor with the lowest cost is selected as the next hop. But only GAHR [9] theoretically introduce the A* [10], a heuristic search algorithm. GAHR tries to solve the problem in the view of graph search, and presents a basic solution for wireless home automation.

In this paper, we propose an enhanced routing scheme by improving GAHR in respects of convergence speed and communication overhead. It employs the heuristic artificial intelligence (AI) algorithms to search for an optimal or suboptimal routing path.

2   Routing Algorithm

2.1   Notations and Assumptions

In this paper, we first consider the GR algorithm in a planar scenario. We assume that the location can be obtained from global position system, like GPS, or other relative position method in [11–13], and denoted as (x, y). We also assume that each node with a ubiquitous ID can be taken as a particle, and have the same commination radius.

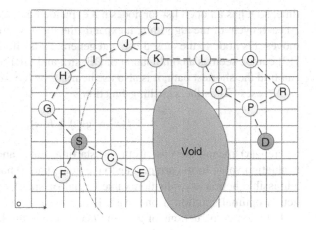

Fig. 1 Communication hole in this topology prevents E from geographic greedy forwarding, so the packet has to be returned back to search for another path

2.2 Problem Description

We take an example to illustrate the greedy forwarding and communication void, as shown Fig. 1. The grid width is 1 unit, and each node's radius is 3 units. All communication links are shown as dash line from one node to another node. S represents the source node, and D the destination node.

Here we use the Euclidean distance between a node and destination node as the greedy forwarding metric. The Euclidean distance function is defined as:

$$dist(m, n) = sqrt\left((m.x - n.x)^2 + (m.y - n.y)^2\right). \tag{1}$$

In Fig. 1, S has three neighbors G, F, and C. We get the distance value of each: $dist(C, D) = 10.05$, $dist(F, D) = 13.15$, and $dist(G, D) = 14.14$, so S would choose C, the neighbor with shortest distance to D, as the next hop. Then repeat this progress: C would choose E as the next hop. Obviously, E, with no neighbor closer to D than E, gets trapped, and then local optimum problem for this greedy geographic routing emerges.

2.3 Heuristic Forward Selection

If we see the topology as a graph, routing protocol aims to find a path from source node to destination node, which involves graph search and AI: routing protocol represents a solution path, nodes the states of problem and edges the moves. Two popular search algorithms are Dijkstra and best-first search (BFS). Dijkstra, an old and classical algorithm, starts with the source node outwards to examine the closest not-yet-examined node repeatedly. It can guarantee that a shortest path could be found if no edge with negative cost. BFS chooses the closest node to expand at one time, so it has an open list for nodes not expanded and a closed list nodes expanded. At each cycle of the algorithm, it expands the most promising node on the open list, moves this node to the closed list, and generates its children until the goal node. A* [13] can be seen as a combination of Dijkstra and GBFS: it is like Dijkstra in that it can find the shortest path; it is also use heuristic value for searching guide like BFS.

A* uses (2) as the searching function:

$$f(x) = g(x) + h(x), \tag{2}$$

where $g(x)$ means the cost from the starting state, and $h(x)$ means the heuristic evaluation value form current state to the goal state. It has been proven that given an admissible heuristic evaluation value (equal or smaller than actual value), A* can get an optimal solution if one exists [14].

Function constructions of $g(x)$ and $h(x)$ become the key part of heuristic search. We have the searching value $f(n)$ in heuristic searching function for geographic routing:

$$f(n) = w_g * g(n) + w_h * h(n), \tag{3}$$

where $g(n)$ is the cost of the least expensive path from the source node to the current node n, $h(n)$ is the estimate cost of the path from current node n to the destination node, w_g and w_h are weights for path cost function and heuristic evaluation function.

In HGR, $g(n)$ is designed as follows:

$$g(n) = g(nexthop) + (N_{traverse} - 1) * dist(n, previoushop), \tag{4}$$

For $h(n)$, to get the exact heuristic value in theoretical, we need to calculate the shortest path between every pair of nodes, which is not feasible. An approximate way is used as follows:

$$h(n) = dist(n, nexthop) + h(nexthop). \tag{5}$$

For weights w_g and w_h, at one extreme, if w_h equals 0, only $g(n)$ plays the role, and A* turns into Dijkstra. At the other extreme, if w_g equals 0, only the $h(n)$ works, and A* becomes GBFS. Here we define a weight ratio $w = w_h/w_g$, which can be used to control the tradeoff between the path cost and heuristic value. It has been studied in [10] that a greater w can make the searching speed faster but with a suboptimal path, so the speed and accuracy is a tradeoff for A* algorithms. We design an unfixed tradeoff in HGR,

$$w_h = w_{h0} - N_{forward} * w_{step} + hole\_index(n) * w_t, \tag{6}$$

where $N_{forward}$ is the number of this node forwarding packet to D ever, and w_t is the step value for $N_{forward}$ and $hole\_index$, w_{h0} and w_{h1} are constant initial values. $hole\_index$ is defined as

$$hole\_index(n) = hole\_index(previous) + 1, \ if \ h(nexthop) > h(n), \qquad (7)$$

$$hole\_index(n) = hole\_index(previous), \ if \ h(nexthop) \leq h(n). \qquad (8)$$

In order to reduce overhead, other neighbors, besides the next hop, can also access the updated searching value of the current node by MAC overhearing. In a hole-free network, the HGR can achieve the same performance with GR greedy algorithms, like GPSR, in respects of hop count, end-to-end delay, and overhead.

3 Simulation and Analysis

To validate the design of our HGR, we conduct several simulations in OPNET Moduler [15]. The network configuration is shown in Table 1

Because heuristic search is an optimization algorithm by iteration, based on dynamic adjustment of heuristic value, it has a convergence speed and may have trouble in fluctuating. Due to space constraints, this paper focuses verification on convergence parameters, like convergence speed or iteration number (the number of packet sent when finding an optimal path steadily) and average hop count. To deeply evaluate the ability to step back from communication hole, we design different holes in several topologies manually. One of them is chosen shown in Fig. 2, where node 2 is the source node and node 1 the sink node. Because a hole is amorphous, a trap is proposed to indicate the degree of difficulty of stepping back. A trap is an area where nodes who return the packet back when facing communication holes.

As shown in Fig. 2, HGR with dynamic weight has the best performance and HGR with constant weight (w is set to 1) the second best: smaller average hop and faster convergence speed compared to GAHR. HGR with dynamic weight fluctuates once and stabilize fast (2 packets). HGR with constant weight also fluctuates once, but need sending 5 packets to be steady. GAHR fluctuates a lot (3 times) and takes long time (11 packets) to be stable. We also test some other topologies with different communication holes, and get same results as that in Fig. 2.

Table 1 Simulation parameters

Name	Parameter
Network	Size: 500 × 500 m
Node	Number: 30 Radio range: 40 m
MAC	Type: 802.11 Bandwidth: 1 Mb/s
Packet	Rate: 1 packet per 0.5 s
Simulation	Time: 10 s $w_{h0} = 0.92$, $w_{h1} = 0.95$, $w_{step} = 0.01$, $w_t = 0.008$

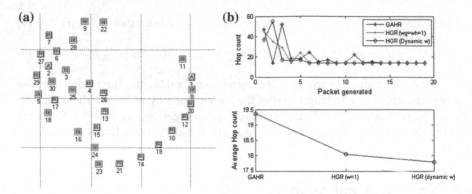

Fig. 2 The results of GR algorithm in (**b**) tested on the topology in (**a**). There are three traps in this topology: the first is around node 26, the second around node 24 and the third around node 22. Hop count and average hop count are used to evaluate the performance

HGR has no communication overhead after overhead optimization, while GAHR has as many as the number of each forwarding nodes' all neighbors.

4 Conclusion

In this paper, we present an enhanced heuristic geographic routing, HGR. It has a well-designed cost and heuristic functions with dynamic weights. Each node chooses the neighbor with the lowest searching value as the next hop to forward the packet and updates the cost and heuristic values. As shown in the simulation results, HGR searches routing path faster (has less average number of hops) and fluctuates less (finds the optimal or sub-optimal path quickly) compared to GAHR. In addition, it has much less communication overhead.

Acknowledgments This work is sponsored by National Basic Research Program of China (973 Program, No. 2012CB315904), and Shenzhen Basic Research (No. JCYJ20140417144423192).

References

1. Ko Y-B, Vaidya NH (2000) Location-aided routing (LAR) in mobile ad hoc networks. Wireless Netw 6(4):307
2. Karp B, Kung HT (2000) GPSR: greedy perimeter stateless routing for wireless network. In: Proceedings of the 6th annual ACM/IEEE international conference on mobile computing and networking (MobiCom 2000)
3. Shu L, Zhang Y, Yang LT et al (2010) TPGF: geographic routing in wireless multimedia sensor networks. Telecommun Syst 44(1–2):79–95

4. Zhang D, Dong E (2015) A bypassing void routing combining of geographic and virtual coordinate information for WSN. In: 22nd International conference on telecommunications (ICT). IEEE
5. Chen W, Li X (2007) Improving routing quality of greedy forwarding in wireless networks. In: Fifteenth IEEE international workshop on quality of service. IEEE, pp 65–73
6. Zhang H, Fan W, Wang L et al (2009) Real-time and reliable greedy geographical routing for mobile wireless sensor networks. J Comput Res Dev 46(5):713–722
7. Park J, Yong NK, Jin YB (2013) A forwarder selection method for greedy mode operation of a geographic routing protocol in a WSN. In: Fifth international conference on ubiquitous and future networks (ICUFN). IEEE, pp 270–275
8. Wang H, Zhang X, Khokhar A (2007) Efficient "Void" handling in contention-based geographic routing for wireless sensor networks. In: IEEE global telecommunications conference, pp 663–667
9. Li XH, Hong SH, Fang KL (2011) WSNHA-GAHR: a greedy and A* heuristic routing algorithm for wireless sensor networks in home automation. Commun IET 5(13):1797–1805
10. Hart PE, Nilsson NJ, Raphael B (1968) A formal basis for the heuristic determination of minimum cost paths. IEEE Trans Syst Sci Cybern SSC4 4(2):100–107
11. Savvides A, Han CC, Strivastava MB (2001) Srivastava dynamic fine-grained localization in ad-hoc networks of sensors. In: Proceedings of the fifth international conference on mobile computing and networking, Mobicom, pp 166–179
12. Li M, Liu Y (2007) Rendered path: range-free localization in anisotropic sensor networks with holes. IEEE/ACM Trans Netw 18(1):320–332
13. Hightower J, Borriello G (2001) Location systems for ubiquitous. Computer 34:57–66
14. Ward A, Jones A, Hopper A (1997) A new location technique for the active office. IEEE Pers Commun 4(5):42–47
15. www.opnet.com

A Content-Aware Expert Recommendation Scheme in Social Network Services

Young-Sung Shin, Hyeong-Il Kim and Jae-Woo Chang

Abstract Because a wide range of professionals utilize Social Network Service (SNS), the SNS users have recently required an expert recommendation service to enable users to perform both cooperation and technical communication with experts. A content-boosted collaborative filtering (CBCF) provides various prediction algorithms which support effective recommendations. However, the CBCF cannot calculates the similarity of items (or users) when the calculation condition is not clearly provided. To solve the problem, we propose a content-aware hybrid collaborative filtering scheme for expert recommendation in SNSs. Finally, we show from a performance analysis that our scheme outperforms the existing method in terms of recommendation accuracy.

Keywords Collaborative filtering · Expert recommendation · Content-aware recommendation · Social network service

1 Introduction

With the development of the internet technologies and the growing needs for the online communication, various Social Network Services (SNSs) have been emerged. The SNSs are platforms to build social networks among people who share interests, activities, and any connections. Meanwhile, there exist SNSs for a specific purpose by sharing information of business or specialties. In the SNSs, some users want to get an advice from an expert. However, it is very difficult to find experts in

Y.-S. Shin · H.-I. Kim · J.-W. Chang (✉)
Department of Computer Engineering, Chonbuk National University, 1-Ga,
Duckjin-Dong, Duckjin-Gu, Jeollabuk-Do Jeonju 664-14, Republic of Korea
e-mail: jwchang@jbnu.ac.kr

Y.-S. Shin
e-mail: twotoma@jbnu.ac.kr

H.-I. Kim
e-mail: melipion@jbnu.ac.kr

SNSs. So, it's necessary to develop an expert recommendation system which enables users to perform both cooperation and technical communication with experts. However, the existing recommendation systems mainly focus on recommending items, such as movies, music, books, news, and web pages, by using the user's preferences. However, there are few works to recommend experts because it is difficult to classify experts based on their interest, preference, career and experiences.

The schemes used in the existing recommendation systems [1–8] can be categorized into content-based method [1, 7, 8] and collaborative filtering method [2, 3, 5]. The content-based method recommends items by analyzing which items a user prefers. If a user defines preferred items, the method recommends items being similar to them. Meanwhile, the collaborative filtering method recommends items by finding other users who have the similar preference with a user. The content-based method can analyze individual preference, but it does not consider similar preferences among users. Meanwhile, the collaborative filtering method can analyze the relationship among users, but it cannot evaluate individual characteristics. In addition, it shows the low recommendation quality when there is no enough information about users.

To solve the problems, hybrid collaborative filtering methods [3, 4, 6] have been proposed. The most typical hybrid method is content-boosted collaborative filtering (CBCF) [9]. CBCF can solve the scarcity problem of the collaborative filtering method by using the content-based technique. However, CBCF shows the low recommendation accuracy when the number of meaningful attributes is much smaller than that of all the attributes.

Therefore, to solve the problem of the CBCF method, we propose a content-aware hybrid collaborative filtering scheme for expert recommendation in social networks services. For this, we devise a new cosine similarity measure by supplementing the Pearson correlation coefficient. In addition, we provide a mechanism to find a proper expert by using user profiles. From a performance analysis, we show that our scheme outperforms the existing CBCF method in terms of service accuracy.

The rest of the paper is organized as follows. Section 2 introduces the related work on collaborative filtering schemes and expert recommendation methods. In Sect. 3, we provide some consideration for an expert recommendation system and propose content-aware hybrid collaborative filtering scheme. In Sect. 4, we compare the performance of our scheme with that of the existing methods. Finally, we conclude this paper with future work in Sect. 5.

2 Related Work

The hybrid collaborative filtering method can accurately predict items by combining the existing collaborative filtering methods. The most typical hybrid method is content-boosted collaborative filtering (CBCF) [9]. CBCF can solve both cold-start problem and scarcity problem by using a content-based technique [10]. With Pearson's correlation coefficient, CBCF recommends items to a user by analyzing the contents of items. For this, it determines items' attributes and assigns weights to each attribute through a regression analysis. A content-based similarity measure, ContentSim (I_i, I_j), between items I_i and I_j is calculated by Eq. (1) [11].

$$ContentSim(I_i, I_j) = \sum_{n=1}^{m} w_n \times f(A_{n_i}, A_{n_j})$$ (1)

Here, w_n is a weight for each attribute and $f(A_{n_i}, A_{n_j})$ is a function to calculate the similarity of the items on an attribute A_n. CBCF also considers both local similarity and global similarity among users. The local similarity indicates a direct relationship among users. The local similarity between users U_a and U_b, CollabSim (U_a, U_b), is calculated by using Eq. (2). Here, γ is a threshold of a weight and sim (a, b) is Pearson's correlation coefficient of U_a and U_b.

$$CollabSim(a, b) = \frac{Min(|I_a \cap I_b|, \gamma)}{\gamma} \times sim(a, b)$$ (2)

The global similarity indicates an indirect relationship between users by considering other users [12]. That is, the global similarity is calculated by using similarities among other users being related with U_a and U_b. Also, CBCF can expand neighboring users who are considered for recommendation. Thus, CBCF can solve not only the scarcity problem, but also achieve high recommendation accuracy. The global similarity is used when the local similarity cannot be computed because there is no direct relationship between users. Meanwhile, Eq. (2) can be used to calculate a similarity between items. In this case, γ can be replaced with δ.

Using the values, scores on items are predicted by using EMDP (Effective Missing Data Prediction) algorithm [13]. Through EMDP algorithm, it is possible to predict scores on missing values. The items with high scores are recommended to the user. However, CBCF has two problems. First, it is difficult to find the optimal values of γ and δ, which are used in Eqs. (1) and (2). Second, CBCF shows the low recommendation accuracy when the number of meaningful attributes is much smaller than that of all the attributes.

3   Content-Aware Hybrid Collaborative Filtering Scheme for Expert Recommendation

In this section, we first describe the overall architecture for our content-aware hybrid collaborative filtering scheme for expert recommendation. Secondly, we discuss the user attributes that should be considered for expert recommendation.

Thirdly, we explain how to apply a cosine similarity measure to analyze relationships among users. Finally, we describe our algorithm for expert recommendation.

3.1 Overall Architecture

Figure 1 shows an overall architecture for our content-aware hybrid collaborative filtering scheme for expert recommendation. Our scheme calculates a content-aware user similarity by utilizing user information stored in SNSs. In addition, our scheme calculates collaborative filtering-based user similarity. For this, we use a rating table containing scores that a user gives on the other users. By using the two similarity values, our scheme estimates missing values based on EMDP [13] and constructs a preference score prediction (PSP) table. Our scheme verifies scores in the PSP table by using the rating table. Finally, our scheme recommends experts with the highest scores.

3.2 User Attributes for Expert Recommendation

To perform a content-aware analysis, user attributes should be defined to calculate similarities among users. For this, we use the user information as shown in Table 1. Among them, interesting field, specialty, origin area and work place are constructed by using the user information in SNSs. Meanwhile, the number of posts, answers, and followers are acquired by using the statistics in SNSs. In addition, a rating attribute is determined by referring to the rating table.

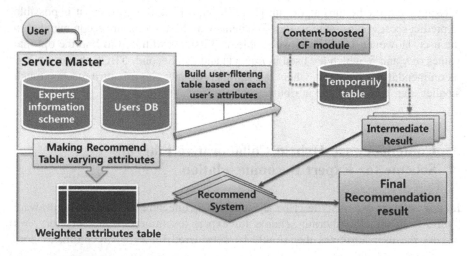

Fig. 1 Overall system architecture

Table 1 Expert attributes

Dimension	Type	Domain	Distance measure
Specialty	String list	Computer, graphic, etc. ([0, 1])	1, 0/$\lvert C_1 \cap C_2 \rvert/C_1$
Interesting field	String list	Computer, graphic, etc. ([0, 1])	$\lvert C_1 \cap C_2 \rvert/C_1$
Origin area	String	Seoul, Pusan, etc. ([0, 1])	1, 0
Work place	String	Samsung, LG, etc. ([0, 1])	1, 0
Number of followers	Integer	[1,)	
Age	Integer	[1, 120]	1/abs or linear function
Number of posts	Integer	[1,)	
Number of answers	Integer	[1,)	
Number of papers	Integer	[1,)	
Rating	Integer	[1, 5]	
Nationality	String	Korea, USA, etc.	1, 0

The specialty, interesting field, the origin area and work place are main attributes to calculate the similarities among users. In case of specialty and interesting field, a similarity is calculated by counting the number of fields that users have in common. For the origin area and work place, a similarity is set as 1 if users reside in the same place (or area), otherwise the similarity is set as 0. The similarities are used in Eq. (1). Meanwhile, the number of papers, posts, answers, and followers are used to calculate the activity scores of users. The activity scores of users are calculated by using Eq. (3).

$$weight_{u,i} = w_1 + (w_2 - w_1) \times \left[\sum_{t=1}^{n} \frac{uservalue(attribute(t))}{maxvalue(attribute(t))} / n \right] \quad (3)$$

Here, w_{min} and w_{max} are the minimum and maximum weights given by a user. For an attribute t, uservalue (t) means the values of users' activity scores while maxvalue (t) is the maximum activity score among all users. As a result, a user with the highest activity score is given w_{max} while a user with the lowest activity is given w_{min}.

With the calculated score, we can measure the recommendation value ($rv_{u,i}$) of a user by using Eq. (4). Here, the $weight_{u,i}$ is used to adjust a preference score calculated by EMDP. Thus, we can regard users with high activity scores as experts.

$$rv_{u,i} = EMDP_{u,i} \times weight_{u,i} \quad (4)$$

3.3 Local User Similarity Based on Cosine Similarity

The existing CBCF calculates a local similarity between items by using Eq. (2). So, if the number of items that U_a and U_u give scores in common is greater than γ, the value of $\frac{Min(|\mathrm{I}_a \cap \mathrm{I}_b|, \gamma)}{\gamma}$ becomes 1 (e.g., γ/γ). Otherwise, the Pearson coefficient between users is computed by multiplying $\frac{|\mathrm{I}_a \cap \mathrm{I}_b|}{\gamma}$. However, the CBCF uses the randomly selected γ value. So, the similarity between users can be different, depending on the value of γ.

To solve the problem, we assign a weight to the Pearson coefficient by using the cosine similarity between users. The cosine similarity between U_a and U_u is calculated by Eq. (5).

$$cosweight(a, u) = \frac{\sum_{i \in I_a \cap I_u} R_{i,a} \times R_{i,u}}{\sqrt{\sum_{i \in I_a \cap I_u}(R_{i,a})^2 \times (R_{i,u})^2}} \qquad (5)$$

Here, $R_{i,a}$ is a preference score of U_a on item i whereas $R_{i,u}$ is that of U_u. The value of cosweight (a, u) is 1 when U_u and U_a has the highest similarity whereas the value is 0 when they have the lowest similarity. We can calculate the local user similarity between U_u and U_a, NewCollabSim (a, u), by using Eq. (6).

$$NewCollabSim(a, u) = cosweight(a, u) \times sim(a, u) \qquad (6)$$

Here, sim (a, u) means the Pearson coefficient between U_a and U_u. By using a cosine similarity to calculate the local user similarity, our scheme has two advantages. First, our scheme can solve the problem that the user similarity can be different, depending on being an arbitrarily selected value. Second, our scheme can achieve the improved recommendation accuracy by reducing the variation of user similarity.

3.4 Content-Aware Hybrid Collaborative Filtering Algorithm for Expert Recommendation

In this section, we explain our content-aware hybrid collaborative filtering algorithm for expert recommendation in SNSs. First, the algorithm reads a rating table and user profile information. Second, by using Eq. (6), it calculates local similarities among all users. If a user does not have enough information to compute the local similarity, the algorithm calculates global similarities for the user. Based on the weights given to the local and global user similarities, it computes the final similarities among users, e.g., u_b. Third, using Eq. (1), the algorithm calculates the content-aware similarities among properties of all the experts. For this, we use properties defined in Table 1. Fourth, by using Eq. (6), the similarities among experts are calculated and the final similarities among experts, e.g., u_i, are calculated. Fifth, for a query issuer, the algorithm checks whether he/she has both u_b and u_i. If the user has both values, the algorithm calculates a prediction score by using the given weight λ. If the user has one of u_b and u_i, the algorithm selects the existing one as a prediction score. If there is no u_b and u_i, it determines the prediction score by using the following two values; an average score given by the query issuer on experts and an average score that other users give on the experts. Finally, by multiplying activity scores, the algorithm calculates the final preference scores and recommends experts whose preference scores exceed a given threshold.

4 Performance Analysis

For the performance analysis, we use both synthetic data and real data. For the synthetic data, we generate 100,000 score data with 1000 users. For the real data, we use MovieLens data extracted from IMDb (The Internet Movie Database) [14]. There are 100,000 score data that 943 users give on 1682 movie contents. To determine weights for the properties of experts, we conduct a survey on 100 persons. Table 2 shows the defined weights for the properties of experts by analyzing the survey data.

To measure the recommendation accuracy of both our scheme and CBCF, we use MAE (Mean Absolute Error). MAE determines the accuracy by measuring the differences between the actual value and the estimated value. So, the smaller MAE value means the higher recommendation accuracy. MAE is calculated by Eq. (7). Here, N is the total number of data. $a_{i,j}$ means the actual score that a user i gives on an item j while $(\bar{a}_{i,j})$ means the estimated value.

$$MAE = \frac{\sum_{i=1}^{N} \sum_{j=1}^{N} |a_{ij} - \bar{a}_{ij}|}{N} \tag{7}$$

Table 3 shows the variables used in the experiments. α is a weight given to the local and global user similarities. β is a weight given to the content-aware similarity and $(1 - \beta)$ is a weight to calculate the collaborative filtering-based similarity. γ and δ are only used in CBCF.

Figure 2a shows the recommendation accuracy of both schemes with varying α on the synthetic data. We set the value of β as 0.6. Overall, our scheme shows about 10 % better recommendation accuracy than that of the CBCF. This is because our

Table 2 Weight for each property of experts

Property	Value	Property	Value
Interesting field	0.3304	Academic background	0.1552
Specialty	0.1779	Office	0.0956
Career	0.174	Working area	0.0668

Table 3 Variables

Variables	α	β	γ	δ	λ
Value	0.3–0.7	0.4–0.8	30	25	0.6

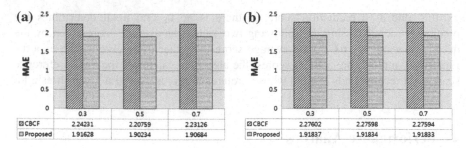

Fig. 2 Recommendation accuracy on the synthetic data **a** with the varying α **b** with the varying β

Fig. 3 Recommendation
accuracy with varying α on
the real data

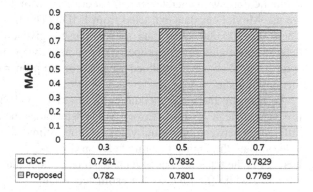

scheme makes use of the cosine similarity measure while the CBCF uses γ being arbitrarily selected value. So, our scheme can analyze relationships among users more accurately. Meanwhile, our scheme shows the best performance when the value of α is 0.5. This implies that the local similarities of users have the same importance for recommending experts as the global similarities of users. Figure 2b shows the recommendation accuracy of both schemes with varying β on the syntactic data. We set the value of β as 0.5. Overall, our scheme shows about 10 % better recommendation accuracy than that of the CBCF. Meanwhile, both schemes show the higher recommendation accuracy as the value of β becomes larger. This means that the content-aware similarities of users are crucial for good recommendation quality.

For real data, we found that the recommendation accuracy is rarely affected by β. So, we only show the performance of both schemes with varying α in Fig. 3. Overall, our scheme shows slightly better recommendation accuracy than CBCF because our scheme can analyze the relationships of users by using a cosine similarity measure.

5 Conclusion

The existing CBCF method has a problem that it uses the randomly selected parameters which degrade the recommendation accuracy. To solve the problem, we proposed a content-aware hybrid collaborative filtering scheme for expert recommendation in SNSs. For this, we devised a new cosine similarity measure to calculate a weight for the local similarities among users. Through the performance analysis, we showed that our scheme achieved the better recommendation accuracy on both the synthetic data and the real data than the existing CBCF. As a future work, we plan to expand our scheme to the distributed computing environment, like Hadoop [15], to efficiently perform our recommendation algorithm.

Acknowledgments This work was supported by the Human Resource Training Program for Regional Innovation and Creativity through the Ministry of Education and National Research Foundation of Korea (NRF-2014H1C1A1065816) and also supported by the Institute for Information & communications Technology Promotion (IITP) grant funded by the Korea government (MSIP) (No. R0113-15-0005, Development of an Unified Data Engineering Technology for Large-scale Transaction Processing and Real-time Complex Analytics).

References

1. Jianshan S, Jian M, Zhiying L, Yajun M (2014) Leveraging content and connections for scientific article recommendation in social computing contexts. Comput J 57:1331–1342
2. Breese JS, Heckerman D, Kadie C (1998) Empirical analysis of predictive algorithms for collaborative filtering. In: Proceedings of the 14th annual conference on uncertainty in artificial intelligence, pp 43–52
3. Su X, Khoshgoftaar TM (2009) A survey of collaborative filtering techniques. Adv Artif Intell 2009
4. Sarwar B, Karypis G, Konstan J, Reidl J (2001) Item-based collaborative filtering recommendation algorithms. In: Proceedings of the 10th international World Wide Web conference, pp 285–295
5. Massa P, Avesani P (2004) Trust-aware collaborative filtering for recommender systems. In: Proceedings of international conference on cooperative information systems, LNCS 3290, Springer, pp 492–508
6. Li W, Wei H (2013) An improved collaborative filtering approach based on user ranking and item clustering. In: Internet and distributed computing systems. Springer, Berlin, pp 134–144
7. Han KT, Park MK, Choi YS (2011) Adaptive and collaborative recommendation using content type. J KIISE (Korean Institute of Information Scientists and Engineers) Softw Appl 38(1):50–56
8. Deshpande M, Karypis G (2004) Item-based top-N recommendation algorithms. ACM Trans Inf Syst 22:143–177
9. Özbal G, Karaman H, Alpaslan FN (2011) A content-boosted collaborative filtering approach for movie recommendation based on local and global similarity and missing data prediction. Comput J 54:1535–1546
10. Papagelis M, Plexousakis D, Kutsuras T (2005) Alleviation the sparsity problem of collaborative filtering using trust inferences. In: Proceedings of the 3rd international conference on trust management, LNCS 3477, Springer, pp 224–239
11. Debnath S, Ganguly N, Mitra P (2008) Feature weighting in content based recommendation system using social network analysis. In: Proceedings of the 17th international conference on World Wide Web, pp 1041–1042

12. Floyd RW (1962) Algorithm 97: shortest path. Commun ACM 5:345–348
13. Ma H, King I, Lyu MR (2007) Effective missing data prediction for collaborative filtering. In: ACM SIGIR'07, pp 39–46
14. The Internet Movie Database (IMDb). http://www.imdb.com
15. Shvachko K et al (2010) The hadoop distributed file system. In: IEEE 26th symposium on mass storage systems and technologies (MSST), pp 1–10

Automated Theorem Finding by Forward Reasoning Based on Strong Relevant Logic: A Case Study in Tarski's Geometry

Hongbiao Gao and Jingde Cheng

Abstract The problem of automated theorem finding is one of 33 basic research problems in automated reasoning which was originally proposed by Wos. The problem is still an open problem until now. To solve the problem, a systematic methodology with forward reasoning based on strong relevant logic has been proposed. This paper presents a case study of automated theorem finding in Tarski's Geometry to show the generality of the methodology.

Keywords Automated theorem finding · Forward reasoning · Strong relevant logic · Tarski's geometry

1 Introduction

The problem of automated theorem finding (ATF for short) [1, 2] is one of 33 basic research problems in automated reasoning which was originally proposed by Wos in 1988: "What properties can be identified to permit an automated reasoning program to find new and interesting theorems, as opposed to proving conjectured theorems?" It is still an open problem [3, 4], although there are some works on automated theorem discovery and automated theorem generation [5–8].

The most important and difficult requirement of the problem is that, in contrast to prove conjectured theorems supplied by the user, it asks for criteria that an automated reasoning program can use to find some theorems in a field that must be evaluated by theorists of the field as new and interesting theorems. The significance of solving the problem is obvious because an automated reasoning program satisfying the requirement can provide great assistance for scientists in various fields [9, 10].

H. Gao · J. Cheng (✉)
Department of Information and Computer Sciences, Saitama University,
Saitama 338-8570, Japan
e-mail: cheng@aise.ics.saitama-u.ac.jp

H. Gao
e-mail: gaohongbiao@aise.ics.saitama-u.ac.jp

© Springer Science+Business Media Singapore 2016   55
J.J. (Jong Hyuk) Park et al. (eds.), *Advanced Multimedia and Ubiquitous Engineering*, Lecture Notes in Electrical Engineering 393,
DOI 10.1007/978-981-10-1536-6_8

To solve the ATF problem, a forward reasoning approach based on strong relevant logic and its systematic methodology [3, 9–11] have been proposed. The systematic methodology is a logic-based reasoning, uses the forward deduction as the reasoning approach, and separates the logic parts and empirical parts of formal theories to do forward deduction. To verify the effectiveness of the methodology, we performed case studies of ATF in NBG set theory, Peano's arithmetic and graph theory, and those case studies shows that forward reasoning approach based on strong relevant logic is hopeful to solve the ATF problem [3, 12].

"In his 1926–27 lectures at the University of Warsaw, Alfred Tarski gave an axiomatic development of elementary Euclidean geometry, the part of plane Euclidean geometry that is not based upon set-theoretical notions, or, in other words, the part that can be developed within the framework of first-order logic" [13]. However, we have not used our methodology to do ATF in the field of geometry which is one of the most important branches of mathematics.

This paper presents a case study of ATF in Tarski's Geometry. The result of the case study shows that the proposed methodology is a general method for ATF.

2   Basic Notions and Notations

A formal logic system L is an ordered pair $(F(L), \vdash_L)$ where $F(L)$ is the set of well formed formulas of L, and $\vdash_L$ is the consequence relation of L such that for a set P of formulas and a formula C, $P \vdash_L C$ means that within the framework of L taking P as premises we can obtain C as a valid conclusion. $Th(L)$ is the set of logical theorems of L such that $\phi \vdash_L T$ holds for any $T \in Th(L)$. According to the representation of the consequence relation of a logic, the logic can be represented as a Hilbert style system, Gentzen sequent calculus system, Gentzen natural deduction system, and so on [11].

Let $(F(L), \vdash_L)$ be a formal logic system and $P \subseteq F(L)$ be a non-empty set of sentences. A formal theory with premises P based on L, called an L-theory with premises P and denoted by $T_L(P)$, is defined as $T_L(P) =_{df} Th(L) \cup Th^e{}_L(P)$ where $Th^e{}_L(P) =_{df} \{A | P \vdash_L A \text{ and } A \notin Th(L)\}$, $Th(L)$ and $Th^e{}_L(P)$ are called the logical part and the empirical part of the formal theory, respectively, and any element of $Th^e{}_L(P)$ is called an empirical theorem of the formal theory [11].

Based on the definition above, the problem of ATF can be said as "for any given premises P, how to construct a meaningful formal theory $T_L(P)$ and then find new and interesting theorems in $Th^e{}_L(P)$ automatically" [11].

The notion of degree of connectives of logic L [11] is defined as follows: Let θ be an arbitrary n-ary $(1 \leq n)$ connective of logic L and A be a formula of L, the degree of θ in A, denoted by $D_\theta(A)$, is defined as: (1) $D_\theta(A) = 0$ if and only if there is no occurrence of θ in A, (2) if A is in the form $\theta(a_1, \ldots, a_n)$ where $a_1, \ldots, a_n$ are formulas, then $D_\theta(A) = \max\{D_\theta(a_1), \ldots, D_\theta(a_n)\} + 1$, (3) if A is in the form $\sigma(a_1, \ldots, a_n)$ where σ is a connective different from θ and $a_1, \ldots, a_n$ are formulas, then $D_\theta (A) = \max \{D_\theta (a_1), \ldots, D_\theta (a_n)\}$, and (4) if A is in the form QB where B is a formula and Q is the quantifier prefix of B, then $D_\theta (A) = D_\theta (B)$.

The notion of degree of logical fragment [11] about logical connectives can be defined as follows: Let $\theta_1, \ldots, \theta_n$ be logical connectives of logic L and $k_1, \ldots, k_n$ be natural numbers, the fragment of L about $\theta_1, \ldots, \theta_n$ and their degrees $k_1, \ldots, k_n$, denoted by $Th^{(\theta_1, k_1, \ldots, \theta_n, k_n)}(L)$, is a set of logical theorems of L which is inductively defined as follows (in the terms of Hilbert style axiomatic system): (1) if A is an axiom of L and $D_{\theta_1} (A) \leq k_1, \ldots, D_{\theta_n} (A) \leq k_n$, then $A \in Th^{(\theta_1, k_1, \ldots, \theta_n, k_n)}(L)$, (2) if A is the result of applying an inference rule of L to some members of $Th^{(\theta_1, k_1, \ldots, \theta_n, k_n)}(L)$ and $D_{\theta_1} (A) \leq k_1, \ldots, D_{\theta_n} (A) \leq k_n$, then $A \in Th^{(\theta_1, k_1, \ldots, \theta_n, k_n)}(L)$, and (3) Nothing else are members of $Th^{(\theta_1, k_1, \ldots, \theta_n, k_n)}(L)$.

The notion of predicate abstract level [3] is defined as follows: (1) Let pal $(X) = k$ denote that an abstract level of a predicate X is k where k is a natural number, (2) $pal(X) = 1$ if X is the most primitive predicate in a target field, (3) pal $(X) = \max (pal(Y_1), pal(Y_2), \ldots, pal(Y_n)) + 1$ if a predicate X is defined by other predicates $Y_1, Y_2, \ldots, Y_n$ in the target field where n is a natural number. A predicate X is called k-level predicate, if $pal(X) = k$. If $pal(X) < pal(Y)$, then the abstract level of predicate X is lower than Y, and Y is higher than X.

The notion of function abstract level [3] is defined as follows: (1) Let $fal(f) = k$ denote that an abstract level of a function f is k where k is a natural number, (2) fal $(f) = 1$ if f is the most primitive function in the target field, (3) $fal(f) = \max (fal(g_1), fal(g_2), \ldots, fal(g_n)) + 1$ if a function f is defined by other functions $g_1, g_2, \ldots, g_n$ in the target field where n is a natural number. A function f is k-level function, if fal $(f) = k$. If $fal(f) < fal(g)$, we call the abstract level of function f is lower than g, and g is higher than f.

The notion of abstract level of a formula [3] is defined as follows: (1) $lfal(f) = (k, m)$ denotes that an abstract level of a formula A where $k = pal(A)$ and $m = fal(A)$, (2) $pal(A) = \max (pal(Q_1), pal(Q_2), \ldots, pal(Q_n))$ where Q_i is a predicate and occurs in A $(1 \leq i \leq n)$, or $pal(A) = 0$, if there is not any predicate in A, (3) $fal(A) = \max (fal(g_1), fal(g_2), \ldots, fal(g_n))$ where g_i is a function and occurs in A $(1 \leq i \leq n)$, or $fal(A) = 0$, if there is not any function in A. A formula A is (k, m)-level formula, if $lfal(A) = (k, m)$.

(k, m)-fragment of premises P, denoted by $P(k, m)$, is a set of all formulas in P that consists of only (j, n)-level formulas where m, n, j and k are natural numbers $(0 \leq j \leq k$ and $0 \leq n \leq m)$ [3].

3 The Systematic Methodology for ATF

The systematic methodology for ATF consists of five phases. Phase 1 is to prepare logical fragments of strong relevant logic for various empirical theories. The prepared logic fragments are independent from any target field, therefore they can be reused for ATF in different fields. Phase 2 is to prepare empirical premises of the target theory and draw up a plan to use collected empirical theorems. In detail, we prepare (k, m)-fragment of collected empirical premises in the target field to define a semi-lattice. A set of the prepared fragments and inclusion relation on the set is a partial order set, and is a finite semi-lattice. Moreover, a set of formal theories with the fragments and inclusion relation on the set is also a partial order set, and is also a finite semi-lattice. Partial order of the set of the prepared fragments can be used for a plan to reason out fragments of formal theories with collected empirical premises. According to the partial order, we can systematically do ATF from simple theorems to complex theorems.

Phase 3 to phase 5 are performed repeatedly until deducing all fragments of formal theory that have been planned in phase 2. In this methodology, loop means doing phase 3 to phase 5 at once. We use one of (k, m)-fragment of collected empirical premises to perform phase 3 to phase 5 in one loop. In detail, we firstly use lowest level fragment of premises to reason out empirical theorems. Then, we enter into phase 4 to abstract deduced empirical theorems, and then enter into phase 5 to find new and interesting theorems from empirical theorems. After that, we go back to the phase 3, and use the next level fragment of premises and theorems obtained in last loop as premises of this loop. Then, we enter into phase 4 and phase 5 to abstract theorems and find interesting theorems again. We repeat the loops until all of the (k, m)-fragment of collected empirical premises have been used.

4 Case Study of ATF in Tarski's Geometry

The purpose of the case study is to show the generality of our methodology. We performed the case study according to our methodology. Phase 1 is to prepare logical fragments of strong relevant logic. We prepared logical fragments in the case study of axiomatic set theory [3] and those logic fragments can be reused in the case study. Phase 2 is to prepare the empirical premises of Tarski's Geometry. Quaife [14] recorded axioms and definitions of Tarski's geometry in his book. In the case study, we chose those axioms and definitions in Quaife's book as empirical premises of the case study. Then, we defined the (k, m)-fragment of collected empirical premises according to the proposed methodology. In detail, first we summarized all of the predicate abstract levels in the formalized definitions as shown in Table 1. Second, we summarized all of the function abstract levels in the formalized definition as shown in Table 2. Third, we defined the (k, m)-fragment of collected empirical premises in Tarski's Geometry as shown in Table 3.

Table 1 Predicate abstract level in Tarski's Geometry

Predicate	Abstract from	Abstract level
≡	None	1
=	None	1
Between	None	1
Collinearity	Between	2

Table 2 Function abstract level in Tarski's Geometry

Function	Abstract from	Abstract level
line	None	1
ext	None	1
innerpasch	None	1
euclid	None	1
euclid'	None	1
cont	None	1
insertion	ext	2
reflection	ext	2

Table 3 The (k, m)-fragment in Tarski's Geometry

(k, m)-fragment	Subset of (k, m)-fragment
$P(1, 1)$	Axiom1–Axiom11
$P(1, 2)$	$P(1, 1)$, definition of reflection, insertion
$P(1, 0)$	Definition of collinearity
$P(2, 1)$	$P(1, 1)$, $P(2, 0)$
$P(2, 2)$	$P(1, 2)$, $P(2, 1)$

Table 4 The results of the case study

Used logic fragments	Obtained empirical theorems
$Th^{(\Rightarrow, 2)}(EeQ)$	56
$Th^{(\Rightarrow, 3)}(EeQ)$	342
$Th^{(\Rightarrow, 2, \neg, 1)}(EenQ)$	74
$Th^{(\Rightarrow, 3, \neg, 1)}(EenQ)$	1767
$Th^{(\Rightarrow, 2, \neg, 1, \wedge, 1)}(EcQ)$	143

From Phase 3 to Phase 5, we performed deduction, abstraction, and finding of theorems. We used the general reasoning engine FreeEnCal [15] as the tool. In detail, we used the prepared logic fragments from small to large according to the defined semi-lattice of strong relevant logic [3] as logic premises, and used (k, m)-fragments of collected empirical premises of Tarski's Geometry from lower abstract level to higher abstract level as empirical premises to perform ATF. Then, we showed the results of the case study in Table 4.

The case study shows that our methodology holds generality. By using our methodology, we defined the (k, m)-fragments of empirical premises of Tarski's Geometry well and the case study were performed systematically in each phase. Besides, the theorems reasoned out in the case study are all based on forward reasoning approach such that we may find unknown theorems in the reasoned out set of theorems. Because our approach provides a continuous and systematic way to prepare the logic fragments and use them to do ATF in geometry, if we do ATF by using our approach continuously, it is possible to find a new and interesting theorem of geometry in the future.

49152

5 Concluding Remarks

We have presented a case study of ATF by using forward reasoning approach based on strong relevant logic in Tarski's Geometry, and showed the generality of our proposed methodology through the case study.

Cheng has proposed a semi-lattice model of formal theories [16], which can support forward reasoning approach based on strong relevant logic to do ATF in multi-fields. The core of the model is strong relevant logic and axiomatic set theory is seen as the minimum element in the semi-lattice, and other formal theories can be established on the axiomatic set theory. We will do ATF in Hilbert's axiomatic geometry, lattice theory, and group theory based on the proposed model in future.

References

1. Wos L (1988) Automated reasoning: 33 basic research problem. Prentice-Hall, Upper Saddle River
2. Wos L (1993) The problem of automated theorem finding. J Autom Reasoning 10(1):137–138
3. Gao H, Goto Y, Cheng J (2014) A systematic methodology for automated theorem finding. Theoret Comput Sci 554:2–21
4. Gao H, Goto Y, Cheng J (2014) Research on automated theorem finding: current state and future directions. In: Proceedings of the 9th FTRA international conference, FutureTech 2014, LNEE, vol 309. Springer, Heidelberg, pp 105–110
5. Colton S, Meier A, Sorge V, McCasland R (2004) Automatic generation of classification theorems for finite algebras. In: Automated reasoning, LNCS, vol 3097. Springer, Heidelberg, pp 400–414
6. McCasland R, Bundy A, Autexier S (2007) Automated discovery of inductive theorems. J Stud Logic Grammar Rhetoric 10(23):135–149
7. Recio T, Velez MZ (1999) Automatic discovery of theorems in elementary geometry. J Autom Reasoning 23(1):63–82
8. Tang P, Lin F (2011) Discovering theorems in game theory: two-person games with unique pure nash equilibrium payoffs. Artif Intell 175(14):2010–2020
9. Cheng J (1994) A relevant logic approach to automated theorem finding. In: The workshop on automated theorem proving attached to international symposium on fifth generation computer systems, pp 8–15
10. Cheng J (1995) Entailment calculus as the logical basis of automated theorem finding in scientific discovery. In: Systematic methods of scientific discovery: papers from the 1995 spring symposium, AAAI Press—American Association for Artificial Intelligence, pp 105–110
11. Cheng J (2000) A strong relevant logic model of epistemic processes in scientific discovery. In: Information modelling and knowledge bases XI. Frontiers in artificial intelligence and applications, vol 61. IOS Press, pp 136–159
12. Gao H, Goto Y, Cheng J (2015) Automated theorem finding by forward reasoning based on strong relevant logic: a case study in graph theory. In: Advanced multimedia and ubiquitous engineering—future information technology, LNEE, vol 352. Springer, Heidelberg, pp 23–30
13. Tarski A, Givant S (1999) Tarski's system of geometry. Bull Symbolic Logic 5(2):175–214
14. Quaife A (1992) Automated development of fundamental mathematical theories. Kluwer Academic, Dordrecht

15. Cheng J, Nara S, Goto Y (2007) FreeEnCal: a forward reasoning engine with general-purpose. In: The 11th international conference on knowledge-based intelligent information and engineering systems, LNCS (LNAI), vol 4693. Springer, Heidelberg, pp 444–452
16. Cheng J (2007) A semilattice model for the theory grid. In: Proceedings of the 3rd international conference on semantics, knowledge and grid, IEEE Computer Society, pp 152–157

The Potential of mCommerce for Seniors in Developed Countries

Petra Maresova and Blanka Klimova

Abstract An important trend in the area of IT at present are mobile technologies and mCommerce. They can be also exploited by seniors who in developed countries are becoming to be perceived as a new group of potential customers and users in all areas of human activities, including ICT. The aim of this article is to describe a potential of mCommerce for seniors whose number in the developed countries will be increasingly rising. The methods used for this study include a retrospective analysis of available sources in the area of the use of ICT by seniors, a data analysis from the world's databases (Eurostat, WHO) and an analysis of the external environment of ICT sector based on the previous studies. The findings show that the main benefits for the seniors in the use of mCommerce seem to be direct and fast accessibility to information, comfortable electronic payment transactions, cuts of variable costs, and thus the overall improvement of quality of life. On the contrary, the main obstacles include security and trust issues, mobile device limitations and marketing challenges.

Keywords ICT · mCommerce · Seniors · SWOT analysis

1 Introduction

An important trend in the area of IT at present are mobile technologies and mCommerce. They can be also exploited by the seniors who in the developed countries are becoming to be perceived as a new group of potential customers and users in all areas including ICT. Current demographic trend, especially in the developed countries, but also globally, is characterized by an aging population. The

P. Maresova · B. Klimova (✉)
Faculty of Informatics and Management, University of Hradec Kralove,
Rokitanskeho 62, Hradec Kralove, Czech Republic
e-mail: blanka.klimova@uhk.cz

P. Maresova
e-mail: petra.maresova@uhk.cz

© Springer Science+Business Media Singapore 2016
J.J. (Jong Hyuk) Park et al. (eds.), *Advanced Multimedia and Ubiquitous
Engineering*, Lecture Notes in Electrical Engineering 393,
DOI 10.1007/978-981-10-1536-6_9

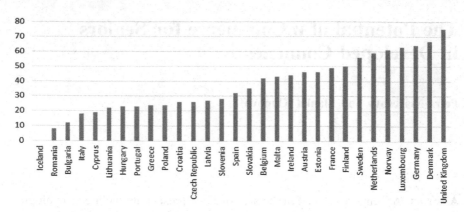

Fig. 1 Individuals having ordered/bought goods or services for private use over the internet in the last three months (in %). *Source* Own according to Eurostat [3]

proportion of people over 80 years will be doubled according to the estimates for 2050. A similar ratio applies to the seniors older than 65 years [1, 2].

The exploitation of mCommerce in the developed countries is becoming increasingly popular. Figure 1 illustrates the use of the Internet by private persons for buying goods and services. This is one of the possible indicators of the development of mCommerce. There are significant differences within the European countries, which is affected by the economic situation and the growth of GDP.

The aim of this article is to describe a potential of mCommerce for the seniors whose number in the developed countries is tremendously rising. Thus, the technologies are characterized with respect to the seniors and their specific needs.

2   Method

In this article the methods of an analysis of the accessible sources in the area of the ICT use by the seniors, a data analysis from the world's databases (Eurostat, WHO) and an analysis of the external environment of ICT sector based on the previous studies [4, 5] are applied. The data from the databases are expressed in histograms and tables. Due to the limited scope of this article, only the main results are described.

3 Mobile Devices and mCommerce for Seniors

3.1 Specification of Mobile Devices and mCommerce and Their Use at Present

A mobile device is a small transmittable electronic wireless device with its own power supply and different applications. It is often equipped with a touch screen or miniature keyboard. The most common mobile devices include smart phones, notebooks, netbooks, PDA and readers of electronic books. There is an increasing number of individuals and companies which own them. In this way they have new possibilities of communication with customers, offering tailored-made services or remote solution to problems, which is particularly what the seniors need.

Mobile business is a relatively new area of computer science, which is connected with the use of mobile networks. The key turning point in its development started in the second half of the 90s of the 20th century. Thus, mCommerce is a set of company's processes performed via mobile technologies. It represents a new communication channel for electronic business, particularly in B2B (business to business) a B2C (business to customer). According to Sadeh [6], mCommerce is a set of applications and services which are accessible from the mobile devices that enable access to the Internet. mCommerce thus represents any transactions with a money value which is carried out via a mobile communication network.

The implementation of mCommerce in company's business activities represents changes in business processes as well as in company's organization. These changes in processes must run with respect to the data security. Also the authorization of the access to the information sources and uniformity of terminal equipment. The advantage is simplicity of the use of the channel for users and interactive data transmission. The first area where mCommerce found its use was a sale of games and music. Gradually, mCommerce expanded its activities into the field of mobile payments, shopping, purchasing, auction, tracking, marketing, navigation or access to the company's network. Moreover, it started to offer a mobile healthcare, which is especially targeted at older generation in order to improve quality of their life.

3.2 mCommerce and Its Use by Elderly People

Benefits of mobile technologies are closely connected with the benefits of mCommerce. Sometimes these two areas from the business point of view are intertwined because the mobile devices themselves without a specific use in business would not record any competitive benefit. The main benefits of mCommerce are thus as follows:

- a higher level of personalization (following the identification),
- a possibility of personal approach to a seniors on the basis of one-to-one marketing,
- increasing comfort and communication with family members,
- shortening of time for handling an order if it is placed in the field.

Of course, there are certain problematic issues in the use of mCommerce. These mainly include limitations on the side of mobile devices:

- a size of display and its resolution,
- uncomfortable data entry (small, reduced keyboard),
- language localization—imperfect localization of operation systems and software applications,
- a relatively big variability of technological platforms—it represents a complication for developers who must adjust mobile applications for a big number of technological platforms,
- impact of connection speed,
- dependence on the device and period of battery life.

At present there are many companies which have already described and measured benefits of the use of mobile devices. For example, a Japanese company selling used cars has increased an amount of its orders by 20–30 % in this way. In addition, companies in the building or health industry have recorded acceleration of some processes and better communication with customers including old people.

4 Results—SWOT Analysis

Mobile devices and m-Commerce may bring a lot of advantages to old people. The following SWOT analysis summarizes these advantages as well as the risks. All factors in individual parts of SWOT analysis have been divided in two subgroups. The first subgroup includes items that characterize the background of mobile technologies/mCommerce in connection to old people in the developed countries. The latter subgroup focuses on the technology itself [7–9] (Table 1).

As the SWOT analysis indicates, there are both positive and negative aspects of the use of mCommerce by the older generation. The key advantages seem to be direct and fast accessibility to information, comfortable electronic payment transactions, cuts of variable costs, and thus the overall improvement of quality of life. On the contrary, the main obstacles include security and trust issues, mobile device limitations and marketing challenges.

Table 1 SWOT analysis of the benefits and risks of the use of mCommerce for the seniors

Strengths	Weaknesses
Macroeconomic factors in the developed countries with respect to the needs of old people: • high market penetration with mobile devices (above all phones)—expansion of offer for the seniors • relatively good ICT infrastructure • educating seniors about the mobile services Qualities of the technology • interaction, dialogue with the older generation • specific tailor-made solutions to the requirements of the seniors • personalization—possibility to react to individual suggestions • possibility to flexibly adjust prices of products • seniors can easily compare prices • access distant shops • speed, efficiency, direct accessibility of data	Macroeconomic factors in the developed countries with respect to the needs of old people: • limited domestic market • limited R&D expenditures • companies lack willingness to risk and invest in new technologies • low focus of research activities on this field Qualities of the technology • limited size of display • insufficient endurance of the accumulator • need for the internet connectivity • limited computing capacity of mobile devices • lower security of transmissions less frequent use of antivirus solutions • not all mobile devices support mCommerce tools • lack of personal contact with the customer/a senior • some products cannot be seen and tested before their purchase
Opportunities	Threats
Macroeconomic factors in the developed countries with respect to the needs of old people: • the Internet and globalization facilitates entering new markets • wider use of mobile technologies by seniors everywhere in the world • gradual reduction of rates for using mobile operators' services • competitiveness of small as well as large companies Qualities of the technology • low input costs and scalability of software • lowering operating costs • possibility of attractive presentation of goods • use of predictive search for goods • use in education • possibility to provide special communication, support and services to the handicapped and seniors	Macroeconomic factors in the developed countries with respect to the needs of old people: • global market is occupied by large companies and well-known brands • disreputable electronic shops • unwillingness to engage in new approaches, aversion to changes (force of habit...) Qualities of the technology • communication via mobile devices can be regarded as spam • fear of data abuse, necessity to solve data security to a wider extent • loss or theft of mobile phone implies a much higher risk • some types of goods have longer terms of delivery than common shops • it is more complicated to lodge a claim • more difficult solution of non-standard and non-defined services • legal limitations

5 Conclusion

Although the seniors still lag in the use of mCommerce behind the younger generation, they are becoming interested in this type of service. The reason is that most of the present seniors aged 55 have been already active users of mobile devices, including smartphones [10]. In addition, trading companies in the developed countries see a big potential in this group of population and attempt to adapt their products and services to the seniors' physical, cognitive, economic and social needs [11].

Acknowledgments This paper is published thanks to the support of the internal projects of University of Hradec Kralove: Economic and Managerial Aspects of Processes in Biomedicine.

References

1. WHO (2012) In dementia a public health priority. Available from http://apps.who.int/iris/bitstream/10665/75263/1/9789241564458_eng.pdf. Accessed 14 Dec 2015
2. OECD (2015) Database data in: population development, historical data and forecast. Available from http://stats.oecd.org/#. Accessed 14 Dec 2015
3. Eurostat (2015) ICT industry. Available from http://ec.europa.eu/eurostat. Accessed 14 Dec 2015
4. Marešová P, Hálek V (2014) Deployment of cloud computing in small and medium sized enterprises in The Czech Republic. E+M Econ Manage 17(4):159–174
5. Marešová P (2013) Potential of ICT for business in the Czech Republic. Professional Publishing
6. Sadeh N (2002) M-commerce: technologies, services, and business models. John Wiley, New York
7. Oganesjan N (2013) Soudobé trendy v oblasti prostředků mobilních informačních a komunikačních technologií, Systémová integrace. Available from http://www.cssi.cz/cssi/soudobe-trendy-v-oblasti-prostredku-mobilnich-informacnich-komunikacnich-technologii. Accessed 14 Dec 2015
8. Felicitta J, Gnana JJ (2009) The impact of M-Commerce in global perspectives A SWOT analysis. In: Proceedings of the 8th WSEAS international conference on electronics, hardware, wireless and optical communications, pp 76–80
9. Niranjanamurthy M et al (2013) Analysis of e-commerce and m-commerce: advantages, limitations and security issues. Int J Adv Res Comput Commun Eng 2:2360–2370
10. Adults' Media Use and Attitudes Report 2014 (2014) Available from http://stakeholders.ofcom.org.uk/market-data-research/other/research-publications/adults/adults-media-lit-14/. Accessed 14 Dec 2015
11. McGaughey RE, Zeltmann SM, McMurtrey ME, Downey JP (2012) M-Commerce and the elderly: the current state of affairs. Available from http://www.swdsi.org/swdsi2012/proceedings_2012/papers/Papers/PA141.pdf. Accessed 14 Dec 2015

A Supporting Environment for Contract-Based Programming with Ada 2012

Bo Wang, Hongbiao Gao and Jingde Cheng

Abstract The latest version of programming language Ada, Ada 2012, has introduced the concept of contract-based programming (CBP) and became the first internationally standardized programming language to include CBP as an intrinsic feature of the language. CBP can strictly stipulate and assure the correctness of programs to enhance the reliability and security of safety-critical systems, due to terrible design and/or programming practice, there is an issue that it might obstruct some other factors of the software quality. Therefore, it is essential to implement a supporting environment for CBP with Ada 2012 in order to not only retain reliability by using CBP, but also avoid taking interference to other factors of software quality. Until now, there is no report for proposing supporting environments or tools for CBP, while most studies focus on how to check the conditions of contracts, i.e., what contracts should do for software engineering activities. To support CBP with Ada 2012, this paper analyzes the issues that CBP disturbs some other factors of software quality, proposes methods to avoid the issues, and shows a supporting environment for CBP in Ada 2012 programs.

Keywords Ada 2012 · Contract-based programming · Supporting environment

B. Wang · H. Gao · J. Cheng (✉)
Department of Information and Computer Sciences,
Saitama University, Saitama 338-8570, Japan
e-mail: cheng@aise.ics.saitama-u.ac.jp

B. Wang
e-mail: wangbo@aise.ics.saitama-u.ac.jp

H. Gao
e-mail: gaohongbiao@aise.ics.saitama-u.ac.jp

© Springer Science+Business Media Singapore 2016   69
J.J. (Jong Hyuk) Park et al. (eds.), *Advanced Multimedia and Ubiquitous Engineering*, Lecture Notes in Electrical Engineering 393,
DOI 10.1007/978-981-10-1536-6_10

1   Introduction

A supporting environment can effectively improve software engineering activities and it is required more and more indispensable to enhance the software quality, which is influenced by reliability, functional suitability, performance efficiency, compatibility, usability, security, maintainability, and portability factors [1, 10].

In order to improve reliability and security of software quality, Contract-Based Programming [11] and Design by Contract™ [9] have been proposed. They can strictly stipulate and assure the correctness of programs, and thus the concept and methodology have been widely studied and adopted in the academic and industrial fields. With regard to CBP, generally speaking, we use the preconditions of the contracts to assure the correctness of parameters of subprograms, and we use the postconditions of the contracts to assure that the values returned from subprograms satisfy the requirements of the callers; Moreover, in many cases, we also use some contract conditions on the types in order to assure the correctness of the constructed objects, for example, type_invariant.

Furthermore, the latest version of the Ada programming language, Ada 2012, has been approved as an ISO/IEC international standard [11]. The most improvement of programming language Ada 2012 is supporting CBP, and more importantly, it is the first and the only one programming language, which makes the concept and methodology of CBP be an international standard [2, 3]. Ada 2012 supports the preconditions and postconditions of contracts for the subprograms (function, procedure). Meanwhile, it supports the Type_Invariant of contracts for the operations of types. In addition, Ada 2012 offers the static_predicate and dynamic_predicate of contracts for subtypes. Using these contract terms, we can better achieve the design goals of the software engineering projects, improve the reliability, safety, and security of the systems, and come out a better specification record. Moreover, the contract-based programming helps us debugging and supporting reuse. It is a prerequisite for software engineering activities.

However, although CBP is important to promote the reliability, security of software quality and is heavily used in practice, due to terrible design and/or programming practice with CBP, we are confronted with some issues [15]: (1) Contracts may expose private data; (2) The variables in contracts may be directly accessed; (3) The logics of contracts may be hardly understood; (4) Contracts that have complex definitions of models may hinder readability and maintainability; (5) Contracts that have unnecessary heavyweight style may obstruct CBP development and degenerate abstraction and readability; (6) Contracts may produce excess of redundant specifications.

With regard to the issues, there is no study about how to resolve them until now. Not only for reliability by using CBP, but also for avoiding taking interference to other factors of software quality, our goal is to provide a supporting environment to maintain and enhance CBP with Ada 2012. Although the contracts are written with specifications of subprograms, they influence the control flow and data flow of programs, because they are made a run-time check in term of a Boolean expression.

Therefore, we have to capture, identify, and analyze them from control flow and data flow.

Cheng has proposed Nondeterministic Parallel Control Flow Net (CFN), and Nondeterministic Parallel Definition-Use Net (DUN) [7], both are arc-classified digraphs, in order to represent concurrent and/or distributed programs. The CFN represents multiple control flows in a concurrent program as well as the single control flow in a sequential program. The DUN is an extension of CFN, such that it represents multiple control flows, definitions and uses of variables, and inter-process synchronization and communication in a concurrent program. Moreover, System Dependence Net [17] is a formal model which can present the program dependences and interprocedural relations in a concurrent program with multiple procedures.

In this paper, we propose a supporting environment for CBP with Ada 2012. Some static analysis tools of the supporting environment are proposed to support CBP with Ada 2012. By means of formal models of DUNs and SDNs, we extend their applications as a DUN generator, an SDN generator, and further there are some applications tools derived from DUN generators and SDN generators.

The rest of paper is organized as follows. Section 2 introduces contract-based programming with Ada 2012 and gives the issues of contracts for Ada 2012 because of bad design and practice. Section 3 shows a supporting environment for contract-based programming with Ada 2012. Finally, Sect. 4 shows concluding remarks.

2   Contract-Based Programming

2.1   Contract-Based Programming with Ada 2012

Programming language Ada, the next generation of the world's premier programming language for engineering safe, secure, and reliable software, has evolved to Ada 2012, i.e., the latest version of the Ada language standard [2, 3, 11]. It is intended for large and long-lived systems, and widely used in the worlds of high-integrity, safety-critical, high-security, which are closely related to commercial, military airborne avionics, air traffic control, railroad systems, and medical equipment [8]. Ada 2012 has a lot of changes and extensions from the previous version of Ada 2005, including a seismic shift for supporting contract-based programming explicitly, which effectively improves the reliability of a program [2, 8].

Robert Dewar gave an explanation as follows: "In the context of Software, a 'contract' is an assertion of some property of a program component reflecting a requirement that the component must meet" [8]. However, the notation came from the Eiffel that is a programming language, designed by Bertrand Meyer [13]. It is the first programming language introduced Design by Contract™ [9, 13]. In spite of this,

Ada is the first programming language that integrated the notion "contract-based programming" into an ISO/IEC international standard [2]. By contract-based programming, Ada can protect the program from incorrect composition at run time [2].

Programming language Ada 2012 introduced five types of contracts, which are precondition, postcondition, type_invariant, static_predicate, and dynamic_predicate, respectively [11]. In Ada 2012, one of the most important points is that using new syntax (using **with**) to introduce aspect specifications which enable certain properties of entities to be stated where they are declared rather than later using representation clauses. It is good to use pre- and postconditions for subprograms and similar assertions for types and subtypes with predicate.

A precondition is an obligation on the caller to ensure that it is true before the subprogram is called and it is a guarantee to the implementer of the body that it can be relied upon on entry to the body [2]; A postcondition is an obligation on the implementer of the body to ensure that it is true on return from the subprogram and it is a guarantee to the caller that it can be relied upon on return [2]; Type_Invariant specify some invariant properties of private types; Static_Predicate and Dynamic_Predicate are used to supply subtype declarations and type declarations as aspect specifications as a type of contracts [3].

2.2 The Issues in Contract-Based Programming

According to ISO/IEC 25010, software quality is required reliability, functional suitability, performance efficiency, compatibility, usability, security, maintainability, and portability to assess software systems for high-quality. Ada introduced CBP into the programming methodology for high-reliability, safety-critical, and security-critical programming, where Ada heavily affects. CBP helps review and understand the program, and facilitates to assure the correctness of safety-critical systems [2, 3, 8]. It is essential features for software development. However, duo to awful design and/or programming practice with CBP, CBP may bring us some issues, i.e., CBP could obstruct some other factors of software quality, which ISO/IEC 25010 requires, such as performance efficiency, compatibility, maintainability, readability, and portability [15].

CBP might cause some issues, which have been proposed in [15], such as: (1) contracts may expose private data, (2) the variables in contracts may be directly accessed; (3) the logics of contracts may be hardly understood; (4) contracts that have complex definitions of models may hinder readability and maintainability; (5) contracts that have unnecessary heavyweight style may obstruct CBP development and degenerate abstraction and readability; (6) contracts may produce excess of redundant specifications.

The first and second issues are that it is quite easy to access private or protected data in contracts, especially, the Type_Invariant contract condition in Ada that is given to private types. Sometimes we need to encapsulate some private types, however, when we use the Type_Invariant to limit invariant conditions of a private type, the internal data might be visible to outside, because developers must specify whether they can be modified or not.

The third issue is that it is quite difficult to understand the contract conditions if they are presented by terrible logics or long specification definitions. In that case, it is impractical for developers to understand the illogical contracts conditions. We need clear, concise, and logical contract conditions.

The fourth issue is that it is quite difficult to maintain and read the problems with CBP. Sometimes we need to maintain, restructure, even add features to some existing programs with CBP, called refactoring.

Refactoring is to change the source code without changing the behavior of the program [4]. In software development, as the creation of the source code advances, design changes and bug fixes tend to be the middle stage. This is becoming redundant. To solve the problem, making a flexibly rework source code accommodate the forthcoming specification of changes, called "refactoring". However, with regard to CBP, the contracts have been written for subprogram or types, that is, when we want to refactor some subprograms, we must remove and/or change the contracts of them. Moreover, the contracts are strongly correlated to subprograms. They result in that it is quite difficult to refactor the programs with CBP. Similarly, when we want to add and/or extend the features to the existing body of code, whose contracts have made some requirements for the bodies, we must tear up the contracts to sign and/or revise the contracts for new features of the bodies. However, the relationships have been proven with strong program dependences in CBP [16], which give rise to hardly adding the features with CBP. The reason is that statements do not independently exist in programs.

The fifth and sixth issues are that it is quite easy to disturb performance efficiency, compatibility, and portability of software quality. Sometimes, we encounter heavyweight contracts in programs, and thus it is hard to improve efficiency, because of run-time cost. Also, we could not process a compatibility issue, even portability issue, because of an excess of heavyweight or redundant contracts. Therefore, we need to achieve lean software development for CBP. Lean software development is about how to achieve breakthrough quality, savings, speed, and business value [14], where it has been defined seven principles to achieve "lean". For lean software development, it is necessary to resolve the issues from CBP.

3 A Supporting Environment for Contract-Based Programming with Ada 2012

3.1 An Overview

A supporting environment is an ideal solution to maintain and enhance contract-based programming with Ada 2012, and aid developers to prevent and/or resolve the issues of CBP. Besides, developers could use CBP as ever, but not to focus on the issues. The supporting environment consists of static tools and dynamic tools. Static tools process some static analysis of control flow and data flow of CBP with Ada 2012. They are represented by graph-theory formal models of DUNs and SDNs.

Based on DUNs and SDNs, one DUN generator and one SDN generator for CBP with Ada 2012, have been developed. They are basic components. From two static tools, furthermore, there are a program slicer and a complexity measure tool for CBP with Ada.

3.2   The Representation of Contract-Based Programming in Definition-Use Nets

Definition-Use Net (DUN) [7] is a graph-theoretical concurrent program representation. It is an arc-classified digraph, which has vertices representing program statements with information about definitions and/or uses of the values of variables, formal parameters of the subprograms, returned values from functions, actual parameters of subprogram call, and inter-process synchronization and communication, and arcs representing deterministic or non-deterministic control flow between vertices.

By exploiting it, we can acquire an explicit representation of control flow and data flow. It is very useful in high-integrated software development activities such as program dependence analysis, testing, debugging, and complexity measuring.

3.3   A Definition-Use Net Generator for Contract-Based Programming with Ada 2012

We present a method that could compute all kinds of vertices and arcs of DUNs of Ada 2012 programs, and then developed an ASIS-based tool to cope with syntax and semantics of Ada 2012. The Ada Semantic Interface Specification (ASIS) [12] is an ISO standard that defines an interface between Ada environments. The tool can gain considerable information, whose interfaces of ASIS installed as an Ada library.

The functions of the DUN generator are to generate DUNs of compilation units in the Ada environment. In order to generate DUNs from Ada 2012 programs, there are 6 functional components in a definition-use generator. The core component, called Ada2DUN, is invoking other five components, such as DUN_Handler, Gela_Ids, Stacks, V_Strings, and Id_List.

3.4 The Representation of Contract-Based Programming in System Dependence Nets

System Dependence Net (SDN) [17] is a formal model to explicitly represent program dependences and interprocedural relations in a concurrent program with multiple procedures. Program dependences are determined by control flow and data flow in the program [5].

Since capturing program dependences between statements of a program is indispensable to many software development activities. For contracts, there are some new program dependences [16], such as precondition dependence, postcondition dependence, and predicate dependence.

3.5 A System Dependence Net Generator for Contract-Based Programming with Ada 2012

When we present the definitions of various types of program dependences and interprocedural relations, we can construct a formal model (SDN) to depict dependence-based program representation explicitly.

The SDN generator can capture various program dependences, representing a data flow for generating program dependences from the result of the DUN generator in Ada 2012 programs.

3.6 A Program Slicer for Contract-Based Programming with Ada 2012

Program slicing is a method for automatically decomposing programs, and has been proven useful in many fields, such as debugging, cohesion measurement, comprehension, re-engineering and maintenance [6].

When there are numerous contracts in an Ada 2012 program, sometimes, we need to examine one or some special contracts, a program slicer that can slice contract-based programming, is needed. The purpose of program slicing is to eliminate the irrelevant parts of a program to a certain criterion to shrink the entire program automatically. With slices, it is easier to grasp main points of specified behaviors. Therefore, a program slicer could effectively resolve heavyweight style and excess of redundant specifications of CBP with Ada 2012. A program slicer for CBP with Ada 2012 should be developed.

4 Concluding Remarks

A supporting environment can effectively improve software engineering activities and it is required more and more indispensable to enhance the software quality, which depends on reliability, functional suitability, performance efficiency, compatibility, usability, security, maintainability, and portability factors.

Although Contract-Based Programming can reinforce the software system reliability, safety, and security, it produces a series of issues to obstruct some other factors of software quality, due to defective design and programming practice. In general, these programs are critical for safety-critical systems, we must pay special attention to these issues, and otherwise it will have a catastrophic impact on personal life safety.

In this paper, we have expounded some issues that might be produced by contract-based programming with Ada 2012, proposed a supporting environment for contract-based programming with Ada 2012, including various tools for contract-based programming with Ada 2012. Using this environment, contract-based programming with Ada 2012 can drastically improve the software quality in Ada 2012 programs.

As a future work, a method of deadlock prevention with CBP for Ada 2012 programs should be implemented.

References

1. Andrew B, Ekembe GN, Kerr A (2016) A dictionary of computer science. Oxford University Press, Oxford
2. Barnes J (2013) Ada 2012 rationale: the language—the standard libraries. Lecture notes in computer science/programming and software engineering. Springer, Berlin
3. Barnes J (2014) Programming in Ada 2012. Cambridge University Press, Cambridge
4. Beck M, Brant K, Opdyke J, Roberts W, Fowler D (1999) Refactoring: improving the design of existing code. Addison-Wesley Professional, Reading
5. Cheng J (1993) Process dependence net of distributed programs and its applications in development of distributed systems. In: Proceedings of 17th annual international computer software applications conference. IEEE Computer Society Press, Washington, DC, pp 231–240
6. Cheng J (1993) Slicing concurrent programs a graph-theoretical approach. In: Fritzson PA (ed) Proceedings of 1st international workshop on automated and algorithmic debugging, AADEBUG'93, Linkoping, Sweden, May 3–5, 1993. Lecture Notes in Computer Science, vol 749. Springer, Heidelberg, pp 223–240
7. Cheng J (1994) Nondeterministic parallel control-flow/ definition-use nets and their applications. In: Joubert GR, Trystram D, Prters FJ, Evans DJ (eds) Parallel computing: trends and applications. Elsevier Science Publishers B. V, North-Holland, pp 589–592
8. Dewar R Ada 2012: Ada with contracts. http://www.drdobbs.com/architecture-and-design/ada-2012-ada-with-contracts/240150569. Accessed at 3 Dec 2015
9. Eiffel software: building bug-free O-O software: an introduction to Design by Contract™ https://www.eiffel.com/values/design-by-contract/introduction/. Accessed at 3 Dec 2015

10. ISO/IEC: ISO/IEC 25010:2011 (en): systems and software engineering—systems and software quality requirements and evaluation (SQuaRE)—system and software quality models (2016)
11. ISO/IEC: ISO/IEC 8652:2012 (en): information technology—programming language—Ada (2012)
12. ISO/IEC: ISO/IEC 15291:1999 (en): Information technology—programming language—Ada semantic interface specification (ASIS) (2013)
13. Meyer B (1992) Applying "design by contract". Computer 25(10):40–51
14. Poppendieck M, Poppendieck T (2003) Lean software development: an Agile Toolkit. Addison-Wesley, Reading
15. Viana T (2013) A catalog of bad smells in design-by-contract methodologies with Java modeling language. J Comput Sci Eng 7(4):251–262
16. Wang B, Goto Y, Cheng J (2013) New types of program dependences and interprocedural relations in Ada 2012 programs. In: Proceedings of 4th IEEE international conference on software engineering and service science. IEEE Press, pp 718–723
17. Zhao J, Cheng J, Ushijima K (1996) System dependence net: an interprocedural program dependence representation for Occam2 programs. In: Noguchi S, Ota M (eds) Correct models of parallel computing. IOS Press, Amsterdam, pp 87–96

Economic and Technological Aspects of Business Intelligence in European Business Sector

Petra Maresova and Blanka Klimova

Abstract The development of ICT goes hand in hand with a rapid growth of company data volume. Much of the data contains valuable information, which can be used for the company's further development. The aim of this paper is to analyze the use of business intelligence in European business sector. Technological and economic aspects of the use of business intelligence will be described. The attention will also be focused on mobile BI. Moreover, in the end they will be summarized in the SWOT analysis. The used methods are analysis of the external environment and the subsequent SWOT (Strengths, Weaknesses, Opportunities, Threats) analysis. The external environment involves forces outside the ICT (information and communication technologies) sector in Europe that can potentially influence the use of business intelligence. The analysis shows that, given the corporate internet facilities in Europe, there is great potential for its use that is not currently used.

Keywords Business intelligence · Technological aspects · Europe · SWOT analysis

1 Introduction

Every company management aims to be fully aware of the current situation in the company. This knowledge consists of a lot of information from different sources—economy, production, trade, inventory, marketing, and so on. The development of ICT goes hand in hand with a rapid growth of company data volume. Much of the data contains valuable information, which can be used for the company's further development. The question remains, though, how to extract this information from

P. Maresova · B. Klimova (✉)
Faculty of Informatics and Management, University of Hradec Kralove,
Rokitanskeho 62, Hradec Kralove, Czech Republic
e-mail: blanka.klimova@uhk.cz

P. Maresova
e-mail: petra.maresova@uhk.cz

© Springer Science+Business Media Singapore 2016
J.J. (Jong Hyuk) Park et al. (eds.), *Advanced Multimedia and Ubiquitous Engineering*, Lecture Notes in Electrical Engineering 393,
DOI 10.1007/978-981-10-1536-6_11

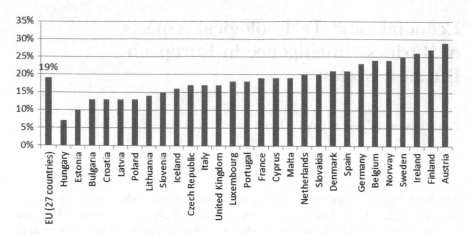

Fig. 1 Enterprises using chosen BI tools (in 2012). *Source* The author according to Eurostat [1]

the gathered data. In recent years the so-called Decision Support Systems (DSS) have gained ground. Tools of Business Intelligence (BI) belong to this category, together with Data Warehouse, which is a sort of data base. These systems enable companies to administer their data and extract strategic information from them.

Business intelligence is a tool which is used above all in companies. In fact, private companies are the main purchaser of these products. Graph 100 illustrates the BI utilization in Europe (Fig. 1).

As far as the utilization of BI tools in companies in the EU is concerned, Austria and Finland are at the top. The Czech Republic is slightly below the EU average with 17 % of companies utilizing these technologies. Hungary, Estonia and Bulgaria are at the bottom. The difference between the EU countries with the highest and lowest BI utilization is not as dramatic as it is in case of some other indicators. The aim of this paper is to analyze the use of business intelligence in European business sector. Technological and economic aspects of the use of business intelligence will be described. The attention will also be focused on mobile BI. Moreover, in the end they will be summarized in the SWOT analysis.

2   Method

The used methods are analysis of the external environment and the subsequent SWOT (Strengths, Weaknesses, Opportunities, Threats) analysis. The external environment involves forces outside the ICT (information and communication technologies) sector in Europe that can potentially influence the use of business intelligence. These analysis and the characteristics of the technology has been described in detail in the context of previous research [2]. Given the scale of this paper only the current situation of business intelligence use is described and then directly so-called SWOT matrix, where are summarized strengths, weaknesses, opportunities and threats of the given segment [3].

3 Technological Aspects of Business Intelligence

Data Warehousing Institute [4], a provider of educational and instructional pro-grammes in the field of Data Warehouse and BI, states that BI includes Data Warehouses, analytic tools and knowledge management. It points out two crucial factors: BI is more than a set of tools. It loses its value without relevant processes and users; the BI value is always realized in relation to a profitable company activity. In other words, if the knowledge that can be used for generating a prof-itable activity ignored, BI loses its significance. BI tools' function is based on certain principles, which are listed below [5–8]:

- multidimensionality—saved data can be viewed from different points of view, on different levels of detail,
- aggregation—it is possible to choose, according to dimensional hierarchy and structure, how detailed the given data representation should be,
- historical data—data is stored in the long term, which enables to use it for various time analyses and predictions,
- subject orientation—only data that is relevant for later analyses is stored.

BI system operates efficiently if certain technical preconditions have been ful-filled [9]: providing sufficient capacity for data storage, guaranteed data security, setting a sufficiently long time for storing data. It is also necessary to utilize methods for assessing whether and to what extent the targets are met. It is also vital to control BI functionality (e.g. by benchmarking). There are also factors that influence the success rate of BI implementation and operation as a [10]: quality of company management, quality of BI vision and strategy, identification of effects of the solution, definition of BI objectives and IS state and production data state. The tools and applications for Business Intelligence are expressed in the Fig. 2 [11].

Currently, it is becoming increasingly topical Mobile Business Intelligence extends traditional BI applications mobile devices. It is a technology suitable for a wide range of users who need access to BI functions also outside their office. Mobile BI solution should serve primarily to support its users' everyday company activities. Mobile BI application focuses on a smaller amount of information, which is chosen for its high utility value, which is limited by time. Mobile BI mission is not to substitute the role of the classical PC and traditional BI tools. It should help use accessible up to date information for immediate decision-making, better cooperation with colleagues, business partners and customers. Important prereq-uisites like high-speed internet connectivity, high-performance appliances, low charges, and other important aspects have become accessible only recently.

Fig. 2 Tools and
applications for business
intelligence. *Source* Own

The key improvements included the following areas:

- mobile phones and tablets—size of display, control, capacity; data transmission speed 2G–4G networks have gradually been increasing this speed; lowering costs (converted to the transmitted volume of data); infrastructure and signal coverage.

The utilization of BI and analytic tools on mobile platforms by means of either application or web interface has not become common, yet. In most companies (53 %) it is used by less than 10 % of users, in another 16 % of companies it is used by 10–25 % of users [12].

4 Use of Business Intelligence—SWOT Analysis in Europe Business Environment

Dubious economic situation emphasized the necessity and advantages of qualified decision making. Therefore, employees at all levels must have instruments facilitating better decision making. The SWOT analysis below lists and describes advantages as well as risks of the BI tools. Chosen parts of the analysis focus in detail on mobile Business Intelligence (Table 1).

The above mentioned analysis shows some recommendations. Companies have to consider what information to share with employees and other stakeholders. The managers have to support positive attitude of employees to business intelligence tools. And connect its use with mobile technologies to reach multiplicative positive effects.

Table 1 SWOT analysis of the benefits and risks of the use of business intelligence

Strengths	Weaknesses
• High penetration of mobile devices in households • Good accessibility of quality internet connectivity • Increased efficiency of labour through the integration of BI and source applications, convergence of technologies and tools • Facilitating faster decision making based on facts • Ability to categorize customers in groups • Possibility to better forecast events in the company • Fast deployment • Access to information in real time *Mobile BI* • Permanent access to up-to-date information and higher efficiency of labour • Simplicity—mobile BI is becoming user friendly. It is caused by limitations of the device as well as their purpose	• Low company investment in innovation • Need for permanent maintenance and information update • Limited utilization for SME • Difficult qualification of returns on investment (ROI) in BI, benefits emerge indirectly thanks to the fact that employees are better informed *Mobile BI* • Smaller display • Lower processing speed • Limited interactivity • Higher security requirements—needed authorization and access control • Need for supplementary infrastructure for implementation and administration
Opportunities	Threats
• People's growing ICT skills • Growing use of mobile devices • Development of social network utilization in business—possibility to aim at given segments and more efficient use of BI • Accessibility and utilization of BI tools from anywhere thanks to mobile technologies	• Underestimation of BI benefits for companies • Employees' resistance to new things • Little knowledge about developing possibilities of BI tools • Insufficient mapping of processes—in case of bad definition the system will not operate correctly • BI can bring additional work with feeding data • Data security

5   Conclusion

The aim of this paper was to analyze the use of business intelligence in European business sector. The fiercely competitive economic environment of the present day requires an emphasis on topical, relevant and reliable information. Business Intelligence shortens the time devoted to activities with low added value like data collecting and data summarization. BI provides the user with aggregated data with a possibility of drill-down view of details. Thus, it at the same time creates new options for the company to further increase its profitability and make adequate decisions. In fact, it is predicted to further develop, particularly in the direction of better accessibility of information in real time.

Acknowledgments This paper is published thanks to the support of the internal projects of University of Hradec Kralove: Economic and Managerial Aspects of Processes in Biomedicine.

References

1. Eurostat, ICT Industry (2015) Available from http://ec.europa.eu/eurostat. Accessed 14 Dec 2015
2. Marešová P, Hálek V (2014) Deployment of cloud computing in small and medium sized enterprises in the Czech Republic, E+ M Ekonomie a Manage 17(4):159–174
3. Marešová P (2013) Potential of ICT for business in the Czech Republic. Professional Publishing
4. Loshin D (2003) Business intelligence—the Savvy manager's guide. Getting onboard with emerging IT. Morgan Kaufmann Publishers, USA
5. Armburst M et al (2009) Above the clouds: a Berkeley view of cloud computing. Available from: http://www.eecs.berkeley.edu/Pubs/TechRpts/2009/EECS-2009-28.html. Accessed 14 Dec 2015
6. Goncalves V, Ballon P (2011) Adding value to the network: mobile operators' experiments with software-as-a-service and platform-as-a-service models. Telematics Inform 28(1):12–21
7. Marston S, Li Z, Bandyopadhyay S, Zhang A, Ghalsasi A (2011) Cloud computing—the business perspective. Decis Support Syst 1(51):176–189
8. Marešová P (2010) Knowledge managemet in the Czech companies. E+ M Ekonomie a Manage 13(1):131–143
9. Slánský D (2004) Řešení úloh Business Intelligence se zaměřením na prostředí telekomunikačních společností. Disertační práce, VŠE-FIS, Praha
10. Novotný O, Pour J, Slánský D (2005) Business intelligence, grada, Czech Republic
11. Business Intelligence: TDWI—The Data Warehousing Institute (2012). Available from: http://tdwi.org/portals/business-intelligence.aspx. Accessed 14 Dec 2015
12. Gartner (2013) Gartner says worldwide business intelligence software revenue to grow 7 percent in 2013. http://www.gartner.com/newsroom/id/2340216. Accessed 14 Dec 2015

A Dual-Process Technique for Risk Decision Making by Implicating Equate-to-Differentiate Approach

Yu Xiang, Lei Bai, Bo Peng and Li Ma

Abstract The mainstream risk decision making models, which follow the maximization rule, are based on the unbounded rationality hypothesis. However, the Equate-to-Differentiate model, which is a heuristic framework and follows the satisfaction rule, challenges these dominating models by proposing a bounded rationality approach. This study contributes to research on dual-process techniques by applying both models for explaining inference strategies that are used in individuals predicting and reasoning behaviors. To test its empirical validity, we demonstrate evidence that our model can account for real practical choices which are anomalies or paradoxes from the point of view of many other risk decision making models.

Keywords Dual-process · Risk decision making · Equate-to-differentiate

1 Introduction

The common denominator of most mainstream risk decision making (RDM) theories of human behavior is the premise that conflicts are mastered in a rational way which makes trade-offs between outcomes associated with each decision alternative and probabilities assigned to these outcomes. Such theories intend to believe that outcomes and related probabilities can be integrated into a compensatory decision value or utility on the basis of two processes known as weighting and summing [1], and intend to maximize the decision value or utility to provide preference ordering over alternatives. The family of integrative models includes Expected Utility Theory (EUT), Subjectively Weighted Utility (SWU),

Y. Xiang (✉) · L. Bai · B. Peng
School of Information Science and Technology, Yunnan Normal University,
Kunming, China
e-mail: iamlionx@126.com

L. Ma
Library of Kunming University of Science and Technology, Kunming, China

© Springer Science+Business Media Singapore 2016
J.J. (Jong Hyuk) Park et al. (eds.), *Advanced Multimedia and Ubiquitous Engineering*, Lecture Notes in Electrical Engineering 393,
DOI 10.1007/978-981-10-1536-6_12

Rank-Dependent Utility (RDU), Rank-and Sign-Dependent Utility (RSDU), original Prospect Theory (OPT), Cumulative Prospect Theory (CPT), Third-Generation Prospect (PT3), Rank Affected Multiplicative Weights (RAM), Transfer of Attention Exchange (TAX), Gains Decomposition Utility (GDU) and many others, which are slower, effortful, resource-dependent, rule-based, and controlled analytic systems [2].

Instead of postulating integration of decision information, some RDM theories are non-compensatory and treat outcomes and probabilities in a bounded rational way to acquire important behavioral decision properties called dimensions. Such theories assume that in making a decision people do not combine information from different dimensions, they only use one dimension at a time and will stop examination when the reasoning information from current dimension is satisficing to make a good-enough choice. Such non-integrative models includes Lexicographic Semi-orders (LS), Priority Heuristic (PH), Single-Dimension Heuristics (SDH) and Equate-to-Differentiate Theory (EtD), etc., which are relatively effortless heuristic systems that rest on prior knowledge, judgmental heuristics, and immediate experience [3, 4].

Although these two kinds of cognitive systems are sharply different in evolutionary histories, neurological substrates, and thinking and reasoning mechanisms, they essentially posit a fundamental idea that the human brain may be a dual system [5–7]. Thus, In recent years, dual-process theories of inference have received a large share of attention and become increasingly influential [8–11]. This is most probably related to the need to explain the apparent anomalies and paradoxes created by the discovery of a series of cognitive biases violating elementary rules of logic of many RDM models. In this paper, we will introduce a specific RDM computational architecture to experiment with the use of both integrative and non-integrative processes that based on EUT and EtD approaches to dominate an inference approximation model.

The following parts of this paper will review background on EUT, represent the semantics and the assessment procedures for EtD approach. Then the dual-process model on the basis of both EtD and EUT approaches will be introduced, and some of its behavioral aspects will be discussed either. Lastly, we will represent the practical operation and behavior of this RDM model and test its empirical validity by demonstrating evidence that it can account for real practical decision choices which are anomalies or paradoxes from the point of view of many RDM models.

2 Making One Decision by Two Minds

2.1 The Expected Utility Decision Making Framework

In 1947, Von Neumann and Morgenstern retained the main idea of the expected value theory and introduced the EUT which models expected utility (EU) by replacing objective monetary amounts with subjective utilities, and describing probabilities of possible outcomes with an objective probability function. EUT believes that, under certain axioms of rational behaviors, when a decision maker faced with risky (probabilistic) outcomes of different choices will behave as if he or she is maximizing the EU which is a totalled products of weights and values for each possible alternative, this means the individual will always prefer choices that maximize EU. For any decision alternative X, there will be a probability p_i assigned to one of its possible outcomes x_i, where $i = 1, \ldots, n$, then the utility value of x_i can be denoted as $u(x_i)$ and the resulting EU of alternative X can be defined as formula:

$$EU(X) = \sum_{i=1}^{n} p_i u(x_i) \qquad (1)$$

2.2 The Equate-to-Differentiate Decision Making Framework

As a non-integrative approach to human decision making, Li proposed the EtD model as a heuristic mean by which the dominance rule can be made applicable in more general cases. The main idea of EtD is called weak dominance strategy which states that if alternative A is at least as good as alternative B on all attributes, and alternative A is definitely better than alternative B on at least one attribute, then alternative A dominates alternative B. The EtD model postulates that, in order to utilize the very intuitive or compelling rule of weak dominance to reach a binary choice between A and B in more general cases, the final decision is based on detecting A dominating B if there exists at least one j and one i (known as the dimensions, where $i \neq j$ and $i,j = 1, \ldots, M$), such that $U_{Aj}(x_j) - U_{Bj}(x_j) > 0$ having subjectively treated all $U_{Ai}(x_i) - U_{Bi}(x_i) \leq 0$ as $U_{Ai}(x_i) - U_{Bi}(x_i) = 0$, and vice versa, where x_j and x_i indicate the objective values of each alternative on dimensions j and i.

The application of EtD principle is straightforward. In a representative RDM task, in order to utilize weak dominance to make a good-enough choice, people have to try hard to "equate" less significant difference between alternatives on either the best possible outcome dimension (BPO) or the worst possible outcome dimension (WPO), thus leaving the greater one-dimensional difference to be differentiated as the determinant of the final choice.

2.3 The Dual-Process Risk Decision Making Framework

It is not long after the EUT landmark book appeared, evidence emerged that people systematically violated EUT, and this evidence has accumulated in the subsequent decades. On the other hand, EtD model concerns only the best and the worst outcome dimensions but probabilities associated with them, which makes it struggle being utilized in RDM tasks. However, In this article, we pursue a new way to react to these disadvantages: to explain choice as the direct consequence of the use of both EUT and EtD processes. Take two-alternative choice problem for example, let X and Y be two alternatives, x_B and y_B be the best possible outcomes (BPO) from them, x_W and y_W be the worst possible outcomes (WPO) from them, p_B and q_B be the probabilities associated with the best possible outcomes (PBPO), p_W and q_W be the probabilities associated with the worst possible outcomes (PWPO). Thus, with four non-integrative dimensions, the dual-process RDM model consists of the following steps:

Step 1. In order to measure outcomes and probabilities in a unified dimensionless unit and facilitate inter-dimension comparisons, all dimensions must be normalized into the corresponding unified dimensions by following formulas:

$$\tilde{x}_{B,W} = \frac{x_{B,W}}{\max(|x_B|, |y_B|, |x_W|, |y_W|)}, \quad \tilde{y}_{B,W} = \frac{y_{B,W}}{\max(|x_B|, |y_B|, |x_W|, |y_W|)} \quad (2)$$

$$\tilde{p}_{B,W} = \frac{p_{B,W}}{\max(|p_B|, |q_B|, |p_W|, |q_W|)}, \quad \tilde{q}_{B,W} = \frac{q_{B,W}}{\max(|p_B|, |q_B|, |p_W|, |q_W|)} \quad (3)$$

Step 2. In order to utilize weak dominance rule to reach a decision, the significant differences between the two alternatives on each dimension must be computed by following formulas:

$$d_{BPO} = |\tilde{x}_B - \tilde{y}_B|, \quad d_{WPO} = |\tilde{x}_W - \tilde{y}_W| \quad (4)$$

$$d_{PBPO} = |\tilde{p}_B - \tilde{q}_B|, \quad d_{PWPO} = |\tilde{p}_W - \tilde{q}_W| \quad (5)$$

Step 3. Screen dimensions by "equating" dimensions with less significant difference and "differentiating" dimensions with the most significant difference, so that amount of information can be ignored, people only need to consult one or few reasons.

Step 4. Choose the alternative with the most attractive gain or probability. Here the term *attractive* refers to the alternative with higher minimum or maximum gain and lower probability of the minimum gain, or with the lower minimum or maximum loss and the higher probability of the minimum loss. More importantly, New integrative dimensions need to be examined to reach the decision while there are more than one non-integrative dimensions being differentiated. By using formula (1), these new integrative dimensions can accordingly be combined from following significant differences:

$$d_{BPO}^l = \tilde{x}_B - \tilde{y}_B, \quad d_{WPO}^l = \tilde{x}_W - \tilde{y}_W \quad (6)$$

$$d_{PBPO}^l = \tilde{p}_B - \tilde{q}_B, \quad d_{PWPO}^l = \tilde{p}_W - \tilde{q}_W \quad (7)$$

$$d_{BOBP}^{A} = \tilde{x}_B \times \tilde{p}_B + \tilde{x}_B \times \tilde{q}_B, \quad d_{BOBP}^{B} = \tilde{y}_B \times \tilde{p}_B + \tilde{y}_B \times \tilde{q}_B \qquad (8)$$

$$d_{BOWP}^{A} = \tilde{x}_B \times \tilde{p}_W + \tilde{x}_B \times \tilde{q}_W, \quad d_{BOWP}^{B} = \tilde{y}_B \times \tilde{p}_W + \tilde{y}_B \times \tilde{q}_W \qquad (9)$$

$$d_{WOBP}^{A} = \tilde{x}_W \times \tilde{p}_B + \tilde{x}_W \times \tilde{q}_B, \quad d_{WOBP}^{B} = \tilde{y}_W \times \tilde{p}_B + \tilde{y}_W \times \tilde{q}_B \qquad (10)$$

$$d_{WOWP}^{A} = \tilde{x}_W \times \tilde{p}_W + \tilde{x}_W \times \tilde{q}_W, \quad d_{WOWP}^{B} = \tilde{y}_W \times \tilde{p}_W + \tilde{y}_W \times \tilde{q}_W \qquad (11)$$

$$d_{BOBWP}^{A} = \tilde{x}_B \times (\tilde{p}_B - \tilde{p}_W), \quad d_{BOBWP}^{B} = \tilde{y}_B \times (\tilde{q}_B - \tilde{q}_W) \qquad (12)$$

$$d_{WOBWP}^{A} = \tilde{x}_W \times (\tilde{p}_W - \tilde{p}_B), \quad d_{WOBWP}^{B} = \tilde{y}_W \times (\tilde{q}_W - \tilde{q}_B) \qquad (13)$$

$$d_{BWOBP}^{A} = (\tilde{x}_B - \tilde{x}_W) \times \tilde{p}_B, \quad d_{BWOBP}^{B} = (\tilde{y}_B - \tilde{y}_W) \times \tilde{q}_B \qquad (14)$$

$$d_{BWOWP}^{A} = (\tilde{x}_W - \tilde{x}_B) \times \tilde{p}_W, \quad d_{BWOWP}^{B} = (\tilde{y}_W - \tilde{y}_B) \times \tilde{q}_W \qquad (15)$$

$$d_{BWOBWP}^{A} = \tilde{x}_B \times \tilde{p}_B + \tilde{x}_W \times \tilde{p}_W, \quad d_{BWOBWP}^{B} = \tilde{y}_B \times \tilde{q}_B + \tilde{y}_W \times \tilde{q}_W \qquad (16)$$

If two outcome or two probability dimensions are differentiated as the determinant of the final choice, depending on which pair of significant difference is compared, the integrative possible outcomes dimension $IPO = \{d_{BPO}^{I}, d_{WPO}^{I}\}$, or the integrative possible probabilities dimension $IPP = \{d_{PBPO}^{I}, d_{PWPO}^{I}\}$ can be defined by Eqs. (6) or (7). Then, people assume to choose the alternative with the most attractive return on IPO or IPP. Similarly, if one outcome and one probability dimensions are differentiated, then, proper significant differences pair can be compared according to Eqs. (8) to (11) to define the utility dimension $IU = \{d_{BOBP}^{A}, d_{BOBP}^{B}\}$, or $IU = \{d_{BOWP}^{A}, d_{BOWP}^{B}\}$, or $IU = \{d_{WOBP}^{A}, d_{WOBP}^{B}\}$, or $IU = \{d_{WOWP}^{A}, d_{WOWP}^{B}\}$. If three dimensions are differentiated, by using Eqs. (12) to (15), $IU = \{d_{BOBWP}^{A}, d_{BOBWP}^{B}\}$, or $IU = \{d_{WOBWP}^{A}, d_{WOBWP}^{B}\}$, or $IU = \{d_{BWOBP}^{A}, d_{BWOBP}^{B}\}$, or $IU = \{d_{BWOWP}^{A}, d_{BWOWP}^{B}\}$. And, by using Eq. (16), $IU = \{d_{BWOBWP}^{A}, d_{BWOBWP}^{B}\}$ when no dimension can be differentiated. People prefer alternative that maximizes the utility on the IU. This step gives the core of our dual-process model: **the more difficult to decide (differentiate), the more rationality be introduced.**

2.4 The Empirical Tests (Evidence)

The Allais Paradox. Following two pairs of choice problems produce violations of the EUT axiom: A(100 million, $p = 1.0$), B(500 million, $p = 0.1$; 100 million, $p = 0.89$; 0, $p = 0.01$), and C(100 million, $p = 0.11$; 0, $p = 0.89$), D(500 million, $p = 0.1$; 0, $p = 0.9$). The dual-process model, in contrast, makes strong prediction by normalizing alternatives to A(0.2, 1; 0.2, 1), B(1, 0.1; 0, 0.01) and C(0.2, 0.122; 0, 0.989), D(1, 0.111; 0, 1), differentiating dimensions PWPO = (1, 0.01) of

A and B, and BPO = (0.2, 1) of C and D, that people assume to chose A over B, and D over C, which accounts for the psychological result of empirical test done by [12].

The Reflection Effect. Here, the choice is between two gains or between two losses respectively: A(200,000, $p = 1.0$), B(400,000, $p = 0.5$; 0, $p = 0.5$), and C ($-200,000$, $p = 1.0$), D($-400,000$, $p = 0.5$; 0, $p = 0.5$). The dual-process mode differs A from B and D from C, which accounts for the psychological result of empirical test done by [13].

The Certainty Effect. Two simple demonstrations are: A(4000, $p = 0.8$; 0, $p = 0.2$), B(3000, $p = 1.0$), and C(4000, $p = 0.2$; 0, $p = 0.8$), D(3000, $p = 0.25$; 0, $p = 0.75$). The dual-process model selects the certain alternative B over A, and C over D, which accounts for the psychological result of empirical test done by [14].

The Possibility Effect. Two pairs of choice problems are: A(6000, $p = 0.45$; 0, $p = 0.55$), B(3000, $p = 0.9$; 0, $p = 0.1$), and C(6000, $p = 0.001$; 0, $p = 0.999$), D (3000, $p = 0.002$; 0, $p = 0.998$). The dual-process mode chooses B over A, and C over D, which accounts for the psychological result of empirical test done by [14].

The Fourfold Pattern. Four pairs of two-branch problems are: A(100, $p = 0.05$; 0, $p = 0.95$), B(5, $p = 1.0$), and C(100, $p = 0.95$; 0, $p = 0.05$), D(95, $p = 1.0$), and E(-100, $p = 0.05$; 0, $p = 0.95$), F(-5, $p = 1.0$), and G(-100, $p = 0.95$; 0, $p = 0.05$), H(-95, $p = 1.0$). The dual-process model chooses A over B, and D over C, and F over E, and G over H, which refers to the phenomenon that people are generally risk averse when the probability of winning is high but risk seeking when it is low, and risk averse when the probability of losing is low but risk seeking when it is high. This result accounts for the empirical test done by [15].

Intransitivities. To differ following five alternatives: A(5.00, $p = 0.29$; 0, $p = 0.71$), B(4.75, $p = 0.33$; 0, $p = 0.67$), C(4.50, $p = 0.38$; 0, $p = 0.62$), D(4.25, $p = 0.42$; 0, $p = 0.58$) and E(4.00, $p = 0.46$; 0, $p = 0.54$). The dual-process model selects A over B, B over C, C over D, D over E, but violates transitivity by selecting E over A, which results in the intransitive circle and accounts for empirical test done by [1]. And this demonstration shows that the dual-process model can also be applied to choose from a number of alternatives by comparing them in pairs to obtain the preference ordering.

3 Conclusion

This research aims to make a dual-process framework for RDM by using both the integrative EUT approach and the non-integrative EtD approach. And to test its empirical validity, feasibility and practicability, we demonstrate evidence that our dual-process model can account for real practical decision choices which are anomalies or paradoxes from the point of view of many other RDM models. Results show that our model typically consults only one or a few reasons without causing more computational burden than other RDM methods. The methodology of this dual-process model can be easily extended to various areas with RDM problems, so the further research may focus on the application of this new model.

References

1. Brandstätter E, Gigerenzer G, Hertwig R (2006) The priority heuristic: making choices without trade-offs. Psychol Rev 113:409–432
2. Birnbaum MH (2008) New paradoxes of risky decision making. Psychol Rev 115:463–501
3. Birnbaum MH (2010) Testing lexicographic semiorders as models of decision making: priority dominance, integration, interaction, and transitivity. J Math Psychol 54:363–386
4. Li S (2004) A behavioral choice model when computational ability matters. Appl Intell 20:147–163
5. Rustichini A (2008) Dual or unitary system? Two alternative models of decision making. Cogn Affect Behav Neurosci 8:355–362
6. Barrouillet P (2011) Dual-process theories of reasoning: the test of development. Dev Rev 31:151–179
7. Evans JSBT (2003) In two minds: dual-process accounts of reasoning. Trends Cogn Sci 7:454–459
8. Jun SH, Vogt C (2013) Travel information processing applying a dual-process model. Ann of Tourism Res 40:191–212
9. Evans JSBT (2010) Thinking twice: two minds in one brain. Oxford University Press, Oxford
10. Evans JSBT (2011) Dual-process theories of reasoning: facts and fallacies. In: Holyoak K, Morrison R (eds) The Oxford handbook of thinking and reasoning. Oxford University Press, New York
11. Gershman SJ, Markman AB, Otto AR (2012) Retrospective revaluation in sequential decision making: a tale of two systems. J Exp Psychol Gen. doi:10.1037/a0030844
12. MacCrimmon KR (1968) Descriptive and normative implications of the decision-theory postulate. In: Borch KH, Mossin J (eds) Risk and uncertainty. St. Martin's Press, New York
13. Rachlinski JJ (1996) Gains, losses, and the psychology of litigation. South California Law Rev 70:113–119
14. Kahneman D, Tversky A (1979) Prospect theory: an analysis of decision under risk. Econometrica 47:263–291
15. Tversky A, Fox CR (1995) Weighing risk and uncertainty. Psychol Rev 102:269–283

A Method for Knowledge Checking Service Selection with Incomplete Weight Information Based on the Grey Related Analysis and Data Envelopment Analysis in Fuzzy Environment

Ming Li, Yuqi Yu and Yingcheng Xu

Abstract The knowledge checking service (KCS) is critical for safeguarding the quality of knowledge. In organizations, there are many knowledge checking services with similar functions but different qualities, in order to select the best KCS, the method which combines grey related analysis (GRA) with data envelope analyzes (DEA) with incomplete weight information in fuzzy environment is proposed. In the method, the evaluation information is given linguistically and processed by the 2-tuple linguistic model and GRA. The DEA model is constructed to derive the precise weight information. Afterwards, by solving DEA model, the order of the alternatives can be derived. In the method, the combination of the advantages of DEA and grey correlation analysis leads to the avoidance of subjectivity and make the selection more accurately. The applicability of the proposed method is validated by an example.

Keywords Grey related analysis · Incomplete weight information · DEA · 2-tuple linguistic model · Knowledge checking service selection

1 Introduction

Knowledge is an important asset for organizations and the knowledge repository is constructed to store these valuable assets [1]. The quality of knowledge in the knowledge repository determines the effects of knowledge reusing. Checking knowledge is a feasible way to safeguard the quality of knowledge. In organiza-

---

M. Li · Y. Yu
School of Business Administration, China University of Petroleum,
Beijing, 102249, China

Y. Xu (✉)
China National Institute of Standardization, Beijing 100191, China
e-mail: politeperson@foxmail.com

© Springer Science+Business Media Singapore 2016
J.J. (Jong Hyuk) Park et al. (eds.), *Advanced Multimedia and Ubiquitous Engineering*, Lecture Notes in Electrical Engineering 393,
DOI 10.1007/978-981-10-1536-6_13

tions, there are many knowledge checking services with similar functions but different qualities. Non-functional QoS properties rely more on the perceptions of users. It is difficult to be assessed precisely with numeric values [2]. The linguistic terms are fitter for the evaluation of non-functional QoS properties [3, 4]. In the evaluation of KCS, the weight information is always given incompletely [5]. It means that the weight information is partially given in the form of linear inequalities such as rankings and interval descriptions instead of precise numbers.

In order to resolve the problem, we propose the KCS selection method in fuzzy environments with incomplete weight information. In the method, the linguistic evaluation information is processed by the 2-tuple linguistic model. The model is to be continuous in its domain and can express any counting of information in the universe of the discourse in fuzzy environments [4]. Similar to the work [5], the grey related analysis (GRA) method are used the aggregate of the linguistic evaluation which is given by group of people from multiple aspects. Based on the work [6], the data envelope analyzes (DEA) method is used to derive the precise weight information based on the incomplete weight information. Finally, the best alternative can be selected. The combination of GRA with DEA not only assures the objectivity when the weight vector is determined, but also ranks alternatives by non-uniform weight [6]. The rest of this paper is organized as follows. The next section constructs the new method. In Sect. 3, an example is given to illustrate the applicability of the proposed method. The final section makes conclusions.

2 The Method Combining Grey Related Analysis with DEA with Incomplete Weight Information in Fuzzy Environment

Let $A = \{A_1, A_2, \ldots, A_m\}$ be the set of alternatives, $C = \{C_1, C_2, \ldots, C_n\}$ be the set of criteria, and $E = \{E_1, E_2, \ldots, E_k\}$ be the set of experts. Suppose $R_k = (r_{ij}^{(k)})_{m \times n}$ is the group decision making matrix, where $r_{ij}^{(k)}$ is linguistic rating value given by the expert E_k, for the alternative A_i with respect to the criterion C_k. The information about criteria weights is incompletely known. Let $w = (w_1, w_2, \ldots, w_n) \in H$ be the weight vector of criteria, where $w_j \in [0, 1]$, $\sum_{j=1}^{n} w_j = 1$. The weight information is partially given in the following forms [7]. For $i \neq j$, form 1: A weak ranking: $w_i \geq w_j$; form 2: A strict ranking: $w_i - w_j \geq \alpha_i, \alpha_i > 0$; form 3: A ranking of differences: $w_i - w_j \geq w_k - w_l, j \neq k \neq l$; form 4: A ranking with multiples: $w_i \geq \beta_i w_j, 0 \leq \beta_i \leq 1$; form 5: An interval form: $\gamma_i \leq w_j \leq \gamma_i + \varepsilon_i, 0 \leq \gamma_i < \gamma_i + \varepsilon_i \leq 1$.

By extending the method [5, 6], the proposed method are given as follows.

Step 1 With the function θ, the linguistic decision matrix $(r_{ij}^{(k)})_{m \times n}$ is transformed into the 2-tuple linguistic decision matrix $R = (r_{ij}^{(k)}, 0)_{m \times n}$.

Step 2 With the arithmetic mean operator, the linguistic decision matrix R is aggregated into collective evaluation information matrix $R_0 = (r_{ij}, a_{ij})_{m \times n}$.

$$(r_{ij}, a_{ij}) = \Delta \left(\sum_{k=1}^{t} \frac{1}{t} \Delta^{-1} \left(r_{ij}^{(k)}, 0 \right) \right), \quad i = 1, 2, 3, \ldots, m; j = 1, 2, \ldots, n \quad (1)$$

Step 3 The fuzzy linguistic positive ideal solution (FLPIS) and fuzzy linguistic negative ideal solution (FLNIS) is defined as

$$(r^+, a^+) = \left((r_1^+, a_1^+), (r_2^+, a_2^+), \ldots, (r_n^+, a_n^+) \right) \quad (2)$$

$$(r^-, a^-) = \left((r_1^-, a_1^-), (r_2^-, a_2^-), \ldots, (r_n^-, a_n^-) \right) \quad (3)$$

For the benefit criterion,

$$\left(r_j^+, a_j^+ \right) = \max_i \{ (r_{ij}, a_{ij}) \}, \quad j = 1, 2, \ldots, n \quad (4)$$

$$\left(r_j^-, a_j^- \right) = \min_i \{ (r_{ij}, a_{ij}) \}, \quad j = 1, 2, \ldots, n \quad (5)$$

For the cost criterion,

$$\left(r_j^+, a_j^+ \right) = \min_i \{ (r_{ij}, a_{ij}) \}, \quad j = 1, 2, \ldots, n \quad (6)$$

$$\left(r_j^-, a_j^- \right) = \max_i \{ (r_{ij}, a_{ij}) \}, \quad j = 1, 2, \ldots, n \quad (7)$$

Step 4 The fuzzy linguistic grey relational coefficient of each alternative from LPIS and LNIS is derived by

$$\left(\rho_{ij}^+, \tau_{ij}^+ \right) = \Delta \left(\frac{\min_i \min_j \left| \Delta^{-1}(r_{ij}, a_{ij}) - \Delta^{-1}(r_j^+, a_j^+) \right| + \rho \max_i \max_j \left| \Delta^{-1}(r_{ij}, a_{ij}) - \Delta^{-1}(r_j^+, a_j^+) \right|}{\left| \Delta^{-1}(r_{ij}, a_{ij}) - \Delta^{-1}(r_j^+, a_j^+) \right| + \rho \max_i \max_j \left| \Delta^{-1}(r_{ij}, a_{ij}) - \Delta^{-1}(r_j^+, a_j^+) \right|} \right)$$

$$(8)$$

$$\left(\rho_{ij}^-, \tau_{ij}^- \right) = \Delta \left(\frac{\min_i \min_j \left| \Delta^{-1}(r_{ij}, a_{ij}) - \Delta^{-1}(r_j^-, a_j^-) \right| + \rho \max_i \max_j \left| \Delta^{-1}(r_{ij}, a_{ij}) - \Delta^{-1}(r_j^-, a_j^-) \right|}{\left| \Delta^{-1}(r_{ij}, a_{ij}) - \Delta^{-1}(r_j^-, a_j^-) \right| + \rho \max_i \max_j \left| \Delta^{-1}(r_{ij}, a_{ij}) - \Delta^{-1}(r_j^-, a_j^-) \right|} \right)$$

$$(9)$$

where, the value of the coefficient ρ is 0.5.

Step 5 The relational degree of each attributes from TLPIS is obtained by

$$\left(\rho_{ij}, \eta_{ij}\right) = \Delta \left(\frac{\Delta^{-1}(\rho_{ij}^+, \tau_{ij}^+)}{\Delta^{-1}\left(\rho_{ij}^+, \tau_{ij}^+\right) + \Delta^{-1}(\rho_{ij}^-, \tau_{ij}^-)} \right), \quad i = 1, 2, \ldots, m \quad (10)$$

Step 6 Establish DEA model for each alternative, then find the optimal solution for the optimal correlation.

$$\max \theta = \sum_{j=1}^{n} \omega_j \Delta^{-1}\left(\rho_{ij}, \eta_{ij}\right)$$

$$\text{s.t.} \begin{cases} \sum_{j=1}^{n} \omega_j \Delta^{-1}\left(\rho_{ij}, \eta_{ij}\right) \leq 1, & i = 1, 2, 3, \ldots, m \\ \omega_j \geq 0 \\ \{\omega_j\} \in H \\ \sum_{j}^{n} \omega_j = 1 \end{cases} \quad (11)$$

In the model, weight coefficient of each observation point is the decision variable, and its optimal value θ is the best relational degree of each alternative.

Step 7 Select the optimal solution

The best relational degree of each alternative is obtained by establishing a linear programming model in Step 6 for each alternative. Then the alternative with the optimal maximum correlation is selected as the optimal solution.

3 Numerical Examples

Let us suppose there is a virtual enterprise that needs to select the knowledge checking services among the set of services with similar functions but different qualities. Three KCSs denoted by A_1, A_2, A_3 are to be selected. The criteria includes runtime (G_1), transaction (G_2), cost (G_3) and security (G_4) [2]. Three experts E_k (k = 1, 2, 3) are invited to participate in decision. Both decision matrix and the incomplete attribute weights information are presented with 2-tuple linguistic terms. The term set S = {S_0 = Definitely Low (DL), S_1 = Very Low (VL), S_2 = Low (L), S_3 = Average (A), S_4 = High (H), S_5 = Very High (VH), S_6 = Definitely High (DH)} is used to give opinions.

The evaluation matrix of the alternatives given by three experts E_k ($k = 1, 2, 3$) are as follows:

$$R_1 = \begin{bmatrix} VH & EH & VL & H \\ H & VH & A & H \\ VH & EL & VH & M \end{bmatrix}, \quad R_2 = \begin{bmatrix} EH & L & M & EL \\ A & L & VH & H \\ VH & A & L & L \end{bmatrix},$$

$$R_3 = \begin{bmatrix} EH & L & L & VL \\ H & A & VL & EL \\ H & VH & A & VL \end{bmatrix}$$

The incomplete criteria weights information is given as follows:

$$\left\{ \begin{array}{c} (s_1, -0.4)w_1 \le (s_1, 0)w_2 \le (s_1, -0.2)w_1 \\ (s_1, 0)w_3 - (s_1, 0)w_2 \le (s_0, 0.2) \\ (s_0, 0.1) \le (s_1, 0)w_4 \le (s_0, 0.3) \end{array} \right\}$$

With Step 1 and Step 2, the collective evaluation information matrix is derived as

$$R_0 = \begin{bmatrix} (S_6, -0.33) & (S_3, 0.33) & (S_2, 0) & (S_2, -0.33) \\ (S_4, -0.33) & (S_3, 0.33) & (S_3, 0) & (S_3, -0.33) \\ (S_5, -0.33) & (S_5, -0.33) & (S_3, 0.33) & (S_2, 0) \end{bmatrix}$$

Then the relational degree of attributes from TLPIS is derived by step 3 to step 6, which is shown in Table 1.

Then the DEA model is construed as follows.

DEA model for A_1:

$$max\, \theta_1 = 0.7500\omega_1 + 0.2994\omega_2 + 0.3003\omega_3 + 0.3333\omega_4$$

$$s.t. \left\{ \begin{array}{c} 0.7500\omega_1 + 0.2994\omega_2 + 0.3003\omega_3 + 0.3333\omega_4 \le 1 \\ \omega_k \ge 0 \quad (k = 1, 2, 3, 4) \\ 0.6w_1 \le w_2 \le 0.8w_1 \\ w_3 - w_2 \le 0.2 \\ 0.1 \le w_4 \le 0.3 \\ \sum_{j}^{n} \omega_j = 1 \end{array} \right.$$

Table 1 Relational degree of each attribute from TLPIS

$\Delta^{-1}(\xi_{11}, \eta_{11})$	$\Delta^{-1}(\xi_{12}, \eta_{12})$	$\Delta^{-1}(\xi_{13}, \eta_{13})$	$\Delta^{-1}(\xi_{14}, \eta_{14})$
0.7500	0.2994	0.3003	0.3333
$\Delta^{-1}(\xi_{21}, \eta_{21})$	$\Delta^{-1}(\xi_{22}, \eta_{22})$	$\Delta^{-1}(\xi_{23}, \eta_{23})$	$\Delta^{-1}(\xi_{24}, \eta_{24})$
0.2500	0.2994	0.6006	0.333
$\Delta^{-1}(\xi_{31}, \eta_{31})$	$\Delta^{-1}(\xi_{32}, \eta_{32})$	$\Delta^{-1}(\xi_{33}, \eta_{33})$	$\Delta^{-1}(\xi_{34}, \eta_{34})$
0.5	0.7006	0.6997	0.4433

Table 2 Result of models

	Weight vector ω_k	Optimal relational degree
A_1	$\omega_1 = \{0.5625, 0.3375, 0, 0.1000\}$	0.5563
A_2	$\omega_2 = \{0.2692, 0.2154, 0.4154, 0.100\}$	0.4146
A_3	$\omega_3 = \{0.2692, 0.2154, 0.4154, 0.100\}$	0.6205

DEA model for A_2:

$$max\,\theta_1 = 0.2500\omega_1 + 0.2994\omega_2 + 0.6006\omega_3 + 0.3333\omega_4$$

$$s.t. \begin{cases} 0.2500\omega_1 + 0.2994\omega_2 + 0.6006\omega_3 + 0.3333 \leq 1 \\ \omega_k \geq 0 \quad (k = 1, 2, 3, 4) \\ 0.6w_1 \leq w_2 \leq 0.8w_1 \\ w_3 - w_2 \leq 0.2 \\ 0.1 \leq w_4 \leq 0.3 \\ \sum_j^n \omega_j = 1 \end{cases}$$

DEA model for A_3:

$$max\,\theta_1 = 0.5\omega_1 + 0.7006\omega_2 + 0.6997\omega_3 + 0.4433\omega_4$$

$$s.t. \begin{cases} 0.5\omega_1 + 0.7006\omega_2 + 0.6997\omega_3 + 0.4433\omega_4 \leq 1 \\ \omega_k \geq 0 \quad (k = 1, 2, 3, 4) \\ 0.6w_1 \leq w_2 \leq 0.8w_1 \\ w_3 - w_2 \leq 0.2 \\ 0.1 \leq w_4 \leq 0.3 \\ \sum_j^n \omega_j = 1 \end{cases}$$

By solving linear programming model, the results of three linear programming models are shown in Table 2.

The ranking all the alternatives accordance with the optimal relational degree of each alternative is $A_3 \succ A_1 \succ A_2$, and thus the most desirable alternative is A_3.

4   Conclusions

This paper provides a method combined GRA and DEA, which helps to select of the best KCS in fuzzy environment. The evaluation information is given linguistically and processed by the 2-tuple linguistic model. In the method GRA, the grey relational coefficient is used to represent the cohesion between ideal target sequence and each comparability sequence. By solving DEA model, not only the precise weight information is derived but also the orders of the alternatives are gotten. The method makes the selection more accurately and objectively.

Acknowledgments The research is supported by the National Natural Science Foundation of China under Grant No. 71101153, 71301152, 71571191 and Science Foundation of China University of Petroleum, Beijing (No. 2462015YQ0722), Humanity and Social Science Youth Foundation of Ministry of Education in China (Project No. 15YJCZH081, 13YJC790112)

References

1. Alavi M, Leidner DE (2001). Review: knowledge management and knowledge management systems: conceptual foundations and research issues. MIS Q 107–136
2. Wang P (2009) QoS-aware web services selection with intuitionistic fuzzy set under consumer's vague perception. Expert Syst Appl 36(3):4460–4466
3. Xu Z (2004) A method based on linguistic aggregation operators for group decision making with linguistic preference relations. Inf Sci 166(1):19–30
4. Herrera F, Martínez L (2000) A 2-tuple fuzzy linguistic representation model for computing with words. IEEE Trans Fuzzy Syst 8(6):746–752
5. Wei GW (2011) Grey relational analysis method for 2-tuple linguistic multiple attribute group decision making with incomplete weight information. Expert Syst Appl 38(5):4824–4828
6. Wu DD, Olson DL (2010) Fuzzy multi-attribute grey related analysis using DEA. Comput Math Appl 60(1):166–174
7. Kim SH, Ahn BS (1999) Interactive group decision making procedure under incomplete information. Eur J Oper Res 116(3):498–507

A Secure Range Query Processing Algorithm for the Encrypted Database on the Cloud

Hyeong-Il Kim, Munchul Choi, Hyeong-Jin Kim and Jae-Woo Chang

Abstract Secure range query processing algorithms have been studied as the range query can be used as a baseline technique in various fields. However, when processing a range query, the existing methods fail to hide the data access patterns which can be used to derive the actual data items and the private information of a querying issuer. The problem is that the data access patterns can be exposed even though the data and query are encrypted. So, in this paper we propose a new range query processing algorithm on the encrypted database. Our method conceals the data access patterns while supporting efficient query processing by using our proposed encrypted index search scheme. Through the performance analysis, we show that the proposed range query processing algorithm can efficiently process a query while hiding the data access patterns.

Keywords Database outsourcing · Database encryption · Encrypted index structure · Secure range query processing · Data access patterns

1 Introduction

With the development of cloud computing, a data owner can outsource his/her database and their managements to a cloud. By outsourcing the database, the data owner can flexibly utilize the resource of the cloud, thus reducing the management

H.-I. Kim · M. Choi · H.-J. Kim · J.-W. Chang (✉)
Department of Computer Engineering, Jeonbuk National University,
Jeonju, South Korea
e-mail: jwchang@jbnu.ac.kr

H.-I. Kim
e-mail: melipion@jbnu.ac.kr

M. Choi
e-mail: oopsmun@jbnu.ac.kr

H.-J. Kim
e-mail: yeon_hui4@jbnu.ac.kr

© Springer Science+Business Media Singapore 2016   101
J.J. (Jong Hyuk) Park et al. (eds.), *Advanced Multimedia and Ubiquitous Engineering*, Lecture Notes in Electrical Engineering 393,
DOI 10.1007/978-981-10-1536-6_14

costs. The cloud not only stores the database, but also provides an authorized user with querying services on the outsourced database. However, if the original database is outsourced to the cloud, the cloud or an attacker can abuse the private information stored in the database. For example, if a real estate agent outsources his/her original database to the cloud, the cloud or an attacker can sell the property information to the other agents. In addition, the private information of a user can be revealed to the attacker. For example, if a user sends a query with his/her location information to use location-based services, the attacker can find places where the user frequently visit.

Meanwhile, a range query, one of the most typical query types, is widely used as a baseline technique in many fields. The range query finds all the data inside a given query range. However, some privacy threat can occur when issuing the range query. This is because a range information is closely related to the interest of a user.

Therefore, researches on the range query processing algorithms which consider the data privacy have been performed [1–5]. However, all the existing works fail to hide the data access patterns during the query processing. The data access patterns are the good source to derive not only the actual data items, but also the private information of a querying issuer. This is the critical problem because the data access patterns can be exposed even though the data and query are encrypted [6]. To the best of knowledge, a scheme proposed in [7] is the only work that hides the data access patterns over the encrypted database. However, the scheme only supports kNN query processing and requires high computation cost. To solve the problem, in this paper we propose a new range query processing algorithm on the encrypted database. Our method conceals the data access patterns while supporting efficient query processing by using our proposed encrypted index search scheme.

The rest of the paper is organized as follows. Section 2 introduces the related work and Sect. 3 presents the overall system architecture and secure protocols. In Sect. 4, we propose our secure range query processing algorithm based on the encrypted index. The performance analysis of our scheme is presented in Sect. 5. Finally, we conclude the paper with some future research directions in Sect. 6.

2 Related Work

Yiu et al. [1] proposed the cryptographic transformation (CRT) method which utilizes encrypted R-tree index. However, CRT cannot preserve the data access pattern as a user hierarchically requests the required R-tree nodes to the cloud. A scheme proposed by Hore et al. [2] partitions the data into a set of buckets and builds indices for buckets. However, a data owner should store and search the indices locally. In addition, the result of schemes in [1, 2] usually contains the false-positives. Wang et al. [3] proposed a scheme which utilizes the encrypted version of R-tree. However, the scheme has a shortcoming that a result contains many false-positives. In addition, the data access patterns are revealed because the cloud returns a set of nodes which intersect the query range. Wang et al. [4]

proposed an encrypted R-tree based range query processing scheme. However, the data access patterns are revealed to a cloud because all the identifiers of the data that satisfy the query are returned by the cloud. Most recently, Kim et al. [5] proposed a range query processing scheme using the Hilbert-curve order based index. However, the scheme has a problem that a user is in charge of index traversal during the query processing. In addition, the scheme leaks the data access pattern and the query result may contain false-positives.

Next, we briefly review the Paillier cryptosystem [8]. The Paillier cryptosystem is an additive homomorphic and probabilistic asymmetric encryption scheme for public key cryptography. The public key pk for encryption is given by (N, g), where N is a product of two large prime numbers p and q, and g is in $Z_{N^2}^*$. The secret key sk for decryption is given by (p, q). Let $E()$ denote the encryption function and $D()$ denote the decryption function. The Paillier crypto system has the following properties. (i) The product of two ciphertexts $E(m_1)$ and $E(m_2)$ results in the encryption of the sum of their plaintexts m_1 and m_2; $E(m_1 + m_2) = E(m_1)*E(m_2)$ mod N^2. (ii) The bth power of ciphertext $E(m_1)$ results in the encryption of the product of b and m_1; $E(m_1*b) = E(m_1)^b$ mod N^2. (iii) Encrypting the same plaintexts with the same public key results in distinct ciphertexts (aka 'semantic security').

3 System Architecture and Secure Protocols

The system consists of four components: data owner (DO), authorized user (AU), and two clouds (C_A and C_B, respectively). The DO owns the original database (T) of n records. A record t_i ($1 \leq i \leq n$) consists of m attributes and jth attribute value of t_i is denoted by $t_{i,j}$. To provide the indexing on T, the DO partitions T by using kd-tree. If we retrieve the tree structure in hierarchical manner, the access pattern can be disclosed. So, we only consider the leaf nodes of the kd-tree and all the leaf nodes are retrieved once during the query processing. Let h denote the level of the constructed kd-tree and F be the fanout of each leaf node. The total number of leaf nodes is 2^{h-1}. From now on, a node means a leaf node. Each node is represented as the lower bound $lb_{z,j}$ and the upper bound $ub_{z,j}$ for $1 \leq z \leq 2^{h-1}$ and $1 \leq j \leq m$. Each node stores the identifiers (id) of data being located inside the node region.

To preserve the data privacy, the DO encrypts T attribute-wise using the public key (pk) of the Paillier cryptosystem [8] before outsourcing the database. So, the DO generates $E(t_{i,j})$ for $1 \leq i \leq n$ and $1 \leq j \leq m$. The DO also encrypts the kd-tree nodes so as to support efficient query processing over the encrypted database. The lb and the ub of each node are encrypted attribute-wise, so $E(lb_{z,j})$ and $E(ub_{z,j})$ are generated for $1 \leq z \leq 2^{h-1}$ and $1 \leq j \leq m$. In the system, we assume that the clouds, C_A and C_B, act as semi-honest adversaries. This is because protocols under the *semi-honest* adversaries are efficient in practice and can be used to design protocols against malicious adversaries. So, the C_A and C_B correctly perform the given protocols and do not exchange unpermitted data. However, an adversary may try to obtain additional information from the intermediate data during executing his/her own protocol.

To support range query processing over the encrypted database, a secure multiparty computation (SMC) is required between C_A and C_B. For this, the DO outsources the encrypted database and its encrypted index to the C_A with pk while the sk is sent to the C_B. The encrypted index includes the region information of each node in cipher-text and the ids of data that are located inside the node in plain-text. The DO also sends pk to AUs to enable them to encrypt a query. At query time, an AU first encrypts a query attribute-wise. Then, the AU sends $E(q.lb_j)$ and $E(q.ub_j)$ for $1 \leq j \leq m$ to C_A. C_A processes the query with the help of C_B and returns a query result to the AU.

As an example, assume that an AU has 8 data in two-dimensional space (e.g., x-axis and y-axis) as depicted in Fig. 1. The data are partitioned into 4 nodes for a kd-tree. To outsource the database, the DO encrypts each data and the information of each node attribute-wise. For example, t_1 is encrypted as $E(t_1) = \{E(2), E(1)\}$.

Meanwhile, our range query processing algorithm is constructed using several secure protocols. We describe the secure protocols that are used in our range query processing algorithm. All the protocols except SBN protocol are performed through the SMC technique between C_A and C_B. SBN protocol can be executed by C_A alone. Due to the space limitation, we first briefly introduce two existing secure protocols that we adopt from [7, 9]. SM (Secure Multiplication) protocol [7] computes the encryption of $a \times b$, i.e., $E(a \times b)$, when two encrypted data $E(a)$ and $E(b)$ are given as inputs. SBD (Secure Bit-Decomposition) protocol [9] computes the encryptions of binary representation of the encrypted input $E(a)$. The output is $[a] = \langle E(a_1), \ldots, E(a_l) \rangle$ where a_1 and a_l denote the most and least significant bits of a, respectively. We use symbol $[a]$ to denote the encryptions of binary representation.

Fig. 1 An example in two-dimensional space

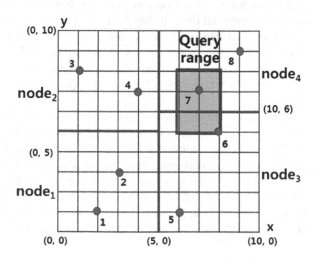

Next, we propose our new secure protocols. First, SBN (Secure Bit-Not) protocol performs the bit-not operation when an encrypted bit $E(a)$ is given as input. The output $E(\sim a)$ is computed by $E(a)^{N-1} \times E(1)$. Here, "-1" is equivalent to "$N-1$" under Z_N.

Second, SCMP (Secure Compare) protocol returns $E(1)$ if $u \leq v$, $E(0)$ otherwise, when $[u]$ and $[v]$ are given as inputs. We devise SCMP by modifying SMIN [7] protocol which outputs $[min]$ between two inputs $[u]$ and $[v]$. The variables generated during SMIN can be categorized into two folds. One set of the variables include hints about what the minimum value is. Another set of the variables is used to securely extract the minimum value. Because we only need the information about whether u is smaller or not, we only compute the former (e.g., W, G, H, Φ, L, L'). The goal of designing SCMP is to make the returned value from C_B be exactly opposite for the same inputs, based on the functionality selected by C_A.

The overall procedure of SCMP is as follows. (i) C_A appends $E(0)$ to the least significant bits of $[u]$ and $E(1)$ to the least significant bits of $[v]$. By doing so, SCMP makes u smaller than v only when two values are the same. (ii) C_A randomly chooses one functionality between $F_0{:}u > v$ and $F_1{:}v > u$. The selected functionality is oblivious to C_B. Then, C_A computes $E(u_i \times v_i)$ using SM and W_i, depending on the selected functionality. In particular, if $F_0{:}u > v$ is selected, C_A computes $W_i = E(u_i) \times E(u_i \times v_i)^{N-1}$. If $F_1{:}v > u$ is selected, C_A computes $W_i = E(v_i) \times E(v_i \times u_i)^{N-1}$. For $F_0{:}u > v$, $W_i = E(1)$ when $u_i > v_i$, and $W_i = E(0)$ otherwise. Similarly, for $F_1{:}v > u$, $W_i = E(1)$ when $v_i > u_i$, and $W_i = E(0)$ otherwise. (iii) C_A performs bit-xor between $E(u_i)$ and $E(v_i)$ and stores the result into G_i. C_A computes $H_i = (H_{i-1})^{r_i} \times G_i$ and $\Phi_i = E(-1) \times H_i$ where $H_0 = E(0)$. Here, r_i is a random number in Z_N. Assume that j is the index of the first appearance of $E(1)$ in G_i. j means the first position where the minimum value between u and v can be determined. (iv) C_A computes $L_i = W_i \times \Phi_i^{r_i}$ where L_i involves the information about which value is smaller between u and v at j. C_A generates L' by permuting L by using a random permutation function π_1 and sends L' to C_B. (v) C_B decrypts L' attribute-wise and checks whether there exists 0 in L_i' for $1 \leq i \leq l$. If so, C_B sets α as 1, and 0 otherwise. After encrypting α, C_B sends $E(\alpha)$ to C_A. By doing so, the returned values by C_B are exactly opposite with the selected functionalities for the same input which coincides with the goal of SCMP protocol. (vi) C_A performs $E(\alpha) = \text{SBN}(E(\alpha))$ only when the selected functionality is $F_0{:}u > v$ and returns the $E(\alpha)$. So, the final $E(\alpha)$ is $E(1)$ when $u \leq v$, regardless of the selected functionality. Note that the only information decrypted during SCMP is L' which is seen by C_B. However, C_B cannot obtain an additional information from $D(L')$ because the selected functionality is oblivious to C_B.

Third, SRO (Secure Range Overlapping) protocol returns $E(1)$ when $range_1$ overlaps $range_2$, $E(0)$ otherwise, when the encryptions of binary representation of two ranges $[range_1]$ and $[range_2]$ are given as inputs. Assuming that both $range_1$ and $range_2$ consist of $[lb_j]$ and $[ub_j]$, where $1 \leq j \leq m$, the two ranges overlap only if two following conditions are satisfied; (i) $E(range_1.lb_j) \leq E(range_2.ub_j)$ for $1 \leq j \leq m$, (ii) $E(range_2.lb_i) \leq E(range_1.ub_j)$ for $1 \leq j \leq m$. SRO determines the conditions by using our SCMP. The overall procedure of SRO is as follows.

(i) C_A initializes $E(\alpha)$ as $E(1)$. (ii) C_A obtains $E(\alpha')$ by performing SCMP([$range_1$. lb_j], [$range_2.ub_j$]) and updates $E(\alpha)$ by executing SM($E(\alpha)$, $E(\alpha')$). C_A repeats this step for $1 \leq j \leq m$. Similarly, C_A computes $E(\alpha')$ by performing SCMP([$range_2.lb_j$], [$range_1.ub_j$]) and updates $E(\alpha)$ by executing SM($E(\alpha)$, $E(\alpha')$) for all attribute values. Only when all conditions are satisfied, the value of $E(\alpha)$ remains $E(1)$. (iii) C_B returns the final $E(\alpha)$. Note that no decryption is performed during SRO except performing SCMP and SM protocols.

Finally, SPE (Secure Point Enclosure) protocol returns $E(1)$ when p is inside the range or on a boundary of the range, $E(0)$ otherwise, when the encryptions of binary representation of a point [p] and [$range$] are given as inputs. The overall procedure of SPE is identical to SRO. This is because if a low bound and an upper bound of a range is the same, the range can be considered as a point. However, we also define SPE protocol to make the relations between inputs clear.

4 Secure Range Query Processing Algorithm

In this section, we present our secure range query processing algorithm (SRange$_I$) using the kd-tree on the encrypted database. SRange$_I$ consists of two steps; encrypted kd-tree search step and result retrieval step.

First, the procedure of the encrypted kd-tree search step is as follows.

(i) C_A computes [$q.lb_j$] and [$q.ub_j$] for $1 \leq j \leq m$ by using the SBD. C_A also computes [$node_z.lb_j$] and [$node_z.ub_j$] for $1 \leq z \leq num_{node}$ and $1 \leq j \leq m$ by using SBD where num_{node} is the total number of kd-tree leaf nodes. Then, C_A securely finds nodes which overlap the query range by executing $E(\alpha_z) \leftarrow$ SRO([q], [$node_z$]) for $1 \leq z \leq num_{node}$. Note that the nodes with $E(\alpha_z) = E(1)$ overlaps the query range, but both C_A and C_B cannot know whether the value of each $E(\alpha_z)$ is $E(1)$.

(ii) C_A generates $E(\alpha')$ by permuting $E(\alpha)$ using a random permutation function π and sends $E(\alpha')$ to C_B. For example, SRO returns $E(\alpha) = \{E(0), E(0), E(1), E(1)\}$ in Fig. 1 as the query range overlaps the $node_3$ and $node_4$. Assuming that π permutes data in reverse way, C_A sends the $E(\alpha') = \{E(1), E(1), E(0), E(0)\}$ to C_B.

(iii) Upon receiving the $E(\alpha')$, C_B obtains α' by decrypting the $E(\alpha')$ and counts the number of α' with the value of 1. The number of $\alpha' = 1$ is stored into c. So, c means the number of nodes that overlaps the query range.

(iv) C_B creates c number of node groups (e.g., NG). C_B assigns to each NG a node with $\alpha' = 1$ and $num_{node}/c-1$ nodes with $\alpha' = 0$. Then, C_B computes NG' by randomly shuffling the ids of nodes in each NG and sends NG' to C_A. For example, C_B can obtain $\alpha' = \{1, 1, 0, 0\}$. However, C_B cannot correctly point out ids of the nodes overlapping the query range because the values in α' were permutated by C_A. As two node groups are required, C_B assigns $node_1$ and $node_2$ to NG_1 and NG_2, respectively. In this example, $num_{node}/c-1$ is calculated as 1 because $num_{node} = 4$ and $c = 2$. So, C_B randomly assigns a node to each node group. Assume that C_B assigns $node_3$ to NG_1 and $node_4$ to NG_2. So, $NG_1 = \{1, 3\}$ and $NG_2 = \{2, 4\}$. Then, C_B randomly shuffles the ids of the nodes in each NG. The result can be like $NG_1' = \{1, 3\}$ and $NG_2' = \{4, 2\}$.

(v) C_A obtains NG^* by permuting the ids of nodes using π^{-1} in each NG'. In each NG^*, there exists only one node overlapping the query range. However, C_A cannot know the correct id of the node because the ids of the nodes in NG^* are shuffled by C_B. Sixth, C_A gets access to one datum in each node (e.g., $node_z$) for each NG^* and performs $E(t'_{i,j}) \leftarrow SM(node_z.t_{s,j}, E(\alpha_z))$ for $1 \leq s \leq F$ and $1 \leq j \leq m$. Here, α_z is the outputs of SPE, corresponding to the $node_z$. If a node has the less number of data than F, it performs SM by using $E(max)$, instead of using $node_z.t_{s,j}$, where $E(max)$ is the largest value in the domain. When C_A accesses one datum from every node in a NG^*, C_A performs a homomorphic addition such as $E(cand_{cnt,j}) \leftarrow \prod_{i=1}^{num} E(t'_{i,j})$, where num means the total number of nodes in the selected NG^*. By doing so, a datum in the node overlapping the query range is securely extracted without revealing the data access patterns. By repeating these steps, all the data in the nodes are safely stored into the $E(cand_{cnt,j})$ where cnt means the total number of data extracted during the index search.

As an example, C_A obtains $NG_1^* = \{2, 4\}$ and $NG_2^* = \{1, 3\}$ by permuting $NG_1' = \{3, 1\}$ and $NG_2' = \{4, 2\}$ using π^{-1}. Then, C_A accesses $E(t_3)$ in $node_2$, $E(t_7)$ in $node_4$ for NG_1^*. The results of SM using $E(t_3)$, e.g., $E(t'_1)$, are $E(0)$ for every attribute because the $E(\alpha)$ value of $node_2$ is $E(0)$. However, the results of SM using $E(t_7)$, e.g., $E(t'_2)$, become $E(7)$ and $E(7)$ for x and y dimension, respectively. So, the results of the attribute-wise homomorphic addition of $E(t'_1)$ and $E(t'_2)$ are $E(7)$ and $E(7)$ for x and y dimension, respectively. Thus, one datum $E(t_7)$ in $node_4$ is securely extracted into $E(cand_1)$. Similarly, values of $E(t_8)$ can be securely extracted into $E(cand_2)$ by using $E(t_4)$ and $E(t_8)$. In the same way, for NG_2^*, all the data in the $node_3$ (e.g., $E(t_5)$ and $E(t_6)$) are securely extracted into $E(cand_3)$ and $E(cand_4)$, respectively.

Second, the procedure of the result retrieval step is as follows. (i) C_A computes $\{([cand_{i,j}] \mid 1 \leq i \leq cnt, 1 \leq j \leq m\}$ by using the SBD. Here, cnt is equal to $F \times$ (the number of node groups).

(ii) C_A securely finds data inside the query range by executing $E(\alpha_i) \leftarrow SPE$ $([cand_i], [q])$ for $1 \leq i \leq cnt$. Note that the data with $E(\alpha_i) = E(1)$ are included in the query range. However, both C_A and C_B cannot know whether the value of each $E(\alpha_i)$ is $E(1)$. For example, when $E(cand) = \{E(t_7), E(t_8), E(t_5), E(t_6)\}$ is given from the step 1, SPE returns $E(\alpha) = E(1)$ for $E(t_7)$ and $E(t_6)$, which are located inside the query range. The data with $E(\alpha) = E(1)$ should be sent to the user. To minimize the computation cost at the user side, it is required to send decrypted results. However, if the cloud decrypts the results, the actual content of the data are revealed to the cloud.

So, (iii) C_A computes $E(\gamma_{i,j}) = E(result_i) \times E(r_{i,j})$ for $1 \le i \le cnt$ and $1 \le j \le m$ by generating a random value $r_{i,j}$. C_A generates $E(\alpha')$, $E(\gamma')$, and r' by permuting $E(\alpha)$, $E(\gamma)$, and r, using a random permutation function π_1. Then, C_A sends $E(\alpha')$ and $E(\gamma')$ to C_B, and r' to AU, respectively. iv) C_B decrypts $E(\alpha_i')$ and $E(\gamma'_{i,j})$ for $1 \le i \le cnt$ and for $1 \le j \le m$. Then, C_B sends α' and γ' corresponding to the $\alpha' = 1$ to AU. Finally, AU computes $\gamma'_{i,j} - r'_{i,j}$ for $1 \le i \le cnt$ and $1 \le j \le m$ only for the corresponding $\alpha_i = 1$.

5 Performance Analysis

There is no existing range query processing algorithm that hides the data access patterns. So, in this section, we compare our $SRange_I$ with a baseline algorithm $SRange_B$ which only performs result retrieval step by considering all the data without using an index. We do the performance analysis of both schemes in terms of query processing time with different parameters. We used the Paillier cryptosystem to encrypt a database for both schemes. We implemented both schemes by using C++. Experiments were performed on a Linux machine with an Intel Xeon E3-1220v3 4-Core 3.10 GHz and 32 GB RAM running Ubuntu 14.04.2. To examine the performance under various parameters, we randomly generated synthetic datasets by following [7]. We set the size of the range as 0.1 which means the relational portion of the range compared to the total domain size (i.e., l). In addition, we set the domain size (l) as 12 and the encryption key size (K) as 1024.

Figure 2 shows the performance of $SRange_I$ for varying the level of kd-tree. Figure 2a shows the performance of $SRange_I$ for varying h and n. Overall, as the n becomes larger, the query processing time increases. Meanwhile, when the n increases, the h that shows the best performance becomes larger. For all cases, when the h is increased, the query processing time decreases for the smaller h while the query processing time increases for the larger h. Figure 2b shows the performance of $SRange_I$ for varying h and m. As the m becomes larger, the query processing time linearly increases. This is because all the protocols including SRO and SPE should process additional data as the m increases. We set the h as 7 in the following

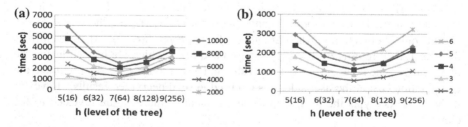

Fig. 2 Performance of $SRange_I$ for varying h. **a** $m = 6$, $K = 1024$, **b** $n = 6$ k, $K = 1024$

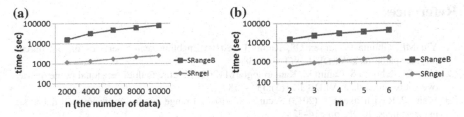

Fig. 3 Comparison of SRange$_I$ and SRange$_B$. **a** $m = 6$, $K = 1024$, **b** $n = 6$ k, $K = 1024$

performance evaluation because SRange$_I$ shows good performance when $h = 7$ in our parameter settings.

Figure 3a shows the performance of both SRange$_I$ and SRange$_B$ schemes varying the n. Overall, as the n becomes larger, the query processing time linearly increases for both schemes. Overall, SRange$_I$ shows much better performance than SRange$_B$, because SRange$_I$ filters irrelevant data by using the index. On average, SRange$_I$ shows about 25 times better performance than SRange$_B$. Meanwhile, Fig. 3b shows the performance of both schemes varying the m. Overall, as the m becomes larger, the query processing time linearly increases for both schemes. However, on average, SRange$_I$ shows about 27 times better performance than SRange$_B$.

6 Conclusion

With the popularity of the outsourced databases, researches on the range query processing methods over the encrypted database have been actively performed. They can preserve the data privacy and the query privacy, but there is no work that hides the data access patterns during the query processing. To solve the problem, we proposed a new secure range query processing algorithm on the encrypted database. Our method conceals the data access patterns while supporting efficient query processing by using our proposed encrypted index search scheme. We showed from our performance analysis that our algorithm achieves efficient query processing performance while hiding the data access patterns. As a future work, we plan to expand our work to support other query types, such as Top-k and skyline queries.

Acknowledgments This work was supported by the Human Resource Training Program for Regional Innovation and Creativity through the Ministry of Education and National Research Foundation of Korea (NRF-2014H1C1A1065816)

References

1. Yiu ML, Ghinita G, Jensen CS, Kalnis P (2010) Enabling search services on outsourced private spatial data. VLDB J 19(3):363–384
2. Hore B, Mehrotra S, Canim M, Kantarcioglu M (2012) Secure multidimensional range queries over outsourced data. VLDB J 21(3):333–358
3. Wang P, Ravishankar CV (2013) Secure and efficient range queries on outsourced databases using R-trees, ICDE, pp 314–325
4. Wang B, Hou Y, Li M, Wang H, Li H (2014) Maple: scalable multi-dimensional range search over encrypted cloud data with tree-based index, ASIACCS, pp 111–122
5. Kim H, Hong S, Chang J (2015) Hilbert curve-based cryptographic transformation scheme for spatial query processing on outsourced private data. Data Knowl Eng. doi:10.1016/j.datak.2015.05.002
6. Vimercati S, Foresti S, Samarati P (2012) Managing and accessing data in the cloud: privacy risks and approaches, CRiSIS, pp 1–9
7. Elmehdwi Y, Samanthula BK, Jiang W (2014) Secure k-nearest neighbor query over encrypted data in outsourced environments, ICDE, pp 664–675
8. Paillier P (1999) Public-key cryptosystems based on composite degree residuosity classes, EUROCRYPT, pp 223–238
9. Samanthula BK, Chun H, Jiang W (2013) An efficient and probabilistic secure bit-decomposition, ASIACCS, pp 541–546
10. Carmit H, Lindell Y (2010) Efficient secure two-party protocols: techniques and constructions, Springer Science & Business Media

Enabling Consumer Trust
Upon Acceptance of IoT Technologies
Through Security and Privacy Model

**Wazir Zada Khan, Mohammed Y. Aalsalem,
Muhammad Khurram Khan and Quratulain Arshad**

Abstract Internet of Things (IoT) has become a popular paradigm by digitizing our physical world, bringing appealing level of conveniences to community. Besides that consumers embrace potential IoT benefits to them, they are much more concerned about the security and privacy of their data. Since, the increased connectivity between devices and the internet in IoT presents security and privacy related challenges, and the data breach of sensitive personal information can be exploited to harm the consumers; the trust of these consumers on the IoT can be tampered. The success of IoT ultimately depends upon the consumer perceptions about security and privacy in IoT and the level of digital trust of its consumers. Since trust has been an important element to influence consumer's behavior, thus, it can be stimulated by increased consumer perceptions of both security and privacy of IoT. In this paper we contribute to identify the evolving features of IoT and identify important security and privacy requirements from consumer perspectives. We propose a conceptual security and privacy model and highlighting important threats and challenges on various stages of this model.

Keywords Internet of things · Security · Privacy · Trust

W.Z. Khan (✉) · M.Y. Aalsalem · Q. Arshad
Farasan Networking Research Laboratory, Faculty of CS and IS,
Jazan University, Jizan, Saudi Arabia
e-mail: wazirzadakhan@jazanu.edu.sa

M.Y. Aalsalem
e-mail: aalsalem.m@jazanu.edu.sa

Q. Arshad
e-mail: brightsuccess_12@yahoo.com

M.K. Khan
Center of Excellence in Information Assurance, King Saud University,
Riyadh, Saudi Arabia
e-mail: mkhurram@ksu.edu.sa

© Springer Science+Business Media Singapore 2016   111
J.J. (Jong Hyuk) Park et al. (eds.), *Advanced Multimedia and Ubiquitous
Engineering*, Lecture Notes in Electrical Engineering 393,
DOI 10.1007/978-981-10-1536-6_15

1 Introduction

The actual term "Internet of Things" was first quoted by Kevin Ashton in 1999 [1]. "Internet of Things (IoT) is a concept and a paradigm that considers pervasive presence in the environment of a variety of things/objects that through wireless and wired connections and unique addressing schemes are able to interact with each other and cooperate with other things/objects to create new applications/services and reach common goals" [2–4].

According to Cisco IBSG [5], the term IoT was born sometime between 2008 and 2009 since there were more connected devices as compared to 2003 when the number of connected things was relatively small and ubiquitous devices such as smartphones were just being introduced. Now recently the Internet of Things has evolved to a huge leap and has become immensely important since it is expected to have 50 billion connected devices by 2020 [6]. Thus, in future IoT is predicted to be the interconnection of billions to trillions of smart things/devices. We define the IoT vision as follows:

> Internet of Things heralds the vison of such a paradigm which connects virtual or physical objects (Anything) and people of any age group (Anyone) through wired or wireless connections (Any network) in order to benefit the consumers (Any service) who are positioned anywhere (Any place) without the involvement of time constraints (Any time).

The above definition demonstrates this vision clearly that Internet of things encompasses three major agents i.e. people, objects and data that are taking part in evolving the notion of IoT. Communications in IoT will take place not only between people i.e. people to people (P2P) and devices/objects i.e. machine to machine (M2M) but also between people and their devices/environment i.e. (P2M).

Consumers embrace the compelling products and services provided by IoT manufacturers but according to a recent survey by Trend Micro, consumers are concerned about both IoT security (75 %) and privacy (44 %). Consumers have access to a wide range of gadgets and smart IoT devices but the convenience provided by these smart devices is accompanied with a lot of security and privacy issues. A hacker/intruder can take control of IoT devices (e.g. smart door locks, smart light bulbs, insulin pumps are vulnerable, connected car can be hacked to remotely allow the control of brakes), steal personal sensitive information (personal fitness information can expose the location of a person to a hacker etc.), or disrupt services (smart refrigerator can send spam emails etc.). On the ignorance of these issues in IoT, undesired consequences will be confronted like non-acceptance and failure of new services and damage to reputation. Despite a plethora of research contributions [7–13] to identifying security and privacy challenges of IoT, the holistic view of arising issues with the growing number of technologies and a range of changing features and in terms of perceived consumer security and privacy in IoT is missing. In this paper we contribute to identify evolving features of IoT which pose serious threats to the consumer security and privacy today, identify security and privacy requirements with respect to consumer perspectives in IoT and finally propose security and privacy conceptual model to achieve consumer trust on technology acceptance of IoT.

We contribute to the above discussion in organizing the rest of the paper into three sections: Sect. 2 identifies some of the important features and characteristics of IoT which pose serious threats to consumer security and privacy. Section 3 presents security and privacy requirements from the consumer perspectives. In Sect. 4 we propose the security and privacy model for achieving consumer trust upon technology acceptance of IoT. Section 5 finally concludes the paper.

2 Evolving IoT Features

In this section we define some of the unique and evolving IoT features that constitute the exclusiveness of the IoT. *Uncontrolled Environment* allows most of the IoT objects/devices to become a part of uncontrolled environment where surroundings are capricious and interactions between devices are trustless due to unstable network connectivity and inconsistent presence. Moreover the sensors can be publically accessible and weak links are created which can be easily exploited by malicious entities or intruders. *Heterogeneity/Interoperability:* The nature of IoT ecosystem is heterogeneous where a multitude of things/objects from various manufacturers with different functionalities on the context of their applications have been integrated. *Constrained Resources:* IoT involves devices/things which have energy and computation constraints e.g. battery powered devices and micro sensors etc. Thus, heavy cryptographic techniques cannot be applied in IoT. *Scalability*: Since billions of IoT devices are sharing information and improving the efficiency of our daily lives by completing tasks, the huge amounts of data are flowed and from the physical world. Thus, current security IoT architectures are designed for relatively small scale IoT islands but with increasing number connected devices, security and privacy issues will also be elevated and new highly scalable security architectures will be required in near future. To tackle with privacy issues using smartphones research is conducted on location based services, detection of privacy breaches [14] and privacy aware architectures for participatory sensing [15].

3 Security and Privacy Requirements from Consumer Perspective

IoT manufacturers and researchers are working productively to add more intelligence and connectivity into objects which results in increasing acceptance of these devices by the consumers, but the reality is that the security and privacy concerns are not considered in any of these devices as analyzed by Symantec [16]. Poor encryption or mostly unencrypted connections for communications, weak passwords, and defective user interfaces in IoT devices leave the consumers potentially exposed and their sensitive private information can be compromised by the hackers. Attacks including brute force attack, DoS and DDoS attacks, sniffing, eavesdropping, malware infection, modification or theft of data, arbitrary code execution attack, spoofing, ransomware, spamming [17, 18] etc.

The increased connectivity between devices and the internet can lead to device level security risks like it may enable the intruders and hackers to access and misuse personal information. Unauthorized access to fitness devices, connected cars, connected home appliances can endanger consumer life since these potential risks can be exacerbated if device level security is not considered in IoT devices. Thus, the designers of IoT devices must provide outbound connections and devices must not have open inbound ports for connecting IoT devices to a secure network. Moreover, when any IoT device disappears or stops sending/receiving data, the owner/consumer must be provided with a facility to monitor the status of his online/offline device since an offline device may result in local tampering by an intruder or there may be power or internet outage. In order to tackle these risks the IoT devices must have in-built tamper resistant hardware. Finally IoT devices must be provided with user friendly setup for running and installing IoT devices and easy to install software and firmware upgrades in order to keep them up to date. The IoT devices must have also anti-theft mechanisms installed on them. If IoT devices are not secured properly, they can give rise to security breaches of both consumer and enterprise data. Ultimately it results in tampering the consumer trust upon the IoT. Thus, there is need that the companies developing IoT products should implement reasonable security by considering the general data security requirements while designing IoT applications. *Availability* ensures the survivability of network services despite attacks. *Authenticity* is a security goal that enables an IoT device to ensure the identity of other IoT device it is communicating with. *Confidentiality* is the assurance that sensitive data is being accessed and viewed only by those who are authorized to see it. *Data Integrity* ensures that the contents of data or correspondences are preserved and remain unharmed during the transmission from the sender to receiver. Third is Communication security of connected devices in IoT environment can be achieved through end-to-end authentication and encryption. For achieving true communication security, the data (generated from IoT devices) itself should be encrypted with the Advanced Encryption Standard (AES) encryption specification.

Personal sensitive information can be about consumer's precise geolocation, financial account numbers, health information, habits, locations, user's mood, stress levels, demographics, smoking habits, sleep patterns and physical conditions over time which may raise privacy risks and hackers may infer to steal such sensitive information very easily. All this personal data can be used by companies (to make credit, insurance or employment decisions) and manufacturers to provide consumers beneficial services but it can be misused in unauthorized by unauthorized individuals if proper privacy measures are not taken. Also a manufacturer, third party service provider or an intruder can also eaves-drop unencrypted personal data generated by personal IoT devices. Data privacy can be achieved by data minimization i.e. storing minimum and only most related personal data on the device or just storing a virtual data in the form of digital shadows. Consumer private data is collected by the IoT manufacturers for two core objectives; for diagnostics purposes and consumer service improvement. But sometimes consumer data is exposed to third party service providers which provide services to IoT manufacturers. Privacy of data sharing can be achieved by minimum sharing of Consumer private data. Consumers must have confidence in how their data are used, stored, and transported and should remain in control of their personal data and must be informed and indicated about their data sharing to third parties.

4 Proposed Security and Privacy Model

This section presents framework to our analysis of security and privacy threats and challenges in the Internet of Things from consumer perspective. We present our security and privacy model with respect to consumer perspectives of security and privacy in IoT for achieving consumer trust upon technology acceptance of IoT. In our model, we consider four entities and four actors. The three entities are *Smart Objects, Connectivity Infrastructure, Data and Services.* The four actors are *Consumer, Vendors/Manufactures* and *Third Party Service Provider* and *Intruder.* SMART objects are augmented with information and communication technology (ICT) and are capable of sensing/actuating, processing, storing and interpreting/ sharing information created within themselves and also around their neighboring world of SMART objects and humans. These SMART objects first sense/actuate through one or multiple sensors, gathering live information from the consumer or his/her environment. Then, these SMART objects start learning their environment or processing by executing instructions or tasks that are fixed or adjustable. After gathering and processing useful information, SMART objects react appropriately and make intelligent decisions. Finally these SMART objects participate in intra-network or inter-network communications and share their information with humans or other SMART objects. The SMART objects need to be connected to the internet through some connectivity infrastructure in order to interact and commu- nicate and provide services to the consumer. The behavior of these smart objects depends on where and how they are used. In our model smart objects can be consumer goods, assembly machinery, logistics and transportation items, ware- houses, retailers' facilities or end-user assets etc.

Consumer in our model is a person who is using the smart objects and thus the main beneficiary of the IoT vision. The data collected by SMART objects can be of two types: consumer driven data (i.e. personal data generated when users/consumers utilize IoT applications and devices for their personal use) and enterprise driven data (i.e. the business related data generated by the organizations or firms when they use IoT based solutions). The consumer driven data is indis- pensable for the manufacturer, the hacker (intruder), third party service providers, employers and insurance companies, government agencies. The manufacturers and

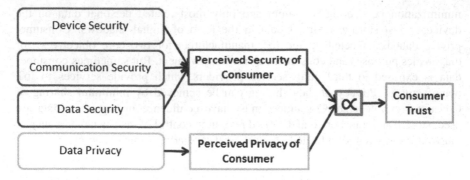

Fig. 1 Conceptual security and privacy model for technology acceptance of IoT

third party companies need consumer data for diagnostics purposes and for product improvement and enhancing customer services. Hackers, intruders or cybercriminals need consumer data for their illegal exploits. Employers or Insurance companies are interested in consumer health related information. The study in [20] reviewed the models for standard security weaknesses, such as hard-coded accounts with default passwords, unencrypted video and audio feeds, commands sent in clear text over the Internet, and the ability to gain unauthorized control through remote shells and similar interfaces. The encryption and password protection we use in financial matters has not yet made it into cars thus a connected car can be hacked and controlled, either putting the owner in danger turns off an engine of a high speed car or exposing confidential information about the owner. According to the study in [19], some of the smart home appliances are vulnerable to access control attacks, SSDP discovery, ARP poisoning. Our proposed security and privacy model is diagrammatically illustrated in Fig. 1. The proposed conceptual model will not only help the IoT developers and manufacturers in reducing the attacks and vulnerabilities but it will also drive the adoption of best practices for IoT security and privacy.

5 Conclusion

The connected IoT devices are creating security and privacy risks like unauthorized persons can access and misuse personal information, a number of attacks can be launched by the intruders etc. In this paper we have identified and highlighted some important security and privacy requirements of IoT from consumer perspective. We have proposed a conceptual security and privacy model for the consumer's perceived security and privacy in IoT which is based on some antecedents. Consumer trust can be built effectively if the consumer's perceived security and privacy requirements are achieved.

References

1. Abowd GD, Dey AK, Brown PJ, Davies N, Smith M, Steggles P (1999) Towards a better understanding of context and context awareness. In: Proceedings of the 1st international symposium on handheld and ubiquitous computing, ser. HUC'99. London, UK; Springer-Verlag, pp 304–307
2. Atzori Luigi, Iera Antonio, Morabito Giacomo (2010) The internet of things: a survey. Comput Netw 54(15):2787–2805
3. Mashal Ibrahim, Alsaryrah Osama, Chung Tein-Yaw, Yang Cheng-Zen, Kuo Wen-Hsing, Agrawal Dharma P (2015) Choices for interaction with things on Internet and underlying issues. Ad Hoc Netw 28:68–90
4. Vermesan O, Friess P (2013) Internet of things: converging technologies for smart environments and integrated ecosystems, River Publishers
5. Evans D (2011) The internet of things how the next evolution of the internet is changing everything, CISCO White paper, Cisco Internet Business Solutions Group (IBSG), April 2011
6. Fortino G, Guerrieri A, Russo W, Savaglio C (2014) Internet of things based on smart objects
7. Atamli AW, Martin A (2014) Threat-based security analysis for the internet of things. In: Secure Internet of Things (SIoT), IEEE, pp 35–43
8. Gang GAN, Zeyong LU, Jun J (2011) Internet of things security analysis. In: Internet technology and applications (iTAP), IEEE, pp 1–4
9. Gazis V, Cordero CG, Vasilomanolakis E, Kikiras P, Wiesmaier A (2014) Security perspectives for collaborative data acquisition in the internet of things. In: International conference on safety and security in internet of things. Springer
10. Roman R, Zhou J, Lopez J (2013) On the features and challenges of security and privacy in distributed internet of things. Comput Netw 57(10):2266–2279, July 2013
11. Sadeghi A-R, Wachsmann C, Waidner M (2015) Security and privacy challenges in industrial internet of things. In: Annual design automation conference, ACM, p 54
12. Sicari S, Rizzardi A, Grieco LA, Coen-Porisini A (2015) Security, privacy and trust in internet of things: the road ahead. Comput Netw 76:146–164
13. Zhang Z-K, Cheng M, Cho Y, Shieh S (2015) Emerging security threats and countermeasures in IoT. In: ACM symposium on information, computer and communications security, ACM, pp 1–6
14. Hornyack P, Han S, Jung J, Schechter S, Wetherall D (2011) These aren't the droids you're looking for: retrofitting android to protect data from imperious applications. Proceedings of the 18th ACM conference on computer and communications security, CCS'11, ACM, pp. 639–652, doi:10.1145/2046707.2046780
15. Khan WZ, Xiang Y, Aalsalem MY, Arshad Q (2013) Mobile phone sensing systems: a survey. Communications Surveys & Tutorials, IEEE 15(1): 402–427
16. Barcena MB, Wueest C (2015) Insecurity in the Internet of Things, Version 1.0 – 12 Mar 2015. [Online]. Available https://www.symantec.com/content/en/us/enterprise/media/security_response/whitepapers/insecurity-in-the-internet-of-things.pdf
17. Internet of things, Privacy & Security in a Connected World, FTC staff report Jan 2015
18. Khan WZ, Khan M, Muhaya F, Aalsalem M, Chao H-C (2015) A comprehensive study of email spam botnet detection. Communications Surveys & Tutorials, IEEE 99
19. Sivaraman V, Gharakheili HH, Vishwanath A, Boreli R, Mehani O (2015) Network-level security and privacy control for smart-home IoT devices. In: Wireless and mobile computing, networking and communications (WiMob), 2015 IEEE 11th International Conference on, IEEE, pp. 163–167
20. Goodin D (2015) 9 baby monitors wide open to hacks that expose users' most private moments [Online] http://arstechnica.com/security/2015/09/9-baby-monitors-wide-open-to-hacks-that-expose-users-most-private-moments/. Last visited 15 Dec 2015

Defects Extraction for QFN Based on Texture Detection and Region of Interest Selection

Kai Chen, Zhisheng Zhang, Yuan Chao, Fuyun He and Jinfei Shi

Abstract On the surface of the quad flat non-lead (QFN) dark-filed images, noise pixels (including textures produced in the molding process) obstruct the defect inspection. To extract defects from QFN surface, a novel method based on texture detection and region of interest selection is proposed. Firstly, a QFN texture direction detector is proposed. Secondly, multilevel thresholding method is used to segment QFN images. Thirdly, according to the image level, the bright defects images and the dark defect images are obtained. Then, the region of interest selection method is applied to reserving defects regions and removing QFN textures and noise pixels. Finally, our method extracts defects by combining the bright and dark defects image. The experiments show that the proposed method can extract defects efficiently.

Keywords Quad flat non-lead (QFN) · Defect extraction · Texture detection · Region of interest selection

1 Introduction

The quad flat non-lead (QFN) package is a type of semiconductor package that connects integrated circuits to PCB board. However, in the production process, kinds of defects are generated on QFN surface. The defects seriously affect the quality of QFN and are potentially harmful to the PCB board. Therefore, it is essential to detect defects from QFN surface.

In the recent years, many researchers are committed to surface defect inspection based on machine vision. Yun et al. [1] proposed a discrete wavelet transform and an adaptive local binarization method to detect defects on steel surface. Song et al. [2]

K. Chen · Z. Zhang (✉) · Y. Chao · F. He
Mechanical Engineering School, Southeast University, Nanjing, China
e-mail: oldbc@seu.edu.cn

J. Shi
Huaihai Institute of Technology, Lianyungang, China

© Springer Science+Business Media Singapore 2016
J.J. (Jong Hyuk) Park et al. (eds.), *Advanced Multimedia and Ubiquitous Engineering*, Lecture Notes in Electrical Engineering 393,
DOI 10.1007/978-981-10-1536-6_16

119

applied a saliency linear scanning morphology method to inspect defects for silicon steel strip. Chiu and Tarng [3] developed an adaptive neuro-fuzzy inference system to detect ring varistors. Karimi and Davud [4] presented a survey on tile surface inspection. Tsai and Luo [5] applied mean-shift technique to detect defects on multicrystalline solar wafer. However, there are few researches worked on QFN surface defect inspection. Wang [6] proposed 2-D maximum entropy based on integral matrix to detect only two kinds of lead defects.

In our previous work [7], the mathematical morphology and modified region growing method were applied to extract defects from QFN surface images which captured with bright-filed illumination. Nevertheless, some defects cannot be fully displayed in QFN bright-filed images. Therefore, QFN images captured with dark-filed illumination are presented as the detection targets in this paper. In order to extract defects from the QFN dark-filed images, a novel method based on texture detection and region of interest selection is presented.

The rest of the paper is organized as follows: in Sect. 2, the proposed method is illustrated. The experiment results and the conclusion are given in Sects. 3 and 4.

2 The Proposed Method

2.1 Multilevel Thresholding Segmentation

Image segmentation is a crucial step for extracting defects. One of the useful segmentation methods is the thresholding method. However, it is a challenge to segment defects from the surface image with a single threshold. To solve the problem, the firefly algorithm with opposition-learning [8] is proposed to search multilevel thresholds. The segmentation results of the multilevel thresholding method are shown in Fig. 1. As a case study, a QFN image with scratch defects is shown in Fig. 1a. The results with 2-thresholds, 3-thresholds and 4-thresholds are illustrated in Fig. 1b–d. Obviously, the result of 4-thresholds reserves more defects than the images of 2-thresholds and 3-thresholds. Therefore, the segmented images with 4-thresholds are carried out in this paper.

(a)   (b)   (c)   (d)

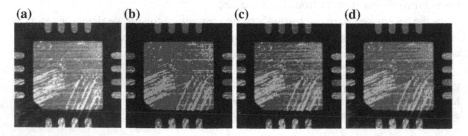

Fig. 1 Segmentation results with 2-thresholds, 3-thresholds and 4-thresholds

(a)   (b)   (c)   (d)

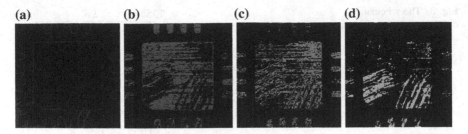

Fig. 2 Four class images divided from the segmented image with 4-thresholds

2.2 Segmentation Post-processing

In order to extract defects, it is necessary to analyse the QFN dark-filed images and the segmented images with 4 thresholds. On the surface of QFN dark-filed images, textures produced in the molding process are displayed on the surface of central board and leads. These textures (hereinafter referred to as QFN textures) are not defects. However, in some cases, these textures may be recognized as defects which affect the defects inspection.

The segmented image with 4-thresholds is partition into 5 classes. The first class is the background. The rest four classes are shown in Fig. 2. From Fig. 2, it can be seen that he third and fourth classes contain the QFN textures which are not defects. The second class (hereinafter referred to as dark defects image) and the fifth class (hereinafter referred to as bright defects image) are useful to extract defects. Therefore, the dark defects image and the bright defects image are the targets to deal with.

From Fig. 2a, d, it can be found that noise pixels (such as QFN textures and pixels around edges) obstruct the extraction defects. Among the noise pixels, the QFN textures are the biggest obstacle of extracting defects. In order to remove the QFN textures, a novel texture direction detector is proposed in the next section.

2.3 QFN Texture Direction Detector

The orientation of a texture image has the characteristics of consistent and uniform. Texture in an image means the changes of the gray value in a certain direction are smaller than the changes in other directions [9]. According to the feature of texture, it is necessary to calculate the changes of gray value in each direction. In this section, four statistical data of the directions (0°, 45°, 90°, 135°) are defined as:

$$S_1 = \sum_{i,j}^{N} |f(i,j+1) - f(i,j)| \tag{1}$$

Fig. 3 The schematic diagram of texture direction

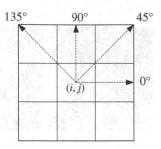

$$S_2 = \sum_{i,j}^{N} |f(i-1,j+1) - f(i,j)| \tag{2}$$

$$S_3 = \sum_{i,j}^{N} |f(i-1,j) - f(i,j)| \tag{3}$$

$$S_4 = \sum_{i,j}^{N} |f(i-1,j-1) - f(i,j)| \tag{4}$$

where $f(i,j)$ is the gray value of the pixel (i,j). The schematic diagram of texture direction is shown in Fig. 3.

For QFN image, the most obvious textures are on the central board. Moreover, the texture directions of the QFN surface images are horizontal and vertical. Hence, the two directions of textures depend on the gray value changes of the central board which can be calculated by Eqs. (1) and (3).

The main steps of detecting QFN texture direction D_{QFN} are as follows:

1. Locate the central board area.
2. Label the connected regions in the central board area, and calculate the mean gray value of each connected region. If the mean value of a connected region is greater than a threshold T_1 or smaller than a threshold T_2, then exclude the connected region.
3. Find the maximum connected region which can meet the rule of Step 2. Calculate the gray value changes of the region in horizontal and vertical direction according to Eqs. (1) and (3).
4. If $S_1 > S_3$, then the texture direction D_{QFN} is detected as horizontal. Otherwise, the texture direction D_{QFN} is detected as vertical.

It is worth mentioning that in Step 2, there is a constraint. In some cases, the scratch and fusion defects may cause a large brighter area on the central board. Moreover, the stain defects may cause a large darker area on the central board. In order to detect the direction of QFN texture, it is necessary to exclude those brighter and darker areas.

2.4 Region of Interest Selection

In the previous section, the method of detecting QFN texture direction is proposed. Then, QFN textures removal and defects regions selection are presented in this section.

Firstly, label the connected regions of the dark defects image and the bright defects image. These connected regions are regions of interest (ROI).

In the second step, in order to detect texture direction of each connected region, calculate the gray value changes in four directions according to Eqs. (1), (2), (3) and (4). The minimum value determines the texture direction of ROI D_{ROI}.

In the third step, select the regions of interest. According to different situations, two operators are applied to the dark defects image and the bright defects image.

For the bright defects image, if the texture direction of ROI is not equal to that of QFN texture, then the region is recognized as defect region. In case of $D_{ROI} = D_{QFN}$, if the mean value of the connected region R_{mean} is greater than the threshold T_1, then reserve the connected region; otherwise, eliminate the connected region.

For the dark defects image, if the texture direction of ROI is not equal to that of QFN texture, then reserve the connected region. In case of $D_{ROI} = D_{QFN}$, there are two conditions. If the mean value of the connected region R_{mean} is smaller than the threshold T_2, then reserve the connected region; otherwise, eliminate the connected region. From Fig. 2a, it can be seen that there are some noise pixels around edges in the dark defects image. Therefore, the eliminating method integrated Canny edge detection and modified region growing method [7] are used to extract defects from the dark defects image.

2.5 The Proposed Method

In order to extract defects from QFN surface, a novel method based on texture detection and region of interest selection method is proposed. The main steps of the proposed method are as follows:

1. Input image.
2. Detect the QFN texture direction.
3. Segment image with 4-thresholds using the multilevel thresholding method based on the firefly algorithm with opposition-learning.
4. Obtain the dark defects image and the bright defect image.
5. Use the region of interest selection method to locate the defects regions.
6. Combine the two images and extract the defects.

The flowchart of the proposed method is shown in Fig. 4.

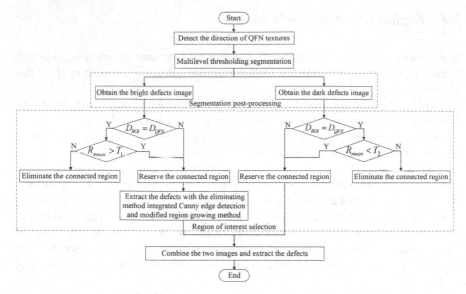

Fig. 4 The flowchart of the proposed method

3   Experiment

In order to verify the effectiveness of the proposed method, six QFN defects images captured from QFN test handler with dark-field illumination were tested in this section. The experiments were implemented in MATLAB on a computer with Intel Core 2.26 GHz and 2 GB of memory. According to the characteristics of QFN defect images, the thresholds T_1 and T_2 were set as 225 and 95.

Figure 5 gives the results of the proposed method. In Fig. 5, the first column and the third column are tested images; the second column and the fourth column are the corresponding defects images of the proposed method. From Fig. 5, it can be found that the proposed method efficiently extract the defects from QFN surface.

4   Conclusion

In this paper, a QFN defect extraction method is proposed. The process of the proposed method includes multilevel thresholding segmentation, segmentation post-processing, QFN texture direction detector and region of interest selection. The main contributions are: 1. According to the characteristics of QFN defects images, QFN texture direction is proposed. 2. Two region of interest selection methods are applied to the bright defects image and the dark defects image, respectively.

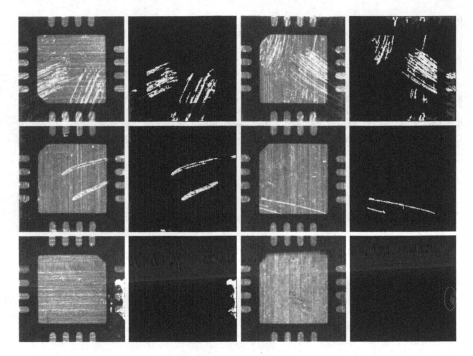

Fig. 5 The results of the proposed method

The experimental results show that the proposed method can extract defects from the QFN surface efficiently. In the future, the defect feature extraction and classification are the research targets.

Acknowledgments This work is supported by the National Nature Science Foundation of China (Grant No.51275090) and the Fundamental Research Funds for the Central Universities and Jiangsu Postgraduate Innovation Program (Grant No.KYLX15_0208).

References

1. Yun JP et al (2014) Defect inspection system for steel wire rods produced by hot rolling process. Int J Adv Manuf Technol 70:1625–1634
2. Song K-C et al (2014) Surface defect detection method using saliency linear scanning morphology for silicon steel strip under oil pollution interference. ISIJ Int 54:2598–2607
3. Chiu Shih-Wen, Tang Kea-Tiong (2013) Towards a chemiresistive sensor-integrated electronic nose: a review. Sensors 13:14214–14247
4. Karimi MH, Asemani D (2014) Surface defect detection in tiling Industries using digital image processing methods: analysis and evaluation, ISA Trans 53:834–844
5. Tsai D-M, Luo J-Y (2011) Mean shift-based defect detection in multicrystalline solar wafer surfaces. IEEE Trans Ind Inf 7:125–135

6. Wang M et al (2009) A fast algorithm for segmenting defects on the surface of QFN packages, International Conference on Information Engineering and Computer Science, ICIECS 2009, IEEE, pp 1–4
7. Chen K et al (2015) Defects extraction for QFN based on mathematical morphology and modified region growing, IEEE International Conference on Mechatronics and Automation (ICMA), pp 2426–2430
8. Chen K et al (2014) Defect image segmentation using multilevel thresholding based on firefly algorithm with opposition-learning. J Southeast Univ (English Edn) 30:434–438
9. Wang Z, Wang ZQ, Mao YW (2002) A description based on texture direction and the clustering and segmentation to directional texture images, J Image Graphics 7:1279–1284

Perceptron: An Old Folk Song Sung on a New Stage

Yuping Li

Abstract Conventional pattern classification aims to improve classification accuracy for the whole dataset. In the time of Big Data, however, there are circumstances in which people may take interest only in those typical instances and other issues like scalability and efficiency take priority. Keeping these issues in mind, in this paper, we revisit the perceptron algorithm. While it is a linear model, we show that with proper objective functions, it can be transformed to a probabilistic learner. The evaluation is carried out with the well known Pima diabetes database. The experimental results indicate that the perceptron algorithm is comparable to other sophisticated sophisticated algorithms in terms of the criteria discussed in this paper.

Keywords Perceptron · Efficiency · Classification

1 Introduction

When it comes to pattern classification or classifiers, two major issues can be distinguished in general, namely, (i) the adopted paradigm and algorithmic approach to classification; (ii) the definition and assessment of similarity of instances to classes [1]. The first issue is about learning process, i.e., when to learn and how to learn. The second issue is about learning subject, i.e., the assumed model for each class that encodes its relationship with instances.

Although classification in general is a rather dignified data mining task, different specialized techniques to enhance classification solutions have been contributed from multiple fields. In this paper, we revisit perceptron, the pioneer of neural networks [2]. The reason is two-fold for selecting this simple yet effective classifier. First, perceptron is simple and thus flexible with respect to the two issues above. As to learning process, perceptron allows for both online and batch mode learning. As

Y. Li (✉)
School of Business Planning, Chongqing Technology and Business University,
Chongqing, China
e-mail: liyuping821@126.com

© Springer Science+Business Media Singapore 2016

127

J.J. (Jong Hyuk) Park et al. (eds.), *Advanced Multimedia and Ubiquitous Engineering*, Lecture Notes in Electrical Engineering 393,
DOI 10.1007/978-981-10-1536-6_17

to learning subject, while perceptron is essentially a linear model, due to the subsequent flexible net function, it can perform maximum a posteriori estimation and output the posterior probabilities. Second, although a number of sophisticated learning algorithms have recently been brought forward in the literature, due to the huge volume of data, many companies still use the simple and fast learning algorithms for their daily task. For them, a small improvement in accuracy, say, 1 % increase in classification rate, is not as vital or necessary as other practical issues such as robustness and quick response [3]. For instance, since users of search engines would only view the top few results from the returned millions of search results, as long as the simple method does not mispredict the ranks of the top few results, to end users, it does not look much different from those sophisticated methods that can accurately predict the rank for every result. On the other hand, the users are more sensitive to issues like repeatability of search results and response time, which may put simple methods at an advantage.

In this paper, we want to shed only some light on these issues during the examination of perceptron. In particular, we demonstrate in detail how the linear perceptron can be transformed into a posterior probability learner. The examination is carried out with the help of the well known Pima diabetes database available on the UCI machine learning repository [4]. Although many studies have been carried out on this dataset, to date it still defies many of the pattern classification algorithms.

The rest of the paper is organized as follows. Sect. 2 briefly reviews perceptron and demonstrates in detail how the linear perceptron can be transformed into a posterior probability learner. Sect. 3 reports the experimental results on the diabetes dataset. Finally, Sect. 4 concludes this paper with some discussion.

2 Perceptron

2.1 Principles

As the pioneer of neural networks, the perceptron algorithm was invented at the Cornell Aeronautical Laboratory by Frank Rosenblatt [5]. The perceptron was intended to be a machine, rather than a program. While its first implementation was in software for the IBM 704, it was subsequently implemented in custom-built hardware as the "Mark 1 perceptron," which was designed for image recognition. Figure 1 gives perceptron's architecture.

The output of perceptron is given by

$$y(x) = f(\text{net}) \tag{1}$$

$$= f(w^T x + b) \tag{2}$$

where x is the input vector, w is the weight vector, b is the bias and f is the transfer function. If we use sign $(\cdot)$ for f, perceptron is essentially a linear function again.

Fig. 1 The perceptron model

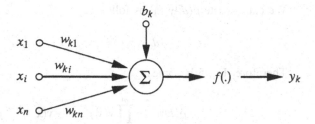

In pattern classification, instead of directly outputting class label w, we want it to output the probability that the current input x belongs to class w, i.e., the posterior probability p (w|x). Hence we often employ a monotonic function with range in [0, 1] for the transfer function f. For instance, we can use the sigmoid function defined as

$$f(\text{net}) = \frac{1}{1 + \exp(-\text{net})} \tag{3}$$

Actually, when using the sigmoid function for classification, e.g., assign x to class 1 if $y > 0.5$, the decision boundary it forms is also linear, since $y > 0.5 \Leftrightarrow net > 0 \Leftrightarrow w^T x + b > 0$.

2.2 Probabilistic Learning

Although perceptron outputs linear class boundaries, below we demonstrate that with particular setting, the output of such a perceptron model can be regarded as the posterior probability.

In binary classification problem (it can be easily extended to multi-class case), although the target is often 1 for the right class and 0 elsewhere, it is reasonable to assume that the perceptron is supposed to learn a nondeterministic binary function $d: X \rightarrow \{0, 1\}$, where $d(x) = 1$ with a certain probability. That is, we seek a function $y: X \rightarrow [0, 1]$ such that $y(x) = p(d(x) = 1)$. To that end, the likelihood function is a useful criterion to measure how good the learned function y fits the data [6–8]. Therefore, given a data sample $D = \{(x_i, d_i)\} \, \underset{i=1}{M}$ where $d_i = 0$ or 1, it makes sense that we wish our function y to maximize the sample likelihood:

$$p(D|y) = \prod_{i=1}^{m} p(x_i, d_i|y) \tag{4}$$

$$= \prod_{i=1}^{m} p(d_i|y, x_i)p(x_i) \tag{5}$$

We can rewrite $p(d_i|y, x_i)$ as follows

$$p(d_i|y, x_i) = y(x_i)^{d_i}(1 - y(x_i))^{1-d_i} \tag{6}$$

Therefore, Eq. 5 becomes

$$p(D|y) = \prod_{i=1}^{m} y(x_i)^{d_i}(1 - y(x_i))^{1-d_i} p(x_i) \tag{7}$$

The function for maximum likelihood (ML) is the one

$$f_{ML} = argmax_f \prod_{i=1}^{m} y(x_i)^{d_i}(1 - y(x_i))^{1-d_i} \tag{8}$$

The last term $p(x_i)$ is dropped, since it is independent of y. By adding the monotonic function ln, we have

$$f_{ML} = argmax_f \sum_{i=2}^{M} d_i \ln(y(x_i)) + (1 - d_i) \ln(1 - y(x_i)) \tag{9}$$

The negative of the expression above is referred to as cross entropy. One can see that when the perceptron is adjusted to minimize the cross entropy, the resultant y is the maximum likelihood estimator to the probabilistic target function d.

As for training, with the sigmoid function in Eq. 3, the likelihood function becomes

$$E = \sum_{i=2}^{M} d_i \ln\left(\frac{1}{1 + \exp(-w^T x_i)}\right) + (1 - d_i) \ln\left(1 - \frac{1}{1 + \exp(-w^T x_i)}\right) \tag{10}$$

where we augment the original d-dimensional x and w to $(d + 1)$-dimensional [x, 1] and [w, b] respectively to incorporate the bias b. To maximize it, we can employ the update rule of gradient ascent [9]

$$w(n + 1) = \left(1 - \frac{a}{n}\right)w(n) + \frac{a}{n}\sum_{i=2}^{M}\left(d_i - \frac{1}{1 + \exp(-w^T x_i)}\right)x^i \tag{11}$$

where the second term is the gradient, _E/_w, and _ is the initial learning rate.

3 Experimental Results

We use the Pima diabetes database to evaluate the perceptron algorithm. This dataset has 768 records about diabetes information of a Pima Indian population living near Phoenix, Arizona, USA. Each record has 9 numerical attributes, for which the first 8 are recordings of some property such as age and blood pressure, and the last is a binary valued variable (class label) indicating whether she has signs of diabetes.

The following is the detail of our experimental setting. The initial w is set to zero. The initial learning rate _ is sampled evenly at a constant interval 0.05 in [0.1, 0.5]. 10-fold cross validation is employed and the training is stopped when we obtain the best test rate. Hence the perceptron algorithm is run 90 times on the diabetes dataset. Figure 2 shows the box plots for these 90 classification rates. In general, the best results are obtained around $\alpha = 0.25$. At this time, the average training rate and the test rate are 0.77 and 0.73 respectively.

4 Discussion

Pima indians diabetes database has been studied with many classification algorithms. Perhaps the most comprehensive one is the StatLog project [10]. They used 12-fold cross validation and logistic discrimination achieved the best test result among many other approaches like CART, C4.5, Bayes Tree, Kohonen network, LVQ, SMART, etc. For comparison, we list in Table 1 the major results from this project (they did not try perceptron). Because they used a larger training set and a smaller test set, it is not surprising that their results of logistic discrimination are better than ours. On the other hand, it must be noted that logistic discrimination, back propagation networks and RBF are all neural network-like algorithms. They are much more complicated than perceptron in structure and hence need more

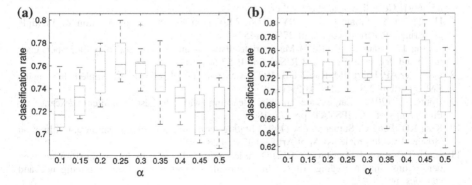

Fig. 2 Perceptron's results on the diabetes dataset. **a** The training rate. **b** The test rate

Table 1 The classification rates on the diabetes dataset obtained in StatLog

Algorithm	Longdisc	RBF	KNN	Discrim	Backprop
Train	0.781	0.782	0	0.780	0.802
test	0.777	0.757	0.676	0.775	0.752

costly optimization procedures. The detailed results depend a lot on the particular optimization methods employed. In our case, however, we simply used the simple gradient ascent method to maximize the likelihood function encoded in the perceptron, which also led to a result close to those complicated ones.

As mentioned earlier, in practice, users may take interest only in the top results rather than all of the results. In classification problems, these top instances often refer to those data that are representative of the class characteristics and thus with higher posterior probabilities. We also run the logistic discrimination and RBF on the diabetes dataset. It is observed that they really share a lot of higher posterior probability instances with perceptron. This speaks to the eligibility of perceptron as an alternative for partial classification, i.e., classifying only those top/typical instances. More recently, the perceptron has also been found helpful to deep learning via its linear transformations [11]. Indeed, in the era of big data, there are more and more emerging applications where the old folk-song, perceptron, can be sung to a new tune.

References

1. Duda RO, Hart PE, Stork DG (2000) Pattern classification, 2nd edn. Wiley, New York
2. Bishop CM (ed) (2006) Pattern recognition and machine learning. Springer, Heidelberg
3. McMahan HB, Holt G, Sculley D (2013) Ad click prediction: a view from the trenches. In: Proceedings of the 19th ACM SIGKDD international conference on knowledge discovery and data mining, pp 1222–1230
4. Newman DJ, Hettich S, Blake CL, Merz CJ (1998) UCI repository of machine learning databases. http://www.ics.uci.edu/_mlearn/MLRepository.html
5. Rosenblatt F (1957) The perceptron-a perceiving and recognizing automaton. Technical report 85-460-1, Cornell Aeronautical Laboratory
6. Hu T, Yu Y, Xiong J, Sung SY (2006) Maximum likelihood combination of multiple clusterings. Pattern Recogn Lett 27(13):1457–1464
7. Rasson JP, Granville V (1995) Multivariate discriminant analysis and maximum penalized likelihood density estimation. J R Stat Soc B 57:501–517
8. Dempster AP, Laird NM, Rubin DB (1977) Maximum likelihood from incomplete data via the EM algorithm. J R Stat Soc B 39:1–38
9. Bottou L (2010) Large-scale machine learning with stochastic gradient descent. In: Proceedings of COMPSTAT, pp 177–186
10. King RD, Feng C, Sutherland A (1995) Statlog: comparison of classification algorithms on large real-world problems. Appl Artif Intell 9(3):289–333
11. Raiko T, Valpola H, LeCun Y (2012) Deep learning made easier by linear transformations in perceptrons. In: Proceedings of the international conference on artificial intelligence and statistics. pp 24–932

Simulation of Explosion Using the Ideal Viscoelastic Object Yield Condition

Byeong-Seok Shin, Gyeong-Su Kim and Su-Kyung Sung

Abstract In particle-based fluid simulations, viscoelastic materials require yield stress for material deformation. We propose an ideal viscoelastic material yield condition developed by modifying the Tresca's condition that can be easily approximated using the difference between the maximum and minimum principal stress, unlike the von Mises condition for which the forces in numerous directions applied to an object should be calculated. The proposed ideal viscoelastic material yield condition assumes the area of the object deformed due to the forces applied to it as the principal stress based on the Tresca yield condition. Using this method, the process through which a viscoelastic material explodes because it cannot endure the critical stress when its interface decreases beyond the ideal yield condition can be realistically expressed.

Keywords Particle-based fluid simulations · Viscoelastic materials · Yield condition

1 Introduction

Fluid simulations are mainly used to express the movements of liquids in movies or computer games. Fluid data consisting of many particles cannot be easily rendered in real time. In general, the smoothed-particle hydrodynamics (SPH) technique is used for the efficient rendering of fluid particles [1]. SPH has been developed in the

B.-S. Shin (✉) · G.-S. Kim · S.-K. Sung
Department of Computer Science and Information Engineering, Inha University,
Incheon, Korea
e-mail: bsshin@inha.ac.kr

G.-S. Kim
e-mail: hoolist1234@naver.com

S.-K. Sung
e-mail: rebirth87@naver.com

© Springer Science+Business Media Singapore 2016
J.J. (Jong Hyuk) Park et al. (eds.), *Advanced Multimedia and Ubiquitous Engineering*, Lecture Notes in Electrical Engineering 393,
DOI 10.1007/978-981-10-1536-6_18

133

field of astrophysics and is an interpolation method applied with the Navier-Stokes equation.

We proposed an explosion simulation method for viscoelastic materials. Among the kinds of forces applied in SPH, the viscous force resists against the acceleration generated by external forces. Particles resisted by external forces other than gravity continuously slow down and when their speed has reached a certain critical point, they agglomerate with the attraction to one another. However, unlike general liquids, viscoelastic materials have elasto-plasticity for returning to their original shapes when they have been impacted. So, SPH-based particle fluid simulations cannot naturally express elasto-plasticity. Studies to express viscoelastic materials using SPH have been conducted. To express the elasto-plasticity, Simon et al. proposed a yield condition under which objects are deformed when subjected to external force exceeding the critical point and are recovered to their original states otherwise [2]. In particular, the yield condition proposed by von Mises was approximated to express resilience by changing the locations of particles subjected to external force by their migration lengths only when their migration lengths exceed the threshold value.

In this study, an ideal viscoelastic material yield condition is made by modifying the Tresca yield condition to express the phenomenon of the explosion of internal viscoelastic materials when they are unable to endure external forces as the interfaces around the materials gradually decrease. That is, the area of viscoelastic materials formed by particles was calculated so that the object would explode when the area decreased to below the threshold size. Although the scope of application of the Tresca yield condition is narrower than that of the von Mises condition because it is for soft objects only, since its calculation formula is not calculated, the association between the Tresca calculated formula and the proposed ideal viscoelastic material yield condition can be proven.

2 Related Work

Since the computation rapidly increases to express fluid advection using the Euler method [3] and this makes processing in real time difficult, the Lagrangian method is used for which the computation is smaller than others [4, 5]. It directly simulates fluid particles by focusing on particles per se rather than environments around fluids. The SPH technique intended to efficiently compute the correlations among all particles is frequently used. SPH uses radially symmetric smoothing kernels. The field values of particles in a kernel are calculated as the average values of particles overlapping with their neighboring kernels. Currently, it is used in many fluid areas, such as fluid-solid deformation simulations [6] and melting fluid simulations [7].

As fluid expression has begun to receive attention, interest in the expression of viscoelasticity fluids has also increased. In particular, attempts have been made to express the elasto-plasticity of viscoelastic fluids that have properties intermediate between fluids and solids when subjected to external forces using yield criteria and stress. Adam et al. approximated the deformation gradient involved in the deformation of the shape of materials when point-based viscoelastic materials are plastic deformed after they are dropped or were impacted [8]. Simon et al. proposed a double-density relaxation technique for the realistic expression of the elasticity of viscoelastic materials subjected to external forces. In addition, the von Mises yield condition was applied to viscoelastic materials' stress.

However, these studies of elasto-plasticity failed to express the exploding property of semi-fluids. Depending on their components, viscoelastic materials may easily lose the shape of objects that are not simply plastic when external forces are applied.

3 Ideal Explosion of Viscoelastic Materials

In viscoelastic material simulations, when objects composed of particles are subjected to external forces from all directions, the density of particles rapidly increases and the pressure rises. When the limit within which the original shape can be maintained is exceeded by strong external forces, the object fails to maintain its shape then explodes.

Stress is the resistance per the unit area occurring inside an object when the object has been deformed by external force. When a fluid receives forces from the outside, forces of the same size act in the opposite direction inside the fluid to maintain the fluid's original shape. Stress comprises *shearing stress* and *normal stress*. Shearing stress refers to the internal force from inside the object due to shearing force and normal stress refers to stress perpendicular to a cross section, which is the force formed in response to vertical loads acting on the cross section. Normal stress is used to express stress occurring perpendicularly to each plane.

Since viscoelastic material simulations should include the properties of both solids and fluids, yield conditions are necessary for materials to receive external force for plastic-deformation. Yield conditions refer to those in which objects receive external force to fail, which were stipulated in relation to the characteristics of materials. Hypotheses that explain yield conditions include the maximum shearing stress theory (Tresca theory) and the maximum shearing deformation energy theory (von Mises theory). The von Mises theory assumes that yield occurs when the deformation energy has reached a certain threshold value. In general, the strength of an object is analyzed using the torsional energy levels at various points of the object to measure the condition in which the relevant object fails. However, the forces received by the object at individual points should be calculated and the amounts of calculations for the resultant value; stress levels are large.

In particle-based fluid simulations, the reference points of viscoelastic materials are not on the xyz-axes of the object, but on the particles that constitute the object. Therefore, whether particles have been deformed is determined based on the distance traveled by particles that received the force. However, the explosion appearing as a result of forces acting in many directions cannot be expressed using methods that approximate changes in objects using particles' travel distances. Explosions are a phenomenon appearing as a result of pressure rapidly increased physically/chemically in closed spaces. To express such pressure, forces received by the planes of objects consisting of many particles should be calculated instead of the force received by one particle. Although the existing travel distance-based approximation is efficient for small numbers of particles, it is not efficient for simulations of large viscoelastic materials in fluid simulations in which many particles are used.

Our proposed method uses the Tresca yield condition under the concept of the maximum stress theory that yield occurs when the maximum stress placed on the object is the same as the maximum stress at the point of yield during tensile tests.

The Tresca yield condition equation is related to the principal stress, meaning that stress occurs due to external forces placed on objects. The Tresca yield condition is expressed as 1/2 of the difference between the maximum principal stress (σ_{max}) and the minimum principal stress (σ_{min}). Although the allowable range values of soft materials according to the conditions are stable in the case of the von Mises yield condition, since the calculations are complicated, the Tresca yield condition shown in (Eq. 1) that expressed the value as an approximate equation is utilized.

$$\tau_f = \frac{S_y}{2} = \frac{\sigma_{max} - \sigma_{min}}{2} \tag{1}$$

Using incompressibility, which is a characteristic of particle-based simulations, an ideal viscoelastic material yield condition is proposed to obtain yield conditions by assuming the principal stress of objects as volumes instead of travel distances as with existing methods. Incompressibility is a state in which the volume does not change, no matter how much the object is compressed. Whereas gas molecules have compressibility, as they are apart from each other, liquid molecules are not compressed, no matter how much force is applied to them because they are connected to each other in ideal neighboring states. To express realistic liquids, particle-based simulations have incompressibility. When the pressure rapidly increased by external forces obstructs the incompressibility of liquids, the reaction force to return to the original state is accumulated in the liquids and explosions occur when this reaction force becomes larger than the external force applied.

An ideal rectangular viscoelastic material that is maintained at a certain volume due to incompressibility is assumed, and the moment at which the material fails to endure and explodes when the incompressibility is obstructed by very strong external forces is defined as the ideal viscoelastic material yield condition. The form that has the minimum principal stress is assumed to be the stabilized state in which incompressibility is maintained.

$$\left| \frac{V_l - V_m}{2} \right| = \tau_f = \Delta v \tag{2}$$

Equation (2) is an equation for the ideal viscoelastic material yield condition proposed in the present paper. V_l is an object that has the minimum principal stress and V_m is the size of an object that has the maximum principal stress. Since the size of the object that has the maximum principal stress is small to the extent that it can be ignored, the size of V_l is assumed as $1 \times 1 \times 1$, which is the smallest volume in the simulation. Eventually, the form where the yield condition is formed leading to explosions is half the size of the one that has the minimum principal stress.

Unlike distance-based approximation, when the same force is applied to the object in several directions, the amount of changes in the entire object is calculated instead of the amount of changes in one particle. As a result, fewer operations are performed and the object is assumed to be an ideal form having the principal stress to show realistic explosions.

4 Experimental Results

The experiment was conducted in a system having an Intel Core i5 3.4 GHz CPU and a main memory of 8 GB. An nVidia GeForce 760 having a memory of 4 GB was used and Blender and Python scripts were used for implementation. To test the viscoelastic material yield condition in 3D spaces, the volume of the object was calculated. To conduct the experiment with an object consisting of viscous materials, an object having a viscosity level approximately 1.6 times higher than that of water was formed. The experiment was conducted with 1000 particles, which is the minimum number of particles for incompressibility to be maintained. The state in which all particles gathered in the hexagonal interface was assumed as the minimum principal stress, and the moment at which the area of the interface became the minimum area $1 \times 1 \times 1$ was assumed as the maximum principal stress. Based on the Tresca yield condition, experiments were conducted in which the yield stress occurred and particles exploded at the moment when the difference between the maximum principal stress and the minimum principal stress became 1/2 of the Tresca yield condition. To compare the existing distance-based yield condition simulations, the form of the object at the moment when the ideal viscoelastic material exploded at the yield condition was measured.

Figure 1 shows the front and side views of a situation in which a hexahedron was thrown to the edge interfaces of six planes in SPH so that the volume of the hexahedron decreased and the viscoelastic material exploded at the critical point when the volume decreased to 1/2 of the original volume. After the object crushed after receiving the initial impact, the bonds among particles were maintained until the volume decreased to 1/2 of the original volume, but the bonds among particles were lost as the volume decreased further so that the object exploded. In the case of existing distance-based viscoelastic yield simulations, when external force exceeded the limit of the yield condition, hair gel that has a viscosity level 1.6 times higher than that of water can be exploded when only general persons' grasping power is imposed on it.

Fig. 1 Movement of particles of a cube-shaped viscoelastic material during explosion

The comparison of frame rates according to the number of particles showed similar results for both the distance-based approximation yield condition and the ideal viscoelastic material yield condition. Frame rates of 20, 20, and 2 fps were shown in the cases of 1000, 2275, and 4000 particles, respectively. During explosions, under the viscoelastic material yield condition, frame rates of 24, 10, and 4 fps were shown in the cases of 1000, 2275, and 4000 particles, respectively.

5 Conclusion

In the particle-based viscoelastic material simulations, material plasticity was determined using the von Mises yield condition suitable for soft materials' stress. However, length-based travel distance change methods could not be applied to the explosions of viscoelastic materials that received forces from many directions. Therefore, in the present paper, the Tresca theory, which is a different yield condition for soft materials than the von Mises yield condition, was referred to make an explosion yield condition for viscoelastic materials. A phenomenon that after the explosion of the object, particles in the vicinity of the object gathered to form a small lump was identified.

Acknowledgment This work was supported by the National Research Foundation of Korea (NRF) grant funded by the Korea government (MSIP) (No. 2015R1A2A2A01008248).

References

1. Müller M, Charypar D, Gross M (2003) Particle-based fluid simulation for interactive applications In: Proceedings of the 2003 ACM SIGGRAPH/Eurographics symposium on Computer animation, Eurographics Association, pp 154–159
2. Clavet S, Beaudoin P, Poulin P (2005) Particle-based viscoelastic fluid simulation, Euro graphics/ACM SIGGRAPH, pp 219–228
3. Foster N, Fedkiw R (2001) Practical animation of liquids. In: Proceedings of the 28th annual conference on computer graphics and interactive techniques, ACM, pp 23–30
4. Stam J (1999) Stable fluids SIGGRAPH, pp 121–128
5. Hirt CW, Cook JL, Butler TD (1970) A lagrangian method for calculating the dynamics of an incompressible fluid with free surface. J Comput Phy pp 103–124
6. Muller M, Schirm S, Teschner M, Heidelberger B, Gross M (2004) Interaction of fluids with deformable solids. J Comput Anim Virtual Words, pp 159–171
7. Muller M, Keiser R, Nealen A, Pauly M, Gross M, Alexa M (2004) Point based animation of elastic, plastic and melting object. In: Proceedings of the symposium on computer animation, pp 141–151
8. Gerszewski D, Bhattacharya H, Bargteil AW (2009) A Point-based method for animating elastoplastic solids In: Proceedings of Eurographics/ACM SIGGRAPH symposium on computer animation, pp 219–228

Distributed Cluster Collaboration Strategy for Object Association and Identification in Large Areas

Sangjin Hong and Nammee Moon

Abstract This paper presents a collaborative strategy of the distributed RFID sensor clusters for object association and identification. The process that converts the group associations to the single associations is also described. The basic association mechanism utilizes two homographic regions that model the RFID fluctuations. The sources of potential generation of false associations are discussed and the techniques for eliminating them with sensor collaboration are presented. The problem with the information inconsistency and its temporal propagation in the large-scale is described, and the mechanism for detecting and correcting such an inconsistency is proposed. The association performance of the proposed strategy is simulated with various parameters.

Keywords Heterogeneous sensor networks · Object association · Collaborative processing · Surveillance systems

1 Introduction

Heterogeneous sensor networks have received much attention in the field of multiple object tracking to exploit advantages of using different functionalities [1–5]. The visual sensor is one of the most popular sensors due to its reliability and ease of analysis [6, 7]. However, the visual sensor based tracking system is limited to detection and tracking for recording the trajectory of objects, and is not suitable for object identification. One of the main difficulties of the visual sensor-based object

S. Hong
Stony Brook University, New York, USA

N. Moon (✉)
Hoseo University, Asan, South Korea
e-mail: mnm@hoseo.edu

© Springer Science+Business Media Singapore 2016   141
J.J. (Jong Hyuk) Park et al. (eds.), *Advanced Multimedia and Ubiquitous Engineering*, Lecture Notes in Electrical Engineering 393,
DOI 10.1007/978-981-10-1536-6_19

tracking is that distinguishable characteristics of the objects are non-trivial to be constructed for all the detected targets due to the similarities in color, size, and shape of the objects. Also, several identification sensors, such as RFID (Radio Frequency Identification), fingerprint, or iris recognition system, have been utilized for object identification. However, the functionality of these sensors is limited to object identification and they are bit suitable for object tracking. They can only alarm human operators of events triggered by identification sensors and cannot make intelligent decisions. Therefore, an identification sensor can only complement the visual sensor based tracking system in the intelligent surveillance system.

There have been some related works regarding the issue of surveillance using heterogeneous sensors such as heterogeneous data association and efficient network architecture. Schulz et al. [8] proposed a method to track and identify multiple objects by using ID-sensors such as infrared badges and anonymous sensors such as laser range finders. Although the system successfully associates the anonymous sensor data with ID-sensor data, the transition between the two phases is heuristically averaging the number of different assignments in Markov chains. Moreover, it does not provide a recovery method against losing the correct ID, and the number of hypotheses grows extremely fast whenever several people are close to each other. Shin et al. [9] proposed the network architecture for a large scale surveillance system that supports heterogeneous sensors such as video and RFID sensors. Although the event-driven control effectively minimizes the system load, the paper does not deal with the association problem of heterogeneous data as well as the mitigation of data overload. Although such approaches can associate data of different formats successfully, they do not provide a recovery method against incorrect identification. Also, the computational cost of probabilistic assignment increases exponentially with the number of neighboring objects. The performances of these approaches, however, can be significantly degraded by the coverage uncertainty of the RFID sensors. The coverage uncertainty is caused by time-varying fluctuation of radio frequency signals. False associations of the objects and/or individuals can occur because visual sensors and identification sensors obtain data in different formats at different sampling times.

In this paper, a collaborative strategy of the distributed RFID sensor clusters for object association and identification is presented. The basic association mechanism at the cluster utilizes two homographic regions that model the RFID fluctuations. The association process is triggered by the events provided by the RFID reader and the visual sensors. The conversion process from the group association to the single association is incorporated at the server. The false associations are minimized through collaboration among the clusters where the server constantly monitors local database at the cluster. Moreover, the problem with the information inconsistency and its temporal propagation in the large-scale is described, and the mechanism for detecting and correcting such an inconsistency is proposed.

2   Object Association Within the Cluster

2.1   Cluster Characteristics

Multiple clusters are placed within the area where the cluster has one RFID reader for the object identification. These clusters locally associate the objects with their identities and the clusters communicate with the server for information collaboration where the consistency of the association is monitored and corrected. The visual sensor network provides visual information for the object association as shown in Fig. 1a. Normally, the visual sensor network performs typical surveillance operations such as detection and tracking of all objects. The visual sensor network maintains unique object ID for all objects as well as their trajectories. The events are generated and transmitted to the clusters if the object enters or leaves the clusters. Upon receiving the events from the visual sensor network, the cluster performs the association process. The clusters maintain the local database while the server maintains the aggregated database.

As illustrated in Fig. 1b, each cluster has a set of homographic regions (outer region and inner region) representing the RFID coverage range. The visual sensor network notifies the cluster if there is any object crossing the homographic regions. The visual sensor network generates four possible events: an object crossing the outer region from outside, an object crossing the outer region from inside, an object crossing the inner region from outside, and an object crossing the inner region from inside. In addition to these four events, the RFID reader associated with the cluster generates two events. RFID appeared within the cluster and RFID disappeared from the cluster. The clusters use the event information from the visual sensor network and the ID registration status from the RFID sensor operation for the object association.

2.2   Association Strategy

For the discussion, it is assumed that the RFID reader coverage is bounded between the inner and outer regions. When the object crosses the outer boundary, the object ID for that object is inserted into the entering object list. Since the boundary does not correspond exactly to the RFID coverage, the RFID registration may not happen at the same time. After the crossing, the RFID may be registered and this RFID is inserted into the entering object list. When the same object crosses the inner boundary, both object ID and RFID are paired and transferred to the cluster local database and the entries are removed from the entering object list. Similarly, when the object currently located inside the inner boundary crosses the inner boundary, the object ID is inserted into the leaving object list. As soon as the RFID disappears from the cluster, the disappeared RFID is inserted into the leaving object list. After the object crosses the outer boundary, the cluster decides that the object left from

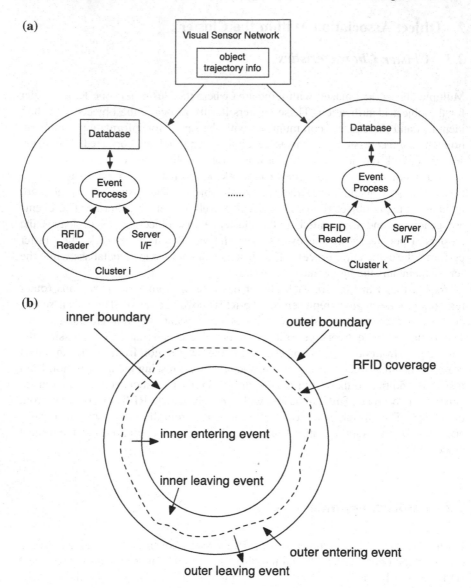

Fig. 1 **a** Visual sensor network monitors the entire areas. Events are generated when the object crosses the homographic regions for object association within the cluster. **b** Illustration of the RIFD reader characterization and representation

the cluster and removes the entry from the cluster local database and the leaving object list. When multiple objects enter the outer boundary, the objects IDs are enlisted into the entering object list. Because both of the objects are inside the clusters, two RFIDs will be registered. If one crosses the inner boundary, the group association (one object ID and two RFIDs) is established since it is impossible to distinguish between the objects due to unknown RFID coverage boundary. In this case, the object ID is removed from the entering object list but both RFIDs remain within the entering object list. When the other object crosses the inner boundary, the group association is again established. Since there is no object in the entering object list, the RFIDs currently in the entering object list are removed. Similar group associations are possible for the objects leaving the cluster.

2.3 Coverage Fluctuation and False Association

When the RFID coverage fluctuates, the RFID creates momentary RFID registration or de-registration even though the object may not be in position to trigger the associations. Also, if the RFID coverage spans outside the outer boundary, the RFID may be registered even before the object crosses the boundary. If other objects are already in the boundary, that object may be associated with the group association. Several situations where false associations may occur due to multiple objects entering the cluster with coverage fluctuations are discussed. Figure 2a illustrates a situation where the object has its own RFID. In this situation, when the objects are entering, the RFIDs are switched leading to false association. However, when they are leaving, the RFIDs are properly associated. While this situation is hard to resolve at the cluster level, it can be resolved by designating their statuses to

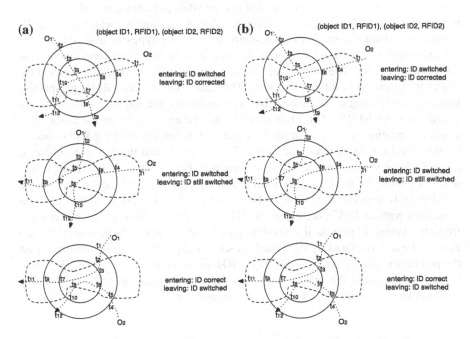

Fig. 2 **a** Illustration of the false associations. **b** Illustration of the wrong ID assignment

group associations. On the other hand, second case illustrates that the wrong assignments were made to both objects and when they leave the cluster, the RFIDs are still switched. The association is consistent so this situation is very difficult to resolve unlike the first situation. The third case is similar to the first case and can be easily resolved by changing the association status to group association. Figure 2b illustrates a situation where one object has its own ID and another object does not. In this situation, when objects are entering, the object without ID is assigned with an ID and the object with ID is not associated with any ID. However, when the objects are leaving, both of the objects are correctly associated. Thus conflicting association is made. On the other hand, the second case illustrates a situation in which wrong assignments are made when the objects enter and no correction is made when they leave. Hence permanent wrong assignment is made without any conflict. The first case is easily resolved by changing the association status to a group association but the second case is not easy to handle since it is difficult to determine if errors occurred or not. Third case is similar to the first case and can be easily resolved by changing the association status to the group association.

3   Cluster Collaboration to Handle False Association

3.1   Handling the Detection and Tracking Problems

The internal server database is organized into two data structures, namely, object ID perspective and RFID perspective structures. The data structure with the object ID perspective maintains the list of associated RFIDs, the types of associations, the cluster in which the last association took place, and the time the object entered and left from the cluster. The same object ID may appear in the list multiple times if the object is associated in different clusters. The data structure from RFID perspective keeps not only similar information but also maintains the object ID history associated with the RFIDs. This data structure is updated whenever the association status information is received from the cluster. If the object tracking failure occurs by the visual sensor network, the object ID associated with the lost track object is removed from the internal database as shown in Fig. 3a. When the visual sensor network regains the tracking, the visual sensor network assigns a new object ID and considers this object as if it has never been associated. If the removed object ID was associated with an RFID, the old object ID is put into the history list and removed from the current. Figure 3a also illustrates a situation when multiple objects are too close to be differentiated by the visual sensor network. In this case, similarly with the previous situation, a new set of object IDs are given to these objects. However, instead of removing the information from the server database, the server simply modifies their association statuses to group association.

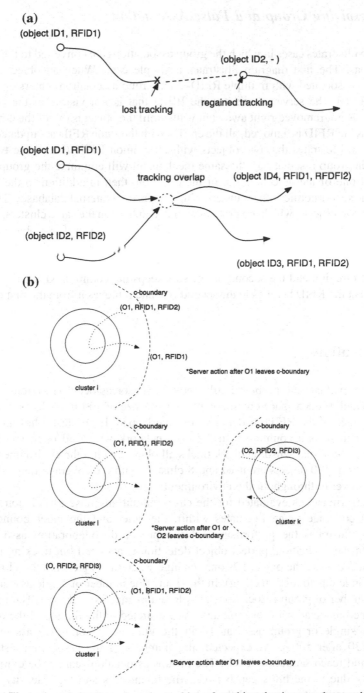

Fig. 3 **a** Illustration of situation where the tracking of an object that is currently associated is lost and regained by the visual sensor network. Illustration of a situation where two objects that are individually associated in the system have been merged and converted their association statuses to the group association. **b** Illustration of the mechanism for converting group associations to single associations. Conversion is triggered after the first object is out of c-region

3.2   Resolving Group and False Association

Figure 3b illustrates cases in which the group associations are converted to the single associations. The first diagram illustrates a simple case. When an object that is previously associated with multiple RFIDs (i.e., group association) enters or leaves from a cluster, the server eliminates the RFID that is not visible in the cluster. The RFID is not removed right away but waits until the object is out of the c-region. As soon as the RFID is removed, all the entries with the same RFID are updated. The second case illustrates that two objects with a common RFID (i.e., these two are partially in group association), the same mechanism will eliminate the group association. If one of the objects is out of the c-region, then in addition to the server update, the server notifies other clusters to update its own internal databases. The last case is for two objects, which are group associated and are in the same clusters. When they are group associated, due to the coverage fluctuation, even if one object leaves the cluster, the other object may still have the same RFID. In this case, the server waits for the first object to leave the cluster and out of the c-region. Once the first object leaves the c-region and the second object still keeps the common RFID, the server declares that the RFID belongs to the second one and removes it from the first object.

4   Evaluations

In order to evaluate the proposed collaborative sensor association system, a simulation model of open space environment with the size of 100 m by 150 m is used. The coverages of the RFID readers are not overlapped. Each cluster has an RFID reader and there is a common visual sensor network where all open spaces are monitored. The visual sensor network tracks all objects within the environment. For the evaluation, 120 objects are used and 8 clusters with the coverage range of 5 m are placed evenly throughout the environment.

The performance is evaluated for the case without any false association where the RFID coverage range fluctuates within the outer and the inner boundaries. Figure 4a illustrates the performance of the proposed collaboration association method. In the evaluation, perfect object detection is assumed but tracking misses are introduced. (i.e., the object IDs only change when the objects are too close and do not change due to miss tracking). In the figure, the number of single associations and the number of group associations are plotted as functions of time. The number of combined associations is also plotted. As illustrated in the figure, all the objects are either single or group associated and the number of combined associations reaches 120 after 500 s. As expected, the numbers of the associations steadily increase and reach saturation levels. The groups associations cannot be eliminated completely due to the finite gap between the boundaries and high density of the objects. However, it is expected that when more clusters are employed, the saturation levels may change where the saturation level of the single associations gets to

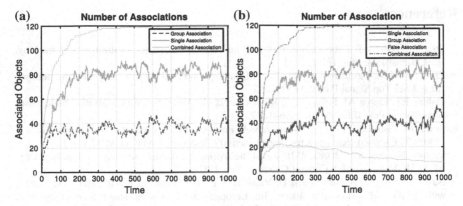

Fig. 4 a Performance of the single and group associations as a function of the time. In the evaluation, 8 clusters are deployed and 120 objects with their own RFID are used. Perfect detection and tracking are assumed **b** Illustration of the association performance when the RFID coverage of the cluster fluctuates. The plot shows the number of false association after the server correction

a higher level. Note that the group associations are still useful for locating the objects in the environment. Figure 4b illustrates the association performance when the server is correcting the inconsistency. As shown in the figure, the number of combined associations reaches 120 around 500 s. Initially, there are may false associations but the level of the number of associations steadily decreases as time progresses indicating the server is correcting the inconsistency. However, the number of false associations does not drop to zero completely since new object IDs are generated due to tracking misses (i.e., when the objects are close to one another). The level of false associations can be maintained at lower level if there are more clusters and the trajectories of the objects are more dispersed.

5 Conclusions

In this paper, a collaborative strategy of distributed RFID sensor clusters for object association and identification is proposed and evaluated. The basic association mechanism utilizes two homographic regions that model the RFID fluctuations. The problem with the information inconsistency and its temporal propagation in large-scale is described, and the mechanism for detecting and correcting such inconsistency is proposed. The proposed mechanism effectively converts the group associations to single associations and reduces the number of false associations resulted from the fluctuations of the RFID reader coverage. The performance of the proposed collaborative mechanism is evaluated with 120 objects with random trajectories within a large area. It is demonstrated that the total number of associations including the single and the group associations is maximized even with the RFID reader coverage fluctuations.

References

1. Strobel N, Spors S, Rabenstein R (2001) Joint audio-video object localization and tracking. IEEE Signal Proc Mag 18(1):22–31
2. Zhou H, Taj M, Cavallaro A (2008) Target Detection and tracking with heterogeneous sensors. IEEE J Sel Top Signal Proc 2(4):503–513
3. Collins RT, Lipton AJ, Fujiyoshi H, Kanade T (2001) Algorithms for cooperative multisensor surveillance. Proc IEEE 89(10):1456–1477
4. Smith JR, Fishkin KP, Jiang B, Mamishev A, Philipose M, Rea AD, Roy S, Sundara-Rajan K (2005) RFID-based techniques for human- activity detection. Commun ACM 48(9)
5. Vaidya N, Das SR (2008) RFID-based networks: exploiting diversity and redundancy. ACM SIGMOBILE Mob Comput Commun Rev 12(1)
6. Isasi A, Rodriguez S, Armentia JLD, Villodas A (2010) Location, tracking and identification with RFID and vision data fusion. In: European workshop on smart objects: systems, technologies and applications (RFID SysTech), pp. 1–6
7. Zhao W, Chellappa R, Phillips PJ, Rosenfeld A (2003) Face recognition: a literature survey. ACM Comput Surv 35(4):399–458
8. Schulz D, Fox D, Hightower J (2003) People tracking with anonymous and ID-sensors using Rao-Blackwellised particle filters. In: Proceedings of the International joint conference on artificial intelligence
9. Shin J, Kumar R, Mohapatra D, Ramachandran U, Ammar M (2007) ASAP: a camera sensor network for situation awareness. In: Proceedings of the International conference on principles of distributed systems

Experimental Study of Real-Time Comprehensive Indoor Air Quality

Kwang-il Hwang and Seung-Kyu Park

Abstract The growing concern about IAQ has accelerated the development of small, low cost Indoor Air Quality (IAQ) monitoring systems. These are capable of monitoring various indoor air pollutants in real-time. However, since most IAQ monitoring systems present the sensed value of the corresponding pollutant as a number, when we read the sensor values it is difficult for not experts but normal users to identify how polluted the air is or what is the pollution criteria of each pollutant. Therefore, for ambient air quality, a comprehensive Air Quality Index (AQI) is already being used in a number of nations to present the polluted level of the air, and thereby people can identify the current status of air quality easily. Nevertheless, since the index calculation is based on ambient air pollutants, and the index presents a section mean of sensed values collected for 1 or 24 h, the AQI used for presenting ambient air quality is not suitable for IAQ representation. Therefore, in this paper, we perform an experiment that applies the AQI directly to IAQ monitoring system that we developed, and derive some problems through the result analysis.

Keywords Indoor air quality · Air quality index · Real-time IAQ monitoring

1 Introduction

The indoor air quality (IAQ) has become a matter of growing concern over the last few decades. This concern was initially triggered by reports of occupants of various indoor environments who complained about a variety of unspecific symptoms, such as irritation or dryness of mucous membranes, burning eyes, headache of fatigue. Because in some cases these symptoms could be related to elevated concentrations of specific pollutants in indoor air, such as formaldehyde, increasing attention was

K. Hwang (✉) · S.-K. Park
Department of Embedded Systems Engineering, Incheon National University,
Incheon, South Korea
e-mail: hkwangil@inu.ac.kr

© Springer Science+Business Media Singapore 2016
J.J. (Jong Hyuk) Park et al. (eds.), *Advanced Multimedia and Ubiquitous Engineering*, Lecture Notes in Electrical Engineering 393,
DOI 10.1007/978-981-10-1536-6_20

devoted to determining climate conditions and chemical compounds in the air of rooms whenever people complained about bad indoor air quality [1].

In addition to the growing concern about IAQ, advances in the Internet of Things (IoT) and sensor technologies enabled the development of small, low cost IAQ monitoring systems [2–4]. These systems can monitor various indoor air pollutants in real-time and thus make users purify indoor air using evacuation or air cleaner systems by indentifying current air quality in real-time. However, since most IAQ monitoring systems present the amount of the sensed value of the corresponding pollutant as a number, it is difficult for not experts but normal users to identify how polluted the air is or what is the pollution criteria of each pollutant. Therefore, for ambient air quality, a comprehensive air quality index (AQI) is already used in a number of nations [5–13] to present the polluted level of the air, and thereby people can identify the current status of air quality easily. Nevertheless, since the index calculation is based on ambient air pollutants, and the index presents a section mean of pollutant values collected for 1 or 24 h, the AQI used for presenting ambient air quality is not suitable for IAQ.

Therefore, in this paper, we first perform an experiment that applies the AQI directly to IAQ monitoring system that we developed, and derive some problems through the result analysis. Based on the result, we also design a real-time comprehensive indoor air quality indicator, and prove the performance superiority of the proposed method through experiment.

2 Comprehensive Air Quality Index

An air quality index (AQI) is a number used by government agencies [14] to communicate to the public how polluted the air currently is or how polluted it is forecast to become [15, 16]. High AQI value means air quality is poor and thus the air can impact people health. Therefore, Different countries have their own air quality indices, corresponding to different national air quality standards, such as Canada [5], Hong Kong [6], Mainland China [7], India [8], Singapore [9], South Korea [10], UK [11], Europe [12], and United States [13]. Even though their specific standards are different a little bit, calculation and representation methods are similar.

Computation of the AQI requires an air pollutant concentration over a specified averaging period, obtained from an air monitor or model. Taken together, concentration and time represent the dose of the air pollutant. Health effects corresponding to a given dose are established by epidemiological research [17]. Air pollutants vary in potency, and the function used to convert from air pollutant concentration to AQI varies by pollutant. Air quality index values are typically grouped into ranges. Each range is assigned a descriptor, a color code, and a standardized public health advisory. South Korea divides the AQI level into four categories: Good, Moderate, Unhealthy, Very Unhealthy.

3 Experiments with CAQI

In this Section, we conduct an initial experiment that applies AQI directly to IAQ monitoring system that we developed. As shown in Fig. 1, in order to collect IAQ information, we developed tiny IAQ system which is capable of sensing Volatile Organic Compounds (VOC), Co, Co_2, Particle Materials (PM) 10, also known as dust, Temperature, and Humidity, respectively. The collected data set is periodically transmitted to server via Wi-Fi. Using the platform, we collected IAQ data, and based on the data we also analyzed distribution of each sensor data.

Since AQI is based on several pollutants affecting ambient air, in order to apply AQI to IAQ only two sensors (Co and PM) should be taken into account. Figure 2 shows the result which AQI is applied to Co and PM sensor, respectively. Measurement interval is 5 min so that AQI is presented by meaning the values collected for 1 h. The result shows that the variation of AQI is significantly sluggish with respect to the rapid changes in AQI. When AQI gets even seriously worse, the AQI did not respond to the recent changes converging to old values. That is, the AQI is not proper for IAQ representation. Therefore, the design considerations for the new indoor air quality are as follows:

- Minimum overhead in processing
- Small memory usage
- Outlier or missing value handling capability
- Indication representing comprehensive pollutants
- Quick response with respect to real-time IAQ changes.

Fig. 1 A prototype of real-time IAQ monitoring system

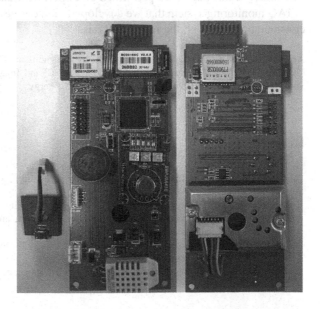

(a)   (b)

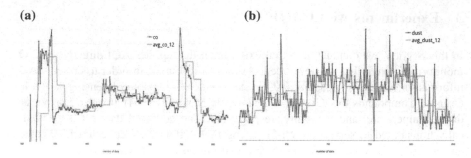

Fig. 2 AQI representation result for indoor air quality **a** Co. **b** Dust

4 Conclusion

Small, low cost Indoor Air Quality (IAQ) monitoring systems are capable of monitoring various indoor air pollutants in real-time. However, since most IAQ monitoring systems present the sensed value of the corresponding pollutant as a number, when we read the sensor values it is difficult for not experts but normal users to identify how polluted the air is or what is the pollution criteria of each pollutant. Therefore, for ambient air quality, a comprehensive Air Quality Index (AQI) is already being used in a number of nations to present the polluted level of the air, and thereby people can identify the current status of air quality easily. Nevertheless, since the index calculation is based on ambient air pollutants, and the index presents a section mean of sensed values collected for 1 or 24 h, the AQI used for presenting ambient air quality is not suitable for IAQ representation. Therefore, in this paper, we performed an experiment that applies the AQI directly to IAQ monitoring system that we developed, and derive some problems and design considerations through the result analysis.

Acknowledgments This work was supported by the Industrial Core Technology Development Program (10049009, Development of Main IPs for IoT and Image-Based Security Low-Power SoC) funded by the Ministry of Trade, Industry and Energy.

References

1. Maroni M, Seifert B,. Lindvall T (1995) Indoor air quality: a comprehensive reference book, vol 3. Elsevier
2. Open source DIY Project: LiV RPi indoor air quality monitor, http://www.livpi.com/
3. Standalone air quality monitor based around Raspberry Pi. http://hackaday.com/2012/12/11/standalone-air-quality-monitor-based-around-raspberry-pi/
4. Homemade arduino based indoor air quality CO2 PPM, temperature, humidity monitor. https://www.youtube.com/watch?v=gBtDGUB8HO8
5. Canada (2008). Environment Canada—air—AQHI categories and explanations. Ec.gc.ca. 16 Apr 2008. Retrieved 11 Nov 2011

6. Hong Kong (2014) Air quality health index. Government of the Hong Kong Special Administrative Region. Retrieved 9 Feb 2014
7. Mainland China (2013) People's Republic of China Ministry of environmental protection standard: technical regulation on ambient air quality index (Chinese PDF)
8. India, Rama Lakshmi (2014). India launches its own Air quality index. Can its numbers be trusted? Washington post. Retrieved 20 Aug 2015
9. Singapore (2011) MEWR—key environment statistics—clean air. 8 June 2011 App.mewr. gov.sg. Retrieved 11 Nov 2011
10. South Korea (2015) What's CAI. Air Korea. Retrieved 25 Oct 2015
11. United Kingdom, COMEAP. "Review of the UK Air Quality Index". COMEAP website
12. Europe, Garcia, Javier, Colosio, Joëlle (2002). Air-quality indices: elaboration, uses and international comparisons. Presses des MINES. ISBN 2-911762-36-3
13. United States (2011) Air quality index (AQI)—a guide to air quality and your health. US EPA. 9 Dec 2011. Retrieved 8 Aug 2012
14. International Air Quality (2015). Retrieved 20 Aug 2015
15. National Weather Service Corporate Image Web Team (2015) NOAA's national weather service/environmental protection agency—United States air quality forecast guidance. Retrieved 20 Aug 2015
16. https://www.gmes-atmosphere.eu/services/raq/raq_nrt/
17. Step 2 (2015) Dose-response assessment. Retrieved 20 Aug 2015

A Development of Streaming Big Data Analysis System Using In-memory Cluster Computing Framework: Spark

Kiejin Park, Changwon Baek and Limei Peng

Abstract In this paper, to deal with stream big data processing issue, we design and implement a big data analysis system using Spark which is an In-memory cluster computing framework. Spark is provided by ASF (Apache Software Foundation) open-source community, and is regarded as a next-generation high performance cluster computing technology. From the performance evaluation of the proposed system, we can see that Spark is 20+ times faster than conventional Mapreduce-based Hive SQL in terms of the response time. According to these results, we can confirm that the proposed system can be applied to solve the soft real-time big data analysis jobs for sensor data generated in a smart factory.

Keywords Cloud · Spark · MapReduce · Hive SQL · Real-time

1 Introduction

The existing RDBMS (Relational Database Management System) is able to realize soft real-time data processing to some extent. However, when using RDBMS, basically all the data that needs processing should be recorded in the standardized tables based on entity-relationship data model. Moreover, with the increasing of records in the table, the data capacity that needs to be processed also increases

K. Park (✉) · L. Peng
Department of Industrial Engineering, Ajou Univserity, Suwon,
Korea
e-mail: kiejin@ajou.ac.kr

L. Peng
e-mail: auroraplm@ajou.ac.kr

C. Baek
Department of ICT Management and Equipment,
Korean National Police Agency, Seoul, Korea
e-mail: baekcw@gmail.com

© Springer Science+Business Media Singapore 2016   157
J.J. (Jong Hyuk) Park et al. (eds.), *Advanced Multimedia and Ubiquitous Engineering*, Lecture Notes in Electrical Engineering 393,
DOI 10.1007/978-981-10-1536-6_21

sharply which makes RDBMS difficult to response and handle all the data promptly. On the other hand, the current data volume generated online is very diverse in data types and huge in capacity which requires vast analysis capability [1]. The existing analysis systems based on RDBMS are showing short in these aspects and novel access methods are needed.

In this paper, to solve the above mentioned problems, we collect a large amount of real-time sensor streaming data with huge amount that is generated online without restriction on capacity and save the data in the cluster in a distributed manner. Then, we develop an analysis system which is able to sense errors of given sensor data by various analysis methods. The proposed system adopts the In-memory process approach which uses one of the latest big data processing framework, say Spark. Spark is developed based on HDFS (Hadoop Distributed File System) that can save/refine/process/analyze/visualize huge data volume [2]. In the performance evaluation, when using In-memory based Spark to process the huge amount of sensor data that are generated at a smart factory, the processing time is shown to be 20+ times faster than Hive which uses existing SQL-on-Hadoop [3]. The construction of this paper is as follows. In Sect. 2, we introduce the analysis of streaming big data and In-memory cluster computing. In Sect. 3, we introduce the system design and analysis process for analyzing the huge amount of sensor data in a soft real-time manner. Section 4 shows the performance evaluation of the proposed system and the analysis result. Section 5 concludes the paper and introduces the future research.

2 Related Research

2.1 Research for Streaming Big Data Analysis

When processing big data, the batch processing method of MapReduce just uses the various combinations of keys and values in the distributed file system made up of the Map and Reduce functions to provide the query results by users [4]. However, even though this can solve the processing for huge formal/informal data, when querying every time, the local HDD (Hard Disc Drive) should be accessed which limit the real-time processing capability [5]. On the other hand, due to the cheap computing resource and the development of network, various existing H/Ws and S/Ws are combined to process data easily.

For example, a cluster resource management framework called YARN (Yet Another Resource Negotiator) which can manage various resources in Hadoop has been proposed (refer to Fig. 2). Via YARN, other various big data computing framework can be added to the computing resource based on HDFS. Among them, Spark is a typical one. In Spark, Spark SQL, Spark Streaming, Mllib, GraphX, etc., are provided [6] (Fig. 1).

(a)   (b)

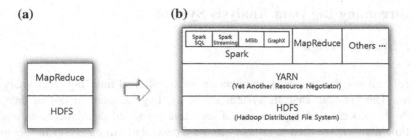

Fig. 1 The change of the big data processing platform from MRv1 to MRv2. **a** Mapreduce version 1(MRv1). **b** Mapreduce version 2(MRv2)

2.2 In-memory Based Cluster Computing: Spark

To achieve quick big data processing, in contrast to reading data from an HDD, it is necessary to read from memory. Comparing to MapReduce which processing data in terms of Job units, Spark uses DAG (Directed Acyclic Graph) and can process finer computing units which is more appropriate to distributed memory processing. The basic data processing units of RDD (Resilient Distributed DataSets) is the data units processed in the distributed memory by Spark [7, 8]. It focuses on the read-only data processed in various distributed memory. RDD classifies all the distributed data as different sets, record the lineage that needs to be processed in memory and can respond to the errors occurred during processing in memory.

In Fig. 2, map and union can process narrow-dependency computing in the same node, groupBy and join can process the required wide-dependency computing among nodes. During practical distribution processing, the phenomenon of shuffling and bottleneck may occur due to sequential processing on jobs in MapReduce. However, Spark DAG scheduling processes each object of RDD in terms of Tasks, so it can process several tasks in the same node simultaneously. The tasks that are processes simultaneously are grouped as the stages in Fig. 2.

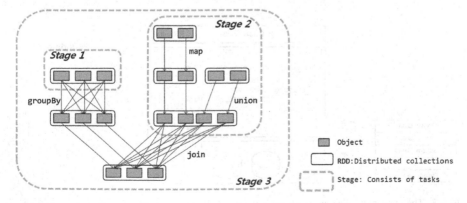

Fig. 2 Spark computing flow divided by stages

3 Streaming Big Data Analysis System

3.1 System Design

Figure 3 shows the proposed architecture of a soft real-time big data analysis system. The big data analysis system saves the huge amount of online data in HDFS. To process such big amount of data that are saved distributedly in a soft real-time manner, we need to connect to the Spark platform based on In-memory cluster computing method [9]. Additionally, to visualize the analysis results, the open source data analysis tool called R is connected. More exactly, we will visualize the refinement, processing, analysis, abnormal detection, and the used patter of saved data consistently.

3.2 Data Processing

Spark does not process the loading data immediately, instead it first construct lineage and then process to increase efficiency. In the module called transformations of Fig. 4, it first construct lineage for RDD that uses various calculations (map, filter, union, join, etc.) and the actual processes are executed after the corresponding commands. In Fig. 4, block ① points to the files saved in HDFS (the file location is set as a parameter). In block ②, map() functions split the data read from block ①, and then calculates the Parsing Map transformations. Like this, after constructing lineage for data sets in the memory, the real data loading and processing actions occur when show() function is called. At this time, we can process more efficiently in the memory with distributed lineage of data sets. Due to this, in the limited space of memory, we can process big amount of data. In case of lacking memory, data can be temporarily saved in HDFS and be loaded to memory when needed. Using this method, we can also prevent data loss during processing.

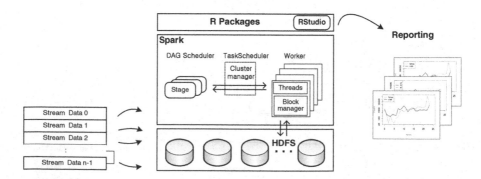

Fig. 3 The conceptual diagram of streaming big data analysis system

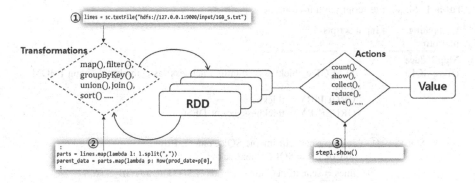

Fig. 4 Spark data analysis flow: transformation and action

4 Performance Evaluation

4.1 System Construction Environment and Experimental Result

The data analyzed in the experiment is collected in a real-time manner by the sensors. To check the difference in the processing speed due to memory size and data file size of In-memory based Spark, we compare memories of 8, 16, 32, and 64 GB. The data file sizes in HDFS are set to be 150, 300, 450, and 1000 MB.

1. Analysis Scripts

The descriptions for Spark(SQL) script are as follows: (1) to execute SparkSql, SQLContext is imported; (2) load the existing special data file in HDF(the data file locations are set as parameters of lines), prepare to construct RDD, and execute the action commands; (3) call map transformation and split them by comma; (4) for the split rows, for every data in different row and columns, we call map transformation; (5) generate parent_data DataFrame; (6) define the executed query; (7) start all the practial Spark Processing in show() actions (Table 1).

2. Compare the processing time of Spark and MapReduce(Hive SQL)

Through comparing the processing speed between In-memory process based Spark and patch processing based Hive SQL, we can see significant difference between the calculation speeds. In this experiment, for both Spark and Hive SQL, the processing time are evaluated when the main memory sizes are set to be 8 and 64 GB, respectively, the same queries are executed, and data file sizes are set to be different. To conduct complex calculation than Sorting, we first use GROUP BY to collect the same values and calculate the number of elements, and then we executed the searching action using ORDER BY.

As shown in Fig. 5, when the data size increases from 150 to 1000 MB, the performance are shown to be increased by a minimum of 4.05 times and a

Table 1 Shows the script input used in the experiment

Computing platform		Input scripts
MapReduce (Hive SQL)		: SELECT c_thickness, count(c_thickness) as c_thickness_count FROM Table 1 GROUP BY c_thickness ORDER BY c_thickness_count DESC :
Spark (SQL)	①	from pyspark.sql import SQLContext, Row sqlContext = SQLContext(sc)
	②	lines = sc.textFile("hdfs://127.0.0.1:9000/input/1GB_S.txt")
	③	parts = lines.map(lambda l: l.split(","))
	④	parent_data = parts.map(lambda p: Row(prod_date=p[0], prod_no=p[1], prod_name=p[2], degree=int(p[3]), mold=p[4], prod=p[5], s_no=int(p[6]), fix_time=float(p[7]), a_speed=float(p[8]), b_speed=float(p[9]), seperation=float(p[10]), s_seperation=float(p[11]), rate_term=int(p[12]), mpa=float(p[13]), load_time=float(p[14]), highpressure_time=int(p[15]), c_thickness=float(p[16])))
	⑤	schemaParentTable = sqlContext.createDataFrame(parent_data) schemaParentTable.registerTempTable("parent_data")
	⑥	step1 = sqlContext.sql("SELECT c_thickness, count(c_thickness) as c_thickness_count FROM parent_data GROUP BY c_thickness ORDER BY c_thickness_count DESC")
	⑦	step1.show()

Fig. 5 A comparison of searching operation speed for Spark and Hive SQL

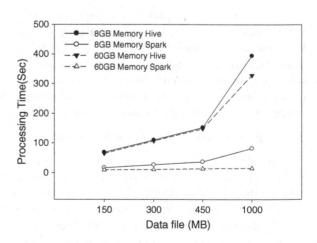

maximum of 21.87 times in Table 2. The maximum performance occurred when the main memory size is 64 GB and data size is 1000 MB. We can conclude that as the increasing of the main memory size and the data file size, the performance improvement also increases.

Table 2 The improvement ratio of searching speed for Spark and Hive SQL

Data file (MB)	Main memory(GB)			
	Hive (8)	Spark (8)	Hive (64)	Spark (64)
150	1	4.05	1	5.50
300	1	4.07	1	9.72
450	1	4.10	1	10.57
1000	1	4.80	1	21.87

5 Conclusion

In this paper, we design a streaming big data analysis system by collecting huge amount of sensor data generated in a smart factory, saving them in a distributed cluster environment with no capacity restriction, and then analyzing many aspects of them in a soft real time manner. In the performance evaluation of the proposed system, the In-memory bases Spark outperformed the existing batch-based MapReduce for 20+ times in terms of the processing time. In the future, efforts on proposing optimum H/W and S/W architecture should be made to analyze the impact of memory size and data file size of Spark cluster nodes.

Acknowledgments This work is partially supported by the National Research Foundation of Korea (NRF) grant funded by the Korean government (2015R1C1A1A02036536).

References

1. Chen L, Ko J, Yeo J (2015) Analysis of the influence factors of data loading performance using Apache Sqoop. KIPS Trans Softw Data Eng 4(2):77–82
2. Shvachko K et al (2010) The hadoop distributed file system. In: Proceedings of the 26th IEEE transactions on computing symposium on MSST, pp 1–10
3. Thusoo A, Sarma JS, Jain N, Shao Z, Chakka P, Zhang N, Antony S, Liu H, Murthy R (2010) Hive—a petabyte scale data warehouse using Hadoop. In: Proceedings of the 26th IEEE international conference on data engineering, pp 996–1005
4. Dean J, Ghemawat S (2004) MapReduce: simplified data processing on large clusters. In: Sixth symposium on operating system design and implementation, pp 137–150
5. Choi H, Lee KY (2014) Efficient processing of an aggregate query stream in MapReduce. KIPS Trans Softw Data Eng 3(2):73–80
6. Zaharia M, Das T, Li H, Hunter T, Shenker S, Stoica I (2013) Discretized streams: fault-tolerant streaming computation at scale, ACM, pp 423–438
7. Zaharia M, Chowdhury M, Das T, Dave A, Ma J, McCauley M, Franklin M, Shenker S, Stoica I (2012) Resilient distributed datasets: a fault-tolerant abstraction for in-memory cluster computing, NSDI
8. Hindman B, Konwinski A, Zaharia M, Ghodsi A, Joseph AD, Katz R, Shenker S, Stoica I (2011) Mesos: a platform for fine-grained resource sharing in the data center, NSDI, pp 295–308
9. Shinnar A, Cunningham D, Herta B, Saraswat V (2012) M3R: increased performance for in-memory Hadoop jobs. Proc VLDB 5(12):1736–1747

Research of Different Mobility Models on Routing Protocol Performance of Ad Hoc Networks

Na An, Lei Tang, Yishui Zhu, Zhiliang Kou, Xinxin Chen
and Zongtao Duan

Abstract We researched the performance of AODV routing protocol based on NS-2 in Ad Hoc networks on the Linux platform. When node's moving speed is changing, the typical Random Way Point mobility model is analyzed by using NS-2. And when the vehicle's running speed is changing, the IDM_LC model is analyzed by using VanetMobiSim and NS-2. The performance of AODV routing protocol is evaluated on the basis of End-to-End Delay, Packet Loss Rate and Throughput. Finally, we compared the performances of AODV routing protocol as the node's moving speed is changing on these models. The results show that different mobility models have different effects on the network performance of AODV routing protocol.

Keywords Ad Hoc networks · Mobile model · AODV protocol · NS-2 · Performance analysis

1 Introduction

In wireless mobile Ad Hoc networks [1], the movement of node makes network topology change continuously, leading to the research of routing protocol faces enormous challenges [2]. At present, the simulation is used to evaluate performance of routing protocol in the research of wireless Ad Hoc networks, and it is better to evaluate the performance of the routing protocol by selecting an appropriate node mobility model. The rest of this paper is organized as follows. Section 2 presents two mobility models, the Random Way Point mobile model of the entity mobile models and the IDM_LC model of the vehicular Ad Hoc networks. Section 3 introduces the simulation platform and analyzes the simulation results, including

N. An · L. Tang · Y. Zhu (✉) · Z. Kou · X. Chen · Z. Duan
School of Information Engineering, Chang'an University, Xi'an 710064, China
e-mail: yszhu@chd.edu.cn

© Springer Science+Business Media Singapore 2016　　　　　　　　165
J.J. (Jong Hyuk) Park et al. (eds.), *Advanced Multimedia and Ubiquitous Engineering*, Lecture Notes in Electrical Engineering 393,
DOI 10.1007/978-981-10-1536-6_22

the overviews of AODV routing protocol, and the definitions of performance indexes and the settings of simulation parameters, and so on. Section 4 concludes the whole paper and prospect for the future.

2   Overview of Mobility Models

Node mobility model illustrates node's movement pattern (including its position, speed and acceleration, etc.), and it can determine how a node moves, which reflects the change of node's position, speed and direction. In this paper, we focus on the entity mobility models and the VANET [3] mobility models. Entity mobile models [4] mainly deal with mobility situation of the independent nodes. At present, the entity mobility models mainly include RWP (Random Way Point movement) model, RDM (Random Direction Movement) model and RWM (Random Walk Movement) model. The VANET mobility models [5, 6] include the synthetic model, the survey-based model, the traffic simulator-based model and the trace-based model. In this paper, we simulated and analyzed RWP model of the entity mobility models and IDM_LC [7] model of the VANET mobility models.

2.1   Random Way Point Movement Model

In study [8, 9], RWP model is proposed by Joshson and Maltz firstly, which is a kind of individual mobility model widely used in MANET. We use the setdest tool to generate node's motion scene directly because RWP model is integrated in NS-2. RWP model can be described as follow: Given a certain region R, a way point P is selected uniformly at random in R, and a destination D1 is selected uniformly at random in R, then the node starts moving from P to D1 with a speed selected uniformly at random in an interval $[V_{min}, V_{max}]$. When the node arrives at destination D1, a pause time at T1 is selected uniformly at random in an interval $[tmin, tmax]$ upon termination of pause time, and a new destination D2 is selected uniformly at random in R. When the node arrives at destination D2, then repeats this process. If the value of V_{max} is very small and Tp is very long, the whole network topology is relatively stable. The schematic diagram of a node movement is shown in Fig. 1.

This model is consistent with the motion characteristics of nodes in most of the situations, but in study [10], there are two drawbacks of this model: the average speed is reduced gradually and the distribution of nodes is not uniform. That is because the node's average speed will decay in the movement process of the node. If the node's minimum speed is smaller, the decay time of the node movement speed will be longer, and the time of system reached steady-state also will be longer, then the network is difficult to reach a stable state. Recently, we can solve these problems by increasing movement speed of nodes those are far away from destination node and reducing movement speed of nodes those are close to destination node.

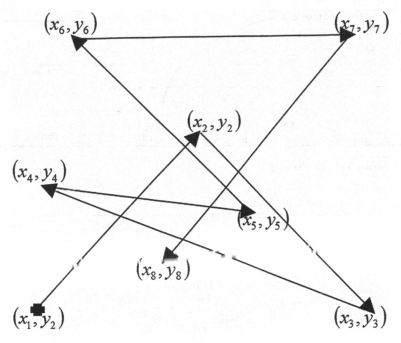

Fig. 1 The schematic diagram of a node movement

2.2 IDM_LC Model

The IDM_LC [7] is an intelligent driver model with lane changing function, it has overtaking and multi-lanes features. Because the numbers of lanes among roads are different, vehicles close to the intersection will get the next road structure according to macro mobility characteristics. The model points out, if changing lane can minimize the number of vehicle braking, the vehicle will change lane and drive in other lanes. Using the following formulas to judge:

$$a_1 - a \pm a_{bias} > p(a_{cu} + a_{new} - a_{1cur} - a_{1new}) + a_{thr} \tag{2.1}$$

$$a_{1new} > -a_{safe} \tag{2.2}$$

In the above formula, a_1, a is acceleration of the vehicle changing lane in the candidate lane and the current lane, a_{cu}, a_{new} is the acceleration of following vehicle before changing lane in the current lane and candidate lane, a_{1cu}, a_{1new} is the acceleration of following vehicle after changing lane in the current lane and candidate lane, a_{thr} is the acceleration threshold, it is the minimum acceleration of the vehicle changing lane, a_{safe} is the acceleration safety value, a_{bias} is the acceleration bias value, p is courtesy factor. When the Eq. (2.1) is established, the model allows the vehicle to enter the first lane. The scenario of the vehicles changing lane is shown in Fig. 2, and the vehicles' movement scenario of the IDM_LC is shown in Fig. 3.

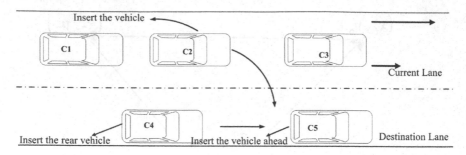

Fig. 2 Scenario of lane changing

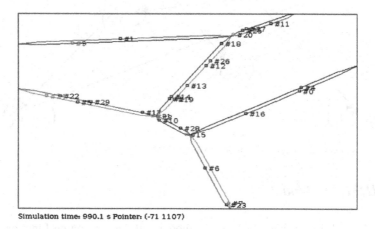

Simulation time: 990.1 s Pointer: (-71 1107)

Fig. 3 The simulation of IDM_IL model

3 Simulation Analysis

In this section, we researched the performance of AODV routing protocol based on NS-2. For RWP model, we simulated and analyzed performances of AODV routing protocol only by using NS-2. Because RWP model is the mechanism integrated in NS-2, so we can use the setdest tool of NS-2 to generate mobile scenarios, then write the TCL script and import into the mobile scenarios, finally do the simulation of RWP model; For IDM_LC model, we simulated and analyzed performances of AODV routing protocol by using VanetMobiSim and NS-2. Firstly, using traffic simulation software VanetMobiSim to generate the mobile scene file we need, then will import it into TCL script prepared, finally completes the simulation of IDM_LC model.

3.1 AODV Routing Protocol

AODV (On-Demand Distance Vector) routing protocol [11] is an on-demand routing protocol of Ad Hoc networks, it is called on-demand distance vector routing protocol. It's a combination of DSDV [12] protocol and DSR [13] protocol, and it adopted the idea of hop by hop routing and periodic updating of routing mainte-nance phase in DSDV protocol. It also uses the mechanism of on-demand establish and maintenance routing as well as support for multi-casts routing QoS [14] in DSR protocol. Based on these characteristics, AODV protocol has become a hot topic in wireless Ad Hoc networks.

3.2 Performance Criteria

Network performance is the embodiment of the characteristics of network, while the network performance parameter [15] is used to describe the characteristics of the network in detail. The formula of several performance parameters are given as below:

$$Averagedelay = \frac{\sum (RevTime - SedTime)}{SumPackets} \tag{3.1}$$

$$AvgThroughput = \frac{SumRevpackets}{Times} \tag{3.2}$$

$$Droprate = \frac{DropPackets}{SendPackets} \tag{3.3}$$

In formula (3.1), *Averagedelay* is average end-to-end delay, which is the average time from date packet is sent by the source node to is received successfully by the destination node. *RevTime* is the time that date packets are received by the desti-nation node, and *SedTime* is the time that date packets are sent by the source node, and *Sumpackets* is the total number of date packets are sent.

In formula (3.2), *AvgThroughput* is the average throughput, which measured that the total number of date packets are received successfully by destination node in the unit time. *SumRevpackets* is the total number of data packets are received by the destination node in a certain period of time, and *Times* is the statistical time.

In formula (3.3), *Droprate* is the packet loss rate, which is the ratio that the total number of data packets are dropped and the total number of data packets are sent. *Droppackets* is the total number of date packets are discarded, and *Sendpackets* is the total number of date packets are sent.

3.3 The Simulation Parameters

For RWP model, we created 10 mobile nodes in one simulation area with dimensions of the 1000×1000 m^2, and the pause time of each node is 1 s and the total time of simulation are 100 s, and taking the maximum movement speed as a variable, and respectively selecting 10, 20, 30, 40, 50 m/s to do five times simulation. For IDM_LC model, we selected the city scene with ranges of 1000×1000 m^2, the lane is usually two-lanes, the number of intersections controlled by traffic lights is 6, the time interval of the traffic lights changing is 10 s, the maximum acceleration and deceleration respectively are 0.6 and 4 m/s^2, the comfortable deceleration is 0.9 m/s^2, the acceleration threshold of lane changing is 0.2 m/s^2, the politeness factor is 0.5. And taking the vehicles' running speed as a variable, and respectively selecting 36, 72, 108, 144 and 180 km/h. To ensure the reliability of data, we can generate ten times mobile scene files randomly in the case of same simulation parameters. Finally, each data point is the average of ten times simulation results. Finally, the moving scene files and business scene files are imported into the network script TCL file. After the simulation, we get the Trace file and Nam visualization file.

3.4 Performance Analysis

In this section, we compared network performance of the routing protocol in different mobile models. The comparisons of simulation results are shown in Fig. 4. The solid column diagram represents the average delay, packet loss rate and throughput of the RWP model, and the column chart of filling slant line represents the average end-to-end delay, packet loss rate and throughput of the IDM_LC model respectively. Figure 4a, b show that when the node's maximum movement speed increases, average end-to-end delay and packet drop rate of RWP model is always larger than those of IDM_LC model. That is because the average speed of RWP model is attenuating in the moving process. If the maximum movement speed of node is increased, the attenuation time of average speed will be longer, and the topology of whole network is changing faster and faster, and efficient routing becomes less and less, this will lead to average end-to-end delay and packet drop rate increased. However, average end-to-end delay of IDM_LC model is almost no change with increase of the maximum movement speed, packet drop rate has a very small change and it reached a maximum at 30 m/s, so the network topology of IDM_LC model is relatively stable. Based on this, compared with RWP model, network performance of IDM_IM model is better. Figure 4c shows that throughput of RWP model is changing with the increase of the maximum movement speed of nodes dramatically, while throughput of IDM_IM model is changing with the increase of the maximum movement speed of nodes smoothly. That is because the network topology of RWP model is changed with the increase of the maximum

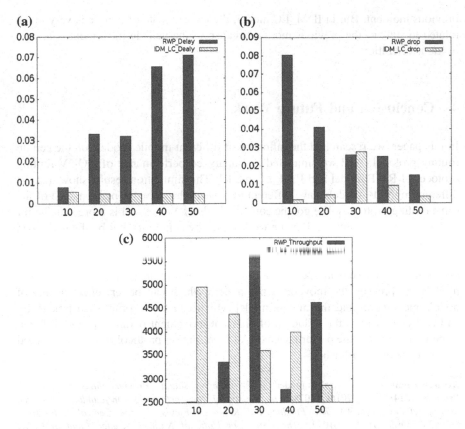

Fig. 4 The comparison of simulation results. **a** Average end-to-end. **b** Packet loss rate. **c** Throughput

moving speed frequently, the network state is quite instability, which leads to the dramatic change of throughput. However, the vehicle's speed of IDM_IM model will not be attenuated in one simulation, so the network topology which is composed of vehicles will not change greatly, and the change of throughput is relatively stable. Moreover, when the node's maximum movement speed is increasing, the throughput variation of RWP model is opposite to IDM_LC model.

In summary, the network performance of IDM_LC model is better than that of RWP model in addition to throughput, and RWP model and IDM_LC model have different effects on the network performance of AODV routing protocol. There are mainly two reasons: (1) the topology of node's trajectories is different in different mobility models. For example, node's movement of RWP model is random in the specified region completely, and the moving trajectory is not subject to any restrictions, but node's movement of IDM_LC model is restricted by the topology of road. (2) the motion states of different mobility models are different. In RWP model, the movement of a node at a time has nothing to do with state of the previous moment. But in IDM_LC model, the current state of a node is very much related to state of the previous motion because of the vehicle movement is limited by its acceleration.

4 Conclusion and Future Works

In this paper, we researched the influence of different mobile models on the certain routing protocol. And we simulated and analyzed performance of AODV routing protocol of RWP model and IDM_LC model. The simulation results show that the different mobility models have different effects on the network performance of the same routing protocols. We got the conclusion that RWP model is more suitable for nodes moving randomly and the network topology is not affected by the node own characteristics, while IDM_IM model and IDM_LC model are more suitable for some traffic scenarios. Next we will study on the effects of the node's pause time and minimum movement speed to the network performance of different mobility models. At present, the movement parameters which can better reflect degree of node's movement, and the mobile model which can be accomplished practically and easily, as well as the influence of different movement parameters and different mobility models on the performance of Ad Hoc routing protocol need to be studied by more scholars in further.

Acknowledgments This work is funded by *The project of Shaanxi Province Industrial Research Projects* (2014K05-28, 2016GY-078); *The Ministry of transport application foundation research project* (2014319812150); *The Fundamental Research Funds for the Central Universities* (310824153405, 310824161012); *The project of National Natural Science Fund of China* (61303041); *The Scientific Research Foundation for The Returned Overseas Chinese Scholars in Shaanxi Province of China* (0308-100702).

References

1. Pelusi L, Passarella A, Conti M (2006) Opportunistic networking: data forwarding in disconnected mobile ad hoc networks. IEEE Commun Mag 44(11):134–141 IEEE
2. Duan Z, Yan Y, Tang L, Chen X, An N, Kou Z (2015) A tutorial survey on delivery of service data in vehicular ad-hoc networks. UIC-ATC-ScalCom-CBDCom-IoP, pp 1417–1424 (Accepted)
3. Chen C, Jin Y, Pei Q, Zhang N (2014) A connectivity-aware intersection-based routing in VANETs. Eurasip J Wireless Commun Netw 2014(1):1–16
4. Liu T (2010) Research on entity mobile models of Ad Hoc Network. Guilin University of Electronic Technology (in Chinese)
5. Djenouri D, Soualhi W, Nekka E (2008) VANET's Mobility models and overtaking: an overview. In: International conference on information and communication technologies: from theory to application, IEEE, pp 1–7

6. Harri J, Filali F, Bonnet C (2009) Mobility models for vehicular ad hoc networks: a survey and taxonomy. Department of Mobile Communications in Institute Eurecom, IEEE Communications Survey and Tutorials, France. IEEE, pp 19–41
7. Lu Z (2010) The research and simulation of VANETs based on VanetMobiSim/NS-2. Wuhan University of Technology (in Chinese)
8. Wang B (2011) The research and implementation of routing algorithm in the opportunity network. South-central University For Nationalities (in Chinese)
9. Davies V (2002) Evaluating mobility models within an ad hoc network [D]. Masters Thesis, Colorado School of Mines
10. Juang P, Oki H, Wang Y, Martonosi M et al (2002) Energy-efficient computing for wildlife tracking: design tradeoffs and early experiences with ZebraNet. In: Proceedings of the 10th annual conference on architectural support for programming languages and operating systems, vol 36, no (10). ACM, pp 96–107
11. Perkins CE, Royer EM (1999) Ad-hoc on demand distance vector routing. IEEE workshop on mobile computing systems and applications (WMCSA), vol 6, no 7. IEEE, pp 90–100
12. Perkins CE, Bhagwat P (1999) Highly dynamic destination sequenced distance vector routing (DSDV) for mobile computers. Acm Sigcomm Comput Commun Rev 24(4):234–244
13. Johnson DB, Maltz DA, Broch J (2002) The dynamic source routing protocol for mobile Ad Hoc networks (DSR). ACM, IETF MANET Working Group, pp 139–172
14. Akkaya K, Younis M (2003) An energy-aware QoS routing protocol for wireless sensor networks. In: International conference on distributed computing systems workshops, IEEE, pp 373–375: 710–715
15. Khairnar MVD, Kotecha K (2013) Simulation-based performance evaluation of routing protocols in vehicular Ad-Hoc network. International review on computers and software, arXiv.org (ISSN 2250-3153)

A Development of Touch Sensing Using a Depth Camera–Projector System

Ji Yeol Park, Jinwon Park, Kyumok Kim, Jon-Ha Lee
and Seung-Won Jung

Abstract In this paper, we develop a touch detection system using the Kinect-projector system. In our system, the touch area is first determined using a user's assistance with the Kinect provided skeleton data, and the touch is then detected within only the touch area to simplify and speed-up the process. In particular, a precise touch location is found considering the user's touch behavior and depth characteristics. Experimental results demonstrate that the proposed system can be used for touch sensing on planar walls without requiring any active touch sensors.

Keywords Depth camera · Projector–camera system · Touch detection · Touch sensing

1 Introduction

As the growth of the display technology, many display devices support detecting users' touch using special touch sensors placed on the panel or cameras amounted around devices' boundaries. Recently, owing to advances in computer vision, another type of touch detection technology has been introduced called a projector–camera-based touch detection technology. Since the technology uses a projector to make a screen and detect users' touch on the projected screen, it does not necessitate special touch sensors or even display devices. Thus, it is highly desirable in various applications. UBI-Interactive, which is a touch screen service using a depth camera–projector, and the Roomalive Toolkit [1] presented in Microsoft Build 2015 are some examples of this technology. In this paper, we develop our own touch detection system, which is based on the conventional method [2], but we present a

J.Y. Park · J. Park · K. Kim · J.-H. Lee · S.-W. Jung (✉)
Department of Multimedia Engineering, Dongguk University,
Seoul, South Korea
e-mail: swjung83@dongguk.edu

© Springer Science+Business Media Singapore 2016   175
J.J. (Jong Hyuk) Park et al. (eds.), *Advanced Multimedia and Ubiquitous Engineering*, Lecture Notes in Electrical Engineering 393,
DOI 10.1007/978-981-10-1536-6_23

new algorithm for a more accurate localization of touch coordinates. Experimental results support the effectiveness of the proposed system.

2 Related Works

Early study on the vision-based touch sensing technology such as Wellner's digital desk [3] and Kruger's Videodesk [4] uses a color camera to detect users' touch [5]. Meanwhile, after the release of Microsoft Kinect, many recent studies have attempted to use depth cameras for many difficult computer vision problems. In particular, by using the Roomalive toolkit [1] and multiple Kinects and projectors, we can now use even non-planar surfaces as the screen. To this end, the conventional dSensingNI (Depth Sensing Natural Interaction) system [6] supports multi-touch sensing and interaction with arbitrary 3D objects. dSensingNI supports a multi-touch table called 'use-Table' as a touch space and detects the touch via three steps. Arm and hand regions are first detected from depth images, finger positions are then located, and the touch location is finally determined from the outline of finger positions. OmniTouch [7] is a wearable touch screen and projection system, which also supports multi-finger touch detection and tracking. On-demand projection is provided by detecting the surface and displaying images with the precise alignment to the surface. The surface can be user's palm, wall, or notepad. In addition, if the image is projected onto the palm, it selects which part of the palm is suitable for display.

3 Proposed Touch Sensing System

We use the Kinect v2, which provide real-time high quality depth images, and extract the skeleton data using the Kinect SDK. Our system assumes that a projection area is flat and the distance between the Kinect and projection area is around 1.5–2 m. Basically, touch is sensed by comparing the depth image of the projection area and the depth image of every depth video frame. Details will be given in the following sub-sections.

3.1 Calibration

In our system, the projection area must be specified before touch detection. To this end, we display the four corner points of the projection area and let the user touch the points as shown in Fig. 1. To detect user's touch on the four corners, we use the skeleton data provided by the Kinect v2 and assume that the touch activity occurs when the position of the hand skeleton does not change during a certain amount of

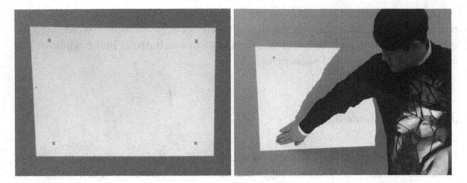

Fig. 1 User needs to specify the projection area by touching red points during calibration

time. The correspondence between the projector and depth camera can be easily found by this user-assisted initialization step. The depth values within the rectangle specified by the four points are then saved and compared with the consequent depth vide frames. In practice, a 10 % larger rectangle is used for the experiment because neighboring depth values are required to detect touch position.

3.2 Touch Sensing

The basic idea of touch sensing is presented by Wilson [2]. If a current depth value in a specific point (x, y), $d_{x,y}$, is within the two threshold values (d_{max}, d_{min}), we can consider the touch action occurs as shown in Fig. 1. Here the two threshold values need to be carefully determined according to the depth value of the projection area (defined as $d_{surface}$) (Fig. 2).

All the pixels satisfying Eq. (1) can be considered as touch pixels.

$$d_{min} < d_{x,y} < d_{max} \tag{1}$$

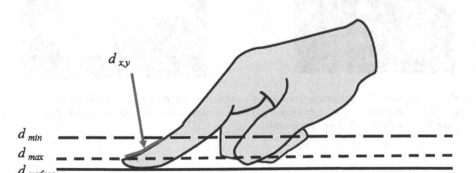

Fig. 2 Two thresholds, d_{min} and d_{max}, are used for touch detection [4]

However, several false positive touch pixels can be detected due to the depth noise. To find an accurate position of the touch, we apply a sliding window to the projection area and find the pixel that has the most touch pixels in the window. We call this touch pixel as 'Touch point (*P*)'.

3.3 Touch Localization

It is very hard work to find an accurate touch position *P* if we use only the method described in Sect. 3.2. We thus suggest a method that can refine touch location by analyzing the pixels near the touch. To this end, we first apply four rectangular windows to four directions (up, down, left, right) as shown in Fig. 3. The touch pixels in each search window are then counted to find the orientation of the user's hand. We can easily guess that window having many touch pixels than other search windows corresponds to the orientation of the user's hand because the pixels in the wrist and palm region also tend to satisfy Eq. (1). The detected touch point P is thus not on or around the fingertip as shown in Fig. 4a. To solve this problem, we shift the touch position toward the direction which is opposite direction of the window with the maximum touch pixels. The amount of shift is determined according to the distance between the Kinect and the wall. Figure 4b shows that the shifted position is closer to the actual touch location.

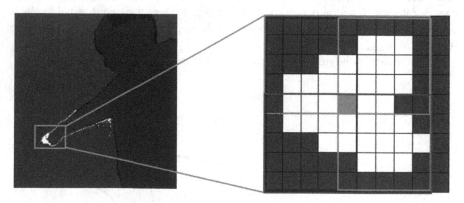

Fig. 3 *Left image* is depth image when a user touches the wall. *Rectangular* windows are applied at Touch Pixel P (*Red dot* in *right image*) and each window color represents direction of window (*blue* left, *red* right, *yellow* up, *green* down)

(a)   **(b)**

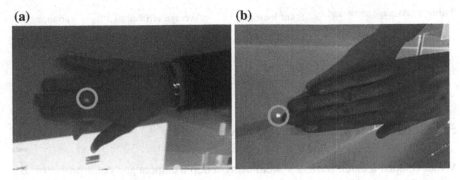

Fig. 4 Touch point P (*red circle*) before (**a**) and after (**b**) applying the proposed touch localization scheme

4 Experiment

In our experiment, we used Kinect v2 as a depth camera and Optoma s316 as a projector. A PC with Intel i5-4210 1.70 GHz CPU and 16 GB RAM was used. In our touch sensing-based drawing application as shown in Fig. 5, depth video frames were processed with 30 fps. d_{max} was set as $d_{surface}$–5 and d_{min} was set as $d_{surface}$–20. The distance between Kinect v2 and projection area was about 1.5 m. The projection area occupied about 90×55 cm^2 when resolution was set as 1080 p. The amount shift for touch localization was empirically set as 5 pixels. We evaluated the distance between the designated point and touch point obtained by the algorithm. From the four designated points located at the left-top, right-top, left-bottom and right-bottom of the wall, the error values were obtained as shown in Table 1. The total average error and variance values were obtained as 1.393 and 0.440, respectively.

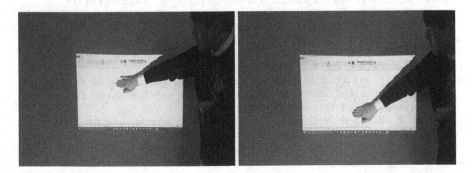

Fig. 5 Touch sensing is operated by using our method

Table 1 Average error and variance of the designated and detected touch points

Point location	Average error (cm)	Variance
Left-top	1.237	0.368
Left-bottom	0.837	0.322
Right-top	1.425	0.560
Right-bottom	1.375	0.410

5 Conclusion and Future Works

We developed a touch sensing system using a depth camera and color projector. By using the proposed system, we can use a wall as a touch pad. There are many remaining work for the improvement. Because the system detect touches for every frame, detection touch points are not temporally stable. Thus we plan to use video frames for better extracting and tracking touch positions. In addition, our user-assisted calibration needs to be automated. By solving these problems, we expect our system can be used as an economical and efficient alternative to existing touch panel systems.

Acknowledgments This research was supported by the MSIP (Ministry of Science, ICT and Future Planning), Korea, under the ITRC (Information Technology Research Center) support program (IITP-2016-H8501-16-1014) supervised by the IITP (Institute for Information & communications Technology Promotion).

References

1. Jones B, Sodhi R, Murdock M, Mehra R, Benko H, Wilson A, Ofek E, MacIntyre B, Raghuvanshi N, Shapira L (2014) Roomalive: magical experiences enabled by scalable adaptive projector camera units. In: Proceedings of ACM UIST
2. Wilson AD (2010) Using a depth camera as a touch sensor. In: Proceedings of ITS
3. Wellner P (1991) The DigitalDesk calculator: tangible manipulation on a desk top display. In: Proceedings of ACM UIST
4. Krueger M (1991) Artificial reality, vol 2. Addison-Wesley, Boston
5. Zhang S, He W, Yu Q, Zheng X (2012) Low-cost interactive whiteboard using the kinect. In: Proceedings of IASP
6. Klompmaker F, Nebe K, Fast A (2012) dSensingNI: a framework for advanced tangible interaction using a depth camera. In: Proceedings of the sixth international conference on tangible, embedded and embodied interaction
7. Harrison C, Benko H, Wilson A (2011) OmniTouch: wearable multitouch interaction everywhere. In: Proceedings of ACM UIST

Fault Localization Method by Utilizing Memory Map and Input-Driven Update Interval

Kwanhyo Kim, Ki-Yong Choi and Jung-Won Lee

Abstract As the importance of automotive ECU (Electronic Control Unit) and its software increase, the systematic testing method is applied to them. However, it takes a lot of time to localize the faults because the developers have not been enough information which can be used for debugging by the nature of the test process for the automotive software. In this paper, we propose a method to reduce the fault-suspicious region in the memory by utilizing the memory map and the correlation between the inputs and the update information. As a preliminary result, we confirmed that the fault-suspicious region is reduced to 17.42(%) of the memory size by using the proposed method.

Keywords Automotive ECU · Automotive software · Fault localization · Embedded testing · Memory map · Memory update

1 Introduction

In recent years, about 90 % of the car innovations are based on ECU and its software [1]. Therefore, the systematic testing method is applied to them. However, the developers perform developing, debugging, and unit testing and the testing group performs system testing independently in a separated environment due to the OEM (Original Equipment Manufacturer) system of the automotive industry as shown in Fig. 1 [2]. The developers have difficulty in debugging through the lack of testing information. Because the testers perform the black-box testing based

K. Kim · K.-Y. Choi · J.-W. Lee (✉)
Department of Electrical and Computer Engineering, Ajou University, Suwon, Republic of Korea
e-mail: jungwony@ajou.ac.kr

K. Kim
e-mail: khyo0317@gmail.com

K.-Y. Choi
e-mail: ki815kaisian@gmail.com

© Springer Science+Business Media Singapore 2016
J.J. (Jong Hyuk) Park et al. (eds.), *Advanced Multimedia and Ubiquitous Engineering*, Lecture Notes in Electrical Engineering 393,
DOI 10.1007/978-981-10-1536-6_24

Fig. 1 The process of developing automotive ECU

on the HiL (Hardware-in-the-Loop) simulation in the environment where a source code is not available, the developers receive the test result which is limited from the tester. The delivered information is only the result of the test process itself such as the time of test, the test suit number, the number of test cases, pass/fail information, etc.

There are few researches related to the fault-localization method for OEM developers in the black-box testing environment. Therefore, we propose a method to reduce the fault-suspicious region in the memory by utilizing the memory map and the update information in the black-box environment where the memory information is available. Firstly, the memory is partitioned by utilizing the memory map, and the fault suspiciousness is computed by the update information in the memory, and then each partition has the score of fault suspiciousness. Finally, the ranking of the fault-suspicious region in the memory is determined based on the weight-added fault suspiciousness using the input-driven update interval.

The reason why we focus on the memory for localizing the faults is following. An update in the memory occurs due to "DU pair" existed in the source code. In DU pair, "D" means "Definition" and "U" means "Use". For example, in the statement "A = B;" of the source code, "A" is defined as "Definition" and "B" is defined as "Use" [3]. The value of the defined variable "A" is stored in the memory when the instruction of memory interface (such as "LOAD", "STORE" or "MOVE") is executed, and this operation means that the value of the specific address is updated [4]. However, since the number of updated addresses is too many, it is impossible to find the fault location by examining all the updated addresses.

To solve this problem, firstly, we target only the data section in the entire memory. It is because each symbol is allocated to the fixed address of the data section during the execution of a program. Therefore, the update information at the specific address is subordinate to the updated event of the symbol. If we can know the time of the fail during the HiL simulation, we can catch the fault candidates which are updated at that time. We can also reduce the range of that time by using the input-driven update interval. In this paper, we propose a method to reduce the fault-suspicious region in the data section by partitioning the data section and applying the update information to the partitioned data section.

2 Related Work

Generally, it takes a lot of time to locate the faults in the debugging process. Therefore, there are various researches for a method to efficiently localize the faults. One of these methods is to utilize a source code [5]. However, this method cannot be utilized for the fault localization where a source code is unavailable. The method applicable in the black-box environment is to utilize the Run-stop debugging. This method is to search the fault-suspicious region by setting the break point in a program [6], but it isn't able to be utilized to the fault localization for automotive ECU because it is common that the automotive ECU doesn't have an external terminal for the Run-stop debugging.

However, it is possible to retrieve the memory information by utilizing an external terminal for the CAN (Controller Area Network) used for communication between the automotive ECUs [7]. Therefore, there are researches for the fault localization by analyzing the memory information. The research for the fault localization by analyzing the memory information was conducted in [8], but this method is unsuitable for the automotive software because it is based on the environment where the memory information is retrieved from various clients in the distributed system. Also, the fault localization by using the memory update information was conducted in [4]. However, there are problems that the number of memory updates is too many and the result of [4] contains only the symbols that mean the signals communicating with an external interface. To solve these problems, we propose a method which can reduce to the fault-suspicious region containing symbols associated with the actual state of the ECU.

3 Reducing Memory Region by Fault Suspiciousness

3.1 The Process of Reducing Memory Region by Fault Suspiciousness

In this section, in order to provide the fault location in the memory to developers, we propose a method to reduce the fault-suspicious region by utilizing the memory map and the update information. The memory map contains the memory size allocated to each section, the memory size in each section allocated to each object file, etc.

The process of proposed method is shown in Fig. 2. Firstly, the memory is partitioned by utilizing the memory map, and each update information is subordinate to each partition depending on the unit of partitioned memory. Then, the fault suspiciousness is calculated by using the update information subordinate to each partition, and the fault-suspicious region in the memory is reduced depending on

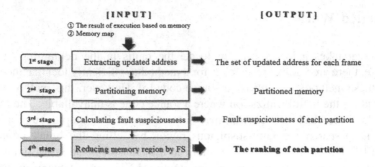

Fig. 2 The process of reducing memory region by fault suspiciousness

the calculated fault suspiciousness. The fault-suspicious region in the memory is reduced over four stages, and the description of each step is as follows.

- **1st stage. Extracting updated address**: The memory information acquired during program execution means the set of value at each address. Thus, the update information is extracted by checking whether a value at each address changed at a particular time.
- **2nd stage. Partitioning memory**: The data section is partitioned by the memory unit allocated to each object file by utilizing the information in the memory map.
- **3rd stage. Calculating fault suspiciousness**: The number of updates is counted in each partition for each frame, then the partitions whose the number of updates is less than average are determined as *FSP* (Fault Suspicious Partition). By repeating this operation for the total frames, the number that each partition is determined as *FSP* is calculated and this is defined as *NFSP* (the Number of Fault Suspicious Partition). Then, *FS* (Fault Suspiciousness) for each partition is calculated by using accumulated *NFSP* given a weighting in the input–driven update interval. That is, *FS* means the degree of correlation between the inputs and the update information.
- **4th stage. Reducing memory region by fault suspiciousness**: The ranking of fault-suspicious region is determined based on *FS* calculated in 3rd stage, and the fault-suspicious region in the memory is reduced in accordance with this ranking.

3.2 Extracting Updated Address

The memory (M) of the program executed for T is captured for $N(=T/P)$ times in a particular period (P) [7]. The terms used in the 1st, 2nd stages of Fig. 2 are as follows.

- Frame (F_i) ≡ {$V_{i,a}$|$V_{i,a}$ is the value of the address a at time $P \times i$, i is a frame number}

- Memory Update$(U_{i,a}) = \begin{cases} 1, |V_{i,a} \neq V_{i-1,a} \\ 0, |V_{i,a} = V_{i-1,a} \end{cases}$ for $1 \leq i \leq N, 1 \leq a \leq M$
- Partition$(PT_j) \equiv$ The partition in data section subordinate to object file j
- Update Count$(UC_{i,j}) \equiv$ The number of $U_{i,a}$ in PT_j for F_i

The update information obtained in this way can be utilized for the fault localization because the addresses with high update frequency when the input is set can be considered as the fault candidate. In [4], *IDUR* (Input-Driven Update Range) is defined as the range that the number of updated addresses is maintained more than the average after the number of updated addresses has increased, and Fig. 3 is an example of *IDUR* obtained using the proposed method in [4] for a particular test case. In the experiment, we use the ranges of frames derived using *IDUR* algorithm in [4].

3.3 Reducing Memory Region by Fault Suspiciousness

The algorithm used in this step is described in Fig. 4. In this algorithm, the average number of updated addresses for each frame is calculated, then the partitions with the number of updated addresses smaller than average are determined as *FSP* and *NFSP* of those partitions is increased. Then, the ratio of *NFSP* in *IDUR* and the ratio of *NFSP* in the total frames are calculated. And the proportion of former to latter is utilized as *FS*. In this connection, the formulas are defined as follows.

- $FSP_{i,j} \equiv \left\{ (PT_j, UC_{i,j}) | 0 < UC_{i,j} < AVG_i, AVG_i = \dfrac{\sum \# \, of \, updated \, addresses \, in \, F_i}{\# \, of \, partitions \, in \, F_i} \right\}$
- $NFSP_j \equiv$ The number of frames that PT_j is determined as *FSP*
- $FS_j = \dfrac{NFSP_j \, in \, IDUR}{The \, number \, of \, frames \, in \, IDUR} \div \dfrac{NFSP_j \, in \, the \, total \, frames}{The \, total \, number \, of \, frames}$

Thus, the ranking of fault-suspicious region is determined depending on *FS*. Therefore, developers can firstly localize the faults in the partitions with higher *FS*.

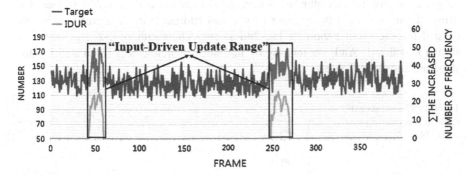

Fig. 3 The example of input-driven update range

Algorithm 1 *The Algorithm of Reducing Memory Region by FS*

INPUT : *UC, the number of updated address in data section for each object file*
         F^{IDUR}, *the range of frames for IDUR*
         F, the range of the total frames
OUTPUT : *FS, the fault suspiciousness for each objet file*

1: $uc_{i,j} \equiv$ *the number of update address in data section for each object file j in frame i of UC*
2: $nfsp_j \equiv$ *the number of frame that partition j is determined as FSP in the total frames*
3: $nfsp_j^{IDUR} \equiv$ *the number of frame that partition j is determined as FSP in IDUR*
4: $fs_j \equiv$ *the fault suspiciousness for each object file j of FS*

5: **FOR** $i = 1$ *to the total number of frames*
6:    *Average* = SUM(uc_i)/SIZE(uc_i)
7:    **FOR** $j = 1$ *to* SIZE(uc_i)
8:       **IF** ($0 < uc_{i,j} < Average$)
9:          **IF** (*i is in IDUR*)
10:            $nfsp_j^{IDUR} = nfsp_j^{IDUR} + 1$
11:         **END IF**
12:            $nfsp_j = nfsp_j + 1$
13:      **END IF**
14:   **END FOR**
15: **END FOR**

16: **FOR** $j = 1$ *to* SIZE(uc_i)
17:    $fs_j = (nfsp_j^{IDUR} \div F^{IDUR}) \div (nfsp_j \div F)$
18: **END FOR**

Fig. 4 The algorithm of reducing memory region by FS

4 Experiment Result

The memory($M = 29,400$ byte) is captured for 400 times(N) with a period of 10 ms (P). The size of data section is 25,228 byte in the memory. Also, the set of *IDUR* ranges by using the algorithm of [4] are 53–74 frames and 253–276 frames. By using this information, the number of updated addresses in each partition is calculated for each frame through 1st, 2nd stages. The result of 1st, 2nd stages is shown in Table 1. And, the ranking by the fault suspiciousness calculated by 3rd stage are shown in Table 2.

Table 1 The number of updated addresses in each object file

Objet file	Frame #1	...	Frame #399
Obj #1	0	...	0
...	...	...	...
Obj #67	3	...	3
Average	1.23	...	1.22

Table 2 The ranking by fault suspiciousness

Rank	Object file	Ratio in IDUR	Ratio in total frame	FS
1	Obj #14	4.3×10^{-2}	0.5×10^{-2}	8.7
	...	...	...	
	Obj #60	4.3×10^{-2}	0.5×10^{-2}	
19	Obj #26	6.5×10^{-2}	1.0×10^{-2}	6.5
20	Obj #42	28.0×10^{-2}	4.7×10^{-2}	5.9

The validity of this result has been verified by comparing this result with the result of [4], and the result of [4] was verified by testers and developers who ran the test and modified faults. Also, the data sections allocated to 13 object files among 20 object files in Table 2 contain symbols that mean the actual state of ECU. And, these symbols receive signals from the symbols in [4]. In this case, it can be more meaningful because the symbols in the result of proposed method are associated with the actual state of ECU while the symbols in [4] are associated with the external interface. In conclusion, the fault-suspicious region in the memory is reduced to $(1879 \div 10,786) \times 100(\%) = 17.42(\%)$ since the size of data sections allocated to 20 object files is 1879 byte and the entire size of partitions that an update occurred is 10,786 byte.

5 Conclusion

In this paper, we proposed a method to reduce the fault-suspicious region in the memory in the environment where the black-box testing using the HiL simulation is performed targeting the automotive ECU and its software. The memory was partitioned by using the memory map, then we confirmed that the fault-suspicious region in the memory was reduced by calculating *FS* of each partition.

The advantages of the proposed method are as follows. Firstly, there is no cost to be consumed for analyzing a source code. Secondly, it is applicable to the environment without an external terminal of ECU for the Run-stop debugging. In the future work, we'll study a method of partitioning memory based on the stack information to reduce the fault-suspicious region in the environment where the memory map is not available.

Acknowledgments This research was supported by Next-Generation Information Computing Development Program through the National Research Foundation of Korea (NRF) funded by the Ministry of Science, ICT & Future Planning (NRF-2014M3C4A7030504).

References

1. Altinger H, Wotawa F, Schurius M (2014) Testing methods used in the automotive industry: results from a survey. In: JAMAICA proceedings of the 2014 workshop on joining AcadeMiA and industry contributions to test automation and model-based testing
2. Siegl S, Hielscher K-S, German R (2010) Model based requirements analysis and testing of automotive systems with timed usage models. In: The 18th IEEE international on requirements engineering conference, pp 345–350
3. Wong WE et al (1995) Effect of test set minimization on fault detection effectiveness. In: The 17th international conference on software engineering, pp 41–50
4. Choi K-Y et al (2015) HiL testing based fault localization method using memory update frequency. In: The 10th KIPS international conference on ubiquitous information technologies and applications, vol 373, no 1, pp 765–772
5. Xie X et al (2010) Spectrum-based fault localization without test oracles. Technical Report UTDCS-07-10
6. Vermeulen B (2008) Functional debug techniques for embedded systems. IEEE Design Test Comput 25:208–215
7. Lee J-W et al (2015) Data cascading method for the large automotive data acquisition beyond the CAN bandwidth in HiL testing. In: The 10th KIPS international conference on ubiquitous information technologies and applications, vol 373, no 1, pp 773–780
8. Wu R et al (2014) CrashLocator: locating crashing faults based on crash stacks. In: The 2014 international symposium on software testing and analysis, pp 204–214

Power Measurement Technique Considering the State Changes of GPS Using Location APIs

Jae-Hyeon Park, Deok-Ki Kim and Jung-Won Lee

Abstract The mobile context-aware service is performed based on the collected data from the various sensors. Additional power is consumed by the operations of the sensors which lead to the reduced battery life. So it is necessary to manage the sensors efficiently for sustainable mobile context-aware service. Among the sensors, GPS is well known as a noticeable battery hog affected by the surrounding environment. The power of the mobile device is consumed unnecessarily due to the operation of the GPS in the place where the locational data is not updated. Therefore, the efficient management of the GPS is required and analysis of the power consumption of the GPS has to be preceded. However, in the existing studies, the GPS has been analyzed with course-grained models such as ON/OFF or enabled/disabled so it is hard to get information enough to identify what the state is causing unwanted power consumption of the GSP. In this paper, we propose a technique for analyzing the power consumption of the mobile device according to fine-grained states of GPS using location APIs.

Keywords Power consumption · Mobile device · GPS · Context-awareness · LBS (location based service)

J.-H. Park · D.-K. Kim · J.-W. Lee (✉)
Department of Electrical and Computer Engineering, Ajou University, Suwon, Republic of Korea
e-mail: jungwony@ajou.ac.kr

J.-H. Park
e-mail: jaehp2560@gmail.com

D.-K. Kim
e-mail: kdk0421@gmail.com

© Springer Science+Business Media Singapore 2016
J.J. (Jong Hyuk) Park et al. (eds.), *Advanced Multimedia and Ubiquitous Engineering*, Lecture Notes in Electrical Engineering 393,
DOI 10.1007/978-981-10-1536-6_25

189

1   Introduction

The mobile device collects data about the surrounding environment using various sensors. Based on the collected data, the mobile device infers the contexts of the user and provides the most suitable service [1]. The context is composed of spatial, temporal and behavioral data such as indoor, outdoor, walk, night and home [2]. To recognize the contexts correctly, it is required to collect the related sensor data and analyze as soon as possible [3]. Thus, additional power is consumed by the operations of the sensors and the increased power consumption leads to reduced battery life. The battery problem makes the mobile context-aware service unpractical. Therefore, it is necessary to manage the operations of the sensors efficiently.

Among the sensors, the GPS gathering the locational data is affected by the environment of receiving the radio waves from the satellites. GPS is the most expensive module in the aspect of power consumption. If the GPS is occasionally unable to receive the radio waves, it could not update the locational data although it works. It causes unnecessary power consumption. To solve this problem, the efficient management of the GPS is required and analysis of the state in which the power is unnecessarily consumed has to be preceded. In this paper, we define the fine-grained states of the GPS so that it can be provided enough information to manage the GPS and propose a technique to analyze power consumption according to status of the GPS using location APIs. Finally, we show that it can trace the change of GPS states by the requests of a location based application.

2   Related Work

Studies for analyzing the power consumption of the mobile device could be roughly divided into hardware approaches and software approaches.

Monsoon [4] is a typical measurement tool using hardware method. Monsoon supplies power to mobile device and measures it. Monsoon is capable of measuring power precisely but it can be only used in a fixed indoor locations. In other studies, NEAT [5] adds hardware to link between a battery and a mobile device, then it measures the power supplied from battery to the mobile device. During the measurement, it is synchronized to the mobile device with periodic signal and records the logs of system. It can be used in analyzing power consumption of the modules using system log in the mobile environment. However, hardware modification is needed for synchronizing the mobile device and NEAT deals with more data than necessary to analyze interesting module normally.

In the studies of using a software method, there are Powertutor [6] and Appscope [7], which use energy models. Appscope detects requests of the operating system to access modules, and it determines usage and status of the modules. Then it calculates power consumption by substituting usage and status into the energy models that have been defined in advance. It confirms power consumption of each modules.

However, it can be only used in the mobile devices having the predefined energy models and the model of GPS among the energy models is designed with only two states (ON/OFF), so it is hard to analyze fine-grained behavior of GPS.

There have been some studies including the previous work [8] for analyzing power consumption of the mobile device. However, they have analyzed the GPS with coarse-grained model, which makes it hard to detect the states causing unwanted power consumption of the GPS. Thus, for providing enough information to manage the GPS efficiently in terms of power, we define GPS states and propose the method for measuring the power consumption of the mobile device according to these states.

3 Design for Analysis of GPS States

3.1 Definition of GPS States

The GPS receives radio waves from satellites and then transmits locational data to applications. Thus, the states of the GPS could vary with surrounding environment in progress of using the GPS. In Android location API, there are callback functions to be called when locational data is updated and status of the GPS module and location provider providing periodic reports of the locational data are changed. These functions represent the status of the GPS and are called when the status of the GPS is changed. Thus, we have used these functions to define GPS states [9].

In callback functions, there are onLocationChanged(), onProviderDisabled(), onProviderEnabled(), onStatusChanged() and onGpsStatusChanged(). Among these functions, onStatusChanged() and onGpsStatusChanged() are called when status of the location provider and the GPS module is changed, and they provide information via arguments. This information includes detailed status of the GPS module and the location provider. We have defined GPS states as the status of the GPS specified by this information and the other functions. The results are shown in Table 1. Table 1 shows GPS states occurred depending on whether locational data is updated, and the status of the location provider and the GPS module are changed.

3.2 Detection of GPS States

In order to observe the GPS states, it is necessary to know when these functions are called. We have been able to know this moment by finding where these function are called in Android System and notifying when these function are executed.

We have finded that onGpsStatusChanged() is called at LocationManager class, and onLocationChanged(), onProviderDisabled(), onProviderEnabled() and onStatusChanged() are called at LocationManagerService (LMS) class [10].

Table 1 GPS states based on location API

Location APIs		GPS state
GpsStatus.Listener	onGpsStatusChanged()	GPS_EVENT_STARTED
		GPS_EVENT_FIRST_FIX
		GPS_EVENT_STOPPED
		GPS_EVENT_SATELLITE_STATUS
LocationListener	onLocationChanged()	onLocationChanged
	onProviderDisabled()	onProviderDisabled
	onProviderEnabled()	onProviderEnabled
	onStatusChanged()	AVAILABLE
		OUT_OF_SERVICE
		TEMPORARILY_UNAVAILABLE

LocationManager provides API for accessing the location service system. GpsStatusListenerTransport class in the LocationManager defines functions that update status of the GPS module. The onGpsStatusChanged() is called by execution of these functions since it has characteristic to be invoked when the status of the GPS module is updated. LMS is one of the system services. It manages connections of the location provider and applications that request locational data. In LMS, there is a class that makes connection between the location provider and the applications. The functions executed in response to change of GPS states are called by internal functions in this class. onLocationChanged() is called at callLocationChangedLocked(), onStatusChanged() is called at callStatusChangedLocked(), and onProviderDisabled() and onProviderEnabled() are called at ProviderEnabledLocked().

And we have modified Android Framework to notify the observer application of the moment these functions are called. Figure 1 shows a method used in our observer application to collect GPS states. When these functions are invoked in LMS and LocationManager, they announce data of GPS states to the observer application. They use the broadcast as means for transmitting data of GPS states. They send data of GPS states with a different key according to their position such as LocationManager or LMS, and the observer application receives and distinguishes the data by using keys.

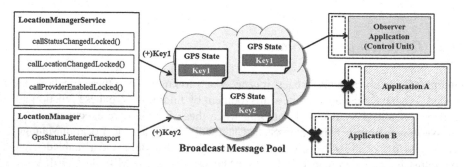

Fig. 1 Process of transmission of GPS states

4 Implementation

Our measurement system has been implemented separately to Measurement Unit and Control Unit. The Control Unit handles the Measurement Unit with commands such as start and stop. And, it observes change of GPS state according to requirements of running applications while operating as service application. The Measurement Unit is developed as a portable power meter. It supplies power to the mobile device and measures it. Sampling rate is determined at 100 Hz based on the research of Dong [11]. It receives data of GPS state from the Control Unit, and records it by combining data of power measurement. They communicate via bluetooth.

5 Evaluation

5.1 Change of GPS States According to Indoor/Outdoor

We compare the power consumption and GPS states associated with indoor and outdoor. Mobile device used in the experiment is Nexus4, and we run test application to operate GPS. The test application requests and releases location service alternately and updates the data at high speed as possible. Figure 2 is a graph of power consumption for using in indoor/outdoor. It is possible to verify change in power associated with change of GPS states through the graph. According to this graph, GPS_EVENT_STOPPED(a) and GPS_EVENT_STARTED(b) of GPS states are detected in indoor, that is, the GPS module is stopped and started. In outdoor, The GPS module is started at (d). After then, GPS_EVENT_SATELLITE_STATUS state continuously occurs and status of reception of the satellites is updated. When

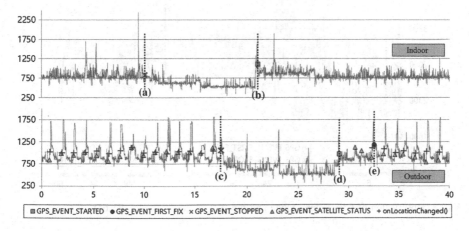

Fig. 2 Observation of GPS states change and power in indoor/outdoor

locational data is updated, onLocationChanged() state occurs and the spikes appear in the graph at this time. When the first location data is updated after the GPS module is started, GPS_EVENT_FIRST_FIX(e) state is verified. It is possible to confirm that locational data and status of the satellites are updated within one-second period and there is a difference in the change of GPS states depending on indoor/outdoor.

5.2 Change of GPS States According to Using Location Based Service Application

We observe the change of GPS state according to the usage of location service based commercial application. Mobile device used in the experiment is Nexus4, and the application used in the experiment performs function of the navigation. The experiment has been conducted outdoors. Figure 3 is a graph of power consumption for the application execution. This graph shows the overall higher power consumption than in the graph of Fig. 2 because of the power consumed by generating continuously graphics for display. The change of the GPS states according to using the application is confirmed through the graph. In the application, it is initialized by stopping and starting GPS module two times in (a), and the status of the satellites is updated in about one-second intervals after (b). Locational update is interrupted in (c) then the GPS is initialized by stopping and starting GPS module immediately. It shows a pattern that repeats updating status of the satellites after (d). Through this pattern, it can be confirmed that the location-based service is executed after (a) and status of the satellites is updated with a period close to one second.

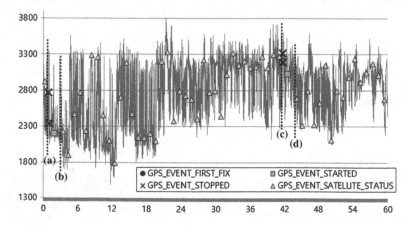

Fig. 3 Observation of GPS states change and power in according to application

6 Conclusion

In this paper, we propose the method for collecting information of GPS states and measuring power consumption in accordance with change of GPS states. For this, we define GPS states based on Android location API, and modify Android Framework layer to transmit information of the GPS state to the Control Unit in Application layer. Furthermore, we show a difference of changing GPS states in outdoor and indoor, and trace the changes of the GPS states according to the requirements of a commercial location-aware application. The method proposed in this paper will be helpful for generating detailed energy model of the GPS and analyzing the unwanted power consumption of the GPS.

Acknowledgments This research was supported by the MSIP (Ministry of Science, ICT & Future Planning), Korea, under the ITRC (Information Technology Research Center) support program (IITP-2015- H8501-15-1006) supervised by the IITP (Institute for Information & communications Technology Promotion)

References

1. Kim DK, Lee JW (2015) GPS state modeling for power consumption estimation of location-aware applications. Korea Computer Congress 2015 (KCC2015), vol 2015, no 6, pp 430–432
2. Tu Y (2008) xTolk—a context-aware mobile application on the nokia N95 8 GB smartphone
3. Perera C et al (2013) Context aware computing for the internet of things: a survey. IEEE Commun Surv Tutorials 16(1):414–454
4. Monsoon Solutions, Inc. http://www.msoon.com/LabEquipment/PowerMonitor
5. Brouwers N et al (2014) NEAT: a nevel energy analysis toolkit for free-roaming smartphones, sensys' 14. In: Proceedings of the 12th ACM conference on embedded network sensor systems, pp 16–30
6. Zhang L et al (2010) Accurate online power estimation and automatic battery behavior based power model generation for smartphones. In: Proceedings 8th IEEE/ACM/IFIP international conference on hardware/software codesign and system synthesis, pp 105–114
7. Yoon C (2012) AppScope: application energy metering framework for android smartphones using kernel activity monitoring. In: Proceedings 2012 USENIX annual technical conference, pp 36
8. Choi KY, Lee JW (2014) Portable power measurement system for mobile devices. J KIISE: Comput Practices Lett 20(3):131–142
9. Android Developers http://developer.android.com/reference/
10. Android Open Source Project http://source.android.com/
11. Dong M, Zhong L (2011) Self-constructive high-rate system energy modeling for battery-powered mobile systems. In: MobiSys '11 Proceedings of the 9th international conference on mobile systems, applications, and services, pp 335–348

A Secure Communication in Web of Things

Jin H. Park, Im Y. Jung and Soon J. Kim

Abstract A technique to communicate with a smart sensor device using the Web is currently being developed. When the user approaches the device, like a beacon, the device sends a URL to the built-in sensor to the user's smartphone. With this URL, the user can communicate with the smart sensor device through a Web interface. When communicating with a beacon using a Web interface, encryption is required for secure communication between the Web browser and beacon. In this paper, we propose secure communication using a symmetric key distribution. Our method prevents malicious applications from eavesdropping on messages and replaying a message. In addition, we evaluated the execution time.

Keywords Bluetooth security · Key agreement · Replay attack · Physical web

1 Introduction

As the number of smart devices is growing at a rapid pace, installing a particular application to communicate with all different types of smart device is impractical. Physical Web is an open project being developed by Google. As the basic concept of this project, users interact with a smart device using a Web browser. For this, URLs are assigned to a smart device such as a smart car, vending machine, or Web camera. This means that a specific application is not required to communicate with a smart device [1–4]. For example, a beacon can broadcast a URL to a user's smartphone when the user arrives at a bus station. From this URL, the user can

J.H. Park · I.Y. Jung (✉) · S.J. Kim
Kyungpook National University, 80 Gaehakro Bukgu,
Daegu 702-701, Republic of Korea
e-mail: iyjung@ee.knu.ac.kr

J.H. Park
e-mail: helloworld@knu.ac.kr

S.J. Kim
e-mail: snjkim@ee.knu.ac.kr

© Springer Science+Business Media Singapore 2016   197
J.J. (Jong Hyuk) Park et al. (eds.), *Advanced Multimedia and Ubiquitous
Engineering*, Lecture Notes in Electrical Engineering 393,
DOI 10.1007/978-981-10-1536-6_26

Fig. 1 Communication with smart car through a browser

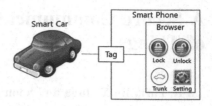

know the arrival time of a particular bus. Because it is quite inconvenient from a user's perspective to install new application for each specific service provided by a smart device, through the realization of such a technique, app management problems can be resolved by utilizing a Web browser instead of specific apps.

Using a Web browser to interact with a smart device can resolve the app management problem. However, a security problem still remains. In particular, if the data to be sent and received between the tag (interface card for beacon) and Web browser are not encrypted, sensitive information such as billing information may be exposed. In Bluetooth security procedures, authentication between a beacon and tag is conducted based on a shared secret key. If authentication is successfully completed, a link key is generated. As another approach, an Elliptic Curve Diffie-Hellman (ECDH) method is used to exchange the link key. This link key is used for encryption and decryption. As a Web browser is used to interact with the beacon, a session key between the beacon and Web browser should be established for secure communication. An application developer may guarantee an application layer security on his/her own development. In web browser, using a TLS (Transport Layer Security) or SSL (Secure Sockets Layer) is alternative way. But, these are great pressure on the resource constrained device like beacon. That is, end-to-end security should be achieved. In addition, replay and injection attacks, known as Bluetooth security threats, may occur more often in a Web environment [5–7].

In this paper, we propose a session key establishment scheme between a beacon and browser. This prevents malicious applications from intercepting a message. Further, using a random number, our method prevents a replay attack. The scenario applied is shown in Fig. 1, which illustrates that a smart car can be connected to a smartphone browser. In Sect. 2, we suggest a potential problem in this environment and suggest a method for solving it. In Sect. 3, we evaluate our method. Finally, some concluding remarks are given in Sect. 4.

2 Secure Communication Between Beacon and Browser

2.1 Problem Statement

When a user enters a beacon service area, the built-in tags in the beacon and smartphone conduct an authentication process using a secret key or ECDH, and generate a link key. This link key is used to encrypt and decrypt messages.

Fig. 2 Data exposure between tag and browser

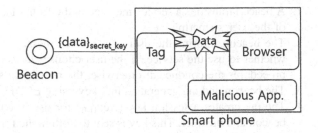

However, the data transmitted to the browser from the tag are exposed in the form of plain text. This problem is shown in Fig. 2. If the smartphone has a security vulnerability, data may be exposed to a malicious application. When a tag is accessible by other applications on the smartphone, the data are exposed to these applications. To resolve this problem, a pre-shared key may be used between the tag and browser, in which case the tag should continuously encrypt and decrypt the messages delivered between them. Therefore, it is necessary to establish a session key for secure communication between the Web browser and beacon.

2.2 Key Distribution Scheme

The proposed scheme assumes that the link key (Key_{Be-T}) between the beacon and tag is established using ECDH. The secret key (Key_{T-Br}) used between the browser and tag is saved in a Trusted Platform Module (TPM). A TPM is a microchip built into the latest smartphones, and is used to maintain a secret key. The cipher used in this paper is the advanced encryption standard (AES), which is a more efficient cipher algorithm than other available algorithms (DESL, HIGHT, SEA, TEA/XTEA). Basically, a random number is provided by the beacon. It is inserted in a structured message format. For the browser to read and write the random number, the browser also uses this format. Figure 3 shows the proposed scheme. The steps shown in Fig. 3 can be described as follows:

Fig. 3 Secure communication between beacon and browser

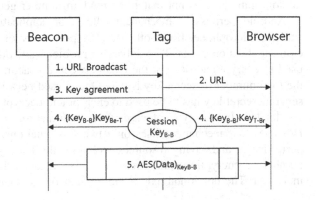

1. A beacon transmits a service message in the form of a URL when detecting a tag of the user's smartphone.
2. The beacon informs the user of a service message. The user then determines whether to use the service. If the user chooses to use the service, the following procedures are conducted; otherwise, the remaining steps are ignored.
3. The beacon and tag generate a link key using ECDH or a pre-shared secret key.
4. The tag creates a session key (Key_{B-B}) for use in communicating between the beacon and browser. This key is sent to both in the form of an encoded message. If a pre-shared key does not exist, Key exchange is conducted through ECDH.
5. The beacon and browser use this key for encrypting and decrypting the message. In addition, to prevent a replay attack, a random number generated by the beacon is included in the message.

3 Evaluation

An evaluation can be categorized into security and performance. The security is improved because messages are concealed from malicious applications, and encrypted messages are verified by checking the random number generated. The performance is improved by reducing the number of computations.

The proposed scheme guarantees secure communication between a Web browser and beacon. To achieve this, the session key is generated by a tag based on a trust relationship between the beacon and tag, and between the tag and browser. After being encrypted by the tag, the session key is delivered to both the beacon and browser. That is, by providing end-to-end message confidentiality, no messages are exposed to malicious applications installed on a smartphone. There are some ways an attacker can try. Those are chosen-message attack, chosen-plaintext attack and chosen-cipher text attack. However, it is no use doing because AES was proven safe against these types of attack.

A 128-bit random number is inserted at the end of the message when the message is transferred, preventing a replay attack. Even if an attacker re-sends an encrypted message to a beacon, the message is rejected by the beacon because its random number does not match the random number generated by the beacon.

Android permission mechanism allows an application to access the data of camera, microphone, Bluetooth, etc. The possibility of eavesdropping by a malicious application exists. To resolve this problem, an additional secret key must be used to encrypt and decrypt the data between a beacon and a browser. Therefore, the total number of secret key is two. One is used between a beacon and a tag. If a separate secret key has to be used to encrypt and decrypt a message, the tag may be overloaded. In this type of case, four computations are executed per message. However, our mechanism uses only two computations, resulting in an improved performance and saving resources including the battery life. Figure 4 shows the number of encryptions and decryptions executed as the number of messages is increased. The horizontal axis is the number of messages. The vertical axis is the

Fig. 4 Number of executions per message

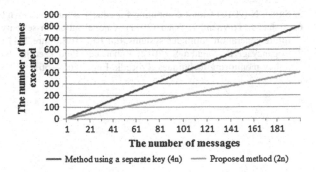

number of algorithms executed. Our method has only 2n and the method using a separate key has 4n, where n is the number of messages. Therefore, our method reduces the number of operations to 1/2.

4 Conclusion

The number of smart devices on the market has been rapidly increasing. Installing specific applications on a smartphone to communicate with all available smart devices is an impractical approach. To address this problem, a technique for interacting with a smart device through a Web browser is being developed. However, many security problems still need to be addressed. Thus, we proposed a secure communication between the tag and browser, this prevents malicious applications from intercepting a message. The proposed scheme also prevents replay attacks. The time to encrypt and decrypt is reduced by half in comparison with using a separate key.

Acknowledgments This work was supported by Institute for Information & communications Technology Promotion (IITP) grant funded by the Korea government (MSIP). [No. 10041145, Self-Organized Software platform (SoSp) for Welfare Devices]

References

1. Khan BH (2000) A framework for web-based learning. Educational Technology Publications, Englewood Cliffs
2. Liaw S-S, Huang H-M, Chen G-D (2007) Surveying instructor and learner attitudes toward e-learning. Comput Educ 49:1066–1080
3. Wang Y-S, Wang H-Y, Shee DY (2007) Measuring e-learning systems success in an organizational context: scale development and validation. Comput Hum Behav 23:1792–1808
4. Chikh Azeddine, Berkani Lamia (2010) Communities of practice of e-learning, an innovative learning space for e-learning actors. Procedia Soc Behav Sci 2:5022–5027

5. Sultan N (2010) Cloud computing for education: a new dawn? Int J Inf Manage 30:109–116
6. Arshad J, Townend P, Xu J (2011) A novel intrusion severity analysis approach for clouds, future generation computer systems. doi:10.1016/j.future.2011.08.009
7. Loganayagi B, Sujatha S (2012) Enhanced cloud security by combining virtualization and policy monitoring techniques. Procedia Eng 30:654–661

An Interactive Virtual Reality System with a Wireless Head-Mounted Display

Shujia Hao, Wei Song, Kaisi Huang, Yulong Xi, Kyungeun Cho and Kyhyun Um

Abstract Virtual reality (VR) with head-mounted display (HMD) device provides an immersive experience for novel multimedia applications. This paper develops an interactive virtual reality system with a wireless HMD to enable a natural VR operation interface. In a server, the system utilizes the Kinect as a motion detection device to estimate VR user's location and gesture information in real time. Through a WiFi network, the user's information is transferred to the HMD as a client, where the user controls an avatar following his motion. The controlled avatar interacts with the virtual environment in real time. The proposed system is implemented using a Samsung Gear VR, Kinect 2.0 and Unity3D environment. This system is compatible with serious games, virtual and physical collaboration, natural user interfaces, and other multimedia applications.

Keywords Virtual reality · Natural user interface · Head-mounted display · Wireless sensor network

1 Introduction

Virtual Reality (VR) technology has been actively researched in various multimedia fields. HMD is widening rapidly in recent years. HMDs allow VR user to observe the virtual environment at both left and right viewports, which generate a stereo image in human's brain [1]. HMD devices are also available for Natural User Interface (NUI) applications, which aim to implement multimedia operation with human gesture controlling [2]. The interdisciplinary projects combining NUI, VR and HMD provide users with natural operation and intuitive observation experience.

S. Hao · W. Song (✉) · K. Huang
Department of Digital Media Technology, North China University of Technology,
Beijing, China
e-mail: sw@ncut.edu.cn

Y. Xi · K. Cho · K. Um
Department of Multimedia Engineering, Dongguk University, Seoul, Korea

© Springer Science+Business Media Singapore 2016
J.J. (Jong Hyuk) Park et al. (eds.), *Advanced Multimedia and Ubiquitous Engineering*, Lecture Notes in Electrical Engineering 393,
DOI 10.1007/978-981-10-1536-6_27

Recently, several human motion sensors are developed for NUI input devices, such as Microsoft Kinect and Leap Motion [3]. The Kinect is a popular body gesture detection device for touch-less operation interface. By combining HMD with the Kinect, this paper proposes a wireless interactive virtual reality system. As computing in a server, the Kinect detects the user's motion information, as an NUI. Different from video stream transmission method, this system only transmit the motion signal and the VR visualization process is generated by the HMD client. This method with small data volume enables the real-time wireless network transmission so as to promote the HMD VR commercialized. The proposed system provides several function interfaces for NUI application, such as serious games, medical experiments, and multimedia lectures.

The remainder of this paper is organized as follows. Section 2 overviews related work. Section 3 discusses the architecture of the interactive virtual reality system. Section 4 develops a serious game using the proposed system. Section 5 concludes this paper.

2 Related Work

Currently, Oculus Rift is a popular display device in VR researching areas. Draganov [4] proposed a disable patient assistant system with the Oculus Rift. In the system, he utilized a sensor glove equipped on the hands for hand gestures recognition, so as to interact with virtual objects. Kenneth [5] utilized a leap motion to develop a molecular graphics controlling toolkit, called Aquaria. By hand motion recognition, the interaction between real and virtual world was visualization in scene of the Oculus Rift display. Avila [6] utilized a Virtuix Omni VR treadmill to extend the user's movement scope by walking, jumping, and strafing on it. The interaction methodologies between real and virtual environments are always detected through wearable sensors, such as data gloves and inertial measurement units. These NUI controllers need data transmission cables to communicate with a server computer. The cables limit the scope of user's movement and reduce the VR immersion.

Some researchers implemented the sensors computation by a computer carried on the user's back. Although this method enable the VR user's free movement, the user felt tired for a long time walking with the heavy computer. These methods with body mounted sensors caused the operation uncomfortable, thus wireless human gesture sensing device is necessary for VR enhancement. To solve this problem, Sony PlayStation VR, a wireless HMD, was developed so that wearable devices were not required for VR development [7]. These technologies transmitted the VR visualization result to the HMD via a wireless network. Due to the limited bandwidth, the display signal was unstable for real-time video transmission, while the user moves. To enhance natural user experience, this paper develops a wireless HMD technology for real-time interactive VR approaches.

3 Interactive Virtual Reality System

We proposed an interactive virtual reality system with wireless HMD, as shown in Fig. 1, which provides VR developers with wireless motion recognition interface. The system is mainly combined with a motion detection server and a wireless HMD VR client.

In the motion detection server, we utilize a Kinect to detect user's skeleton motion and analyze gesture information from infrared video sequences. We display the user's location and gesture information in a monitor. The system delivers the computed motion and gesture datasets to the wireless HMD via WiFi network. Different from transmitting large dataset of the VR visualization buffers, the delivery dataset size by this method is within 1 KB per frame.

In the wireless HMD VR client, an avatar is controlled by the received gesture data. The avatar interacts with virtual objects computed by the smart phone, which is installed in a HMD. We utilize the Unity Legacy Integration, provided by Oculus, to realize the immersive experience for VR display. The virtual environment is captured by left and right virtual cameras, which provide a stereo scene to the VR user.

4 Experiments

Using the proposed system, we developed a serious game, shown in Fig. 2. We utilized Microsoft Kinect 2 to detect user's gesture on a server, which is a 2.60 GHz Intel® Core™ i5-4210 M CPU laptop with a GeForce GTX 850 M graphics card and 4 GB RAM. The client is implemented on a Samsung Gear VR with a Samsung

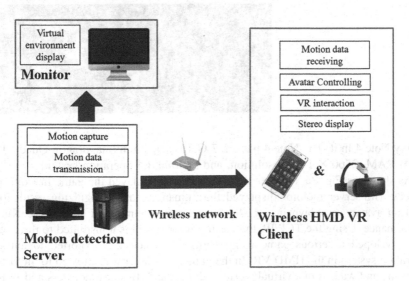

Fig. 1 The architecture of the proposed interactive virtual reality system

Fig. 2 A serious game
development using the
proposed interactive VR
system. **a** Real world capture.
b Avatar controlling. **c** Avatar
in HMD VR. **d** Game sense

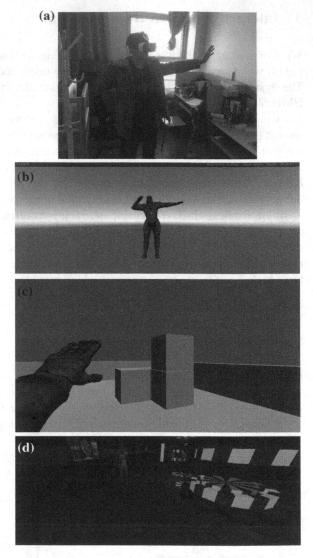

galaxy Note 4 in it. The Note 4 has a 2.7 GHz Qualcomm Snapdragon Quad CPU, 3 GB RAM, 2560 × 1440 resolution, and android 4.4 operation system.

As shown in Fig. 2a, the user wore the HMD and played the game in front of a Kinect. The server monitor displayed the human gesture recognizing result joint with an avatar, as shown in Fig. 2b, in order to monitor and correct the Kinect performance. Using the TCP/IP, the gesture information is transmitted to the client. We developed a serious game using Unity3D, which was exported to android operation system in the HMD VR. In the game, the player was allowed to hit virtual monsters and walked in a virtual world with his hand. Besides monsters and virtual environment, the player was able to see his avatar body at the first person viewport, as shown in Fig. 2c, d.

The proposed system allows users to interact the virtual objects by their gestures, without wearing any motion detection device. It has a bright prospect in digital media technologies, such as entertainment, gaming, film and video, and education.

5 Conclusions

To provide a natural and convenient interface for the HMD VR, this paper described an interactive VR System using the Kinect, as a gesture detection sensor. By transmitting the gesture information from the server to the HMD VR client, the system realized that the user interacted with the virtual environment by his gesture operation. The user was able to control and browse his avatar in the HMD VR in real time due to the small transmission datasets. The developed serious game verified that such wireless NUI operation approach enhanced the immersive experience.

In our system, the obstacles in the real world are not visualized in the VR scene, thus the user is easy to hit and knock onto the obstacles. In future, we will reconstruct the real world to a virtual 3D background model using a LiDAR sensor. The VR scene will provide obstacle warning graphics interface to show the point clouds of the real world.

Acknowledgments This research was supported by the National Natural Science Foundation of China (61503005), and by SRF for ROCS, SEM.

References

1. Gordon NS, Merchant J, Zanbaka C et al (2011) Interactive gaming reduces experimental pain with or without a head mounted display. Comput Hum Behav 27:2123–2128
2. Song W, Cai X, Xi Y et al (2015) Real-time single camera natural user interface engine development. Multimedia Tools Appl, pp 1–17
3. Beattie N, Horan B, McKenziea S (2015) Taking the LEAP with the oculus HMD and CAD— plucking at thin air? Procedia Technol 20:149–154
4. Draganov IR, Boumbarov OL (2015) Investigating oculus rift virtual reality display applicability to medical assistive system for motor disabled patients. In: The 8th IEEE international conference on intelligent data acquisition and advanced computing systems: technology and applications, pp 24–26
5. Kenneth S, Christian S, Bruce T et al (2013) The molecular control toolkit: controlling 3D molecular graphics via gesture and voice. In: 2013 IEEE symposium on biological data visualization, pp 49–56
6. Avila L, Bailey M (2014) Virtual reality for the masses. Comput Graph Appl 34:103–104
7. Ito M, Kihara K, Yoshida S et al (2015) Patient's self-monitoring of transurethral surgical images using a head-mounted display. Urol Case Rep 3:27–29

Programming Practice and Digital Textbook on Smartphone

Kwang Sik Chung, Hye Won Byun and HeonChang Yu

Abstract As information technology service matures to an even higher level and as sensor technology becomes embedded on person's life, the needs to support and satisfy instant personal learning activity on own life without the limitation of time, space, and additional complement have become a vital point to everyday lives. Especially smartphone users are increased in a short-term lesson and exercise, and instant and short learning contents on mobile learning model. And programing subjects for distance learning are limitedly supported, since virtual practice environment is not appropriate for tutoring service. Programming practices lesson has frequent program errors and needs error correction by oneself or by a tutor. But on distance learning, it is almost impossible for a learner to be guided or correct lesson from a tutor. In this paper, well-formed programming practice scenarios, by that a learner could follow and learn program practice lesson, are supported and delivered by small-bite size learning contents. For well-formed programming practice scenarios, small bite learning contents are 10–15 min length and consists of lecture video, synchronized lecture slides video with lecture video, digital textbook, sample program execution drills, and modifiable program execution drills. Programming Exercise, a mobile learning app, provides learners with interactions between the learners and the contents by program practice.

Keywords Virtual laboratory · Virtual programming practice · Smart phone · Smart learning

K.S. Chung (✉)
Department of Computer Science, Korea National Open University,
Seoul, Korea
e-mail: kchung0825@knou.ac.kr

H.W. Byun
Department of English Language and Literature, Sejong University,
Seoul, Korea
e-mail: wonnyb@sejong.ac.kr

H. Yu
Distributed and Cloud Computing Lab, Korea University, Seoul, Korea
e-mail: yuhc@korea.ac.kr

© Springer Science+Business Media Singapore 2016
J.J. (Jong Hyuk) Park et al. (eds.), *Advanced Multimedia and Ubiquitous Engineering*, Lecture Notes in Electrical Engineering 393,
DOI 10.1007/978-981-10-1536-6_28

1 Introduction

E-learning or blended learning is common and reasonable among many companies and many formal education institutions, because of e-learning's economical advantage over existing off-line learning environment. Especially mobile learning environment is appropriate for lifelong educations, since almost learners have their current jobs [1]. Mobile learning for lifelong educations enables learners' autonomous learning as they can adjust their learning time and learning place and always access learning contents. Various learning contents delivered through mobile devices (notes or pad type computer, smartphones, etc.) are becoming more and more practical and effective to learners across contexts with many advantages [2–4].

First, using smartphones enables instant access to learning contents regardless of place and time. Second, smartphones provide various learner's interaction or learning activity with various built-in sensors, which could consolidate the cost and usage of infrastructures for providing practice and drills to computer science or computer engineering students. Generally, programming practices provided to computer science or engineering majors in offline environment require numbers of programming, debugging, execution ground, and subsidiary facilities. But these requirements have to be built by a learner on e-learning environment and these requirements are big burden to a learner. To address the aforementioned issues, we design and develop virtual programming practice mobile learning contents based on Android platform. These contents are expected to overcome the constraints of learner's location and time, to reduce practice environment construction burden of a learner, to allow more learners to easily take programming practice, and to deliver all-in-one learning contents(lecture video, synchronized lecture slides video with lecture video, sample program execution drills, digital textbook and modifiable program execution drills). Developed virtual programming practice mobile learning contents are developed for smartphones based on Android platform, and to generate interactions between learners and develop virtual programming practice mobile learning contents by using built-in JVM and program execution interface. The virtual programming practice mobile learning contents also take the advantage of GUI and touch interface for users to understand their tasks easily. This following sections will first discusses current literature related to the efficacy and development of simulation-based learning. Second, we will describe the design and developmental processes of virtual programming practice mobile learning contents. Finally we will conclude the paper by providing insights and future research and development agenda derived from the virtual programming practice mobile learning contents.

2 Related Works

'Virtual Practice' intends to realize the objective of delivering virtual practice environment through the virtual programming practice mobile learning contents. The virtual programming practice mobile learning content was designed to simulate the actual programming practices environments. In simulation-based Virtual Practice, learners will be able to develop indirect practice and execution experiences by interacting with concepts, principles, mutual relations, machine's operating procedures and instructions in real learning situations [5]. As like the previous works [4], virtual programming practice mobile learning contents also utilizes portable simulation environment on certain aspects of the program lessons, to mimic the compiling and execution machine. As a result, learners may perceive increased motivation through interacting with simulated high-fidelity problem-solving tasks [6]. With virtual programming practice mobile learning contents, learners can easily experience program coding, program modification and program execution through smartphone application, which does not need program compiler download, program complier install and execution environment configuration for program lesson.

The virtual programming practice mobile learning contents has classification matrix as like dimensionality, learner motion frame of reference, multimodal interaction, and virtual experiment contents driving person [1, 7]. The virtual programming practice mobile learning contents have characteristics of flat dimensionality of interaction, dynamic learner activity, inside-out of references, multimodal interactions between learners and learning contents, and learner driving virtual experience. And the virtual programming practice mobile learning contents are similar with tutorial learning model. But the virtual programming practice mobile learning contents provide interactions with learners and contents and immediate feedback (program execution results), according to learner's reactions (program modification).

3 The Developed Virtual Learning Contents

Based on the learning model and development method [8], we developed virtual programming practice mobile learning contents on a smartphone that stimulates learners' interactions with the intended program coding instruction (sample program and modifiable program). Several important concepts on effective learning were considered when designing the virtual programming practice mobile learning contents for program practice. Design factors such as well-framed sample program with lecture, execution environment feasibility, execution scenarios, especially the convergence of lecture, lecture video and program practice were taken into account to enhance the interactions between learners and the contents. The following section describes the steps learners should take, in order to interact with the virtual programming practice mobile learning contents.

At the introduction stage, learners should read and keep in mind the goal and introduction of practices, and be motivated by the one-bite session of the virtual programming practice mobile learning contents. In the introduction stage, a learner can take a class with introduction lecture video, true-or-false questions for introductory pretest, and terminology definitions. At the lecture stage, learners could become to know program coding methods and program grammar by watching lecture video and synchronized lecture slides video with lecture video or reading digital textbook. The digital textbook is more detail contents about program grammar and attribute explanation. The lecture video, lecture slides video and digital textbook. At practice stage, if a learner would like to practise sample program, the learner can execute sample program and modifiable sample program and confirm execution results of sample program and modifiable sample program. The modifiable sample program can be modified and executed by a learner and explained in the lecture video, synchronized lecture slides video with lecture video. The sample program and modifiable sample program executions. At summary stage, learners should answer the questions and finish each stage. First of all, a learner read and reconfirm terminology definitions of this contents. And a learner watch the summary lecture video. Lastly a learner answer post test (multiple selection questions) and confirm answer explanation. The post tests are objective test and related with pretest.

3.1 User-Centered Interaction Design

A survey was conducted after the experiment. All the participants completed the 28 questionnaires. The survey was divided into three parts. First, recognition, on how easy it was to use the overall system was questioned. Second, usability, on how easy or practical the system appeal to the users were questioned. Finally, cognitive load for the users, both positive and negative effects were asked.

The questionnaire contains 28 questions, each with a 5-point rating scale (1 = Strongly Disagree 5 = Strongly Agree), with higher points indicating greater satisfaction associated with the ease and accessibility of use. However, for the negative aspects on the cognitive load, point 1, strongly disagree indicates that the users didn't experience any or little discomfort or negative affect upon use. The numbers were added and each part was analyzed with linear graphs.

Figure 1 shows the overall usage of the digital textbook. The questions asked how the experiment helped their overall study. The graph indicates that overall experiment was generally positive for the users. Specially, nearly 80 % of the participants responded positively to the fact that this experiment helped them in understanding the given context. The participants were less satisfied with the

Fig. 1 Overall usage of the digital textbook

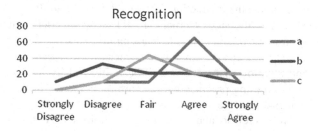

Fig. 2 Usability of this experiment

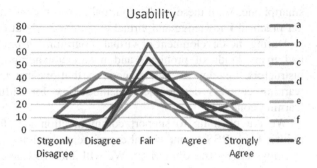

organizational part of the content. Improvements could be made to enhance navigational aspect of the screen.

Figure 2 shows the usability of this experiment. The results shows that interaction and motivation was the most encouraging factor about this experiment. The participants felt that this experiment provided interactive learning and were able to encourage their learning environment. However, the screen did not provide enough information for the users. Effective information could be provided to the learners to guide their use and also visual enhancement could be made as 'visual attractiveness' was one of the least satisfactory aspect of the textbook. No participants responded positively about the visual attractiveness of the screen.

4 Conclusion

In recent years, mobile devices have been commonly used for various contents and services. Especially smartphones have become the most important devices or tools for mobile contents, mobile communications and especially mobile learning, which has several characteristics that are not supported by desktop computers. Smartphones can provide seamless and instant learning environment and can be the best fit for mobile learning. Virtual programming practice contents for mobile learning needs frequent learners' interaction, in order to introduce programming class. And smartphones interface and mobility can extract programming interests and improve learning effects for learners, with one-bite size instant learning contents.

The primary objective of this research is to develop a virtual programming practice learning contents for engineering and science learners for smartphones and exploit smartphones' mobility and portability for learning interactions and instant and casual learning environment. The second objective is to develop the virtual programming practice learning contents according to digital textbook development methodology [8]. In this research, learning interactions factors and instant and casual learning environment enhancing learning effects and flows were developed and serviced with the by virtual programming practice learning contents of a smartphone. With these kinds of virtual learning contents and advantages, learners get practical knowledge and virtual experiences about offline programming class.

During the development of virtual programming practice learning contents, we had many kinds of problems and misunderstanding among a lecturer, content instructors, developers and learners so that we try to develop virtual practice learning contents development methodology for virtual programming practice learning contents.

We are planning to support communication and feedback function such as twitter, blog, RSS to our virtual experiments learning contents. And we managed learning activity tracking server. We will analyze learning activities of learners.

Acknowledgments This work was supported by 2015 Korea National Open University Research Fund.

References

1. Chung KS et al (2011) Design of integrated interactive mobile and e-learning (I2ME) system for Open University Malaysia. Proc AAOU
2. Chung KS et al (2009) Design and development of arithmetic operating learning management system based on PDA. J Korea Assoc Comput Educ
3. Chung KS et al (2009) Design and development of a learning management system for mobile learning environment with PDAs. Proc ICDE
4. Chung KS, Kwon S, Huang WH (2013) Design and development of sensor-based virtual experiment for smart phone. J Digital Contents Soc 14(2)
5. Lee KH, Park WH (2001) A study on the development of simulated CAI program for photosynthetic experiment. J Sci Edu Cent 27
6. Jeon J, Woo AJ (2002) Development and the application of web based simulation program about acid-base titration in the general chemistry. 6(2)
7. Wickens CD, Barker P (1995) Cognitive issues in virtual reality. In: Furness TA, Barfield W (eds) Virtual environments and advanced interface design, 3rd edn. Oxford University Press, New York
8. Chung KS et al (2010) Study on the methodology of digital textbook design and development for KNOU. Proc WorldComp

Researching Apache Hama: A Pure BSP Computing Framework

Kamran Siddique, Zahid Akhtar and Yangwoo Kim

Abstract In recent years, the technological advancements have led to a deluge of data from distinctive domains and the need for development of solutions based on parallel and distributed computing has still long way to go. That is why, the research and development of massive computing frameworks is continuously growing. At this particular stage, highlighting a potential research area along with key insights could be an asset for researchers in the field. Therefore, this paper explores one of the emerging distributed computing frameworks, Apache Hama. It is a Top Level Project under the Apache Software Foundation, based on bulk synchronous parallel model. We present an unbiased and critical interrogation session about Apache Hama and conclude research directions in order to assist interested researchers.

Keywords Apache hama · Bulk synchronous parallel · Bsp · Distributed computing · Hadoop · Mapreduce

1 Introduction

Nowadays, one of the largest technological challenges in computing systems research is to provide mechanisms for storage, information retrieval, and manipulation on massive amount of data. The need for research and development of big

K. Siddique · Y. Kim (✉)
Department of Information and Communication Engineering,
Dongguk University, Seoul, Korea
e-mail: ywkim@dongguk.edu

K. Siddique
e-mail: kamran@dongguk.edu

Z. Akhtar
Department of Mathematics and Computer Science,
University of Udine, Udine, Italy
e-mail: zahid.akhtar@uniud.it

© Springer Science+Business Media Singapore 2016
J.J. (Jong Hyuk) Park et al. (eds.), *Advanced Multimedia and Ubiquitous Engineering*, Lecture Notes in Electrical Engineering 393,
DOI 10.1007/978-981-10-1536-6_29

215

data processing frameworks is tremendously increasing. This paper presents our efforts towards writing a first focused paper on one of the emerging open source software frameworks, Apache Hama. It is a Top Level Project under the Apache Software Foundation but still it has a very limited documentation and research resources, which may be intimidating for newcomers in the initial phase of research. Therefore, highlighting a potential research area along with concise and significant insight could be of interest to researchers in the field. Hama is a distributed computing framework based on Bulk Synchronous Parallel (BSP) computing techniques for massive scientific computations e.g., graph, matrix and network algorithms [1, 2]. Our idea to contribute in this particular area is motivated by the key observation of the current trends in large scale data processing and at the same time, by observing the search log about Apache Hama over several research platforms [3, 4].

This paper provides an unbiased and critical interrogation session about Hama and our work is mainly directed to:

- Investigate research direction in big data processing using Hama;
- Researchers and graduate students intended to explore Hama in a record time;
- Practitioners, and users interested in acquainting themselves with thorough analysis of Hama.

The next section of the paper presents a questions and answers session followed by conclusion and future direction in Sect. 3.

2 Interrogation Session

In this section, we formulate the most significant, focused and unbiased questions and answers about Apache Hama that serves the basis for extracting research directions.

2.1 What Is Hama?

Hama, previously known as HAdoop MAtrix and short for Apache Hama, is a top-level project of Apache Software Foundation. Hama is a distributed computing framework based on the BSP programming model [1, 2]. It is designed to run on massive datasets, which are stored in the Hadoop Distributed File System (HDFS), and to solve scientific problems based on graphs, matrices, machine learning and networks. It is written in Java, deployed on HDFS and therefore fully compatible with Hadoop clusters.

2.2 What Is the Architecture of Hama and How It Works?

The architecture of Hama is very analogous to Apache Hadoop, since the underlying distributed file system is same. It consists of the following three major components [5]:

BSP Master is responsible for scheduling jobs and assigning the tasks to a Groom Server. This master component maintains the Groom Server status and the job progress information. It disseminates execution class across Groom Servers. The BSP Master controls the supersteps in a cluster and takes care if a job fails on a Groom Server. Moreover it also provides a cluster control interface for users.

Groom Server acts as a slave component in Hama architecture and it runs BSP peer tasks, assigned by the BSP Master. Each Groom Server pings BSP Master to undertake tasks and acknowledge its status to BSP Master by using periodical piggybacks. The BSP Peer slots are configurable and they should match the number of threads that a work is able to run in parallel. For best performance and data locality concept of Apache Hadoop, a Groom Server and a data node should run on the same machine.

Zookeeper or synchronization component is responsible for managing barrier synchronization tasks efficiently. The Zookeeper and BSP Master are launched parallel because of central barrier synchronization.

Figure 1 illustrates the architecture and working of Hama. When a user submits a job, the BSP JobClient establishes the communication channel with BSP Master by using Hadoop RPC framework. In this process, it partitions the input and stores the input splits to HDFS and then submit a new job to BSP Master. It is locally executed by the client and sends status updates about the submitted job and superstep count. The BSP Master reads all the information and then schedules the

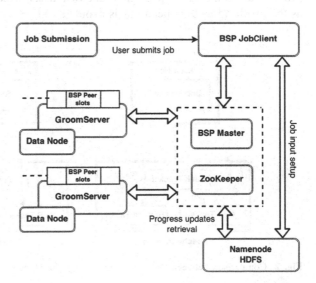

Fig. 1 Hama architecture and its working

jobs. The BSP JobClient updates itself with the job progress and also periodically informs the user for the same. Once, a task is assigned to Groom Server, it continues its execution until the last superstep is executed. During this process, the job rescheduling is not done on a different Groom Server. In case of failure, the job is marked failed and gets killed. The Zookeeper is responsible for barrier synchronization of BSP Peer tasks.

2.3 What Makes Hama Different From Other Big Data Computing Frameworks?

Hama is a pure BSP model, inspired by the work on Google Pregel. It is more focused towards processing complex computation-intensive tasks rather data-intensive tasks, which makes it different from other frameworks. In spite of Hama's similar architecture with Apache Hadoop and an inspiration from Google Pregel work, yet it has significant differences. Hama framework aims to provide a more general-purpose framework than Pregel and Apache Hadoop, supporting massive scientific computations such as matrix, graph, machine learning, business intelligence and network algorithms. It is not only restricted to graph processing; it provides a full set of primitives that allows the creation of generic BSP applications. The main difference in the architecture of Hama and Hadoop can be seen in Fig. 2. In Hama, the BSP tasks can communicate with each other, while the communication between Map and Reduce tasks is forbidden in Hadoop [6]. Moreover, in MapReduce model, the only form of communication between the tasks is through the persistence of data on the disk because this model enforces all Map tasks to finish their execution before the execution of any Reduce task. Whereas Hama provides direct message exchange for the BSP tasks, which leads to better efficiency as the overhead of I/O operations is avoided.

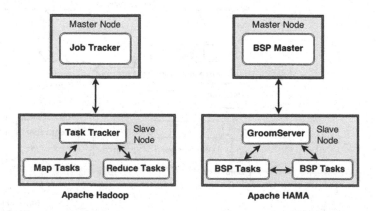

Fig. 2 Comparison between the architecture of Apache Hadoop and Apache Hama

2.4 What Are the Strengths of Hama?

Following are the strengths of Hama [6]:

- Hama supports diverse massive computational tasks. It is not just limited to large scale graph processing.
- Hama provides BSP primitives instead of graph processing APIs, which enables it to operate at a lower level.
- Hama provides explicit support to message passing.
- It has a simple, small and flexible API.
- As a result of following the BSP model, it does not suffer with conflicts and deadlines during the communication.
- Hama is primarily proposed to be used with Java, but Hama pipes also enable programmers to write programs in C++.
- Hama is not just limited to Hadoop Distributed File System (HDFS); it is flexible enough to be used with any distributed file system.
- Hama supports General-Purpose computing on Graphics Processing Units (GPGPU) acceleration.

2.5 What Are the Shortcomings of Hama?

The shortcomings of Hama are given below [6, 7]:

- For graph partitioning, Hama does not use any special algorithm which results in causing unnecessary communication between the nodes.
- There is a lack of graph manipulation functions in Hama's API.
- BSP Master is a single point of failure and if it dies, the application will stop.

2.6 In Which Application Domains Hama Can Be the Most Suitable Choice?

Hama is a general purpose solution for large-scale computing and it can be more suitable to use for intensive iterative applications. Hama is able to outperform MapReduce frameworks [8] in such application domains because it avoids the processing overhead of MapReduce approach such as sorting, shuffling, reducing the vertices etc. MapReduce inherits this overhead in each iteration and of course there exist at least millions of iterations. Hama provides a message passing interface and each superstep in BSP is faster than a full job execution in MapReduce framework, such as Hadoop.

2.7   Could Hama Be Applied to Deep Learning Frameworks?

Recent advances in deep learning hold the promise of allowing machine learning algorithms to extract discriminative information from big data without labor-intensive feature engineering. Though, few giant companies such as Google, Microsoft have developed distributed deep learning systems, these systems are closed source software. However, latest Apache Hama provides open source distributed training of an Artificial Neural Network (ANN) using its BSP computing engine. In Hama, two kinds of components are involved in the training procedure: (i) master task (merging the model, updating information and sending model updating information to all groom tasks); (ii) groom task (calculating the weight updates according to the training data). Hama's ANN is presently data parallel only. Researchers are afoot for supporting both data and model parallelism.

2.8   Who Is Using Hama?

Hama is currently being used by both small and large enterprises across a wide range of industries. It is currently being used and sponsored by SAMSUNG electronics [3]. A well-known Chinese search engine named Sogou is also using Hama with the following specifications [9, 10]:

- Runs 7200 cores Hama cluster for SiteRank;
- Data set is approximately 400 GB;
- Over 6 Billion edges.

3   Conclusions

In this paper, we highlighted and explored Apache Hama as a potential research area in the field of computing. It is evident that research on big data processing using Apache Hama is in its early stage and there is a need to identify its future directions by providing an in-depth and critical analysis. In order to accomplish this task, we formulated the most significant and focused questions about Hama in Sect. 2 and answered them with the help of research literature. The extraction of such questions reveals some of the promising areas of Hama that probably deserves further exploration and development; such as specialized graph partitioning algorithms, optimization of memory usage and fault tolerance mechanism. In our future work, we intend to come up with the performance comparison of Apache Hama with other massive computing frameworks. It may further help to forecast Apache Hama's future and to open new doors for intended researchers. Finally, to the best of our knowledge and belief, this kind of up-to-date work about Apache Hama is missing from the current bibliography and we hope that it will help researchers who want to devote in this particular research area.

Acknowledgment This research was supported by the MSIP (Ministry of Science, ICT and Future Planning), Korea, under the ITRC (Information Technology Research Center) support program (IITP-2016-H8501-16-1015) supervised by the IITP (Institute for Information & communications Technology Promotion).

References

1. Apache Hama (2015) http://www.apache.org/. Accessed: 20 Nov 2015
2. Illecker M (2014) Scientific computing in the cloud with Apache Hadoop and Apache Hama on GPU, Master thesis, Faculty of Mathematic, Computer Science and Physics, University of Innsbruck
3. Apache Hama (2015) https://blogs.apache.org/Hama/. Accessed 06 Sept 2015
4. Mailing List Archives (2015) http://mail-archives.apache.org/mod_mbox/Hama-user/. Accessed 26 Feb 2015
5. Apache Hama Design Document V0.6 (2015) Available http://people.apache.org/~tjungblut/downloads/hamadocs/ApacheHamaDesign_06.pdf. Accessed 10 Apr 2015 (Online)
6. Cordeiro D, Goldman A, Kraemer A, Junior, FP (2015) Using the BSP model on clouds. Available: http://ccsl.ime.usp.br/baile/sites/ime.usp.br.baile/files/chapter_0.pdf. Accessed 20 Mar 2015 (Online)
7. Luo S, Liu L, Wang H, Wu B, Liu Y (2014) Implementation of a parallel graph partitioning algorithm to speed up BSP computing, In: Proceedings of 11th international conference on fuzzy systems and knowledge discovery, IEEE, China, 19–21 August 2014, pp 740–744
8. Ting IH, Lin CH, Wang CS (2011) Constructing a cloud computing based social networks data warehousing and analyzing system. In: Proceedings of international conference on advances in social networks analysis and mining, IEEE, Kaohsiung, Taiwan, 25–27 July 2011, pp 735–740
9. DataSayer (2015) http://datasayer.com/hama.php. Accessed 12 Feb 2015
10. Yoon EJ (2015) Available online: http://hadoop.co.kr/2013/HIS2013_edwardyoon.pdf. Accessed 12 Jan 2015

Interactive Lecture System Based on Mixed Reality with Transparent Display

Yulong Xi, Seoungjae Cho, Simon Fong, Byong kwon Lee,
Kyhyun Um and Kyungeun Cho

Abstract This paper proposes the interactive lecture system based on mixed reality using a transparent display that enables interaction with the users watching the display. This system unlike existing remote video lectures, will allow students to participate progressively in the lectures by enabling the interaction between the instructor and students. Furthermore, this system also improves the reality in such a way that, during the visualization of the real-time video lectures on the transparent display, it seems that the instructor is in the same place with the students. This paper experiments and implements the proposed system based on the transparent display, 2D camera, and 3D sensors.

Keywords Transparent display · Remote lecture · Interactive lecture · Natural user interface

1 Introduction

The equipment used for the transparent display and its application system have been continuously investigated and developed [1, 2]. The transparent display can visualize both contents and background on the other side of the screen simultaneously and can enable face-to-face interaction between more than two users [3].

Generally, remote multimedia lectures are based on video lectures and support only simple interaction using devices like a mouse. This paper describes a real-time remote lecture system using the features of a transparent display. This system enables an instructor to give remote lectures to students in several different areas.

Y. Xi · S. Cho · B.k. Lee · K. Um · K. Cho (✉)
Department of Multimedia Engineering, Dongguk University-Seoul,
26 Pildong 3 Ga, Jung-Gu, Seoul 04620, Korea
e-mail: cke@dongguk.edu

S. Fong
Department of Computer and Information Science, University of Macau, Taipa 3000, Macau,
China

© Springer Science+Business Media Singapore 2016

223

J.J. (Jong Hyuk) Park et al. (eds.), *Advanced Multimedia and Ubiquitous Engineering*, Lecture Notes in Electrical Engineering 393,
DOI 10.1007/978-981-10-1536-6_30

Moreover, the system will lead the progressive participation of students and improve the efficiency of learning by making the instructor and students interact based on the gestures that are used in the system proposed in this paper.

The system visualizes an instructor on the transparent display in a classroom by taking a picture of the instructor in a remote place in real time, eliminating the background, and then transferring the picture to the classroom in a remote place. It then enhances the reality through the transparent display in such a way that it seems the instructor is in the same place as students. This paper experiments and implements the lecture system, thus enabling students on the other side of the transparent display to practice experiments using the test experiment tools based on mixed reality.

2 Related Work

The research related to remote lecture and virtual classroom enabling interaction has been continuously executed in [4–7].

Hariharan [4] enabled students to expand a scene in a 2D video image by a simple motion based on Kinect. This function allows the interaction among students during a remote lecture. However, the research does not support the interaction between an instructor and a student.

Inoue [5] proposed the remote lecture system based on cloud enabled interaction by a simple motion. However, since the system supports only one-on-one lecture, it is difficult to implement this research in a single lecture where the students are located at different remote places simultaneously.

Sharma [6] proposed the remote lecture system, which enables several users in a virtual environment to participate simultaneously. This system uses Kinect to turn a user's motion to be reflected on a virtual character. However, it is difficult to make several users participate in a single lecture presented in one place because each user needs one Kinect in this system.

Anand [7] proposed the remote lecture system based on video. An instructor can give a lecture to several students in different places using this system. However, the reality of this system is inferior to the lectures in a real classroom because the system uses only 2D video.

This paper proposes the system enabling interaction between an instructor and the students based on natural user interface (NUI), which uses human motions. In addition, the efficiency of lectures is enhanced by improving the reality of remote lectures using the transparent display [3]. Furthermore, the rich contents of a lecture are secured by implementing the practice environment for lectures combining virtual and real environment.

3 Lecture System Configuration

The proposed lecture system enabling interaction between an instructor and the students is represented in Fig. 1 that illustrates the device configuration in a remote classroom system. The remote classroom system comprises of several Kinects and a transparent display. The transparent display visualizes the image of an instructor and the contents of lecture in real time.

Furthermore, this system implements the algorithm recognizing motions of students using several Kinects.

Figure 2 presents the device configuration of a remote instructor system. The system comprises of a projector screen and a Kinect. The project screen visualizes the students in remote classrooms and the contents of a lecture simultaneously. Using this system, an instructor can check the results of recognition of motions of students. Moreover, an instructor can control the contents of a lecture as the system recognizes an instructor's motions by a Kinect.

Figure 3 is the layout of the remote lecture system proposed in this paper. The instructor controls the contents of lecture by simple gestures from a remote place. The results that include recognizing gestures of students are delivered to the instructor in a remote place. The server transfers the images of an instructor after clearing the background and the screen on the contents of lecture to each client in real time.

The clients visualize the images on the contents of lecture, and images of an instructor transferred from the server to the students. The students can then ask a

Fig. 1 Device configuration in a remote classroom

Fig. 2 Device configuration
in a remote instructor system

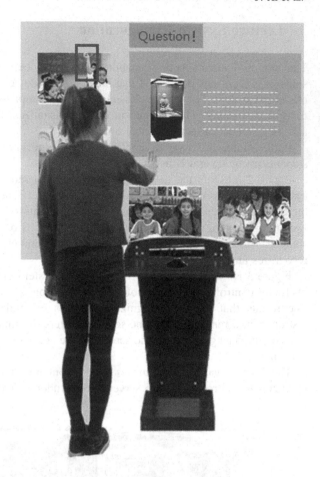

question to an instructor by making gestures or interacting with the contents of the lecture. Each client transfers the data including the images of students, results of gesture recognition, and the concentration of students to the server in real time. Gestures of the students are recognized by using multiple Kinects.

4   Experiment

This paper implements the remote lecture system using the transparent display and develops two types of lecture contents. In the first type, an instructor remotely gives lectures to students using the lecture contents including how to use a fire extinguisher and a microscope. In the second type, an instructor can observe students participating in the lecture in real time. Furthermore, an instructor can control the lecture contents using gestures and guide students to participate in the experiments.

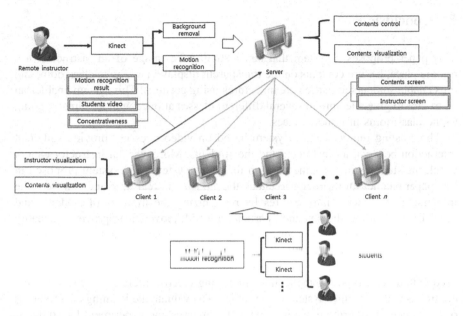

Fig. 3 Overall remote lecture system layout

The students can see the lecture contents along with the image of an instructor in a remote place through the transparent display and make the gesture by raising an arm to participate in the lecture contents. Figure 4 presents the scene of experimental lecture comprising of a virtual lecture contents and the actual experiment tools on the transparent display.

Fig. 4 Mixed reality-based experiment scene

5 Conclusion

This paper proposes a system that can visualize the image of an instructor in a remote place, lecture contents on the transparent display in a remote classroom, and thus enable students to participate in lectures using gestures. This system enables an instructor to give a lecture to several different classes at once without directly going to the classrooms in remote places.

The existing remote lecture system based on video does not provide sufficient interaction between an instructor and the students. Moreover, an instructor cannot check the students in real time through the video system. The system proposed in this paper enables an instructor to check the students in real time and enhances the immersion of students into lectures by recognizing the motions of students and accordingly, leading the students' participation. Moreover, it improves the reality by visualizing the image of an instructor in a remote place through the transparent display in such a way that it seems as though the instructor and students have participated in a lecture in the same place. The system proposed in this paper can be used with diverse types of applications including video conference and smart home control as well as lecture system in the future. To evaluate the learning effectiveness of the system, furthermore, we will define the metrics and experiment for students.

Acknowledgments This research was supported by the MSIP (Ministry of Science, ICT and Future Planning), Korea, under the ITRC (Information Technology Research Center) support program (IITP-2016-H8501-16-1014) supervised by the IITP (Institute for Information and communications Technology Promotion).

References

1. Su CW, Liao CC, Chen MY (2016) Color transparent display using polymer-dispersed liquid crystal. Display Technol J 12(1):31–34
2. Sharma A, Liu L, Maes P (2013) Glassified: an augmented ruler based on a transparent display for real-time interactions with paper. In: Proceedings of the adjunct publication of the 26th annual ACM symposium on user interface software and technology, pp 21–22
3. Moon B, Yoo S (2014) A study on the evaluation of UX elements for users' selective. Arch Design Res 27(2):183–197
4. Hariharan BSP, Uma G (2014) Gesture recognition using Kinect in a virtual classroom environment. In: Proceedings of 2014 4th international conference on digital information and communication technology and it's applications (DICTAP), pp 118–124
5. Inoue A, Schlittenhart I (2012) Intelligent autopilot for remote classroom: A cloud based solution. In: Proceedings of 2012 joint 6th international conference on soft computing and intelligent systems (SCIS) and 13th international symposium on advanced intelligent systems (ISIS), pp 1414–1419
6. Sharma S, Chen W (2014) Multi-user VR classroom with 3D interaction and real-time motion detection. In: Proceedings of 2014 international conference on computational science and computational intelligence (CSCI), 2:187–192
7. Anand S, Jayahari KR, Bijlani K, Vijayan V, Chatterjee S (2014) Pedagogy-based design of live virtual classroom for large-scale training. In: Proceedings of 2014 IEEE 6th international conference on technology for education (T4E), pp 195–201

Interaction Engine Design for Virtual Experiments by Multi-users

Yeji Kim, Yulong Xi, Seoungjae Cho, Simon Fong, Changhwan Yi,
Kyhyun Um and Kyungeun Cho

Abstract For scientific educational purposes, many types of chemical experiments are conducted in academic institutions. However, these experiments in real classroom environments can be quite dangerous and can potentially harm students. To instruct students in conducting experiments safely, virtual chemical experiment applications were developed. However, existing virtual science experiment applications are mostly limited to having only one participant. To solve this limit, this paper describes the design of an interaction engine, enabling interaction among multiple users and implements the virtual science experiment application based on that interaction engine.

Keywords Virtual experiment · Multi-user interaction · Hand gesture recognition

1 Introduction

Science experiments generally involve a number of materials in real classroom environments, and so expend substantial resources in acquiring and preparing those materials. Furthermore, some science experiments have potential hazards, which can lead to injuries or death. Since it can be difficult for students to directly conduct many science experiments, they indirectly experience the experiments mainly through books or videos. For dealing with these situations, a variety of virtual science experiment applications have been developed. However, existing virtual science experiment applications tend to have been developed for only one user.

Y. Kim · Y. Xi · S. Cho · C. Yi · K. Um · K. Cho (✉)
Department of Multimedia Engineering, Dongguk University-Seoul, 26 Pildong 3 Ga,
Jung-gu, Seoul 04620, Korea
e-mail: cke@dongguk.edu

S. Fong
Department of Computer and Information Science, University of Macau, Taipa 3000, Macau,
China

© Springer Science+Business Media Singapore 2016   229
J.J. (Jong Hyuk) Park et al. (eds.), *Advanced Multimedia and Ubiquitous Engineering*, Lecture Notes in Electrical Engineering 393,
DOI 10.1007/978-981-10-1536-6_31

This paper proposes an engine structure enabling interaction among multiple users. The engine realizes the interaction among multiple users based on hand gestures in virtual 3D space. Moreover, this paper describes the development of the virtual science experiment engine based on the engine explained above.

2 Related Work

A variety of virtual applications were developed for students to experience hazardous science experiments [1–3]. These applications utilizes keyboard and mouse mostly, and the experiment can be performed by only one user [4–6].

Kim [4] developed a 3D video education system based on gesture interface. The system acquired image, audio, and joint data for a user using the Kinect device and defined 27 gestures using both hands based on the azimuth. Furthermore, the location of a user was mapped in a virtual 3D space based on the user's 3D coordinates acquired by motion sensors. This system enabled up to five users to receive instruction through 3D video communication based on image and audio using the 3D video education system. The system is not intuitive and uses simple gestures. It tends to reduce the concentration of users. Moreover, the spatial scope of gestures is restricted in order to prevent the recognition of unnecessary gestures.

Hwang [5] introduced a multimedia service for remote learning. The server includes a database for English learning such as textbooks, dictionaries, boards, and repeat. The users of this server send or receive data using TCP/IP through RAS. The server applies the multi-thread approach for efficient data exchange. The multi-thread of the server comprises an input/output thread for loading files from the learning database, a thread for saving the live broadcast, and the main thread. Whenever the server has a new access from a user, it generates one user service thread. The server supports audio chatting among the users and deals with the extraordinary events that may happen during the connection of audio chatting between two users. In addition, live broadcast was implemented by sharing broadcast data between a broadcaster and a listener.

Jang [6] proposed a group-based remote learning system. This system reduced the load on the server system by distributing the server functions to the client PCs and enabled the remote learning in real time. Similarly, on the network, the group communication platform generates the group when clients get access to the server and the users in a group can interact with each other. The server transfers the service control authority to users establishing a group for discussion or lecture. Moreover, other users who want to use the group can get the PC information of the user establishing the group and get access to the relevant group.

The research above supports the access of multiple users. However, since the interaction among users was mainly chatting, it does not have the sufficient progressive interaction required for learning.

This paper proposes an engine structure enabling bi-directional interaction among multiple users by adopting the server-client communication structure.

Furthermore, this paper describes the development of an application enabling multiple clients to share an experimental environment in one 3D virtual space using the proposed engine.

3 Interaction Engine Design

This paper describes the design of an interaction engine for multiple users based on the virtual experiment framework. The engine adopted the server-client communication structure for executing the communal experiment by recognizing the interaction data among multiple users at the same time. On the basis of the server-client communication structure, the engine comprises a data exchange function, an access control function for multiple clients, a function to save data acquired from gesture recognition devices, and a function to define gestures depending on applications. The engine also adopted an approach for synchronizing data on the server and exchanging data between the server and clients using TCP/IP, enabling interaction among multiple users. Figure 1 illustrates the interaction engine structure for multiple users.

The multiple client access and communication management module manages server access by clients and data exchange between the server and clients. The multiple client collision management module manages collisions, which can occur during interaction among clients on one object. The multiple client data management module extensively manages user input data from each client. Each client transfers user input data to the server after getting access to it and receives data on other clients from the server.

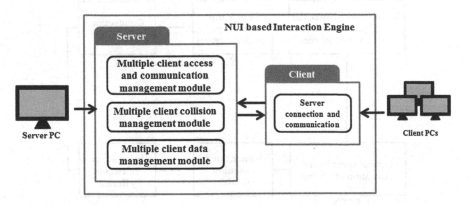

Fig. 1 Interaction engine structure diagram for multiple users

4 Experiment and Results

This paper describes the implementation of the virtual chemical experiment application for verifying the feasibility of interaction among multiple users using the engine proposed here. The application was implemented using the Unity3D game engine and the experiment was executed using the Windows 7 operating system. Multiple users observed the virtual 3D experiment environment using each user's computer monitor and conducted the experiment through interaction using a tracking device. Such applications can enhance the concentration of users involved in virtual experiment lectures.

The experiment used seven computers. One computer acted as the server, the main computer and other six computers acted as the clients representing each user, the sub-computers. The main computer generated the virtual 3D laboratory on the server and received the user access request from multiple clients. At this point, both the main computer and sub computers implemented the function to recognize gestures. The main computer and sub-computers were connected to each tracking device. The server extensively manages the data on the interaction by sub-computers transferred from clients and the interaction executed in the main computer. The users of the main computer and sub-computers can check the interaction results on their monitors in real time. Figure 2 presents the experiment flow chart using this application.

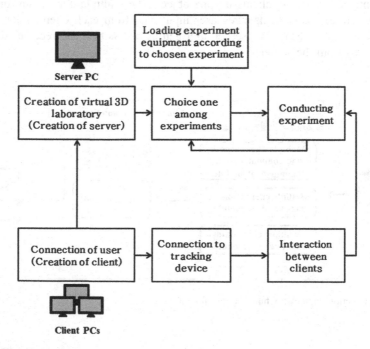

Fig. 2 Virtual chemical experiment application flow chart

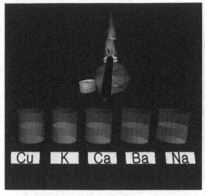

Fig. 3 Virtual chemical experiment screen

This paper describes the execution of the virtual chemical experiment with multiple users accessing the server. The actual experiment used a virtual alcohol lamp and metal aqueous solutions of Cu, K, Ca, Ba, and Na. The users executed the experiment by holding and moving a stick with their hands. The students could observe the chemical reactions easily and safely through the virtual science experiment without any anxiety due to the use of hazardous substances. While the multiple users grabbing and moving a stick, there were no scramble to obtain it between users. This could be achieved by multiple client collision management module that assigns an authority to control an object by only one user. Figure 3 illustrates the screen executing the virtual chemical experiment using the application.

5 Conclusion

This paper described the design of an interaction engine enabling multiple users to conduct an experiment together and described the implementation of the virtual chemical experiment application based on the engine. The engine was designed for multiple users to communicate on the basis of the server-client structure. Furthermore, this paper defined the module that manages the input data from multiple clients and the collision management module preventing collision among multiple users. This paper verified that multiple users could execute the experiments together and interact with each other.

Acknowledgments This research was supported by the MSIP (Ministry of Science, ICT and Future Planning), Korea, under the ITRC (Information Technology Research Center) support program (IITP-2016-H8501-16-1014) supervised by the IITP (Institute for Information & communications Technology Promotion) and by Basic Science Research Program through the National Research Foundation of Korea (NRF) funded by the Ministry of Science, ICT and future Planning (NRF-2015R1A2A2A01003779).

References

1. Matsuda H, Shindo Y (2008) Virtual chemical experiment using cyber assistant professor: CAP. In: Eighth IEEE international conference on advanced learning technologies 2008, ICALT'08, pp 977–981
2. Lee SA (2001) Design and implementation of the virtual experimental laboratory for common science. Thesis, Hanseo University
3. Chung KS, Kwon S, Huang W-H (2013) Design and development of sensor-based virtual experiment contents for smart phone. J Digital Contents Soc 14:161–169
4. Kim J-O, Jung J-S, Kim D-H, Kwon S-O, Lee J, Ju S, Park C, Jang R-H, Yoo K-H (2014) Development of interactive 3D video education system based on gesture interface. J HCI Soc Korea 551–554
5. Hwang K, Choi CY (1998) Design and implementation of multimedia server for distance learning. KIISE Trans Comput Practices 325–336
6. Jang SW, Jeon YJ (2000) Design and Implementation of a Group-based Real-time Distance Learning System. KIISE Trans Comput Practices 6(5):543–554

3D Eye-Tracking Method Using HD Face Model of Kinect v2

Byoung Cheul Kim and Eui Chul Lee

Abstract Despite the extensive research into 3D eye-tracking methods, such methods remain dependent on many additional factors such as the processing time, pose, illumination, image resolution, and calibration procedure. In this paper, we propose a 3D eye-tracking method using the HD face model of Kinect v2. Because the proposed method uses accurate 3D ocular feature positions and a 3D human eye scheme, it can track an eye gaze position more accurately and promptly than previous methods. In an image captured using a Kinect v2, the two eye-corner points of one eye are obtained using the device's high-definition face model. The 3D rotational center of the eyeball is estimated based on these two eye-corner points. After the center of the iris is obtained, the 3D gaze vector that passes through the rotational center and the center of the iris is defined. Finally, the intersection point between the 3D gaze vector and the actual display plane is calculated and transformed into pixel coordinates as the gaze position. Angle kappa, which is the gap between the actual gaze vector and the pupillary vector, is compensated through a user-dependent calibration. Experiment results show that the gaze estimation error was an average of 47 pixels from the desired position.

Keywords Kinect v2 · HD face · Natural user interface · 3D eye tracking

B.C. Kim
Department of Computer Science, Graduate School, Sangmyung University, Seoul, Republic of Korea

E.C. Lee (✉)
Department of Computer Science, Sangmyung University, Seoul, Republic of Korea
e-mail: eclee@smu.ac.kr

© Springer Science+Business Media Singapore 2016
J.J. (Jong Hyuk) Park et al. (eds.), *Advanced Multimedia and Ubiquitous Engineering*, Lecture Notes in Electrical Engineering 393,
DOI 10.1007/978-981-10-1536-6_32

235

1   Introduction

Based on the recent developments of computer hardware and software, the natural user interface (NUI) field has been extended. For example, body gestures, touch screens, facial and eye-gaze tracking, and speech recognition have been adopted as NUI methods. Among them, because eye-tracking methods are regarded as the most intuitive and comfortable, they have been widely researched and used as a navigation interaction method.

Previous researches on gaze tracking can be categorized into two types of methods: remote and head-mounted. The former normally uses cameras, such as narrow- and wide-view cameras [1, 2], or stereo cameras with multiple illuminators [3]. In addition, a head-mounted method uses another wearable device such as a pair of glasses. Because there is no need to wear any particular device, a remote gaze-tracking method is convenient for users. However, a high system cost, high level of complexity for users, and complicated calibration steps are required for such a method. Murphy-Chutorian et al. [4] proposed a remote gaze-tracking system. They use a single high-resolution camera to obtain the face region, and calculate the gaze position based on the image of the face and eye(s). However, the resolution of the face image is low, and is affected by the illumination and other factors. Consequently, the accuracy in determining the gaze position is inadequate.

Previous researches can also be classified into 2D- [1, 4] and 3D-based [2, 3] gaze-tracking methods. A 3D-based method is more accurate than a 2D-based one; however, a high cost and long processing time are required. In contrast, a 2D-based method is simpler and cheaper than a 3D-based one, but is less accurate and requires more complicated calibration steps. Because the accuracy is regarded as the most important issue in accordance with the increasing computational power of conventional computers, 3D-based methods have recently been considered a good approach. A method for tracking a 3D eye-gaze direction was developed using multiple cameras and light sources [5]. Another method was proposed for tracking facial feature points based on the color of human skin [6]. However, these methods also present many problems such as limitations in terms of the tracking accuracy owing to errors in the sensing data and inconvenience when undergoing the calibration step, which is affected by the pose, self-occlusions, or other external factors.

To solve these problems inherent to previous methods, a new remote 3D eye-tracking method is proposed. Our proposed method is convenient and requires only simple calibration steps. In addition, it is accurate when using the high-definition face model provided by Kinect v2 SDK. The rotational center of the eyeball is estimated based on the two eye corner points. Moreover, the iris center of the eye is defined using depth data provided by Kinect v2. The gaze vector passing through both the iris and rotational centers is calculated. Finally, the intersection between the gaze vector and display is adopted for the eye-gaze tracking. Because the subject's face is detected automatically without being affected by their posture or other external factors, accurate key points are detected. In addition, an additional calibration step is not required, allowing the possibility of simple and accurate eye-gaze tracking.

2 Proposed Method

Our proposed method is processed through the flow shown in Fig. 1.

2.1 Geometric Calibration

In the visible image captured from the Kinect device, because the X and Y values of an arbitrary pixel's coordinates are obtained from the RGB camera of the Kinect v2, they are same as the camera space coordinates of the image. However, the Z value is obtained using the 3D depth sensor of the Kinect v2, and is therefore not the same as the arbitrary pixel coordinates obtained from the RGB camera. The exact X, Y, and Z values of the 3D camera space coordinates can be obtained from the coordinate mapper provided by Kinect v2 SDK.

To conduct eye-tracking of a display, the camera space coordinates should be transformed into the display coordinates. The principal point between the camera space and display is not the same as shown in Fig. 2. The principal point of the

Fig. 1 Flow diagram of the proposed method

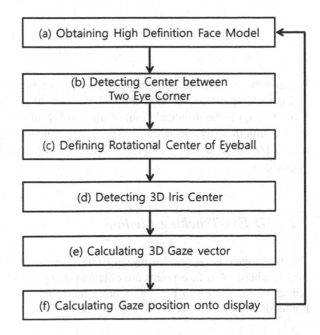

(a) Obtaining High Definition Face Model

(b) Detecting Center between Two Eye Corner

(c) Defining Rotational Center of Eyeball

(d) Detecting 3D Iris Center

(e) Calculating 3D Gaze vector

(f) Calculating Gaze position onto display

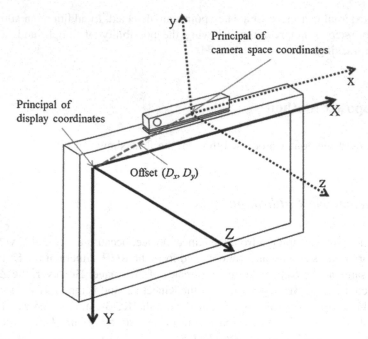

Fig. 2 Geometric relation between camera-space and display coordinates [8]

display coordinates is located in the top-left area of the display. The transformation is conducted according to the following equations [7].

$$x_d = x_c + D_x \tag{1}$$

$$y_d = y_c + D_y \tag{2}$$

Because the Z value of arbitrary pixel coordinates is the same between the display and camera space coordinates, a transformation of the Z value is not conducted. Here, (x_d, y_d) is the principal point of the display, and (x_c, y_c) is the principal point of the camera space. In addition, (x_d, y_d) is transformed into (x_c, y_c) by adding offsets (D_x, D_y). In our system configuration, D_x and D_y are 250 and 70 mm, respectively.

2.2 3D Eye-Tracking Method

The face image is captured using an RGB camera. We now proceed to step (a) in Fig. 1, where 1436 face points are obtained using the HD face model provided by Kinect v2, as shown in Fig. 3a. Among them, we use the inner and outer corner points of the eye, as shown in Fig. 3b. In addition, the center point between the

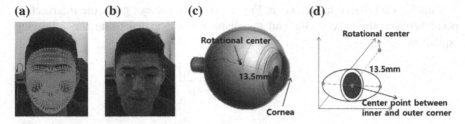

(a) **(b)** **(c)** **(d)**

Fig. 3 **a** HD face model, **b** inner and outer corner points, **c** 3D eyeball, and **d** translation of center point to rotational center

inner and outer corners is calculated (step (b) in Fig. 1). Generally, the rotational center of the eyeball is located 13.5 mm behind the surface of the cornea, as shown in Fig. 3c [9]. The rotational center of the eyeball is defined by translating the center point direction in the rear 13.5 mm of the Z axis, as shown in Fig. 3d (step (c) in Fig. 1).

Next, we proceed to step (d) in Fig. 1. In the image captured from the RGB camera, the eye region is obtained using the HD face model provided by Kinect v2, as shown in Fig. 4a. To extract the iris center, the eye region image is transformed into a gray image. Binarization (Threshold: 23) is applied to detect the iris region, as shown in Fig. 4b. When the binarization is conducted, two types of noises, pepper and salt, occur. Pepper noise in the background is removed through component labeling, as shown in Fig. 4c. In addition, morphological operations (erode and dilate) are conducted to remove salt noise within the iris region, as shown in Fig. 4d. Then, to extract an accurate iris center point, the iris region is replaced with a square model, as shown in Fig. 4e. The center of the square model is regarded as the iris center point of the eye, as shown in Fig. 4a. The extracted iris center is transformed into the camera space coordinates using the Kinect depth sensor.

The gaze vector is calculated according to the following equations (step (e) in Fig. 1), and is defined as a vector passing through two points, such as the rotational center and the iris center.

$$\frac{x - x_i}{x_r - x_i} = \frac{y - y_i}{y_r - y_i} = \frac{z - z_i}{z_r - z_i} \tag{3}$$

Here, (x_r, y_r, z_r) is the rotational center coordinate of the eyeball, and (x_i, y_i, z_i) is the iris center coordinate of the eye.

(a) **(b)** **(c)** **(d)** **(e)** **(f)**

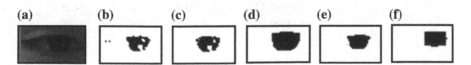

Fig. 4 **a** Detected iris region and iris center point, **b** binarization of the image, **c** component labeling, **d** morphology operation (dilate), **e** morphology operation (erode), and **f** square model

Finally, we proceed to step (f) in Fig. 1. To track the eye gaze, the intersection point between the gaze vector and the display is calculated using the following equations.

$$x_c = x_i + \frac{-z_i(x_r - x_i)}{(z_r - z_i)} \tag{4}$$

$$y_c = y_i + \frac{-z_i(y_r - y_i)}{(z_r - z_i)} \tag{5}$$

Here, (x_c, y_c) is the intersection point within the camera space coordinates. Through the geometric calibration, (x_c, y_c) is transformed into a physical tracking point. In addition, the length of the gaze direction differs for each individual. Thus, angle kappa, which is the gap between the actual gaze vector and the pupillary vector, is compensated through a user-dependent calibration. A user-dependent calibration is conducted by translating the offsets between the predefined position and the user-dependent position.

3 Experiment Results

To validate the feasibility of our proposed method, experiments were conducted to measure the accuracy of the eye-tracking system. During the experiments, the tracking accuracy for the right direction was measured for five different subjects. Each subject gazed toward five predefined positions. The indication order was assigned randomly. The measurement results are shown in Table 1.

As shown in Table 1 and Fig. 5, we confirmed that the RMS error between the tracking point and the experiment point is about 47 pixels, thereby confirming the feasibility of the proposed eye-tracking method.

Table 1 Experiment results (*unit* pixel)

Reference point	Tracking point		RMS error
	X-axis	Y-axis	
#1 (320,270)	342.4	292	31.39
#2 (320,810)	345.2	784	36.20
#3 (960,540)	930.2	559	35.34
#4 (1600,270)	1595.2	324	54.21
#5 (1600,810)	1680	806	80.09

Fig. 5 Experiment conducted to measure the accuracy of the tracking direction

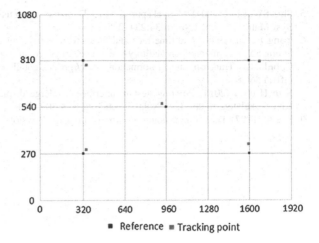

■ Reference ■ Tracking point

4 Conclusion

In this paper, a new 3D eye-tracking method using the Kinect v2 HD face model was proposed. To track the eye gaze, the iris and rotational centers were extracted. Moreover, the gaze vector, which passes through the both iris and rotational centers, was calculated. Consequently, the eye-tracking was conducted using the intersection point between the gaze vector and display.

In future studies, we will develop a new 3D eye-tracking method by considering the 3D facial orientation using Kinect v2 as an NUI interface.

Acknowledgments This research was supported by the Ministry of Science, ICT and Future Planning (MSIP), Korea, under the Information Technology Research Center (ITRC) support program (IITP-2015-H8501-15-1014) supervised by the Institute for Information & Communications Technology Promotion (IITP).

References

1. Yoo DH, Chung MJ (2005) A novel non-intrusive eye gaze estimation using cross-ratio under large head motion. Comput Vis Image Underst 98(1):25–51
2. Wang JG, Sung E (2002) Study on eye gaze estimation. IEEE Trans Syst Man Cybern B Cybern 32(3):332–350
3. Shih SW, Liu J (2004) A novel approach to 3-D gaze tracking using stereo cameras. IEEE Trans Syst Man Cybern B Cybern 34(1):234–245
4. Murphy-Chutorian E et al (2007) Head pose estimation for driver assistance systems: a robust algorithm and experimental evaluation. In: Proceedings IEEE ITSC, pp 709–714

5. Shin SW, Liu J (2004) A novel approach to 3-D gaze tracking using stereo cameras. IEEE Trans Syst Man Cybern B Cybern 34:234–245
6. Yang J et al (1998) Real-time face and facial feature tracking and applications. In: AVSP'98 international conference on auditory-visual speech processing, pp 79–84
7. Coordinates Transformation Information https://groups.google.com/forum/#!topic/open-kinect/ihfBIY56Is8
8. Kim H et al (2014) Pointing gesture interface for large display environments based on the Kinect skeleton model. Lect Notes Electr Eng 309:509–514
9. Lee C (1997) Three dimensional position of the eye. Psychol Issues 4:255–278

A Fault-Tolerant Intersection Control Algorithm Under the Connected Intelligent Vehicles Environment

Mourad Elhadef

Abstract In this paper, we introduce a fault-tolerant inVANETs-based intersection control algorithm which relies on vehicle-to-vehicle or vehicle-to-infrastructure communications to control the traffic and grant the privilege to cross the intersection. The primary-backup approach is adopted in this work, where a backup controller is added to monitor the primary controller and to take on once it discovers that it has failed. The proposed solution guarantees that the safety, liveness, and fairness properties are satisfied all the time.

Keywords Fault-tolerance · inVANETs · Intersection traffic control · Intelligent transportation systems · Distributed mutual exclusion

1 Introduction

Future smart cities will rely heavily on intelligent transportation systems (ITS) in order to cope with the ever-increasing traffic congestion, accompanied with unpredicted accidents and emergencies [1, 2]. Various solutions have been proposed to automatically control the traffic at intersections. The traditional ones focused more on optimizing the scheduling of lights to maximize traffic flow and reduce congestions [3]. While, recent approaches have been focusing on more smart and adaptive traffic light scheduling relying on computational intelligence such as evolutionary genetic [4], fuzzy logic [5], neural networks [2], and machine learning [6]. Readers are referred to the survey [7] by Zhao et al. for more details. In Wu et al. [8], developed a centralized algorithm that assumes the existence of a traffic controller which role is to grant the privilege of passing the intersection

This work is supported by ADEC Award for Research Excellence (A²RE) 2015 and Office of Research and Sponsored Programs (ORSP), Abu Dhabi University.

M. Elhadef (✉)
College of Engineering, Abu Dhabi University, Abu Dhabi, UAE
e-mail: mourad.elhadef@adu.ac.ae

© Springer Science+Business Media Singapore 2016
J.J. (Jong Hyuk) Park et al. (eds.), *Advanced Multimedia and Ubiquitous Engineering*, Lecture Notes in Electrical Engineering 393,
DOI 10.1007/978-981-10-1536-6_33

to requesting vehicles. In [9], more advanced communication and sensing technologies have been used to enable real-time traffic-response green light traffic control, by scheduling traffic lights following a certain control strategy inferred from real-time traffic data and preselected logic rules. A completely different approach, *the trajectory maneuver*, has been studied in [6]. It is based on an intersection controller which objective is to optimally manipulate vehicles' trajectories based on nearby vehicles' conditions in order to avoid potential overlaps. In trajectory maneuver, the vehicles can move smoothly without stopping, and hence, this approach improves the efficiency of the system. Various methods have been studied to calculate the optimal trajectories, including cell-based [10], merging [9], fuzzy-logic [11], scenario-driven [12], global adjusting and exception handling [4]. As it is the case for optimal traffic light control, trajectory maneuver is a hard problem due to the complexity of trajectory calculation. Moreover, the dependence on centralized controller makes the approach costly and prone to single point of failure.

In this paper, we extend, by making it fault-tolerant, the inVANETs-based intersection control algorithm introduced in [13]. This algorithm relies on vehicle-to-vehicle or vehicle-to-infrastructure communications to control the traffic and grant the privilege to cross the intersection. The *primary-backup* approach is adopted in this work, where a backup controller is added to monitor the primary controller and to take on once the primary fails.

The rest of the paper is organized as follows. Section 2 provides the system model and basic definitions. The fault-tolerant intersection control algorithm is detailed in Sect. 3. Finally, Sect. 4 concludes and presents future research directions.

2 Preliminaries

Without loss of generality, consider as an example a typical four directions intersection as shown in Fig. 1, where lanes are numbered l_0–l_7. The traffic intersection rules state that vehicles with crossing paths, e.g., lanes l_0 and l_6, must mutually exclusively pass the intersection. Such lanes are said to be *conflicting,* and denoted by $\propto$. While, vehicles with non-crossing paths, e.g., l_0 and l_4, can simultaneously pass the intersection. These vehicles and their lanes are said to be *concurrent,* and denoted by $\approx$. Following this definition, we have for example $l_0 \propto l_6$ and $l_0 \approx l_4$. Wu et al. [8] represented the concurrency/conflict relationship using a conflict graph which could be generalized to any type of intersection. The small dashed square is the *core area* and the large one will be referred to us as the *queueing area.* Any vehicle that enters the core area will be in the *CROSSING* state; while in the queuing area it will be in the *WAITNG* or *QUEUING* state.

Each vehicle is autopilot driven and has a unique *id*. The vehicles are equipped with GPS, sensors and other devices that help the autopilot to navigate and to avoid collisions. The vehicle's positioning system, e.g., GPS, and the sensors that are

Fig. 1 A typical four-way
traffic intersection

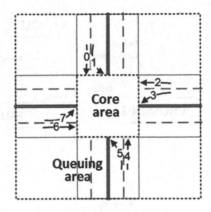

deployed at the boundaries are used as well to detect the core/queuing areas'
boundaries. Furthermore, vehicles can communicate with each other
(vehicle-to-vehicle communication, V2V) or with the intersection infrastructure
(vehicle-to-infrastructure communication, V2I) using their wireless communication
devices. This provides vehicles with a wireless FIFO channel. Messages transmission is assumed to be reliable, and the transmission range of the communicating
devices covers an area larger than the queuing area. This results in all vehicles,
inside the queuing area, forming a one-hop ad hoc network and any pair of vehicles
can communicate directly. In addition, the intersection is managed by a central
controller installed close to the crossing area. Vehicles can communicate directly
with the controller using V2I communication messages in order to request permission to cross the intersection.

Each vehicle transitions between four states when crossing an intersection
(*IDLE, WAITING, QUEUING, CROSSING*), and a fifth state when it fails
(*FAULTY*). Each vehicle starts initially in the *IDLE* state while it is out of the
intersection area. When the vehicle enters the queuing area its state changes to
WAITING. In this state the vehicle has sent its request to access the crossing area to
the controller and it is waiting for the controller's approval. The vehicle's state
changes to *QUEUING* once the controller grants the vehicle access to the core area.
All vehicles in the *QUEUING* state can only cross the core area in a FIFO fashion.
Vehicles that have been delayed and can no longer cross the core area within the
specified time period, will see their state changed back to *WAITING*. In addition,
a vehicle that changes position to a conflicting lane while in the *QUEUING* state,
will have its state updated to *WAITING*, and will be requested by the controller to
wait. Once a vehicle enters the core area, its state is changed to *CROSSING*. Finally,
once the vehicle crosses the intersection and leaves the core area, its state is set back
to *IDLE*. Figure 2 depicts the vehicle's state transition diagram.

Any vehicle is subject to various types of failure whether at the hardware level or
the software level. We assume that each vehicle is equipped with a fault detection
system which main duty is to monitor the vehicle state and to detect any mal-
function that could incapacitate it from crossing the intersection. The

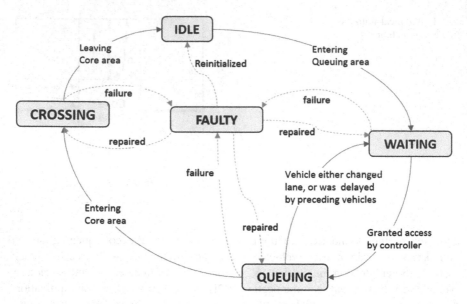

Fig. 2 Vehicles' state transition diagram

implementation of the fault detection system is outside the scope of this paper, but we assume that this subsystem will trigger the event *failure* to announce a failure. This results in the vehicle state being changed to *FAULTY*. Once the event *repaired* occurs, the vehicle state is changed back to its last state or to the original IDLE state in case the vehicle has been towed away. Vehicles that cannot proceed because they are blocked by a faulty car will be able to inform the controller allowing him hence to grant access to other lanes until the problem is fixed. Once the blocked vehicles announce to the controller that the problem has been solved, the controller will give them priority depending on the delays they experienced.

The intersection traffic control has been formalized as a vehicle mutual exclusion for intersections (VMEI) problem [8]. The VMEI problem states that each vehicle at the intersection requests to pass the intersection along the direction as it wants. As a result, vehicles will queue up at the corresponding lanes when they enter the queue area. Vehicles can pass the intersection simultaneously if and only if they are in concurrent lanes or the same lane to avoid collision or congestion. Three properties must be satisfied by any correct solution to meet the VMEI problem: *safety*, *liveness*, and *fairness* [8]. The *safety* property guarantees the mutual exclusion and states that at any moment, no conflicting vehicles can be in the core area. That is, if there is more than one vehicle in the core area, they must be concurrent with each other. The *liveness* property guarantees that the solution is deadlock free. It states that any waiting vehicle will be granted access to the core area in a finite time. Finally, the *fairness* property asserts that each vehicle must be able to pass the intersection after a finite number of vehicles did so, i.e., no lane is given priority over another. The fairness property guarantees that the solution is *starvation free*.

3 A Fault-Tolerant inVANETs-Based Traffic Control Algorithm

The controller-based approach for traffic control relies on locks to grant or deny access to the intersection. Any waiting vehicle can only cross the intersection only after the conflicting lanes have been locked by the controller successfully. Once a vehicle reaches the queueing area it immediately sends a request to lock the conflicting lanes. The controller managing the locks will be able to reply back with a message to grant access to the intersection. The controller objective is to guarantee that all the three properties, i.e. safety, liveliness, and fairness, are satisfied all the time, while maximizing the throughput of the intersection. The locking mechanism works as follows. The controller maintains one lock per lane, and hence, for the intersection depicted in Fig. 1, eight locks will be used. Table 1 shows the complete correct locking scheme. For example, a vehicle on lane 2 can cross the intersection only after the controller locks the lanes 1, 2, and 7.

The notation used throughout this paper is as follows. $State_i$ indicates the state of the vehicle which includes: *IDLE*, *WAITING*, *CROSSING*, *QUEUING*, and *FAULTY*. The state *IDLE* indicates that the vehicle is outside the intersection area; While the state *WAITING*, is reached once the vehicle has requested permission to cross the intersection and still waiting for the controller command. The state *CROSSING* is used when the vehicle is crossing the intersection, and the state *QUEUING* shows that the vehicle has been granted access by the controller but it needs to wait for all preceding vehicles to cross first. A vehicle in the QUEUING state may be moved back to the *WAITING* state if it moves into a new lane that conflicts with its current one, or if ordered by the controller to wait due to delays resulting from preceding vehicles. $lane_i$ denotes the lane of the vehicle. *crossingList* refers to the list of vehicles the controller granted permission to cross the intersection. Any vehicle in this list can now proceed to cross the intersection. $locks_i$ denotes the set of lanes to be locked for vehicle i (see Table 1). *Locked* refers to the set of lanes locked by the controller at any given point of time.

The fault-tolerant approach we are proposing relies on the *primary-backup* approach. That is, there is a *primary controller* which main duties are to manage the intersection and to synchronize with the *backup* controller. The backup controller is synchronized with the primary controller at all time and it is kept updated with all traffic information relevant to this intersection. If the primary controller fails (crashes) the backup takes on and guarantees that the traffic control at the intersection is kept under control. In this work, we consider only permanent crash failures, i.e. once the controller crashes it stops sending and receiving messages and

Table 1 Locking mechanism for a typical four-way traffic intersection	Vehicle's lane	0	1	2	3	4	5	6	7
	Lanes to be locked	0	1	1	0	1	2	3	1
		5	3	2	3	3	5	5	4
		7	6	7	5	4	7	6	7

loses its internal state. Our fault-tolerant inVANETs-based intersection control algorithm comprises three tasks: the *vehicleTask*, the *primaryControllerTask*, and the *backupControllerTask*.

The following five messages are exchanged between the vehicles and the controllers. *<ALIVE>* message is transmitted periodically by the primary controller to the backup to indicate that it is alive and working fine. *<REQUEST, i, lane_i>* message is sent by vehicle i to the controller to indicate its lane and that it wants to cross the intersection. *<CROSS, vehiclesList, duration>* message sent by the controller to order waiting vehicles in *vehiclesList* to cross the intersection within the specified *duration*. *<DELAYED, i, lane_i>* transmitted by vehicle i to inform the controller that it did not succeed in crossing the intersection within the specified duration. *<NEWLANE, i, lane_i>* message indicates that vehicle i moved into a new lane conflicting with its old position. *<CROSSED, i>* message sent by vehicle i to inform the controller that it has crossed. Finally, *<FAILED, i>* message indicates to the controller that the vehicle i is experiencing problems and it has failed. The controller needs to block the lane of this vehicle until it is fixed and allows other lanes to proceed.

3.1 VehicleTask *Operations*

We first start by describing the vehicle view and show what are the main steps followed by any vehicle before crossing the intersection. Figure 3 summarizes these steps and the interaction between the *vehicleTask* and the *primaryControllerTask*. Upon reaching the queueing area the vehicle i sends the message *<REQUEST, i, lane_i>* to the controller asking for permission to cross the intersection (step 1.1). The vehicle's state changes to *WAITING* which means that the vehicle is waiting for the controller to grant it access to the intersection. While waiting to receive the permission to cross the intersection, the vehicle may move into a new lane that may conflict with the old position that was sent to the controller. In that case, the message *<NEWLANE, i, lane_i>* is sent to the controller to inform it about this change (step 1.5). Any vehicle i can be either in the queuing area, or in the intersection area while crossing it, or outside the intersection area upon crossing it, as a result the state of the vehicle changes accordingly (step 1.2). Any vehicle i can cross the intersection only upon reception of the message *<CROSS, vehiclesList, duration>* and i is listed in *vehiclesList* (step 1.3). The *duration* period sets the maximum time for a vehicle to cross the intersection. In real-life scenarios we may have situations in which vehicles are delayed because of a failure, a slow driver, or congestion, resulting hence in delaying all vehicles on that lane. Once this duration expires any vehicle i, that was delayed moves back to the state *WAITING* until it is granted access again. Any vehicle which did not succeed in crossing the intersection will receive the message *DELAYED* (step 1.4) informing it that it has been moved back to the waiting state.

Fig. 3 *VehicleTask*
algorithm

Algorithm 1 *VehicleTask*

Initialization //tasks performed by vehicle i
$\quad State_i = IDLE$; $crossingList = \emptyset$;
CoBegin
$\quad$ **1.1.** **Vehicle i enters the queueing area:**
$\quad\quad$ Send ($<REQUEST, i, lane_i>$, $Controller$);
$\quad\quad$ $oldLane_i = lane_i$;
$\quad\quad$ $State_i = WAITING$; // wait for message *CROSS*
$\quad$ **1.2. Vehicle i's GPS position changed:**
$\quad\quad$ **if** (i's position in IntersectionArea)
$\quad\quad$ $State_i = CROSSING$;
$\quad\quad$ **else if** ($State_i = CROSSING$ & i's position out
$\quad\quad\quad\quad\quad\quad\quad\quad$ IntersectionArea)
$\quad\quad$ $State_i = CROSSED$;
$\quad$ **1.3. Receive($<CROSS, vehiclesList, duration>$):**
$\quad\quad$ **if** ($State_i = WAITING$ & $i \in vehiclesList$) {
$\quad\quad\quad$ $State_i = QUEUING$;
$\quad\quad\quad$ $crossingList = vehiclesList$;
$\quad\quad\quad$ SetTimer($crossingTimer, duration$);
$\quad\quad\quad$ Move and cross the intersection; }
$\quad$ **1.4. Receive ($<DELAYED, vehiclesList>$):**
$\quad\quad$ **if** ($State_i = QUEUING$ & $i \in vehiclesList$) {
$\quad\quad\quad$ $State_i = WAITING$;
$\quad\quad\quad$ StopTimer($crossingTimer$); }
$\quad$ **1.5. Lane change detected:**
$\quad\quad$ **if** ($State_i = QUEUING$ & $oldLane_i \propto lane_i$) {
$\quad\quad\quad$ Send ($<NEWLANE, i, lane_i>$, $Controller$);
$\quad\quad\quad$ $oldLane_i = lane_i$;
$\quad\quad\quad$ $State_i = WAITING$; }
$\quad$ **1.6. $State_i = CROSSED$ //Vehicle i crossed:**
$\quad\quad$ Send ($<CROSSED, i>$, $Controller$);
$\quad\quad$ StopTimer($crossingTimer$);
$\quad\quad$ $State_i = IDLE$;
$\quad$ **1.7. Timeout of $crossingTimer$:**
$\quad\quad$ **if** ($State_i = QUEUING$) {
$\quad\quad\quad$ $State_i = WAITING$;
$\quad\quad\quad$ Send ($<DELAYED, i, lane_i>$, $Controller$); }
$\quad$ **1.8. Failure detected:**
$\quad\quad$ $State_i = FAULTY$;
$\quad\quad$ Send ($<FAILED, i>$, $Controller$);
$\quad$ **1.9. Failure repaired OR vehicle towed away:**
$\quad\quad$ Send ($<REPAIRED, i>$, $Controller$);
$\quad\quad$ $State_i = IDLE$;
$\quad\quad$ Perform step 1.1 if vehicle was repaired
CoEnd

In [1, 8], Wu et al. assumed that the last vehicle to cross the intersection is the one that will inform the controller by sending the message *RELEASE*. Since now we are taking into consideration that vehicles may be delayed and not being able to cross within the allocated time period, we have changed the algorithm in a way that any vehicle upon crossing the intersection must send the message *CROSSED* to the controller (step 1.6). Hence, the controller will be able to know which vehicles crossed, and which ones have been delayed as they will be sent *DELAYED* messages.

3.2 PrimaryControllerTask *Operations*

The main steps of the *primaryControllerTask* are described in Fig. 4. Upon receiving the message <*REQUEST, i, lane$_i$*> from any vehicle *i* requesting to cross the intersection (step 2.1), the primary controller checks first if the set of lanes to be locked for vehicle *i* are already locked. If they are already locked then vehicle *i* is added to the list *crossingList* of vehicles with granted access, and the message <*CROSS, crossingList*> is broadcasted to inform all the vehicles in *crossingList* that they can now cross the intersection (see procedure *GrantNextWaiting* in Fig. 5). If, on the other hand, no lane is locked, then vehicle *i* and any vehicle on a lane not conflicting with *lane$_i$* can cross the intersection. Otherwise, vehicle *i* is added to the waiting list. Note that the controller sets the *crossingTimer* to a particular duration, granting hence the access to the intersection only for limited time period.

The primary controller may also receive the message <*NEWLANE, i, newLane*> from a vehicle that changed lane. In that case the controller updates the information it stores in the waiting list. If the new lane conflicts with the old one, and the controller already granted this vehicle *i* access to the intersection, i.e. $i \in crossingList$, then the vehicle is moved back to the waiting list (step 2.2). Upon receiving the message <*CROSSED, i*> (step 2.3) the primary controller learns that the vehicle *i* just crossed the intersection. In such a case, the primary controller updates the crossing list, and if it becomes empty it grants access to the next vehicle in the waiting list.

To implement the fairness property the primary controller uses the *crossingTimer*. The fairness property means that any vehicle will have the chance to cross the intersection after a certain period of time (step 2.4). When the timer expires, the controller checks first if there are vehicles waiting to cross. If so, it checks if all the vehicles previously granted access have crossed the intersection. If some have been delayed then the controller will send them the message <*DELAYED, crossingList*> to inform them they need to wait for the next round. To handle the situation in which some vehicle may be already in the crossing area, the timer waits for another *crossDuration* before granting other vehicles access to the intersection. Finally, if no vehicle is waiting then the controller can extend the crossing duration to the delayed vehicles. Step 2.5 deals with the failure of any vehicle and step 2.6 announces to the primary controller that the vehicle which has been announced previously as faulty has been repaired or towed away. The last step (step 2.7) allows the primary controller to inform the backup that it is alive and monitoring the traffic.

Algorithm 2 *ControllerTask (controllerRole)*

Initialization //tasks performed by the primary controller
    crossingList = waitingList = locked = failedList = $\varnothing$;
    role = controllerRole;
    SetTimer(*aliveTimer, aliveDelay*);
CoBegin
    2.2. Receive (<*REQUEST, i, lane$_i$*>) from vehicle *i*:
        if (*locks$_i$ $\subset$ locked*) {
            crossingList = crossingList $\cup$ {i};
            if *(role = PRIMARY)*
                Broadcast (<*CROSS, crossingList, duration*>); }
        else if (*locked = $\varnothing$*)
            GrantNextWaiting (i);
        else *waitingList = waitingList $\cup$ {i}*;
    2.2. Receive (<*NEWLANE, i, newLane*>) from vehicle *i*:
        if (*i $\in$ crossingList & lane$_i$ $\propto$ newLane*) {
            crossingList = crossingList - {i};
            waitingList = waitingList $\cup$ {i}; }
        Update *lane$_i$* in *waitingList* using *newLane*;
    2.3. Receive (<*CROSSED, i*>) from vehicle *i*:
        crossingList = crossingList − {i};
        if (*crossingList = $\varnothing$*)
            *GrantNextWaiting (*first vehicle in *waitingList);*
    2.4. Timeout of *crossingTimer* OR
        Receive (<*DELAYED, i*>) from vehicle *i*:
        if (*waitingList $\neq$ $\varnothing$*)
            if (*crossingList $\neq$ $\varnothing$*) {
                Broadcast (<*DELAYED, crossingList*>);
                Wait(*crossDuration*); }
            *GrantNextWaiting (*first vehicle in *waitingList);}*
        else if (*crossingList $\neq$ $\varnothing$*)
            ResetTimer(*crossingTimer, duration*);
    2.5. Receive (<*FAILED, i*>) from vehicle *i*:
        failedList = failedList $\cup$ {i};
        blockedLanes = blockedLanes $\cup$ {lane$_i$};
        *delayedList = all vehicles in *waitingList* on a same
                          lane as vehicle *i*
        if *(role = PRIMARY)*
            Broadcast (<*DELAYED, delayedList*>);
    2.6. Receive (<*REPAIRED, i*>) from vehicle *i*:
        failedList = failedList - {i};
        if *(there is no other faulty vehicle on lane$_i$)*
            blockedLanes = blockedLanes - {lane$_i$};
    2.7. Timeout of *aliveTimer*:
        if *(role = PRIMARY)* Send (<*ALIVE*>, *Backup*);
        else role = *PRIMARY*; // backup becomes primary
        ResetTimer(*aliveTimer, aliveDelay*);
CoEnd

Fig. 4 *PrimaryControllerTask* algorithm

Fig. 5 Procedure
GrantNextWaiting

```
Procedure GrantNextWaiting (vehicle j) {
    locked = locksⱼ;
    crossingList = vehicles in waitingList and on lanes
                              concurrent to laneⱼ;
    if (role = PRIMARY)
    Broadcast (<CROSS, crossingList, duration>);
    ResetTimer(crossingTimer, duration);
}
```

3.3 BackupControllerTask *Operations*

The backup controller has two main duties. First, it needs to keep all the information related to the traffic synchronized with the primary controller. That is at any moment the traffic information known to the primary controller is identical to that maintained by the backup controller. This can be easily implemented as all vehicles and the primary controller communicate with each other by broadcasting. The second duty is to monitor the primary controller. Once it detects that the primary controller has failed it will take on and ensure that traffic control continues. The backup controller algorithm is almost identical to the primary controller algorithm with minor differences. This explains why we combined them in the same algorithm shown in Fig. 4. When starting the primary controller it will be given the role *PRIMARY* so that it acts as a primary controller, and the backup will be started with a role *BACKUP*. Note from the algorithm, e.g., steps 2.1, 2.3, and 2.4, that the transmission of messages are conditioned by the role of the controller. Only the primary will be able to send. In step 2.7, if the role is *PRIMARY* the task will send *ALIVE* message to announce that the primary is alive, otherwise, the role is *BACKUP* and since the alive timer expired it means the primary is down. In this case, the role of backup changes to *PRIMARY* and it starts acting as a primary.

4 Conclusion

In this paper, we have proposed a fault-tolerant centralized intersection control for intelligent transportation systems. Our algorithm uses the primary-backup approach and relies on intelligent vehicular ad hoc networks. The backup controller keeps monitoring the primary controller and once it detects it is down it takes on and guarantees that the safety, liveness, and fairness properties are satisfied all the time. In future work, we working on simulating our algorithm on real scenarios to be able to compare it with existing ones, e.g. Wu et al. in [8]. In addition, we are extending our work by making fully distributed, where only vehicle-to-vehicle communications are used to grant the privilege of passing the intersection.

References

1. Ni W, Wu W (2014) A message efficient intersection control algorithm based on VANETs. Internet Veh Technol Serv 8662:31–41 (Lecture Notes in Computer Science)
2. Srinivasan D, Choy MC, Cheu RL (2006) Neural networks for real-time traffic control system. IEEE Trans Intell Transp Syst 7(3):261–272
3. Lertworawanich P, Kuwahara M, Miska M (2011) A new multiobjective signal optimization for oversaturated networks. IEEE Trans Intell Transp Syst 12(4):967–976
4. Lee J, Park B (2012) Development and evaluation of a cooperative vehicle intersection control algorithm under the connected vehicles environment. IEEE Trans Intell Transp Syst 13(1): 81–90
5. Qiao J, Yang ND, Gao J (2011) Two-stage fuzzy logic controller for signalized intersection. IEEE Trans Syst Man Cybern A Syst Hum 41(1):178–184
6. Zhou B, Cao J, Zeng X, Wu H (2010) Adaptive traffic light control in wireless sensor network-based intelligent transportation system. In: Proceedings IEEE vehicular technology conference fall
7. Zhao D, Dai Y, Zhang Z (2012) Computational intelligence in urban traffic signal control: a survey. IEEE Trans Syst Man Cybern C Appl Rev 12(1):485–494
8. Wu WG, Zhang JB, Luo AX, Cao JN (2015) Distributed mutual exclusion algorithms for intersection traffic control. IEEE Trans Parallel Distrib Syst 26(1):65–74
9. Raravi G, Shingde V, Ramamritham K, Bharadia J (2007) Merge algorithms for intelligent vehicles. In: Proceedings GM R&D workshop, pp 51–65
10. Dresner K, Stone P (2008) A multiagent approach to autonomous intersection management. J Artif Intell Res 31(1):591–656
11. Milans V, Perez J, Onieva E, Gonzalez C (2010) Controller for urban intersections based on wireless communications and fuzzy logic. IEEE Trans Intell Transp Syst 11(1):243–248
12. Glaser S, Vanholme B, Mammar S, Gruyer D, Nouveliere L (2010) Maneuver-based trajectory planning for highly autonomous vehicles on real road with traffic and driver interaction. IEEE Trans Intell Transp Syst 11(3):589–606
13. Elhadef M (2015) An adaptable inVANETs-based intersection traffic control algorithm. In: Proceedings of the 13th IEEE international conference on pervasive intelligence and computing (PICom 2015), pp 2387–2392. Liverpool, UK

QSL: A Specification Language for E-Questionnaire, E-Testing, and E-Voting Systems

Yuan Zhou, Hongbiao Gao and Jingde Cheng

Abstract E-questionnaire, e-testing, and e-voting are the essential ingredients of modern communities as the methods for a group to express a choice, a preference, or an opinion by an e-paper. Many kinds of e-questionnaire, e-testing, and e-voting systems are implemented to provide e-questionnaire, e-testing, and e-voting services on the Internet. However, there is a gap manifested in difficult communications among questioners, developers, and systems. To cover the gap, this paper proposes QSL, the first specification language with a standardized, consistent, and exhaustive list of requirements for specifying various e-questionnaire, e-testing, and e-voting systems such that the specifications can be used as the premise of automatically generating e-questionnaire, e-testing, and e-voting systems. This paper also presents QSL structure satisfying stability and extensibility, shows various QSL applications for providing convenient QSL services to questioner and developer.

Keywords QSL · Specification language · E-questionnaire · E-testing · E-voting · Web service

1 Introduction

E-questionnaire, e-testing, and e-voting are the essential ingredients of modern communities as the methods for a group to express a choice, a preference, or an opinion by an e-paper. Over a decade, there are many kinds of e-questionnaire,

Y. Zhou · H. Gao · J. Cheng (✉)
Department of Information and Computer Sciences,
Saitama University, Saitama, Japan
e-mail: cheng@aise.ics.saitama-u.ac.jp

Y. Zhou
e-mail: shuugen@aise.ics.saitama-u.ac.jp

H. Gao
e-mail: gaohongbiao@aise.ics.saitama-u.ac.jp

© Springer Science+Business Media Singapore 2016   255
J.J. (Jong Hyuk) Park et al. (eds.), *Advanced Multimedia and Ubiquitous Engineering*, Lecture Notes in Electrical Engineering 393,
DOI 10.1007/978-981-10-1536-6_34

e-testing, and e-voting systems implemented to provide e-questionnaire, e-testing, and e-voting services on the Internet. According to intents and purposes by different companies, organizations, and individuals, different requirements for different types of e-questionnaire/e-testing/e-voting can thus derive different e-questionnaire/ e-testing/e-voting systems.

There are four difficult problems on communications among questioners, developers, and systems. If existing e-questionnaire/e-testing/e-voting systems cannot conduct an e-questionnaire/e-testing/e-voting a questioner wants, the questioner may need a new system. On communication between questioner and developer, firstly, it is difficult for questioner to clearly describe specifications for the new system, since he/she does not know what are necessary. Secondly, it is also difficult for developer to understand the specifications for the system from a questioner because the questioner may be not able to clearly describe the specifications and developer is not a specialist in questioner's field. Thirdly, on communication between questioner and the systems, it is a big burden to learn how to use a new system if questioner does not know the usage of the system. At last, it is inconvenient that data cannot be generally reused, if a questioner wants to use downloaded data from an e-questionnaire/e-testing/e-voting system in others. It is desirable to automatically generate e-questionnaire, e-testing, and e-voting systems for satisfying what questioner wants, providing convenience, and saving labor cost and time.

Therefore, it is necessary to provide a specification language as a formalized specification. The specification language should specify necessary requirements for e-questionnaire, e-testing, and e-voting systems with a unique precise definition, because providing a specification language for both questioner and developer can make questioner to clearly describe the requirements for the system, and developer can also clearly understand what questioner needs. In addition, developer can implement the system, which provides e-questionnaire, e-testing, and e-voting services. Communication between questioner and e-questionnaire/e-testing/e-voting system, it will be easy because of only one method for questioner. Meanwhile, it is convenient that specification language provides questioner with data by a unique format that can be reused. Figure 1 shows the relationship of designer of a specification language, questioner and developer of e-questionnaire, e-testing, and e-voting systems. Besides, the ideal state is that a tool as a complier to automatically generate e-questionnaire, e-testing, and e-voting systems for questioner. With the feedbacks from questioner and developer, designer revises the language.

This paper proposes QSL, the first specification language for e-questionnaire, e-testing, and e-voting systems that serves as a formalized specification for specifying various e-questionnaire, e-testing, and e-voting systems with a standardized, consistent, and exhaustive list of requirements, such that the specifications can be used as the premise of automatically generating e-questionnaire, e-testing, and e-voting systems. The rest of the paper is organized as follows: Chap. 2 presents the primitive elements of e-questionnaire, e-testing, and e-voting systems. Chapter 3 presents QSL structure. QSL applications for providing convenient QSL services are presented in Chap. 4. Finally, some concluding remarks are given in Chap. 5.

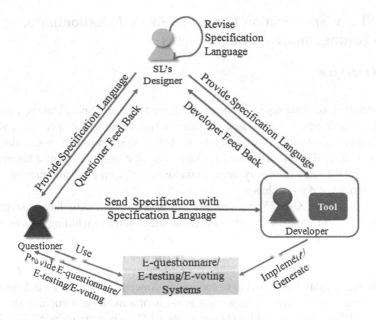

Fig. 1 Relationships among designer, questioner, and developer

2 Primitive Elements of E-Questionnaire, E-Testing, and E-Voting Systems

In order to specify various e-questionnaire, e-testing, and e-voting systems, the basic idea is to find out the primitive elements of e-questionnaire, e-testing, and e-voting systems by surveying various e-questionnaire systems and represent various e-questionnaire, e-testing, and e-voting systems by combining the elements. The primitive element is an element used to combine into various e-questionnaire, e-testing, and e-voting systems with its independent attribute, as well as the basis of design of the questionnaire specification language.

We investigated 30 e-questionnaire systems, 20 e-testing systems, and 20 e-voting systems [2, 5]. We found the similarities and differences among e-questionnaire, e-testing, and e-voting systems. We extracted elements from all the functions of the systems and classified them according to the similarities and differences. The primitive elements of e-questionnaire, e-testing, and e-voting systems consists of entity and representation. Entity is uniquely identified regardless of changing representation, which will be designed as an element in QSL. Representation is to express the corresponding entity that will be designed as the attribute or value of the element.

There are 45 primitive elements [1] classified into 6 independent groups: participant, questionnaire/examination paper/ballot (*paper* for short), function of an e-questionnaire/e-testing/e-voting (*function* for short), server, software, and phase.

3   QSL: A Specification Language for E-Questionnaire, E-Testing, and E-Voting Systems

3.1   Overview

As a specification language, we designed Questionnaire Specification Language (QSL for short), and it serves as a formalized specification for specifying various e-questionnaire, e-testing, and e-voting systems. QSL provides vocabulary and notation to describe various desirable functions of e-questionnaire, e-testing, and e-voting systems, and necessary items to make description clear and precise, and to use as format for data exchange.

QSL is based on XML [3] because XML is a versatile markup language, capable of labeling the information content of diverse data sources including structured and semi-structured documents that allow us to use the structure of XML intelligently and express the complete specification of e-questionnaire, e-testing, and e-voting systems. Furthermore, XML provides a standard way produced by W3C so that there are many tools and software to support it. Since the XML schema language is a formalization of constraints, expressed as rules or a model of structure, that apply to class of XML documents [4]. The grammar of QSL is defined by XML schema.

3.2   QSL Structure

According to the primitive elements of e-questionnaire, e-testing, and e-voting systems, we design QSL structure. Figure 2 illustrates QSL structure of relationship overview among e-questionnaire, e-testing, and e-voting.

In order to extend and upgrade QSL easily without changing the whole configuration, we design that QSL structure has 3 layers. In the innermost layer, QSL defines core elements. Specifying any e-questionnaire, e-testing, and e-voting system must specify all the core elements. The core element consists of the combinations of the elements in the middle layer. The elements in middle layer are

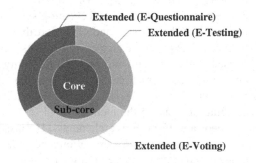

Fig. 2 Relationship overview among e-questionnaire, e-testing, and e-voting

called sub-core elements. In the outermost layer, there are 3 isolated ranges, which are for e-questionnaire, e-testing, and e-voting, respectively. The elements in this layer are called extended elements. For example, if a user wants to specify an e-voting system, he/she shall specify all the elements in the innermost layer and middle layer, and specify all or part of the elements in the outermost layer depending on the security level.

In order to well define the combinations of core elements, sub-core elements, and extended elements, we use double-digit to mark the elements. In the ten's place, 0, 1, and 2 stands for core element, sub-core element, and extended element, respectively. Table 1 shows the list of the elements with the double-digit numbers. In the one's place, 0 stands for a special mark. The elements are associated with the

Table 1 Core elements, sub-core elements, and extended elements

Group	No	Element	Configuration
Core	00	QSL	–
	01	Security	Phase, Server, Software, Participant
	02	System	Phase, Function, Server, Software
	03	EPaper	Phase, Paper, Participant
	04	Data	Phase, Paper, Participant
Sub-core	11	Phase	SettingUp, Distributing, Collecting, Submitting, etc.
	12	Paper	Arrangement, Text, Media, Question, Option, etc.
	13	Function	Func-Import, Func-Export, Func-Distribute, etc.
	14	Server	RAServer, PSServer
	15	Software	CSSoftware, CTSofteware
	16	Participant	Sponsor, Questioner, Analyst, Monitor, Respondent
Extended (E-Q)	21q	Logic	Skipping, Piping, Extraction
	22q	RateControl	–
	23q	Ranking	–
Extended (E-T)	21t	Marker	Marker, Score, SampleAnswer
	22t	Score	–
	23t	SampleAnswer	–
	24t	Formula	–
Extended (E-V)	21v	Authentication	Secret, Token, Biometrics
	22v	Anonymisation	Seal, Channel
	23v	Auditing	–
	24v	CAServer	ID, Link
	25v	ATSoftware	Version, ID, Link, Solution
	26v	Candidate	ID, Name, Affiliation, Proposer

namespace defined using **QSL**. As the configuration of core elements, it gives a combination relationship of sub-core elements. In addition, some major elements for constructing sub-core elements and extended elements are shown below.

To ensure stability and extensibility, we design QSL based on its configuration, such that it provides the phase isolation to easily revise elements in middle and outermost layers without changing the general structure.

4 QSL Applications

Considering providing conveniences to both questioner and developer, it is hopeful to implement a series of applications for QSL. There are 2 kinds of applications that should be prioritized. Figure 3 illustrates QSL implementation cycle. Questioner design an e-questionnaire/e-testing/e-voting system using a specific QSL structure editor to mutually transform between requirement list and QSL specification, and to create and edit error-free QSL specifications according to QSL grammar coupled with a read-helper to hint each element's meaning. QSL structure editor output a valid QSL document. Developer can read easily this QSL document by the assistant from QSL editor, and implement an e-questionnaire/e-testing/e-voting system. A QSL compiler can read QSL document and automatically generate e-questionnaire, e-testing and e-voting systems for questioner.

Fig. 3 QSL implementation cycle

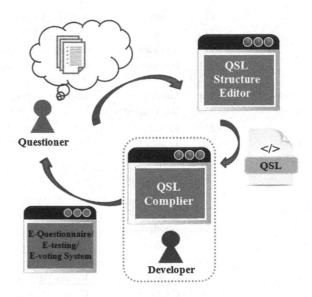

5 Conclusion

This paper proposed QSL: a first specification language for e-questionnaire, e-testing, and e-voting systems for generating e-questionnaire, e-testing, and e-voting systems automatically. In addition, the paper presented QSL structure that satisfies stability and extensibility, and showed various QSL applications for providing convenient QSL services to questioner and developer.

In the future, we continue improving QSL through case studies. We will implement a QSL structure editor for mutual transformation between requirement list and QSL specification, and a QSL compiler system to automatically generate e-questionnaire, e-testing and e-voting systems for conveniently reusing specifications.

References

1. AISE Lab, Saitama University (2014) QSL manual (ver. 1.5). http://www.aise.ics.saitama-u.ac.jp/QSL
2. Wang Z, Zhou Y, Wang B, Goto Y, Cheng J (2015) An extension of QSL for e-testing and its application in an offline e-testing environment. In: Park JJ et al (eds) Advanced multimedia and ubiquitous engineering, Lecture notes in electrical engineering, vol 352. Springer, Berlin, pp 7–14
3. W3C: Extensible markup language (XML) 1.0 (fifth edn). http://www.w3.org/TR/2008/REC-xml-20081126/
4. W3C: XML schema. https://www.w3.org/XML/Schema
5. Zhou Y, Goto Y, Cheng J (2014) QSL: a specification language for e-questionnaire systems. In: Proceedings of the 5th IEEE international conference on software engineering and service science (ICSESS 2014), Beijing, China, pp 224–230. IEEE, NY

Predicting New Attacks: A Case Study in Security Analysis of Cryptographic Protocols

Da Bao, Kazunori Wagatsuma, Hongbiao Gao and Jingde Cheng

Abstract Knowledge about attacks is a necessary foundation for security analysis of information systems or cryptographic protocols. Current security verification methods for improving the security of target systems or the soundness of cryptographic protocols has limitations because they are all based on the assumptions from known attacks, while the attackers are trying every possible attacks against the information systems. Once a new-style attack was found by adversaries earlier, it would bring severe loss to the target systems. Therefore, it is essential to understand and take measures against new attacks previously. A new method has been proposed for predicting new attacks, but it lacks experimental results to prove its effectiveness. This paper confirms the effectiveness of the proposed method by a rediscovery experiment that shows several known attacks on cryptographic protocols rediscovered successfully. The paper also shows issues of the approach for predicting new attacks.

Keywords Information security · Predict new attacks · Attack analysis · Forward reasoning · Cryptographic protocols

D. Bao · K. Wagatsuma · H. Gao · J. Cheng (✉)
Department of Information and Computer Sciences, Saitama University, Saitama, Japan
e-mail: cheng@aise.ics.saitama-u.ac.jp

D. Bao
e-mail: baoda@aise.ics.saitama-u.ac.jp

K. Wagatsuma
e-mail: wagatsuma@aise.ics.saitama-u.ac.jp

H. Gao
e-mail: gaohongbiao@aise.ics.saitama-u.ac.jp

© Springer Science+Business Media Singapore 2016
J.J. (Jong Hyuk) Park et al. (eds.), *Advanced Multimedia and Ubiquitous Engineering*, Lecture Notes in Electrical Engineering 393,
DOI 10.1007/978-981-10-1536-6_35

1   Introduction

Knowledge of attacks is a necessary foundation for security analysis of information systems or cryptographic protocols. The traditional approaches [1, 4] to improve the security of target systems or protocols is that developers make some assumptions according to the known attacks and then verify the corresponding countermeasures against the attacks. Such kind of approach is limited because all the assumptions come from the known attacks. Developers can only prove their systems insulated against the known attacks and almost has none capabilities against unknown attacks.

However, the security of target systems is as strong as the weakest link [9]. Once a new attack was found by attackers earlier than developers did, it would bring severe loss to the target systems. It is essential to predict new unknown attacks beforehand for the target information systems or secure protocols.

A method [3] has been proposed for predicting new attacks. The method considered that the attacks are consisting of some primary tactics and by combining those primary tactics can obtain some new attacks. But the proposed method lacks experimental results to prove its effectiveness.

This paper confirms the effectiveness of the proposed method by a rediscovery experiment that shows several known attacks on cryptographic protocols rediscovered successfully. The paper also shows issues of the approach for predicting new attacks. The rest of this paper is organized as follows: Sect. 2 presents the approach for predicting new attacks. Section 3 discusses the case study of predicting new attacks on cryptographic protocols. Section 4 gives a discussion about the case study. Finally, some concluding remarks are given in Sect. 5.

2   Basic Approach for Predicting New Attacks

The proposed method [3] for predicting new attacks considered that attacks are composed with some primary tactics. The primary tactics of attacks do not only involve the components of target systems and theirs links, but the resource belonging to attackers, assets of systems (the targets of attacks), authentication mechanism to the assets and the countermeasures should be also considered as the primary tactics at least.

As the first step of predicting new attacks, the primary tactics of attacks on the target systems should be clarified, and then we can attempt to combine primary tactics in different the patterns to obtain some new attacks. It is helpful to classify the known attacks because each primary tactics has its own characteristics. Although some tactics of attacks may be common among different kinds of information systems, primary tactics should be analyzed in the circumstances where the attacks happen.

3 Predicting New Attacks on Cryptographic Protocols

We confirm the effectiveness of the proposed method by simulating the process of predicting new attacks on protocols for authentication and key establishment. This section explains our consideration about the attacks on the protocols and the detailed steps of rediscovering known attacks, which is with the aid of a reasoning-based formal analysis method [15].

3.1 Analysis of Attacks on Cryptographic Protocols

To clarify the primary tactics of attacks on cryptographic protocols, we analyzed a classification of attacks on cryptographic protocols has been proposed [6]. It distinguishes attacks in 10 categories.

These kinds of attacks are as following: (1) Eavesdropping: the intruder captures the message that are exchanged among the principals. (2) Modification: the intruder alters the message that are exchanged among principals. (3) Replay: the intruder records messages and then send it to the same and/or a different principal. If necessary, the intruder would start a new run of protocols. (4) Preplay: the intruder engages in a run of the protocol before a run by the legitimate principals. (5) Reflection: the intruder just sends messages back to the principals who sent them. (6) Denial of Service: the intruder prevents or hinders legitimate principals from completing the protocol. (7) Typing Attacks: the intruder replaces a part of message with other part of message. The two parts of message has different type. There is no limit to the two parts coming from the same message. (8) Cryptanalysis: the intruder get useful information from the protocol runs to make the cryptanalysis easier. (9) Certificate Manipulation: the intruder chooses or modifies certificate information to hinder one or more protocol runs. (10) Protocol Interaction: the intruder chooses a different protocol to interact with a known protocol.

By analyzing these 10 categories of attacks, we can summarize 3 primary tactics of attacks: (1) The intruders can choose to be a legitimate principal or not. To be a principal is active way that allow the intruders to archive their goals by exchanging message with other principals, while choosing not to be a legitimate principal is a passive way that does not need the intruder to disturb the protocols runs by the legitimate principal. (2) The intruders can perform several runs of protocols in parallel. The runs cannot be only from the same protocol, but runs from different protocols can also be performed together. (3) The intruders can alter their sending message as possible as they can, but the altered message must comply with the formats defined in the protocol specification.

According to the primary tactics, we can reorganize the 10 categories of attacks. Eavesdropping, Denial of Service and Cryptanalysis are passive ways for intruders; Modification is a passive way but the exchanging message should be altered as intruders' wish; Replay, Preplay, Reflection and Certificate Manipulation need intruders execute protocol run in parallel, meanwhile, they also need altering messages in appropriate way; Typing Attacks need intruders to alter messages in appropriate way; Protocol Interaction need intruders to choose appropriate protocols and run them in parallel. Although we have got the primary tactics that consist of attacks, yet it is necessary to choose a suitable method for deducing new attacks.

3.2   A Reasoning-Based Formal Method for Analysis of Protocols

A concept of formal analysis with reasoning for information security, which can be used to analysis cryptographic protocols, has been proposed [10]. With the proposed method, analysts can formalize principals and intruders' behavior of target protocol, and deduce attacks by intruder by forward reasoning. If those deduced attacks succeed, the target cryptographic protocol is not secure. In the method, strong relevant logics [8, 10] are appropriate for logic systems underlying forward reasoning because strong relevant logics are assured that conclusions that are not related to premises are not deduced. Figure 1 shows the overview of the reasoning-based formal method.

Analysts do not need to enumerate target attacks by intruder before doing the analysis in formal analysis method with reasoning. Analysts analyze deduced attacks in order to detect success of attacks by intruder. As the result, it is possible to detect attacks that analysts did not assume previously. Therefore, formal analysis method with reasoning can support to detect attacks that analysts did not enumerate. Until now, a detailed method of formal analysis with reasoning for key exchange protocols has been proposed [15].

Furthermore, a forward reasoning engine, which can automatically perform the reasoning process, has been proposed and developed [11]. This engine is named as FreeEnCal and has capability to handle any logic system and formal theory by input vocabulary, configuration rules, axiom, and inference rule of logical formulas. With the support of FreeEnCal, logical formulas can be automatically deduced from input logical formulas as premises.

However, attack prediction capability of the proposed method depends on behavior models of intruders. Current behavior models of intruders do not give a

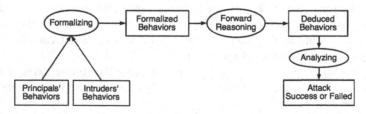

Fig. 1 Overview of the formal analysis method with reasoning

behavior that who can decode which encrypted data by which mathematical computation with which data. The shortcoming of the method can be made up by adding our primary tactics which can enrich the set of intruders' behavior so that the capabilities of the method can be improved.

3.3 Rediscovering Attacks on Cryptographic Protocols

Rediscovering attacks means using the proposed approach to discover those known attacks again. In order to investigate whether the approach is effective for predicting new attacks, a way is to rediscovery some known attacks on a certain cryptographic protocols because from the viewpoint of the mechanism of deducing theorems, "rediscovery" is actually identical with "discovery".

With the reasoning-based method, the following three sets should be firstly formalized into logical formulas according to strong relevant logic. The formulas will be putted into the FreeEnCal [11], a forward reasoning engine for general purpose, to execute the deduction.

Behaviors of Participants: It represents a set of rules among actions in each step that is represents as if a participant receives a certain data, then the participant sends an other data.

Behaviors of Intruders: It represents a set of rules what actions an intruder performs in a communication process of a protocol. In the proposed method, behavior of an intruder is based on Dolev-Yao Model [13]. Current behavior model of intruders is not enough for detecting the flaw in the protocols, because the generation of falsified message is not complete for intruders who want to try sending any appropriate message to principals. To solve this problem, we can add the primary tactics for attacks to this behavior set and formal it with the model. These primary tactics can extent the ability described by intruders' behavior model.

Common Behavior among Participants and an Intruder: It represents a set of rules except for behavior about sending and receiving data by participants and an intruder. For example, decryption of encrypted data is included in this target.

Secondly, analysts use FreeEnCal to perform forward reasoning automatically and new logical formulas would be generated. In tasks of forward reasoning, analysts use FreeEnCal for forward reasoning about each step of the target protocol and check whether the formulas that represents success of attack are included in deduced logical formulas after the removal. If specific formulas are included, it can be said that attacks by an intruder succeed in the target cryptographic protocol. Formulas that represent successful completion of a protocols mean that any participant sent or got data in forward reasoning about last step of protocol. Analysts check whether an atomic formula is deduced or not in forward reasoning about last step of target protocol.

We choose two protocols for authentication and key establishment for rediscovering the attacks: Otway-Rees protocol [14] and Wide-mouthed-frog protocol.

Otway-Rees Protocol

1. A → B: M, A, B, $\{N_A, M, A, B\}K_{AS}$
2. B → S: M, A, B, $\{N_A, M, A, B\}K_{AS}$, $\{N_B, M, A, B\}K_{BS}$
3. S → B: M, $\{N_A, K_{AB}\}K_{AS}$, $\{N_B, K_{AB}\}K_{BS}$
4. B → A: M, $\{N_A, K_{AB}\}K_{AS}$

An attack on Otway-Rees protocol was found [5]. The complete process of the attacks shows as following.

1. A → B: M, A, B, $\{N_A, M, A, B\}K_{AS}$
2'. C_B → S: M, A, C, $\{N_A, M, A, B\}K_{AS}$, $\{N_C, M, A, B\}K_{CS}$
3'. S → C_B: M, $\{N_A, K_{AB}\}K_{AS}$, $\{N_C, K_{AB}\}K_{CS}$
4'. C_B → A: M, $\{N_A, K_{AB}\}K_{AS}$

If the trusted third party (S) does not check the plaintext "M, A, C" and the contents in ciphertext "$\{N_C, M, A, B\}K_{CS}$" in the second step, S would recognize the ciphertext being altered. Then the run of protocol would continue and the session key would be distributed to A and the intruder C who is masquerading as B. This attack can have been rediscovered in our experiment, because the intruder used the third primary tactic that has been explained in Sect. 3.1.

Wide-mouthed-frog Protocol

1. A → S: A, $\{T_A, B, K_{AB}\}K_{AS}$
2. S → B: $\{T_S, A, K_{AB}\}K_{BS}$

The intention of wide-mouthed-frog protocol [7] is that the timestamp "T_S" used to provide freshness assurance to S and B, that is, the "K_{AB}" can match with only one timestamp. However, the attack on this protocol [12, 2] can let the session key match more than one timestamp. The complete process of the attacks shows as following.

1. A → S: A, $\{T_A, B, K_{AB}\}K_{AS}$
2. S → B: $\{T_S, A, K_{AB}\}K_{BS}$
1'. I_B → S: B, $\{T_S, A, K_{AB}\}K_{BS}$
2'. S → I_A: $\{T_{S'}, B, K_{AB}\}K_{AS}$
1". I_A → S: A, $\{T_{S'}, B, K_{AB}\}K_{AS}$
2". S → B: $\{T_{S''}, A, K_{AB}\}K_{BS}$

In this attack, the intruder executes three runs of the protocol. When the third run is complete, the session key K_{AB} held by B would match two timestamp, T_S and $T_{S''}$. This would make K_{AB} an invalid key for principal B, so that A and B cannot establish a secure channel for their communication. This attack is rediscovered in our experiment because the intruder taken the second primary tactic of attack that is explained in Sect. 3.1.

Except attacks, already known ones, are found by analyzing on the deduction results. In our case study, we rediscovered those known attacks on cryptographic protocols according to the proposed approach combining with the reasoning-based method. Therefore, our experiment result can show that the approach is effective for predicting new attacks on cryptographic in the sense that from the viewpoint of the mechanism of deducing theorems, "rediscovery" is as same as "discovery".

4 Discussion

The results of the rediscovery experiment have shown the effectiveness of our approach for predicting new attacks. During the case study, we also shown that our approach can help the reasoning-based formal method improve its capability of analyzing security of cryptographic protocols. With adding the primary tactic of attacks into the intruder behavior model, it extends the deduced result that are used to analyze cryptographic protocol. This extension makes the reasoning method better.

However, there is a gap between rediscovery of attacks and discovery of attacks. Although we have rediscovered several known attacks on cryptographic protocols, there are some issues for real "discovery" which we have to do in the future. Firstly, we rediscovered those attacks only based on low degree fragment of strong relevant logic. If we can make the higher degree fragment of strong relevant logic, we can archive more logical theorems. More logical theorems mean that we can discover more empirical theorems, which would bring more new attacks. Secondly, if we want to discovery some unknown attack, we should consider what kind of results are "new". It is not easy to filter out the really useful for all the deduced results.

5 Concluding Remarks

In our case study, we rediscovered those known attacks on cryptographic protocols according to the proposed approach. The experiment result shows the effectiveness of the approach for predicting new attacks by showing several known attacks on protocols rediscovered successfully. The paper also shown issues of the approach for real predicting new attacks.

In the future, we will use the approach to predicting unknown attacks on the cryptographic protocols. In other security-concern field, such as intrusion detecting system, we will apply our approach to predicting intrusions that are typically attacks on the information systems.

References

1. Abadi M, Fournet C (2001) Mobile values, new names and secure communication. In: Proceedings of the 28th ACM SIGPLAN-SIGACT symposium on principles of programming languages, pp 104–115, ACM
2. Anderson RJ, Needham RM (1995) Programming Satan's computer. In: van Leeuwen J (ed) Computer science today: recent trends and developments. LNCS, vol 1000. Springer, Heidelberg, pp 426–440

3. Bao D, Goto Y, Cheng J (2014) Predicting new attacks for information security. In: Park JJ et al. (eds) Computer science and its applications, ubiquitous information technologies. LNEE, vol 330. Springer, Heidelberg, pp 1353–1358

4. Bau J, Mitchell J (2011) Security modeling and analysis. IEEE Secur Priv 9(3):18–25

5. Boyd C, Mao W (1994) On a limitation of BAN logic. In: Helleseth T (ed) EUROCRYPT 1993. LNCS, vol 765. Springer, Heidelberg, pp 465–474

6. Boyd C, Mathuria A (2003) Protocols for authentication and key establishment. Springer, Heidelberg

7. Burrows M, Abadi M, Needham R (1990) A logic of authentication. ACM Trans Comput Syst 8(1):18–36

8. Cheng J (2006) Strong relevant logic as the universal basis of various applied logics for knowledge representation and reasoning. In: Kiyoki Y, Henno J, Jaakkola H, Kangassalo H (eds) Information modelling and knowledge bases XVII. Frontiers in artificial intelligence and applications, vol 136. IOS Press, Amsterdam, pp 310–320

9. Cheng J (2014) New challenges in future software engineering. In: Park JJ, Pan Y, Kim C, Yan Y (eds) Future information technology, FutureTech 2014. LNEE, vol 309. Springer, Berlin, pp 31–36

10. Cheng J, Miura J (2006) Deontic relevant logic as the logical basis for specifying, verifying, and reasoning about information security and information assurance. In: Proceedings of 1st international conference on availability, reliability and security, IEEE Computer Society, pp 601–608

11. Cheng J, Nara S, Goto Y (2007) FreeEnCal: a forward reasoning engine with general-purpose. In: Knowledge-based intelligent information and engineering systems, LNAI, vol 4693. Springer, Berlin, pp 444–452

12. Clark J, Jacob J (1996) Attacking authentication protocols. High Integr Syst 1(5):465–473

13. Dolev D, Yao A (1983) On the security of public-key protocols. IEEE Trans Inf Theory 29:198–208

14. Otway D, Rees O (1987) Efficient and timely mutual authentication. Oper Syst Rev 21(1):8–10

15. Wagatsuma K, Goto Y, Cheng J (2015) A formal analysis method with reasoning for key exchange protocols. J Inf Process Soc Jpn 56(3):903–910 (in Japanese)

A Dynamic Traffic Data Visualization System with OpenStreetMap

Wei Song, Jiaxue Li, Yifei Tian, Simon Fong and Wei Wang

Abstract This paper proposes a dynamic traffic data visualization system with OpenStreetMap (OSM). The system connects server database to client web browser by a Transmission Control Protocol/Internet Protocol (TCP/IP) to access remote traffic data. In order to reduce the computation consumption of the server, the traffic estimation and prediction from large datasets is analyzed in the client. We implement a Graphic Processing Unit (GPU) programming technology to implement the data mining process in parallel for real-time approach. To provide an intuitive interface to the users, the system renders the data mining results with the OSM mid-ware, which provides geographic data of the world.

Keywords Traffic visualization · TCP/IP · GPU programming · Data mining · Openstreetmap

1 Introduction

With the continuous urban population and increasing traffic pressure, the reasonable analysis of traffic data is key to solve the traffic pressure, and the concise visualization of traffic information is convenient to users to browse the traffic situation. Traditionally, the traffic information is displayed in the form of simple 2D/3D diagrams, such as trend chart, bidirectional flow diagram, pie chart and so on [1].

W. Song (✉) · J. Li · Y. Tian
Department of Digital Media Technology, North China University of Technology,
Beijing, China
e-mail: sw@ncut.edu.cn

S. Fong
Department of Computer and Information Science, University of Macau,
Macau, China

W. Wang
Guangdong Electronic Industry Institute, Dongguan, China

© Springer Science+Business Media Singapore 2016   271
J.J. (Jong Hyuk) Park et al. (eds.), *Advanced Multimedia and Ubiquitous Engineering*, Lecture Notes in Electrical Engineering 393,
DOI 10.1007/978-981-10-1536-6_36

By these methods, it is not convenient to find the relation between the data and its geographical location in an intuitive view.

Recently, the data visualization technologies in earth maps have been widely researched, such as Google Maps and OpenStreeyMap (OSM) [2]. To present the traffic datasets intuitively, we need to solve the problem that such datasets are huge and constantly updating. The traditional data mining and visualization processes are implemented by CPU sequential programming methods, which are difficult for processing big data in real time and cause a low computation speed [3].

This study builds a web server via Myeclipse, which accesses remote data from database using a Transmission Control Protocol/Internet Protocol (TCP/IP). In the client, we apply Graphic Processing Unit (GPU) technology to analyze and render data mining processes in parallel for the real-time approach. For intuitive data visualization, we render the traffic datasets and analyzing results corresponding to their geographical location in an OSM as the background. The visualization results are presented in web browsers intelligibly.

2 Related Works

Data visualization via the Web browser is a challenging task in the big data and cloud computing researching areas. Kopeć [4] utilized WebGL to visualize a color mesh for geological data representation. The distributed users were able to view the remote multidimensional information through the Web browser, that provided a convenient interface of data analyzing. Weichselbraun [5] proposed a Web intelligence framework of contextualization and semantic knowledgebase for opinion mining. He visualized the knowledgebase with their geographic data in the Google map. To extend the data visualization applications to mobile device, Mohamed [6] proposed a clutter-aware clustering visualiser algorithm on a Google map of Android mobile phone. This method provided a adaptive strategy by allowing users interact the cluster results iteratively so as to satisfy the data mining requirements.

Besides the Google maps, OSM was developed as a geographic knowledge collective [7]. The geographical information systems (GIS) packages were able to be edited using a Java OpenStreetMap Editor (JOSM). Lots of commercial, educational and political projects based on geographic location were developed using OSM. For example, Rifat [8] developed a location based information system as a road guider. For big data mining approaches, it was difficult to apply these method to analyze and visualize the stream datasets in real time. To present a traffic big data in real time, this paper proposes a dynamic traffic data visualization system with OpenStreetMap.

3 The Dynamic Traffic Data Visualization System

In this section, we propose a dynamic traffic data visualization system, as shown in Fig. 1. In the system, the traffic datasets are acquired from remote database using TCP/IP. After delivered to the client, the datasets are analyzed and converted color and geometric information buffer by GPU computation. By a TCP/IP memory transmission, the visualization buffer is converted from C to Java language programming environment so as to access the Web browser by MyEclipse. As the geometry background, OSM is imported in the MyEclipse environment, which provides geographic location information. After merging the visualization buffer and OSM, the user is able to browse the traffic data on a Web-based geographic map.

To realize real-time data mining, we utilize GPU programming technology to implement the data mining process in parallel for real-time approach, as shown in Fig. 2. Firstly, the traffic datasets is loaded into the GPU memory from the CPU memory. Next, we apply the GPU programming technology to realize the data mining algorithms from large datasets in parallel, such as clustering and prediction. Then, each data is converted to a color and graphic unit, which combines into a visualization result buffer, which is copied from the GPU memory to the CPU memory. Finally, as a foreground image, the visualization buffer is masking onto the browser so as to integrate with the OSM buffer.

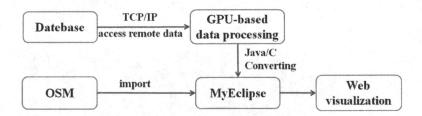

Fig. 1 The architecture of the dynamic traffic data visualization system

Fig. 2 The GPU-based data mining and visualization process

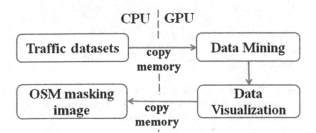

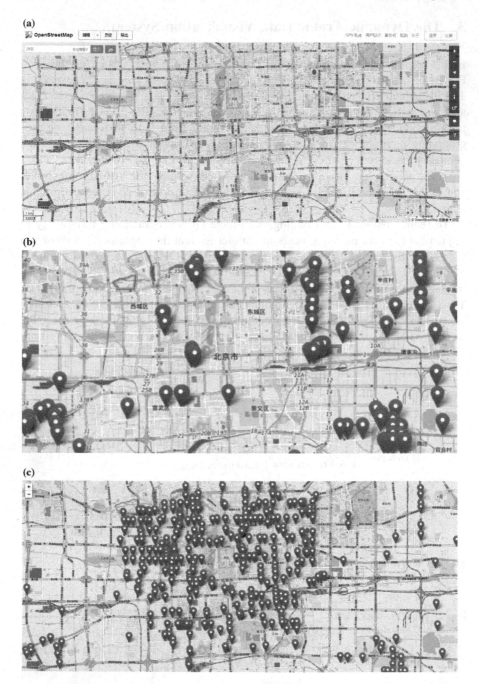

Fig. 3 The traffic data visualization results. **a** The OSM background image. **b** A visualization fragment from 500-line datasets. **c** A visualization fragment from 1000-line datasets. **d** A visualization fragment from 1500-line datasets

(d)

Fig. 3 (continued)

4 Experiments

To illustrate our proposed system, we analyzed and demonstrated the vehicle GIS packets in Beijing city, as shown in Fig. 3. The experiments were implemented on a 3.20 GHz Intel® Core™ Quad CPU computer with a GeForce GT 770 graphics card, and 4 GB RAM. The GPU-based parallel computation is implemented using the CUDA toolkit. We installed JDK 1.8.0_60 to configure Java environment, MySQL Server 5.5 to access data by SQLyog, and MyEclipse Professional 2014 to realize the Web visualization.

As shown in Fig. 3a, OSM was imported in the MyEclipse environment as the geometry background. Then we accessed and rendered vehicle GIS datasets of different counts, as shown in Fig. 3b–d. The data mining and visualization processing speed by GPU computation was 3.3 s on averagely.

5 Conclusions

The traditional visualization methods of statistical traffic information present datasets in text and table forms, which are difficult to query the useful information quickly. In this paper, we proposed a dynamic traffic visualization system with OSM, which provided an intuitive interface to the users conveniently. By the GPU programming technology, the traffic data mining and visualization methods were processed in parallel so as to realize real-time approach. In future, we will accomplish the data mining algorithms and data visualization models in this system.

Acknowledgment This research was supported by the National Natural Science Foundation of China (61503005), and by SRF for ROCS, SEM.

References

1. Song W, Wu D, Fong S et al (2015) A real-time interactive data mining and visualization system using parallel computing. In: The tenth international conference on digital information management, pp 10–13
2. Chen B, Sun W, Vodacek A (2014) Improving image-based characterization of road junctions, widths, and connectivity by leveraging OpenStreetMap vector map. In: IEEE international geoscience and remote sensing symposium, pp 4958–4961
3. Song W, Cai X, Xi Y et al (2015) Real-time single camera natural user interface engine development. Multimed Tools Appl. doi:10.1007/s11042-015-2986-6
4. Kopeć A, Bała J, Pięta A (2015) WebGL based visualisation and analysis of stratigraphic data for the purposes of the mining industry. Proc Comput Sci 51:2869–2877
5. Weichselbraun A, Gindl S, Scharl A (2014) Enriching semantic knowledge bases for opinion mining in big data applications. Knowl-Based Syst 69:78–85
6. Mohamed MG, Shonali K, Brett G et al (2013) Interactive self-adaptive clutter-aware visualisation for mobile data mining. J Comput Syst Sci 79:369–382
7. Haklay M, Weber P (2008) OpenStreetMap: User-generated street maps. IEEE Pervasive Comput 7:12–18
8. Rifat MR, Moutushy S, Ahmed SI, Ferdous HS (2011) Location based information system using OpenStreetMap. In: IEEE Student Conference on Research and Development, pp 397–402

Face Recognition Based on Deep Belief Network Combined with Center-Symmetric Local Binary Pattern

Chen Li, Wei Wei, Jingzhong Wang, Wanbing Tang and Shuai Zhao

Abstract Human face recognition performances usually drops heavily due to pose variation and other factors. The representative deep learning method Deep Belief Network (DBN) has been proven to be an effective method to extract information-rich features of face image for recognition. However the DBN usually ignore the local features of image which are proven to be important for face recognition. Hence, this paper proposed a novel approach combined with local feature Center-Symmetric Local Binary Pattern (CS-LBP) and DBN. CS-LBP is applied to extract local texture features of face image. Then the extracted features are used as the input of Deep Belief Network instead of face image. The network structure and parameters are trained to obtain the final network model for recognition. A large amount of experiments are conducted on the ORL face database, and the experimental results show that compared with LBP, LBP combined with DBN and DBN, the proposed method has a significant improvement on recognition rates and can be a feasible way to combat with pose variation.

Keywords Face recognition · Pose variation · CS-LBP · DBN

1 Introduction

As a biometric technology, face has many distinct advantages compared with other biometric characteristics: it can be captured from a long distance which is friendly and convenience especially for the information security or access control application and it also has a wealthy structure and relatively larger area which is not easily

C. Li (✉) · J. Wang · W. Tang · S. Zhao
College of Computer Science, North China University of Technology,
Beijing, China
e-mail: lichen@ncut.edu.cn

W. Wei
College of Electronic and Information Engineering, North China
University of Technology, Beijing, China

© Springer Science+Business Media Singapore 2016

277

J.J. (Jong Hyuk) Park et al. (eds.), *Advanced Multimedia and Ubiquitous Engineering*, Lecture Notes in Electrical Engineering 393,
DOI 10.1007/978-981-10-1536-6_37

to be occluded. Hence face recognition has becoming an indispensable biological authentication method and attracting many attentions.

During the last decades, many face recognition approaches have been proposed and can be roughly divided into two types: pixel-based approach and feature-based approach [1]. The Principle component analysis (PCA), Linear Discriminant Analysis (LDA) and Independent Component Analysis (ICA) methods are the most typical pixel-based methods and have been proved to be effective for recognition with large databases. The feature-based approach mainly include Local Binary Pattern (LBP), Gabor, SIFT and their modified approaches. Most the above methods can achieve satisfying recognition result upon frontal and high resolution face image. However the feature extraction methods usually rely on artificial selection. Besides, to extract more robust deep-level features in order to express face information more effectively is still difficult. Hence face recognition performances usually drops heavily due to pose variation and other factors under unconstrained environment, which is still a challenging task for researchers [2, 3].

Deep Learning [4] has become an important research area in computer vision. Deep Belief Network (DBN) is a typical Deep learning method with strong learning and expression ability. It can learn essential data feature from small samples and extract feature automatically without artificial selection. However, when pixel level image are import to DBN directly, the recognition performance normally decline since DBN ignores the local features of the images [5]. In order to make full use of the learning ability of DBN, proposed a novel approach combined with local feature and DBN is proposed. This paper is organized as follows: Sect. 2 describes the proposed technique, Experiment results are demonstrated in Sect. 3. Then we conclude the paper in Sect. 4.

2 Technical Approach

2.1 Center-Symmetric Local Binary Pattern (CS-LBP)

Local binary pattern (LBP) is an feature descriptor proposed by Heikkila which has been proven to be effective at texture feature description. And it can be seen as a standard approach for extract structural model of texture information. However texture features extracted by LBP is usually too nuanced to be robust for flat area of images [6]. To compensate the shortage, CS-LBP is proposed. It encode the change of the image from four different direction with center symmetric principle. The CS-LBP features can be described with Eqs. (1) and (2):

$$CS - LBP_{R,N,T}(X, Y) = \sum_{i=0}^{\left(\frac{N}{2}\right)-1} S\left(n_i - n_{i+\left(\frac{N}{2}\right)}\right)2^i \qquad (1)$$

$$s(x) = \begin{cases} 1, & x > T \\ 0, & \text{otherwise} \end{cases} \qquad (2)$$

where n_i and $n_{i+(N/2)}$ correspond to the gray value of center-symmetric area pixels, N represents the pixel numbers on a circle of radius R. To enhance the robustness of CS-LBP feature on flat image regions, a threshold T is set for the change of image intensity. Compared with the traditional LBP, CS-LBP has lower dimension and lower computational complexity. Also it is more robust to noise interference. Hence CS-LBP is used for feature extraction to preserve more useful information of the image and reduce the impact of noises like pose variation.

2.2 Deep Belief Network

Since the deep learning architecture is proposed, it has drawn much interests. The deep learning architecture normally consist of feature detector units arranged in layers. Simple features are extracted by lower layers and put into higher layers to extract more complex features [7]. One of the most typical deep architectures DBN is proposed by Hinton in 2006 [8]. It is a multi-layer generative model composed of unsupervised Restricted Boltzmann Machine which consists of a visible layer as well as a hidden layer. It is build to detect more complex features which can reveal hidden information and higher-order correlations of the data.

To demonstrate its basic principle, a DBN model is shown in Fig. 1. As shown on the left part of Fig. 1, vi (i = 1, 2, …) represents the vector of visible layer; hi (i = 1, 2, …) represent the vector of the hidden layer. As shown on the right part of Fig. 2, a RBM [9] is composed of a visible layer and a hidden layer. The number of the visible units in the lower RBM equals to the number of the hidden units in next higher RBM. Pre-training the DBN model consists of learning the RBMs one by one, during which the learned features of one RBM are put into the next RBM as the input 'data'.

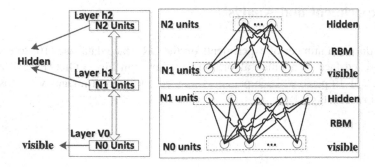

Fig. 1 DBN structure containing two RBMs

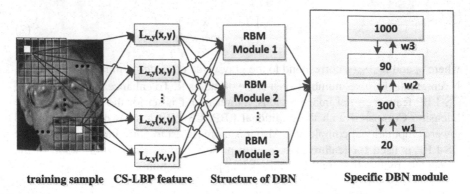

training sample CS-LBP feature Structure of DBN   Specific DBN module

Fig. 2 Process of the proposed algorithm

2.3 DBN Combined with CS-LBP Based Face Recognition

Applying DBN to realistic-sized images is challenging because pixie-level face images are high-dimensional which will cause very high computationally complexity to the training algorithm. Besides DBN usually ignore the local features of images which is important for recognition. Hence the DBN Combined with CS-LBP algorithm is proposed in this part.

As shown in Fig. 2, firstly the local features of the input images are extracted by CS-LBP. Secondly, the obtained features are feed into the DBN instead of original face images as the input of the visible layer. Thirdly, pre-training the DBN from the bottom layer to the top layer. The main process is: training the first layer's network parameters and use its output as the second layer's input data and so on. To obtain the best net parameters, the Back Propagation (BP) algorithm is applied to fine tune the pre-trained DBN. In this paper, the final DBN model contains 3 layers and the number of iterations for each layer is 20. Finally, the Euclidean distance classifier is applied for classifying the face images accurately.

3 Experiment and Analysis

We conducted a number of experiments on the ORL face database [10] to evaluate the proposed face recognition algorithm. As shown in Fig. 3 ORL face databases consisted of 40 persons. Each person contained 10 different images with pose and expression variation.

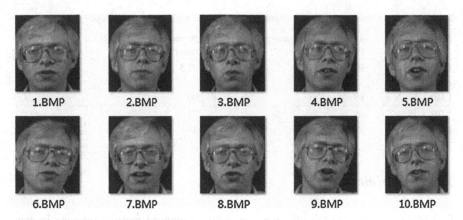

Fig. 3 Images example of ORL database

3.1 Experiment 1

We selected the approximate frontal face image of each person to form the test dataset, and the remaining 9 images of the same person to form the training dataset. The training dataset consist of 360 images, and test dataset contains 40 images. The recognition results are shown in Fig. 4.

Figure 4 shows the comparison between the proposed method and other 3 methods including LBP combined with PCA, LBP combined with DBN and DBN. The experimental result shows that: the rank1 recognition rate of the proposed method is 97.5 %. It is at least 7.5 % higher than the rank1 recognition rate of the other 3 typical algorithm as shown in Fig. 4b–d. Hence, the proposed methods gains obvious performance improvement over the other three typical methods.

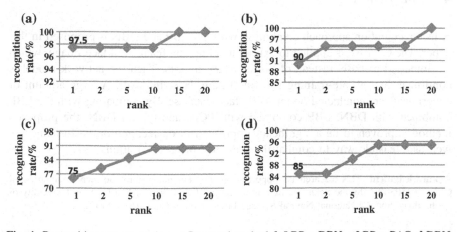

Fig. 4 Recognition rate comparison. a Proposed method. b LBP + DBN. c LBP + PAC. d DBN

Table 1 Comparison of different recognition method on multi-pose face image

Method	Multi-pose face recognition rate (%)	Approximate frontal face recognition rate (%)
Proposed method	92.78	97.5
LBP + DBN	87.89	90
LBP + PCA	65	75
DBN	81.5	85

3.2 Experiment 2

To further demonstrate the effectiveness of the proposed method on face images with pose variation, several other experiments are conducted. Since each person has 10 images with pose variation of different degree, each image of the same person is used to be the test image in turn, which means 10 group of test datasets and training datasets is formed. Then the proposed algorithm is performed on these 10 datasets. The final recognition rate is the average of these ten experiments, which demonstrate the recognition rate of the proposed method on multi-pose face images. Table 1 shows the result.

As shown in Table 1, when employing the face images with pose variation as the test set, the performance of the four algorithm all degrade to a certain extent. However, the proposed method still achieve the highest rank1 recognition rate 92.78 % which is at least 5 % higher than the other three methods. This verifies the proposed algorithm combining the local features and the advantage of DBN gains obvious performance improvement over the multi-pose face image.

4 Conclusion

A face recognition approach combining with CS-LBP and DBN is proposed in this paper. The CS-LBP is applied to extract local texture features of face image, which are imported to DBN instead of original face images. Then the network model is confirmed through pre-training and fine tuning layer by layer. A large amount of experiments are conducted on the ORL face database. By comparing with the LBP combined with DBN, LBP combined with PCA, and typical DBN, the proposed method is proven to be a significant improvement on recognition performance as well as a feasible way to combat the influence of pose variation.

Acknowledgment This research is supported by the National Natural Science Foundation of China (61503005), by the Scientific Research Starting Foundation of North China University of Technology, and the National Natural Science Foundation of China (61371142).

References

1. Klare B, Jain AK (2010) Heterogeneous face recognition: matching NIR to visible light images. In: Pattern recognition international conference on IEEE, pp 1513–1516
2. Shuicheng Y, Dong X, Benyu Z et al (2007) Graph embedding and extension: a general framework for dimensionality reduction. IEEE Trans Pattern Anal Mach Intell 29:40–51
3. Jian Y, David Z, Frangi AF et al (2004) Two-dimensional PCA: a new approach to appearance-based face representation and recognition. IEEE Trans Pattern Anal Mach Intell 26:131–137
4. Arel I, Rose DC, Karnowski TP (2010) Deep machine learning—a new frontier in artificial intelligence research [Research frontier]. IEEE Comput Intell Mag 5:13–18
5. Liang SF, Liu YH, Li-Chen LI (2014) Face recognition under unconstrained based on LBP and deep learning. J Commun 35:154–160
6. Coates A, Ng AY (2011) Selecting receptive fields in deep networks. Adv Neural Inf Process Syst, 2528–2536
7. Lee H, Grosse R, Ranganath R et al (2009) Convolutional deep belief networks for scalable unsupervised learning of hierarchical representations. In: International conference on machine learning, pp 609–616
8. Hinton GE, Salakhutdinov RR (2006) Reducing the dimensionality of data with neural networks. Science 313:504–507
9. Schölkopf B, Platt J, Hofmann T (2007) Greedy layer-wise training of deep networks. Adv Neural Inf Process Syst 19:153–160
10. [Online] Available: http://www.cl.cam.ac.uk/research/dtg/attarchive/facedatabase.html

A Proposal of Methods for Extracting Temporal Information of History-Related Web Document Based on Historical Objects Using Machine Learning Techniques

Jun Lee and YongJin Kwon

Abstract When searching for historical topics on Web search engines, the query results are not displayed in chronological order of documents content. Hence the user has to manually navigate through the search result in order to plot the documents on a time axis. If documents can be sorted in contextual chronological order automatically, it would have various practical applications. To test if this concept is feasible, we analyzed the Annals of the Joseon Dynasty, which is a compilation of daily journals spanning six hundred years, and applied various approaches of machine learning algorithms to estimate the approximate temporal information of historical documents written in modern period. Our experiment showed the accuracy as high as 64 %, suggesting that estimating temporal information based on document text is feasible.

Keywords Temporal information · Temporal extraction · Machine learning · Historical information · Historical object

1 Introduction

In information retrieval process through search engine, some users want to retrieve several documents that are corresponding with specific time period situation. For example, if user wants to search a document that contains the situation before 'Japanese invasions of Korea era', he may use the keyword 'Japanese invasions of Korea' by using searching query. Then, search engine gives all of documents about

J. Lee · Y. Kwon (✉)
Department of Telecommunication and Information Engineering,
Korea Aerospace University, Goyang-City, Gyeonggi-do, Korea
e-mail: yjkwon@kau.ac.kr

J. Lee
e-mail: jun@grrc.kau.ac.kr

© Springer Science+Business Media Singapore 2016
J.J. (Jong Hyuk) Park et al. (eds.), *Advanced Multimedia and Ubiquitous Engineering*, Lecture Notes in Electrical Engineering 393,
DOI 10.1007/978-981-10-1536-6_38

285

'Japanese invasions of Korea' disregarding time period in order. It makes user to do an additional work. In addition, a large percentage of cases which is related to historical documents have different time period between generation date of a document and record time of contents. If time period in document contents can be extracted, it may facilitate effective information for retrieval and various applications. Consequently, we pursue a research extracting time period of Joseon era's historical documents by using historic literature for Joseon era in order to deduct the time period corresponding with document content in this paper. We define historical objects based on historic literature that was collected from web and confirm a possibility of extracting time period of web document by machine learning techniques. Finally, we'll evaluate the result of temporal indexing accuracy and improvement.

2   Data for Training and Testing

This section introduces the ancient journal set used machine learning in our method and presents a definition of historical objects, which are identified during data preprocessing. Ancient documents record what was happening at the time of recording, hence the temporal information is assumed to be accurate. The Annals of the Joseon Dynasty used in our study has daily recordings of events, thus time information retrieval is straightforward and thus appropriate as a training data.

For machine learning, we define historical objects and use them for preprocessing. The training and test data are analyzed to identify morphemes and filter out unused words to extract historical objects. Modern historical documents are then processed to determine their temporal information based on historical objects.

2.1   Data Set for Machine Learning

The following explains the details of training and testing data used in our machine learning algorithm. We used the Annals of the Joseon Dynasty written over 517 years (1394–1911) for training. This daily journal records the events and facts surrounding the kings during the Joseon Dynasty, and it comprises of 1893 separate books. Events taking place in the government were recorded for each day in chronological order, hence it could function as a great source of temporal information.

The entire volume of the Annals has been previously translated to the modern Korean and put in a digital format. This has been made available for public view, and we created a wrapper tailored for the Annals to extract the text and temporal information, which were stored in a database for machine learning.

Next, we also retrieved modern historical web documents from search engines to test with our temporal information extractor. Documents containing fewer than 10 historical objects were determined to be incorrectly retrieved for reasons of homophones and the like, hence these documents were excluded from preprocessing.

We then used historical objects as search words and collected 100 web documents per query. The collected documents were preprocessed for morpheme analysis. Out of the preprocessed documents, we randomly selected 50 paragraphs for testing and estimated their temporal information. The results were checked against their true values to evaluate the estimation performance.

2.2 Data Preprocessing for Historical Object

The focus of preprocessing in our work is historical objects that appear in the ancient journals. These objects are used as keywords in query. Historical objects are of the following types in our work: individuals, historic items, place names, and events. This is based on the observation of most popular historical encyclopedias in use. For example, the Integrated Korean History Database organizes the data in the broad categories of individuals, maps, historic items, books, and research papers. The Korean Folk Culture Encyclopedia has its glossary organized in the categories of individuals, place names, books, and events. For data preprocessing, we used the Korean Morpheme Analyzer (KLT) [15], and picked nouns, from which non-historical objects were excluded. We were able to identify approximately 28 K historical objects.

Historical objects are used in estimating the temporal information of the input text. The decision of using historical objects in this is based on a survey result that readers of history use the same strategy as shown in Fig. 1.

We polled 10 individuals who are non-experts in history. We provided 10 randomly selected historical paragraphs and asked them the type of clues they used in guessing the temporal information. As shown in Fig. 2, most of the participants used the name of the king. The next most frequently used item was the name of events. Some used prepositions or postpositions for clues. We held an assumption based on the survey results that people use historical objects in estimating the temporal information of a given text.

Fig. 1 Our survey result of how people determine the temporal information of a given text

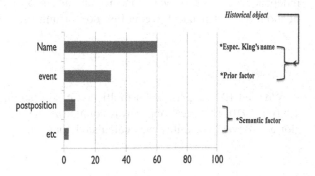

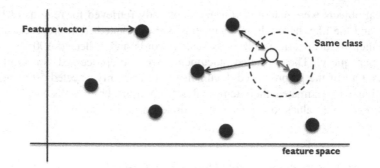

Fig. 2 K-NN algorithm

3 Extracting Temporal Information from Modern Historical Documents Using Machine Learning Algorithm

This section describes how we applied machine learning algorithms to extract temporal information from text. We employed a host of machine learning algorithms to test the feasibility of accurate temporal information extraction: Naive Bayes Classifier as a supervised learning algorithm, Co-EM as a semi-supervised learning algorithm, and K-NN, which is object-based. A similarity filtering method is also presented to enhance the result. The Joseon Dynasty period from 1934 to 1911 was divided for each decade and this was the smallest unit of temporal information for training and testing. Fifty separate texts were collected for testing and our estimate results were checked against their true values.

3.1 Temporal Information Extraction Using Naive Bayes Classifier

The Naive Bayes Classifier is based on Bayes' theorem that assumes strong independence between events and it generally shows solid performance in classification. For independent events that do not influence each other, Eq. (1) holds:

$$p(C|F_1, \ldots F_n) = \frac{p(C)p(F_1, \ldots F_n|C)}{p(F_1, \ldots F_n)} \tag{1}$$

We used 10-year periods for multiclass-case, resulting in 63 different cases from 1390 to 1910. Historical object was counted in the Annals for each 10-year period slot and Bayes probability was calculated for each historical object. Then the test data was analyzed for historical objects. The object with the highest Bayes probability in the input text was used in determining the temporal information.

$$classify(f_1,\ldots,f_n) = argmax_c p(C_k = c_k) \prod_{i=1}^{n} p(F_i = f_i | C_k = c_k)$$

(2)

$$C_k : year, \; F_i : objects$$

Historical objects have already been calculated for probability for each decade based on the Annals, and this probability is reflected in estimating the temporal information of the test data. If a decade has a high count of a historical object and this object is seen often in an input text, then that decade is likely to be assigned as the temporal information of the input text. A decade that satisfies Eq. (2) is selected as the temporal information for input text; probability for each decade is calculated as in Eq. (3).

$$P(C|F_n) = argmax \left(\prod_{i=1}^{n} P(F_i|C_k) \right)_{k=1390}^{1910}$$

(3)

As noted above, there is an assumption behind Naive Bayes Classifier that the appearance of each historical object is independent. We addressed the zero probability value problem by assigning 1 as the minimum count for each historical object for all decade periods.

Our implementation of Naive Bayes Classifier correctly estimated 46 % of the input, or 23 texts out of 50. Despite the low accuracy, the result is meaningful because it shows temporal information extraction in this approach is indeed feasible.

Out of the 23 correctly estimated test cases, we could observe that there were more than 10 occurrences of historical objects in the 22 test cases implying that a higher number of historical objects improved accuracy. This finding is consistent with our finding with the survey that historical objects are used in temporal information inference.

3.2 Temporal Information Extraction Using Co-EM Algorithm

The next algorithm we used was Co-EM as a semi-supervised learning algorithm. Co-EM uses expectation maximization for semi-supervised learning, and two sets of data are mixed together repeatedly and applied for training a classifier. The algorithm is detailed in Table 1 [16].

Table 1 Co-EM algorithm

Co-EM algorithm
1 Labeled data set L, unlabeled data set U, let U1 be empty, let U2 = U
2 Iterate the following
1 Train a classifier h1 from the feature set (instance) X1 of L and U1
2 Probabilistically label all the unlabeled data in U2 using h1
3 Train a classifier h2 from U2
4 Let U1 = U, probabilistically label all the unlabeled data in U1 using h2
3 Combine h1 and h2

First, a classifier, h1, is trained using training data. Afterwards, unsupervised data is applied for training. With the unsupervised data, another classifier, h2, is trained. This process is performed repeatedly.

Co-EM algorithm was initially designed to handle only two sets of data, but we modified it to accommodate the dozens of 10-year periods in the Joseon Period

$$P(Y|X_1 = k) = \sum_j P(Y|X_2 = j)P(X_2 = j|X_1 = k)$$

$$P(Y|X_2 = j) = \sum_j P(Y|X_1 = k)P(X_1 = k|X_2 = j)$$

$$(4)$$

$$X_1 = unlableddata(historical\ objects\ in\ web\ document's)$$

$$X_2 = labeleddata(each\ year's\ historical\ objects)$$

$$r = 1390 - 1910(per\ 10\ year)$$

First, the test data is defined as a set, h2, and then each 10-year period of the rest of the Joseon Period as a set, h1. Based on the historical objects that appear in the test data, the object occurrence probability is calculated using the update rule of Eq. (4). This maximize probability value each 10-year period's sets. Afterwards, the probability for each 10-year period is multiplied by test data probability to determine the temporal information.

$$classify(X) = argmax\,P(Y|X_1) \times P(Y|X_2)$$

$$(5)$$

Our implementation of Co-EM algorithm correctly retrieved temporal information for 32 test cases out of 50, a 64 % accuracy. The result is superior to what we obtained with Naive Bayes Classifier, but it has to perform Co-EM algorithm for each 10-year period for each historical object to calculate probability, hence the time complexity is higher. Nonetheless, the performance of 64 % is promising to be employed for practical use. Semi-supervised learning algorithms are known to be heavily influenced by non-supervised training data, hence we expect to improve the accuracy after more data is collected in the future, which we will work on in a later work.

3.3 Temporal Information Extraction with Object-Based Training

In contrast with the two probability-based algorithms above, this section describes an object-based machine learning algorithm for temporal information retrieval.

K-NN algorithm shows economic time complexity and reasonable performance. We chose this over other object-based algorithms such as the Lazy Algorithm because there are multiple target sets and classification is performed in a multi-dimensional space.

In K-NN algorithm, the target set is constructed with feature vectors, which are placed in feature space. Then test data consisting of feature vectors are also placed in feature space. The closest target set is determined as the class that the test data belongs to, as illustrated in Fig. 2.

Here, K signifies the number of target sets that the test data can be classified to. Since we only need one result which is a ten-year period, we set $K = 1$ and 1-NN algorithm is used. The most important point to consider in using K-NN algorithm is converting target sets to feature vectors to place in feature space.

In our work, we used TF/IDF (term frequency/inverse document frequency) to accomplish this. TF/IDF indicates how often a specified item appears in a given document and it signifies the importance of the item. If an item appears often within the document set, then it implies the item is not really important. This is called document frequency (DF), the inverse of which is called inverse document frequency (IDF).

Capturing on this characteristic of TF/IDF, we assigned negative weights to the more frequently used words throughout the Annals for IDF; words more frequently used for specific 10-year periods were given weight (word occurrence count) for TF. The feature vector constructed this way can be expressed as in Eq. (6).

$$F_y = w_1x_1, w_2x_2, \ldots, w_nx_n$$

$$Weight\, w_i = 1 - |norm(x_i\, total\, sum\, frequency)|\, (0\, to\, 1) \qquad (6)$$

$$Instance\, value\, x_i = |norm(x_i\, current\, year\, frequency)|\, (0\, to\, 1)$$

Here, weight is equivalent to IDF. If a specific object appears frequently throughout the Annals, then it is given a negative weight. Instance value is used as TF, and the occurrence for each 10-year period was used as weight.

The feature vector for each period as in Eq. (6) was placed in the feature space and the same was performed for test data, and the feature set that has the closest vector distance was classified as the final temporal information.

Our implementation of 1-NN algorithm to estimate temporal information showed an accuracy of 24 %, or 12 cases out of 50. The reason behind this significantly lower accuracy over the two previous methods is due to the characteristic of object-based learning that requires a large number of test data. The 1-NN algorithm as implemented is not ideal for practical use, however, K could be raised

J. Lee and Y. Kwon

to 3 for another set of training, which may enhance the accuracy. One important historical object is individuals. The average lifespan of a person during Joseon Period was 50–60 years, and they usually appear in the Annals for about 30 years, which may also have contributed to the disappointing accuracy. We then included the second and third feature vectors after applying 1-NN algorithm, and the accuracy was boosted to 65 %. These points all will be addressed in our future work.

4 Conclusion and Suggestion for Further Research

In this paper, we tested the feasibility of extracting temporal information by means of a few machine learning algorithms including Naive Bayes Classifier, Co-EM algorithm, and K-NN. The Annals of the Joseon Dynasty was referenced as a training data to test other modern historical documents. We chose to use supervised, semi-supervised and object-based learning methods to find out the feasibility since research work on temporal information is just starting to draw attention.

Despite the relatively low performance of the algorithms, this paper is significant in showing the feasibility of temporal information extraction from document text. In doing so, we used the Annals of the Joseon Dynasty as the formal data to estimate the temporal information of modern web documents. We further enhanced the proposed methods by extending with similarity filtering and this enhanced both accuracy and time complexity, which we verified through experiments. Historical objects were defined that help estimate temporal information by capturing on how humans do when no immediate temporal data is suggested, and we implemented this over machine learning algorithms.

In our future work, we will focus on semi-supervised learning algorithms for temporal information extraction and indexing in order to improve the estimation accuracy. The object-based learning algorithm as implemented in this paper will also be worked on to identify further possibilities.

We will also extend the work to non-formal web documents such as news articles or weblog posts to retrieve temporal information. Such advances will help develop data search services to add time-axis to their keyword-based searches, and it will also have many applications such as identifying reflex points where data content changes.

Acknowledgments This work was supported by the GRRC program of Gyeonggi province. [GRRC2015-B01 Ambient mobile broadcasting service system development]

References

1. Allen JF (1983) Maintaining knowledge about temporal intervals. Commun ACM 26 (11):832–843
2. Alonso O, Gertz M, Baeza-Yates R (2007) On the value of temporal information in information retrieval. SIGIR Forum 41(2):35–41
3. Pustejovsky J, Castãno JM et al (2008) TimeML: robust specification of event and temporal expressions in text. In: Proceedings of the AAAI spring symposium on new directions in question answering, pp 28–34
4. Alonso O, Strotgen J, Baeza-Yates R, Gertz M (2011) Temporal information retrieval: challenges and opportunities. In: International temporal web analytics workshop, pp 1–8
5. Kolomiyets O, Moens M-F (2009) Meeting TempEval-2: shallow approach for temporal tagger. In: Proceedings of the workshop on semantic evaluations: recent achievements and future directions (SEW '09), pp 52–57
6. Alonso O, Gertz M, Baeza-Yates R (2009) Clustering and exploring search results using timeline constructions. In: Proceedings of the 18th ACM international conference on information and knowledge management (CIKM '09), pp 97–106
7 Makkonen J, Ahonen M, Ito H (2003) Following temporal information in topic detection and tracking. In: Proceedings of 7th European conference on research and advanced technology for digital libraries (ECDL '03), pp 393–404
8. Alonso O, Baeza-Yates R, Gertz M (2009) Effectiveness of temporal snippets. In: Proceedings of the workshop on web search result summarization and presentation (WSSP 09), pp 1–4
9. Qamra A, Tseng B, Chang E (2006) Mining blog stories using community-based and temporal clustering. In: Proceedings of the 15th ACM international conference on information and knowledge management (CIKM '06), pp 58–67
10. Swan R, Allan J (2000) TimeMine: visualizing automatically constructed timelines. In: Proceedings of the 23rd annual international ACM SIGIR conference on research and development in information retrieval (SIGIR '00), p 393
11. Jatowt A, Kanazawa K, Oyama S, Tanaka K (2009) Supporting analysis of future-related information in news archives and the web. In: Proceedings of the 9th joint conference on digital libraries (JCDL '09)
12. Shaparenko B, Caruana R, Gehrke J, Joachims T (2005) Identifying temporal patterns and key players in document collections. In: Proceedings of the IEEE ICDM workshop on temporal data mining: algorithms, theory and applications (TDM '05), pp 165–174
13. Toyoda M, Kitsuregawa M (2006) What's really new on the web? Identifying new pages from a series of unstable web snapshots. In: WWW2006: Proceedings of the 15th international world wide web conference. ACM Press, Edinburgh, Scotland, pp 233–241
14. Strotgen J, Gertz M, Popov P (2010) Extraction and exploration of spatio-temporal information in documents. In: Proceedings of the 6th workshop on geographic information retrieval (GIR '10), pp 1–8
15. Kang S-S, Zhang B-T (1996) A general morphological analyzer and spelling checker for the Korean language using syllable characteristics. J KIISE (B) 23(5)
16. Nigam K, Ghani R (2000) Analyzing the effectiveness and applicability of cotraining. In: Proceedings of the workshop on information and knowledge management

Mobility-Aware TAC Configuration in LTE-Based Mobile Communication Systems

Hyung-Woo Kang and Seok-Joo Koh

Abstract In LTE-based mobile communication systems, a Tracking Area Code (TAC) defines a group of cells for a paging area. In mobile networks, the paging performance is a critical factor to be considered, since it may give large impacts on paging response time as well as paging traffic load in the mobile system. This paper proposes a mobility-aware TAC configuration scheme to increase the paging success rate in mobile communication systems. We first construct an optimization model for TAC configuration by considering the mobility (handover) patterns of mobile users as well as the TAC size and the capacity of paging traffic. Then, we propose the tow algorithms for TAC configuration to maximize the paging success rate, while some constraints are satisfied. From the performance analysis with real traffic data of SK Telecom in Korea, we can see that the proposed TAC configuration provides larger paging success rates than the existing TAC configuration.

Keywords Mobile communication · Paging · Tracking area code · Optimization · Algorithms

1 Introduction

With the advent of smart phones, mobile communication system has been rapidly evolved to the Long Term Evolution (LTE) technology [1, 2]. In the design of the LTE-based mobile system, the paging performance is one of the important factors to be considered. The paging operation is initiated to locate a mobile user in the network, when a call request to the user arrives. In the LTE-based mobile systems, a paging area is defined by a Tracking Area Code (TAC) [3, 4].

H.-W. Kang · S.-J. Koh (✉)
School of Computer Science and Engineering, Kyungpook National University,
Daegu, Korea
e-mail: sjkoh@knu.ac.kr

H.-W. Kang
e-mail: hwkang0621@gmail.com

© Springer Science+Business Media Singapore 2016
J.J. (Jong Hyuk) Park et al. (eds.), *Advanced Multimedia and Ubiquitous Engineering*, Lecture Notes in Electrical Engineering 393,
DOI 10.1007/978-981-10-1536-6_39

In this paper, we address the TAC configuration for paging optimization. In the existing TAC configuration, a network operator arbitrarily constructs a TAC with a group of cells, in which only the geographical topology information of cells is considered. However, this scheme tends to incur low paging success rate, which induces large paging response time and large paging traffic loads.

In this paper, we propose a new mobility-aware TAC configuration scheme for paging optimization. The proposed scheme is based on a mathematical optimization model for TAC configuration, in which we consider the mobility (handover) patterns of mobile users as well as the TAC size and the capacity of paging traffic. Then, we propose the two algorithms for TAC configuration to maximize the paging success rate, while some constraints are satisfied.

This paper is organized as follows. In Sect. 2, we discuss the TAC optimization and the paging operations. In Sect. 3, we describe an optimization model for TAC configuration and propose the TAC configuration algorithms. Section 4 analyzes the paging performance of the existing and proposed schemes in term of the paging success rate, with the real traffic data of SK Telecom. Finally, Sect. 5 concludes this paper.

2 TAC Configuration and Paging Operations

Usually, when a mobile user is connected to a cell in network attachment phase, the user is assigned to the TAC in which the cell is contained. Given a TAC configuration, when a paging is required for a mobile user, the paging process is performed as follows.

If the user was registered with a TAC, then a gaging signal will be broadcast to all of the cells contained in the TAC. This is called the *first* paging. If the first paging request fails (i.e., no response to the paging request from the user), then the *second* paging is performed. In the second paging, the paging request will be broadcast to all of TACs in the area, in which a large amount of paging messages are generated in the network and the paging response time will also get larger. Therefore, it is very important to optimize the TAC configuration so as to maximize the paging success rate for the first paging.

However, at present, most of the mobile operators configure TACs in an arbitrary way. In this TAC configuration, only the geographical location information of cells in the network is considered, and a network manager manually configures a group of cells as a TAC. That is, the mobility or handover pattern was not considered in the TAC configuration. So, if the user has already moved to another cell during a dormant mode, the actual TAC of the user may be changed and thus it is likely that the first paging process fails.

In this paper, we propose a new TAC configuration scheme for paging optimization. The proposed scheme is designed by considering the mobility (handover) patterns of mobile users as well as the TAC size and the capacity of paging traffic.

3 Proposed TAC Configuration Scheme

3.1 Optimization Model for TAC Configuration

We first construct a mathematical optimization model for TAC configuration. Given a network area with many cells, the goal is to find an optimal TAC configuration (mapping from a group of cells to a TAC) by considering the paging traffic and the user mobility between cells. The paging success rate (PSR) will be used as an objective function of the optimization model. The PSR represents the success probability for the first paging.

To derive the optimization model of TAC configuration, we define the following variables and parameters:

- h_{ij}: handover ratio that a user moves from cell i to cell j, where $\Sigma_{j \in N} h_{ij} = 1$;
- λ_i: average paging traffic load for cell i, which is calculated as the number of LTE connections established in the cell,
- d_{ij}: geographical distance between cell i and j;
- N: a group of total cells in the area, with the size of n;
- M: a group of TACs in the area, with the size of m;
- S_{TAC}: the maximally allowable number of cells for a TAC;
- C_{TAC}: the maximum paging traffic load allowable for a TAC;
- D_{TAC}: the maximally allowable distance between two cells contained in a TAC; and
- x_{ik}: a decision variable, $x_{ik} = 1$ if cell i is assigned to TAC k, $x_{ik} = 0$ otherwise.

Based on these variables and parameters, we can make an optimization model for TAC optimization, as shown in Fig. 1.

In the model, the objective function represents the PSR that is defined as the ratio of $\lambda_i \times h_{ij}$ in which a user moves cell i to cell j, and both i and j are assigned to the same TAC k (i.e., $x_{ik} = 1$ and $x_{jk} = 1$).

In addition, we consider the following four constraints:

1. TAC *assignment*: each cell should be assigned to one TAC;
2. TAC *size*: the number of cells assigned to a TAC cannot exceed S_{TAC};

$$\text{Maximize} \quad \Sigma_{k \in M} \Sigma_{i \in N} \Sigma_{j \in N} \lambda_i \times h_{ij} \times x_{ik} \times x_{jk}$$

Subject to (constraint conditions)

$$\Sigma_{k \in M} x_{ik} = 1, \text{ for all } i \in N \tag{1}$$
$$\Sigma_{i \in N} x_{ik} \leq S_{TAC}, \text{ for all } k \in M \tag{2}$$
$$\Sigma_{i \in N} \lambda_i \times x_{ik} \leq C_{TAC}, \text{ for all } k \in M \tag{3}$$
$$d_{ij} \times x_{ik} \times x_{jk} \leq D_{TAC} \text{ for all } i, j \in N, k \in M \tag{4}$$
$$x_{ik} = 1 \text{ or } 0, \text{ for all } i \in N, k \in M \tag{5}$$

Fig. 1 TAC Optimization Model

3. *Paging traffic capacity*: the paging traffic load for a TAC cannot exceed C_{TAC}; and

4. *Distance*: the distance between any pair of two cells within a TAC cannot exceed D_{TAC}.

It is noted that this optimization problem is similar to the knapsack problem [5], which is known as an NP-complete problem. The TAC optimization problem can be reduced to the knapsack problem by considering only a single TAC (i.e., m = 1) and by taking only the constraints (3) and (5). Accordingly, we need to design some heuristic algorithms to solve the TAC optimization problem.

3.2 Optimization Model for TAC Configuration

To solve the TAC optimization problem, we propose the two algorithms: *TAC reconfiguration* and *local improvement*. We apply these two algorithms sequentially and iteratively, until no further improvement of the PSR objective function is made.

3.2.1 TAC Reconfiguration with a Center Cell

Given a TAC configuration, we first find a *center* cell for each TAC. Such a center cell will be determined by calculating the distances from a candidate center cell to the other cells within the TAC. Then, we define a center cell as the cell with the minimum distance to the other cells.

In the next step, a feasible TAC will be gradually configured, starting from the initial center cell. for each TAC k, let $S(k)$ be the set of cells contained in TAC k. We also define S^* as the set of the remaining cells that have not been assigned to any TAC. Initially, $S(k)$ contains only the center cell of TAC k. Then, we select a cell $j \in S^*$ that gives the largest mobility rate from the cells in $S(k)$, $\Sigma_{i \in S(k)} \lambda_i \times h_{ij}$. Now, the selected cell j will be assigned to TAC k (i.e., $S(k) = S(k) + \{j\}$), if the inclusion of cell j satisfies the constraints (2), (3), and (4) of Fig. 1. These operations will be repeated until all cells are assigned to one of the TACs in the area.

3.2.2 Local Improvement by TAC Change

The local improvement algorithm is used to find a more optimal solution, based on the TAC configuration obtained in Sect. 3.2.1. For the given TAC configuration, we try to change the TAC of a cell into another TAC. A trial of TAC change will be accepted, only if the PSR value is improved and the resulting TAC configuration satisfies the constraints (2), (3), and (4) of Fig. 1. Otherwise, we do not change the TAC of the cell. These procedures are performed until no improvement of PSR is made for all cells.

4 Experimental Results

4.1 Test Networks

In experiments for performance analysis, we use the real-world data of network topology, user paging traffic, and mobility rates, which are given by *SK Telecom* in Korea. The proposed TAC configuration scheme was applied to a total of 20 target areas, and we calculate the PSR values.

For experiments, the default parameter values are set as follows: $S_{TAC} = 150$, $C_{TAC} = 2100$, $D_{TAC} = 1/2 *$ the maximum distance between cells in target area.

4.2 Results and Discussion

In experiments, the distance between two cells is calculated by using the Euclidean distance. As a performance metric, we calculate the *paging success probability (PSP)* = PSR/$\Sigma_{i \in N} \lambda_i$, which represents the ratio of successfully paged traffics over total paging traffics in the network. Table 1 shows the results of the existing and proposed TAC configuration schemes for the target area 27, which has n (total number of cells) = 1498 and m (the number of TACs) = 15.

Table 1 TAC configurations for target area 27

TAC Index	Existing configuration			Proposed configuration		
	# of cells	Maximum distance	PTL	# of cells	Maximum distance	PTL
2700	146	13040	1151	97	17750	677
2701	145	9378	838	100	17020	662
2702	142	17778	1126	100	32191	913
2703	138	10249	1184	100	8938	652
2704	125	4139894	1090	100	11799	635
2705	145	8811	926	100	13202	1229
2706	171	35699	941	99	99153	336
2707	135	90849	821	100	18925	307
2708	141	4989	1074	100	4501	782
2709	152	4144829	429	100	12687	580
270A	2	0	0	100	11385	535
270B	54	95494	48	99	19922	390
270C	1	0	34	100	18619	850
270D	2	1121	0	99	17411	524
270E	5	3837	0	104	90164	589
PSP	72.66 %			87.30 %		

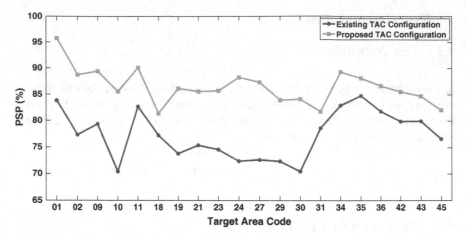

Fig. 2 Paging success probability for 20 target areas (color figure online)

For the existing TAC configuration in the table, we can see that TAC 2706 contains 171 cells, whereas TAC 270A, 270C, 270D, 270E have smaller than 10 cells. This implies that the existing TAC configuration is severely unbalanced in terms of the TAC size. We can also see such unbalanced configuration in the viewpoint of the maximum distance between cells in TAC and the paging traffic load (PTL) per TAC. Overall, this result gives the PSP of 72.66 %.

In the table, on the other hand, we can see that the proposed scheme leads to a balanced TAC configuration. Most of the TACs have the TAC size of a minimum 97 cells and up to 104 cells. In the proposed scheme, the maximum distance between cells and PTL in TAC are also equally distributed for all TACs. Finally, the proposed TAC configuration provides the PSP of 87.30 %, which is higher than the existing scheme by 14.64 %.

Finally, Fig. 2 compares the PSP values of the 20 target areas for the existing and proposed TAC configuration schemes. From the figure, we can see that the proposed scheme provides greater PSPs than the existing scheme. Overall, it seems that the proposed TAC configuration scheme can improve the PSPs of the existing scheme by 10.16 % on the average and 15.16 % in the maximum.

5 Conclusions

In this paper, we presented a new TAC configuration scheme to maximize the paging success rates in LTE-based mobile communication networks, with a mathematical optimization model. The proposed scheme consists of the two algorithms: TAC reconfiguration with a center cell and local improvement by TAC change.

By experimentations with real-world data of SK Telecom in Korea, the proposed scheme is compared with the existing scheme in terms of the paging success rate.

From the results, we can see that the proposed scheme provides more optimized TAC configurations than the existing scheme by maximizing the paging success rate. It is also noted that the proposed scheme can give much more balanced TAC configurations, compared to the existing scheme.

Acknowledgments This study was supported by the BK21 plus project (SW Human Resource Development Program for supporting Smart Life) funded by the Ministry of Education, School of Computer Science and Engineering, Kyungpook National University, Korea (21A20131600005).

References

1. David Astély et al (2009) LTE: the evolution of mobile broadband. IEEE Commun Mag 47 (4):44–51
2. 3GPP TS 36.300 (2008) Evolved universal terrestrial radio access (E-UTRA) and evolved universal terrestrial radio access network (E-UTRAN). Overall Description Stage 2
3. Lyberopoulos GL et al (1995) Intelligent paging strategies for third generation mobile telecommunication systems. IEEE Trans Veh Technol 44(3):543–554
4. Amotz Bar-Noy et al (2013) Paging mobile users in cellular networks: optimality versus complexity and simplicity. Theoret Comput Sci 470:23–35
5. Johnsonbaugh R, Marcus Schaefer M (2004) Algorithms. Prentice Hall

Two-Stage Estimation Filtering for Temporarily Uncertain Systems

Pyung Soo Kim

Abstract In this paper, a two-stage estimation filter is proposed to consider both nominal system and temporarily uncertain system by applying infinite memory structure (IMS) and finite memory structure (FMS) estimation filters selectively. One of two filtered estimates is selected as the valid estimate according to presence or absence of uncertainty. A detection rule is developed to indicate presence or absence of uncertainty and select the valid filtered estimate from IMS and FMS filtered estimates. The detection rule consists of uncertainty presence and absence detections. Two kinds of test variables for the detection rule are defined using the chi-squared distribution with one degree of freedom. Finally, to verify the proposed two-stage estimation filter, computer simulations are performed. Simulation results show that the proposed two-stage estimation filter works well for both nominal system and temporarily uncertain system.

Keywords Finite memory structure filter · Infinite memory structure filter · Two-stage estimation · Detection rule

1 Introduction

The infinite memory structure (IMS) filter such as the well-known Kalman filter has been used generally and widely for the optimal state estimation using all past measurements and thus applied successfully for various areas [1, 2]. As an alternative to the IMS filter, the finite memory structure (FMS) filter has been developed [3, 4] and also applied successfully for various areas [5–8]. It has been known that the FMS filter has some good properties such as unbiasedness and deadbeat, which cannot be obtained by the IMS filter. Moreover, in contrast to the IMS filter, the

P.S. Kim (✉)
System Software Solution Lab, Korea Polytechnic University,
237 Sangidaehak-ro, Siheung-si, Gyeonggi-do 429-793, Korea
e-mail: pskim@kpu.ac.kr

© Springer Science+Business Media Singapore 2016   303
J.J. (Jong Hyuk) Park et al. (eds.), *Advanced Multimedia and Ubiquitous Engineering*, Lecture Notes in Electrical Engineering 393,
DOI 10.1007/978-981-10-1536-6_40

FMS filter is inherently bounded input/bounded output stable and more robust against temporary modeling uncertainties and round-off errors.

As shown in [3, 4], IMS and FMS filters have shown that there could exist the trade-off between the estimation error and the tracking ability for temporarily uncertain systems. Of course, the IMS filter can outperform the FMS filter for the nominal system that has no temporary uncertainty. However, for the temporarily uncertain system, the estimation error of the FMS filter is smaller than that of the IMS filter on the interval where modeling uncertainty exists. In addition, the convergence of the estimation error for the FMS filter is much faster than that of the IMS filter after temporary modeling uncertainty disappears, which shows the superiority of the FMS filter in terms of the tracking ability. Therefore, the FMS filter can outperform the IMS filter when applied to temporarily uncertain systems, although the FMS filter is designed with no consideration for robustness. One possible explanation for this is that the estimation error and the tracking ability of the estimation filter might be closely related to the memory length for past measurements. It can have smaller estimation error as the memory length increases, which improves the filtering performance. However, as the memory length increases, the convergence time of a filtered estimate becomes long.

Therefore, this paper proposes a two-stage estimation filter to consider both nominal system and temporarily uncertain system by applying IMS and FMS estimation filters selectively. One of two filtered estimates is selected as the valid estimate according to presence or absence of uncertainty. A detection rule is developed to indicate presence or absence of uncertainty and select the valid filtered estimate from IMS and FMS filtered estimates. The detection rule consists of uncertainty presence and absence detections. Two kinds of test variables for the detection rule are defined using the chi-squared distribution with one degree of freedom. Finally, the proposed two-stage estimation filter is verified by computer simulations. Simulation results show that the proposed two-stage estimation filter works well for both nominal system and temporarily uncertain system.

2 IMS and FMS Estimation Filtering

Consider the following linear discrete-time state-space signal model:

$$x_{i+1} = Ax_i + Gw_i, \ z_i = Cx_i + v_i, \tag{1}$$

where $x_i \in R^n$ is unknown state vector and $z_i \in R^q$ is a measured observation vector. At the initial time i_0 of system, the state x_{i_0} is a random variable with a mean $\bar{x}_{i_0}$ and a covariance Σ_{i_0}. The system noise $w_i \in R^p$ and the observation noise $v_i \in R^q$ are zero-mean white Gaussian whose covariances Q and R.

The infinite memory structure (IMS) filter such as the well-known Kalman filter provides an optimal state estimate $\hat{x}_i^{ims}$ for the system state x_i as follows [12]:

$$\hat{x}_{i+1}^{ims} = A(I + \Sigma_i C^T R^{-1} C)^{-1} (\hat{x}_i^{ims} + \Sigma_i C^T R^{-1} z_i),$$
$$\Sigma_{i+1} = A(I + \Sigma_i C^T R^{-1} C)^{-1} \Sigma_i A^T + GQG^T, \tag{2}$$

where $\hat{x}_{i_0}^{ims} = \bar{x}_{i_0}$ and Σ_i is the error covariance of the estimate $\hat{x}_i$ with initial value Σ_{i_0}. The IMS filter has been used generally and widely for the optimal state estimation using all past measurements and thus applied successfully for various areas. However, the IMS filter tends to accumulate the estimation error as time goes and can show even divergence phenomenon for temporary modeling uncertainties and round-off errors because it utilizes all past measurements accomplished by equaling weighting and has a recursive formulation.

Thus, as an alternative to the IMS filter, the finite memory structure (FMS) filter has been developed under a weighted least square criterion using only the most recent finite measurements on the window $[i - M, i]$. The window initial time $i - M$ will be denoted by i_M hereafter for simplicity The FMS filter provides an optimal state estimate $\hat{x}_i^{fms}$ for the system state x_i as follows [3, 4]

$$\hat{x}_{i+1}^{fms} = \Omega_M^{-1} \hat{\eta}_i$$
$$\hat{\eta}_{i_M + j + 1} = \left[I + A^{-T} (\Omega_j + C^T R^{-1} C) A^{-1} GQG^T \right]^{-1} A^{-T} [\hat{\eta}_{i_M + j} + C^T R^{-1} z_{i_M + j}],$$
$$\Omega_{i+1} = \left[I + A^{-T} (\Omega_j + C^T R^{-1} C) A^{-1} GQG^T \right]^{-1} A^{-T} (\Omega_j + C^T R^{-1} C) A^{-1},$$
$$0 \leq j \leq M. \tag{3}$$

The FMS filter has been developed and also applied successfully for various areas. It has been known that the FMS filter has some good properties such as unbiasedness and deadbeat, which cannot be obtained by the IMS filter. Moreover, in contrast to the IMS filter, the FMS filter is inherently bounded input/bounded output stable and more robust against temporary modeling uncertainties and round-off errors.

3   Two-Stage Estimation Filtering

Sometimes, temporary modeling uncertainties can be considered in actual situations. For the temporarily uncertain system, the estimation error of the FMS filter is smaller than that of the IMS filter on the interval where modeling uncertainty exists. In addition, the convergence of the estimation error for the FMS filter is much faster than that of the IMS filter after temporary modeling uncertainty disappears, which shows the superiority of the FMS filter in terms of the tracking ability. Therefore, the FMS filter can outperform the IMS filter when applied to temporarily uncertain systems, although the FMS filter is designed with no consideration for robustness.

In this section, a two-stage estimation filter is proposed to consider both nominal system and temporarily uncertain system by applying IMS and FMS estimation filters selectively. One of two filtered estimates is selected as the valid estimate according to presence or absence of uncertainty. That is, the IMS filtered estimate $\hat{x}_i^{ims}$ is selected as the valid estimate $\hat{x}_i$ for the nominal system and the FMS filtered estimate $\hat{x}_i^{fms}$ is selected as the valid estimate $\hat{x}_i$ for the temporarily uncertain system as follows:

$$\begin{array}{ll} \hat{x}_i^{ims} & \text{if norminal system} \\ \hat{x}_i^{fms} & \text{if temporarily uncertain system} \end{array}$$

To indicate presence or absence of uncertainty and select the valid filtered estimate from IMS and FMS filtered estimates, a detection rule is developed. The detection rule consists of uncertainty presence and absence detections. The uncertainty presence means that the uncertainty occurs from the nominal system. A test variable t_i^{ims} for the uncertainty presence detection is defined by the estimation error of IMS filtered estimate $\hat{x}_i^{ims}$ as follows:

$$t_i^{ims} = \left(x_i - \hat{x}_i^{ims}\right)^T \Sigma_i^{-1} \left(x_i - \hat{x}_i^{ims}\right)$$

where Σ_i is the estimation error covariance of $x_i - \hat{x}_i^{ims}$ and obtained from (2). The uncertainty absence means that the uncertainty disappears. A test variable t_i^{fms} for the uncertainty absence detection is defined by the estimation error of FMS filtered estimate $\hat{x}_i^{fms}$ as follows:

$$t_i^{fms} = \left(x_i - \hat{x}_i^{fms}\right)^T \Omega_M^{-1} \left(x_i - \hat{x}_i^{fms}\right)$$

where Ω_M is the estimation error covariance of $x_i - \hat{x}_i^{fms}$ and obtained from (3).

Note that two test variables are in the chi-squared distribution with one degree of freedom. Therefore, when an uncertainty appears in proportion to the power of the uncertainty, the test variable t_i^{ims} increases from the chi-squared distribution. On the other hand, when an uncertainty disappears in proportion to the power of the uncertainty, the test variable t_i^{fms} decreases from the chi-squared distribution. Thus, presence or absence of uncertainty can be detected by comparing the test variable t_i^{ims} or t_i^{fms} to a threshold value γ. The probability of false alarm (PFA) of the test variables can be easily determined using the chi-squared distribution with one degree of freedom function as follows:

$$PFA = 1 - P_{\chi^2}(\gamma_*) = 1 - \frac{1}{2.5066} \int_0^{\gamma_*} \varepsilon^{-1/2} e^{-\varepsilon/2} d\varepsilon$$

where γ_* stands for the threshold value.

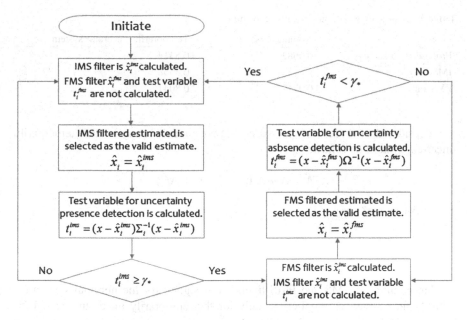

Fig. 1 Operation flow for two stage estimation filtering (color figure online)

Thus, when $t_i^{ims} \geq \gamma_*$, the FMS filtered estimate $\hat{x}_i^{fms}$ is selected as the valid estimate $\hat{x}_i$, which means that the uncertainty occurs. And then, when $t_i^{fms} < \gamma_*$, the IMS filtered estimate $\hat{x}_i^{ims}$ is selected as the valid estimate $\hat{x}_i$, which means that the uncertainty disappears as follows (Fig. 1):

$$\hat{x}_i = \begin{cases} \hat{x}_i^{ims} & if \ t_i^{ims} \geq \gamma_* \\ \hat{x}_i^{fms} & if \ t_i^{fms} < \gamma_* \end{cases}.$$

4 Computer Simulations

Computer simulations are performed for a discrete-time state-space signal model. The nominal system for the state-space signal model is as follows:

$$A = \begin{bmatrix} 1.54 & -0.7379 \\ 0.7379 & 0 \end{bmatrix}, \quad G = \begin{bmatrix} 1 \\ 1 \end{bmatrix}, \quad C = [1 \quad 1]. \tag{4}$$

The IMS filter (2) and the FMS filter (3) are designed for this nominal system (4). System and measurement noise covariances are taken as $Q = 0.25$ and $R = 1$, respectively. The window length is taken as $M = 10$. When temporary uncertainties

Table 1 Total average for simulations of 40 runs

Filters	Nominal system	Temporarily uncertain system
Proposed two-stage	0.0682	0.5314
IMS only		0.5358
FMS only	0.0747	0.8041

are considered, the actual state-space signal model becomes the temporarily uncertain system as follows

$$\bar{A} = A + \Delta A, \quad \bar{C} = C + \Delta C, \tag{5}$$

where ΔA and ΔC are

$$\Delta A = \begin{bmatrix} \delta_i & 0 \\ 0 & \delta_i \end{bmatrix}, \quad \Delta A = [0.5\delta_i \quad 0.5\delta_i], \quad \delta_i = 0.1 \quad for \ 100 \leq i \leq 150.$$

Hence, although IMS and FMS filters are designed for the nominal system (4) with A and C, they are applied actually for the temporarily uncertain system (5) with $\bar{A}$ and $\bar{C}$. To make a clearer comparison of estimation performances, simulations of 40 runs are performed and each single simulation run lasts 400 samples. For both nominal system (4) and temporarily uncertain system (5), the filtering performance is compared by the mean of root-squared estimation error for simulations of 40 runs. Table 1 shows the total average for simulations of 40 runs. For the nominal system (4) that has no temporary uncertainty all the time, the proposed two-stage estimation filter can outperform the FMS filter. For the temporarily uncertain system (5), the proposed two-stage estimation filter can outperform the IMS filter. Therefore, the proposed two-stage estimation filter can work for both nominal system and temporarily uncertain system.

5 Concluding Remarks

This paper has proposed a two-stage estimation filter to consider both nominal system and temporarily uncertain system by applying IMS and FMS estimation filters selectively. One of two filtered estimates is selected as the valid estimate according to presence or absence of uncertainty. A detection rule has been developed to indicate presence or absence of uncertainty and select the valid filtered estimate from IMS and FMS filtered estimates. The detection rule consists of uncertainty presence and absence detections. Two kinds of test variables for the detection rule have been defined using the chi-squared distribution with one degree of freedom. Computer simulations have shown that the proposed two-stage estimation filter works well for both nominal system and temporarily uncertain system.

References

1. Simon D (2011) Kalman filtering with state constraints: a survey of linear and nonlinear algorithms. IET Control Theory Appl 4(8):1303–1318
2. Faragher R (2012) Understanding the basis of the Kalman filter via a simple and intuitive derivation. IEEE Signal Process Mag 29(5):128–132
3. Kim PS (2010) An alternative FIR filter for state estimation in discrete-time systems. Digit Signal Proc 20(3):935–943
4. Zhao S, Shmaliy YS, Huang B, Liu F (2015) Minimum variance unbiased FIR filter for discrete time-variant systems. Automatica 53(2):355–361
5. Cho SY, Lee HK (2012) Modified RHKF filter for improved DR/GPS navigation against uncertain model dynamics. ETRI J 34(3):379–387
6. Kim PS (2013) A computationally efficient fixed-lag smoother using recent finite measurements. Measurement 46(1):846–850
7. Promarico-Franquz J, Shmaliy YS (2014) Accurate self-localization in RFID tag information grids using FIR filtering. IEEE Trans Industr Inf 10(2):1317–1326
8. Kim PS (2015) An estimation filtering for packet loss probability using finite memory structure strategy. Lect Notes Electr Eng 373:301–307

MAC Protocol with Priority to Urgent Data in Wireless Healthcare Monitoring Sensor Networks

Jeong Gon Kim and Rae Hyun Kim

Abstract The WBSN is a network environment in which various types of bio-signals generated directly or indirectly inside and outside the body are measured and processed for transmission to monitor the condition of the patient. The conventional DTD (Decrease of Transmission Delay)—MAC protocol transmits general and emergency data without any classification. As a result, the average delay and packet loss rate increase. Hence, in order to mitigate this performance degradation, we propose two types of adaptive MAC protocols to deal with emergency data separately in the system. The first proposed protocol reduces the delay by prioritizing emergency data over other general data by sending them first. The second proposed protocol applies the maximum delay requirement to emergency data to reduce the packet loss of both general and urgent data packets at the same time.

Keywords WBSN · DTD-MAC · MED MAC · CSMA/CA · TDMA

1 Introduction

WBSN (Wireless Body Sensor Networks) is a kind of special network that was developed from WBAN (Wireless Body Area Network) environment [1], which allows the communication within a body based on wireless sensor networks (WSNs) [2]. It is an environment where the condition of a patient is monitored in real time by collecting bio-signal data from the tools or node transplanted inside or outside the body. In near future, the WBSN is expected to replace the existing wired environments of medical surveillance or monitoring [3]. Carrier sensed multiple access/collision avoidance (CSMA/CA) [4] is a widely known MAC protocol, and

J.G. Kim (✉) · R.H. Kim
Department of Electronic Engineering, Korea Polytechnic University,
Siheung, Kyunggi Do 429-793, Korea
e-mail: jgkim@kpu.ac.kr

R.H. Kim
e-mail: hjkl525@naver.com

© Springer Science+Business Media Singapore 2016   311
J.J. (Jong Hyuk) Park et al. (eds.), *Advanced Multimedia and Ubiquitous Engineering*, Lecture Notes in Electrical Engineering 393,
DOI 10.1007/978-981-10-1536-6_41

is used when a number of nodes are transmitted in such a sensor network environment, and triggers extremely high consumption of energy of application systems through high frequency of idle listening and packet collision. Therefore, there had already been many researches that announced the advantages of the time division multiple access (TDMA) method considering electricity consumption and reduction in delayed transmission of nodes or devices [5, 6]. Meanwhile, general and urgent data are the two types of data transmitted by each node, and the urgent data should especially be processed quickly without any delay. The IEEE 802.15.4 MAC protocol [7] is a hybrid method that applies both the competition-oriented method, which is universally applied for data processing in the WBAN and WBSN environments, and schedule-oriented method. However, the GTS (Guaranteed Time Slot) allocation method of the IEEE 802.15.4 MAC protocol applies the first in first service (FIFS) queuing method where the channels are allocated in the order the arrival of packets, that causes inevitable delay in transmission and making it inadequate for transmission of urgent data [8]. In this paper, we propose a MAC protocol to reduce the average delay and packet loss rate when the ratio of emergency data over general data is varied. It improves the quality of urgent data transmission and reduces the packet loss of general data due to high traffic congestion and prioritized transmission between general and emergency data.

The structure of this paper is as the following. In Sect. 2, the existing method of DTD-MAC protocol [9] that reduces transmission delay and packet loss considering the data process in the WBSN environment will be discussed. In Sect. 3, Management of Emergency Data (MED)-MAC protocols, which reduce the average packet delay that results from the increase of total traffic and ratio of urgent data, is proposed and will be discussed in detail. In Sect. 4, the MAC protocols proposed in this paper will be examined, and its features will be analyzed. Finally, in Sect. 5, the conclusion and future research topics will be proposed.

2 Related Research

Each node attempts to transmit data for channel allocation and when it reaches the maximum transmission delay of 250 ms, we allocate a channel before other nodes regardless of the priority decided by the coordinator. In addition, the original priority of each node comply with WBAN standard but none of the nodes transmit data for channel allocation, a temporary change in priority ranking occurs when the buffer data of each node reaches 250 ms, and the delayed node is guaranteed with transmission prior to others (Fig. 1).

On the other hand, the packets of nodes that failed to transmit data till the last moment are added up to the transmission delay or packet loss. The DTD-MAC protocol has a principle of transmitting data within 250 ms, the maximum

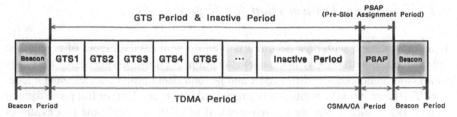

Fig. 1 The super-frame of conventional DTD-MAC protocol (color figure online)

transmission delay from its occurrence. However, the DTD-MAC protocol only considered the environment where there is no urgent data, which leads to a lack of flexible response in processing the mixed urgent data and general data.

3 Proposed MAC Protocol

Figure 2 shows the structure of the super-frame in proposed MED-MAC protocol.

The proposed MAC protocol attained the flexibility in processing urgent data by adding the urgent period (UP) frame to the original super-frame of the DTD-MAC protocol. The proposed MAC protocol adopts the variable super-frame structure where the structure changes according to the relative occurrence rate of urgent and general data. Therefore, the UP frame will allow flexible variation of frame lengths according to the amount of emergency data Node measured at PET. The main topic to be considered will be to obtain a solution to yield the optimized transmission function by controlling the adaptable processing method according to the occurrence rate of urgent data through the two suggested methods.

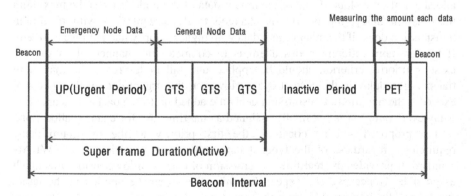

Fig. 2 The super-frame of the proposed MED-MAC Protocol (color figure online)

3.1 Prioritized Transmission for Urgent Data

In an environment with high occurrence rate of urgent data, all types of urgent data are guaranteed with priority in channel allocation and transmission before the nodes of all other general data when urgent and general data compete for channel allocation. Therefore, prior transmission is guaranteed for urgent data for fast processing of urgent data, which improves the requirement of QOS and real-time processing of urgent data transmission. However, the delay requirement of maximum 250 ms is still applied for general data. Hence, it is expected that there is an increase of packet loss in general data transmission. Therefore, it is expected that this scheme can be effective for the target system, in which the the urgent data processing is more important than other factors for the system operation and maintenance.

3.2 Delay Limitation for Urgent Data Packet Transmission

In situations where urgent and general data of each node compete for channel allocation, all the data is classified according to the priority standards, (ECG > EEG > EMG), and the urgent data should be transmitted within 100 ms, the maximum transmission delay for real time transmission. If the urgent data is not transmitted within 100 ms, it results in transmission delay and packet loss. Even though general data acquires time slots as compared to urgent data while competing for channel allocation, it should be transmitted within 250 ms by WBAN delay requirement. If it fails, data flows into the buffer and are kept in standby condition, and the transmission delay in the buffer is also added up to the total transmission delay in the final delay calculation. When the general data had reached the maximum transmission delay of 250 ms, it has the priority of transmission over the urgent data if none of urgent data reach the maximum transmission delay in that channel allocation. When the urgent data competes with another urgent data for channel allocation, the same priority criterion (ECG > EEG > EMG) is also applied for the allocation of time slots. If one of the urgent data of the node reaches the maximum transmission delay, the priority is changed to the urgent data with maximum transmission delay if the other urgent data with higher priority had not reached them. If two or more different nodes attempts to compete for channel allocation, the existing priority criterion should be applied until all nodes reach the maximum transmission delay in the current cycle. However, the urgent data of the node that exceeded the maximum transmission delay are added up to the packet loss and total delay even though it is not finally assigned as the time slot for channel allocation.

The proposed scheme considers the first priority to the maximum delay requirement regardless of the type of data and priority criterion of the WBAN standard. It provides the real-time transmission of data with lower priority as much as possible. Hence, we can expect that this scheme can be applied to the target system, and the important factor is the prevention of increased delay and packet loss.

4 Performance Comparison

In this paper, the WBSN network environment was composed of star-topology, and the length of one time-slot was defined as 50 ms. Each cycle was composed of 100 time slots, and the average collected from 100 cycles was calculated. The priority of general data was ECG > EEG > EMG, and the occurrence rate of EEG, ECG, and EMG are similar in this paper. The maximum transmission delay of each node was assumed as 250 ms from the starting time of initial transmission. When the transmission was not succeeded within 250 ms, it is added up to the total transmission delay and packet loss. The occurrence rate of urgent data was defined as 10, 20, 30, and 50 % for competition with general data. The assessment for function was executed under assumption that the general and urgent data will occupy 240 % of the current traffic environment of data. In addition, the maximum transmission delay was defined as 100 ms for the urgent data, the transmission of urgent data is always prior to the general data, and other competitive conditions with general data are applied for the criterion, which is evaluated with the original DTD-MAC protocol.

We evaluate the average time delay and the amount of packet loss when the ratio of emergency data has a value of 10, 20, 30, and 50 % over the total data traffic. Tables 1 and 2 present the values of average transmission delay of general data and urgent data, and the values of data packet loss, respectively.

Here, MED-MAC (1), which is the proposed scheme in Sect. 3.1, is the transmission method of both prioritized allocation and reducing the average time delay, and MED-MAC (2), which is the proposed scheme in Sect. 3.2, shows the results of transmission method by reducing the amount of packet loss of urgent data and general data. From the two tables, the transmission delay of MED-MAC (1) attains the smallest value of average time delay in all the variation cases of general and

Table 1 Average data transmission delay for the urgent and general data packets

Ratio of urgent data	Bio data	DTD-MAC		MED-MAC (1)		MED-MAC (2)	
		G.D.	U. D.	G.D.	U. D.	G.D.	U. D.
10 %	ECG	0	0	0	0	0	0
	EEG	999	959.12	640.34	22.12	936.23	962.5
	EMG	5634.2	5270.8	1791.71	42.47	6628.5	7180.8
20 %	ECG	0	0	0	0	0	0
	EEG	955.1	883.57	467.72	53.31	1014.30	1076.17
	EMG	6317.9	5164.38	1206.3	107.24	6214.00	5467.16
30 %	ECG	0	0	0	0	0	0
	EEG	918.6	901.63	387.18	96.34	995.15	1036.60
	EMG	5850.6	6160.95	984.31	226.72	6838.70	6596.32
50 %	ECG	0	0	0	0	0	0
	EEG	961.4	978.76	359.66	164.22	962.10	994.80
	EMG	5747.2	5679.6	989.81	484.10	6457.30	6397.45

Table 2 The number of packet loss for the urgent and general data packets

Ratio of urgent data	Bio data	DTD-MAC		MED-MAC (1)		MED-MAC (2)	
		G.D.	U. D.	G.D.	U. D.	G.D.	U. D.
10 %	ECG	0	0	0	0	0	0
	EEG	6222	628	5318	74	6506	514
	EMG	7619	764	7012	102	7842	151
20 %	ECG	0	0	0	0	0	0
	EEG	6271	1261	4643	252	1014.30	1018
	EMG	7837	1526	6521	107.24	456	323
30 %	ECG	0	0	0	0	0	0
	EEG	6352	2093	387.18	4096	702	1679
	EMG	7702	2571	984.31	6373	1249	568
50 %	ECG	0	0	0	0	0	0
	EEG	6233	3129	359.66	4084	1582	2555
	EMG	7653	3805	989.81	6407	2550	836

emergency data. Particularly, it also shows that much reduction of delay of the urgent data, and hence, this implies its effectiveness in prior processing of the urgent data. From Table 2, the packet loss for MED-MAC (2) is decreased compared with DTD-MAC and MED-MAC (1) when the ratio of emergency data exceeds 20 % of the total data traffic. It indicates that MED-MAC (2) can be applied to the target system, in which the packet loss needs to be restricted or minimized even if they have a lower priority data packet.

5 Conclusion

In this paper, two types of MAC protocol for the reduction of time delay and packet loss of urgent data in the WBSN environment were suggested and evaluated. The DTD-MAC protocol that was considered for previous research in the WBSN environment does not have any standard related to processing of urgent data. Namely, if the urgent data were processed using the same criterion of transmission delay for general data, it may result in an inevitable increase in transmission delay and a lot of packet loss for urgent data, which requires real-time processing.

The first proposed MAC protocol provides a method where the urgent data are given absolute priority with no restriction of urgent and general data, and the second proposed MAC protocol guarantees the consistent transmission of urgent data by restricting the maximum transmission delay of urgent data to 100 ms.

The simulation results show that the first prioritized transmission was very effective in all the cases of urgent data rate in reducing the time delay for urgent data. In terms of packet loss, two proposed schemes attain the lower packet loss over the DTD-MAC protocol, and particularly, the second proposed MAC protocol achieves much reduction of packet loss for the data with lower priority when the urgent data rate is increased in three types of signal based healthcare monitoring Wireless sensor networks.

References

1. Choi JS, Kim JG (2014) An Improved MAC protocol for WBAN through modified frame structure. Int J Smart Home 8(2)
2. Kim JS, Lee JH, Rim KW (2010) Energy efficient key management protocol in wireless sensor networks. Int J Secur Appl 4(2):1–12
3. Morchon OG, Baldus H, Sanchez DS (2006) Resource efficient security for medical body sensor networks. In: IEEE International Workshop on Wearable and Implantable Body Sensor Networks
4. LAN-MAN Standards Committee of the IEEE Computer Society (1997) Wireless LAN Medium Access Control (MAC) and Physical Layer (PHY) specification. In: IEEE, New York
5. Gopalan SA, Park J (2010) Energy efficient MAC protocols for wireless body area network. In: Survey, 2010 International Congress on Ultra Modern Telecommunications and Control Systems (ICUMT), pp 739–744
6. Kwon H, Lee S (2009) Energy-efficient multi-hop transmission in body area networks. In: IEEE 20th International Symposium on Personal, Indoor and Mobile Radio Communications, pp 2141–2146
7. IEEE 802.15.4 Standard-2003: Part 15.4 (2003) Wireless Medium Access Control (MAC) and Physical Layer (PHY) specifications for Low-Rate Wireless Personal Area Network (LR-WPANs). In: IEEE Computer Society
8. Lee HG, Lee KH, Shin YT (2012) A priority based MAC protocol for emergency data transmission in wireless body area networks. Telecommun J Inst Electron Eng Korea 49(4)
9. Kim RH, Kim JG (2015) Delay reduced MAC protocol for bio signal monitoring in the WBSN environment. In: 6th International Workshop on Networking and Communication, pp 42–46

Buffer-Aided Relay Selection with Primary Sensing in Underlay Cognitive Radio Networks

Su Min Kim and Junsu Kim

Abstract In this paper, we propose a buffer-aided relay selection scheme with primary sensing ability in an underlay cognitive radio network. The proposed relay selection scheme is evaluated in terms of outage probability, compared with the conventional max-min and max-ratio relay selection schemes through simulations. The results show that the proposed scheme significantly improves the outage performance with a low primary activity and a short sensing period.

Keywords Buffer-aided relaying · Underlay CR · Primary sensing

1 Introduction

Cognitive radio (CR) is one of promising technologies to resolve radio resource shortage by allowing a secondary system to access the license bands of primary systems [1]. There are three main types of CR networks (CRNs): overlay [2], interweave [3, 4], and underlay [5] CRNs. In overlay CRN, concurrent primary and secondary transmissions are allowed by using powerful coding techniques such as dirty paper coding. In interweave CRN, the secondary system first performs channel sensing for primary systems before transmission and then, it transmits data only if the primary channel is idle, while in underlay CRN, the secondary system can transmit data at any time if it satisfies a required interference limit at the primary receiver.

On the other hand, cooperative relaying is another promising technology for future wireless communication networks since it can improve both spectral efficiency and spatial diversity [6]. So far, there have been extensive studies on data forwarding protocol for single-relay networks and relay selection (RS) for multiple-relay networks. Among various RS schemes, it is well-known that the

S.M. Kim · J. Kim (✉)
Department of Electronics Engineering, Korea Polytechnic University, Siheung, Korea
e-mail: junsukim@kpu.ac.kr

© Springer Science+Business Media Singapore 2016
J.J. (Jong Hyuk) Park et al. (eds.), *Advanced Multimedia and Ubiquitous Engineering*, Lecture Notes in Electrical Engineering 393,
DOI 10.1007/978-981-10-1536-6_42

max-min RS scheme [7] is the best scheme for half-duplex (HD) multiple-relay networks.

Recently, it has been shown that employing a buffer at the relay gives us an additional opportunity to improve both resource efficiency and spatial diversity [8]. Accordingly, there have been many studies on buffer-aided relaying in multiple-relay networks [9–12]. Among the studies, the max-link RS scheme [9] asymptotically achieves the full-diversity gain as buffer size increases by releasing two-phase operation. Most recently, the max-ratio RS scheme [12], which modifies the max-min RS criterion and applies to an underlay CRN by additionally considering the interference temperature at the primary receiver, has been proposed. However, it has been inherently devised for interference-limited environments, since the selection criterion is based on signal-to-interference ratio (SIR) by neglecting noise.

In this paper, we propose a buffer-aided RS scheme with primary sensing for an underlay CRN. Our proposed RS scheme is based on signal-to-noise-and-interference ratio (SINR) such that it can well-operate even for noise-limited environments, which might be common for CRNs. In addition, we employ a primary sensing functionality, often used in interweave CRNs, in order to detect the primary activity by sacrificing some portions of resource, although we consider an underlay CRN. This approach is reasonable for CRNs because the basic concept of CR is to improve resource efficiency by exploiting under-utilized radio resources. That is, in meaningful CR environments, the primary activity would be low since otherwise, the secondary system cannot secure sufficient radio resource from the primary CRN.

This paper is organized as follows. In Sect. 2, the system model is presented. In Sect. 3, a buffer-aided RS scheme with primary sensing is proposed. The performance of the proposed RS scheme is evaluated in terms of outage probability, compared with the conventional schemes, through simulations in Sect. 4. Finally, conclusive remarks are presented in Sect. 5.

2 System Model

Figure 1 shows an underlay CRN, which consists of a primary network and a relay-assisted secondary network, considered in this paper. The primary network has a source and a destination, which requires satisfying a certain interference limit. The secondary network consists of a source, a destination, and multiple HD decode-and-forward (DF) relays with buffer. Since we consider HD transmissions in a two-hop relay network, there are two types of links in the secondary network: (a) source-to-relay ($S \rightarrow R_k$) link and (b) relay-to-destination ($R_k \rightarrow D$) link. We assume that there is no direct link from the source to the destination for the secondary network, and the primary and secondary networks interfere with each other.

Fig. 1 System model (color figure online)

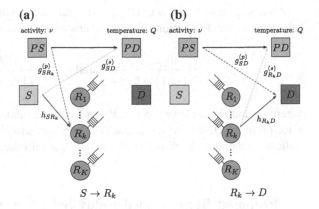

Let us denote a secondary channel gain from node α to node β by $h_{\alpha\beta}$, where $\alpha \in \{S\}$ or $\{R_1, \ldots, R_K\}$, $\beta \in \{R_1, \ldots, R_K\}$ or $\{D\}$, and K denotes the number of relays. Additionally, we denote a cross-interference channel gain from node α in network z to node β by $g_{\alpha\beta}^{(z)}$ where $\alpha \in \{S\}$ or $\{R_1, \ldots, R_K\}$, $\beta \in \{R_1, \ldots, R_K\}$ or $\{D\}$, and $z \in \{p, s\}$ in which p and s denote 'primary' and 'secondary', respectively. We assume independent and identically distributed (i.i.d.) Rayleigh block fading so that all channel gains follow circular symmetric complex Gaussian distributions, i.e., $h_{\alpha\beta} \sim CN(0, \sigma_{\alpha\beta})$ and $g_{\alpha\beta}^{(z)} \sim CN(0, \rho_{\alpha\beta}^{(z)})$ where $\sigma_{\alpha\beta}$ and $\rho_{\alpha\beta}^{(z)}$ denote the average channel gains of the secondary channel and cross-interference channel, respectively. For simplicity without loss of generality, we assume that both the peak power and noise variance are unity so that the channel gains are equivalent to SNRs in this work.

Since we consider an underlay CRN, a secondary transmitter has to guarantee the interference level less than or equal to the interference temperature (Q) at the primary receiver. In this work, we additionally consider primary activity (ν) since the concept of CR is generally meaningful when primary radio resource is under-utilized. Let us denote the peak power by $P_{\max}$. We assume that the primary transmitter always uses the peak power (i.e., $P_S^{(p)} = P_{\max}$) when it is active and the secondary transmitter adjusts its transmit power satisfying the interference temperature at the primary destination according to the cross-interference channel gain. Then, the transmit powers of the secondary source (P_S) and of the secondary relay R_k (P_{R_k}) are determined by

$$P_S = \min\left\{\frac{Q}{|g_{SD}^{(s)}|^2}, P_{\max}\right\} \text{ and } P_{R_k} = \min\left\{\frac{Q}{|g_{R_kD}^{(s)}|^2}, P_{\max}\right\}, \tag{1}$$

where $g_{SD}^{(s)}$ and $g_{R_kD}^{(s)}$ denote the channel gains from the secondary source to the primary destination and from the secondary relay R_k to the primary destination, respectively.

Assuming unit peak power ($P_{\max} = 1$) and unit variance noise, the SINRs at the relay R_k and the destination of the secondary network are derived, respectively, as:

$$\gamma_{SR_k} = \frac{|h_{SR_k}|^2 P_S}{\mathbb{I}\{V = 1\}|g_{SD}^{(p)}|^2 + 1} \text{ and } \gamma_{R_kD} = \frac{|h_{R_kD}|^2 P_{R_k}}{\mathbb{I}\{V = 1\}|g_{SR_k}^{(p)}|^2 + 1}, \quad (2)$$

where P_S and P_{R_k} are given in (1), V is a Bernoulli random variable with parameter v for primary activity, which is one if active and zero if inactive, $\mathbb{I}\{\cdot\}$ denotes the indicator function, which is one if true and zero if false.

3   Proposed Buffer-Aided Relay Selection with Primary Sensing

In this section, we propose a buffer-aided RS scheme with primary sensing (BARS-PS) in an underlay CRN. Figure 2 show the basic frame structure used in this work. In conventional max-min RS [7] and max-ratio RS [12] schemes, a single frame is utilized for source-to-relay or relay-to-destination transmission, while in the proposed BARS-PS scheme, a sensing period (τ) additionally exists before data transmission. Thus, the data transmission period in the proposed scheme is reduced to $(1 - \tau)$, while it is one in the conventional schemes. For simplicity, we assume perfect sensing, i.e., $P_{\text{detect}} = 1$, such that there are no mis-detection and no false alarm.

In conventional max-min and max-ratio RS schemes, a single frame is utilized for source-to-relay or relay-to-destination transmission, while in the proposed BARS-PS scheme, a sensing period (τ) additionally exists before data transmission. Thus, the data transmission period in the proposed scheme is reduced to $(1 - \tau)$, while it is one in the conventional schemes. We first define the outage probability as:

$$P_{\text{out}} = \Pr\left\{\frac{1}{2}\log_2\left(1 + \gamma_{\alpha\beta}\right) < r_0\right\}, \quad (3)$$

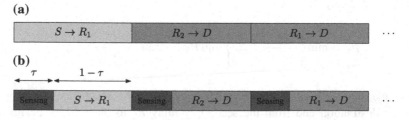

Fig. 2 Basic frame structure: **a** conventional structure **b** proposed structure (color figure online)

where $\gamma_{\alpha\beta}$ is the SINR of $(\alpha \rightarrow \beta)$ link, r_0 denotes the target rate, which is equivalent to a fixed transmission rate at each link, and the factor $1/2$ is because two time slots are effectively required in the end-to-end perspective. Note that in the max-ratio RS scheme, instead of SINR, SIR is used in the outage definition by ignoring noise. However, it is only applicable to interference-limited regime, which is not desirable in underlay CR environments since the performance of secondary CRN is so limited under strong interference conditions. Due to the sensing period, the target rate in the proposed scheme should be increased to $r_0' = r_0/(1 - \tau)$. Instead, the proposed scheme can recognize the primary activity so that it neglects interference from the primary source in RS when primary CRN is inactive.

In buffer-aided relaying, each relay is equipped with a buffer $(B_k, k \in \{1, \ldots, K\})$ with finite size L. Since we consider the fixed rate transmission assuming channel state information at receiver (CSIR), buffer occupancy is equivalent to the number of packets. Thus, the buffer size L means that maximum L packets can be stored in a buffer. Let us denote the buffer length of the k th relay n_k by $\psi(B_k)$. Then $\psi(B_k) = 0$ implies buffer empty and $\psi(B_k) = L$ implies buffer full.

Similar to the conventional max-link RS scheme [9] and max-ratio RS scheme [12], we select the best link among all $2K$ links at every time slot assuming global CSI and buffer state information in the secondary system. However, our proposed BARS-PS scheme selects the best relay based on SINRs with primary activity information given in (2). Employing an integer link variable l (1: $S \rightarrow R_k$ link, 0: $R_k \rightarrow D$ link), in the proposed BARS-PS scheme, the best link and relay pair is determined by

$$(l^*, k^*) = \underset{l \in \{0,1\}, k \in \{1, \cdots, K\}, \psi(B_k) \neq L \text{ for } l=1, \psi(B_k) \neq 0 \text{ for } l=0}{\mathrm{argmax}} \left\{ l\gamma_{SR_k} + (1 - l)\gamma_{R_kD} \right\} \quad (4)$$

where $\psi(Q_k)$ denotes the number of packets in the kth buffer B_k, and γ_{SR_k} and γ_{R_kD} are obtained in (2), but the transmit powers are set to $P_{\max}$ when $V = 0$, while they follow (2) when $V = 1$. After successful transmission, the buffer state of the selected relay is updated by $B_{k^*} = B_{k^*} + 1$ if $l^* = 1$ and $B_{k^*} = B_{k^*} - 1$ if $l^* = 0$.

4 Numerical Results

In this section, we evaluate the proposed BARS-PS scheme in terms of outage probability through simulations, compared with two conventional RS schemes: (1) max-min RS scheme [7], which is the best HD RS scheme without buffer, and (2) max-ratio RS scheme [12], which has been proposed for a buffer-aided relay-assisted CRN as an extended version of the max-link RS scheme [9].

Figure 3 shows the outage probability for varying primary activity when the average cross-interference channel gains are 3 dB, the average secondary channel gains are 20 dB, the interference temperature (Q) is 0 dB, the number of relays (K) is 3, the target rate (r_0) is 1 bits per channel use (bpcu), and the sensing period (τ) is 0.1, which leads to the effective target rate (r_0') as about 1.1 bpcu for the proposed scheme. Basically, as the primary activity increases, the outage performance is degraded since more interference from the primary source affects the performance with increasing the primary activity. The proposed BARS-PS scheme is more sensitive in the primary activity than the conventional schemes, since it exploits the activity information. Thus, the proposed scheme with $L = 1$ achieves the same performance as the max-ratio RS scheme when $v = 1$. However, for $L \to \infty$, the proposed BARS-PS scheme significantly improves the outage performance, especially, at low activity (e.g., $v < 0.1$), it surprisingly improves the outage performance.

Figure 4 shows the outage probability for varying sensing period. As expected, the proposed scheme degrades the outage performance as the sensing period increases since increasing sensing period results in the reduced data transmission period, which leads to increased effective target rate. There are tradeoffs with the conventional schemes when $\tau > 0.3$ with $L = 1$ and when $\tau > 0.45$ with $L \to \infty$, respectively. However, in interweave CRNs, the typical value of sensing period is less than 0.1. Hence, our proposed BARS-PS scheme is practically effective since it significantly outperforms the conventional schemes at short sensing period (e.g., $\tau < 0.1$).

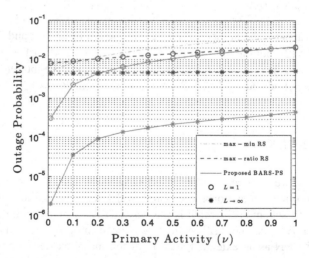

Fig. 3 Outage probability versus primary activity (color figure online) ($K = 3, r_0 = 1$ bpcu, $Q = 0$dB, $\rho_{SD}^{(s)} = \rho_{R_kD}^{(s)} = \rho_{SR_k}^{(p)} = \rho_{SD}^{(p)} = 3$dB, $\sigma_{SR_k} = \sigma_{R_kD} = 20$ dB, and $\tau = 0.1$)

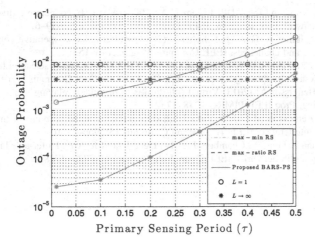

Fig. 4 Outage probability versus sensing period (color figure online) $(K = 3, r_0 = 1 \text{ bpcu},$
$Q = 0\text{dB}, \rho_{SD}^{(s)} = \rho_{R_kD}^{(s)} = \rho_{SR_k}^{(p)} = \rho_{SD}^{(p)} = 3\text{dB}, \sigma_{SR_k} = \sigma_{R_kD} = 20 \text{ dB, and } v = 0.1)$

5 Conclusion

In this paper, a buffer-aided RS scheme with primary sensing was proposed for underlay cognitive radio networks. Thanks to additional sensing ability, the proposed scheme can obtain the activity information so that it exploits the information in an RS criterion. Through simulations, the performance of the proposed scheme was evaluated in terms of outage probability, compared with the conventional max-min and max-ratio RS schemes. The results show that the proposed scheme significantly improves the performance with a low primary activity and a short sensing period.

References

1. Haykin S (2005) Cognitive radio: brain-empowered wireless communications. IEEE J Sel Areas Commun 23:201–220
2. Srinivasa S, Jafar SA (2007) The throughput potential of cognitive radio: a theoretical perspective. IEEE Commun Mag 45:73–79
3. Kim SM, Kim J (2014) Adaptive sensing period based distributed medium access control for cognitive radio networks. IEICE Trans Commun E97-B:2502–2511
4. Kosugi T, Fujii T (2015) Efficient spectrum sharing with avoiding spatial fragmentation of white space. ICT Express 1:55–58
5. Ban TW, Choi W, Jung BC, Sung DK (2009) Multi-user diversity in a spectrum sharing system. IEEE Trans Wirel Commun 8:102–106
6. Laneman JN, Tse DNC, Wornell GW (2004) Cooperative diversity in wireless networks: efficient protocols and outage behavior. IEEE Trans Inf Theory 50:3062–3080

7. Bletsas A, Khisti A, Reed DP, Lippman A (2006) A simple cooperative diversity method based on network path selection. IEEE J Sel Areas Commun 24:659–672
8. Zlatanov N, Ikhlef A, Islam T, Schober R (2014) Buffer-aided cooperative communications: opportunities and challenges. IEEE Commun Mag 52:146–153
9. Krikidis I, Charalambous T, Thompson JS (2012) Buffer-aided relay selection for cooperative diversity systems without delay constraints. IEEE Trans Wirel Commun 11:1957–1967
10. Kim SM, Bengtsson M (2013) Virtual full-duplex buffer-aided relaying—relay selection and beamforming. Proc IEEE PIMRC 1748–1752
11. Kim SM, Bengtsson M (2016) Virtual full-duplex buffer-aided relaying in the presence of inter-relay interference. IEEE Trans Wirel Commun 15:2966–2980
12. Chen G, Tian Z, Gong Y, Chambers J (2014) Decode-and-forward buffer-aided relay selection in cognitive radio networks. IEEE Trans Veh Technol 63:4723–4728

A Cursor Using Limited Range of Motion for Persons with Visual and Motor Impairment

Jong Won Lee, Kang Hyoun Kim and Jin Gon Shon

Abstract Persons with visual impairment have low and tunnel vision, and the persons with motor impairments have muscle weakness and hand tremor. Selecting an object requires constant use of hands and fingers. This increases fatigue and eventually causes muscle damage and strain. As a result, visual and motor impaired persons give up selecting the target object. Traditional cursors are designed to aid quick selection and to reduce error. However, it is insufficient to reduce the fatigue on hands and fingers. In this paper, we suggest a cursor using limited range of motion, CLROM, for persons with visual and motor impairments. CLROM reduces muscle fatigue and prevents muscle damage by limiting the movements of the joints in outer range and middle range. CLROM prevents the losing of the cursor position and overshooting by limiting the motion range to the area cursor. Consequently, CLROM helps to acquire the target object easily and reduces error and muscle fatigue.

Keywords Cursor · Visual impairment · Motor impairment

1 Introduction

According to World Health Organization (WHO), 285 millions of people are estimated to be visually impaired and hundreds of millions of people are affected by neurological disorders worldwide [1, 2]. Selecting a target among objects is essential and most frequently used task in graphic user interfaces. With the development of the resolution and screen size of display, objects such as windows, icons, menus, and

J.W. Lee · K.H. Kim · J.G. Shon (✉)
Department of Computer Science, Graduate School,
Korea National Open University, Seoul, Korea
e-mail: jgshon@knou.ac.kr

J.W. Lee
e-mail: hosori@bohun.or.kr

K.H. Kim
e-mail: khkim@knou.ac.kr

© Springer Science+Business Media Singapore 2016
J.J. (Jong Hyuk) Park et al. (eds.), *Advanced Multimedia and Ubiquitous Engineering*, Lecture Notes in Electrical Engineering 393,
DOI 10.1007/978-981-10-1536-6_43

pointers are smaller and closer on desktop display. Therefore, persons with visual and motor impairment consume more time and effort in acquiring the target object from the objects. Moreover, when they fail to select the target object and choose a wrong object, they would have to repeat the process in order to recover from the error, requiring more time and effort in completing their task. The repeating actions due to errors cause muscle fatigue. This might even damage their muscle tissues and ultimately discourage them from continuing acquiring the target object. People with visual impairments have poor eyesight and tunnel vision and people with motor impairments have tremor and muscle weakness. In both cases, overshooting arises. As a result, a cursor is mislocated and it is not easy to bring it back to the right position. In order to solve the problem, this paper recommends a cursor suitable for visual and motor impaired people.

2 Range of Motion and Traditional Cursor

2.1 Range of Motion

Range of motion is the linear or angular distance of a joint movement from full flexion to full extension. Range of motion is divided into inner range, middle range, and outer range. Inner range is from full flexion to the middle, outer range is from full extension to the middle, and middle range is from center of inner range to center of outer range [3]. It is difficult for the visual and motor impaired people to choose an object far from the cursor. In the process of doing so, hyperextension is often caused on wrist and finger muscles. Hyperextension of muscles increases possibility of strain and damage to the muscles [4]. In order to reduce the risk of hyperextension of muscles, wrists and fingers should move in the middle range and the cursor should be designed to limit the movements of the hand. The visually impaired takes longer time to select the object because they have difficulty locating the cursor once it is moved out of their sight. In the case of the motor impaired person, the movement of the cursor should be more limited than the middle range, since the tremor causes the cursor to move away from the object and make it difficult to select the object correctly. Once the muscle contracts and then relaxes, the muscle recovers the original length without further contraction. Elastic recoil of the muscle is caused due to the elasticity of the muscle. Elasticity of the muscle can reduce the muscle fatigue in the process of selecting the object and thus limiting the range of motion.

2.2 Traditional Cursor

Drag-and-Pop and Drag-and-Pick systems analyzed the directional movements of cursor. Traditional System temporarily brings virtual proxies of the potential selectable targets to the cursor. In these systems, when the target is far from the cursor, the object is brought near to the cursor, enabling selection of the target object [5]. However, to activate it, one must perform a drag, causing a fatigue on the hand. Also they do not consider the situation of dragging an object from closely packed environment. Moreover, in order to select the object brought by dragging, wrist and finger muscles must be contracted further.

Click-and-Cross, Cross-and-Cross, and Adaptive Click-and-Cross are circular area cursors. These systems move the mouse to the target object. The cursor becomes fixed and the objects under the area cursor are separately positioned when the cursor passes the activated area or when the mouse is clicked. During the process, the object is selected when the cursor passes the target object. 'Click-and-cross' and 'cross-and-cross' separate the objects and secure the space between the objects [6]. The 'Adaptive Click-and-Cross' secures space between the objects and increases the width of the object [7]. These cursors reduce error by securing space between the objects and enlarging it. However, when the cursor overshoots the object, the cursor returns to the center of the area cursor slowly. The slow movement of the cursor is time consuming. Also they do not consider the position of the separated objects.

3 Cursor Using Limited Range of Motion

Cursor using limited range of motion; CLROM, is an enhanced cursor for people with low vision [8]. CLROM is a cogwheel shaped area cursor. CLROM has two types of cursors. One is a cogwheel shaped area cursor and the other is the secondary cursor moving within the area cursor. In the process of selecting the object, the visual or motor impaired person uses the wrist and finger muscles frequently, thus increasing muscle fatigue. Frequent use of the hand and finger muscles creates repetitive stress to the muscle, causing muscle damage. Therefore it is essential to design a cursor system that limits the range of motion to reduce fatigue.

3.1 Prevention of Hyperextension in Outer Range

Hyperextension occurs at the edge of the outer range. The positions of the objects are changed in consideration of the elastic recoil, which uses the elasticity of the muscle, thus preventing hyperextension. The object is positioned at the counter direction of the processing direction of the cursor. The elastic recoil decides the order of the positions of the objects on the rim of the area cursor. This process reduces the muscle fatigue. Figure 1 shows the method of positioning the objects to reduce fatigue.

The visual or motor impaired person moves the cursor in the direction where the target object is located. Once the objects are located under the area cursor, the

Fig. 1 Positioning method of
objects (color figure online)

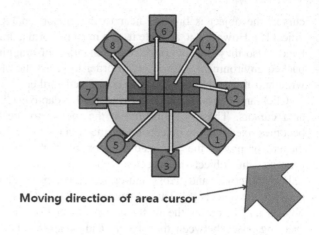

Moving direction of area cursor

objects are separated and located at the rim of the area cursor. The objects are
located in counter direction of the movement of the cursor and the separated objects
are placed on the rim of the area cursor. Thereby, the target object on the rim of the
area cursor can be easily selected without hyperextension. The elastic recoil due to
elasticity of the muscle makes the selection of the objects easy. As a result, one can
click the object with less muscle contraction than the objects that are located in the
direction of the cursor, thus reducing the muscle fatigue.

3.2 Limitation of Cursor Movement Within Middle Range

Unlike limiting the movement in the outer range, the limitation of cursor movement
within middle range selects an object using the elastic recoil of the elasticity of the
muscle. Even in this case, the separated objects are located on the rim of the area
cursor in the counter direction of the processing direction of the cursor. This process
reduces muscle contraction and fatigue. It also helps to select the objects efficiently
and reduce error. The visual and motor impaired people would feel as if the objects
are being dragged to the position when the objects in front of the cursor are located
in counter direction of the cursor. One of the advantages is that the selecting method
and the movement of the cursor can be cognitively coincided.

3.3 Limitation of Cursor Movement Within Area Cursor

As shown in the Fig. 2, the limitation of cursor movements within area cursor
prevents the secondary cursor from getting away from the range of the area cursor.
Overshooting occurs when the cursor moves out of sight due to a false movement of

Fig. 2 Limitation cursor
movement within area cursor
(color figure online)

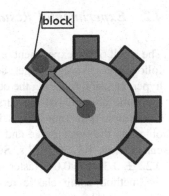

the cursor when trying to select the object. Computer users with low vision would lose the sight of the cursor even when the size of the cursor is large because of tunnel vision. For the motor impaired users, the tremor could result in overshoot and it would take lot of time and effort to select the target object.

Consequently, limiting the movements within area cursor can prevent from making serious errors in the process of object selection.

4 Performance Evaluation

4.1 Experimental Design

The participants for the experiment on prevention of hyperextension in outer range were regular computer users, 23 male and 9 female adults, who were 27.06 ± 4.72 years old. The participants for the experiment on limitation of cursor movement within middle range were regular computer users, 23 male and 20 female adults, with average age of 28.98 ± 1.07. There were two groups for the experiment on limitation of cursor movement. One group limited the cursor movement and the other did not. The group that limited cursor movement consisted of forty five adults, 35 male and 10 female, with average age of 32.22 ± 7.0. The other group consisted of forty five adults, 25 male and 20 female, with average age of 33.11 ± 6.73. Both groups had visual impairment and neurological disorder. Experiments were conducted using 17″ LCD monitors with resolution 1280 × 1024 pixels, connected to desktops running Window XP. Microsoft comparable mouse devices were used under default cursor speed setting. The participants started the experiment in comfortable sittings and the distance between the participant and the monitor was maintained within 40 cm. T-test with double blind method was used to examine mean comparison between acquisition time and error rate. And SPSS version 15 for Windows was used for statistical analysis.

4.2 Experimental Result

The result of the experiment on prevention of hyperextensions in outer range was as follow; the average target acquisition time (HE) to click the object causing hyperextension (clicking the object in the outer range and then clicking the object in the same direction of the cursor) was 2.08 ± 0.41 s, whereas the average target acquisition time (non-HE) selecting the object using elastic recoil (clicking the object in the outer range and then selecting the object in counter direction of the cursor) was 1.87 ± 0.37 s. Selecting objects using elastic recoil was on average 0.22 ± 0.34 s (<0.01) faster than the method which caused hyperextension. Also the method using elastic recoil prevented hyperextension and reduced muscle fatigue and damage.

The error rate and mean time to select the target object between drag-and-pop and CLROM were compared in the limitation of cursor movement within middle range experiment. The result of the experiment was as follow; The average time (DR) taken to drag to the certain point in the middle range and then to select among the objects which have been dragged in the same direction and within $180°$ range was 2.07 ± 0.43 s (<0.01). On the other hand, the average time (C-DR) taken to drag to a certain point in the middle range and then to select among the objects which have been dragged in the opposite direction and within $180°$ range was 1.89 ± 0.46 s. The method using elastic recoil in middle range, moving in the same direction as the cognitive direction, was 0.19 ± 0.51 s faster. The error rate for CLROM was 10 % and drag-and-pick was 14 %. The error rate in CLROM was lower.

The error rate and mean time to select the target object between CLROM and click-and-cross were compared in the limitation of cursor movement within area cursor experiment. The result of the experiment was as follow; When the movement was limited to area within the area cursor, the average time (LAC) took to select the target object was 3.39 ± 1.01 s. When there were no constraints, on average (non-LAC) time taken was 4.45 ± 3.38 s. Limited the movement within the area of

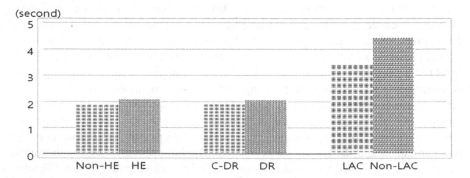

Fig. 3 Result of performance evaluation about limited range of motion

Table 1 Target acquisition time

Parameter	M ± SD	p-value
HE–Non-HE	0.22 ± 0.34	0.001
DR–C-DR	0.19 ± 0.51	0.000
non-LAC–LAC	0.74 ± 2.60	0.063

the area cursor was 0.74 ± 2.60 s faster, but it was not statistically significant (>0.01) and there was no error in both cases. However when the overshooting of the secondary cursor occurred the user with low vision lost the cursor and the person with motor impairment had difficulty relocating the cursor to the target object in the case where there was no constraint. Figure 3 illustrates the performance evaluation. The results are given in Table 1.

5 Conclusion

A Cursor using limited range of motion for persons with visual and motor impairment reduced fatigue, risk of repetitive stress injury, error rate, and object acquisition time. CLROM had the following contributions. It reduced muscle fatigue on hands and fingers, risk of repetitive stress injury, and object acquisition time by preventing hyperextension in outer range and limiting the cursor movement within middle range. It also prevented users from losing their cursor position. Cursor overshooting their intended target object is prevented by limiting the cursor movement within area cursor. Thereby reduced the object acquisition time further. According to the performance comparison, CLROM could make faster object acquisition, reduce error rate, and muscle fatigue of hand and finger for persons with visual and motor impairments. Consequently, persons with visual and motor impairments do not need to give up completing the pointing task and can enjoy better accessibility than before in graphical user interface by using the CLROM.

References

1. World Health Organization (2016) Visual impairment and blindness. http://www.who.int/mediacentre/factsheets/fs282/en. Accessed 05 Jan 2016
2. World Health Organization (2016) What are neurological disorders? http://www.who.int/features/qa/55/en/. Accessed 26 Jan 2016
3. Clarkson HM (2012) Musculoskeletal assessment, 2nd edn. Lippincott Williams & Wilkins, Philadelphia
4. Wahlstrom J (2005) Ergonomics, musculoskeletal disorders and computer work. Occup Med 55 (3):168–176
5. Baudisch P et al (2003) Drag-and-pop and drag-and-pick: techniques for accessing remote screen content on touch- and pen-operated systems. In: Proceedings of Interact, pp 57–64

6. Findlater L et al (2010) Enhanced area cursors: reducing fine pointing demands for people with motor impairments. In: Proceedings of the 23th annual ACM symposium on User Interface Software and Technology (UIST), pp 153–162
7. Li L, Gajos KZ (2014) Adaptive click-and-cross: adapting to both abilities and task improves performance of users with impaired dexterity. In: Proceedings of the 19th international conference on Intelligent User Interfaces (IUI), pp 299–304
8. Lee JW, Park JS, Lee JI, Shon JG (2015) Development of a cursor for persons with low vision. Lect Notes Electr Eng 373:529–534

Efficient Semantic Image Processing Mechanism for Automatic Context-Aware Based on Cloud Infrastructure

Seok-Hyeon Han, Hyun-Woo Kim, Boo-Kwang Park, Yoon-A. Heo and Young-Sik Jeong

Abstract In recent years, fusion studies such as context-aware, multimedia contents and cloud computing in information technology (IT) have been on the rise through the technological development of hardware and software. The automatic context-aware technology using multimedia image data requires high computation. Cloud computing has played a role in meeting the requirements of high computation. The automatic context-aware technology utilizing previously developed multimedia image data has lacked user-defined semantic inference capabilities considerably. This paper proposes a Semantic Image Processing Mechanism for Automatic Context-Aware (SIPM-ACA) based on cloud computing. Semantic inference is done through user-created multimedia contents images. Image's semantics are verified by analyzing texts created by other users. Content-Based Image Retrieval (CBIR) is utilized to find the relationship between image similarities. Through this, proactive context-awareness according to user's context can be inferenced.

Keywords Cloud computing · Semantic · Image retrieval · Context-Aware

---

S.-H. Han · H.-W. Kim · B.-K. Park · Y.-A. Heo · Y.-S. Jeong (✉)
Department of Multimedia Engineering, Dongguk University,
Seoul, Korea (Republic of)
e-mail: ysjeong@dongguk.edu

S.-H. Han
e-mail: shhan0226@gmail.com

H.-W. Kim
e-mail: hwkim@dongguk.edu

B.-K. Park
e-mail: pbg0517@dongguk.edu

Y.-A. Heo
e-mail: hyagood@dongguk.edu

© Springer Science+Business Media Singapore 2016
J.J. (Jong Hyuk) Park et al. (eds.), *Advanced Multimedia and Ubiquitous Engineering*, Lecture Notes in Electrical Engineering 393,
DOI 10.1007/978-981-10-1536-6_44

1   Introduction

In recent years, a number of studies on multimedia contents and automatic context-aware technologies in information technology (IT) have been underway through the technological development of hardware and software [1–4]. Multimedia contents have been used in many areas. Among them, multimedia image data have been utilized in automatic context-awareness. The automatic context-aware technology using multimedia image data requires high computation. The cloud computing environment provides resources and high computation that are required by automatic context-aware technology. The context-awareness shall verify all interactive pieces of information related to objects beyond simple judgments about events [5]. Existing studies showed difficulties in semantic judgment because semantic inference is conducted by using limited specific elements between objects.

This paper proposes a Semantic Image Processing Mechanism for Automatic Context-Aware (SIPM-ACA). The SIPM-ACA reasons semantic meaning in images. The SIPM-ACA collects similar semantical images using Content-Based Image Retrieval (CBIR) that utilizes color, texture, and shape contained in multimedia image data. In order to verify the meaning in images, user's experience about each of images is collected. User's experience and user-defined semantic image are matched with each other. As a result, contexts from collected images can be classified according to user-definition and semantic inference is provided.

2   Related Works

Previous studies on image retrieval employ one-dimensional method that searches images through image index. The accuracy of image retrieval through indexing is very low. Context-Based Image Retrieval (CBIR) searches similar images based on contents that images have [6, 7]. An image is composed of color, texture, shape, and composition. CBIR verifies similarity between different images using the contents in the images. This simple comparison of image similarity cannot provide verification of relationship between images.

To verify image relationship, several studies have been conducted as follows: Fuzzy c-means clustering [8], hierarchical clustering [9], and K-means clustering [10]. The above studies verified relative similarity between different images. Through the identified similarity, an image cluster is composed. Each cluster represents a relationship between images.

Since a study on image clustering analyzes contents contained the images, it has difficulties in semantic inferencing although image classification and search can be possible. To solve the difficulties, this paper proposes a scheme of user-defined semantic inference that image has. As previous studies on user-defined semantic inference, SentiWordNet [11] and OpenHangul [12] are utilized.

3 Scheme of SIPM-ACA

The Semantic Image Processing Mechanism for Automatic Context-Aware (SIPM-ACA) in this study is shown in Fig. 1 in which context-awareness is done using user's image experience.

The multimedia image data collection and search in the SIPM-ACA can be done as follows:

- A variety of multimedia image data that user created and user experiences are transferred via the cloud.
- Multimedia images required for automatic context-awareness are uploaded.
- Content-Based Image Retrieval (CBIR) is used to search similar multimedia images from the uploaded multimedia images.
- The searched multimedia images are expressed via user experiences. Figure 2 shows the user experience as a format of XML.
- Using the user experience, user definition is classified into semantic inference.

Figure 3 shows how to classify user definition into semantic inference.

In the figure, the X axis refers to a positive value and the Y axis refers to a preference value. Since semantic image is matched through user experience, more objective foundation can be made with more user experiences obtained.

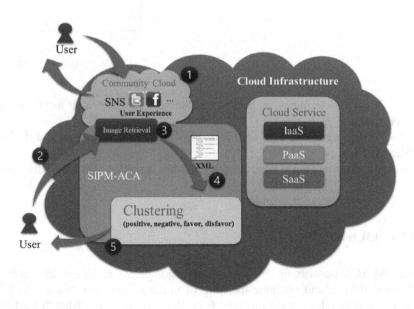

Fig. 1 Overview of SIPM-ACA

Fig. 2 XML for user experience

```
<image id=" ">
    <Experience><!-- User Experience Value -->
        <positive><!-- Positive Experience -->
            <value/>
        </positive>
        <negative><!-- Negative Experience -->
            <value/>
        </negative>
        <favor><!-- Favor Experience -->
            <value/>
        </favor/>
        <disfavor><!-- disfavor Experience -->
            <value/>
        </disfavor>
    </Experience>
</image>
```

Fig. 3 Clustering for user experience

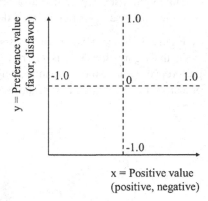

- The X axis determines a positive value via positive and negative user experiences.
- The Y axis determines a preference value via positive and favor and disfavor user experiences.
- Semantic classification is conducted by dividing a section into four subsections.

4 Design of SIPM-ACA

The SIPM-ACA consists of "user interface" through which images are received from smart devices and semantic meaning of image is provided, "image retrieval manager" that searches image received from the user through CBIR, "cloud data manager" that provides images required for retrieval, and "clustering manager" that inferences image's semantic meaning through semantic classification. Figure 4 shows the architecture of the SIPM-ACA.

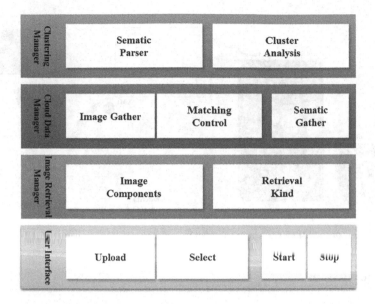

Fig. 4 SIPM-ACA architecture

The operation of user interface consists of image selection used in semantic image processing, upload of the selected image, start and termination of semantic image processing. Image retrieval manager consists of retrieval kind to select a method required for CBIR and image components for image data configuration definition. Cloud data manager consists of image gather that reads images required for image retrieval, semantic gather that reads image's semantic meaning, and matching control that matches image and semantic meaning. Clustering manager consists of semantic parser that analyzes semantic meaning of the retrieved images and cluster analysis that classifies images according to semantic viewpoints.

5   Implementation of SIPM-ACA

The implementation screen of the SIPM-ACM proposed by this paper is shown in Fig. 5. Figure 5 ① creates an image of arbitrary object using a smart device. Figure 5 ② uploads the created image to the cloud system through the Internet. Figure 5 ③ shows how user definition is classified into semantic inference using user experiences. Figure 5 ④ provides a semantic meaning of context aware from the image to the user.

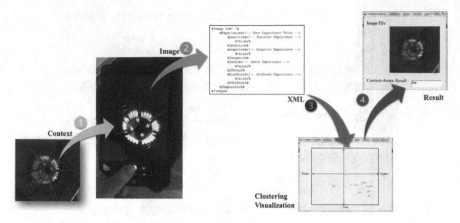

Fig. 5 Screen of the SIPM-ACA implementation

6 Conclusions

This paper proposed a semantic inference scheme using user definition in order to overcome previous context-aware schemes using only components of multimedia image data. The SIMPM-ACA collects similar images using components in images. It also collects user definitions through user experiences. Image inference can be done based on collected information. In the future, we will study not only semantic identification for context-awareness but also objective judgment via automated system based on expert's subjective judgements in the business sector.

Acknowledgments This research was supported by Basic Science Research Program through the National Research Foundation of Korea (NRF) funded by the Ministry of Education (NRF-2014R1A1A2053564). And also this research was supported by the MSIP (Ministry of Science, ICT and Future Planning), Korea, under the ITRC (Information Technology Research Center) support program (IITP-2015-H8501-15-1014) supervised by the IITP (Institute for Information and communications Technology Promotion).

References

1. Luo H, Shyu M-L (2011) Quality of service provision in mobile multimedia—a survey. Hum-Cent Comput Inf Sci 1(5):1–5
2. Sanna G, Angius A, Concas G, Manca D, Pani FE (2015) PCE: a knowledge base of semantically disambiguated contents. J Converg 6(2):10–18
3. Jeong J-S, Bang D-W (2014) An unified representation of context knowledge base for mobile context-aware system. J Inf Process Syst 10(4):581–588
4. Benlamri R, Zhang X (2014) Context-aware recommender for mobile learners. Hum-Cent Comput Inf Sci 4(12):1–34
5. Dey A (2001) Understanding and using context. Pers Ubiquit Comput 5(1):4–7

6. Datta R, Joshi D, Li J, Wang JZ (2008) Image retrieval: ideas, influences and trends of the new age. ACM Comput Surv 40(2):1–60
7. Mangijao Singh S, Hemachandran K (2012) Content-based image retrieval using color moment and gabor texture feature. Int J Comput Sci Iss 9(1):299–309 (Issue 5)
8. Krinidis S, Chatzis V (2010) A robust fuzzy local information C-means clustering algorithm. IEEE Trans Image Process 19(5):1328–1337
9. Wang Q, Chen L, Yap P-T, Guorong W, Shen D (2010) Groupwise registration based on hierarchical image clustering and atlas synthesis. Hum Brain Mapp 31(8):1128–1140
10. Karthikeyan M, Aruna P (2013) Probability based document clustering and image clustering using content-based image retrieval. Appl Soft Comput 13(2):959–966
11. Baccianella S, Esuli A, Sebastiani F (2010) SentiWordNet 3.0: an enhanced lexical resource for sentiment analysis and opinion mining. In: Proceedings of the 7th conference on international language resources and evaluation, Valletta, Malta, 17–23 May 2010, pp 2200–2204
12. An J, Kim H-W (2015) Building a Korean sentiment lexicon using collective intelligence. J Intell Inf Syst 21(2):49–74

Real-Time Barcode Objects Localization by Combining Frequency and Corner Features

Myeongsuk Pak and Sanghoon Kim

Abstract A 2D barcode region localization system for the automatic inspection of logistics objects has been developed. For the successful 2D barcode localization, frequency of the pixel distribution within average 2D barcodes is modeled and the average model of 2D barcode is combined with the corner features to localize the objects having high possibility of 2D barcode candidates An automatic 2D barcode localization software was developed with frequency and corner features and we tested our system on real camera images of several popular 2D barcodes. It improves on runtime of our previous method.

Keywords 2D barcode localization · Barcode detection

1 Introduction

1D or 2D barcode systems are very important in logistics, product packaging and other various commercial applications. Due to the limited capacity of 1D barcodes, 2D barcode systems have been widely used in recent years. In the two-dimensional barcode symbols, data are encoded in both the height and width of the symbol, and the amount of data that can be contained in a single symbol is significantly greater than that stored in a one dimensional symbol. Obviously, the main advantage of using 2D barcodes is that possibly a large amount of easily- and accurately-read data can "ride" with the item to which it is attached. Common examples of 2D barcodes include Data Matrix, PDF417, Aztec Code, CodaBlock, MaxiCode and QR Code. In Japan, the QR Code has been widely used to exchange messages in daily life. The Taiwan High Speed Rail system uses a QR Code on train tickets to prevent the use of fake tickets. 2D barcodes are now deployed extensively by several tagging systems in the life sciences, and for agricultural product portfolios, semiconductors, and electronic products [1].

M. Pak · S. Kim (✉)
Department of Electrical Electronic and Control, Hankyong National University,
327, Jungang-ro, Kyonggi-do Anseong, Korea
e-mail: kimsh@hknu.ac.kr

© Springer Science+Business Media Singapore 2016
J.J. (Jong Hyuk) Park et al. (eds.), *Advanced Multimedia and Ubiquitous Engineering*, Lecture Notes in Electrical Engineering 393,
DOI 10.1007/978-981-10-1536-6_45

2D barcode systems require imaging sensors for scanning and acquisition. Many image-based methods for barcode detection have been proposed. Ouaviani et al. [2] adopted some image processing techniques to segment some of the most common 2D barcodes, including the QR Code, MaxiCode, DataMatrix, and PDF417. Parikh and Jancke [3] introduced a new technique in 2D barcode localization and segmentation by using a process of thresholding, orientation prediction and then corner localization. Kato et al. [4] developed a recognition algorithm which first finds the location of the finder patterns. Then search for the L-shape guide bar (part of the 2D barcode), and performing projective mapping to correct symbol distortion to localize the barcode region. Hu et al. [5] localized the barcode region using texture direction analysis and hough transform. Xu and McCloskey [6] focused on solving the localization and de-blurring problem of motion-blurred 2D barcodes using corner feature and motion direction estimation. Liu et al. [7] analyzed four features of color, geometric structure, gradient and regional "L-type" edge in each connected region to select the barcode region. Lin and Lin [1] used modified run length smearing algorithm for locating multi-symbology and multiple barcodes.

Most other techniques in literature usually work for single 2D barcode, and rely on finding the unique pattern, or are based on the assumptions that 2D barcodes are close to the scanning cameras. But our researches are focused on to increase the detection accuracy of 2D barcode area candidate even when the scanning cameras are in distant from the printed barcodes as in practical barcode inspection application systems.

In this research, a 2D barcode region localization system for the automatic inspection of logistics objects has been developed. For the successful 2D barcode localization, frequency of the pixel distribution within average 2D barcodes is modeled and the average model of 2D barcode is combined with the corner features to localize the final 2D barcode candidates. An automatic 2D barcode localization software was developed with frequency and corner features and we tested our system on real camera images of several popular 2D barcodes. It improves on runtime of our previous method [8].

2 2D Barcode Localization System

This research uses two features to localize 2D QR Code from an image. Firstly, the captured color camera image is converted to grayscale. Then frequency model of the average 2D QR Codes is calculated to characterize the normal QR Codes based on the frequency of the distribution of the pixels included in 2D QR Code. And then using the model of frequency feature, we scan the whole input image with the 50×50 window to verify the similarity between the frequency distribution and the corresponding scanning area. The detected candidate areas are finally combined with the corner features detected results [6] to increase the detection accuracy of 2D barcode.

2.1 Corner Features for 2D Barcode Localization

We employed corners as low-level features for localizing 2D barcode. A 2D barcode is a pattern comprised of small, rectangular black patches on a white background. As a result, its gradient orientation histogram has two strong peaks at orthogonal orientations. Corner features, whose own localization is determined by orthogonality in local gradient orientation distribution, provides a natural tool for us to localize barcode area from this gradient prior [6]. We use the Harris corner detector [9] for corner detection.

2.2 Frequency Distribution Model

Compared to the other patterns in image, all pixel values within 2D barcodes have obvious gray level distribution of black and white group. They are keeping very high and uniform frequency in gray level changes. Figure 1 shows 2D barcode pixel value changes. So we describe the Frequency Model of the average QR Codes to show the general features of the QR Codes.

For calculating the frequency, global thresholding is applied to remove bright pixels and to retain only dark pixels firstly. Then, the pixel value changes are measured by the direction from 0° to 90°. We defined total pixel value changes as below equation:

$$Freq_{direction} = \sum_i N_i \tag{1}$$

where N_i is the number of pixel value changes along a scanline i in one direction.

In our research, the size of QR Code basic cell captured has the range of 2–5 pixels because QR Code is usually being captured badly from a long distance camera in the logistics environment, therefore we suppose that the size of QR Code is more than 40×40 and frequency search window is more than 50×50. For low computation complexity, the search window slides by 5–10 pixels.

Fig. 1 Example of 2D barcode color pattern

2.3   *Estimation of Final QR Code Region*

We estimate the barcode region with the above model. First, a barcode region has a very high frequency of black/white changes, thus we define S_1 as:

$$S_1 = Freq_0 + Freq_{90} \tag{2}$$

where $Freq_0$ and $Freq_{90}$ is the frequency on direction of $0°$ and $90°$. Then, a barcode region must be a concentration of corners, thus we define S_2 as:

$$S_2 = \sum_{(x,y) \in C(P)} M(x,y) \tag{3}$$

where $C(P)$ is the set of all detected corners in the patch P, $M(x, y)$ is the corner strength (magnitude) map.

Based on the modeling and score description of QR Code candidates region above, we finally chosen the region by simply adding the two scores (S_1, S_2) numerically and we give a candidate definition window only to the region with the all 2 score values.

3   Experiments

We tested the proposed algorithm on 100 test images captured in practical packaged objects printed with QR Codes. The proposed algorithm is implemented using Visual C++ programming environments and the test image size is 640×480 and 1280×720 with 24 bits color.

Table 1 summarized the detection accuracy and runtime. It showed that the proposed method has satisfactory accuracy and runtime. The proposed method showed faster runtime than previous works while maintaining still high accuracy as our previous method [8], which achieved more than 98 % in accuracy better than the other works.

Several examples are shown in Fig. 2 and the results shows the algorithm is working well even when there are many similar patterns are existing. Each image may contain different numbers of QR Codes.

4   Conclusion

A 2D barcode region localization system for the automatic inspection of logistics objects has been developed. For the successful 2D barcode localization, frequency of the pixel distribution within average 2D barcodes is modeled and the average model of 2D barcode is combined with the corner features to localize the objects

Table 1 Average performance of four algorithms

		Lin et al. [1]	Xu et al. [6]	Pak et al. [8]	Proposed method
Accuracy (%)		93.06	94.56	98.93	98.91
Runtime (ms)	640 × 480	157	60	71	63
	1280 × 720	731	113	189	116

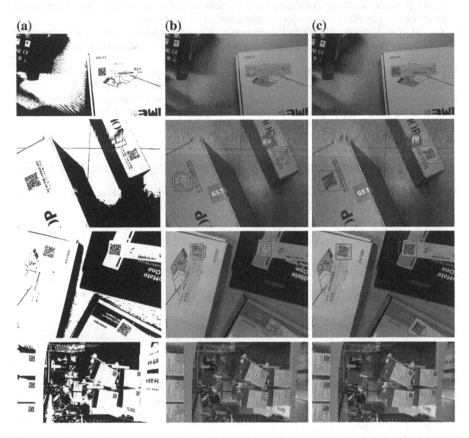

Fig. 2 Barcode localization examples. **a** binary image, **b** detected features and **c** final located region

having high possibility of 2D barcode candidates. An automatic 2D barcode localization software was developed with frequency and corner features and we tested our system on real camera images of several popular 2D barcodes. It improves on runtime of our previous method.

Acknowledgments This research was supported by Basic Science Research Program through the National Research Foundation of Korea (NRF) funded by the Ministry of Education (2015R1D1A1A01057518).

References

1. Lin DT, Lin CL (2013) Automatic location for multi-symbology and multiple 1D and 2D barcodes. J Mar Sci Technol 21(6):663–668
2. Ouaviani E, Pava A, Bottazzi M, Burnelli E, Caselli F, Guerrero M (1999) A common image processing framework for 2D barcode reading. In: 7th international conference on image processing and its applications, vol 2, pp 652–655
3. Parikh D, Jancke G (2008) Localization and segmentation of a 2D high capacity color barcode. In: Proceeding of IEEE workshop on applications of computer vision, pp 1–6
4. Kato H, Tan KT, Chai D (2008) Development of a novel finder pattern for effective color 2D-barcode detection. In: International symposium on parallel and distributed processing with applications, pp 1006–1013
5. Hu H, Xu W, Huang Q (2009) A 2D barcode extraction method based on texture direction analysis. In: Fifth international conference on image and graphics, pp 759–762
6. Xu W, McCloskey S (2011) 2D barcode localization and motion deblurring using flutter shutter camera. In: IEEE workshop on applications of computer vision, pp 159–165
7. Liu Z, Guo X, Cui C (2012) Detection algorithm of 2D barcode under complex background. Int Proc Comput Sci Inf Technol 53(1):116–122
8. Pak M, Kim S (2015) 2D barcode localization using multiple features mixture model. In: Advances in computer science and ubiquitous computing, LNEE. Springer, Berlin, vol 373, pp 677–682
9. Harris C, Stephens M (1988) A combined corner and edge detector. In: Proceedings of the 4th Alvey vision conference, pp 147–151

Study and Comparison of Virtual Machine Scheduling Algorithms in Open Source Clouds

Nandimandalam Mohan Krishna Varma and Eunmi Choi

Abstract Cloud computing is a widely used technology in software industry. In cloud computing, virtualization technique is used to provide most of the services. Mostly cloud providers use Virtual machines to satisfy the user requests. Efficient scheduling of virtual machines is an important job in cloud computing. In this paper, we study Eucalyptus, Open Nebula, and OpenStack cloud virtual machine scheduling algorithms. Eucalyptus cloud uses Round Robin and Greedy virtual machine scheduling algorithms. Open Nebula uses match making scheduling algorithm and filter scheduling algorithm is used for virtual machine scheduling in OpenStack. Round Robin, Greedy, Match making, and Filter scheduling algorithms are compared in this paper.

Keywords Cloud computing · Virtualization · Scheduling · Openstack

1 Introduction

Cloud computing [1] is a most extensively used system, where computers are networked to deliver computing, storage, and application services using virtualization technology. Cloud computing satisfies five necessary features, such as on demand service, access network, resource pooling, elasticity and measured services. To achieve these, cloud computing provide three kinds of basic service models, such as Software as a Service (SaaS), Platform as a Service (PaaS) [2] and Infrastructure as a Service (IaaS) [3]. Customer relationship management applications are commonly used in the SaaS. PaaS delivers application platform for developers. PaaS is used to develop and deploy the user code. Cloud Foundry, google app engine, amazon elastic beanstalk and Microsoft azure environments can be used for PaaS. IaaS can be used to build private infrastructure or deliver

N.M.K. Varma · E. Choi (✉)
School of Business IT, Kookmin University, Seoul, South Korea
e-mail: emchoi@kookmin.ac.kr

N.M.K. Varma
e-mail: nmohankv@kookmin.ac.kr

© Springer Science+Business Media Singapore 2016 349
J.J. (Jong Hyuk) Park et al. (eds.), *Advanced Multimedia and Ubiquitous Engineering*, Lecture Notes in Electrical Engineering 393,
DOI 10.1007/978-981-10-1536-6_46

infrastructure for public. Usage of IaaS can reduce the installation budget. IaaS can provide resources such as computation, storage and communication with the help of virtualization. Eucalyptus [4], Open Nebula [5], and OpenStack [6] environments can be used to provide IaaS. Virtual Machine (VM) scheduling algorithms in these IaaS environments are explained in this paper. In this paper we compare VM scheduling features with a number of aspect, such as VM support, component, container, controller, management, middleware, etc.

In this paper, Sect. 2 shows virtual machine scheduling in different clouds, comparison of scheduling algorithms is given in Sects. 3 and 4 concludes the paper.

2 Virtual Machine Scheduling in Cloud Computing

Cloud computing uses virtual machines for provisioning of resources and services. Resources are allocated to users by scheduling of virtual machines to various hosts located in different geographical locations. Selecting a particular host to virtual machine is called virtual machine scheduling. In this section virtual machine scheduling techniques in various open source clouds are explained in detail.

2.1 Eucalyptus Cloud Virtual Machine Scheduling Algorithms

Eucalyptus [7] is an open source cloud software, which is used to build private cloud computing environment. It was designed with user classes, such as administrators and clients. Eucalyptus supports different hypervisors and Linux operating systems. It consists of five mandatory components, such as Cloud Controller, Walrus, Cluster Controller, Storage Controller, and Node Controller. Cloud controller makes high-level scheduling decisions and send requests to the Cluster controllers. It is responsible for managing the virtualized resources. Walrus stores and accesses virtual machine images and user data. Cluster controller schedules virtual machine execution on specific nodes and manages the virtual machine instances. Storage controller works with cluster controller. Node controller is responsible for starting and stopping of virtual machines.

Eucalyptus uses Greedy or Round Robin scheduling algorithms for scheduling of virtual machines in the cloud. Round Robin virtual machine scheduling algorithm focuses on distributing the load equally to all the hosts. In this algorithm, scheduler allocates one virtual machine to each host in a cyclical method. Round Robin virtual machines scheduling is similar to the round robin process scheduling. The scheduler starts assigning virtual machines to each host and moves to next virtual machine to place into the next host. This algorithm is repeated for all the hosts until each host have at least one virtual machine. After placing virtual

Table 1 Advantages and disadvantages of eucalyptus cloud scheduling algorithm

Scheduling algorithm	Advantages	Disadvantages
Round robin algorithm	Load balancing maintained Response time is less Fairness is good	Power consumption is more
Greedy algorithm	Less power consumption Response time is less	No fairness No load balancing

machines to all hosts it will go to the first host and repeat the same process for next virtual machine placements. The main advantage of round robin virtual machine scheduling algorithm is that it consumes all the resources in a balanced order. Equal number of virtual machines are allocated to all the hosts which guarantee fairness. Major drawback of using round robin virtual machine scheduling algorithm is that the power consumption will be high as many hosts will be kept turned on for a long time. Whereas Greedy round robin virtual machine scheduling algorithm chooses first node which can meet the initial requirements. For this reason power consumption is less in Greedy but load balancing is not achieved. Advantages and disadvantages of round robin and greedy algorithms are shown in Table 1.

2.2 Open Nebula Cloud Virtual Machine Scheduling Algorithm

Open Nebula is an open source private cloud environment. It supports different hypervisors and operating systems. Open Nebula has five components such as front-end, hypervisor enabled hosts, data stores, service network, and virtual machine network. Front-end executes the Open Nebula services. Hypervisor enabled hosts provide the resources needed by the virtual machine instances. Data stores hold the base images of the virtual machines. Service Network is used to support interconnection of the storage servers and Open Nebula control operations. Virtual machine networks are physical networks that support Virtual LANs for the virtual machines.

Open Nebula uses match making algorithm for scheduling for virtual machines in the cloud. Open Nebula default scheduler provides a rank scheduling policy that places virtual machines on physical hosts as per the rank. Open Nebula uses immediate lease provisioning to schedule cloud resources using match making algorithm. The match making algorithm allocates hosts with a higher rank expression first to virtual machines. Rank expression is important in applying placement policies like packing, striping and load aware policy. Packing policy minimizes the number of hosts in use by using allocating more virtual machines to hosts. Striping policy maximizes the resources available to virtual machines in a host. Load aware policy uses hosts with minimum load. Table 2 shows the policy and its tasks of Open Nebula scheduling algorithm.

Table 2 Open nebula scheduling algorithm

Policy	Task
Packing	Minimizes the number of hosts in use
	Packs virtual machines in hosts to reduce fragmentation
	Selects the hosts with more virtual machines running
Striping	Maximizes the resources available to virtual machines
	Spread the virtual machines to hosts
	Selects the hosts with less virtual machines running
Load aware	Maximizes the resources available to virtual machines
	Selects nodes with less load
	Select the nodes the less CPU load

2.3 OpenStack Cloud Virtual Machine Scheduling Algorithm

The OpenStack Cloud consists of different components, such as Dashboard, Compute, Networking, Object storage, Block storage, Identity service, Telemetry, Orchestration, Database service and Image Services. Dashboard service is named as Horizon in OpenStack. Horizon provides a web based portal to interact with other OpenStack services, such as starting instances, assigning IP addresses and stopping instances. Compute service is named as Nova and it is the core part of the OpenStack cloud to manage the instances of virtual machines and networking. Networking service is named as Neutron and it enables network connectivity for other OpenStack services such as Nova. Object Storage service is named as Swift and it stores and retrieves unstructured data objects from scalable system. Block storage service is named as Cinder and it provides persistent block storage to running instances. Identity service is name as Keystone, it provides authentication and authorization service for other OpenStack services. Telemetry service is name as Ceilometer, it monitors and meters the OpenStack cloud for billing, scalability, and statistical purposed. Orchestration service is named as Heat and it orchestrates multiple composite cloud applications. Database service is name as Trove and it provides scalable and reliable cloud database as service functionality for bother relational and non-relational database engines. Image Service is named Glance, it stores and retrieves virtual machine disk images.

Nova makes use of Glance during instance provisioning. OpenStack can be deployed and runs on different Linux environments. It supports KVM, XEN [8], and Hyper-V hypervisors. Nova services can be deployed on same host with other OpenStack components or can be installed on different compute node hosts. OpenStack network consists of public and private networks. IP addresses from the public network are associated with instances of virtual machines to be accessed from the Internet, whereas private network is used for internal web service communication. OpenStack components uses Rabbit Message Queue Protocol for internal communication. Nova API processes virtual machine requests with the help of Queue. Virtual machine scheduling done via nova-scheduler. Nova-scheduler

Table 3 Filter scheduling algorithm

Stages	Class	Functionality
Filtering	Disk filter	Compute node hosts with sufficient disk space are filtered
	Ram filter	Filters the compute node hosts based on the available RAM
Weighing	Disk weigher	Compute node hosts are weighted and sorted based on the free disk space
	Ram weigher	Computes the weight based on the available RAM on the compute node host
	Metrics weigher	Computes the weight based on the compute node host's various metrics
Filter scheduling	Host manager	Passes the compute node hosts which are filtered and weighed
	Filter scheduler	Assigns the virtual machines to appropriate compute node hosts

maps nova-API calls to the suitable OpenStack components. Nova scheduler is responsible for scheduling of virtual machines in OpenStack. Nova scheduler uses filter scheduling algorithm by default. Filter scheduling algorithm uses filtering and weighing process to schedule the virtual machines in nova compute node hosts. Filtering of compute node hosts will be done based on the filter parameters. Based on the filtered hosts weighing process will be started. Weighing process can compute the weight based on the compute node host metrics. Hosts are weighted and sorted with the least weighing compute node host first and high weighing compute node host last. Least weighing compute node host will be select to schedule the virtual machine. Filter scheduling algorithm is written in python. Table 3 shows the each stages in filter scheduling, corresponding classes, and functionality of each class.

Other than disk filter and ram filter there are various filters like core filter, computer filter, image properties filter, availability zone filter, compute capabilities filter, and so on. Among the filters compute filter, ram filter, and availability zone filters are default filters. Other filters can be used along with or instead of default filters. Filter scheduler takes the compute node hosts that remain after the filters have been applied. After that applies one or more cost function to each compute node host to get numerical scores for each compute node host and the cost score is multiplied by a weighing constant.

3   Comparison of VM Scheduling Algorithms in Different Clouds

Table 4 compares the Round Robin, Greedy, Match making, and Filter scheduling algorithms of Eucalyptus, Open Nebula, and OpenStack clouds.

Round robin algorithm is time efficient, because it automatically selects the next host for scheduling of virtual machine. Greedy virtual machine scheduling

Table 4 Scheduling algorithms

Cloud environment	VM scheduling algorithm	Property
Eucalyptus	Round robin	Time efficient
	Greedy	Power saver
Open Nebula	Match making	Cost effective
OpenStack	Filter scheduling	Memory aware

algorithm is power saver, because it places all the possible virtual machines in the first host, so remaining hosts can save the power consumption. Match making virtual machine scheduling algorithm is cost effective, because it optimizes the resource most suitable for the virtual machine.

4 Conclusions

This paper aims to study the various virtual machine scheduling algorithms in open source private cloud environments such as Eucalyptus, Open Nebula, Nimbus, and OpenStack. Brief introduction is given about the Eucalyptus, Open Nebula, Nimbus, and OpenStack cloud components. Round Robin and Greedy virtual machine scheduling algorithms of Eucalyptus and Nimbus clouds are explained. Open Nebula cloud's match making virtual machine scheduling algorithm details are given. Detailed explanation of OpenStack Nova's filter scheduling algorithm is give in this paper. Comparison of Round Robin, Greedy, Match making, and Filter scheduling algorithms are given. Filter scheduling algorithm is memory aware, because it can filter the host based on the ram filter and weights can be calculated based on the memory.

Acknowledgments This research was supported by Basic Science Research Program through the National Research Foundation of Korea (NRF) funded by the Ministry of Education. (Grant Number: 2011-0011507).

References

1. Rimal BP, Choi E, Lumb I (2009) A taxonomy and survey of cloud computing systems. In: International joint conference on INC, IMS and IDC 5, pp 44–51
2. Hossny E, Khattab S, Omara F, Hassan H ((2013)) A case study for deploying applications on heterogeneous PaaS platforms. In: International conference on cloud computing and big data, CloudCom-Asia, pp 246–253
3. Varma NMK, Choi E (2013) Extending grid infrastructure using cloud computing. In: Ubiquitous information technologies and applications. Springer, Netherlands, pp 507–516

4. Nurmi D, Wolski R, Grzegorczyk C, Obertelli G, Soman S, Youseff L, Zagorodnov D (2009) The eucalyptus open-source cloud-computing system. In: Cluster computing and the grid (CCGrid), IEEE/ACM international symposium, vol 9, pp 124–131
5. Ristov S, Gusev M (2013) Security evaluation of open source clouds. In: EUROCON, pp 73–80
6. Teixeira J (2014) Developing a cloud computing platform for big data: the openstack nova case. In: International conference on big data, pp 67–69
7. Varma NMK, Choi E (2012) A scalable grid infrastructure in the eucalyptus cloud environment. In: The second international conference on computers, networks, systems, and industrial applications, pp 286–289
8. Varma NMK, Min D, Choi E (2011) Diagnosing CPU utilization in the Xen Virtual Machine Environment. In: The 6th international conference on computer sciences and convergence information technology, pp 58–63

Forensic Approach for Data Collection in Guest Domain Based on Mobile Hypervisor

Kyung-Soo Lim, Jeong-Nye Kim and Deok-Gyu Lee

Abstract A variety of new security technology has emerged in the mobile security area recently, especially domain isolation technique is widely used, such as TrustZone, Samsung KNOX, etc. By storing user sensitive information and business data in a secure domain, which is isolated from normal domain, may not be exposed to unexpected security accident or unauthorized access. When the security incidents occurred on these devices, it might be impossible to collect data from secure domain, because common forensic tools cannot be accessed in isolated domain. Therefore, it is necessary to research data collection techniques on the device based on domain separation technology. This paper discusses data collection techniques in the secure domain applied by mobile hypervisor-based separation technology.

Keywords Mobile hypervisor · Data collection · Domain separation technology · Forensic acquisition

1 Introduction

In February 2015, Google launched the "Android for Work" enterprise solutions that support the device security, separate domains (personal/business), business services which is including apps to take advantage of smart work. The android for work provides a SE Linux-based security, data encryption, enterprise business app

K.-S. Lim (✉) · J.-N. Kim
Electronics and Telecommunications Research Institute, 218 Gajeong-ro, Yuseong-gu, Daejeon, South Korea
e-mail: lukelim@etri.re.kr

J.-N. Kim
e-mail: jnkim@etri.re.kr

D.-G. Lee
Seowon University, 377-3 Musimseoro, Chungbuk Heungdeok-gu, Cheongju, South Korea
e-mail: deokgyulee@gmail.com

© Springer Science+Business Media Singapore 2016 357
J.J. (Jong Hyuk) Park et al. (eds.), *Advanced Multimedia and Ubiquitous Engineering*, Lecture Notes in Electrical Engineering 393,
DOI 10.1007/978-981-10-1536-6_47

(a separate app market only for android for work), and separate personal/business data isolation, device management console, etc. In the past, Samsung has announced KNOX solution which provides security features that enable business and personal content to coexist on the same handset. The user presses an KNOX icon that switches from Personal to Work area with no delay or reboot wait time, which is based on ARM TrustZone techniques [1]. The manufacturer has claimed this feature will be fully compatible with Android and Google and will provide full separation of work and personal data on mobile devices [2]. The similarities of two services is just the domain separation for normal and business areas (also as called as domain or world). Nowadays, there are various separate domain technologies has emerged and researched in response to the malicious attacks on mobile devices recently.

Unlike logical separation based on separated app market like these solutions, the hypervisor-based domain isolation with traditional virtualization techniques are being widely researched and announced [3, 4]. A hypervisor-based mobile virtualization technology is a technology that isolates plurality of virtual machines generated by single piece of physical mobile equipment and allows communication between the virtual machines to be performed over only an authenticated channel, thereby ensuring a secure execution environment [5]. Figure 1 shows general structure of mobile devices which is mobile hypervisor has been applied. Host and guest OS are separated on two different domains by the hypervisor. As we mentioned above, a way to access and collect information from guest OS uses particular inter-domain communication channel based on the device drivers.

In this case, different operating systems (OSs) may be installed on the guest domain. For example, Secure Execution (SE) is a technique to ensure the secure

Fig. 1 An example of type 2 mobile hypervisor structure

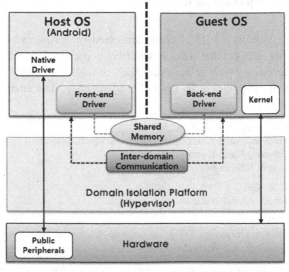

execution environment by making possible to communicate isolated through an authorized channel created by each of the multiple virtual machines [6]. Corresponding to the malicious attacks, SE are separated by isolated domains using virtualization. Most of cases, the security domain is used to store user-sensitive information (such as contacts, call history, photos), secure execution, illegal access protection and so on. Furthermore, financial transactions, mobile banking are operated in secure domain. Several ongoing techniques are following: an open source project Xen-ARM [2], TeeMo by the ETRI [3, 4], MVP (Mobile Virtualization Platform) by VMware and others [7].

However, in the mobile device to which a domain separation technology has been applied, general digital evidence collection tools based on the normal domain cannot be accessed and acquired from the isolated secure domain, furthermore, collecting digital evidence may be impossible by conventional forensic tools. Thus, forensic techniques, corresponding to operating environment (OS) in the isolated secure domain, is necessary to collect digital evidence in the secure domain.

In this paper, we describe a design of forensic collection tool for providing data collection on the isolated secure domain especially which is based on mobile hypervisor. Specifically, the proposed technique are based on live forensics. In case of a particular type 2 hypervisor, data storage of guest OS exists in volatile memory of the host OS. It means an investigator cannot collect user information when the target device was powered off. Which is why we've described our approach is based on live forensic techniques.

2 Forensic Approach for Data Collection in Guest Domain Based on Mobile Hypervisor

This chapter describes a forensic approach for providing forensic acquisition in a domain separation-based mobile device in order for an investigator to collect digital evidence in the secure domain of a target mobile device. The suggested design of evidence collection tool includes a collection module, a control module, and a transmission module.

The collection module includes a filesystem analysis unit, a file duplication unit, a memory dump unit, and a deleted file recovery unit. The filesystem analysis unit acquires a file record and metadata as digital evidence by analyzing the metadata information of the filesystem of secure domain in accordance with domain separation-based mobile device. The file duplication unit collect an identical file corresponding to an original file by performing duplicating physical file data allocation (such as clusters, pages, etc.), in which the data of the file has been stored, based on metadata of the filesystem because integrity may be damaged by simple file copying in the focus of digital forensics. The memory dump unit provides a memory dump function when the memory analysis, used in secure domain of the domain separation-based mobile device, is required. The deleted file recovery unit recovers a deleted file using filesystem metadata of the deleted file which is based on the result of the filesystem analysis unit.

The control module includes a digital evidence metadata generation unit, a log management unit, and an integrity verification unit. The digital evidence metadata generation unit creates the metadata of the collected digital evidence. That is, the digital evidence metadata generation unit creates and manages important metadata, such as the path, size and timestamps information of the collected evidence file. The log management unit generates and manages log history regarding information on which a digital evidence collection function has been performed. The integrity verification unit provides functions of calculating and comparing the cryptographic hash values between the collected file and the original file to determine whether they match each other. The transmission module includes a data encryption unit and an authentication management unit. The data encryption unit and the authentication management unit. The data encryption unit performs the function of encrypting collected digital evidence based on a security key issued by the authentication center server and unique to the target device. Our earlier research paper [7] describes the issuing key with the authentication mechanism. The authentication management unit provides a management function for the authentication of an investigator and the maintenance of a session upon transmission the remote evidence management server over a network.

Figure 2 shows a flowchart illustrating digital evidence collection in a domain separation-based mobile device [8]. At first, the target device information collection module of target device for conducting forensic investigation, collects user identification information (e.g., a user name, a telephone number, and a communication service provider, a target device manufacture serial number, etc.) by analyzing the corresponding domain separation-based mobile device. The target device information collection module transfers the collected user identification information to the control module. It transfers the investigator authentication key value and received user identification information of the corresponding domain separation-based mobile device to the authentication center server over a network in order to allow the investigator permission and the target device registration. Accordingly, the authentication center server confirms the investigator, and then transfers a security key which is generated by user identification information of the target device in accordance with domain separation-based mobile device. In this case, the control module receives and stores the security key.

Thereafter, the target device information collection module collects the system feature information (for example, a manufacturer, an OS platform and version, a processor chipset type, kernel-related information, installed software information, etc.) of the corresponding domain separation-based mobile device under the control of the control module. The target device information collection module transfers the collected system feature information to the control module. The control module transmits the received system feature information to the evidence management server over a network. Accordingly, the evidence management server starts analysis

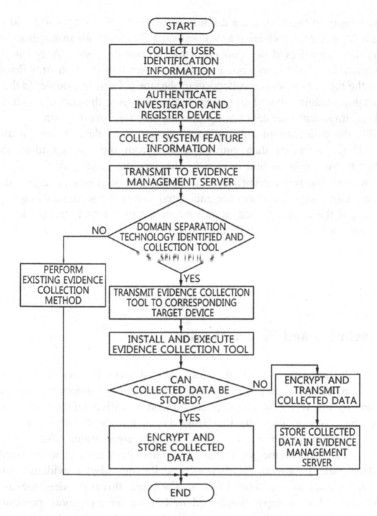

Fig. 2 A flowchart illustrating a method of collecting digital evidence in a domain separation-based mobile device

based on the received system feature information. Identifying a domain separation technology applicable to the corresponding domain separation-based mobile device based on the system feature information, determining whether the technology has been actually applied, and selecting a suitable evidence collection tool. Especially, a hypervisor-based mobile virtualization technology may be identified by installed kernel module and drivers which are required to execute a hypervisor in the normal domain.

If, as a result of the analysis, a domain separation technology will be identified and a suitable evidence collection tool is selected. The evidence management server transfers the selected evidence collection tool to mobile device. Accordingly, the control module of the corresponding domain separation-based mobile device transfers the received evidence collection tool to the collection module. In this case, the collection module is based on mobile hypervisor. And this module collects files and related important user data for conducting forensic investigation.

Finally, the collection module transfers the collected data to the transmission module. If the collected data can be stored from the corresponding domain separation-based target mobile device to the separate storage device, the transmission module receives a security key from the control module, encrypts the data using the security key, and stores the encrypted data in the separate storage device. In contrast, if the collected data cannot be stored in external storage device, the transmission module receives a security key from the control module, encrypts the data using the security key, and transmits the encrypted data to the evidence management server. Accordingly, the evidence management server stores the received collected data.

3 Conclusion and Future Works

Currently, the security technologies for smart devices has developing domain separation techniques to improve reliability and security. Supporting trusted execution environments for secure application and sensitive information could be protected against malicious attacks. However, in the mobile device to which a domain separation technology has been applied, conventional digital evidence collection tools based on the general domain cannot be accessed and acquired from the isolated secure domain, furthermore, collecting digital evidence may be impossible by conventional forensic tools. Therefore, this paper describes forensic approach for a domain separation-based mobile device and, more particularly a forensic tool design, in order for an investigator to collect digital evidence in the secure domain of a target mobile device. We also have been researching a project to develop military-grade security mobile solution based on security platform with mobile hypervisor. The suggested technique is applied to this research project for collecting digital evidence in the event of the infringement incident occurred.

Acknowledgments Foundation item: This work was supported by the ICT R&D program of MSIP/IITP, Korea. [R0101-15-0195(10043959), Development of EAL 4 level military fusion security solution for protecting against unauthorized accesses and ensuring a trusted execution environment in mobile devices]

References

1. Frenzel T, Lackorzynski A, Warg A, Härtig H (2010) ARM TrustZone as a virtualization technique in embedded systems. In: 12th real-time linux workshop
2. Samsung KNOX from Wikipedia. https://en.wikipedia.org/wiki/Samsung_Knox
3. Kim Y, Lee Y, Kim J (2012) TeeMo: a generic trusted execution framework for mobile devices. In: International conference on computer, networks, systems, and industrial applications (CNSI), pp 579–583
4. Andrus J, Dall C, Van't Hof A, Laadan O, Nieh J (2011) Cells: a virtual mobile smartphone architecture. In: Proceedings of the 23th ACM symposium on operating systems principles
5. Kim K, Kim C, Jung S, Shin H, Kim J (2008) Inter-domain socket communications supporting high performance and full binary compatibility on Xen. In: Proceedings of the fourth ACM SIGPLAN/SIGOPS, pp 11–20
6. Colp P, Nanavati M, Zhu J, Aiello W, Coker G, Deegan T, Loscocco P, Warfield A (2011) Breaking up is hard to do: security and functionality in a commodity hypervisor. In: Proceedings of 23rd ACM symposium on operating systems principles
7. Lim K, Jeon Y, Kim J, Lee D (2015) A methodology for live forensic acquisition in secure domain based on domain separation technology. AISC Appl Comput Eng 362:1113–1123
8. Lim K, Park S, Kim J, Lee D (2015) Functional considerations in military-grade security platform using a mobile hypervisor. Comput Sci Appl Lect Notes Electr Eng 330:1413–1418

Modeling and Simulation of PV Modules Based on ANFIS

Ziqiang Bi, Jieming Ma, Wanjun Hao, Xinyu Pan, Jian Wang, Jianmin Ban and Ka Lok Man

Abstract This work presents an optimized method to simulate the modeling of photovoltaic (PV) modules with measured data of PV array. The current-voltage (I-V) characteristics are estimated via adaptive neuro-fuzzy inference system (ANFIS). The proposed ANFIS method takes advantages of no need of internal parameters of PV model and can achieve a more accurate estimation of PV characteristics. By compared with Villalva's model, radial basis function neural networks (RBFNN) and support vector machine (SVM) method, the results predicted by the proposed ANFIS approach show the best estimation performance in terms of root mean squared error (RMSE), mean absolute percentage error (MAPE) and coefficient of determination (R^2).

Keywords ANFIS · Modeling · Characteristic estimation

1 Introduction

PV model is a performance prediction tool that estimates current-voltage (I-V) or power-voltage (P-V) characteristics via environmental conditions. In the last few years, several analytical modeling methods, utilizing mathematical expressions, have been proposed to determine the I-V relations of PV modules [1–5]. Although analytical modeling methods are easy to use, it normally requires primary knowledge of the used PV modules. In 2009, Villalva et al. [5] proposed a comprehensive approach that fits the I-V curve by using the data available in manufacturer's

Z. Bi · J. Ma (✉) · W. Hao · X. Pan · J. Wang · J. Ban
School of Electronic and Information Engineering, Suzhou University of Science and Technology, Suzhou 215009, China
e-mail: jieming84@gmail.com

K.L. Man
Department of Computer Science and Software Engineering, Xi'an Jiaotong-Liverpool University, Science Building, No. 111, Ren'ai Road Suzhou Industrial Park, Suzhou 215123, Jiangsu, China

© Springer Science+Business Media Singapore 2016   365
J.J. (Jong Hyuk) Park et al. (eds.), *Advanced Multimedia and Ubiquitous Engineering*, Lecture Notes in Electrical Engineering 393,
DOI 10.1007/978-981-10-1536-6_48

datasheet, such as open-circuit, short-circuit current, maximum output power, voltage and current at the maximum power point (MPP).

Since artificial intelligence (AI) algorithms showed high accuracy and flexibility in the prediction of non-linear systems, recently, the AI-based methods have been introduced in the field of PV modeling. A radial basis function neural network (RBFNN) based PV model was proposed by Bonanno et al. [6] in 2012 to improve the accuracy of the prediction. Shi et al. [7] applied support vector regression (SVR), a regression technique based on Vapnik's concept of support vectors [8], in forecasting the power output of photovoltaic systems. Simulation results showed the RBFNN and SVR models are effective and promising in performance estimation.

This paper is to present a more accurate and efficient PV model based on adaptive neuro-fuzzy inference system (ANFIS). The ANFIS was first introduced by Jang [9] in 1993, and has been widely used in MPPT [10], face recognition [11] and object tracking [12]. The proposed ANFIS-based model takes advantages of no need of any model parameters. Its accurateness is verified by applying the model to three modules using different PV technologies (multi-crystalline, mono-crystalline and thin-film). It is envisaged that the proposed work can be useful for circuit simulator developers and PV system designers who require a simple and accurate model.

The rest of the paper is organized as follows: the next section introduces the proposed ANFIS modeling method. The results and the validated performance of the proposed method are given in Sect. 3. Section 4 summaries this work.

2 ANFIS-Based PV Model

ANFIS is a fuzzy inference system based on Takagi-Sugeno fuzzy modeling [13]. ANFIS combines the fuzzy inference and neural network algorithms. It overcomes the limitations of fuzzy inference that the identification procedure of the parameters of membership functions (MFs) is not efficient for complex systems.

Considering there are two inputs x, y and one output f, and they obey the following rules:

$$\text{If } x \text{ is } A_i \text{ and } y \text{ is } B_i$$
$$\text{Then } f_i = p_i x + q_i y + r_i (i = 1, 2)$$

where $\{p_i, q_i, r_i\}$ is the parameter set. The architecture of ANFIS is shown in Fig. 1.

Every node in layer 1 has a node function

$$O_i^1 = \mu_{A_i}(x), \ i = 1, 2$$
$$O_i^1 = \mu_{B_{i-2}}(y), \ i = 3, 4 \tag{1}$$

Fig. 1 The architecture for ANFIS

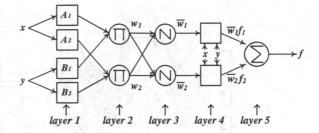

The $\mu_{A_i}(x)$ or $\mu_{B_i}(y)$ is usually chosen to be generalized bell function.

$$\mu_{A_i}(x) = \frac{1}{1 + \left[\left(\frac{x - c_i}{a_i}\right)^2\right]^{b_i}}$$

$$\mu_{B_i}(y) = \frac{1}{1 + \left[\left(\frac{y - c_i}{a_i}\right)^2\right]^{b_i}}$$

(?)

where $\{a_i, b_i, x_i\}$ is the parameter set of the generalized bell function.

Layer 2 is a general function that multiplies the input values.

$$\omega_i = \mu_{A_i}(x)\mu_{B_i}(y) \tag{3}$$

The output of layer 2 need to be normalized by layer 3, the output of the normalization layer is

$$\bar{\omega}_i = \frac{\omega_i}{\sum_i \omega_i} \tag{4}$$

The node function of the nodes in layer 4 is to multiply the outputs of layer 3 and the related supposed function.

$$O_i^4 = \bar{\omega}_i f_i = \bar{\omega}_i(p_i x + q_i y + r_i) \tag{5}$$

The last layer computes the overall output as the summation of the outputs of layer 4.

$$O^5 = \sum_i O_i^4 = \sum_i \bar{\omega}_i f_i \tag{6}$$

The ANFIS architecture for the proposed model is shown in Fig. 2. The input data of the ANFIS model for the photovoltaic estimation model includes the irradiance (G), the ambient temperature (T) and the operating voltage (V), while the output is the current of the PV module.

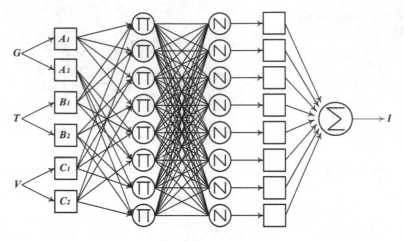

Fig. 2 The ANFIS architecture for the proposed PV model

3 Results and Discussions

In this work, three different statistical indicators were applied in order to evaluate the performance of different kinds of estimation approaches, that include root mean squared error (RMSE), mean absolute percent error (MAPE) and coefficient of determination (R^2). The mathematical expression of these three indicators are given as follows.

$$RMSE = \sqrt{\frac{1}{n}\sum_{i=1}^{n}(\hat{I}_i - I_i)^2}$$

$$MAPE = \frac{1}{n}\sum_{i=1}^{n}|\frac{\hat{I}_i - I_i}{I_i}|$$

$$R^2 = 1 - \frac{\sum_{i=1}^{n}(\hat{I}_i - I_i)^2}{\sum_{i=1}^{n}(\hat{I}_i - \bar{I}_i)^2} \tag{7}$$

where $\hat{I}_i$ is the predicted current, I_i is the measured one and $\bar{I}$ is the mean of the measured currents.

The RMSE is frequently used to measure the differences between the values predicted by the model and the related experimental data. MAPE is also used to measure the errors but it differs in values from module to module because the short-circuit current varies with different PV models. The R^2 evaluates how well the predicted data fits the measured one. $R^2 = 1$ indicates that the predicted values and the measured values are perfectly fitted, while $R^2 = 0$ indicates that the predicted values do not fit the measured values at all.

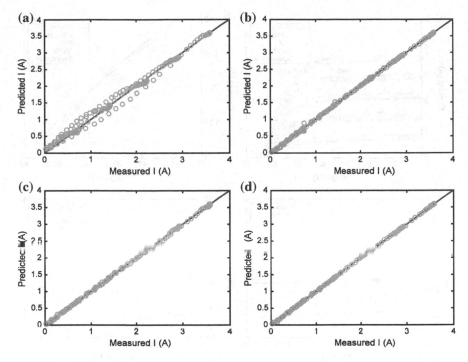

Fig. 3 Operating current predicted by different modeling approaches versus the measured data **a** Villalva's model **b** RBFNN **c** SVM **d** ANFIS (color figure online)

A comparative experiment has been done among the I-V curves of TS-150C1 (Thin Film) predicted by Villalva's model, RBFNN, SVM and the proposed ANFIS models. The results are shown in Fig. 3. Figure 3 depicts the median deviation in 100 runs of the current predicted by four approaches from the measured current of TS-150C1, which is extracted from the datasheet. If the red circle is below the unit-slope straight line, then it indicates that the predicted value is smaller than the measured one, and vice versa. As can be seen, the estimation results of RBFNN model are much better than that of Villalva's model. However, some red circles can be found to deviate from the unit-slope straight line, indicating that some big errors still exist in the predicted I-V curve. It is hard to distinguish the estimation capability of SVM and ANFIS models from Fig. 3.

Figure 4a depicts the photovoltaic I-V curves of TS-150C1 predicted by the methods mentioned above and the measured data extracted from datasheet. Figure 4b–d show the details in the appointed areas. As can be obviously observed that the predicted curve from ANFIS is relatively close to the measured one.

Table 1 lists the mean results of three mathematical indicators for three different modules including mono-crystalline 'SUNTECH STP265S-20' 265 W PV module,

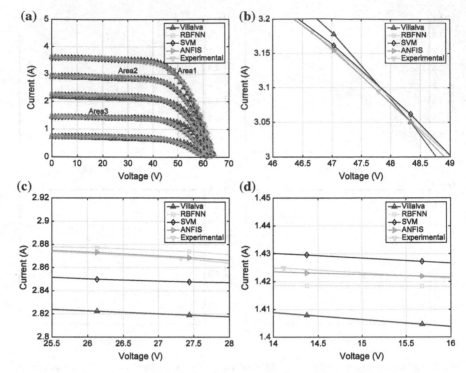

Fig. 4 *I-V curves* of TS-150C1 obtained by different approaches **a** overall view **b** area 1 **c** area 2 **d** area 3 (color figure online)

Table 1 Mean results in 100 runs of different PV models

Method	STP265S-20 (MONO)			KC200GT (POLY)			TS-150C1 (CIGS)		
	RMSE	*MAPE*	R^2 (%)	*RMSE*	*MAPE*	R^2 (%)	*RMSE*	*MAPE*	R^2 (%)
Villalva	0.7015	0.1998	94.45	0.1967	0.0468	99.27	0.1007	0.1386	99.04
RBFNN	0.1251	0.0228	99.65	0.0722	0.0127	99.82	0.0759	0.0263	97.54
SVM	0.0651	0.0336	99.94	0.0375	0.0080	99.95	0.0208	0.0244	99.96
ANFIS	0.0369	0.0173	99.97	0.0294	0.0059	99.95	0.0122	0.0140	99.98

poly-crystalline 'KYOCERA-Solar KC200GT' 200 W PV module and thin-film 'TSMC-Solar TS-150C1' 150 W PV module in 100 runs of four different estimation approaches. It is observed that the ANFIS based method obtains the lower RMSE and MAPE values and higher R^2 value, indicating the more accurate prediction capability.

4 Conclusions

In this paper, an adaptive neuro-fuzzy inference system (ANFIS) based approach has been proposed to estimate the photovoltaic characteristics of various PV modules. The proposed ANFIS based method estimates I-V relations of PV modules with environmental conditions, and does not need any primary knowledge of the used PV modules. The robustness of the proposed method has been evaluated with modules of different PV technologies. Three modeling approaches, Villalva's model, RBFNN and SVM, have been used to benchmark the proposed method. The simulation results show that the proposed ANFIS model obtains the lowest RMSE, MAPE and highest R^2.

Acknowledgments The authors would like to thank the anonymous reviewers for their constructive comments and suggestions to improve this paper. This research is supported by the Natural Science Research Project of Higher Education of Jiangsu (Grant No. 15KJB480002), the National Natural Science Foundation of China (Grant No. 31477109) and the Science and Technology Project of Ministry of Housing and Urban-Rural Development (Grant No. 2016-K1-19, 2014-K1-040).

References

1. Brano VL, Orioli A, Ciulla G, Gangi AD (2010) An improved five-parameter model for photovoltaic modules. Sol Energy Mater Sol Cells 94:1358–1370
2. Brano VL, Orioli A, Ciulla G (2012) On the experimental validation of an improved five-parameter model for silicon photovoltaic modules. Sol Energy Mater Sol Cells 105:27–39
3. Ma J, Ting TO, Man KL, Zhang N, Guan S-U, Wong PWH (2013) Parameter estimation of photovoltaic models via cuckoo search. J Appl Math 2013:8
4. Chin VJ, Salam Z, Ishaque K (2015) Cell modelling and model parameters estimation techniques for photovoltaic simulator application: a review. Appl Energy 154:500–519
5. Villalva MG, Gazoli JR, Filho ER (2009) Comprehensive approach to modeling and simulation of photovoltaic arrays. IEEE Trans Power Electron 24(5):1198–1208
6. Bonanno F, Capizzi G, Graditi G, Napoli C, Tina GM (2012) A radial basis function neural network based approach for the electrical characteristics estimation of a photovoltaic module. Appl Energy 97:956–961
7. Shi J, Lee W-J, Liu Y, Yang Y, Wang P (2011) Forecasting power output of photovoltaic system based on weather classification and support vector machine. In: Proceedings of IEEE Industry Applications Society Annual Meeting, pp 1–6
8. Drucker H, Burges CJC, Kaufman L, Smola A, Vapnik V (1996) Support vector regression machines. Adv Neural Inf Process Syst 28(7):779–784
9. Jang JR (1993) ANFIS: adaptive-network-based fuzzy inference system. IEEE Trans Syst Man Cybern 23(3):665–685
10. Kharb RK, Shimi SL, Chatterji S, Ansari MdF (2014) Modeling of solar PV module and maximum power point tracking using ANFIS. Renew Sustain Energy Rev 33:602–612
11. Sharma R, Patterh MS (2015) A new pose invariant face recognition system using PCA and ANFIS. Optik 126:3483–3487
12. Choi IH, Pak JM, Ahn CK, Lee SH, Lim MT, Song MK (2015) Arbitration algorithm of FIR filter and optical flow based on ANFIS for visual object tracking. Measurement 75:338–353
13. Takagi T, Sugeno M (1985) Fuzzy identification of systems and its applications to modeling and control. IEEE Trans Syst Man Cybern 15:116–132

Non-negative Kernel Sparse Model for Image Retrieval

Yungang Zhang, Lei Bai and Bo Peng

Abstract Sparse representations of signals have become an important tool in computer vision. In this paper, we propose a non-linear non-negative sparse representation model: NNK-KSVD. In the sparse coding stage, a non-linear update rule is proposed to obtain the sparse matrix. In the dictionary learning stage, the proposed model extended the kernel KSVD by embedding the non-negative sparse coding. The proposed non-negative kernel sparse representation model was evaluated on two public image datasets for image retrieval, promising image retrieval performance was obtained.

Keywords Non-negative sparse coding · Kernel · Dictionary learning · Image retrieval

1 Introduction

In recent years, sparse representations of signals have become an important tool in computer vision. In many applications in computer vision, such as image denoising, image super-resolution and object recognition, sparse representations have produced remarkable performance [1–3]. It has also been verified that sparse representation or sparse coding can achieve good outcomes in many image retrieval tasks [4–6].

In sparse-based computer vision tasks, one often needs to learn a dictionary from given sample images [7]. Many algorithms have been proposed to tackle the problem of dictionary learning, the method of optimal directions (MOD) [8] and the KSVD algorithm [9] are two of the most well-known methods.

Y. Zhang (✉) · L. Bai · B. Peng
School of Information Science and Technology, Yunnan Normal University,
Kunming 650092, China
e-mail: Yungang.zhang01@gmail.com

© Springer Science+Business Media Singapore 2016
J.J. (Jong Hyuk) Park et al. (eds.), *Advanced Multimedia and Ubiquitous Engineering*, Lecture Notes in Electrical Engineering 393,
DOI 10.1007/978-981-10-1536-6_49

The dictionaries learned by MOD and KSVD are linear representations of the data. However, in many computer vision applications, one has to face non-linear distributions of the data, using a linear dictionary learning model often leads to poor performance. Therefore several non-linear dictionary learning methods have been proposed. Among them, a recently proposed method kernel KSVD (KKSVD) [10] has shown its ability to obtain better image description than the linear models.

Although the kernel KSVD can outperform its linear counterparts by introducing the non-linear learning procedure, the learned sparse vector and the dictionary yet comprise both additive and subtractive interactions. From the perspective of biological modeling, the existence of both the additive and subtractive elements in the sparse representations of signals is contrary to the non-negativity of neural firing rates [11, 12]. Moreover, the negative and positive elements in the representations may induce the 'cancel each other out' phenomenon [13]. Therefore, many researchers have claimed to use non-negative sparse representations in vision-related applications [14–17]. The non-negative sparse representations are based on the constraints that the input data Y, the dictionary D, and the sparse vector x are all non-negative. Nevertheless, these non-negative sparse representations are all based on linear learning models, therefore their ability to capture the non-linear distributions of data is limited.

Motivated by this drawback of the existing non-negative sparse representation models, in this paper, we propose a non-linear and non-negative sparse model: non-negative kernel KSVD (NNK-KSVD), which integrates the distinctive features of the non-linear models and the non-negative models. In NNKKSVD, the non-negative constraints are embedded into the kernel KSVD for sparse coding and dictionary learning. With the non-negative constraints, the new update rules for sparse vector searching and dictionary learning of kernel KSVD are introduced. The proposed NNK-KSVD sparse model was tested on several benchmark image datasets for the task of image retrieval, state-of-the-art results were obtained.

2 The Non-negative Kernel KSVD

The non-negative sparse coding (NNSC) stresses both the non-negativity and sparseness for data representation. Therefore, given a set of data Y, the NNSC can be defined as the following minimization problem:

$$\text{argmin } Y - DX^2 \; s.t.$$

$$\|x_i\|_0 \leq T, \|d_j\|_2 = 1. D_{ij} \geq 0, X_{ij} \geq 0, \forall i, j. \tag{1}$$

where X is the sparse matrix containing sparse vectors, D is the dictionary and T is the sparse threshold.

In NNSC data representation procedure, the first stage is to optimize the sparse matrix X. The global minimization can be obtained by quadratic programming or gradient descent. In the second stage, the dictionary D is learned. The obtained sparse matrix X is fixed here, then D can be obtained by dictionary learning algorithms.

With the non-negative constraint, the dictionary atoms become sparser and converge to the building blocks of the training samples [18]. However, the existing non-negative sparse models are all based on the linear learning algorithms, their inability to capture the non-linear data distribution inspires us to embed the non-negativity into the non-linear sparse models.

The kernel KSVD proposed in [10] is used here for non-linear data description. As we try to make the kernel KSVD produce the non-negative dictionaries and coefficient matrices, it is necessary to vary the original kernel KSVD model. With the non-negative and non-linear constraints, now the goal of the sparse coding changed to:

$$\min_X \|\varphi(Y) - \varphi(Y)AX\| \ s.t. X \geq 0. \tag{2}$$

where $\varphi(\cdot)$ is the kernel function to make the non-linear mapping and A is the non-linear dictionary. In the sparse coding stage, an iterative pursuit algorithm is proposed in order to keep the coefficients non-negative:

$$x^{t+1} = x^t .* \left(A^T K(Y,Y)\right)./\left(A^T K(Y,Y)Ax^t + \lambda\right) \tag{3}$$

where $K(\cdot)$ is the kernel matrix, t represents the iteration number, $.*$ and $./$ represent entry-wise multiplication and division.

In the dictionary update stage, the dictionary atoms must be kept nonnegative as well. Use the same techniques of the kernel KSVD, under the nonnegative constraint, the minimization problem in (2) now has been changed to:

$$\min_{a_k, x_R^k} \left\|\varphi(Y)E_k^R - \varphi(Y)a_k x_R^k\right\|_F^2, \ s.t. \ a_k, x_R^k \geq 0. \tag{4}$$

In (4), one can see that it has the same nature with KSVD, we try to find the best rank-1 matrix which can approximate the error matrix E_k^R. However, in order to keep the non-negativity and to reach the local minima, the KSVD cannot be used direcctly. An iterative algorithm is proposed here, as illustrated in Algorithm 1.

Algorithm 1 Iterative algorithm for non-negative approximation for E_k^R

Initialization: Set

$$a_k = \begin{cases} 0 & if\ u(i) < 0 \\ u(i) & otherwise \end{cases}, \quad x_R^k = \begin{cases} 0 & if\ v(i) < 0, \\ v(i) & otherwise \end{cases}$$

where $u = \sigma^{-1} E_k^R v_1$, $v = \sigma^{-1} v_1^T$. σ^{-1} and v_1 can be obtained by SVD [10].

Repeat step 1 to 2 for J times:

1: Update $a_k = \frac{E_k^R x_R^k}{(x_R^k)^T x_R^k}$, if $a_k(i) < 0$, set $a_k(i) = 0$. Otherwise, keep $a_k(i)$ unchanged. i runs for the every entry of the vector.

2: Update $x_R^k = \frac{(a_k)^T E_R^k}{(a_k)^T a_k}$, if $x_R^k(i) < 0$, set $x_R^k(i) = 0$. Otherwise, keep $x_R^k(i)$ unchanged. i runs for the every entry of the vector.

Output: a_k, x_R^k.

Given this non-negative approximation algorithm for the dictionary and the coefficient matrix, now the proposed non-negative kernel KSVD (NNK-KSVD) algorithm for learning the dictionary A and the sparse coefficient matrix X is given in Algorithm 2:

Algorithm 2 The NNK-KSVD algorithm

Input: Training sample set Y, kernel function $\psi \kappa$.
Initialization: Find a random position in each column of $A^{(0)}$, set the corresponding element to 1. Normalize each column of $A^{(0)}$ to a unit norm. Set the iteration number $J = 1$.
1: *Sparse coding:* Use the iterative update rule in Eq. (3) to obtain the sparse coefficient matrix X(J) with the dictionary $A^{(J-1)}$ fixed.
2: *Dictionary update:* Use the kernel KSVD algorithm to obtain
3: Update $a_k^{(J)}$ and $x_R^k(J)$ with Alg. 1.
4: Set $J = J + 1$ and repeat step 1 to 4 until a stopping criterion is met.
Output: A, X.

3 Experiments and Results

The proposed non-negative kernel sparse model was applied to two image datasets for the tasks of image retrieval. The datasets used in our experiments are Brodatztexture dataset [19] and Corel-1000 image dataset [20].

The SIFT feature is used as image feature in our experiments. For two images I_1 and I_2, the SIFT features are first extracted, then by using the proposed NNK-KSVD algorithm two dictionaries D_1 and D_2 are obtained. D_1 and D_2 are then used to reconstruct image I_2, respectively, two reconstruction errors E_1 and E_2 can be obtained. The similarity between I_1 and I_2 is calculated as follows:

$$\text{Sim}(I_1, I_2) = \frac{E_1 - E_2 + 1}{2} \tag{5}$$

The larger $\text{Sim}(I_1, I_2)$ is, the more similar the images are.

The proposed sparse model was first evaluated on the Brodatztexture dataset. The dataset contains 111 different texture categories, each category has 9 images, some sample images from the dataset can be seen in Fig. 1.

The precision and recall accuracy obtained by the proposed method can be seen in Fig. 2. The average recall accuracy of our proposed method is 76.4 %, and the state-of-the-art on the same dataset is 76.2 % [6].

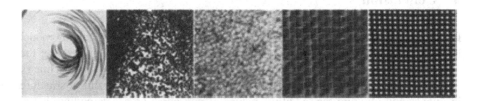

Fig. 1 Sample images from Brodatztexture dataset

Fig. 2 Precision and recall curve of the proposed NNK-KSVD on Brodatztexture dataset

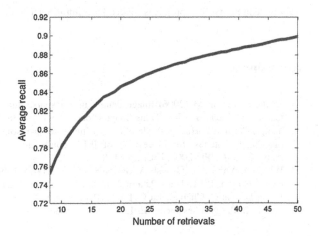

Table 1 Comparison of precision obtained by the proposed model with other methods

Category	Proposed NNK-KSVD	Simplicity [20]	Multi-feature [21]	FIRM [22]
Africa	0.74	0.48	**0.83**	0.47
Beaches	**0.65**	0.32	0.60	0.35
Buildings	0.52	0.35	**0.56**	0.35
Bus	0.77	0.36	**0.86**	0.60
Dinosaur	**0.96**	0.95	0.88	0.95
Elephant	0.72	0.38	**0.87**	0.25
Flower	**0.76**	0.42	0.72	0.65
Horses	**0.87**	0.72	0.85	0.65
Mountain	**0.42**	0.35	0.38	0.30
Food	**0.68**	0.38	0.67	0.48

The best performance of each category is shown in bold

The Corel-1000 image dataset contains 1000 images from ten categories, the categories are: Africa, Beach, Buildings, Buses, Dinosaurs, Flowers, Elephants, Horses, Food and Mountains. Table 1 lists the comparison of precision obtained by the proposed model with other methods.

4 Conclusion

In this paper, we propose a non-linear and non-negative sparse coding model NNK-KSVD. The proposed model extended the kernel KSVD by embedding the non-negative sparse coding. The proposed model was tested on two benchmark image datasets, experimental results show that by exploiting the non-linear structure in images and utilizing the 'additive' nature of non-negative sparse coding, better image retrieval performance can be expected.

Acknowledgments The project is funded by Natural Science Foundation China 61462097.

References

1. Elad M, Aharon M (2006) Image denoising via sparse and redundant representations over learned dictionaries. IEEE Trans Image Process 15(12):3736–3745
2. Yang J, Wright J, Huang T, Ma Y (2008) Image super-resolution as sparse representation of raw image patches. In: Proceeding of IEEE conference on computer vision and pattern recognition. CVPR 2008, IEEE, pp 1–8
3. Wright J, Yang AY, Ganesh A, Sastry S, Ma Y (2009) Robust face recognition via sparse representation. IEEE Trans Pattern Anal Mach Intell 31(2):210–227
4. Wang L, Hsu C, Chen H, Lu C, Lin C, Pei S (2011) Feature-based sparse representation for image similarity assessment. IEEE Trans Multimedia 13(5):1019–1030

5. Thiagarajan JJ, Ramamurthy KN, Sattigeri P, Spanias A (2012) Supervised local sparse coding of sub-image features for image retrieval. In: Proceedings of IEEE conferences on image processing. ICIP 2012, IEEE, pp 3117–3120
6. Guha T, Ward RK (2014) Image similarity using sparse representation and compression distance. IEEE Trans Multimedia 16(4):980–987
7. Mairal J, Bach F, Ponce J (2012) Task-driven dictionary learning. IEEE Trans Pattern Anal Mach Intell 34(4):791–804
8. Engan K, Aase SO, Husoy JH (1999) Method of optimal directions for frame design. In: Proceedings of IEEE international conference on acoustics, speech, and signal processing, vol 5, pp 2443–2446
9. Aharon M, Elad M, Bruckstein AM (2006) The K-SVD: an algorithm for designing of overcomplete dictionaries for sparse representation. IEEE Trans Signal Process 54(11):4311–4322
10. Nguyen HV, Patel V, Nasrabadi N, Chellappa R (2013) Design of non-linear kernel dictionaries for object recognition. IEEE Trans Image Process 22(12):5123–5135
11. Lee DD, Seung HS (1999) Learning the parts of objects by non-negative matrix factorization. Nature 401(6755):788–791
12. Hoyer PO, Hyvärinen A (2002) A multi-layer sparse coding network learns contour coding from natural images. Vis Res 42(12):1593–1605
13. Hoyer PO (2002) Non-negative sparse coding. In: Proceedings of IEEE workshop on neural networks for signal processing, pp 557–565
14. Hoyer PO (2004) Non-negative matrix factorization with sparseness constraints. J Mach Learn Res 5:1457–1469
15. Zass R, Shashua A (2007) Nonnegative sparse PCA. In: In Neural information processing systems, pp 1–7
16. Guthier T, Willert V, Schnall A, Kreuter K, Eggert J (2013) Non-negative sparse coding for motion extraction. In: The 2013 International Joint conference on neural networks (IJCNN), pp 1–8
17. Zhang C, Liu J, Liang C, Xue Z, Pang J, Huang Q (2014) Image classification by non-negative sparse coding, correlation constrained low-rank and sparse decomposition. Comput Vis Image Underst 123:14–22
18. Aharon M, Elad M, Bruckstein AM (2005) K-SVD and its non-negative variant for dictionary design. Proc SPIE Wavelets XI 5914:327–339
19. http://www.ux.uis.no/~tranden/brodatz.html
20. Wang JZ, Li J, Wiederhold G (2001) SIMPLIcity: semantics-sensitive integrated matching for picture libraries. IEEE Trans Pattern Anal Mach Intell 23(9):947–963
21. Chen Q, Ding Y, Li H, Wang X, Wang J, Deng X (2012) A novel multi-feature fusion and sparse coding based framework for image retrieval. In: Proceedings of IEEE conferences on image processing. ICIP 2012, IEEE, pp 2391–2396
22. Chen Y, Wang JZ (2002) A region-based fuzzy feature matching approach to content-based image retrieval. IEEE Trans Pattern Anal Mach Intell 24(9):1252–1267

Feature Pooling Using Spatio-Temporal Constrain for Video Summarization and Retrieval

Jie Ren and Jinchang Ren

Abstract A content-based video retrieval via visual feature pooling is proposed in this paper. Since these visual words represent local features extracted from frame images, spatio-temporal constrains are applied to solve the ambiguity of the model towards effective retrieval of semantic video clips. Both shot level and segment level processing are employed, and the latter is found more robust in dealing with complex scenes where accurate video segmentation may fail. Our experimental results have shown that the constrained scheme help to improve 5 % average matching accuracy. In addition, it suggests that summarized videos at 25–30 % of original size can still maintain a viewing quality of 70–80 % towards fast content delivery.

Keywords Semantic video retrieval · Feature pooling · Content-adaptation · Video summarization

1 Introduction

In the recent two decades, content-based retrieval (CBR) techniques have been proposed for effective indexing and retrieval of digital multimedia, especially for image and video. As CBR can overcome the drawbacks of conventional text-based methods, it has been applied in many applications for its flexible nature and huge commercial potential [1, 2]. One fundamental task of CBR is how to achieve semantic based query.

J. Ren (✉)
College of Electronics and Information, Xi'an Polytechnic University, Xi'an, China
e-mail: renjie@xpu.edu.cn

J. Ren
Department of Electronic and Electrical Engineering, University of Strathclyde, Glasgow, UK
e-mail: jinchang.ren@strath.ac.uk

© Springer Science+Business Media Singapore 2016   381
J.J. (Jong Hyuk) Park et al. (eds.), *Advanced Multimedia and Ubiquitous Engineering*, Lecture Notes in Electrical Engineering 393,
DOI 10.1007/978-981-10-1536-6_50

A video contains a linear structure which is composed of frames in series, where a hierarchical representation can also be extracted via segmentation of video shots and video scenes. Transitions between shots and scenes can be regarded as structuring events which can be detected via analysis of low level features and then used for shot- or event- level retrieval [1–4]. In our paper, rule-based reasoning and machine learning is combined to improve the robustness in extracting these semantics.

With extracted semantics, videos can be retrieved using their associated semantic contents. To represent the video in a short version while keeping the most important contents, content adaptive video summarization is desired in which original videos are represented by either image storyboard or clip skimming for efficient content-access, browsing and retrieval of large video databases [5–7]. In our paper, content of interests are defined using a proposed extracted semantics hence the summarized videos are capable of keeping these semantics for consistency in video retrieval and delivery.

Semantic video retrieval depends on effective extraction of video semantics such as meaningful objects and concepts, and these semantics can then be employed for automatic annotation and content indexing for further retrieval applications. Although global features may be sufficient for separating scenes with significant differences in the global properties, they may not be discriminative enough in most other cases [8]. As a result, representing an image by a set of local image patches has become very popular in visual recognition and retrieval [9–11]. Interest operators are then applied to detect/filter interest points (or regions) based on some spat-temporal saliency [12].

Often, bag-of-features is utilized to represent the "visual texture" of image parts containing objects [13], which is also namely bag of visual words [9], or visual treasures [12, 14]. Many local operators such as Harris' corner detector, Hessian detector and SUSAN detector [15] are rotation invariant. One extension of these detectors is apply them to filtered images using Laplacian of Gaussian (LoG), which lead to corresponding scale invariant detectors. Further details of these detectors as well as application of machine learning approaches like neural network, decision trees and genetic algorithm in this field can be found in [15].

Fig. 1 Diagram of the proposed system

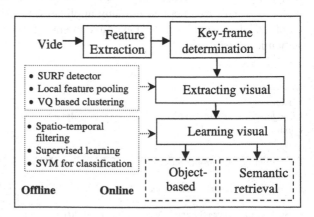

To illustrate how our system works, a block diagram is given in Fig. 1. This contains two main parts namely offline processing and online retrieval, and both of them share majority common modules.

2 Feature Extraction and Keyframe Determination

In our system, the input data is MPEG video, in which block-based motion estimation and data representation forms the fundamental structure. A macroblock of 16×16 pixels is the basic element for analysis and coding, as motion vectors are defined using these macroblocks. In addition, each macroblock is further divided into four 8×8 sub-blocks, on which the DCT and IDCT are applied. Hence there is one DC coefficient and 63 AC coefficients for every sub-block [16].

Based on the block-based DCT, we define $\mu(i)$ and $\sigma(i)$ as the mean and standard derivation for each DC-differencing image $D(i)$, and $p(i)$ is defined as a proportion which represents the percentage of pixels in $D(i)$ that are larger than the given threshold $\lambda(i)$. Then we introduce a combined cut likelihood ℓ_i which related to $\mu(i)$, $\sigma(i)$ and $p(i)$ for cut detection.

$$\ell_i = [1 - \mu(i-1)/[3\mu(i)] + 1 - \sigma(i-1)/[2\sigma(i)] + \sqrt{p(i)}]/3 \qquad (1)$$

After video segmentation, within each shot several keyframes are determined as salient points in both spatial and temporal domains below. Parameters t is used to specify a temporal window of 10 frames; w_μ and w_e are employed to weight the effects of changed intensity and edges in the spatial domain.

$$\kappa^* = \underset{1 \le t < 10}{\operatorname{argmax}}(S_j - S_{j+t})$$
$$S_j = w_\mu \mu_j + w_e(H_j + V_j) \qquad (2)$$

3 Feature Pooling for Visual Object Extraction

In this Section, pooling of visual features is utilized in extracting semantic objects. First, content of interest is extracted from each keyframe, using the Speeded-Up Robust Features (SURF) detector [15]. With the extracted content of interest (COI), we simply divide the whole image into two parts, i.e. COIs and non-COIs. Features are then extracted from all the COIs and stored for further content indexing and matching.

Visual features utilized for pooling include edges, colour features and motion information. In most videos, human activity is the focus. Consequently, in our system, human objects are also determined via skin pixels detection. To model general semantic concepts such as outdoor/indoor, building, the sky, etc., discriminative features are employed for different semantic concept, i.e. edge information is used to classify outdoor/indoor scenes as it is suggested that intensive parallel lines indicate more likely indoor scenes. For the sky, it appears blue and is located to the up-side of the image.

Then, supervised learning is applied which needs image regions with known tags specified in labeled training data or querying images with text descriptions. Support vector machine (SVM) is utilised for supervised training for its good generalisation capacity. The whole image is partitioned into non-overlapped sub-images, and features collected from each sub-image are inputted into the SVMs for training and testing purposes. For each semantic concept, a separate SVM is learnt to make a binary decision. Rule-based reasoning is useful to combine the outputs from individual SVMs to form a final decision, using the dependency as analyzed above.

4 Content-Adaptive Video Summarization and Retrieval

With the extracted human objects and semantic concepts, semantic retrieval of video is achieved for query by these concepts. Content-adaptive summarisation is used for fast delivery of the retrieved results. The strategy for semantic content indexing and retrieval involves two main steps, i.e. extracting semantics for content indexing and semantic retrieval. The contents used for indexing include the detected shot (transition) events, human objects and four semantic concepts, i.e. outdoor, indoor, the building and the sky. The latter five are then employed for shot-level video retrieval applications.

For each retrieved video shot, it contains essential information including frame-based local activity level ℓ_i and associated human objects and semantic concepts. The local activity indicates excitement degree of the frame, and the associated semantics refer to the importance/relevance of the frame to users. Next, we will discuss how to generate effective summarization to adapt with these motion/semantic contents.

Denote $s_k(i)$ as the presentence of human objects and semantics concepts in frame i, where $k = human, outdoor, indoor, sky, building$, also we denote $l_k(i)$ as a new activity level to reflect these objects/concepts which can be defined as follows:

$$l_k(i) = \begin{cases} l_i^{1/(1+s_k)}, & if \quad query \quad kth \quad concept; \\ l_i^{(1+s_k)}, & otherwise. \end{cases} \tag{3}$$

Finally, an overall activity measure $r(i)$ is determined by:

$$r(i) = \prod_k l_k(i) \tag{4}$$

In fact, $r(i)$ is employed to determine the importance of the frame to be included in the summarization. To achieve this, we firstly calculate the accumulated activity measure R_m over the whole sequence, i.e.

$$R_m = \sum_{i=i_{m1}}^{i_{m2}} r(i) \tag{5}$$

where i_{m1} and i_{m2} are the frame boundaries of the clip.

5 Experimental Results

To validate the effectiveness of the proposed system, quantitative evaluations are performed in terms of shot detection, semantics extraction, semantic retrieval and delivery. These are discussed in details as follows.

In total 20 video clips are used for the test, which are all MPEG-1 sequences with a frame size of 352×288. These sequences cover three main topics including news, movies and sports. To enable quantitative evaluations, the two commonly criteria, recall rate R_c and precision rate R_p, are employed. Ground truth maps are manually extracted to define the shot transitions and semantics within the video. For simplicity, human objects and semantic concepts in the video are only defined for I-frames. These can be taken as the average results for all the frames in a group of pictures.

The results on keyframe determination are illustrated in Table 1, which contains results respectively referring to shot-based and clip-based keyframe extraction. In the prior scheme, keyframes are determined for each detected shot; and in the latter one, keyframes are determined in evenly segmented small video clips of 500 frames. For comparison purpose, the result of shot detection is also given.

Regarding the extraction of semantics, the results are quite promising as shown in Table 2. As seen, in general about 90 % of the semantics can be successfully extracted.

As shown in Table 3, a summarisation ratio at about 25–30 % can produce nearly 70–80 % of quality index.

Table 1 Average precision and recall rates for detection keyframe and video shots

	Num.	Detect	Missed	False	Pre. (%)	Recall (%)
Shots	451	466	16	31	93.3	96.5
Keyframe 1	3528	3710	111	243	92.1	95.1
Keyframe 2	3563	3688	84	251	94.3	94.1

Table 2 Average precision and recall rates for semantics extraction

	Num.	Detect	Missed	False	Pre. (%)	Recall (%)	(%)
Outdoor	832	837	70	42	91.0	87.1	89.0
Indoor	1090	1117	76	53	90.8	90.6	90.7
Building	1211	1214	82	61	93.0	88.4	90.7
Sky	908	915	76	40	91.0	88.0	89.4
Road	794	816	63	34	89.6	90.6	90.1
Average	4835	4899	367	230	91.2	89.0	90.1

Table 3 Summarisation ratio vs. average quality index

Ratio (%)	10	15	20	25	30	35	40
Quality (%)	34.2	48.8	61.4	70.2	79.3	84.5	88.7

6 Conclusion

In this paper, we have presented an effective system for semantic video retrieval, where local feature points are determined using SURF detector with objects extracted from keyframes. Pooling of visual features is employed where human objects and several semantic concepts are determined. Considering the spatio-temporal constraints, much improved matching of object COIs can be achieved than using simple nearest neighbor criterion. An improvement of more than 5 % is achieved in semantic video retrieval. The content-adaptive video summarisation has been proved effective in efficient delivery of retrieved results while maintaining a high relevance score ranked by users. This provides useful applications in network applications for online retrieval of videos.

References

1. Cotsaces C, Nikolaidis N, Pitas I (2006) Video shot detection and condensed representation: a review. IEEE Signal Proc Mag 23(2):28–37
2. Ren J, Jiang J, Chen J (2009) Shot boundary detection in MPEG videos using local and global indicators. IEEE Trans Circ Syst Video Tech 19(8):1234–1238
3. Ren J, Jiang J (2009) Hierarchical modelling and adaptive clustering for real-time summarization of rush videos. IEEE Trans Multimedia 11(5):906–917
4. Yuan Y, Wang H, Xiao et al (2007) A formal study of shot boundary detection. IEEE Trans Circ Syst Video Tech 17(2):168–186
5. Ngo CW, Ma YF, Zhang H-J (2005) Video summarization and scene detection by graph modeling. IEEE Trans Circ Syst Video Tech 15(2):296–305
6. Chang S-F, Vetro A (2005) Video adaptation: concepts, technologies, and open issues. Proc IEEE 93(1):148–158
7. Hanjalic A, Xu L-Q (2005) Affective video content representation and modeling. IEEE Trans Multimedia 7(1):143–154

8. Qin J, Yung HC (2010) Scene categorization via contextual visual words. Pattern recognition
9. Everingham M, Gool LV, Williams CKI, Winn J, Zisserman A (2010) The pascal visual object classes (VOC) challenge. In: Int J Comput Vis (IJCV)
10. Tuytelaars T, Lampert CH, Blaschko MB, Buntine W (2010) Unsupervised object discovery: a comparison. IJCV
11. van Gemert JC, Veenman CJ, Smeulders AWM, Geusebroek JM (2010) Visual word ambiguity. IEEE Trans, PAMI
12. Rapantzikos, K., Tsapatsoulis, N., Avrithis, Y., and Kollias, S. 2010, Spatiotemporal Saliency for Video Classification, Signal Processing: Image Communication
13. Zhang J et al (2007) Local feature and kernels for classification of textures and object categories: a comprehensive study. IJCV 73(2):213–238
14. Spyrou E, Tolias G, Mylonas Ph, Avrithis Y (2009) Concept detection and keyframe extraction using a visual thesaurus. Multimed Tools Appl 41(3):337–373
15. Tuytelaars T, Mikolajczyk K (2008) Local invariant feature detectors: a survey. Found Tr Comput Gr Vis 3(3):177–280
16. Jiang J, Qiu K, Xiao G (2008) A block-edge-pattern-based content descriptor in DCT domain. IEEE Trans Circ Syst Video Tech 18(7):994–998

An Output Grouping Based Approach to Multiclass Classification Using Support Vector Machines

Xuan Zhao, Steven Guan and Ka Lok Man

Abstract Support Vector Machine (SVM) classifiers are binary classifiers in nature, which have to be coupled/assembled to solve multi-class problems. One-Versus-Rest (1-v-r) is a fast and accurate method for SVM multiclass classification. This paper investigates the effect of output grouping on multiclass classification with SVM and offers an even faster version of 1-v-r based on our output grouping algorithm.

Keywords Multiclass classification · Support vector machine · Decomposition method · Output grouping

1 Introduction

Support Vector Machine (SVM) is a popular supervised machine learning algorithm for solving problems in classification and regression. An SVM takes a set of training samples (known observations belonging to a certain class/category) and yields a set of decision functions to determine which class a test sample (unknown observation) belongs to [1].

However a novel SVM classifier only solves two-class problems. To solve a multi-class problem, multiple binary SVM classifiers are coupled or assembled as a multi-class SVM. Such a decomposition method plays an important role on the multi-class SVM's generalization performance and time consumption. One-Versus-One (1-v-1), One-Versus-Rest (1-v-r) and ECOC are three of the most commonly

X. Zhao (✉) · S. Guan · K.L. Man
Xi'an Jiaotong-Liverpool University, Suzhou, China
e-mail: xuan.zhao@xjtlu.edu.cn

S. Guan
e-mail: steven.guan@xjtlu.edu.cn

K.L. Man
e-mail: ka.man@xjtlu.edu.cn

© Springer Science+Business Media Singapore 2016 389
J.J. (Jong Hyuk) Park et al. (eds.), *Advanced Multimedia and Ubiquitous Engineering*, Lecture Notes in Electrical Engineering 393,
DOI 10.1007/978-981-10-1536-6_51

used ensemble methods [2, 3]. Empirical result shows 1-v-r is the fastest method in predicting unknown samples [4–6] with good performance.

This paper and investigates the effect of output (class) grouping, which were previously researched in neural networks [7–9], in multiclass SVM classifiers. Finally we offer an even faster version of 1-v-r with the help of the output-grouping algorithm.

2 Background

Output grouping is a learning strategy being applied in neural networks to improve the accuracy and reduce training cost. The strategy is based on observation of class correlation. In previous study in neural networks, strong correlation between two classes i, j implies high similarity. Then i, j can be trained together for better precision [8].

2.1 One-Versus-Rest (1-v-R)

The idea of 1-v-R classification is to build N classifiers for each of the classes. In the training process all the training data is used for every one of the N classifiers. If a classifier is built for class i then the classifier is trained with the samples that belong to class i against the rest of the samples from the training data set.

Once the model is built, an unknown sample goes through all the N classifiers. Each classifier decides whether or not this sample belongs to the corresponding class. Ideally one and only one classifier should respond 'yes' to the unknown sample and the corresponding class will be the class that the sample belongs to, otherwise there is either a clash or a total miss. Under such a circumstance the unknown sample goes to the class with the most training samples.

2.2 Output Grouping

For SVM classifiers, if samples from two classes are 'mixed' together then it is difficult for SVM to draw a line or plane to distinguish the two classes. In the case of 1-v-r, suppose a class i needs to be distinguished from the remaining classes (the 'rest'). If another class j among the rest is highly similar to i then it will also be difficult to tell i and the rest apart, even if other classes among the rest (excluding class j) are easy to be separated from i. As a result, such interaction, correlation or similarity between classes i and j would contribute to a complex but less accurate model.

We tested this hypothesis using the UCI Iris dataset. We duplicated all samples from class 3 and labelled them as class 4, train a linear SVM model using 1-v-r

Iris	Baseline	3 duplicated as 4	3 and 4 grouped
Model size	112	336	256
Accuracy (%)	94.40	65.86	72.57

Table 1 Iris 1-v-r SVM classification performance

method, ran a prediction on training set and ran a 10-fold cross prediction with classifier and the data set. We then merged samples from classes 3 and 4 and labelled them as a new class (grouping), trained and validated an additional 3-versus-4 classifier and merged the results from both classifiers (Table 1).

If the classifier cannot tell 3 and 4 apart, then the best chance of classification error between 3 and 4 should be 50 % (random guessing). Then the cross validated accuracy should be around 71 % instead of 65.86 %. In other words, the strong similarity between class 3 and 4 should not but has affected the performance of other classification tasks. While with class 3 and 4 grouped, we seem to eliminate such undesirable interference.

2.3 Output-Grouping-One-Versus-Rest (OG) Algorithm

We propose an algorithm, OG, which aggregates outputs (classes) by their 'similarity' in groups, then treats the groups as new classes and performs 1-v-r learning.

The algorithm has six components: (1) similarity scorer, (2) class grouper, (3) 1-v-r trainer, (4) intra-group classifier trainer, (5) 1-v-r predictor and (6) intra-group predictor (Figs. 1 and 2; Table 2).

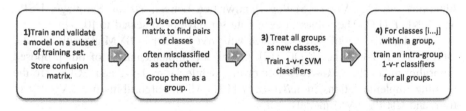

Fig. 1 Training components (1–4) of OG

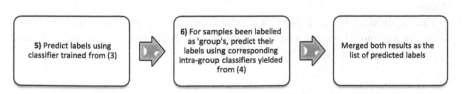

Fig. 2 Prediction components (5 and 6) of OG

Table 2 Grouping algorithm of OG

Input L_sig, list of pair of classes that often been misclassified as each other, sorted by the descending order of mutual misclassification rate. Pairs with misclassification rate lower than the average (or average multiplied by a regularisation parameter) are excluded from the list.
Output G: [], list of groups containing grouped classes

```
while len(L_sig) > 0:
        first_itm = L_sig.pop(0)
        c1, c2 = first_itm[0], first_itm[1]
        group= set().add(c1).add(c2)
        idx = 0
        while 0 <= idx < len(L_sig):
                itm = L_sig[idx]
                if itm[0] or itm[1] in group:
                        pitm = L_sig.pop(idx)
                        group.add(pitm[0]).add(pitm[1])
                        idx = 0
                else: idx += 1
        G.append(group)
```

OG attempts to group "hard-to-tell-apart" classes together so that it should be able to reduce the model complexity, improved the accuracy and further increase the prediction speed. However the speed-up is at the cost of an additional training/prediction, grouping and result merging.

3   Experiments

The OG was evaluated on seven different data sets: UCI Iris Plant, UCI Glass Identification, UCI Vowel, Statlog Handwritten Letters, Statlog Satimage, USPS and MNIST [11]. The values in each data set have been scaled to [0, 1].

Each data set was trained and tested with five multiclass SVM algorithms: OG, OGPG, 1-v-r, 1-v-1 and ECOC [12]. OG is the implementation of our proposed algorithm under the *scikit-learn* framework, while 1-v-r, 1-v-1 and ECOC are the existing implementations in *scikit-learn* [13]. All the algorithms use SVC [2] to train and test the SVM models.

To further address the effectiveness of grouping, we introduce a variant of OG, OG with pre-computed group (OGPG), by supplying the algorithm pre-computed groups.

The experiment for each method ran 50 times for the averaged measurements. Each time the model was trained by randomly-spit 2/3 of the data set and validated on the remaining 1/3 (Table 3).

Table 3 Experiment data sets, parameters and pre-computed groups (OGPG only)

	Size	Classes	Features	Kernel	C	Groups
Iris	150	3	4	RBF	100	(2, 3)
Glass	214	6	9	Poly	100	(1–3, 5)
Vowel	10	11	10	RBF	1000	(4, 5, 10)
Letter	20,000	26	16	Poly	100	(3, 4, 6)
Satimage	7435	6	36	Poly	100	(4, 6, 8–10, 16)
USPS	7291	10	256	Poly	100	(5, 8, 10)
MNIST	10,000	10	780	Poly	100	(7, 9)

4 Results

The accuracy is close for all algorithms except for ECOC in some occasions across all the datasets. OG and OGPG perform slightly better than 1-v-r algorithm on smaller datasets (*iris*, *glass* and *vowel*). However we cannot conclude which algorithm is the best in terms of accuracy (Table 4).

On large data sets (*satimage*, *usps* and *mnist*) OG and OGPG slightly reduced the training time and significantly reduced the prediction time by 0.8–29.2 % and 5.4–30.6 % respectively, compared with 1-v-r method. OGPG is the fastest in terms of prediction, seconded by OG.

Table 4 Averaged accuracy, model size and time consumption of OG, 1-v-r, 1-v-1 and ECOC

		Accuracy (%), StDev/mean	# Support vectors	Training CPU time (ms)	Prediction CPU time (ms)
Iris	OG	**97.25** (2.98)	14	10.8	1.6 (59.06)
	OGPG	**97.25** (3.00)	**13**	10.1	1.4 (180.84)
	1-v-r	97 (2.90)	23	7.2	**0.5** (64.41)
	1-v-1	**97.25** (3.00)	18	6.3	1 (120.51)
	ECOC	90.25 (13.16)	22	**5.2**	2.4 (279.18)
Glass	OG	67.01 (6.72)	238	22	25 (49.64)
	OGPG	67.17 (7.18)	239	22	24 (36.87)
	1-v-r	66.55 (6.57)	241	**17**	**17** (97.77)
	1-v-1	**68.49** (7.40)	**204**	35	62 (39.62)
	ECOC	65.96 (7.34)	511	21	50 (261.80)
Vowel	OG	96.29 (1.97)	**348**	71	71 (28.14)
	OGPG	96 (1.78)	365	74	**58** (58.31)
	1-v-r	95.76 (1.93)	375	**69**	**58** (40.03)
	1-v-1	**96.53** (1.71)	683	135	387 (19.96)
	ECOC	92.71 (2.80)	1507	461	161 (102.60)

(continued)

Table 4 (continued)

		Accuracy (%), StDev/mean	# Support vectors	Training CPU time (ms)	Prediction CPU time (ms)
Satimage	OG	89.09 (0.90)	1739	2107	264 (10.06)
	OGPG	89.09 (0.89)	1731	2037	**259** (7.19)
	1-v-r	**89.16** (0.90)	1810	2983	373 (7.71)
	1-v-1	88.58 (0.93)	**1077**	**560**	488 (6.04)
	ECOC	88.36 (3.28)	3903	7156	799 (19.34)
Letter	OG	94.46 (0.34)	10776	28328	3288 (4.29)
	OGPG	**94.48** (0.33)	**10504**	28164	**3136** (4.95)
	1-v-r	**94.48** (0.34)	10872	28535	3316 (4.40)
	1-v-1	94.8 (0.33)	17813	**4077**	13559 (4.05)
	ECOC	91.62 (0.43)	94667	461447	30190 (12.01)
Usps	OG	98.02 (0.29)	**2086**	19591	4564 (8.91)
	OGPG	98.05 (0.30)	2160	19575	**4230** (6.84)
	1-v-r	97.99 (0.30)	2118	19886	4495 (6.17)
	1-v-1	**98.15** (0.31)	3204	**4666**	10882 (3.46)
	ECOC	97.88 (0.32)	7126	80958	21593 (19.36)
Mnist	OG	96.31 (0.35)	**4866**	50274	21472 (5.36)
	OGPG	96.3 (0.34)	5057	47507	**19809** (2.10)
	1-v-r	**96.35** (0.32)	5018	50759	22781 (2.64)
	1-v-1	96.08 (0.39)	6466	**13038**	55331 (1.79)
	ECOC	95.73 (0.47)	16928	181370	79754 (8.33)

With standard deviation divided by average in the bracket
Bold are the best measured performance among five methods for each data set

On smaller data sets, OG and OGPG's worse speed performance were caused by the fact that the overhead of additional grouping and merging dominates the time consumption of SVM training and prediction.

Even though OG performs an additional training/prediction to determine the grouping on another 33–50 % of the training set, its training time is still less than 1-v-r. The model size is also slightly decreased for all data sets except for *usps* and *mnist*.

5   Discussions and Conclusions

To our disappointment neither OG nor OGPG did improve the accuracy. Our speculation during the experiment shows that the accuracy tends to be *saturated* at a certain point when the number of training samples is *large enough* or the parameters of SVM are *fairly well* optimised.

We may conclude that OG and OGPG improve the speed performance of 1-v-r method even at the cost of performing additional classification tasks.

Our findings show that output grouping is effective at reducing the training complexity of 1-v-r multi-class classification tasks using support vector machines. Nevertheless output grouping can be used to boost the prediction speed of multiclass SVMs with no extra cost. We are now investigating the cause of the *saturated* accuracy and working on combining input and output grouping methods [8, 9, 14–17] for better classification accuracy.

References

1. Chang C-C, Lin C-J (2011) Libsvm. ACM Trans Intell Syst Technol 2(3):1–27
2. svm@scikit-learn.org (2016). Available: http://scikit-learn.org/stable/modules/svm.html
3. Hsu C-W, Lin C-J (2002) A comparison of methods for multi-class support vector machines. IEEE Trans Neural Networks 13(2):415–425
4. Mehra N, Gupta S (2013) Survey on multiclass classification methods. Int J Comput Sci Inf Technol 4(4):572–576
5. Rifkin R (2008) Multiclass classification
6. Tewari A, Bartlett PL (2007) On the Consistency of multiclass classification methods. J Mach Learn Res 8:1007–1025
7. Guan S-U, Li S (2002) Parallel growing and training of neural networks using output parallelism. IEEE Trans Neural Netw 13(3):542–550
8. Yang S, Guan S-U, Guo SJ, Zhao LF, Li WF, Xue HX (2013) Neural Network output partitioning based on correlation. J Clean Energy Technol 1(4):342–345
9. Yang S, Guan SU, Li WF, Zhao LF (2013) Low-interference output partitioning for neural network training. J Clean Energy Technol 1(4)
10. Bordes A, Ertekin S, Weston J, Bottou L (2005) Fast kernel classifiers with online and active learning. J Mach Learn Res 6:1579–1619
11. LIBSVM data: classification, regression, and multi-label. Available https://www.csie.ntu.edu.tw/~cjlin/libsvmtools/datasets/. Accessed on 03 Feb 2016
12. Dietterich TG, Bakiri G (1994) Solving multiclass learning problems via error-correcting output codes. J Artif Intell Res 2:263–286
13. multiclass@scikit-learn.org (2016). Available: http://scikit-learn.org/stable/modules/multiclass.html
14. Guo SJ, Guan S-U, Yang S, Li WF, Zhao LF, Song JH (2013) Input partitioning based on correlation for neural network learning. J Clean Energy Technol 1(4):335–338
15. Guo S, Guan S-U, Li W, Man KL, Liu F, Qin AK (2013) Input space partitioning for neural network learning. Int J Appl Evol Comput 4(2):56–66
16. Guo S, Guan SU, Li W, Zhao L, Song J, Cao M (2012) Promotion-based input partitioning of neural network. In: International conference on computer, communication, automation and control 2012 (CCAC 2012)
17. Guo S, Guan SU, Li W, Zhao L, Song J, Cao M (2014) Promotion-based input partitioning of neural network. In: Proceedings of the 9th international symposium on linear drives for industry applications, vol 3, pp 179–186

Maximum Power Point Estimation for Photovoltaic Modules via RBFNN

Jieming Ma, Ziqiang Bi, Yue Jiang, Xiangyu Tian, Yungang Zhang,
Eng Gee Lim and Ka Lok Man

Abstract Quantitative information of maximum power point (MPP) is crucial for
controlling and optimizing the output power of photovoltaic (PV) modules.
However, it is difficult to obtain the voltage at MPP through direct measurements.
A novel approach of radial basis function neural network (RBFNN) is proposed to
achieve maximum power point estimation in this study. The proposed method has
the capability of determining the MPP of PV arrays directly from the measured
current–voltage data of PV modules, and takes advantages of no need of internal
parameters of PV model. The experimental results show that the proposed approach
can obtain the optimal power output in high accuracy.

Keywords RBFNN · PV modules · Maximum power point estimation

J. Ma (✉) · Z. Bi · Y. Jiang · X. Tian
School of Electronic and Information Engineering, Suzhou University of Science
and Technology, No. 1 Ke Rui Road, Suzhou High-Tech Zone, Suzhou 215009, China
e-mail: jieming84@gmail.com

Y. Zhang
School of Information Science and Technology, Yunnan Normal University,
Kunming 650092, China

E.G. Lim
Department of Electronic and Electrical Engineering, Xi'an Jiaotong-Liverpool University,
No. 111 Ren'ai Road, Suzhou Industrial Park, Suzhou 215123, Jiangsu Province, China

K.L. Man
Department of Computer Science and Software Engineering, Xi'an Jiaotong-Liverpool
University, Science Building No. 111 Ren'ai Road, Suzhou Industrial Park, Suzhou 215123,
Jiangsu Province, China

© Springer Science+Business Media Singapore 2016   397
J.J. (Jong Hyuk) Park et al. (eds.), *Advanced Multimedia and Ubiquitous
Engineering*, Lecture Notes in Electrical Engineering 393,
DOI 10.1007/978-981-10-1536-6_52

1 Introduction

PV modules obtain non-linear current-voltage (I-V) characteristics [1]. Due to the varying atmospheric condition, namely temperature and solar insolation, the power-voltage (P-V) characteristic curve exhibits only one maximum power point (MPP) that varies nonlinearly with these conditions-thus posing a challenge for estimating the locus of MPP.

Maximum power point tracking (MPPT) is a conventional method setting the system operating point to the optimum. Various MPPT methods, such as the perturb-and-observe [2, 3], particle swarm optimization [4, 5] and hybrid method [6, 7], have been proposed. These methods iteratively find the MPP and respond to changes in solar irradiance accordingly, and thus it is difficult for them to quickly acquire the MPPs. In [1], Rodriguez et al. presented an analytic solution of a point in a close neighborhood of the MPP based on the mean value theorem. It was thoroughly proved that this point is enclosed in a ball of small radius that also contains the MPP and therefore can practically be considered as the MPP. A circuit was implemented to demonstrate the feasibility of the non-iterative scheme. To facilitate the efficiency of the MPPT algorithm, Wang [8] proposed a simple and direct-prediction method based on the p-n junction semiconductor theory. The simulation results showed the method can directly determine from an I-V characteristic curve and has a low calculation burden.

The aforementioned analytical methods predict the locus of MPP by using the single-diode model, which includes several parameters. In recent years, the artificial intelligence-based methods have been introduced in the field of PV modeling. Shi et al. [9] applied support vector regression (SVR), a regression technique based on Vapnik's concept of support vectors [10], in forecasting the power output of photovoltaic systems. Abdul Hadi et al. [11] first introduced neuro-fuzzy models to predict solar cell short-circuit current and open-circuit voltage, followed by coordinate translation of a measured I-V response. Celik [12] applied a generalized regression neural network to predict the operating current of PV modules. The operating current was predicted from both neural network. Simulation results showed these models are effective and promising in performance estimation.

Radial basis function neural network (RBFNN) has non-linear approximation features, and they are capable of modeling complex mapping, which perceptron neural networks can only model using multiple intermediary layers [13]. In this paper, an efficient RBFNN-based maximum power point estimation method is proposed to directly predict the voltage at MPP. It takes advantages of no need of any model parameters, and its accurateness is verified by applying the method to four modules using different PV technologies. It is envisaged that the proposed work can be useful for power optimization of a PV generator.

The rest of the paper is organized as follows: the next section introduces the proposed RBFNN based maximum power point estimation method. The results validating the performance of the proposed method are given in Sect. 3. Section 4 summaries this work.

2   Maximum Power Point Estimation Using RBFNN

Artificial neural networks (ANNs) are algorithms which are able to learn from experience, improve their performance and adapt themselves to the changes in the environment [14]. Radial basis function neural networks (RBFNN) is one kind of ANNs consisting of an input layer, a single hidden layer and an output layer, as shown in Fig. 1. All hidden units are constructed by a number of radial basis functions.

The input layer obtains two-dimensional vector $\mathbf{X}$, whose elements are the terminal current $\mathbf{I}$ and voltage $\mathbf{V}$. The output layer has single element, the voltage at MPP $\mathbf{Vmpp}$. For a data set consisting of N input vectors together with the corresponding output currents, the nth $1 \leqslant n \leqslant N$ input and output vector can be represented as Eqs. (1) and (2), respectively:

$$\mathbf{X^n} = \begin{bmatrix} \mathbf{V^n} \\ \mathbf{I^n} \end{bmatrix} \tag{1}$$

$$\mathbf{Y^n} = \mathbf{V^n_{mpp}} \tag{2}$$

In the hidden layer, there are L radial basis neurons $\phi_i (1 \leqslant i \leqslant L)$ connecting directly to all the elements in the input layer [4]. The hidden unit can be expressed as a matrix:

$$\phi = \begin{vmatrix} \phi_1^1 & \phi_2^1 & \cdots & \phi_L^1 \\ \phi_1^2 & \phi_2^2 & \cdots & \phi_L^2 \\ \vdots & \vdots & \ddots & \vdots \\ \phi_1^N & \phi_2^N & \cdots & \phi_L^N \end{vmatrix} \tag{3}$$

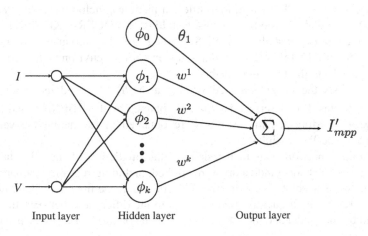

Fig. 1 The structure of radial basis function neural network

Connections between the input and hidden layers have unit weights, denoted as $\mathbf{W} = [w^1, w^2, \ldots, w^L]^T$. The hidden layer transforms the data from the input space $\mathbf{X^n}$ to the hidden space using a non-linear function. The one commonly used is a non-linear Gaussian function as:

$$\phi_i(\mathbf{X^n}) = e^{-\frac{\|x^n - \mu_i\|^2}{2\sigma_i^2}} \tag{4}$$

where $\mu_i(1 \leqslant i \leqslant L)$ represents the center of the RBF, and σ_i is the spread width defining the width of an radial basis function. The centers can be randomly sampled from some set of examples, or they can be determined via a principled clustering technique to find a set of RBF centers which more accurately reflect the distribution of the data points.

A third backpropagation step can be performed to fine-tune all of the RBF net's parameters. The response of each hidden neuron is scaled by its weight, and then is summed to produce the predicted current at MPP I'_{mpp}. The structure of the selected networks leads to the expression of the I'_{mpp} as functions of the terminal current and voltage.

$$I'_{mpp} = f(I, V) \cong \sum_{i=1}^{N} w_i e^{-\frac{(V-\mu_i)^2 + (I-\mu_i)^2}{2\sigma^2}} \tag{5}$$

It is worth pointing out that radial basis networks can require more neurons than standard feedforward.

3 Results and Discussions

In this section, the MPP locus of four different modules, including multi-crystalline 'BP MSX60' 60W PV module, multi-crystalline 'KYOCERA KC200GT' 200W PV module, mono-crystalline 'Shell SQ150' 150W PV module, and thin film 'TSMC TS-150C1' 150W PV modules under various environmental conditions was estimated via the proposed method.

Table 1 lists the mean predicted voltage at MPP V'_{mpp} and its relative error (RE) in 100 runs. It is observed that the RE obtained by the RBFNN based method is below 9 %. More accurate results were obtained in estimating the values of multi-crystalline PV modules.

The trained network was then tested for the prediction of the all data series. Three different statistical indicators were applied, including root mean squared error (RMSE), mean absolute percent error (MAPE) and coefficient of determination (R^2). The RMSE is frequently used to measure the differences between the values predicted by the model and the related experimental data. The MAPE is also used to

Table 1 Mean relative error of V'_{mpp} in 100 runs for different PV modules

Method	MSX60 (multi)			KC200GT (multi)			SQ150 (mono)			TS-150C1 (thin-film)		
	V_{mpp}	V'_{mpp}	RE (%)	V_{mpp}	V'_{mpp}	RE (%)	V_{mpp}	V'_{mpp}	RE (%)	V_{mpp}	V'_{mpp}	RE (%)
STC	17.10	16.78	1.8	26.30	26.65	1.3	34.0	31.44	7.2	7.60	8.42	8.1
NOCT	17.60	17.99	2.2	27.10	27.85	2.8	35.10	35.2	0.3	7.70	8.57	8.7

Conditions at STC: 1000 W/m^2, module temperature 25 °C, AM 1.5
Conditions at NOCT: 800 W/m^2, module temperature 20 °C, AM 1.5

measure the errors but it differs in values from module to module because the short-circuit current is varying from different PV models. The R^2 evaluates how well the predicted data fits the measured one.

The RBFNN was trained with a set of input [$\mathbf{I}$, $\mathbf{V}$] and related target output $\mathbf{I_{mpp}}$, where the solar irradiation G is ranging from 200 to 1000 W/m^2 under a temperature T between 0 and 75 °C. Figure 2 shows the predicted voltage at the MPP of different PV modules. If the red circle is below the unit-slope straight line, then it indicates that the V'_{mpp} is smaller than the measured one, and vice versa. As can be seen, the proposed method provided a correct response with less than 4 % of RMSE.

Figure 3 shows the variation curves of ratios V_{mpp}/V_{oc} and I_{mpp}/I_{sc} under different temperatures and an irradiation intensity of 1000 W/m^2. The V_{oc} and V_{mpp} both linearly decrease with the increase in temperature, while both I_{sc} and I_{mpp} increases lightly with temperature. The temperature coefficient of V_{mpp}/V_{oc} is about -0.081 %/°C, and the temperature coefficient of I_{mpp}/I_{sc} is about 0.015 %/°C. It can also be seen in the inset of Fig. 3 that the I_{sc} and I_{mpp} satisfy the linear proportional relationship $I_{mpp} = 0.9145 \times I_{sc}$.

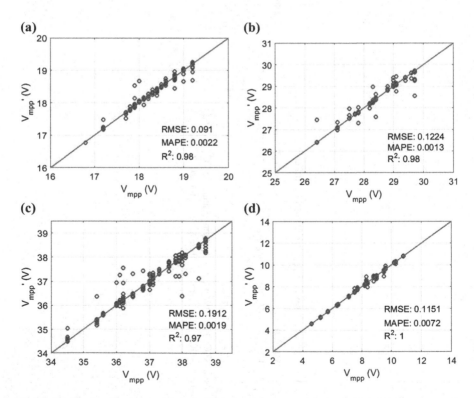

Fig. 2 Predicted voltage at the MPP of different PV modules. **a** MSX60, **b** KC200GT, **c** SQ150, **d** TS150

Fig. 3 The characteristic ratios of V_{mpp}/V_{oc} and I_{mpp}/I_{sc} under different temperatures and an irradiation intensity of 1000 W/m². The *inset* shows the relationship between the short-circuit current I_{sc} and the current I_{mpp} at the MPP for the PV arrays under different temperatures and an irradiation intensity of 1000 W/m²

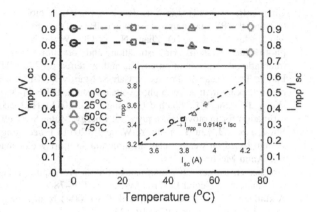

4 Conclusions

A new, simple, and accurate maximum power point estimation method has been presented in this paper. The feasibility of the proposed RBFNN based method for various PV modules subject to different irradiation intensities and temperatures was investigated. It estimates I-V relations of PV modules with environmental conditions, and does not need any primary knowledge of the used PV modules. The experiments demonstrate that the RBFNN based method is capable of predicting the voltage at the MPP in high accuracy. In the future work, the proposed method can also be applied to the optimization of output power.

Acknowedgments The authors would like to thank the anonymous reviewers for their constructive comments and suggestions to improve this paper. This research is supported by the Natural Science Research Project of Higher Education of Jiangsu (Grant No. 15KJB480002), the National Natural Science Foundation of China (Grant No. 51477109) and the Science and Technology Project of Ministry of Housing and Urban-Rural Development (Grant No. 2016-K1-19, 2014-K1-040).

References

1. Rodriguez C, Amaratunga GA (2007) Analytic solution to the photovoltaic maximum power point problem. IEEE Trans Circ Syst I 54(9):2054–2060
2. Hua C, Lin J, Shen C (1998) Implementation of a DSP-controlled photovoltaic system with peak power tracking. IEEE Trans Industr Electron 45(1):99–107
3. Gow JA, Manning CD (2000) Controller arrangement for boost converter systems sourced from solar photovoltaic arrays or other maximum power sources. Proc Inst Electr Eng Electr Power Appl 147:15–20
4. Ishaque K, Salam Z, Amjad M, Mekhilef S (2012) An improved particle swarm optimization (PSO)-based MPPT for PV with reduced steady-state oscillation. IEEE Trans Power Electron 27:3627–3638

5. Chen L-R, Tsai C-H, Lin Y-L, Lai Y-S (2010) A biological swarm chasing algorithm for tracking the PV maximum power point. IEEE Trans Energy Convers 25(2):484–493

6. Ma J, Man KL, Ting TO, Zhang N, Lei CU, Wong N (2013) A hybrid MPPT method for photovoltaic systems via estimation and revision method. In: Proceedings of IEEE international symposium on circuits and systems, pp 241–244

7. Fan Z, Thanapalan K, Procter A, Carr S, Maddy J (2013) Adaptive hybrid maximum power point tracking method for a photovoltaic system. IEEE Trans Energy Convers 28(2):353–360

8. Wang J-C, Su Y-L, Shieh J-C, Jiang J-A (2011) High-accuracy maximum power point estimation for photovoltaic arrays. Sol Energy Mater Sol Cells 95(3):843–851

9. Shi J, Lee WJ, Liu Y, Yang Y, Wang P (2011) Forecasting power output of photovoltaic system based on weather classification and support vector machine. In: Proc IEEE Ind Appl Soc Annu Meeting, pp 1–6

10. Drucker H, Burges CJC, Kaufman L, Smola A, Vapnik V (1996) Support vector regression machines. Adv Neural Inf Proc Syst 28(7):779–784

11. AbdulHadi M, Al-Ibrahim AM, Virk GS (2004) Neuro-fuzzy-based solar cell model. IEEE Trans Energy Convers 19(3):619–624

12. Celik AN (2011) Artificial neural network modelling and experimental verification of the operating current of mono-crystalline photovoltaic modules. Sol Energy 85(10):2507–2517

13. Bors AG (2001) Introduction of the radial basis function (rbf) networks. In: Online symposium for electronics engineers, pp 1–7

14. Goda HM, Shokir EM, Eissa M, Fattah KA, Sayyouh MH (2003) Prediction of the PVT data using neural network computing theory. In: Nigeria annual international conference and exhibition: society of petroleum engineers, pp 85650–85669

Meta-learning with Empirical Mode Decomposition for Noise Elimination in Time Series Forecasting

David O. Afolabi, Sheng-Uei Guan, Ka Lok Man and Prudence W.H. Wong

Abstract In time series forecasting, noise can have a cumulative effect on the prediction of future values thus impacting the accuracy of the model. A common method of machine learning in time series problems is to provide a number of past output values in the series so it can learn to predict the next value, however, other modes of time series forecasting also include one or more input series. This enables the application of the proposed technique in this study to provide additional meta-information to the model to guide learning and improve the prediction performance of the model. We identified the components of two time series datasets using empirical mode decomposition and trained a non-linear autoregressive exogenous model to compare its performance with the traditional approach. Two methods for processing the signal components for noise reduction were proposed and the result from the summed combination significantly outperforms the traditional technique.

Keywords Empirical mode decomposition · Interference-less machine learning · Nonlinear autoregressive model · Time series forecasting

1 Introduction

Machine learning has been applied in the area of time series forecasting problems which basically entails learning ordered data that is continuous over a specified time interval and correctly predicting future values. The Artificial Neural Network (ANN), Hidden Markov Model, and Dynamic time warping are tools that are commonly applied in time series regression and classification tasks such as:

D.O. Afolabi (✉) · S.-U. Guan · K.L. Man
Computer Science and Software Engineering, Xi'an Jiaotong-Liverpool University, Suzhou, China
e-mail: David.Afolabi09@xjtlu.edu.cn

D.O. Afolabi · P.W.H. Wong
Department of Computer Science, University of Liverpool, Liverpool, UK

© Springer Science+Business Media Singapore 2016
J.J. (Jong Hyuk) Park et al. (eds.), *Advanced Multimedia and Ubiquitous Engineering*, Lecture Notes in Electrical Engineering 393,
DOI 10.1007/978-981-10-1536-6_53

weather/natural phenomena forecasting, stock market prediction, sign language identification, human activity classification and control engineering. The performance quality of a model is dependent on the quality of the data being processed, in essence, noisy data can only be detrimental to the machine learning process as the algorithm tries to make sense of the trends within the data.

In order to address the issue of noisy data, algorithms and time series models such as the Autoregressive Integrated Moving Average (ARIMA) have been extended to deal with examples containing a fundamental series and an error series by developing the ARIMA-NOISE (ARIMAN) model [1]. Although this technique is well developed, it can only be applied in the context of a repetitive time series, and the model is based on observation of a repeated time period in order to facilitate an accurate forecast of the data.

Additionally, data smoothing methods have been explored as a means to detect anomalies or outliers and impute values for the detected noise. The Forward Search (FS) method is an example of such methods which can be applied when other traditional robust estimators fail to detect noise in data with noise percentage over certain threshold. The main disadvantage being that subsampling methods can increase the chance of samples with outliers; and secondly, excess sensitivity to noise if parameters are not chosen correctly [2].

Thus in this study, we propose the application of Empirical Mode Decomposition (EMD) for noise reduction during machine learning in both non-linear autoregressive model (NAR) and nonlinear autoregressive exogenous model (NARX) neural networks [3]. The following section in this paper expounds on the Empirical Mode Decomposition; next in Sect. 3, we detail the various types of Non-linear Autoregressive Neural Networks which were used in this study. The result and discussion section are presented followed by concluding section.

2   Empirical Mode Decomposition

The empirical mode decomposition [4] technique was developed to iteratively decompose a signal into a number of base signals named intrinsic mode functions (IMF). It utilizes the Hilbert transform to perform spectral analysis after which frequency-information on time and variation are provided from the instantaneous frequency computation [5, 6].

Significant research has been carried out to improve the robustness of the EMD algorithm such as: stopping criterion, extrema interpolation, and boundary effects [5]. The original non-stationary and nonlinear time series can be reconstructed by summing the derived IMFs. This iterative process of extracting from the high-frequency IMF until the low-frequency IMF is knows as sifting [7] and the steps are shown below for a signal $y(t)$:

STEP 1   Let $h_i(t) = y(t)$, and $i = 1$.
STEP 2   Find some local minima and maxima in $h_i(t)$.

STEP 3 Connect all identified maxima and minima by a cubic spline as the upper envelope $up_i(t)$ and lower envelope $low_i(t)$, and calculate local mean as $m_i(t) = [up_i(t) + low_i(t)]/2$.

STEP 4 Update as $h_i(t) = h_i(t) - m_i(t)$.

STEP 5 Ensure $h_i(t)$ fulfils the requirement of IMF. If not, then redo STEP 2 to STEP 5. If done, then $IMF_i(t) = h_i(t)$, $i = i + 1$ and $h_i(t) = y(t) - IMF_{i-1}(t)$.

STEP 6 Check if $h_i(t)$ is a monotonic function or not. If it is not, then redo STEP 2 to STEP 5 for the next IMF. If it is monotonic then $h_i(t) = rc(t)$ and end the EMD process.

After the EMD process, the result will consist of c IMF functions and a residue, $rc(t)$, shown in Eq. 1 as:

$$y(t) = \sum_{i-1}^{c} IMF_i(t) + rc(t) \tag{1}$$

Therefore each IMF and the final residue all have equal number of data points with respect to the original time series data which enables a straightforward data preprocessing for the time-delayed artificial neural network (ANN) training. Therefore they are transferred into a matrix and used as the exogenous input in the NARX model. Inspired by the incremental contribution based learning model in [8], we are able to devise an algorithm to selectively include attributes—in this case: component IMFs—that enhance the machine learning process. In the experiments, we tested two methods:

1. The selected IMFs are include directly for training in a NARX neural network, and
2. The selected IMFs are summed before being passed as input to the NARX neural network.

3 Nonlinear Autoregressive Model

The nonlinear autoregressive model (NAR) and nonlinear autoregressive exogenous model (NARX) neural networks are capable of predicting future values of a time series after learning past values of that series. These two time series learning models both a need data sequence over a continuous time interval to predict future values with the main difference being that NAR model has only one series in which the future value, y(t), is predicted based on past values:

$$y(t) = f(y(t-1), \ldots, y(t-d)) \tag{2}$$

While in NARX an additional external input series is used along with the original series past values and is expressed as follow:

$$y(t) = f(x(t-1), \ldots, x(t-d), y(t-1), \ldots, y(t-d)) \qquad (3)$$

4 Method

The two time series datasets selected in this study are the Istanbul stock exchange data [9] and the Sunspot numbers data [10]. In the Istanbul stock exchange data (ISE), only a single column, which is the "TL based return index" was used, giving us a time series data of 1×536 (Fig. 1); while in the Sunspot numbers data (SOL) we have a time series of 1×2899 values (Fig. 2). The data division scheme involves sequentially partitioning the time series by assigning the first 70 % for the training, the following 15 % for validation, and the final 15 % for testing.

For noise identification and elimination, each series is processed as follow:

STEP 1 Run the EMD routine on the time series data using default parameters in [5]. Let N be total number of IMFs produced and set the number of neural network hidden neuron to 75 % of N (rounded up).

STEP 2 Based on use-case, set the input and feedback delays (i.e. number of past values presented to the NARX or NAR model for prediction).

Fig. 1 Original Istanbul stock exchange data

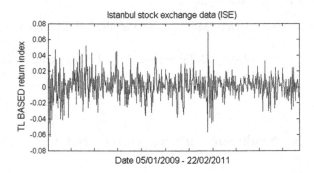

Fig. 2 Original sunspot numbers data

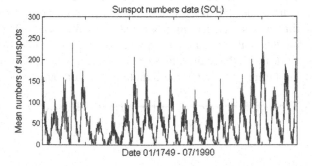

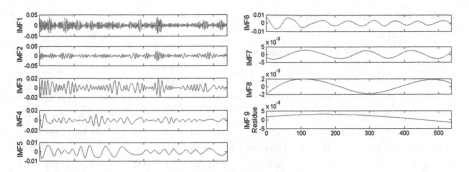

Fig. 3 Empirical mode decomposition of the ISE data

STEP 3   Create N combinations of all IMF whilst progressively excluding higher frequency IMF in each combination.

STEP 4   Create a modified input series $x(t)$ from the remaining IMF in each combination which will either be summed (e.g. SUMtrain, SUMtest in Figs. 4 and 5) or included directly into the input (e.g. INCtrain, INCtest in Figs. 4 and 5).

STEP 5   Train the NARX model with each combination and test the performance to reveal combinations that contribute to noise reduction.

STEP 6   If noise reduction threshold is not met, decrease N and repeat from STEP 3.

Figure 3 is an example of the EMD process on the ISE data showing its component IMFs and the residue. Only for ease of naming/labelling, the residue may be referred to as the last IMF in figures and Sect. 0.

5   Results and Discussions

The algorithm was tested on a high performance computing platform with a hexa-core Intel® Xeon® E5-1660 CPU at 3.3 GHz and 8 GB of RAM. The implementation was completed in MATLAB® with the aid of rParabEmd.m script from [5]. Each test was repeated 300 times to calculate the statistical significance of any enhancements, and then the average training time and mean squared error (MSE) performance during training and testing were record and are shown in Tables 1 and 2 for ISE and SOL time series respectively.

Table 1 Istanbul stock exchange performance

	Average						p-value	
	Training MSE		Testing MSE		Training time (s)			
Original	3.077E−04		2.060E−04		0.38		1.00E+00	
Method	INC	SUM	INC	SUM	INC	SUM	INC	SUM
IMF [1to9]	1.457E−04	3.092E−04	2.960E−04	2.069E−04	0.56	0.49	8.76E−09	1.03E−01
IMF [2to9]	1.539E−04	1.456E−04	3.438E−04	1.111E−04	0.57	0.66	2.31E−10	0.00E+00
IMF [3to9]	2.082E−04	2.022E−04	3.968E−04	1.610E−04	0.55	0.52	1.32E−12	5.24E−220
IMF [4to9]	2.730E−04	2.564E−04	5.468E−04	1.827E−04	0.54	0.52	3.63E−11	1.55E−192
IMF [5to9]	2.863E−04	2.741E−04	7.198E−04	1.937E−04	0.54	0.52	1.18E−09	1.17E−75
IMF [6to9]	3.082E−04	2.925E−04	7.896E−04	1.967E−04	0.52	0.49	1.36E−08	7.57E−51
IMF [7to9]	3.189E−04	3.051E−04	8.677E−04	2.015E−04	0.52	0.47	2.61E−24	2.67E−07
IMF [8to9]	3.080E−04	3.039E−04	1.046E−03	2.535E−04	0.52	0.51	4.59E−13	7.26E−07
IMF [9]	3.295E−04	3.656E−04	1.011E−03	1.071E−03	0.48	0.47	5.82E−31	1.65E−25

5.1　ISE Analysis and Discussion

By training on the Istanbul stock exchange time series data using a NAR model, we get a standard measure of the default performance that can be expected from a traditional approach in time series forecasting. The result shows an average training mean squared error of 3.077×10^{-4}, and average test mse at 2.060×10^{-4} with average training time of 0.384 s from the 300 trials. Using the error reduction method proposed in Sect. 4, Fig. 4 reveals that including the IMF[1to9] directly into a NARX model improves the training mse performance significantly but further iteration shows rapid rise in the test performance error (INCtest). On the other hand, summing the selected IMF components before using it as input in the NARX model shows that elimination of the first intrinsic mode function gave the best performance on the SUMtest and SUMtrain plot in Fig. 4 at IMF[2to9] with a training mse of 1.456×10^{-4} and test mse of 1.111×10^{-4}. With a p-value of 0, it highlights the statistical significance of the noise reduction. Further iterations also show slight improvement over the original time series data in the INCtrain and INCtest result until it begins to erode important meta-information around the 7th iteration. Training time does not reveal any trends except for the fact that the simpler original NAR model required the shortest training time but with poorer performance compared to the best combination, IMF[2to9], on the NARX model which took the longest time.

Table 2 Sunspot numbers performance

	Average						p-value	
	Training MSE		Testing MSE		Training time (s)			
Original	2.345E+02		4.886E+02		2.202		1.00E+00	
Method	INC	SUM	INC	SUM	INC	SUM	INC	SUM
IMF [1to10]	5.198E+02	2.345E+02	4.843E+03	4.558E+02	2.625	2.766	2.24E−02	1.72E−01
IMF [2to10]	6.434E+02	1.032E+02	4.086E+03	2.431E+02	2.511	2.870	2.07E−05	9.10E−23
IMF [3to10]	2.605E+02	1.315E+02	3.140E+04	2.344E+02	2.525	2.718	8.42E−02	3.73E−20
IMF [4to10]	9.280E+02	1.549E+02	1.172E+04	1.099E+03	2.513	2.640	5.36E−03	2.82E−01
IMF [5to10]	5.727E+02	1.703E+02	6.607E+05	2.651E+03	2.397	2.461	3.15E−01	3.24E−01
IMF [6to10]	1.039E+03	2.514E+02	7.053E+04	1.608E+03	2.413	2.286	6.50E−02	3.51E−02
IMF [7to10]	1.250E+03	6.486E+02	7.071E+04	1.544E+03	2.393	2.383	3.95E−02	1.01E−01
IMF [8to10]	1.447E+03	2.404E+02	3.330E+04	1.042E+03	2.271	2.520	3.80E−02	3.10E−01
IMF [9to10]	1.269E+03	2.321E+03	5.731E+04	8.387E+03	2.267	2.282	8.47E−02	5.71E−14
IMF [10]	1.329E+03	2.040E+03	7.556E+04	2.714E+04	2.366	2.405	3.69E−02	1.51E−06

5.2 SOL Analysis and Discussion

In the Sunspot number analysis, the NAR traditional forecasting model took an average of 2.2 s for training on each trial with an mse of $2.345 \times 10^{+2}$ and a testing mse of $4.886 \times 10^{+2}$. From Fig. 5, it can be observed that the direct inclusion of the separate IMF series in a NARX model as source of meta-information is incapable of noise reduction and therefore it performs worse than the original NAR model. Correspondingly, as in the case of the Istanbul stock exchange time-series data, the SUMtrain and SUMtest trend lines in Fig. 5 show lower mean squared errors after a few iterations; having the best performance at IMF[3to10] with an mse of $2.344 \times 10^{+2}$. It was expected that the mse will steadily rise as extra IMF components were not summed but after the IMF[5to10] combination a decline in error was noticed. This spike at the 5th IMF indicates that lower frequency component can also contain noise and further refinement to the algorithm can potentially address this issue. More training time was utilized by NARX model with higher number of exogenous input and also in cases where the summed IMF provide better meta-information to boost training.

Fig. 4 Performance error
comparison plot of the ISE
data

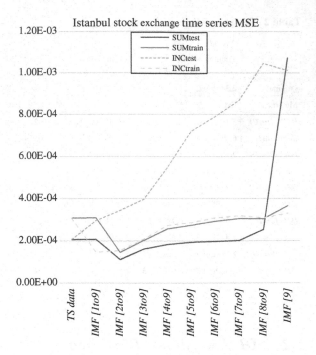

Fig. 5 Performance error
comparison plot of the SOL
data

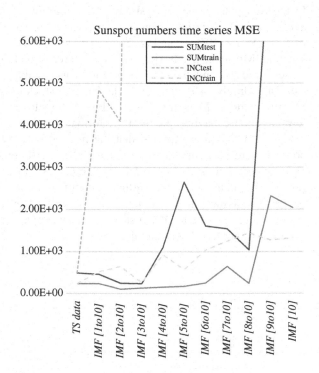

6 Conclusion and Further Research

In this study, we achieve the noise reduction in time series forecasting by iteratively summing selected IMF components created through the Empirical Mode Decomposition technique. We discovered that direct inclusion the IMFs as multiple input into the NARX model will not provide optimal performance; thus further research will seek to identify reasons for the neural network not being capable of detecting the proper mathematical operation on all input attributes to perform comparably to the summed method.

Finally, the method for partitioning the time series in this study for the model training assigns the initial series sequence to the train set and then validation set and finally testing set; but this method forces the model to predict values many steps ahead with gaps which may also induce additional error. An interleaving data division method will be extended for potential enhancement to our proposed algorithm

References

1. Wong W, Miller RB (1990) Repeated time series analysis of ARIMA–noise models. J Bus Econ Stat 8:243–250
2. Pesentia M, Pirasa M (2008) A modified forward search approach applied to time series analysis. Int Arch Photogramm Remote Sens Spat Inf Sci, vol XXXVII
3. Neural network time series prediction and modeling—MATLAB and simulink. http://www.mathworks.com/help/nnet/gs/neural-network-time-series-prediction-and-modeling.html
4. Huang NE, Shen Z, Long SR, Wu MC, Shih HH, Zheng Q, Yen NC, Tung CC, Liu HH (1998) The empirical mode decomposition and the Hilbert spectrum for nonlinear and non-stationary time series analysis. In: Proceedings of the royal society of London A: mathematical, physical and engineering sciences (pp 903–995). The Royal Society
5. Rato RT, Ortigueira MD, Batista AG (2008) On the HHT, its problems, and some solutions. Mech Syst Signal Process 22:1374–1394
6. Kim D, Oh H-S (2009) EMD: a package for empirical mode decomposition and hilbert spectrum. R J 1:40–46
7. Sun TY, Liu CC, Jheng JH, Tsai TY (2009) An efficient noise reduction algorithm using empirical mode decomposition and correlation measurement. In: International symposium on intelligent signal processing and communications systems, 2008. ISPACS 2008, pp 1–4
8. Guan S-U, Liu J, Qi Y (2004) An incremental approach to contribution-based feature selection. J Intell Syst 13:15–42
9. Akbilgic O, Bozdogan H, Balaban ME (2014) A novel Hybrid RBF neural networks model as a forecaster. Stat Comput 24:365–375
10. Hertz P, Feigelson ED (1979) A sample of astronomical time series. Citeseer

Examining Performance Issues of GUI Based Android Applications

Jung-Hoon Shin, Mesfin Abebe, Suntae Kim, Cheol Jung Yoo
and Kwang-Yoon Jin

Abstract Android platform applications are the most dominant technologies in the mobile markets. These applications have a wide range of functionalities such as Game, Business, Education, Entertainment, Shopping, Travel and Weather etc. However, most of these applications have a performance problem in their Graphical User Interfaces (GUIs) since the mobile application GUI testing is daunting and too expensive. In this study, we investigated the severity of the Android applications GUI performance problem by examining a sample of freely downloadable applications from Google Store and analyzed performance issues of the applications.

Keywords Android applications · User interface · Performance improvement

J.-H. Shin · S. Kim (✉) · C.J. Yoo
Department of Software Engineering, CAIIT, Chonbuk National University, 567
Baekje-daero Deokjin-gu, Jeollabuk-do, Jeonju-si, Republic of Korea
e-mail: stkim@jbnu.ac.kr

J.-H. Shin
e-mail: shinjh@jbnu.ac.kr

C.J. Yoo
e-mail: cjyoo@jbnu.ac.kr

M. Abebe
Department of Computing, Adama Sience and Technology University, Adama, Ethiopia
e-mail: mesfinabha@gmail.com

K.-Y. Jin
Department of Computer Engineering, Kangwon National University, Joongang-ro,
Kangwon-do, Samcheck-si, Republic of Korea
e-mail: kyjin@kangwon.ac.kr

© Springer Science+Business Media Singapore 2016
J.J. (Jong Hyuk) Park et al. (eds.), *Advanced Multimedia and Ubiquitous Engineering*, Lecture Notes in Electrical Engineering 393,
DOI 10.1007/978-981-10-1536-6_54

1   Introduction

As operating Android applications is different from PC-based software in terms of limited resources such as memory or power supply, developers have to consider these constraints during the design and implementation of the applications [1]. Generally, it is frequently necessary to debug, test and optimize the applications to enhance and maintain the GUI performance. Testing the applications with the worst and best possible configuration such as screen resolution, pixel density etc. is the common way to identify the GUI performance problems; since it is impossible to test the applications with all existing devices and configurations [2].

In addition to the limitation of the hardware devices, the complexity of the Android platform and the functionality of the applications are constantly increase these days [3]. These continuous changes and the urge to release the applications to the market dare the developers to allot time and effort for performance improvement. However, the majority of the developers are not well-trained to apply existing techniques, methods and concepts to develop quality applications.

Considering all these challenges, we analyzed eight free downloadable Android applications from *Google Play Store*. The samples have different sizes, types and functionalities. In the analysis, we identified that GUI performance problems are common in most of the applications. The result compliant with a previous research finding that said "one in five Android users experiences an application crush" [4]. After identifying the performance problems, we took five layouts (screens) from the sample applications and inspected their GUIs performance issues in detail using Android SDK tools.

The remaining parts of the study are structured as follows: Sect. 2: gives an overview of Android application development and common application problem types. Section 3: describes the methodology and procedure of the study. Finally, Sect. 4: states the conclusion and proposes future study areas.

2   Background: Android Application Problem Types

Android is a mobile operating system from Google Software Company that is an open source product provided to the public for free [5]. Generally, there are two ways to develop Android applications: as a *client-side* native application which is the commonly used and as a *web* application. Most client-side Android applications suffer from basic performance issues such as *Streamline the GUIs, Shrink the APIs,* and *identifying memory issues* [6]. Therefore, Android application development needs to consider various dimensions of performance improvement techniques to develop applications that can be acceptable by the end users [7].

Alternatively, most end users need an easy-to-navigate application that delivers the key functionalities and services through an intuitive and entertaining user interface. They further expect the applications to identify their device type and provide them the right set of options and functionalities. Nowadays, the majority of

Table 1 Common mobile application problem types [6]

No.	Types of problem	Percentage
1	The applications crashed/froze/displayed an error	62
2	The app was slow to lunch	47
3	The app would not launch	40
4	The app didn't function as expected	37
5	None of these	1

the users (85 %) prefer mobile applications than mobile website, since they believe that mobile applications are more continent, fast and easy to navigate. However, study shows that only 28 % of the mobile applications offer good user experience [8]. In another survey study 56 % of the application users reported about problems in using mobile applications in the past half year. The type of the problems and the percentage of each problem type are shown in Table 1.

Additionally, most studies proved that users pay more attention to the perfor mance of the application than any other feature of the applications. For example; 85 % of users reported that performance is very or somewhat important feature in mobile application [9]. Presently, there are many bad reviews about the GUIs performance of Android applications on Google store. Therefore, developers have to put grate effort at every stage of the design and implementation phase of the applications to provide good user experience to the users.

3 Examining Performance Issues of GUI-Based Android Applications

This section introduces performance issues of GUI-based Android applications by using the following three steps. As the first step, Android application source code and resource files are gathered after downloading the sample Android applications (*apk*) from *Google Play Store*. Then, we analyze application performance as the second step by using Android SDK tools for GUI performance measure. Finally, the performance issues are grouped in terms of its types.

3.1 Gathering Android Applications

In order to start the investigation of the performance issues, we downloaded eight Android applications from *Google Play Store*. The applications are taken from different categories such as: business, communication, education, entertainment, and Shopping. The sample applications are free downloadable and have high

Table 2 List of the sample Android applications for the empirical study [10]

No.	Name of the apps	Package	Size (MB)
1	Facebook Pages Manager	com.facebook.pages.app	30.829
2	KakaoTalk: Free Calls and Text	com.kakao.talk	23.139
3	Telegram	org.telegram.messenger	11.929
4	HelloTalk Language Exchange	com.hellotalk	21.947
5	Tom Loves Angela	com.outfit7.tomlovesangelafree	40.732
6	Akinator the Genie FREE	com.digidust.elokence.akinator.freemium	33.901
7	MagicBook: Hearthstone	com.nekmit.magichearthstone	30.930
8	Bee'nGo—Loyalty and Coupons	com.mobeam.beepngo	9.392

download rate. Table 2 indications the name of the applications, the package name of the apk files and the size of the applications.

Next, we extracted the Java source code and the XML files from the apk files of the sample applications. To extract the apk files into Java source code and XML files, we used the following four software tools: *DEX2Jar*, *Java Decompiler*, *APK Tool* and *APK Installer*. The extracted Java source code and XML files imported to the Android studio IDE for further GUIs performance analysis and applying the best practices.

3.2   Analyzing the Applications Performance

We analyzed GPU rendering performance and various performance issues of the gathered applications using the aforementioned tools. For the first step, we imported the sample applications to the Android Studio IDE to examine the GUIs of the applications for *overdraw*. *Overdraw* describes how many times each pixel redrawn during rendering period to build the views on the screen. The overdraw test allows to validate the amount of overdraw, so that it helps developers to determine the performance of the user interfaces. To do this, we have turn on the GPU overdraw debug setting; since it is off by default. The overdraw test identified that most of the sample applications have different level of overdraw problems as summarized in Table 3. Furthermore, we used the GPU rendering to measure how long the applications take to render all the GUI elements using the Profiling GPU rendering tool. The result of the two experiments showed that many of the applications screens need performance tuning to minimize the high overdraw to an acceptable level of *1X Overdraw* and to keep the rendering activity within the 16 ms/frame default target.

As the second step, we analyzed the code and resources using statistic code analysis. A good graphical user interface design should consider a number of issues

Table 3 The overdraw analysis result of the sample applications

No.	Overdraw	Description	# Screens
1	No overdraw (true color)	No overdraw	7
2	1X Overdraw (blue color)	Overdraw once	32
3	2X Overdraw (green color)	Overdraw twice	47
4	3X Overdraw (pink color)	Overdraw three times	196
5	4X+ Overdraw (red color)	Overdraw four or more times	94
Total Number of layouts (Screens)			376

such as *Functionality*, *Layout Design*, and *Interaction* [11]. At this stage, we used the Lint static code analysis tool to analyze the application for potential bugs that specify the need for performance optimization. The tool has the ability to indicate poorly structured code that can affect the reliability and efficiency of the applications. For instance, XML resource that has unused namespace consumes space and unnecessary processing time. In addition, deprecated elements or APIs might fail to achieve the functionality of the application. Hence, the tool can tell us how the sample applications developers are effectively used this tool to optimize their application.

The Android Studio Lint tool detects the possible performance problems along their descriptions and severity levels. The Lint information can be used to optimize the *correctness*, *performance*, *security*, and *usability* of the applications. Though some of the problems are less important such as *spellings* and *general*; however, there are good performance problem indicators like *Android Lint*, *XML* and *Declaration*. The result indicates the presence of unsolved design problems in the applications, especially with their layout files and resources that can significantly affect the user interface performance. This can be easily inferred from the higher percentage of *Android Lint*, *Declaration redundancy*, and *XML* problems. Generally, this motivates us to further review the source code and XML files for GUI performance problems.

4 Conclusion

This paper presented performance issues of GUI-based Android applications. In order to investigate it, we gathered eight open and free android applications. Firstly, we analyzed overdraw of the screen by using GPU-overdraw debugging feature, and showed the sampled applications has the overdraw issue. Secondly, we carried out the static code analysis and presented various performance issues. Based on the performance issues that we investigated in this paper, we are planning to search the best practices and apply them into the sampled applications for improving its performance.

Acknowledgments This research was supported by Next-Generation Information Computing Development Program through the National Research Foundation of Korea(NRF) funded by the Ministry of Science, ICT and Future Planning (NRF-2014M3C4A7030503)

References

1. Liu CH, Lu CY et al. (2014) Capture replay testing for android applications. In: International symposium on computer and control
2. Canfora G, D'Angelo M et al. (2013) A case study of automating user experience oriented performance testing on smartphones. In: IEEE, verification and validation
3. Dong C, Liu X (2013) Development of android application for language studies. Sci Direct 4:8–16
4. Screen and UI Performance (2015) https://www.safaribooksonline.com/library/view/high-performanceandroid/9781491913994/ch04.html
5. Application Fundamentals (2015) http://code.google.com/android/intro/anatomy.html
6. The Statistics Portal (2015) http://www.statista.com/statistics/276623/number-of-apps-available-in-leading-app-stores. Number of apps available in leading app stores as June 2015
7. Screen and UI Performance (2015) https://www.safaribooksonline.com/library/view/high-performanceandroid/9781491913994/ch04.html
8. Mobil Apps: What Consumers Really Need and Want (2013) https://info.dynatrace.com/rs/compuware/images/Mobile_App_Survey_Report.pdf
9. Ali Z, Ismail R (2013) Design and development of android mobile application for students of engineering education in Saudi Arabia. In: International conference of information society, pp 228–233
10. APK Downloader. http://apps.evozi.com/apk-downloader/
11. Smartphone OS Market Share, IDC Analyze (2015) http://www.idc.com/prodserv/smartphone-os-market-share.jsp

Feature Vectors for Performance Test Case Classification

Calvin G. Mangeni, Suntae Kim and Rhan Jung

Abstract This paper proposes a feature-vector for characterizing performance test cases. The feature-vector is composed of six attributes such as use of thread, measuring elapsed time and counting successful and failed number of test cases. In order to identify the feature vector, we thoroughly examined the test cases from five open source projects and extracted performance cases. After then, we established the common feature vector discovered from the performance test cases, and analyzed distribution of the feature vector in the performance as well as general test cases to show the validity of the feature-vector.

Keywords Test case · Performance testing · Feature vector

1 Introduction

A test case is intended to support testing a system's functionality and quality attributes such as performance, availability and security. Since a test case plays a key role in unit and integration tests, it should be carefully maintained by a software developer throughout the entire software development and maintenance lifecycle. In reality, the test case for testing functionality tends to be maintained according to

C.G. Mangeni · S. Kim (✉)
Department of Software Engineering, CAIIT, Chonbuk National University,
567 Baekje-daero, Deokjin-gu, Jeollabuk-do, Jeonju-si 54896, Republic of Korea
e-mail: stkim@jbnu.ac.kr

C.G. Mangeni
e-mail: man.calvin2004@gmail.com

R. Jung
Department of Computer Engineering, Kangwon National University, Joongang-ro,
Kangwon-do, Samcheck-si, Republic of Korea
e-mail: jungran@kangwon.ac.kr

© Springer Science+Business Media Singapore 2016
J.J. (Jong Hyuk) Park et al. (eds.), *Advanced Multimedia and Ubiquitous Engineering*, Lecture Notes in Electrical Engineering 393,
DOI 10.1007/978-981-10-1536-6_55

update of the system features. However, test cases for validating quality attributes are not maintained carefully, and not explicitly managed without separating them from functionality test cases [1]. This may causes the system not to provide appropriate QoS (Quality of Service) to users and other systems. This is mainly attributed to the large amount of test cases and the limited resources [2].

In this paper, we suggest the feature vector for characterizing performance test cases. A performance test case among the quality attribute test cases is a test case for determining how a system properly performs in terms of responsiveness [3]. The feature vector is the essential set of attributes of a test case for supporting automatic classification [4], composing of six attributes such as use of thread, measuring elapsed time and counting successful and failed number of test cases. In order to identify the feature-vector, we thoroughly examined the test cases from five open source projects and extracted performance cases first. After then, we established the common feature vector discovered from the performance test cases, and analyzed distribution of the feature vector in the performance as well as general test cases to show the validity of the feature vector. The suggested feature vector can contribute to support automatic classification of performance test cases and it is also used to give an appropriate guidance for authoring test cases.

The remaining part of this paper is organized as follows: Sect. 2 presents related work. Section 3 introduces steps for identifying feature vectors from five open source projects and shows the distribution analysis. Section 4 concludes this paper and discuss future work.

2 Related Work

Gil and Maman [5] defined the notion of traceable patterns when they introduced micro patterns in java that are recognizable and stand at implementation level of abstraction. Based on the micro pattern, they statistically analyzed the patterns in the open source code. However, it can hardly apply to characterizing test cases, because it capture general implementation patterns without considering features of the test cases. Similar to Gil and Maman, I. Lee et al. [6] introduced a technique for extracting characteristic vectors from the source code for characterizing java method. In their research, the characteristic vectors are intended to support analyzing the relationship between the method signature and its method body implementation, which is not suitable for describing test cases. Pornchai and Nakornthip [7] suggested the idea of clean code selection for their approach based on software metrics for enhancing software maintainability. As they analyzed source code using software metrics, they only focused on quantitative measure such as Number of Line of Code (NLOC), Number of Parameter (NOP), which are too general to characterize the test cases.

3 Feature Vectors for Performance Test Cases

In order to identify feature vectors and show validity of the vectors, we apply the following three steps as shown in Fig. 1. We first start from extracting performance test cases from five open source code. The extracted test cases are then extensively investigated to establish features that form patterns amongst them as a second step. In the third step, we sampled the general test cases and performance test cases and analyzed the test cases in terms of the feature vector, and analyzed the distribution of the feature vector of the two groups.

3.1 Extraction of Performance Test Cases

In order to establish feature vector, we first collected performance test cases from five popular open source projects as shown in Table 1. As the test case for the quality attributes is hard to define only with test case source code, we identified the performance test cases based on the class or method identifiers with explicit tags (e.g. "*Performance*", "*perf*"). As a result, we gathered 42 performance test cases for identifying feature vectors.

3.2 Identifying Feature Vectors for Performance Test Cases

As a second step, we intensively investigated the extracted test cases to extract common characteristic features to differentiate performance test cases from general

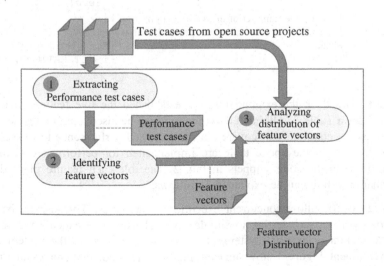

Fig. 1 Overall process to identify feature vector for performance test cases

Table 1 Open source projects for extracting test cases

Name	Version	Description
Apache tomcat	8.0.1	Implementation of the Java Servlet and JavaServer pages
Apache Log4j 2	2.3	Upgrade to logging framework Log4j
Apache JMeter	2.13	A framework for supporting load test
Apache HTTP client	4.2.5	the core HTTP protocol functionality
Apache commons collections	4.0	It contains types that extend and augment the Java collections framework

Table 2 Feature vector for performance test case

Feature	Description	Implementation
Thread	Enables concurrent execution of activities by implementing the runnable interface	`new Thread()` `.start()` `.join()`
Loop	Allows multiple sequential execution of the test case statements, or group of statements until they meet the test condition	`for, while, do while,`
Elapsed time measure	Measures the program execution time in nanoseconds or milliseconds	`timer.start();` `timer.stop();` `timer. getElapsedNanoTime ();` `System.nanoTime();` `System. currentTimeMillis()`
Logging	Records activity	`EventLogger. logEvent(msg); logger.isEnabled (Level.DEBUG);`
Large number of iteration	Executes the same set of instructions a given large number of times or until a specified result is obtained	`int ITERATIONS = 100000; for (int i = 0; i < ITERATIONS; i++)`

test cases. Based on the examination, we established the five feature vectors as summarized in Table 2. Although these features can be discovered in a general test cases, they are commonly discovered in the extracted performance test cases.

The features in the above table are implemented for performance testing as demonstrated in the code snippets in Fig. 2. The role each feature plays during performance testing can be explained as follows:

- The *thread(s)* allow concurrent execution of activities. Threads can be used during performance testing to simulate virtual users that execute the specific code section or external systems that request to process to the system under development. Figure 2 shows an example of source code that creates an array of threads and starts the threads.

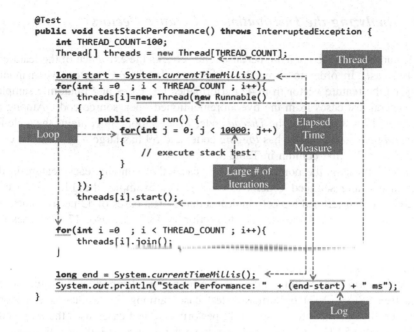

```
@Test
public void testStackPerformance() throws InterruptedException {
    int THREAD_COUNT=100;
    Thread[] threads = new Thread[THREAD_COUNT];

    long start = System.currentTimeMillis();
    for(int i =0  ; i < THREAD_COUNT ; i++){
        threads[i]=new Thread(new Runnable()
        {
            public void run() {
                for(int j = 0; j < 10000; j++)
                {
                    // execute stack test.
                }
            }
        });
        threads[i].start();
    }

    for(int i =0  ; i < THREAD_COUNT ; i++){
        threads[i].join();
    }

    long end = System.currentTimeMillis();
    System.out.println("Stack Performance: "  + (end-start) + " ms");
}
```

Fig. 2 Source code snippets for performance test case features

- The *loop* statements such as for and while are reserved words that are easily discovered in the performance and general test cases. Performance test case generally tend to iterate specific part of the code intensively by using the loop statement. In contrast, the general test case tend to execute the specific code section once, as it just check if the function provides valid features.
- The response time of the system under test or an activity is determined by *measuring the elapsed time*. This is vital and fundamental to performance testing, because performance testing is originally intended to minimize the execution time. Figure 2 shows an representative example that measure the elapse time by using the System.currentTimeMillis() method.
- The *logging* function records and prints the results of a performance test case to the console, file, output stream or remote system. Writing log records to the console or file enables the tester to establish if the test case meets its intended performance purpose. Figure 2 shows the case that remains a log message in a console.
- Unlike a functional test case that run once from start to finish, a performance test case is run many times by the same virtual user in a single scenario. The *number of iterations* are defined to as a termination condition in the *loop* if or after the specified result or condition is attained. In Fig. 2, the loop for executes its body segment 10,000 times.

3.3 Analyzing the Distribution of Feature Vectors

All feature's types are *boolean*, because it just checks the existence of the feature in the test case. In order to show the validity of the feature vector, we manually analyzed the feature vector from 42 performance test cases and randomly sampled 203 general test cases from the five aforementioned open source code. Among all test cases, 17 test cases use the *Thread* code, 71 uses loop, 39 contains the code for *measuring elapsed time*, 41 has *logging* code, and 59 has large *# of iteration* code as shown in the first column in Table 3.

Table 3 presents the portion of the test cases that contains each feature in the performance and sampled general test cases. For example, the 14(33.3 %) cell, which is the first left and top cell, indicates that 14 test cases of 42 performance test cases contain the *Thread* code and its portion is 33.3 %. Also, 17 test cases use thread in all test cases, and 14(82.35 %) of the 17 test cases were performance test cases and 3(17.65 %) were general test cases. Based on this, the feature *Thread* is valuable to characterize performance test case.

For the *loop* feature, this feature is commonly used regardless of type of test cases (see 38(53.52 %) performance test cases among 71 test cases use loop). However, 38(90.48 %) test cases of 42 performance test cases uses the *loop* code, while only 4(9.52 %) test cases does not have the feature. It indicates that most of the performance test case use the *loop* feature.

For measuring the elapsed time, 37 test cases of the 39 test cases that contains the code for measuring the elapsed time were performance test cases, accounting for 94.9 %. Meanwhile, only 2 general test cases has the code for measuring the elapsed time. In addition, all performance test cases contains the logging feature, while the general test cases does not have the logging feature in the sampled code. Lastly, for the large number of iteration, 39(92.85 %) performance tests used a large number of iteration in their loop code, indicating that this feature is appropriate for characterizing the performance test cases.

Table 3 Feature distribution in performance and general test cases

Feature	Performance T. Case (42)		General T. Case (203)	
	With	W/O	With	W/O
Thread	14(33.3 %)	28(66.6 %)	3(1.48 %)	200(98.82 %)
17	14(82.35 %)		3(17.65 %)	
Loop	38(90.48 %)	4(9.52 %)	33(16.25 %)	170(83.74 %)
71	38(53.52 %)		33(46.48 %)	
E. time Measure	37(88 %)	5(11.9 %)	2(0.09 %)	201(99.01 %)
39	37(94.9 %)		2(5.1 %)	
Logging	41(97.6 %)	1(2.4 %)	0(0 %)	203(100 %)
41	41(100 %)		0(0 %)	
# of iteration	39(92.85 %)	3(7.15 %)	20(9.8 %)	183(90.2 %)
59	39(66.1 %)		20(33.2 %)	

4 Conclusion and Future Work

In this paper, we proposed the feature vector for characterizing performance test cases. In order to show the feasibility of the feature vector, we extracted performance cases from five open source projected and used it to define feature vector. Then, we randomly sampled general test cases to analyze the distribution of each feature. Based on the analysis, we showed list of features that can characterize performance test cases sufficiently. As future work, we have a plan to automatically extract the features from the source code and automatically classify performance test cases using machine-learning.

Acknowledgments This research was supported by Next-Generation Information Computing Development Program through the National Research Foundation of Korea (NRF) funded by the Ministry of Science, ICT and Future Planning (NRF-2014M3C4A7030503)

References

1. Cem Kaner JD (2003) What is a good test case? Florida Institute of Technology Department of Computer Sciences
2. Liu Y, Xu C, Cheung SC (2014) Characterizing and detecting performance bugs for smartphone applications. In: Proceedings of the 36th international conference on software engineering
3. Bass L, Clements P, Kazman R (2012) Software architecture in practice, 3rd edn. Addison-Wesley Professional, Boston
4. Suphapala P, Leelanuntkul U, Ngamarowaros N, Sophatsathit P (2007) Test case classification using category-partition finite state machine. NECTEC Tech J 7(18):61–68
5. Gil Y, Maman I (2005) Micro patterns in java code. In: The 20th annual ACM SIGPLAN conference on object-oriented programming, systems, languages, and applications, pp 97–116
6. Lee I, Kim S, Park S, Cho Y (2005) Attributes for characterizing java methods. Advanced multimedia and ubiquitous engineering, LNEE 354, p 9
7. Lerthathairat P, Prompoon N (2011) An approach for source code classification to enhance maintainability. In: Proceedings of the 8th international JCSSE

Hierarchical Semantic Classification and Attribute Relations Analysis with Clothing Region Detection

Jingjin Zhou, Zhengzhong Zhou and Liqing Zhang

Abstract Describing semantic attributes of clothing is an important technique for many applications. In this paper, we investigate problems of predicting the high-level semantic attributes by making use of features learned from middle-level semantic attributes and analyzing the hierarchical relations among the semantic attributes. In order to crop clothing regions from original images under various conditions, a modified Faster-RCNN [1] is implemented. We propose a novel hierarchical semantic tree-structure deep neural network to model the relations between middle-level and high-level semantic attributes, which improves the prediction accuracies of high-level semantic attributes. A large number of experiments are performed to verify different contributions of middle-level semantic features to the high-level semantic attributes.

Keywords Clothing detection · Hierarchical semantic network · Attribute relations analysis · Deep neural network

1 Introduction

In the research community of computer vision, much attention has been paid to clothing classification, retrieval and recommendation [2, 3] in recent years. A large number of clothing images and their relevant information are available due to the expansion of the online shopping markets. Most of the relevant information belongs to semantic attributes. However, little work has been devoted to the study of

J. Zhou (✉) · Z. Zhou · L. Zhang
Department of Computer Science and Engineering,
Shanghai Jiao Tong University, Shanghai, China
e-mail: zhoujingjin@sjtu.edu.cn

Z. Zhou
e-mail: tczhouzz@sjtu.edu.cn

L. Zhang
e-mail: zhang-lq@cs.sjtu.edu.cn

© Springer Science+Business Media Singapore 2016   429
J.J. (Jong Hyuk) Park et al. (eds.), *Advanced Multimedia and Ubiquitous Engineering*, Lecture Notes in Electrical Engineering 393,
DOI 10.1007/978-981-10-1536-6_56

hierarchical relations among semantic attributes. For example, clothing attributes like *clothing type*, *style* are relatively higher semantic attributes than *color*, *length*, *sleeve type*, etc., which can be easily distinguished. In contrast to low-level visual features, we can denote them as high-level semantic attributes and middle-level semantic attributes respectively.

We explore the following questions: (1) How can we predict high-level semantic attributes precisely with the features learned from original images and middle-level semantic attribute labels? (2) What is the relation between the high-level semantic attributes and middle-level semantic attributes?

To tackle these problems, a necessary pre-processing module is a clothing detector which crop the clothing regions from the original images in order to get rid of various bad conditions. A body detector based on R-CNN is used in [2]. However, the method is time-consuming both in phases of training and testing due to multi-stage pipelines. We apply a modified Faster-RCNN detector which enjoys both efficiency and accuracy. To integrate multi semantic attributes of clothing into one holistic model, a tree-structure convolutional neural network for feature learning is proposed in [3], but the different levels of semantic attributes are not taken into consideration. In this paper, a hierarchical semantic tree-structure deep neural network is proposed to model the relations of different semantic feature levels, which results in more accurate prediction of all high-level semantic attributes. With the hierarchical tree-structure network, we are able to explore the contributions of middle-level semantic features to some certain high-level semantic attributes.

2   Clothing Detection

As a pre-processing module, a clothing detector which aims to crop the foreground clothing area from the original clothing image is necessary to deal with various conditions. For example, some clothing may be worn on people or mannequins, while others may be portrayed in isolation. Challenges also come from difference of lighting, background, pose, view point of camera, size of foreground, etc.

We modify the Faster-RCNN framework for the clothing detection. The region proposal network (RPN) is first implemented on the input image to generate around 500 proposals after non-maximum suppression (NMS). Then, the Fast RCNN detection network is implemented. Through Region of Interest (RoI) layer, each proposal is mapped into certain region of the last convolutional feature map, and then fed into two paths of fully connected layers. The output of the softmax indicates the confidence of being the clothing region, and the bounding-box regressor indicates the localization information of clothing region. In our specific implementation of clothing detection, we make some modifications: (a) For RPN, we change the sizes of anchors to 128^2, 256^2, 384^2 pixels, and the aspect ratios to 1:1.5, 1:2, 1:2.5, which are selected according to the training set as prior knowledge. (b) We set a higher NMS threshold (i.e., 0.8) and a relative larger set of proposals (i.e., 500 per image). (c) Instead of auto-selecting a positive threshold for the detection network, we choose the proposal with highest confidence as our final predict clothing region, since we only want to get exactly one clothing region from each image. The detector performs better after adopting the modifications fore-mentioned.

3 Hierarchical Semantic Classification

With the large fine-grained dataset and accurate clothing detector, each attribute label of a certain clothing image can be predicted using CNN models. A simple way is to train N CNN models for each of N attribute categories. However, this approach is time-consuming, and more importantly, it discards the relations among the attributes. As a multi-label learning problem, a tree-structure network is adopted in [2] to integrate visual features and various semantic features. However, all of the semantic attributes are treated equally and the semantic hierarchy is ignored.

In this paper, 11 attribute categories are collected and divided into two levels:

- Middle-level semantic attributes (8): color, pattern, length, sleeve type, collar type, buttonhole placket, thickness, material.
- High-level semantic attributes (3): type, style, appropriate crowd.

Middle-level semantic attributes can be distinguished easily and usually related to certain region of clothing area, while high-level semantic attributes are relatively abstract and hard to distinguish, which agree with our intuition.

We pay attention to those high-level semantic attributes and aim to make full use of the visual features as well as middle-level semantic features. Inspired by [2], we build a novel hierarchical semantic tree-structure deep neural network to model the hierarchical relations among semantic attributes, as shown in Fig. 1.

The network is similar to AlexNet [4]. The low-level visual features are learned and shared among semantic attributes. The FC1 layer is the conjunction layer [2],

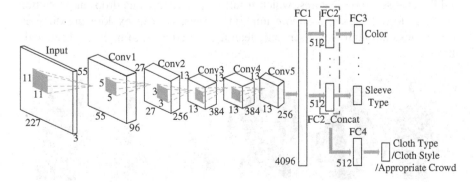

Fig. 1 Hierarchical semantic tree-structure deep neural network

which connects the visual features in lower layers and semantic features in higher layers. N (number of middle-level semantic attributes, i.e., (8) branches follow with FC1, each of which models one middle-level semantic attribute. Notably, we concatenate all of the FC2 branches to form the layer FC2_Concat, which presents for the fusion of low-level visual features and various middle-level semantic features. Following with a 512-dimension fully-connected intermediate layer, FC4 is the final fully-connected layers with the number of neurons equal to that of attribute values. Softmax is then implemented to predict the high-level semantic attributes.

4 Attributes Relations Analysis

As can been seen in Fig. 2, each FC2 layer corresponding to each middle-level semantic attribute concatenates and passes forward to another two fully-connected layers, and finally feeds into the softmax to get the prediction of high-level semantic attribute. The model reveals that middle-level semantic features make contribution to high-level semantic features, which coincides with our intuition. For example, clothes with short sleeves or round collars are less likely to belong to the type of suit.

In order to analyze which middle-level semantic features contribute more to certain high-level semantic feature, we enforce certain FC2 layer to zero, which is equivalent to make every component interval of FC2_Concat zero one by one, as shown in Eq. 1.

$$FC2\_Concat = [\alpha_1 FC2_1^T, \alpha_2 FC2_2^T, \ldots, \alpha_N FC2_N^T]^T$$
$$\text{s.t. } \Sigma\, \alpha_i = N\text{-}1,\ \alpha_i = 0 \text{ or } 1 \tag{1}$$

When certain α_i is set to zero, the corresponding neurons of $FC2_i$ are forced inactive, meaning that features learned by certain middle-level semantic attribute cannot pass forward, and the high-level semantic attribute is predicted without the corresponding information of middle-level semantic attribute. We reevaluate the high-level semantic prediction results in such way for all possible conditions. Those middle-level semantic features, which result in a more obvious drop on prediction precision if set to zeros, are more important. Thus, we can explore the different contributions of middle-level semantic features to prediction of high-level semantic attributes.

Fig. 2 Some clothing detection results with our modified Faster-RCNN

5 Experiment

5.1 Data Preparation

We crawled 207,795 upper-body garment images (with resolutions at least 350×350) from several online shopping stores. In addition to the images, the corresponding surrounding information is also extracted and parsed to ⟨*key*, *value*⟩ pairs. Each *key* represents for a certain attribute category (e.g. color) and each *value* specifies an attribute value (e.g. red). For a certain image, some of its corresponding attributes may be missing. Those attribute categories which more than half of the images miss are discarded. 11 attribute categories are finally collected and there are totally 189 attribute values. Following studies and experiments are based on the large fine-grained dataset.

5.2 Experiments for Clothing Detection

20,000 clothing images are annotated manually with clothing bounding boxes. Note that detected bounding boxes only cover the tutor regions which means sleeves/arms are not within the bounding boxes in case of various human poses.

We randomly sample 15,000 images for training and the other 5000 for testing. Average Precision (AP) is used to evaluate different clothing detectors. Since the performance of clothing detector is important for the following training of classification network, a stricter intersection over region (IoU) threshold (i.e., 0.7) is selected. We compare the performance of Deformable Part-based Model (DPM) [5], the Selective Search (SS) plus Fast-RCNN, and origin Faster-RCNN (see Table 1).

We can see that the DPM model performs the worst. Selective Search plus Fast-RCNN gains more accuracy thanks to more region proposals (about 2 k per image) with various sizes and aspect ratios. Our modified Faster-RCNN, with highest AP and least processing times, outperforms all other detection models. Some detection results of our modified Faster-RCNN are presented in Fig. 2.

Table 1 AP and average processing time of detection models, running on the same computer with Intel i5-4460 CPU (@ 3.2 GHz) with 4 cores, with one GTX 745 GPU card

Detection model	AP (%)	Time (s)
DPM	54.0	8.41
SS + Fast-RCNN	91.2	1.79
Faster-RCNN	83.8	0.38
Modified Faster-RCNN	**93.0**	**0.36**

Table 2 Predicition results of high-level semantic attributes

	Men		Women	
	TS-Net (%)	HS-Net (%)	TS-Net (%)	HS-Net (%)
Clothing type	83.8	**84.8**	78.7	**79.9**
Clothing style	56.8	**57.6**	36.9	**37.7**
Appropriate crowd	80.0	**80.4**	–	–

Data corresponding to appropriate crowd of women are missing

5.3 Experiments for Hierarchical Semantic Classification

The original tree-structure network in [3] is used as the baseline. We denote the baseline as **TS-Net** and our hierarchical semantic network as **HS-Net**. Both of the two classification models fine-tune from the pre-trained caffenet (an improved version of AlexNet) with lower learning rate (start from 0.01, drop 1/10 per epoch) for 10 epochs. The ratio of train set to test set is 3:1. The images put into the network are the enlarged (in the direction of width by a carefully-chose ratio, i.e., 0.2) clothing regions. Considering that the distribution of some attributes for men's clothes and women's clothes are quite different, the two kinds of clothes are trained separately. The prediction results can be seen in Table 2, and as can be seen in Table 2, our hierarchical semantic network performs better than the original tree structure network.

5.4 Experiments for Attribute Relations Analysis

It has been shown that high-level semantic features can be learned directly from the combination of middle-level semantic features. We can further study the different importance of the middle-level semantic features to the high-level semantic

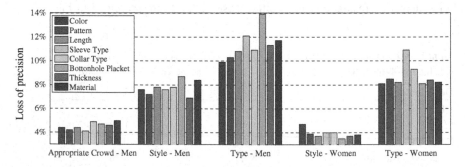

Fig. 3 Loss of prediction of various high-level semantic attributes when setting certain middle-level features zero

attributes. Keeping the whole weights of trained network unchanged, we set the FC2 of middle-level semantic to zero one after another and record how much the prediction accuracy drops. The numerical results are illustrated in Fig. 3.

Results show that missing different middle-level semantic features causes different precision loss. The more loss of precision, the more contribution certain middle-level semantic feature makes to certain high-level semantic feature. Taking this insight to the result, we can find that some of the relations are quite intuitive and comprehensible. For example, features corresponding to *buttonhole placket* relates most to *type* of men's clothes. It is in accordance with the common sense that clothes belong to *down jacket* usually have zippers instead of buttons, and T-shirts always have non zippers nor buttons. Other relations can be seen directly from Fig. 3.

6 Conclusion

We have crawled a large dataset of clothing images and corresponding attributes, and annotated the boundary boxes for part of the dataset. A modified Faster-RCNN has been trained to detect the clothing regions from original images, which is proved both efficient and accurate. We have also proposed a novel hierarchical semantic tree-structure deep neural network to model the hierarchical relations between different levels of semantic attributes. Improved prediction results of high-level semantic attributes are presented by adopting our network. We have also proposed a method to study the relations among different level of semantic attributes.

Acknowledgments The work was supported by the National Basic Research Program of China (Grant No. 2015CB856004), the Key Basic Research Program of Shanghai (15JC1400103) and the National Natural Science Foundation of China (Grant No. 91420302, 61272251).

References

1. Ren S, He K, Girshick R, Sun J (2015) Faster R-CNN: towards real-time object detection with region proposal networks. In: Neural Information Processing Systems (NIPS)
2. Chen Q, Huang J, Feris R, Brown LM, Dong J, Yan S (2015) Deep domain adaptation for describing people based on fine-grained clothing attributes. In: Proceedings of the IEEE conference on computer vision and pattern recognition, pp 5315–5324
3. Huang J, Xia W, Yan S (2014) Deep search with attribute-aware deep network. In: Proceedings of the ACM international conference on multimedia, ACM, pp 731–732
4. Krizhevsky A, Sutskever I, Hinton GE (2012) Imagenet classification with deep convolutional neural networks. In: Advances in neural information processing systems, pp 1097–1105
5. Felzenszwalb PF, Girshick RB, McAllester D, Ramanan D (2010) Object detection with discriminatively trained part based models. IEEE Trans Pattern Anal Mach Intell 32(9): 1627–1645

A Method of Image-Based Water Surface Reconstruction

Ling Zou, Yue Qi and Guoping Wang

Abstract Natural phenomena simulation has attracted a spurt of research attention and interest in both computer graphics and virtual reality technology domains. Water is one of the most common phenomena in real world. Acquisition and modeling of different water movements have become one of the important research topics in recent years. In this paper, we design an acquisition system for capturing dynamic water surface. We also present an image-based method for water surface reconstruction. The goal of water surface reconstruction is to compute 3D coordinates and normals of dynamic water surface.

Keywords Data acquisition · Image-based reconstruction · Water surface reconstruction

1 Introduction

The simulation of liquid has attracted lots of attention from computer graphics researchers [1]. As an important topic in liquid simulation area, reconstructing time-varying water surface has essential research significance and scientific value in

L. Zou (✉) · G. Wang
Graphics and Interaction Lab, School of Electronics Engineering
and Computer Science, Peking University, Beijing 100871, China
e-mail: zouling@pku.edu.cn

G. Wang
e-mail: wgp@pku.edu.cn

Y. Qi
State Key Laboratory of Virtual Reality Technology and System,
Beihang University, Beijing 100191, China
e-mail: qy@buaa.edu.cn

G. Wang
Beijing Engineering Technology Research Center of Virtual Simulation
and Visualization, Peking University, Beijing 100871, China

© Springer Science+Business Media Singapore 2016   437
J.J. (Jong Hyuk) Park et al. (eds.), *Advanced Multimedia and Ubiquitous
Engineering*, Lecture Notes in Electrical Engineering 393,
DOI 10.1007/978-981-10-1536-6_57

many fields ranging from fluid mechanics to oceanography. Most water surface reconstruction methods are either procedural or physics-based. However, the physics-based approaches suffer from their inefficiency and huge computational expense.

With the rapid development of computer hardware and image acquisition devices, image-based reconstruction has become a new research orientation [2]. By utilizing images of fluid motion captured by acquisition devices, accurate dynamic 3D water surfaces can be reconstructed based on refraction and reflection principles which should be obeyed on the interface between air and water and throughout the whole water body. This method can reserve more details and sharp features of water surface while the model calculation can be carried out more efficiently.

2   Related Work

Current modeling methods for dynamic water surface can fall into two main categories: physics-based and image-based methods.

The purpose of physics-based methods is to simulate the dynamics of liquid surface by accurately solving incompressible Navier-Stokes equations. In the simulation of liquid with free surface, accuracy of surface tracking is a critical factor for the quality of simulation.

Image-based modeling methods proposed in recent years. Most of recent research is focused on the use of refraction for the purpose of simplicity. Early research on this topic was conducted by Hohle [3] and in his work the objects beneath the surface of refractive medium are reconstructed. After that, Maas [4] tried to reconstruct the objects by positioning a camera beneath or above the water surface.

In [5, 6], Murase employed the refraction principle of liquid to reconstruct transparent water surface. In his work, a camera is positioned perpendicularly above a tank filled with water at the bottom of which a pattern is attached. The camera obtains a sequence of distorted images when the water surface varies dynamically. The optical flow methods are applied to analyze these images to obtain the trajectory of each point from the optical flow sequence. By averaging each point trajectory and calculating the surface normal, the water surface can be further constructed.

Morris et al. [7, 8] proposed a dynamic water surface reconstruction method. Two cameras are used to build up a stereo camera system. A fixed pattern (chessboard) is used for feature tracking. Ambiguities from single camera capture process are resolved in this method [9]. Besides, this method can obtain the water surface by accurately calculating the coordinate and normal of each pixel. In this method, the refractive index is not necessary to be known. This method also solves the problem of surface occlusion and has the advantage in robustness.

To solve the problem of distortion and blur caused by refraction and reflection, Ding et al. [10] designed a camera array acquisition system. The camera array is divided into two groups and the trigger for each group is interleaved to double the frame rate. At any moment, if a camera loses track of the feature points at a frame, this method will use the rest of the cameras to first approximate the surface and then ray-trace the surface to locate the missing feature points in problematical camera so that the points can be continually tracked.

3 Water Surface Reconstruction

In this paper, we present a method for water surface reconstruction based on images. We design a multi-camera acquisition system which is built up with high-speed cameras, photography luminaire, pattern board, water container and some other equipment for capturing dynamic water surface data. The output of acquisition system is several calibrated high-resolution image sequences which will be used to reconstruct dynamic water surface. As the output of reconstruction step, accurate dynamic 3D water surfaces can be reconstructed based on refraction and reflection principles of water.

3.1 Acquisition Setup

For the purpose of data acquisition, we design a system to capture the detailed movement of water surface which are varying all the time. The hardware setup of our acquisition system is shown in Fig. 1, including cameras, lighting, data storage, etc.

Fig. 1 Water surface acquisition system

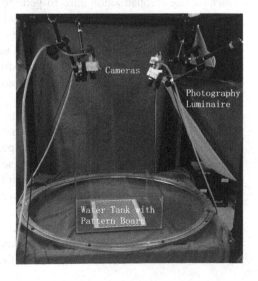

High-speed camera: Several high-speed cameras (OPAL-1000c/Q) with CameraLink interface from Adimec Inc. are used in our system. This kind of camera is able to acquire images (256 grey levels) with resolution of 1024×1024 at 120 fps. All cameras should be fixed to capture the entire water surface. The vertical distance from each camera to pattern board is in the range of 100–150 cm. The horizontal distances between different cameras are about 50 cm. **Lighting**: There are several requirements for lighting: (1) Lighting should be bright enough to ensure the quality of images at frame frequency of 30 fps. (2) Lighting should be stable during the whole period of capturing. (3) Spotlight or line light that may cause disturbing reflections on water surface should be avoided. In most circumstances, indoor natural light can satisfy the above requirements. If requirement (1) is not satisfied, a photography luminaire can make environment brighter when the light is insufficient. **Pattern board**: We print a black-white chessboard on regular paper as the pattern board, make it waterproof, and then attach it at bottom of the tank. It is used for both camera calibration and water surface acquisition.

The capture procedure consists of two main steps: camera calibration and image acquisition. Since the visible regions of our cameras have large overlapping regions, we used Zhang Zhengyou's method [11] for calibration by reusing the checkerboard pattern. When there is any disturbance on the water surface, the captured images of pattern board will be distorted. We can capture a series of images from a certain angle by each camera and these images are synchronized. As the input of our water surface reconstruction algorithm, these images have the same lighting to improve the robustness of feature point matching process.

3.2 Image-Based Water Surface Reconstruction

Water surface reconstruction aims to generate the height field and normal field of water surface using image sequences captured by the calibrated cameras. The distorted feature points are tracked over time and across cameras, spatial-temporal correspondence maps are obtained and then used for specular carving to reconstruct the time-varying water surface. The reconstruction consists of the steps of feature detection, mapping of image pixels to 3D coordinates, voxel carving and so on.

Based on the settings of system described in Sect. 3.1 and assuming the refractive index has the value of r, we compute a pattern-to-pixel correspondence function, $C(q, t)$, that maps the 3D coordinate of an arbitrary point on the pattern to a certain pixel q on the corresponding captured image at time t. We use Harris Corner Detection Method to find the correspondence between chessboard corners and pixels at sub-pixel resolution. Bilinear interpolation is applied on all pixels in a square to get the corresponding 3D positions on chessboard, based on four corners of this square which has already been solved.

Let p be a point on water surface where refraction happens, and assume the normal at p is n. The line from q to p can stand for the incident ray (denoted as q-p), and we represent the angle between n and the incident ray as α. Similarly, the line

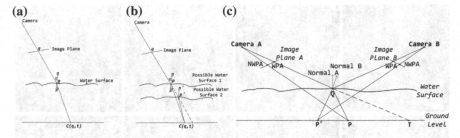

Fig. 2 Water surface refraction. **a** Refraction principle **b** Surface ambiguity **c** Double cameras used for reconstruction

from p to $C(q, t)$ stands for refractive ray (denoted as p-$C(q, t)$), and β represents the angle between n and the refractive ray. The definition of these variables can be depicted by Fig. 2a.

According to Snell's Law [12] in physics, the following relations can be achieved:

1. Incident ray q-p and refractive ray p-$C(q, t)$ are on the same plane.
2. $sin\ \alpha = r * sin\ \beta$ holds for α, β and r.

However, unique solution of p-n pair cannot be guaranteed based on the above two relations. As shown in Fig. 2b, when the distance d between point p and point $C(q, t)$ changes, another pair of p-n values can also exist which still obeys the above relations. Therefore, there might be a set of values for p-n pairs as possible solutions. This leads to the ambiguity in water surface modeling using only one single camera.

To deal with this problem, we adopt the solution proposed in [9] by introducing more cameras to tackle the ambiguity induced by only one camera. First, we capture water surface simultaneously from two cameras. Second, a set of p-n pairs for each camera need to be solved under the assumption that the refractive index of water remains constant. The unique p-n pair can be found once the two solved values of normal n on point p from different cameras are the same. In this case, we can decide this point p is a water surface vertex. The diagram of solution is depicted in Fig. 2c.

4 Experiment Results

Using the method described in Sect. 3, several water surface structures are recorded by our multi-camera acquisition system in experiment, animating as ripples caused by a water drop. Figure 3 shows some snapshots of water surface captured by one camera. These captured image sequences are used as input in our reconstruction method.

The results of one frame water surface reconstruction including surface normal and surface height field. Water surface can be reconstructed using either the height

Fig. 3 Captured images

field or normal map. Using normal map can generate water surface with less noise. From the reconstruction result, we can conclude that our method can correctly compute the height field of water surface and the normal information.

To evaluate the efficacy of our method, we performed simulations in a virtual scene which closely matches the experimental conditions in the lab. Figure 4 demonstrates the evolution of ripples caused by a water drop, until the water surface is back to still gradually. It shows that our algorithm can accurately reconstruct the dynamics of water surface. Figure 5 shows the results of rendered with different light conditions and viewpoints.

Fig. 4 Rendering of water surface construction

Fig. 5 Rendering from different lights and viewpoints

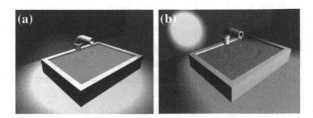

In another word, the above experiments show that using images of pattern board from different cameras, height map and normal map of the water surface can be precisely calculated, by applying still water refractive index and Snell's rules. All of these contribute to the successful construction of water surface.

5 Conclusion

A method of image-based water surface reconstruction is proposed in this paper. Acquisition system is designed for water surface data acquisition, in order to reconstruct water surface by image-based reconstruction method. In experiments, the water surfaces reconstructed from captured images are first demonstrated and satisfactory results are obtained using our approach.

The experiments have shown the feasibility and effectiveness of our approach. However, the shortcoming is obvious in our acquisition system, within which only two high-speed cameras are used. Using multi-camera acquisition system to support more accurate model calculation is our future work.

Acknowledgments This research was supported by Grant No. 2013BAK03B07, 2014BAK18B01 from The National Key Technology Research & Development Program of China, and Grant No. 61232014, 61421062, 61173080, 61472010, 61272348, 61572054 from National Natural Science Foundation of China.

References

1. Zhao Q (2011) Data acquisition and simulation of natural phenomena. Sci China Inf Sci 385–416
2. Zou L, Qi Y, Zhao Q (2013) Review on liquid acquisition and modeling techniques. J Comput Res Dev 50(11):2472–2480
3. Hohle J (1971) Reconstruction of the underwater object, Photogrammetic engineering and remote sensing. ASPRS, Maryland, pp 948–954
4. Flach P, Maas H (2000) Vision-based techniques for refraction analysis in applications of terrestrial geodesy. International archives of photogrammetry and remote sensing, pp 195–201
5. Murase H (1992) Radiometry. Jones and Bartlett Publishers, New York
6. Murase H (1992) Surface shape reconstruction of a nonrigid transport object using refraction and motion. In: IEEE transactions on pattern analysis and machine intelligence, pp 1045–1052
7. Morris N, Kutulakos K (2011) Dynamic refraction stereo. In: IEEE Transactions on pattern analysis and machine intelligence, Washington, DC, pp 1518–1531
8. Morris N (2004) Image-based water surface reconstruction with refractive stereo. University of Toronto, Toronto
9. Sanderson A, Weiss L, Nayar S (1988) Structured highlight inspection of specular surfaces. In: IEEE transactions on pattern analysis and machine intelligence, pp 44–55
10. Ding Y, Li F, Ji Y (2011) Dynamic fluid surface acquisition using a camera array. In: IEEE international conference on computer vision. IEEE Computer Society, pp 2478–2485
11. Zhang Z (2000) A flexible new technique for camera calibration. In: IEEE transactions on pattern analysis and machine intelligence, pp 1330–1334
12. Snell's Law. http://en.wikipedia.org/wiki/Snell's_law

Reversible Image Data Hiding with Local Adaptive Contrast Enhancement

Ruiqi Jiang, Weiming Zhang, Jiajia Xu, Nenghai Yu
and Xiaocheng Hu

Abstract Recently, a novel reversible data hiding scheme is proposed for contrast enhancement by Wu (IEEE Signal Process Lett 22.1:81–85, 2015). Instead of pursuing the traditional high PSNR value, he designs the message embedding algorithm to enhance the contrast of the host image. In this paper, an extended scheme is proposed to not only adaptively enhance the contrast of the image, but also to keep the PSNR value high meanwhile. Firstly, the original host image is divided into non-overlapping blocks, such that the local contrast of the image can be enhanced adaptively. Secondly, we classify the pixels of each block into two sets, the "referenced" set and the "embedded" set, and then processing them alternatively such that additional side information is eliminated. Experimental results demonstrate that our proposed algorithm achieves increased local visual quality and performs better than Wu et al.'s scheme with keeping image's PSNR high as criterion for RDH.

Keywords Local adaptive · Contrast enhancement · Histogram modification · Reversible data hiding

1 Introduction

Data hiding is applied extensively in the community of signal processing, such as ownership protection, fingerprinting, authentication and secret communication. The most classical data hiding technique leads to permanent distortions. In last decades, reversible data hiding (RDH) [1–11] as a new type of information hiding technique, has received much attention. RDH provides not only extracting embedded data precisely, but also restoring the original cover image without any error. This special

R. Jiang · W. Zhang (✉) · J. Xu · N. Yu · X. Hu
Key Laboratory of Electromagnetic Space Information,
Chinese Academy of Sciences,
Hefei, China
e-mail: zhangwm@ustc.edu.cn

© Springer Science+Business Media Singapore 2016
J.J. (Jong Hyuk) Park et al. (eds.), *Advanced Multimedia and Ubiquitous Engineering*, Lecture Notes in Electrical Engineering 393,
DOI 10.1007/978-981-10-1536-6_58

445

property has been found much useful in many sensitive fields, such as medical imagery, military imagery and law forensics, where any change on the host signal is not allowed.

The classic RDH algorithms mainly adopt three techniques, histogram shifting (HS) [3], difference expansion (DE) [4] and prediction-error expansion (PEE) [5]. There are two important metrics to evaluate the performance of a RDH algorithm: the embedding capacity and the distortion. In fact, we always keep the balance between this two metrics, because a higher embedding capacity often cause more distortion and decrease the distortion will result in a lower embedding capacity, so we usually use the Peak-Signal-to-Noise-Ratio (PSNR) to evaluate the performance of algorithm.

Recently, Wu et al. proposed a new RDH algorithm with contrast enhancement [1]. They deemed that the improvement of visual quality is more important than keeping the image's PSNR high. By using some pairs of peaks, the histogram of pixels values is modified to achieve histogram equalization, thus leading to the image contrast enhancement while RDH is realized. The method provides a new direction for the research of RDH.

Contrast enhancement is a meaningful application by RDH, but in real life, local adaptive contrast enhancement is more widely used, such as military images, medical images, etc. In this paper, we considerably extended Wu et al.'s method in order to have a better performance. Firstly, we proposed to cut the original image into several blocks, by manipulating the more centrally distributed block histogram, local adaptive contrast enhanced effect can be achieved. Meanwhile however, if we do the same histogram shifting operation as Wu et al.'s method, we need 16 excluded pixels to record the side information for extracting embedded information and recovering image completely for each individual block, which will loss pure payloads for data embedding. Considering this limitation, the other improved method, double-layered histogram shifting, designed. We divide the pixels of each block into two sets, the referenced set and the embedded set, because the histogram of this two sets are similar, we can shift histogram of the embedded set according to the bins of the referenced set, and then operate histogram of the referenced set based on the bins of the modified embedded set. Since the histogram of the referenced set keeps no changed when embedding the message bits into the embedded set, we do not need 16 pixels to record the value of last two peaks. The experimental results demonstrate that our proposed method achieves increased local visual quality and performs better than Wu et al.'s scheme with keeping image's PSNR high as criterion for RDH.

The rest of the paper is organized as follows: Sect. 2 discusses the important issues regarding Wu et al.'s method, and Sect. 3 describes the detail about our proposed RDH algorithm featured by adaptive local contrast enhancement. The experimental results compared to the previous method demonstrated in Sect. 4. Finally, a conclusion is drawn in Sect. 5.

2   RDH Algorithm with Contrast Enhancement

In Wu et al.'s paper, they tend to enhance the contrast of a host image to improve its visual quality instead of trying to keep the PSNR high, and at the process of embedding data, the side information is embedded into the host image along with the message so that the original image can be recovered completely. Before manipulating the pixel histogram, a pre-processing is used to prevent the overflow and underflow. For a given 8-bit gray-level image I, supposing that the amount of peak-pairs to be spilt is L, excluding the first 16 pixels in the bottom row, all pixels values from 0 to L-1 are added by L. Also, the pixels value from $256-L$ to 255 arc subtracted by L. The position information of modified pixels in the operation has been record in a location map. And then, the image histogram can be calculated by counting the pixels, h(i) represents the numbers of pixels with gray level value i. Based on image histogram, we choose the highest two bins and the corresponding smaller and higher values are denoted by I_S and I_R, respectively. Then the bins with value between this two peaks keep unchanged while the outer ones are shifted outward so that I_S and I_R can be spilt into two adjacent bins for information embedding. The data embedding process performs by:

$$
i' = \begin{cases}
i-1, & \text{for} & i < I_S \\
I_S - b_k, & \text{for} & i = I_S \\
i, & \text{for} & I_S < i < I_R \\
I_R + b_k, & \text{for} & i = I_R \\
i+1, & \text{for} & i > I_R
\end{cases}
\tag{1}
$$

where i' is the modified pixel-value, and b_k is the k-th message bit (0 or 1) to be hidden. We can embed the amount of $(h(I_S) + h(I_R))$ bits into the image by Eq. (1). To increase the embedding capacity, same process repeat by selecting more peak-pairs in the modified histogram until meeting the requirement. The compressed location map is embedded into the image before message bits to be hidden, the side information including the value of L, the size of the compressed location map, the least significant bits (LSBs) and the previous peak values is embed using the last two peaks to be spilt. At last, the LSBs of the 16 excluded pixels in the bottom row are replaced by the value of the last two peaks. With this embedding process, histogram equalization achieved, which leads to contrast enhancement.

$$
b'_k = \begin{cases}
1, & \text{if} & i' < I_S - 1 \\
0, & \text{if} & i' = I_S \\
0, & \text{if} & i' = I_R \\
1, & \text{if} & i' = I_R + 1
\end{cases}
\tag{2}
$$

The extraction and recovery process as follows:

(1) By retrieving the LSBs of the 16 excluded pixels in the bottom row, we get the values of the last two spilt peaks.

(2) The value of L, the length of the compressed location map, the original LSBs of 16 excluded pixels, and the previously spilt peak values are extracted by using Eq. (2).

(3) The recovery operations are carried out by processing all the pixels except the 16 excluded ones with Eq. (3) from previous spilt and then repeated until all of the spilt peaks are restored and the data embedded with them are extracted.

(4) Knowing the length of the compressed location map, the compressed location map obtained from the extracted binary values decompress to the original size.

(5) From the location map, those pixels modified in preprocess are identified, and pixel value is subtracted by L if it is less than 128, or increased by L otherwise.

$$i = \begin{cases} i' + 1, & \text{for} & i' < Is - 1 \\ Is, & \text{for} & i' = Is - 1 \text{ or } i' = Is \\ I_R, & \text{for} & i' = I_R \text{ or } i' = I_R + 1 \\ i - 1, & \text{for} & i' > I_R + 1 \end{cases} \tag{3}$$

3 Our Proposed RDH Algorithm

3.1 Adaptive Block Division

Compared to Wu et al.'s algorithm, we adopted two improved method to achieve better performance. First, we cut the original image into several blocks, usually the size of block is 16×16 or 32×32, and then operate each individual block histogram using Wu et al.'s method, as result, local adaptive contrast-enhanced effect can be realized. For each individual block, the gray level of pixels relatively will be more close to, that is, the histogram will be steeper than that of the original image, in this way, the embedding capacity can be increased in a big range.

3.2 Double Layered Embedding

If using Wu et al.'s method for information embedding after blocking, we need to exclude 16 pixels to record the last two peaks for each individual block, which will loss pure payload for data embedding. At the same time, we find that, if we divide the pixels in a block into two sets, the pixel histogram of them are very similar, as shown in Fig. 1.

Considering this two aspects, we design the other improved method: double-layered embedding. We use Fig. 2 to example the process of double-layered embedding operation:

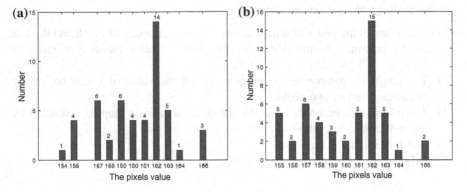

Fig. 1 Histogram of the reference set and the embedded set for one block of "Lena"

(1) Given the original image divides into several 10 × 10 blocks by adaptive block division operation, and then we divide all the pixels in a block into the referenced set (Fig. 1a) and the embedded set (Fig. 1b);

(2) Based on the histogram of referenced set, we pick out the highest two peaks and then operate the histogram of the embedded set using Wu et al.'s method as IS and IR are the pixels whose value equal to the two peaks on the referenced set, the histogram of embedded set (Fig. 1b) changes to (Fig. 2a);

(3) Selecting the highest two peaks on the modified histogram of embedded set, then operating the histogram of referenced set using Wu et al.'s method as I_S and I_R, are the pixels with the same value of the two adopted peaks, in this way, the histogram of referenced set (Fig. 1a) changes to (Fig. 2b);

(4) Utilizing the same process for all the blocks and repeating several rounds until finish embedding the bits stream, which includes compressed location map and messages to be hidden;

(5) The side information including the value of L rounds and the length of compressed location map embed at the last round.

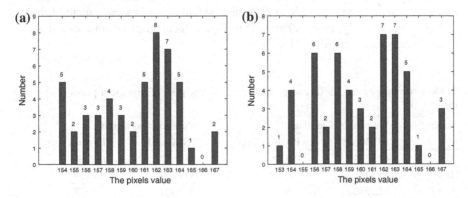

Fig. 2 The modified histogram of the reference set and the embedded set for one block of "Lena"

The extract and recovery process are as follows:

(1) According to the protocol sender and receiver set, the size of block and the last set for information embedding can be obtain, usually the size of block is 16×16 or 32×32.
(2) The length of compressed location map and the value of L can be get by extracting the last two peaks.
(3) The information embedded and the compressed location map are extracted by using Wu et al.'s method.
(4) The location map can be get.
(5) Original image is recovery completely.

4   Experimental Results

Our proposed method compared to the method of Wu et al., using typical 512×512 grayscale images (i.e. Lena, Tank, Barbara) with the experimental environment of MATLAB R2014 under windows 7. For all images, the performance of our proposed method is better.

Besides our block and dividing algorithm, the embedding method in these two algorithms keeps the same thing. As shown in Table 1, for these two algorithm, the payload are both increased by using more peak-pairs for data embedding, that is, increasing the parameter L; and because our proposed algorithm manipulate more centrally contribute histogram in each individual block, the pure hiding rate (Payload) is better than Wu et al.'s method in a big range. What's more, from the PSNR-to-Payload curve in Fig. 3, we also can get a conclusion that our method can embed more data when leads to the same distortion, and if we embed the same amount of data, the host image can be modified less, which means that our embedding performance is superior to Wu et al.'s method.

We select several grayscale images to compare the contrast-enhanced visual quality, due to space limitation, only the result of image "kidney" shown in this paper. The marked image in Wu et al.'s method and in our proposed method shown in Fig. 4, respectively. From (c) and (d) in Fig. 4, local adaptive contrast-enhanced visual quality is observed, obviously.

Table 1 Comparing the PSNR and payload for different pairs of histogram peaks of this two method

Lena	Wu et al.'s algorithm		Our proposed algorithm	
	PSNR (dB)	Payload (bpp)	PSNR (dB)	Payload (bpp)
L = 2	42.1844	0.0309	43.0228	0.2066
L = 4	36.7746	0.0694	37.0637	0.2999
L = 6	33.2580	0.1061	33.5421	0.3627

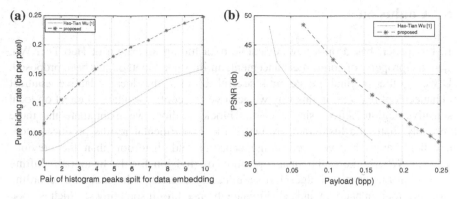

Fig. 3 Comparison about two methods for image "Lena"

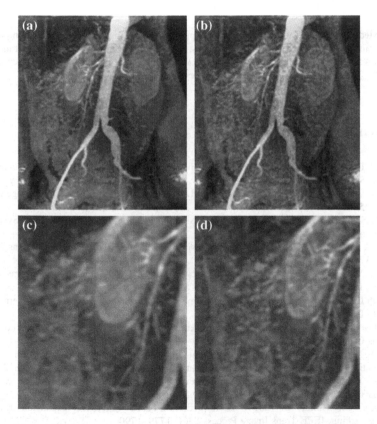

Fig. 4 **a** The marked image in Wu et al.'s method **b** The marked image in proposed method **c** local detail in Wu et al.'s method **d** local detail in proposed method

5   Conlusion

In this paper, based on a new reversible data hiding algorithm of Hao-Tian Wu, with the property of contrast enhancement, an improved method has been proposed. Dividing the original image into several blocks, the local adaptive contrast enhancement realized, in this way we achieve the contrast-enhanced effect on local sensitive region. After using a classic block method, we manipulate the more centrally distribute histogram, by which the experimental results produces more excellent ration between embedding capacity and distortion than the previous scheme. What's more, the smart operation of division for the histogram shifting method in our proposed algorithm significantly decreases the space for recording side information and may indeed eliminate the need for it sometimes, which is good for embedding capacity. Experimental results show that our proposed algorithm has better performance on local visual quality, embedding capacity and hiding distortion, compared to the algorithm of Hao-Tian Wu.

Acknowledgments This work is supported in part by the Natural Science Foundation of China under Grant 61170234 and Grant 60803155, by the Strategic Priority Research Program of the Chinese Academy of Sciences under Grant XDA06030601, and by the Funding of Science and Technology on Information Assurance Laboratory under Grant KJ-13.

References

1. Wu HT, Dugelay JL, Shi YQ (2015) Reversible image data hiding with contrast enhancement. IEEE Signal Process Lett 22(1):81–85
2. Celik MU et al (2005) Lossless generalized-LSB data embedding. IEEE Trans Image Process 14.2:253–266
3. Ni Z, Shi YQ, Ansari N, Su W (2006) Reversible data hiding. IEEE Trans Circuits Syst Video Technol 16(3):354362
4. Tian J (2003) Reversible data embedding using a difference expansion. IEEE Trans Circuits Syst Video Technol 13(8):890–896
5. Lu TC, Tseng CY, Deng KM (2014) Reversible data hiding using local edge sensing prediction methods and adaptive thresholds. Sig Process 104:152–166
6. Thodi DM, Rodrguez JJ (2007) Expansion embedding techniques for reversible watermarking. IEEE Trans Image Process 16(3):721–730
7. Sachnev V et al (2009) Reversible watermarking algorithm using sorting and prediction. IEEE Trans Circuits Syst Video Technol 19.7:989–999
8. Li X, Yang B, Zeng T (2011) Efficient reversible watermarking based on adaptive prediction-error expansion and pixel selection. IEEE Trans Image Process 20(12):3524–3533
9. Yang Y et al (2009) A contrast-sensitive reversible visible image watermarking technique. IEEE Trans Circuits Syst Video Technol 19.5:656–667
10. Dragoi IC, Coltuc D (2014) Local-prediction-based difference expansion reversible watermarking. IEEE Trans Image Process 23(4):1779–1790
11. Jung SW, Ko SJ (2011) A new histogram modification based reversible data hiding algorithm considering the human visual system. IEEE Signal Process Lett 18.2:95–98

Practical Tools for Digital Image Forensic Authentication

Jinhua Zeng, Wei Lu, Rui Yang and Xiulian Qiu

Abstract In this paper, we introduced the state-of-the-art techniques for digital image forensic authentication. A novel system was presented which consisted of the advanced tools for digital image forensic authentication. The tools offered in the system had the functions including the image file header analysis, device identification, re-compression analysis, copy-paste detection, resampling analysis, etc. The system performance has been tested under practical cases of forensic image examination. The experimental data and results have proven the advancement of the proposed system which could be widely applied in forensic image examination and other forensic applications.

Keywords Forensic image authentication · File header · Image re-compression · Device identification · Copy-paste detection · Image resampling

1 Introduction

In forensic science, how to examine digital image authentication is a big problem. In Chinese, expert opinions and images are both important classes of legal evidence. In order to be used as legal evidence in court, images should be authenticated that they are not tampered.

J. Zeng · X. Qiu
Institute of Forensic Science, Ministry of Justice, Shanghai 200063, China
e-mail: zengjh@ssfjd.cn

W. Lu (✉)
School of Data and Computer Science, Guangdong Key Laboratory
of Information Security Technology, Sun Yat-sen University,
Guangzhou 510006, China
e-mail: luwei3@mail.sysu.edu.cn

R. Yang
School of Information Management, Sun Yat-sen University,
Guangzhou 510006, China

© Springer Science+Business Media Singapore 2016
J.J. (Jong Hyuk) Park et al. (eds.), *Advanced Multimedia and Ubiquitous Engineering*, Lecture Notes in Electrical Engineering 393,
DOI 10.1007/978-981-10-1536-6_59

Lots of techniques were proposed to solve the authentication of images. In here, we focused on the methods for forensic authentication of digital images. The topic of digital image forensics has mass findings. In the recent review work [1, 2], the whole digital image life cycle was considered and used as the midline to classify the outcomes in the domain, which consisted of the image acquisition, coding and editing [1]. Farid [3] reviewed the digital image forensic techniques according to tampering artifact types, such as format, camera, pixel, and statistical based forensics. The findings in digital image forensic authentication are advanced and the corresponding techniques are mature, but the practical system and tool in the forensic science application is still immature and deficient.

In this paper, we introduced a novel system for image forensic authentication which consisted of the functions including the image file header analysis, device identification, re-compression analysis, copy-paste detection, resampling analysis, etc. These functions have covered the entire life period of the image generation, storage and operation. The performance and experimental results have been described in details in the paper. The remainder of the paper was organized as follows: Sect. 2 introduced the image file header analysis technique used in the system and its experimental results. Section 3 presented the used device identification method. Section 4 described other tampering artifact detection in the images such as copy-paste, re-compression, resampling, etc. The experimental data and results were given in each corresponding sections.

2 File Header Analysis of Digital Images

Digital images had their specific formats which could be revealed in coding format, file header data, Meta data, etc. For file header analysis, we focused on the images with JPEG compression. The JPEG header contains some important signatures for image authentication that are the image size, camera information, quantization table, and Huffman code, etc. [3]. In the practical cases, the quantization table and Huffman code are valuable information. There are not specific quantization table and Huffman code used in the JPEG compression standard, but the main image editors actually uses certain quantization table or Huffman code to balance compression and quality in images. By summarizing features of the main image editors, such as Photoshop, etc. the system could accurately identify the images modified by main image editors. One example of the experiments was shown as follows:

(1) One image was captured by a SONY video recorder (HDR-XR160E), its quantization table and Huffman code was shown in Fig. 1.
(2) We used the Adobe Photoshop CS5 software to load and then resave the above image, its quantization table and Huffman code was shown in Fig. 2. As shown in Fig. 2, its quantization table was the one typically used in the Photoshop software.

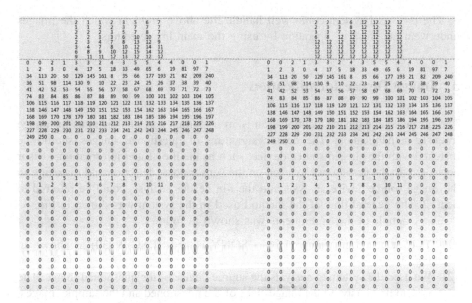

Fig. 1 The quantization table and Huffman code used in the image. The *first row* was the quantization table, the *second* and *last rows* were AC and DC Huffman codes

Fig. 2 The quantization table and Huffman code used in the image resaved by the Photoshop. The *first row* was the quantization table, the *second* and *last rows* were AC and DC Huffman codes

The proposed system could well handle the above problem which the images underwent the "resave" operation by using the main image editors.

3   Image Device Identification

The image source device identification is an important part of signatures for image forensic authentication. The device signature of questioned images should be matched with the alleged source device, such as the file header information, sensor noise, etc. In the system, we focused on the sensor noise detection and matching in the image source device analysis and the file header analysis could be referred to Sect. 2. The general flow of the method used in the system was shown in Fig. 3.

One example of the experiments was shown as follows:

(1) Two images were captured by a SONY camera (DSC-W830) as shown in Fig. 4.
(2) We used the system to analysis the source device of the questioned image. The system first analyzed the image sizes of the questioned and the sample images, and then further calculated the operations depicted in Fig. 3. The experimental result was shown in Fig. 5.

4   Other Tampering Artifact Detection

Except for the above functions, the system also had the techniques including copy-paste detection, re-compression analysis, resampling analysis, etc.

For the copy-paste detection, the SIFT-like (SIFT, scale-invariant feature transform) feature matching method was applied in the system. The SIFT-like method had the disadvantage of sparse feature representation of images; we further proposed affine transformation based image copy-paste detection which could achieve high accuracy in practical cases, one example of the affine transformation based copy-paste detection in the system was shown in Fig. 6. As shown in Fig. 6,

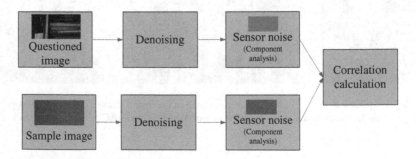

Fig. 3 The general flow of the image source device identification

Fig. 4 Two images captured by the SONY camera. The *left one* was used as the questioned image and the *right one* as the sample image

Fig. 5 The corresponding sensor noises of the images in Fig. 4

Fig. 6 The affine transformation based copy-paste detection in the system. The *left image* was the questioned image, and the *right one* was the result

the affine transformation based copy-paste detection method could accurately measure the similarity of images.

For the re-compression analysis, we focused on the images with JPEG compression. Usually, a digital forgery had undergone a "resave" operation in the tampering. In the experiments, we have observed that the re-compression of JPEG images would change the statistical distribution feature of their DCT transform coefficients, especially in the re-compression operation with different quality factors. Based on the above phenomenon, we developed an efficient tool for re-compression detection of JPEG images. Similar statistical features could be observed in the image resampling and other tampering artifacts.

5 Conclusions

In this paper, a novel system for digital image forensic authentication was presented. The system' functions included the image file header analysis, device identification, re-compression analysis, copy-paste detection, resampling analysis, etc. The whole functions covered the entire image processing period. Each function performances have been described in the corresponding sections, and the results have shown the feasibility and efficiency in digital image authentication. The system could be widely used in forensic image examination and other forensic applications.

Acknowledgments This work is supported by the Grants from the Ministry of Finance, China 106 (GY2014G-2), the Natural Science Foundation of Guangdong (No. 2016A030313350), the Special Funds for Science and Technology Development of Guangdong (No. 2016KZ010103), and the Fundamental Research Funds for the Central Universities (No. 16lgjc83).

References

1. Piva A (2013) An overview on image forensics. ISRN Signal Process 2013:22
2. Singh V, Jain NK (2015) Digital image forensics in multimedia security: a review. J Int J Eng Res Technol 4:1232–1237
3. Digital image forensics. http://www.cs.dartmouth.edu/farid

Parallel Detection Algorithm of Covered Primitives Based on Geometry Shadow Map

Hua Li, Huamin Yang, Cheng Han, Jianping Zhao and Yuling Cao

Abstract In this paper we present a method to generate high-quality hard shadows in real-time based on geometry shadow map. The method focuses on addressing the aliasing artifacts due to the large number of overlapping primitives which cannot be stored sufficiently and yields error of depth reconstruction. We call it Covered Primitives Parallel Detection algorithm (CPPD). In CPPD, a parallel detection algorithm according to the texel edges is proposed without increasing storage of different triangles. Experiments show that CPPD algorithm can improve the accuracy of depth reconstruction and reduce the jagged shadows effectively.

Keywords Shadow map · Anti-aliasing · Primitives · Detection algorithm

1 Introduction

Shadows are essential elements in computer-generated scenes. It provides visual cues to assist in understanding the geometric relationships. Shadow mapping and shadow volume are the two of famous methods to generate hard shadows in

H. Li · H. Yang · C. Han · J. Zhao (✉) · Y. Cao
Department of Computer Science and Technology, Changchun University
of Science and Technology, Changchun 130022, China
e-mail: zhaojpin@aliyun.com

H. Li
e-mail: lihua@cust.edu.cn

H. Yang
e-mail: yhm@cust.edu.cn

C. Han
e-mail: hancheng@cust.edu.cn

Y. Cao
e-mail: caoyuling@cust.edu.cn

© Springer Science+Business Media Singapore 2016
J.J. (Jong Hyuk) Park et al. (eds.), *Advanced Multimedia and Ubiquitous Engineering*, Lecture Notes in Electrical Engineering 393,
DOI 10.1007/978-981-10-1536-6_60

461

real-time. In contract to shadow volume algorithm, shadow mapping is a flexible and efficient method with the feature of independent to the object's complexity. But it suffers from aliasing caused by mismatch of different sample distribution. Inspired by the fact that the depth value can be reconstructed by an occluding primitive stored in the geometry shadow map, the mismatch of different sample distribution can be reduced greatly. However, the storage of overlapped triangles in each texel is an infeasible overhead for the system. In CPPD, a parallel detection algorithm on texel edges is proposed to identify overlapped triangles, which reconstructs shadow boundaries with thin details. CPPD increase the precision of depth reconstruction and reduce the jagged shadow boundary effectively with little overhead to the standard shadow mapping.

2   Related Work

Many algorithms have been proposed to solve the aliasing issues of shadow mapping. Good surveys [1, 2] have comprehensively reviews of the related research work. In distortion shadow map [3], a sample redistribution method is presented so that the geometric silhouette regions in the shadow map can be covered by more texels. Adaptive Shadow Maps (ASMs) [4] and Dynamic Adaptive Shadow Maps on Graphics Hardware [5] use an adaptive method to store the shadow map within a hierarchical representation. Perspective Shadow Maps (PSMs) [6] generates shadow in the post-perspective space to address the perspective aliasing. Light Space Perspective Shadow Maps (LiSPSMs) algorithm [7] expands the idea to split up the whole depth range into different distance from the viewpoint according to different aliasing distribution. Related to our work, Reconstructable Geometry Shadow Maps (RGSM) [8] proposes a method to find the occluding triangle for shadow test. Sub-Pixel Shadow Mapping [9] (SPSM) improves the idea by storing a fixed-size partial representation of the scene geometry and uses the conservation rasterization reducing aliasing and bias issues. Our method can be viewed as a drop-in extension for anti-aliasing mechanism in geometry-based shadow map.

3   Covered Primitives Parallel Detection Algorithm

3.1   Overview

In Reconstructable Geometry Shadow Mapping, the depth inquiry may cause artifact due to the fact that a view-sample might be incorrectly classified when the projection is actually outside a triangle. Common anti-aliasing methods as increasing the resolution of shadow map can hardly handle this type of issue because it will lead to huge impact on memory and fill rate consumption. According to the fact that shadow aliasing always happens in the depth-discontinuous regions, the core of reconstruction depth is to increase the accuracy of identification of the different primitive border. In this paper we introduce covered primitive parallel detection algorithm (CPPD), a new method based on shadow map generating hard shadows with sub pixel precision and high temporal consistency. Similar to the works of reconstructable geometry shadow mapping, CPPD algorithm is enforced based upon extracts and stores geometry information of a plurality of occluding geometry of object's front face from light source's point of view. Projecting each view sample into light space and proceeding to depth estimation by the detection of edges intersection so that a precisely depth is built. The rendering pass will estimate shadowing from partial geometry. According to the requirement of shadow silhouette precisely, we perform a Conservative Rasterization to force the generation of the fragments for every pixel touched by a primitive.

3.2 Conservative Shadow Map

Conservative rasterization [10] guarantees each fragment being produced for any triangle intersecting the texel area. It utilizes a slight forward motion of triangle edges in their normal direction to extend a length of half pixel width, as shown in Fig. 1a. In this paper, we use the minimum conservation depth with a compactness scheme of storage triangle information to fit in a single RGBA texel as small as possible [9]. Figure 1b illustrates one texel being covered by triangles, for a view sample is projected into the Texel_c should be reconstructed by triangle T_3, but the area outside of T_3 will be error estimated without the overlapped triangle detection. Our method focuses on the triangle detection of those are stored in adjacent texel but not limited in the 8 adjacent texel. A per-pixel shadow silhouette test will be enforced for shadow boundary recovering in Sect. 3.3.1.

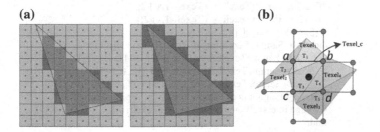

Fig. 1 a Conservative rasterization turn off (*left*) Conservative rasterization turn on (*right*). **b** Texel-covered recognition

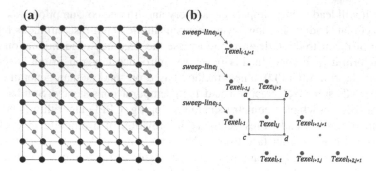

Fig. 2 **a** Line-sweep geometry *shadow* map. **b** Edge ab, ac, cd and bd of Texel$_{ij}$

3.3 Covered Primitives Parallel Detection Algorithm

3.3.1 Identification of Texel Edges and Depth Reconstruction

Line-sweep was introduced by Ville Timonen in Line-Sweep Ambient Obscurance [11]. CPPD algorithm guarantees texel edges intersection with triangles along the direction are captured. In Fig. 2a, we use small dot represent the center of texel and big dot represent four vertexes of texel edges. The Identification of texel edges is enforced based upon the connected texel center, where the midpoint of every two texels center is calculated. CPPD algorithm sweeps the geometry-based shadow map in a dense set of parallel lines and incrementally tracks the triangle profiles. Each parallel line is spaced one texel width S_0 and the lines are traversed $\sqrt{2}S_0$ width step at a time as shown in Fig. 2b, where S_0 is the reciprocal of the resolution.

```
 Algorithm1
Line-sweep shadow map
{
While (SampleTexelLine--)
{for each texelline
  float3 tc[i].x = (Texeli .x +Texeli-1.x )/2;
  float3 tc[i].y = (Texeli .y +Texeli-1.y)/2;}
if (SampleTexel[i][j])
then {ab=SampleTexelLine of {tc[i][j] , tc[i+1][j+1]};
      bd= SampleTexelLine of{ tc [i+1][j+1],tc [i+1][j]};
      dc= SampleTexelLine of { tc [i+1][j] , tc [i-1][j-1]};
      ca= SampleTexelLine of { tc [i-1][j-1] , tc [i][j]};
  Read 4 neighbors of SampleTexel[i][j] for intersection;
If ( edge intersect) then detect SampleTexel[i][j];
End.
  }
```

Equation (1) shows $d_{\tilde{p}}$ on triangle plane derivation for a view sample $P(p_x, p_y)$:

$$d_{\tilde{p}} = \tilde{z} + (p_x - c_x)\frac{d\tilde{z}}{dx} + (p_y - c_y)\frac{d\tilde{z}}{dy} \qquad (1)$$

where c_x and c_y are the vertices coordinates of triangles, $\tilde{z}$ is the depth of texel center of the exact triangle where a view sample p projected.

3.3.2 Per Pixel Shadow Silhouette Test

Tangent estimation of the shadow silhouette is very important for shadow boundary anti-aliasing. It requires consistent depth for shadow test. Unless the triangle fully covers the texel, we generate bias for each fragment with a estimating tight bias bound. Our method classifies the cover pattern as five predetermined pattern and, which simplify tangent estimation. All the predetermined patterns are computed by the half of the relative intersection edge as the tangent plan. In order to product the right self-shadow, we enforce the optimal depth bias to shift the fragments just above their potential occlude using an epsilon presented in Adaptive Depth Bias for Shadow maps [12]. In Fig. 3a, b shows the pattern of two adjacent edges of one texel are intersected by the corresponding triangle. (c) shows two non-adjacent edges situation; (d) and (e) shows three and four edges situation. We use the mid-value of each corresponding edges as a fast tangent estimation.

For the issue of false self-shadowing, we use standard OpenGL depth compression function and a tight bias bound method presented in adaptive depth bias for shadow maps [12]. The naive approach of depth derivatives maps the depth values of near and far clipping plane distance to [0, 1] by a depth compression function. According to the slope angle, the depth is derived by formula (2):

$$\theta_{x|y} = \arctan\left(\frac{d\tilde{z}}{d_{x|y}}\right) \qquad (2)$$

For some precision issues at grazing angles especially at angle near domain bounds of $[-\pi/2, +\pi/2]$, we use standard depth compression function and a

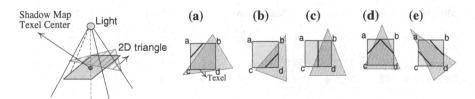

Fig. 3 On the *left* is 2D illustration of tangent estimation for a given fragment lying on the planar surface. On the *right* is five different predetermined pattern set of tangent estimation

constant K (we compared different K in our experiment), which slows down the growth of depth derivatives. According to the derivatives quantization strategy of [9], we use a non linear quantization of Eq. (3):

$$f(x) = K \times x^n \qquad (3)$$

4 Implementations

We implemented our method using CUDA and GLSL with the environment of Intel (R) Xeon(R) CPU E5620@ 2.40 GHz and NVIDIA GeForce GTX580. We compared the CPPD with the standard shadow mapping (SSM) and sub-pixel shadow mapping (SPSM) at 1024^2 resolution of shadow map as shown in Fig. 4. Our method got a better anti-aliasing effect with only a small computational overhead. Rendering time of three objects is shown in Table 1 with 1024^2 and 2048^2 of shadow map respectively.

Figure 5 shows thin objects rendering by SSM and CPPD at 512^2 and 1024^2 resolution of shadow map. Our method does better when render with lower resolution of shadow map compared with SSM. Figure 6a shows self-shadow rendered with different coefficient K. The precise of self-shadow anti-aliasing goes better and (b) shows the effect of CPPD at different resolution of shadow maps.

Fig. 4 Comparisons of SSM, SPSM and our CPPD algorithm at 1024^2 resolution of *shadow* map

Table 1 Comparisons of rendering time (ms). Timings include both shadow map generation and scene rendering time

Models	Polygons	Edges	Vertices	SSM		SPSM		CPPD	
				1024^2	2048^2	1024^2	2048^2	1024^2	2048^2
Object1	76,768	153,536	76,600	7.1	8.6	9.9	12.1	10.1	12.7
Object2	61,260	122,520	58,652	6.4	8.2	9.4	11.2	9.8	12.0
Object3	19,968	39,936	19,872	5.9	7.9	8.9	10.9	9.4	11.8

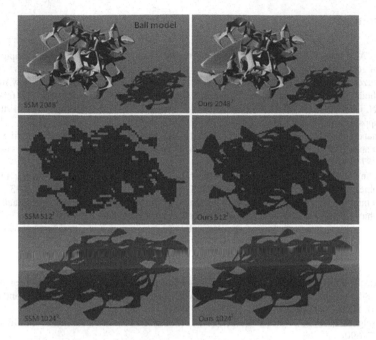

Fig. 5 Comparisons of SSM with our method at different resolution of *shadow* maps

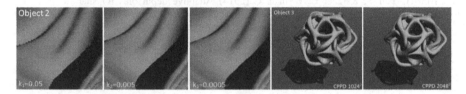

Fig. 6 Self-shadow with different coefficient *K* (*left*) and effect of CPPD rendering (*right*)

5 Conclusions

Covered primitives parallel detection algorithm is an improvement of reconstructable geometry shadow mapping. It achieves high quality hard shadows in real-time. Our method can be extended and used in variety rendering algorithm based on shadow maps.

Acknowledgments This work was financially supported by development project of Jilin province science and technology (20140204009GX) and major scientific and technological plan of Changchun City (14KG008).

References

1. Woo A, Poulin P, Fournier A (1990) A survey of shadow algorithms. IEEE Comput Graph Appl 10(6):13–32
2. Scherzer D, Wimmer M, Purgathofer W (2011) A survey of real-time hard shadow mapping methods. In: Computer graphics forum, vol 30(1). Blackwell Publishing Ltd, pp 169–186
3. Jia N, Luo D, Zhang Y (2013) Distorted shadow mapping. In: Proceedings of the 19th ACM symposium on virtual reality software and technology. Singapore, pp 209–214
4. Fernando R, Fernandez S, Bala K et al (2001) Adaptive shadow maps. In: Proceedings of the 28th annual conference on computer graphics and interactive techniques. ACM, Los Angeles, pp 387–390
5. Lefohn A, Sengupta S, Kniss J, Owens, JD (2005) Dynamic adaptive shadow maps on graphics hardware. In: ACM SIGGRAPH 2005 sketches. ACM, Los Angeles, p 13
6. Stamminger M, Drettakis G (2002) Perspective shadow maps. In: ACM transactions on graphics (TOG), vol 21(3). ACM, Redwood City, pp 557–562
7. Wimmer M, Scherzer D, Purgathofer W (2004) Light space perspective shadow maps. Rend Tech 15
8. Dai Q, Yang B, Feng J (2008) Reconstructable geometry shadow maps. In: Proceedings of the 2008 symposium on interactive 3D graphics and games. ACM, Redwood City, p 4
9. Lecocq P, Marvie JE, Sourimant G et al (2014) Sub-pixel shadow mapping. In: Proceedings of the 18th meeting of the ACM SIGGRAPH symposium on interactive 3D graphics and games. ACM, New York, pp 103–110
10. Hasselgren J, Akenine-Möller T, Ohlsson L (2005) Conservative rasterization. GPU Gems 2:677–690
11. Timonen V (2013) Line-sweep ambient obscurance. In: Computer graphics forum, vol 32(4). Blackwell Publishing Ltd, pp 97–105
12. Dou H, Yan Y, Kerzner E, Wyman, C (2014) Adaptive depth bias for shadow maps. In: Proceedings of the 18th meeting of the ACM SIGGRAPH symposium on interactive 3D graphics and games. ACM, San Francisco, California, pp 97–102

A Density-Aware Similarity Join Query Processing Algorithm on MapReduce

Miyoung Jang, Youngho Song and Jae-Woo Chang

Abstract Recently, the amount of data is rapidly increasing and thus MapReduce has attracted much interest as a new paradigm for such data-intensive applications. Similarity join is an essential operation for data analytics, including record linkage, near duplicate detection, document clustering. However, the performance of MapReduce is limited when applied on complex data analytical task involving joins of multiple datasets. Hence, workload-aware data partitioning techniques are required, which ensure the balance of computation of each machine. In this paper, we propose a similarity join algorithm using MapReduce that provides scalability and high performance by using grid-based data mapping technique for joining datasets. From the experiment analysis, we prove that our algorithm outperforms the existing algorithm under various data size and similarity thresholds.

Keywords Cloud computing · Bigdata analysis · Similarity join · MapReduce · Grid-based partitioning

1 Introduction

Recently, the amount of data is rapidly increasing with the popularity of the Social Networking Services (SNS) and the development of mobile technology. Enterprises and governments analyze big data and leverage them to support effective decision making and marketing. Analytical join queries become important due to their applicability for decision making applications [1–3]. For such data-intensive

M. Jang · Y. Song · J.-W. Chang (✉)
Department of Computer Engineering, Chonbuk National University, Jeonju 560-785,
Republic of Korea
e-mail: jwchang@jbnu.ac.kr

M. Jang
e-mail: brilliant@jbnu.ac.kr

Y. Song
e-mail: songyoungho@jbnu.ac.kr

© Springer Science+Business Media Singapore 2016   469
J.J. (Jong Hyuk) Park et al. (eds.), *Advanced Multimedia and Ubiquitous Engineering*, Lecture Notes in Electrical Engineering 393,
DOI 10.1007/978-981-10-1536-6_61

applications, MapReduce [4] has attracted much interest as a new paradigm of data processing framework. However, MapReduce does not consider the join operation of multiple datasets, which is an important operation in the advanced data analysis.

Among the analytical join queries, similarity joins have been considered as key operations in many data analysis tasks. The goal of similarity join is to find all pairs of records that have scores greater than a predefined similarity threshold (θ) under a given similarity function. The latest work is done by Okcan and Riedewald [5]. They proposed a ClusterJoin to compute similarity joins based on metric distance functions in MapReduce. The authors make two key contributions to prune away a large fraction of candidate pairs. First, they design a general filter that can prune away candidate pairs without actually computing their similarities. This general filter works for any metric distance functions. Second, they propose a dynamic load balancing scheme that is adaptive to data distribution and skewness, with good load balancing. It guarantees that the size of each partition does not exceed the desired threshold with high probability. However, the hash-based data partitioning of ClusterJoin may cause data skewness in some partitions. The random anchor selection method also generate large overlap regions among clusters where the data is densely populated.

In this paper, we propose a grid-based similarity join query processing algorithm. To determine a grid partitioning threshold, we compute distances among sampled data. For this, the data space is primarily divided into equal-sized regions for each dimension and the number of data is counted for the regions. From we perform data partitioning such that the difference between the number of data in a partition and one in another partition is the minimum. Moreover, to guarantee the correctness of similarity join result, we allow overlap between partitions. For this, each partition is expanded by similarity threshold value and stores the data located in the expanded area. So all the data within the similarity threshold for each partition can be assigned into the same reducer.

This paper is organized as follows. Section 2 summarizes the motivation and presents our similarity join query processing algorithm. Section 3 provides the comparison of our join algorithms with the existing join algorithms and finally Sect. 4 concludes the paper.

2   Grid-Based Similarity Join Algorithm

2.1   *Motivation*

To achieve the goal of balanced data partitioning, the processing of theta-joins using a MapReduce job is first studied in [6]. The proposed algorithm uses a matrix to map regions for the assignment of balanced reduce tasks. In [7], the authors consider processing a multi-way theta join in a single MapReduce job and identify when a join should be processed by a single or multiple MapReduce jobs. They propose a set of rules to decompose a multi-way theta-join query and propose a suitable cost model that estimates the minimum cost of each decomposed query plan and select the most efficient one by using one MapReduce job.

Recently, Sarma et al. [5] proposed the ClusterJoin to perform a similarity join of large-scale data sets on MapReduce. The ClusterJoin differentiate itself by proposing a general framework to compute metric distances, whereas most of the existing similarity join algorithms focus on string similarity measures. For this, they proposed a filter that can prune away candidate pairs by using a bisector-based data clustering. Furthermore, the authors proposed a dynamic load balancing scheme that is adaptive to data distribution and skewness, by using a hash function. However, because of the characteristics of the hash function, there is a high possibility that the data skewness is not fully solved when the density is high. Also, the bisector-based clustering algorithm using randomly sampled data may cause high data duplication among clusters.

To solve the problems in this work, we propose a grid based similarity join algorithm to evenly distribute data into clusters and to perform a join in a parallel way. To this end, we first design a dynamic grid index that evenly distribute data to MapReduce jobs by considering data distribution. Secondly, to guarantee the accuracy of the join result, we allow overlap among partitions based on the similarity threshold. This can reduce unnecessary data computation and communication costs by sending only similar data to the same reducer when perform a join.

2.2 Grid-Based Similarity Join Algorithm

The overall system architecture and the query processing flow of the proposed algorithm are illustrated in Fig. 1. Our similarity join algorithm contains a preprocessing step and a MapReduce job. First, in the preprocessing step, our algorithm selects samples to generate a histogram. For this, we divide data R and S into equal-sized regions for each dimension and the number of data for the regions is counted. Note that using data samples to partition the data space tends to distribute data evenly across data partitions, because the sampled data represent the underlying data distribution with more samples in dense regions and fewer in sparse regions. Then, we perform data partitioning such that the difference between the

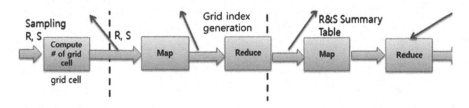

Fig. 1 Cloud computing system

Fig. 2 Determination of
partition axis

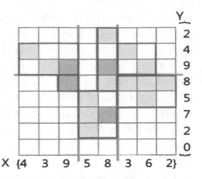

number of data in a partition and one in another partition is the minimum. The
algorithm computes the density of each cells and if there is a cell whose density
exceeds the threshold, we perform an extra partitioning on the cell with the same
method. Moreover, to guarantee the correctness of similarity join result, we allow
overlap between partitions. For this, each partition is expanded by the similarity
threshold value and stores the data located in the expanded area. By this means, all
the data within the similarity threshold can be assigned into the same reducer.
Figure 2 shows an example of data partitioning. For 2-dimensional data, the
deviation of data density among temporal partitions for x-axis is 5.1 whereas one
for y-axis has 9.1. Hence, the algorithm divides the data space from the x axis, and
then continues the division for y axis. When the data space is divided into partitions, we expand the partitions based on the similarity threshold θ to guarantee the
accuracy of query result. For the data located in the overlapped region between
partition A and B, it is stored as $\langle$cluster id_A, [ID, value]$\rangle$ and $\langle$cluster id_B, [ID,
value]$\rangle$. The maximum number of data duplication is 4 times, if the data is located
near to one of the partition vertexes.

Finally, in the 1st MapReduce job, mappers receive pairs of similar data partitions for join and generate intermediate. In the reduce phase, each similarity data
partitions are joined and the final result is sent to users. Figure 2 shows the pseudo
code of join phase. Map function computes a corresponding cluster ID for the
dataset (line 1). The result of map phase is sent to the reducer, in the form
of $\langle$cluster id, (PID, x, y)$\rangle$ (line 2). In the shuffle phase, the intermediate result is
sorted and grouped based on the cluster ID (line 3–4). Each data in a cluster is
compared their similarity in a reduce function (line 5–13) and the union of the
output of all reducers is the result of the similarity join (line 14–15) (Fig. 3).

Fig. 3 Pseudocode of the
proposed join algorithm

Algorithm 4. 2ⁿᵈ MapReduce
\<Map phase\>   Input: Query R. SummaryTableS. RealData S, N. NN_Cell_Info 　　　Table   Output: \<RCellNN id. SCell id. pid. x. y\>
1:　For each tuple in R and S
2:　　If data = R,
Insert R into Grid
Return \<Rcid. pid. x. y\>
3:　　Else if data = S,
Insert S into Grid
Retrieve NN Grid Cell ids in NN_Cell_Info
4:　　For i =0 to Number of NN Cell
Return \<RCell_id. SCell_id. pid. x. y\>
\<Reduce phase\>   Input: cell group CGi of S. grid index of R   Output: k−NN Join result
5:　Aggregate k−NN join results for all tuples Check the   　　number of POI(Pₐ) in its cell
6:　Retrieve k−NN POI from q and calculate distance Dk   　　between (k−NN r_q)
7:　Expand Check(r_q. Grid Cell info. k−NN)
8:　For each {NE. NW. SE. SW } directions
Count bit of the enclosing cells
Return the cell_direction with count
9:　If Dvi−q \<= Dk && SumCount != NULL
Expand Cell from the vertex direction
Retrieve all POIs in the expanded area and add them to   　　the list
10:　Else
Retrieve all POIs within the Dk and add them to the   　　result list
11:　Else if Pn\>k
Expand the query cell where Dist(vi) is NN &&   　　SumCount is large
12:　repeat 2 2−3 for k−NN result retrieval
13:　Retrieve all POIs in the expanded area and add them to the   　　list
14:　Aggregate k−NN results for all tuples and return
15:　Return result to the user

3　Experimental Analysis

In this section, we analyze the performance of our similarity join algorithm with
ClusterJoin proposed by Sarma et al. [5]. For this, we measure the query processing
time of two algorithms under different settings, such as data size, similarity
threshold and the number of data partitions. We evaluate the performance of
similarity join on the synthetic dataset with 100,000 tuples and a real dataset of
Northern East America (NE) containing 119,898 point of interests (POIs) by using
4 computing nodes. The Hadoop cluster consists of 1 master node and 4 data nodes.

The experimental setup of the nodes includes 2.9 GHz Quad-Core Intel Core CPU with 4 GB memory on Ubuntu 12.04.

Figure 4a shows the query processing time of the similarity join algorithms with varying data size. When the number of tuple is 10 M, the query processing time of our algorithm is about 2181 s whereas ClusterJoin requires about 2913 s. From the result, it is shown that our algorithm achieves up to 2 times better performance than ClusterJoin by distributing dataset with our sophisticated data clustering algorithm, which computes data partitions based on the data distribution. Figure 4b shows the query processing time of the algorithms with varying similarity threshold (θ). When the similarity threshold is 0.08, the query processing time of our algorithm is about 9953 s whereas ClusterJoin requires about 20,535 s. From the result, it is shown that our algorithm achieves up to 2.5 times better performance than ClusterJoin. As the similarity threshold increases, there is high possibility that the number of duplicated data among clusters is greatly increased. In case of ClusterJoin, this trend leads to a radical performance deterioration because the hash-based partitioning shows worse performance with densely populated data. On the other hand, our grid-based partitioning algorithm relatively samples data based on the data distribution and generate clusters by using the sampled dataset.

Figure 4c shows the query processing time of the similarity join algorithms with varying number of data partitions. The number of partition indicates the number of clusters used to assign data in the MapReduce. Hence, it is important to find an appropriate number of clusters to process a query in a distributed manner. Our algorithm shows the best performance when the number of cluster is set from 10 to 100, whereas ClusterJoin shows the best performance when the number of cluster is 10. This indicates that ClusterJoin suffers from the data skewness and high

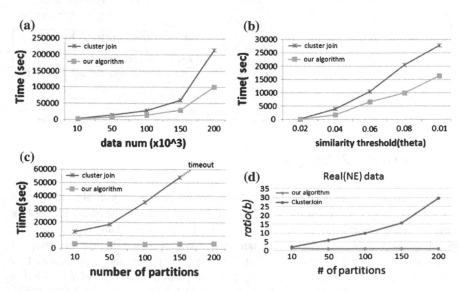

Fig. 4 Performance of the proposed similarity join algorithm. **a** Data size. **b** Similarity threshold. **c** Number of data partitions. **d** Efficiency of the partitioning methods in real dataset

duplication among clusters when the number of cluster increases. In Fig. 4d, we compare the distribution of data in partitions in order to show that our method provides more balanced data partitioning than that of the ClusterJoin. For this, we measure the ratio (b) by dividing the average number of data in partition by the maximum number of data in a partition. Having the value close to 1 means balanced distribution of data among partitions. Our algorithm shows smaller ratio than that of the ClusterJoin when the number of partition is varied from 10 to 200.

4 Conclusion

In this paper, we proposed a grid-based similarity join algorithm to evenly distribute data into clusters and to perform a join in a parallel way. To this end, we first design a dynamic grid index that evenly distribute data to MapReduce jobs by considering data distribution. Secondly, to guarantee the accuracy of the join result, we allow overlap among partitions based on the similarity threshold. This can make us to reduce unnecessary data computation and communication costs by sending only similar data to the same reducer when perform a join.

Acknowledgments This work was supported by the Human Resource Training Program for Regional Innovation and Creativity through the Ministry of Education and National Research Foundation of Korea (NRF-2014H1C1A1065816) and also supported by Institute for Information & communications Technology Promotion(IITP) grant funded by the Korea government(MSIP) (No. R0113-15-0005, Development of an Unified Data Engineering Technology for Large-scale Transaction Processing and Real-time Complex Analytics).

References

1. Lappas T, Gunopulos D (2010) Efficient confident search in large review corpora. In: Machine learning and knowledge discovery in databases. Springer, pp 195–210
2. Levandoski JJ, Mokbel MF, Khalefa ME (2010) Preference query evaluation over expensive attributes. In: Proceedings of the 19th ACM international conference on information and knowledge management. ACM, pp 319–328
3. Lee J, Hwang SW, Nie Z, Wen JR (2010) Navigation system for product search. In: Proceedings of the 26th international conference on IEEE. IEEE, pp 1113–1116
4. Dean J, Ghemawat S (2008) MapReduce: simplified data processing on large clusters. Commun ACM 51(1):107–113
5. Okcan A, Riedewald M (2011) Processing theta-joins using MapReduce. In: Proceedings of the 2011 ACM SIGMOD international conference on management of data. ACM, pp 949–960
6. Zhang X, Chen L, Wang M (2012) Efficient multiway theta-join processing using MapReduce. Proc VLDB Endow (PVLDB) 5(11):1184–1195
7. Das Sarma A, He Y, Chaudhuri S (2014) ClusterJoin: a similarity joins framework using map-reduce. Proc VLDB Endow 7(12):1059–1070

Futures/Option Electric Power Pricing in Smart Grid Using Game Theory and Hybrid AMI Based on Weather Clearness

Jun-Ho Huh and Kyungryong Seo

Abstract Recently, due to the activation of internet networks and development of wireless systems that can establish a network independently, the technical fields where the game theory plays an important role are increasing continuously, solving the decision-making problems in the computer networks. Meanwhile, the development speed of Smart Grids, Micro Grids and IoT-related technologies is also increasing backed by the major IT companies to provide more efficient power management and control services. The game theory used in these technologies allow consumers to check their power usage patterns for better consumption behavior. The power companies use the game-theoretic approaches in their applications and one such example is the 'Demand Response' technology for the Smart Grids, which informs hourly or periodic dynamic prices to the power users. Future energy shortage is a global problem and an inevitable consequence for the Republic of Korea as well. Without the ground-breaking power sources and technologies being available, it is expected that the power companies will offer more segmented power prices depending on the time zones and seasons to save power or to reduce the energy consumption rate. Thus, in this paper, we present a game theory-based pricing approach in a Smart Grid and a hybrid AMI which considers the weather conditions. With this AMI, the future, spot and option prices will be determined based on the decision-making process and by applying the process to the Smart Meter System, an efficient monitoring and management will become possible.

Keywords Energy harvesting · Hybrid AMI · Smart grid · ESS · PLC · Future price of electric power · Option price of electric power · Weather clearness

J.-H. Huh
SUNCOM Co., Busan, Republic of Korea
e-mail: 72networks@pukyong.ac.kr

K. Seo (✉)
Department of Computer Engineering, Pukyong National University,
Busan, Republic of Korea
e-mail: krseo@pknu.ac.kr

© Springer Science+Business Media Singapore 2016   477
J.J. (Jong Hyuk) Park et al. (eds.), *Advanced Multimedia and Ubiquitous Engineering*, Lecture Notes in Electrical Engineering 393,
DOI 10.1007/978-981-10-1536-6_62

1 Introduction

The game theory was originally developed by Von Neuman in 1944 and adopted in various types of decision-making processes in a competitive environment where one's decision affects another's decision-making process. Since then, a variety of mathematical models for the game theory-based decision making processes have been designed and grafted onto political, economic, social and engineering fields. The effectiveness of the game theory was widely recognized by the academia and business world by the middle of 1990s when three game theorists received the Nobel Prize in 1994 [1]. Five others received the same prize afterwards, including John M. Smith who adapted the theory to biology, by which he won the Crafoord Prize.

This theory has been applied to diverse industries and businesses for the decision-making processes and proven its effectiveness in solving the problems in a computer network. Within in the internet network, there are many decisions to be made by the relevant applications to produce deductive conclusions such that devising a logical and effective game theory suitable for the wireless internet system has become an essential task in establishing an efficient Smart Grid, Micro Grid, or IoT system.

The application fields for the game theory continued to expand and during the last ten years, the theory has been actively applied to the engineering field as the problems in this fields became more and more complex and convergent. Some examples can be found in the models that deal with routing and traffic congestion control problems in the internet networks [1–9]. Using the game theory in a wireless environment would mean suitably allocating the limited resources (i.e., wireless spectrums or power resources) in a distributed environment [1] and devising an efficient routing method, both of which are critical in constructing an ideal IoT system for the smart homes.

Recently, the government of the Republic of Korea has made an announcement that they are preparing a medium and long-term promotional plan for the trading market that deals with demand resources, especially focusing on the conserved surplus electric powers. According to the plan, it seems that the Smart Grid, which manages a small-scale power control/distribution system that deals with a variety of power resources produced by using new and renewable energies, is the very core of their scheme. Following the announcement, the major companies in the Republic of Korea such as Samsung Electronics, LG Electronics, LG U-plus, SK Telecom, Korea Telecom and Korea Electric Power Corp (KEPCO) have expended their efforts to develop the IoT-based smart homes concentrating on the issues related to 'Smart Power Management' and 'Power Saving' goals. Another main area of their interest was how to design an effective and efficient system that can be flexible in responding to the 'Demand Response'. The 'Demand Response' refers to the unusual power consumption pattern of the user in response to power company's certain instructions or compensations. That is, the power companies guides consumers to change their power consumption behaviors by offering them with dynamic power prices depending on the time slots or seasons for the better. In most cases, such efforts resulted in power saving behavior of the user.

At this point, the energy-related issues are becoming increasingly important in worldwide commodity markets and a new paradigm that seeks to integrate wireless communication technology with the energy technology is being discussed intensively among the engineers and researchers. The Energy Harvesting' technology is based on the concept of harnessing various ambient energies in the earth environment such as solar radiation, geothermal heat and wind. Such often neglected energies are used to produce eco-friendly electric power. Energy harvesting also includes a technology that delivers electric power to other locations through the wireless energy transmission system where Smart Grids and Micro Grids play a vital role in the process. Once the 5th generation communication networks are realized and IoT becomes a common technology, there will be many more terminal devices which require continuous supply of power such that the studies concerning the wireless energy harvesting technologies and independent power systems carry enormous significance for the engineers and researchers working in the communication field.

2 Transactions in Deregulated Environment

The generation cost is represented as $C(i) = a(i) + b(i)P(i) + c(i)P(i)^2$ with a linear incremental cost function. Correspondingly, price curves for each generator in participating utilities are defined by a straight line with slope m(i) as in (Fig. 1). The linear price curve introduces non-linearities in the problem, however, it is a more realistic representation of price than that of a fixed price for power.

Fig. 1 Price offer in generator i

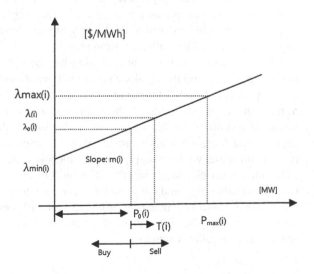

In (Fig. 1), participants increase the generation beyond $P_0(i)$ if the market price is greater than $\lambda_0(i)$ (i.e. the marginal cost of electricity at the gene $P_0(i)$ ration level $P_0(i)$. $T(i)$ the net interchanged power; if $T(i)$ is positive (negative), the participant is selling power to (buying power from) the Pool, $-P_0(i) \leq T(i) \leq P_{max}(i) - P_0(i)$.

Each generator will produce $P(i) = P_0(i) + T(i)$ to supply loads. In this model, Pool participants interact by means of price signals, while the cost coefficients are shared only on a voluntary basis. Once the transactions are set, transmission charges are computed as a percentage of revenues [3].

3 Hybrid AMI (Advanced Metering Infrastructure)

As mentioned earlier, Republic of Korea will face the power shortage problem in the future as many other nations so that it will be inevitable and necessary for them to segmentalize the price of electricity to let the users be conscious of their power usage patterns and to make the best use of conserved powers. For such purposes, we have designed a 'Hybrid AMI' which can be used to optimize Future/Option prices and consumption behaviors of the users by adopting the game theory. In the article, the section describing the spot price is the same as the one in the preceding research [3] so that it will not be repeated.

3.1 Design of Hybrid AMI Using the Game Theory and Power Usage Patterns

The power usage (consumption) patterns of a certain person were studied over a 24-h period and a week [4] and represented in (Fig. 2). At the same time, both the peak and off season prices are calculated. The target power (i.e., conserved or surplus power) will be stored in the Energy Storage System (ESS) temporarily until any sales or self-consumption is decided.

The game theory is useful in analyzing the strategic situations which the traditional supply-demand theory alone cannot deliver an adequate solution. By creating a mathematical model(s) for the analysis, an optimal Production-Distribution condition can be deduced even if there are just a few methodological options and available resources are insufficient for a decision-making process. For instance, suppose that there are a large number of power lines and only three lines are to be used. In this case, with the supply-demand theory, we can infer that there will not be much effects on the power supply situation. On the other hand, if there are only twenty available lines and the same three lines are to be used for the operation, one has to worry about the impacts or problems that will present. Then, the game theory will assesses the situation and produce an adequate solution by determining the optimal consumption behavior.

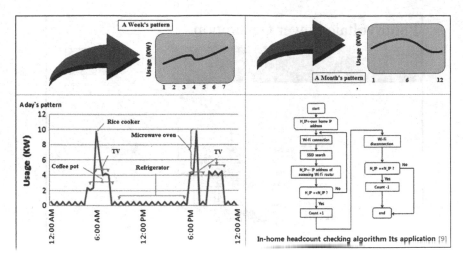

Fig. 2 User's power usage patterns studied in a day and during a week

3.2 Test Bed Environment of Hybrid AMI Based on the Weather Clearness

(Figure 3) describes the current Smart Grid system in Jeju island, Republic of Korea and a test bad experiment for the system was carried out with one PLC (Power Line Communication) server, four PLC Clients (each Client placed in four rooms separately) and one ESS. Electrical power will be traded depending on the spot prices here. But in our approach proposed in this paper adopts the game theory to present economic feasibility and further, we plan to apply daily and weekly usage patterns as well as futures and option prices in the test bed environment to see how the game theory makes judgments and provide solutions. The clearness indexes will also be reflected on the Hybrid AMI to let the photovoltaic power generation system to decide whether to store the power in the ESS on a clear day (high clearness) or buy the power from a certain seller to use it after storing it in a battery when the weather is non-clear (cloudy). Another future task is to upgrade or revise involved parameters while modeling the clearness with the server.

The futures trading can be defined as a sort of market transaction in the Commodity Exchange where a seller and a buyer make a sales contract prior to actual product delivery which could extend from 3 months to a year. The price, purchase amount and delivery term will be set at the time of the contract. The seller (buyer) can also resell (repurchase) his/her product to (from) other party any time before the delivery is made. This transaction system may help in avoiding the risks resulting from future price fluctuations but it can also cause grave monetary damages if either of them makes a wrong decision. A futures option contract, or an option on a futures contract, gives the holder the right to enter into a specified futures contract. If the option is exercised, the initial holder of the option would

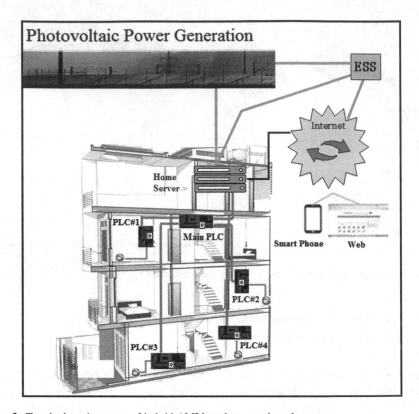

Fig. 3 Test bed environment of hybrid AMI based on weather clearness

enter into the long side of the contract and would buy the underlying asset at the futures price. A short option on a futures contract lets an investor enter into a futures contract as the short who would be required to sell the underlying asset on the future date at the specified price. The futures and option prices of conserved or surplus electricity may be important indexes as the crude oil prices in the Commodity Exchange but they can be influenced by the government's policy change.

4 Conclusion and Future Work

In our study, we described the game theory and its application possibility for the Smart grids, Micro grids and IoT systems to bring out the optimal power consumption patterns for the consumers. At the same time, we have briefly explained the importance of demand response technology for better allocation of resources and introduced the energy harvesting technology as another meaningful power generation and supply option. The Hybrid AMI introduced here considers various levels of weather clearness to use them as the indexes for the decision-making process in the Commodity Exchange where futures, option, and spot prices are offered and thereby conserved electricity is traded. More simulations should be carried out with improved parameters in the future so that we may be able to develop a better and more sophisticated platform technology for the Smart Metering technology that plays an important part in Smart Grid or Micro Grid-based smart homes.

Acknowledgments The first draft of this article was presented in International Symposium on Advanced Engineering 2015 (Post Session), 2015.10.22-24, with KSES 2015 Autumn Annual Conference (Post Session) 2015.10.22-23, Pukyong National University at Yongdang, Republic of Korea. I am grateful to 3 anonymous commentators who have contributed to the enhancement of the article's completeness with their valuable suggestions at the Symposium with Conference.

References

1. Mo JH et al (2009) Game theory and network meeting. J Korean Inst Commun Sci 26(7):17–23 (In Korean)
2. Kelly F (1997) Charging and rate control for elastic traffic. European Trans Telecommun 8 (1):33–37
3. Ferrero RW, Shahidehpour SM, Ramesh VC (1997) Transaction analysis in deregulated power systems using game theory. IEEE Trans Power Syst 12(3):1340–1347
4. Yang YH (2013) Distributed message verification for smart grid. M.S. thesis, Korea University, Republic of Korea, pp 1–40 (In Korean)
5. Huh JH, Seo K (2015) Hybrid AMI design for smart grid using the game theory model. Adv Sci Technol Lett 108:86–92 (SERSC ASTL, Mechanical Engineering)
6. Huh JH, Seo K (2015) Hybrid advanced metering infrastructure design for micro grid using the game theory model. Int J Softw Eng Appl 9(9):257–268 (SERSC)
7. Huh JH, Seo K (2015) RUDP design and implementation using OPNET simulation. Computer science and its applications. Lecture notes in electrical engineering, vol 330. Springer Verlag Berlin Heidelberg, pp 913–919
8. Huh JH, Lee D, Seo K (2015) Implementation of graphic based network intrusion detection system for server operation. Int J Secur Appl 9(2):37–48 (SERSC)
9. Huh JH, Lee DG, Seo K (2015) Design and implementation of the basic technology for realtime smart metering system using power line communication for smart grid. Advances in computer science and ubiquitous computing. Lecture notes in electrical engineering, vol 373. Springer Singapore, pp 663–669

Design for Network Attack Forensic System Based on HTTP Evasive Behavior

Wenhao Liu, Haiqing Pan, Gang Xiong, Zigang Cao and Zhen Li

Abstract The network traffic generated by humans and various devices is one of the most important data sources in network forensics. The main challenge in investigating and collecting evidence in network traffic is handling the huge amounts of data streams caused by the rapid growth of network bandwidth and applications, as well as preserving the useful information for further analysis. HTTP, as the most popular protocol on the Internet, is usually exploited to carry malware and evasive attacks besides the normal services. In this paper, we study how malware and network attacks in real-world exploit HTTP to hide their malicious activities and present an Evasive Network Attack Forensic System (ENAFS), which is able to effectively discover evasive network attacks on HTTP and integrally draw attack the samples and their metadata for further analysis. We believe that our work will benefit the research in the network forensics field in the future.

Keywords Network forensics · HTTP · Evasive attack · Abnormal behavior

1 Introduction

Nowadays, HTTP holds a quite large portion of the network traffic volume. Many attackers and malware exploit HTTP to hide their malicious activities due to its popularity and flexibility [1]. A typical kind of behavior is that one Content-Type is declared in the HTTP header while in fact the actual data is of another different type in order to evade security inspections. Such kind of behavior has been observed in some famous malware, such as Zeus, Torpig, Bredolab [2]. Some Advanced Persistent Threat (APT) attacks, like APT30 [3] and APT Operation Poisoned Helmand [4], also used this trick to bypass detection. Therefore, designing a forensic system to record and analyze the malware and APT attacks behind the

W. Liu · H. Pan · G. Xiong · Z. Cao · Z. Li (✉)
Institute of Information Engineering, Chinese Academy of Sciences, Beijing, China
e-mail: lizhen@iie.ac.cn

© Springer Science+Business Media Singapore 2016
J.J. (Jong Hyuk) Park et al. (eds.), *Advanced Multimedia and Ubiquitous Engineering*, Lecture Notes in Electrical Engineering 393,
DOI 10.1007/978-981-10-1536-6_63

evasive behaviors are very valuable for discovering potential network threat and enhancing the network security.

However, the Content-Type mismatches in HTTP take 35 % of the total HTTP volume [5], and most of them are caused by innocent configuration mistakes. Therefore, it is not a sensible way to simply detect the mismatch by a general rule since there must be a lot of false positives. Meanwhile, the traditional rule-based intrusion detection systems (IDS), e.g. Snort, can only detect limited known Content-Type mismatch attacks based on their rules with few clew in logs which is helpless to investigate and trace these attacks.

To mitigate the problem, we design Evasive Network Attack Forensic System (ENAFS) to record the HTTP Content-Type mismatch data and automatically analyze the latent evasion behaviors. We've deployed the proposed system on a real-world network. The system processed 1.2 billion HTTP requests per day, found 166 million mismatch data and recorded thousands of latent evasive attack samples.

The main contributions of this paper are as follows:

- A novel network attack traffic forensic system is proposed and implemented to record traffic samples and detect evasive network attacks.
- The proposed system is deployed in the real-world network. From 1607 mismatch types recorded by the system, several specific mismatch types that network attacks tend to use to hide their activities have been found.
- Some previously-unseen malware have been detected in the real-world network traffic. These malware activities and samples have been preserved by the system for further analysis.

2 Related Work

Mukkamala and Sung [6] use two artificial intelligence techniques, (Artificial Neural Networks (ANNs) and Support Vector Machines (SVMs), to identify significant features for offline network intrusion analysis, and test them with 1999 DARPA intrusion data. However, this technique is not suitable for real-time network traffic detection. Kaushik and Joshi [7] propose a network forensic system for ICMP attacks and just focus on some specific attacks on ICMP protocol. This system can only detect known attacks since it is based on rules. Cohen [8] proposes a network forensic framework to reassemble streams, parse HTTP protocol and list the traffic content visually. Pilli and Joshi introduce and compare 11 Network Forensic Analysis tools [9], and mention two tools, Infinistream and OmniPeek, which have real-time analysis capabilities. Our work is also based on the real-time traffic analysis. But we further research on the mismatch scenarios and apply it in the proposed ENAFS to detect and trace the latent evasion attacks.

3 Our Approach

In this section, the ENAFS is described in detail, including suspicious HTTP traffic collection, sample detection, and attack tracing. The framework of ENAFS is shown in Fig. 1 and explained below.

3.1 Traffic Collection

ENAFS aims at discovering the latent evasive attack using a fake HTTP content-type header. Therefore, we first need to find out the real HTTP payload type and compare it with the HTTP content-type header.

To achieve this goal, we extract HTTP packets based on PF_RING and use *libmagic* (file type determination library in GNU/Linux) to identify the HTTP payload MIME type and perform a string comparison between libmagic's results and content-type header.

In most of the cases, the comparison results are correct, but sometimes they are not accurate when meeting the following situations.

- Network transmission errors may cause libmagic fail to detect the HTTP payload header and make it return a general type application/octet-stream.
- Libmagic returns the same MIME type with the Content-Type header, but in different description. With Microsoft Application, for example, libmagic

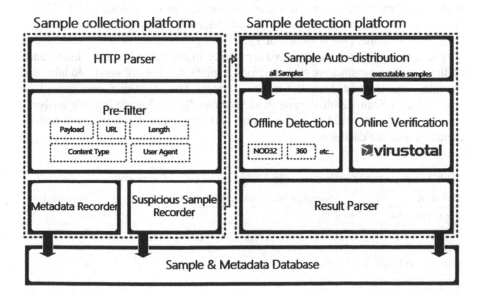

Fig. 1 Network attack forensic system framework

describe it as the type "application/x-dosexec", while Content-Type header describe it as "application/x-msdownload".

- In the Text, Media, and Image classes, libmagic and the Content-Type header agreed on the general category of the type (e.g., image) but disagree on the actual file format (JPEG vs. PNG).
- HTTP payload with *gzip* compression may cause the result inaccurate.

In order to reduce false positive in comparison, we decompress the payload zipped with *gzip* protocol and create a hash map to handle the inaccurate comparison results to make sure that the results are performing as expected.

After comparison, ENAFS will rerecord the metadata of content mismatched HTTP sessions, including source and destination IP address and port, URI, User-Agent and Server field in the HTTP header. In addition, the complete payload sample will also be reassembled and stored with a hash value for further detection.

3.2   Sample Detection and Attack Tracing

Two methods are implemented to detect the suspicious malicious samples. One is offline scanning and the other is online verification.

For offline scanning, five anti-virus software such as 360 Antivirus, Avira, ClamAV, ESET NOD32, and Kaspersky are used. 360 Antivirus is the most famous Antivirus in China, so we choose it to represent free Antivirus software in China. ClamAV is the most famous open source Antivirus software, and we choose it to be representative of open source Antivirus software. We also pick up three widely used and with well performance Antivirus, Avira Antivirus, ESET NOD32 Antivirus, and Kaspersky Antivirus to our detection system. The information of these five Antivirus [10] is shown in Table 1.

These five Antivirus are deployed separately in separate virtual machines, each of them receives suspicious samples from Sample Auto-distribution Module, and executes scanning automatically by the scripts. After scanning, results will be transferred to Scan Result Parsing module. Scan Result Parsing module analyzes scan result files received from Antivirus, and then store the scan result and its metadata into the database.

Table 1 Information of antivirus used by ENAFS sample detection platform

Antivirus	Signature-based scanning	Heuristic scanning	Open source
Avira antivirus	Yes	Yes	No
360 antivirus	Yes	Yes	No
ClamAV	No	Yes	Yes
ESET NOD32 antivirus	Yes	Yes	No
Kaspersky antivirus	Yes	Yes	No

For online verification, we choose VirusTotal, a well-known online scan service which aggregates 55 antivirus products and 61 online scan engines [11] to check for viruses. The offline detection has a better performance while the online verification has a higher recall rate but is relatively slow. Hence, the offline detection is used to scan all the samples that system recorded but only highly suspicious samples will be uploaded for online verification. Currently the system only uploads all the executable samples for online verification.

After sample detection, analysts can take advantage of the comprehensive and well-organized information in database to trace back the attacks. For example, the *URI* and *IP* address can be used to locate the victim and C&C server, *User-agent* field can tell us victim's device (e.g. Mobile or PC) and OS type. *Sample hash* can be used to reveal the relationship of the same attack from different sources.

4 Result Analysis

An offline data set from third part is used to verify our detecting system. The VRT Lab [2] has provided some malicious malware traffic contains evasive attack activities which are suitable for use as benchmark of ENAFS. As is presented in Table 2, our system holds a highly reliable result for detecting malicious malware in third-party.

ENAFS was also used in our network board to detect malicious attack activities. We deployed ENAFS on the boarding entry of CERNET network for 7 days, which serves China's research institution and universities. As a result, ENAFS processed over 8.4 billion HTTP sessions and found out more than 110 million mismatch instances, covering 1607 different kinds of type mismatches. All these mismatch HTTP metadata and payload samples were stored in the attack tracking database. After scanning and analyzing these samples, two types of evasive attacks had been found. One is that malware use image headers or text to hide its executable attribute. The other is that malicious scripts, such as webshell, claims as image to cheat the server-side format verification.

Finally, we tried to trace back the origin of a typical evasive attack recorded by the system. This attack sample was captured on a lottery website. It is an executable

Table 2 ENAFS offline data set detection results

Malware	Attack type	Content-type, Payload-type	Unique samples	Detection rate
Zeus	botnet	application/x-dosexec, image/jpg	40	100 %
Bredolab	botnet	application/x-dosexec, text/php	10	100 %
Tro-downloader	evasive Trojan downloader	application/x-dosexec, image/x-icon	120	100 %

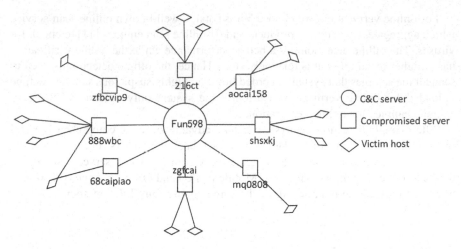

Fig. 2 Evasive network attack tracing graph

file named as *favicon.ico*, which is a common name for a web server, to disguise its real malicious purpose. When victims visit the lottery website, it will trigger drive-by downloads and infect the host. The system also captured other similar instances for *favicon.ico*. There are 15 samples in 8 websites trying to evade detection in such way, and all of them come from illegal lottery sites. Among them, two samples are previously-unseen malware which passed the antivirus scanning. Further analysis showed that all of these malware have relation with the domain *fun598.com*. Figure 2 shows the source tracing graph of the attack generated by ENAFS records.

5 Conclusion and Future Work

In the paper, we developed ENAFS to discover evasive network attacks on HTTP, which is able to integrally preserve attack samples and their metadata from the live traffic. We use several techniques to reduce the false positive system generated. With the help of sample auto-detection platform integrated in ENAFS, analysts can quickly discover the evasive network attack behind the traffic, analyze its sample and trace back its source.

The proposed ENAFS was evaluated on the ISP network for 7 days, during which the system handled 8.4 billion HTTP sessions, downloaded and scanned 110 million samples. From the detection results, we found a typical attack and revealed its malicious activity through our system.

Currently we are analyzing samples that the system has collected, expecting to find more HTTP Evasive behavior and add these features into our system. In the future, we would like to extend our system to support more protocol.

Acknowledgments This work is supported by the National Science and Technology Support Program (No. 2012BAH46B02), Xinjiang Uygur Autonomous Region Science and Technology Project (No. 201230123) and the Strategic Priority Research Program of the Chinese Academy of Sciences (No. XDA06030200).

References

1. Invernizzi L, Miskovic S, Torres R, Saha S, Lee SJ, Kruegel C, Vigna G (2014) Nazca: detecting malware distribution in large-scale networks. In: Proceedings of the ISOC network and distributed system security symposium
2. VRT Labs (2014) Content-type mismatch. https://labs.snort.org/papers/contentmi-smatch.html
3. FireEye (2015) APT30 and the mechanics of a long-running cyber espionage operation. https://www2.fireeye.com/rs/fireye/images/rpt-apt30.pdf
4. Operation Poisoned Helmand (2014) https://www.threatconnect.com/operation-poisoned-helmand/
5. Schneider F, Ager B, Maier G, Feldmann A, Uhlig S (2012) Pitfalls in HTTP traffic measurements and analysis. In: Passive and active measurement. Springer, Berlin, pp 242–251
6. Mukkamala S, Sung AH (2003) Identifying significant features for network forensic analysis using artificial intelligence techniques. Int J Digital Evid IJDE 3
7. Kaushik AK, Joshi RC (2010) Network forensic system for ICMP attacks. Int J Comput Appl 2(3):14–21
8. Cohen M (2008) PyFlag—an advanced network forensic framework. Digital Inv 5:112–120
9. Pilli ES, Joshi RC, Niyogi R (2010) Network forensic frameworks: survey and research challenges. Digital Inv 7(1/2):14–27
10. Comparison of antivirus software (2016) https://en.wikipedia.org/wiki/Comparison_of_antivirus_software
11. VirusTotal (2015) https://en.wikipedia.org/wiki/Virus-Total

A Fine-Grained Large-Scale NAT Detection Method

Bin Yan, Liang Huang, Gaopeng Gou, Yuanbo Guo and Yibao Bao

Abstract With the explosive growth of mobile terminal access to the Network and the shortage of IPv4, the Network Address Translation (NAT) technology has become more and more widely used. The technology not only provides users with convenient access to the Internet, but also brings trouble to network operations and regulatory authorities. This system NAT detection using NetFlow data, is often used for monitoring and forensics analysis in large networks. In the paper, in order to detect NAT devices, an Out-in Activity Degree method based on network behavior is proposed. Our approach works completely passively and is based on NetFlow data only. Our approach gets accuracy of 91.2 % in real large-scale network for a long time.

Keywords Network address translation · Network security · Netflow · Out-in activity degree

1 Introduction

Network Address Translation (NAT) technology is a double-edged sword. On the one hand, NAT technology has brought great convenience and benefits for users. On the other hand, it brought potential security issues for network management. For example, unauthorized users can illegally access the network through NAT.

B. Yan · Y. Guo · Y. Bao
State Key Laboratory of Mathematical Engineering and Advanced Computing,
Zhengzhou, People's Republic of China

G. Gou (✉)
Institute of Information Engineering, Chinese Academy of Sciences, Beijing,
People's Republic of China
e-mail: gougaopeng@iie.ac.cn

L. Huang
National Computer Network Emergency Response Technical Team/Coordination Center
of China, Beijing, People's Republic of China

© Springer Science+Business Media Singapore 2016   493
J.J. (Jong Hyuk) Park et al. (eds.), *Advanced Multimedia and Ubiquitous
Engineering*, Lecture Notes in Electrical Engineering 393,
DOI 10.1007/978-981-10-1536-6_64

Furthermore, if NAT devices are used by hackers to attack other computers, it will be more difficult to trace them than without NAT technology, which results in great threats to network security.

NetFlow traffic, which has no payload and does not carry any high-layer information, is widely used in monitor and forensics analysis in large scale networks. The information contained in standard NetFlow traffic is able to meet the needs of Out-in Activity Degree method Out-in. This method can accurately detect the NAT devices, and effectively figure out the scale of the devices. In order to determine the number of NATed hosts, we retain three fields in the flow records: User-Agent field, Cookie ID field and thunder ID field.

The contribution of our work consists of the following:

(i)   We propose a method based on the Out-in Activity Degree which could recognize different size NAT;
(ii) We improve the NAT detection rate of traditional DPI method by combining Out-in Activity Degree;
(iii) We take the measurement of different NAT in the real network for 20 days, and the experimental results are accurate and in strong practicability.

2   Related Work

Existing NAT traffic identification methods are generally based on passive detection. This method judge source IP address by detecting network traffic. The NAT passive detection methods are divided into two categories based on features in TCP/IP (Transmission Control Protocol/Internet Protocol) protocol and application layer information. Besides, in recent years, with the developments in machine learning (ML) field, many ML algorithms are imported to the NAT network traffic detection problem.

The method based on features in TCP/IP protocol was widely adopted which through analyze the difference of equipment to identify NAT. Bellovin et al. [1] presents a method relying on analysis packet header of IP Identification(ID) fields in SIGCOMM 2002. Straka et al. [2] who used the difference of Time-To-Live (TTL) value under the same conditions of network packets to detect NAT. Kohno et al. [3] present a method to detect NAT based on passively fingerprinting devices by detecting clock skews in physical devices.

Moreover, Rui et al. [4, 5] proposed approaches to NAT detection and the size of estimating the internal network using Support Vector Machine (SVM) and directed acyclic graph SVM. In Krmicek et al. [6], a NetFlow based system for NAT detection is presented. In contrast to all previously mentioned methods, our approach is simple and easily deployed for it is based on NetFlow data only.

In the next section, we describe three Deep Packet Inspection (DPI) based on NAT detecting methods, and propose NAT detection techniques based on Out-in

Activity Degree method. Experimental results show 91.2 % of NAT devices can be detected.

3   NAT Detection Methods

This section describes five methods for NAT detection by using NetFlow data. Three of them (User-Agent, Cookie ID and Thunder ID method) were previously proposed and they have been modified to adopt NetFlow data as input. Furthermore, we present other two methods for NAT detection based on NetFlow data.

3.1   Methods Based on DPI

Various feature information of application layer is used to detect the IP data packet based on based on detection method of application layer, so that the recognition of NAT can be identified and the scale are determined. The experiment adopts the User-Agent identification, Cookie ID identification and thunder ID identification to determine NATed hosts.

3.2   Methods Based on Out-in Degree Activity

In the flow data, a host is identified by IP address. Host connection reflects the behavior between the hosts which establish a network connection that is one of the most important properties. In this section, we proposed Out-in Activity Degree detection method based on network behavior. And this method includes out-in degree and specific characteristics. To better understand the behavior of the host, we given the following definitions:

Definition 1 the out degree is the number of connections of source IP on the right side.

Definition 2 the in degree is the number of connections to destination IP on the left side.

Definition 3 activity refers active condition of the host in unit time, in the paper it includes active condition per day and total activity.

Generally speaking, the smaller the time interval, the better the description of IP active cases; and the larger the time interval, the smaller the value and significance of its existence. In practice, the time interval is not the smaller the better, because small time interval means more complex calculations and rules.

In experiments, we found that the most appropriate time interval is 30 min. Traffic processing platform judges the direction of a net flow, and then marks out-in degree in the source and destination IP, we counted all IP out-in degree and identify all IP activity every 30 min.

3.2.1 Out-in Degree

According to the analysis method of connection between the host behavior, we do not need to parse network packets. Only extracting the relationship between the host connection established, can it calculate the number of the host, which was extracted host properties. We capture different sizes of NAT network traffic in a different location.

The experiment includes three types of NAT: (1) Large NAT, (2) Medium NAT, (3) Small NAT. Each type of experiment selected 10 groups, then computed the average number. We first measured large-scale NAT, it is generally accepted that, the out-in degree increase when the number of hosts after NAT is pretty large. We combine the method based on DPI, to accurately measure the number of hosts after NAT. The results are shown in Fig. 1, ordinate represents the number of connections.

We have observed large-scale NAT for 20 days, the average out-in degree showed in Fig. 1. The abscissa is the time interval, the ordinate is out-in degree. We found that out-degree and in-degree have a similar track. There may be a mathematical relationship between them. Next, we measure medium NAT, illustrated in Fig. 2.

We found that the out-degree and the in-degree have a similar trend in Fig. 2, but the value of out-in degree is smaller than large NAT. It also confirms our previous assumptions about the relationship between number of the out-in degree and the scale of NAT. Next, we measured small NAT, shown in Fig. 3.

We found that out-in degree goes small in **Fig.** 3 although out-degree and in-degree have a similar trend. It is not as good as the large or medium NAT. Next,

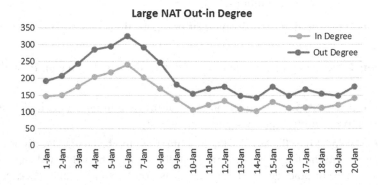

Fig. 1 Large NAT out-in degree

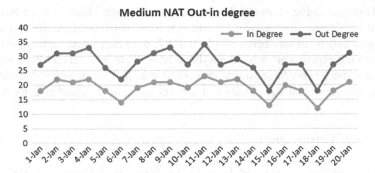

Fig. 2 Medium NAT out-in degree

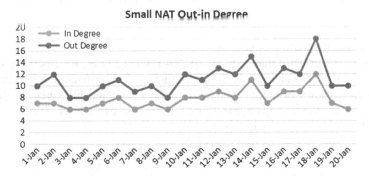

Fig. 3 Small NAT out-in degree

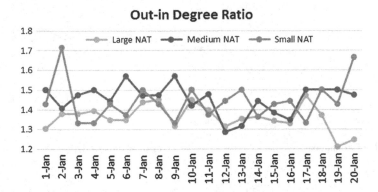

Fig. 4 Three kinds of NAT out-in degree change map

we have calculated the ratio of out-degree and in-degree to estimate the number of out-in degree. As is shown in Fig. 4.

As is shown in Fig. 4, out-in degree ratio has less sensitivity in large NAT and medium NAT, basically between 1.3 and 1.5, while small NAT out-in degree ratio has large changes, mostly between 1.2 and 1.7, because of small amount of data.

During the experiments, we did not distinguish client with server effectively. We find that some servers have similar characteristics. So, we present the concept of activity. We guess that NAT hosts and servers are quite different in daily action.

3.2.2 NAT Activity Degree

In order to further describe the behavior of hosts, we introduce the concept of activity. IP activity mainly composes of two indicators: continuous activity and total activity. In experiments, we counted hosts activity per 30 min, continuous activity refers to the maximum consecutive time interval. We first measured different NAT activity and it is generally believed that, the number of hosts after NAT is large when the activity is high. Results of total activity shown in Fig. 5, ordinate represents the host activity duration.

We have observed different types of NAT for 10 days, total activity change shown in Fig. 5. The abscissa is the time interval. The ordinate is the number of activity, as is shown in Fig. 5, total activity value becomes big when the scale of NAT increases. Next, we have measured continuous active NAT. Results of continuous host activity shown in Fig. 6.

Fig. 5 NAT total activity

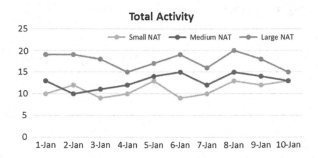

Fig. 6 NAT continuous activity

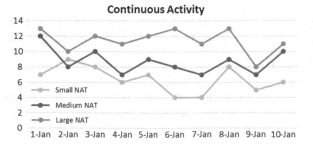

Figure 6 shows that with the scale of NAT decreasing, the continuous activity is further reduced. But the overall still maintains at a higher value.

This experimental takes 20 days long, the accuracy rate reaches 91.2 %. We get a comfortable threshold of out-in degree, when out-in degree is ranged from 1.3 to 1.5, meet any of the following conditions can be identified as NAT:

(i) The continuous activity is ranged from 5 to 12 h.
(ii) The total activity is ranged from 10 to 20 h.

4 Conclusion and Future Work

In the paper, an NAT detection method based on host out-in degree activity is proposed. We have built an appropriate model for NAT properties by continuously adjusting the threshold of host out-in degree activity. Our method also could distinguish NAT and proxy which is much similarity with NAT. The experiments demonstrate that our method is suitable for the large-scale NAT detection.

Acknowledgments This work is supported by the National Science and Technology Support Program (No. 2012BAH46B02) and the Strategic Priority Research Program of the Chinese Academy of Sciences (No. XDA06030200).

References

1. Bellovin SM (2002) A technique for counting NATted hosts. In: Proceedings of the 2nd ACM SIGCOMM workshop on internet measurement, IMW 2002. ACM, New York, pp 267–272
2. Straka K, Manes G (2006) In international federation for information processing. In: Oliver M, Shenoi S (eds) Advances in digital forensics II. Springer, Boston, pp 239–246
3. Kohno T, Broido A, Claffy KC (2005) Remote physical device fingerprinting. IEEE Trans. Dependable Secure Comput. 2(2):93–108
4. Rui L, Hongliang Z, Yang X, Yixian Y, Cong W (2009) Remote NAT detect algorithm based on support vector machine. In: International conference on information engineering and computer science, ICIECS 2009, pp 1–4
5. Rui L, Hongliang Z, Yang X, Shoushan L, Yixian Y, Cong W (2009) Passive NATted hosts detect algorithm based on directed acyclic graph support vector machine. In: International conference on multimedia information networking and security, MINES 2009, vol 2, pp 474–477
6. Krmicek V, Vykopal J, Krejci R (2009) Netflow based system for NAT detection. In: Proceedings of the 5th international student workshop on emerging networking experiments and technologies CoNext student workshop 2009, pp 23–24

Infrared Human Posture Recognition Method Based on Hidden Markov Model

Xingquan Cai, Yufeng Gao, Mengxuan Li and Kyungeun Cho

Abstract The movement of human action recognition technology is the key to human-computer interaction. For the movement of human action recognition problem, this paper has studied the theoretical basis of hidden Markov models including their mathematical background, model definition and hidden Markov model (HMM). After that, we have built the establishment of human action on hidden Markov models and train the model parameters. And this model can effectively target human action classification. Compared with conventional hidden Markov model, the method proposed in this paper to solve the movement of human action recognition problem attempts to establish a model of training data according to the characteristics of human action itself. And according to this, the complex problem is decomposed, thus reducing the computational complexity, to the practical applications to improve system performance results. Through the experiment in the real environment, the experiment show that the model in the practical application can be identification of the different body movement actions by observing human action sequence, matching identification and classification process.

Keywords Human-computer interaction · Feature extraction · Hidden markov models · Human action recognition

X. Cai (✉) · Y. Gao · M. Li
School of Computer Science and Technology, North China University of Technology,
Beijing, People's Republic of China
e-mail: xingquancai@126.com

K. Cho
Department of Multimedia Engineering, Dongguk University, Seoul, Korea

© Springer Science+Business Media Singapore 2016   501
J.J. (Jong Hyuk) Park et al. (eds.), *Advanced Multimedia and Ubiquitous Engineering*, Lecture Notes in Electrical Engineering 393,
DOI 10.1007/978-981-10-1536-6_65

1 Introduction

In recent years, with the development of computer and virtual reality, augmented reality, interactive multimedia and other technology, the demand for increasingly high human-computer interaction(HCI) and the requirements will also be more high than before [1, 2]. In order to achieve the effect of the interaction between human and computer, it needs to make the computer understand people's command. Therefore, use the computer to identify the action of human body has been a one of the hotspots in recent years.

At present, the probabilistic network method used in human action recognition is mainly dynamic Bayesian network [3] and hidden Markov model. This paper has mainly studied the hidden Markov model based on the movement human action recognition method and implement simple human action recognition.

2 Related Work

First of all, in terms of the current study, the human action recognition method is mainly template matching method and probability network method. Among them, the template matching method using an earlier. This method is simple, low computational complexity, but sensitive to the motion interval change and noise. Probability network method has a good stability in time and space of the sequences of actions, but its computational complexity is also high.

In addition, there are the following successful methods for action recognition. In 2012, Zhao [4] presented a recognition algorithm of human action based on multi-features fusion. But because of its own model of the problem in the face of similar actions prone to false. Wu [5] presented a method Using shape descriptors structural relationship of the local key positions for effective expression. In 2014, Chen [6] presented a novel method on action recognition by combining Bayesian Network model with high-level semantic concept. In 2015, Liang [7] presented an action recognition method in the motion process of human's lower limbs In order to control the wide range motion of virtual human. But with the increase of the number of action types and the training data [8], the training time of SVM will increase greatly [9], and the accuracy rate will be reduced under the condition of training parameters. However, just as Zhu [10] shows, there are still some shortcomings in accuracy, robustness and computational efficiency in the process of human complex behavior modeling in the past.

3 Method of Human Action Recognition Based on Hidden Markov Model

3.1 The Basic Principle of Hidden Markov Model

Markov process can be defined as if a stochastic process under a state only with the previous state, and has nothing to do with the previous state, this stochastic process is called first order Markov process. Therefore, at the time, the choice of the state is only related to the previous state, which is called a first order Markov model, as shown in the formula (1).

$$X(t+1) = f(X(t)) \tag{1}$$

Among them, $X = (X_1, X_2, \ldots, X_T)$ is a kind of random sequence.

Markov chain to describe such a status switch, each state is the only decided by the front of a finite number of States. It is a special case of Markov stochastic process, which is defined as follows: is a set of state sequences, at any time, are in a state is a set of states. It is at the moment the state probabilities, this probability only with it in time before the state probability value, and it has nothing to do in the moment before the state probability, such as formula (2) shown in:

$$P(X_{t+k} = q_{t+k} | X_t = q_t, \ldots, X_1 = q_1) = P(X_{t+k} = q_{t+k}) \tag{2}$$

Markov hypothesis can greatly simplify the problem, but it may also be a very bad assumption at the same time, because it may lead to a lot of important information loss.

Hidden Markov model is the extension of the Markov model, the state direct observation is invisible, but it can be through a series of observation vector sequence observed. In which each observation vector can be through some probability density distribution respectively, the performance of various states. Each observation vector is generated by a sequence of States, which has a corresponding probability density distribution. Therefore, the hidden Markov model is a double stochastic process, the hidden Markov chain with a certain number of States and the set of random function set [8].

The hidden Markov model is a five tuple, and a standard hidden Markov model can be represented as a formula (3):

$$\lambda = (N, M, \pi, A, B) \tag{3}$$

Among them, the parameters are expressed respectively:

N is the number of hidden states in the model. M on behalf of the hidden Markov model in each hidden state of the corresponding number of observations. Π represents the initial state of the probability vector. A represents the state of the transition-probability matrix. B indicates the probability distribution matrix of the observation value.

3.2 Establish a Hidden Markov Model for the Movement of the Action Human Body

This chapter will be the recognition of human behavior as a time-varying data classification. In the process of classification every human action will be defined as a state at first. The link between the various states is done by probability. The action that the user makes in the scene is called a series of observations. Each action of the user is composed of motion sequences, each of state is equivalent to a traversal of the various states defined before. This process by calculating the joint probability, and the maximum value of the joint probability as a criterion to identify the behavior of the human body to make a classification of the behavior of the scene.

In this paper, the relationship between the human action recognition methods in the adjacent state is established by the hidden Markov model. And the observation sequence is assumed to be a random state mechanism, which is composed of a fixed number of hidden states.

The model parameter $\lambda = (N, M, \pi, A, B)$ of human behavior recognition is described in Sect. 3.1, N said the behavior of the class book, and M said the basic behavior of the database contains a number of key gestures. That is the size of the code. For each movement, this article uses 4 key gestures to describe, then $M = 4N$.

3.3 Model Parameter Training

Hidden Markov model parameter training plays an important role in the process of behavior recognition, which is also called parameter estimation. Whether the parameter estimation is reasonable or not directly affects the accuracy of the model to the result of behavior recognition. Therefore, before the behavior recognition processing, the known behavior sequence must be defined to train the parameter $\lambda = (\pi, A, B)$ set.

The training process of the model parameters has the following steps: At first, set the initial parameters. And then, the parameters should be reasonable and effective training. In this paper, the estimation of model parameters is completed by the Baum-Welch algorithm. Using forward algorithm to calculate the output probability, if $\log P(O|\lambda) - \log P(O|\lambda_0) < \Delta$, the algorithm process is completed. Otherwise, reset the parameter to make the $\lambda_0 = \lambda$, and repeat the algorithm.

4 Results

In order to verify the feasibility and validity of the hidden Markov model to recognize the action of human motion, the method is designed and implemented in the laboratory.

In this paper, we will get different series of observations on the behavior of the human body, different observation sequences show different action of the human body. Each action in the observation sequence is defined as a state. When the people in the scene to make the movement, by calculating the probability of the maximum probability of state and observation sequence matching, you can on human motion classification, so as to achieve the purpose of human action recognition. Figure 1 shows the sequence of the human body's extended left arm. Similar to sequence of the extended right arm of the human body. Figure 2 shows an observation sequence for the pause indication. Figure 3 shows a sequence of observations to restart the instruction.

As shown in Fig. 4, when the body reaches the left arm, the tank is turning left. Similar to when the human body reaches the right arm, the tank turns to the right. And when the moving tank receives the suspension of the instructions issued by the human body, the tank stopped running, as shown in Fig. 5. When the stop in the tank received instructions to restart, the tank began to move again, as shown in Fig. 6.

Fig. 1 Observation sequence of extended *left arm*

Fig. 2 Observation sequence of pause indication

Fig. 3 Restart the sequence of observations

Fig. 4 Human body extend the *left arm*, the virtual tank to turn *left*

Fig. 5 Human body has made a pause to indicate, driving tank stop

Fig. 6 Human body makes the start instructions, the stop tank start again

5 Conclusions and Future Work

Compared with conventional hidden Markov model, the method proposed in this paper to solve the movement of human action recognition problem attempts to establish a model of training data according to the characteristics of human action itself. And according to this, the complex problem is decomposed, thus reducing the computational complexity, to the practical applications to improve system performance results.

Through the experiment in the real environment, the experiment show that the model in the practical application can be identification of the different body movement actions by observing human action sequence, matching identification and classification process.

Acknowledgments This research was supported by Project of National Science and Technology Support Plan (2012BAF84F02).

References

1. Wang XY, Dai GZ, Zhang XW, Zhang FJ (2008) Recognition of complex dynamic gesture based on HMM-FNN model. J Softw 19:2302–2312
2. Su HY, Chen QA, Wu HT (2015) Human activity recognition based on combined SVM&HMM. Comput Modernization 237:1–8
3. Du YT, Chen F, Xu WL (2009) Approach to human activity multi-scale analysis and recognition based on multi-layer dynamic bayesian network. Acta Automatica Sinica 35: 225–227
4. Zhao HY, Li CY (2012) Human action recognition based on multi-features fusion. Appl Res Comput 29:3169–3172
5. Wu QX, Deng FQ, Kang WX (2012) Human action recognition in complex scenes based on fuzzy integral fusion. J S China Univ Technol (Nat Sci Ed) 40(1):146–151
6. Chen WQ, Xiao GQ, Lin X, Qiu KJ (2014) On a human behaviors classification model based on attribute-bayesian network. J S China Univ Technol (Nat Sci Ed) 39
7. Liang F, Zhang ZL, Li XY, Tong Z (2015) Action recognition of human's lower limbs in the process of human motion capture. J Comput Aided Des Comput Graph 27:2419–2426
8. Li C, Xu JY, Ding GT (2012) CHMM-based background subtraction algorithm. Comput Eng Des 33(9):3517–21
9. Jin P, Bouman CA, Sauer KD (2015) A model-based image reconstruction algorithm with simultaneous beam hardening correction for X-ray CT. IEEE Trans Comput Imaging 1 (3):200–216
10. Zhu XD, Liu ZJ (2012) Human abnormal behavior recognition based on topic hidden Markov model. Comput Sci 39:251–255

Multiple Heterogeneous JPEG Image Hierarchical Forensic

Xiangwei Kong, Bo Wang, Mingliang Yang and Yue Feng

Abstract Since image processing software is widely used to tamper or embed data into JPEG images, the forensics of tampered JPEG images now plays a considerable important role. However, most existing forensics methods that use binary classification can hardly deal with multiclass image forensics problems properly under network environments. In this paper, we propose a hierarchical forensics scheme against multiple heterogeneous JPEG images. We introduce a compression identifier based on Markov model of DCT coefficients as the first hierarchical section and then develop a tampering detection and steganalyzer separately as the second phase. We conduct a series of experiments to testify the validity of the proposed method.

Keywords Image forensics · Heterogeneous images · Classification

1 Introduction

With the popularity of image editing tools such as Photoshop and steganography software, it becomes more convenient to modify digital images without leaving any perceptible artifacts. That makes digital image forensics become an increasingly heated issue.

X. Kong (✉) · B. Wang · M. Yang · Y. Feng
School of Information and Communication Engineering, Dalian University of Technology,
Dalian 116024, People's Republic of China
e-mail: kongxw@dlut.edu.cn

B. Wang
e-mail: bowang@dlut.edu.cn

M. Yang
e-mail: yangml@mail.dlut.edu.cn

Y. Feng
e-mail: fy2012@mail.dlut.edu.cn

© Springer Science+Business Media Singapore 2016   509
J.J. (Jong Hyuk) Park et al. (eds.), *Advanced Multimedia and Ubiquitous Engineering*, Lecture Notes in Electrical Engineering 393,
DOI 10.1007/978-981-10-1536-6_66

As illustrated in [1], binary-classification image forensics has made much progress [2] detected whether the part of an image was initially compressed at a lower quality than the rest [3–6] are put forward to distinguish single and double JPEG compression. Another branch of binary-classification image forensics is steganalysis forensics, a way to distinguish the original images and stego images that hide secret messages. The experimental results of [7] and [8] show that the detection accuracy attains above 90 % even for the low embedding rate of 10 %. However, images on network are not limited to binary-classification. So the existing image forensics algorithms cannot obtain high detection accuracy when the images are mainly from heterogeneous and multiclass source.

This paper focuses on the forensics of multiple heterogeneous images based on a hierarchical forensics scheme that aims at dealing with double compression,. followed by a tampering detection and steganalysis separately to forensics single compression level and double compression level.

2 The Proposed Hierarchical Forensics Scheme

From the view of forensics, JPEG images operation can be roughly divided into four classes. The first is the original JPEG images coming from camera or transformed from lossless images. The second is to scale or recompress and then resave in JPEG format. It happens when the images are uploaded to the social network. The above processed images can be considered as normally edited image whose content is not changed. The third is forged images whose content and information are changed. The forth is steganography that embeds data into images. These four classes can be further divided into binary classes. The original images have been compressed only once. As for the stego images, since the compression will destroy the secret messages, most steganographic algorithms are based on single compressed images. So they could also be regarded as single compressed. The other kind of images is edited or forged images. Double compression occurs when the image is originally stored in JPEG format and then resaved as a JPEG after tampering, because the second compression quality factor is different from the original one. Thus an image should be firstly detected whether is single or double compression.

As this hierarchical principle, we put forward the mechanism of hierarchical forensics. The first hierarchical layer is a compression identifier, which can identify the single compressed images and the double compressed images. The second layer is the forensics of single compressed images and double compressed image respectively.

3 Compression Identifier

As is proposed in [9], the first digits of DCT coefficients follow a generalized Benford's law for the single compression case, while for the double compression case, the distribution shows violation to the logarithmic trend. So the probability distribution of the first digits of DCT coefficients was used directly as features in [9] to classify double compressed images. However, the formed feature is first order statistics, which cannot reflect the correlations between adjacent DCT coefficients. So we model the distribution as a Markov chain and use one-step transition probability matrix to characterize this process. Being different from [9] and [10], we include 0 in the range of the first digits in order to retain information as much as possible. Matrix $F(i, j)$ represents the elements of the first digits of DCT coefficients in the position of ith row and jth column. The transition probability matrix for along the horizontal direction can be defined by:

$$
p\{F(i,j+1) = v | F(i,j) = u\} = \frac{\sum_{i=1}^{m}\sum_{j=1}^{n-1}\delta(F(i,j)) = u, F(i,j+1) = v)}{\sum_{i=1}^{m}\sum_{j=1}^{n-1}\delta(F(i,j)) = u)}. \tag{1}
$$

where m and n are the numbers of rows and columns respectively, and $\delta(x)$ equals one when x is true, equals zero otherwise.

According to the stochastic processes theory, if a Markov chain has state space S and transition probability matrix p, the stationary distribution π will be unique when:

$$
\lim_{n\to\infty} p^n(x, y) = \pi(y), y \in S. \tag{2}
$$

In this case, π can be calculated by solving the following equations:

$$
\begin{cases} \pi = \pi p\,, \\ \sum_{j} \pi_j = 1\,. \end{cases} \tag{3}
$$

where π is a 10-dimensional vector since there are 10 finite-states in the proposed Markov model. Since the stationary distribution π of a Markov model is unique, it will be used as features for double compression detection in the proposed method.

As stated above, for a given image the DCT coefficients of the Y channel are extracted first in order to reduce the dimensionality. Then the first digits of DCT coefficients are calculated from the first 20 individual AC modes as stated in [10]. After that, each stationary distribution will be calculated according to (3) as features. As a result, a feature vector of $10 \times 20 = 200$ elements is obtained for each given image. And then the feature will be fed to the Support Vector Machine (SVM) classifier [11].

4 Tampering Detection and Localization

Figure 1 shows a classical image forged scenario. A region from a JPEG image (red lines) is pasted onto a host image (gray lines) and then recompressed in JPEG format (blue lines). The forged region usually exhibits the presence of non-aligned double JPEG (NA-JPEG) artifacts. As illustrated in Fig. 1b, the forged region is misaligned with the final JEPG compression block grid by shift (x_f, y_f), while the background region is misaligned with the final JEPG compression block grid by shift (x_b, y_b). Basing on the theory above, we can utilize the shift to locate the forged region.

When it comes to the relationship between shift and the DCT coefficients, let m represent the number of 8×8 DCT blocks and $n(j)$ represent the sum of zero JPEG coefficients in the jth component. The percentage of zero JPEG coefficients in the jth component and the average percentage of zero JPEG coefficients are as follows:

$$p(j) = \frac{n(j)}{m}, j = 1, 2, \ldots, 64, \text{ AVERAGE} = \frac{\sum_1^{64} p(j)}{64}. \tag{4}$$

To illustrate the relationship between AVERAGE and NA-JPEG compression shift, we crop a given JPEG image I with quality factor QF along a block shift (i, j) and compress it a second time with the same quality factor to get image $I\_shift(i, j)$. We define the Double Block Shift Matrix (DBSM) of the given image I as:

$$DBSM(i, j) = \text{AVERAGE}(I\_shift(i, j)), \ 0 \le i, j \le 7 \tag{5}$$

We can find out that the position of the peak value in DBSM coincides with the JPEG block shift of NA-JPEG image. The given image is divided into overlapped image blocks in size of $N \times N$ with Step M. After that, we can use the shift (i, j) of every block to get the forged location of the given image.

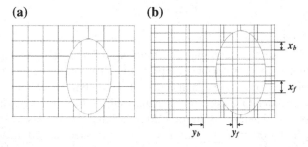

Fig. 1 **a** Block artifacts before resaving; **b** block artifacts after resaving in JPEG format

5 Experiment and Discussion

We carried out our experiments on the BOSSbase database, which consists of 10,000 grayscale RAW images. We selected 500 images from randomly and compressed them in JPEG format with quality factor QF1 = {65, 75, 85, 95} respectively to generate 2000 single compressed images as the original JEPG images. The stego images were obtained by embedding a fixed relative payload of 0.1 bits per nonzero DCT coefficient (bpnc) with two steganographic algorithms, OutGuess [12] and F5 [13], generating 4000 stego images. Then each set of the original images are decompressed, cropped by 64 shifts (i, j) $(0 \leq i, j \leq 7)$ separately, and compressed with QF2 = {65, 75, 85, 95, 99}. Finally we generated 640,000 double compressed JPEG images.

5.1 Compression Identifier Analysis

We use SVM to classify the double and single compressed images. For each group, we randomly choose 50 % of the images as training data and the remaining for testing. To ensure the effectiveness and stability of the proposed method, the experiments are repeated 5 times with the training sets and testing sets chosen randomly. We made [10] as our comparison because in [1], it has been compared with other methods and it outperforms other previous methods such as [14] when it comes to distinguishing between single and double compression.

We can see from Table 1 that both [10] and our proposed method work well when QF2 > QF1. But for the situation of QF2 < QF1, our proposed method outperforms [10] in most cases. This is mainly because the artifacts can be magnified when considering the correlations between the neighbor DCT coefficients with Markov model.

Table 1 Detection results of the compression identification (by %)

QF2 QF1	Method	65	75	85	95	99
65	Our method	–	100	100	100	100
	Work [10]	–	97	97	98	99
75	Our method	99	–	99	100	100
	Work [10]	93	–	95	99	99
85	Our method	99	100	–	100	100
	Work [10]	89	89	–	96	98
95	Our method	95	97	100	–	100
	Work [10]	76	83	89	–	94

5.2 Tampering Location

For the cropped forged images, we compute the accuracy of each condition by averaging the accuracy of all the 64 shifts. The results are reported in Table 2. The accuracy in the case of QF2 > QF1 is much higher than in the case of QF2 ≤ QF1. This is because the block artifacts of the previous compression is weakened after the post compression when QF2 ≤ QF1.

5.3 Steganalysis

For JPEG images steganalysis, the CD-PEV feature vector [7] and the DCTR feature vector [15] are used to construct a SVM classifier. However, the performance of the method has a severe degradation for heterogeneous images. Table 3 shows the steganalysis will take the double compressed images as the stego images. So it is necessary to pick out the single compressed cover and stego images from the mixed images before the steganalysis classifier. Compared to binary classifier, the proposed method could successfully pick up the stego images from the mixed images.

Table 2 Average accuracy (%) of the block shift estimate of the proposed method under different QF1 and QF2

QF2 QF1	65	75	85	95	99
65	25.3	68.7	98.7	100	100
75	20.3	27.7	83.7	100	100
85	16	19	28.3	97.7	100
95	21	15.7	19.3	28	100

Table 3 Detection accuracy (%) of steganalysis

QF	Method	CD-PEV [7]		DCTR [15]	
		OutGuess	F5	OutGuess	F5
65	Our method	93	90	95	97
	Binary classifier	50	50	49	50
75	Our method`	95	92	96	96
	Binary classifier	50	50	50	50
85	Our method	96	94	96	96
	Binary classifier	50	49	50	47
95	Our method	97	97	96	96
	Binary classifier	47	47	50	50

6 Conclusion

In this paper, a scheme was proposed for the mixed images classification. We proposed to utilize the Markov model of DCT coefficients to identify the double compression. Experimental results show that our proposed method performs well even when QF2 < QF1. Then we presented an efficient method to locate the forged part in a tampered image. The proposed method does not need a classifier like a machine learning model and robust to common forgery processing such as resizing and blurring. After analyzing the double compression, the performance of the steganalysis can significantly outperform traditional steganalyzers in mixed images scenario.

Acknowledgments The work is supported by the Foundation for Innovative Research Groups of the NSFC(Grant No. 71421001), NSFC (Grant No. 61172109).

References

1. Alessandro P (2013) An overview on image forensics. ISRN Sig Proc
2. Farid H (2009) Exposing digital forgeries from JPEG ghosts. IEEE Trans Inf Forensics Secur 4(1):154–160
3. Pevny T, Fridrich J (2008) Detection of double-compression in JPEG images for applications in steganography. IEEE Trans Inf Forensics Secur 3(2):247–258
4. Huang FJ, Huang JW, Shi YQ (2010) Detecting double JPEG compression with the same quantization matrix. IEEE Trans Inf Forensics Secur 5(4):848–856
5. Feng XY, Doerr G (2010) JPEG recompression detection. Proc SPIE 7541:75410J
6. Chen CH, Shi YQ, Su W (2008) A machine learning based scheme for double JPEG compression detection," In: 19th international conference on pattern recognition, pp 1–4
7. Pevný T, Fridrich J (2007) Merging Markov and DCT features for multi-class JPEG steganalysis. In: Proceedings SPIE security, steganography, and watermarking of multimedia contents, San Jose, CA, vol 6505, pp 1–13
8. Fridrich J (2005) Feature-based steganalysis for JPEG images and its implications for future design of steganographic schemes. In: Fridrich J (ed) Information hiding, 6th international workshop, volume 3200 of lecture notes in computer science, pp 67–81
9. Fu D, Shi YQ, Su W (2007) A generalized Benford's law for JPEG coefficients and its applications in image forensics. In: Proceedings of SPIE conference on electronic imaging, security and watermarking of multimedia contents, San Jose, USA
10. Li B, Shi YQ, Huang JW (2008) Detecting doubly compressed JPEG images by using mode based first digit features. In: IEEE international workshop on multimedia signal processing, pp 730–735
11. Chang CC, Lin CJ (2001) LIBSVM: a library for support vector machines, 2001. http://www.csie.ntu.edu.tw/~cjlin/libsvm
12. Provos N (2001) Defending against statistical steganalysis. In: 10th USENIX security symposium, Washington, D.C., pp 323–336
13. Westfeld A (2001) F5-a steganographic algorithm: high capacity despite better steganalysis. In: Proceedings of international workshop information hiding (IWIH), Pittsburgh, PA, pp 289–302

14. Chen YL, Hsu CT (2011) Detecting recompression of JPEG images via periodicity analysis of compression artifacts for tampering detection. IEEE Trans Inf Forensics Secur 6(2):396–406
15. Holub V, Fridrich J (2014) Low complexity features for JPEG steganalysis using undecimated DCT. IEEE Trans Inf Forensics Secur 10(2):219–28

Research on the Forensic Direction of Social Networking Software

Guocheng Pu, Yonghao Mai, Jingwu Liu and Lingxu Shuang

Abstract Today, with the increasing development of science and technology, social network software is accepted by more and more people. For most of the people, exchanging information and instant messaging are the function of social software. That makes people's lives very convenient. But it has also become the powerful tool for criminal activities. Therefore, the evidence of social network software has also become an effective evidence to prove the crime.

Keywords Social networking software · Forensic

1 Research Background

With the popularity of the computer in our work and daily life. Internet plays a more and more important role in the communication of society, economy, culture and life. There are many instant message platforms, like AIM, Skype, YAhoo, Messenger, etc. Nowadays, instant message is the most popular way in communicating. The number of the users of each system is no less than 100 million. As of June, 2015, there are 628 million net citizens in China. Computer penetration rate is 48.8 %. Mobile commerce applications develop at a high speed, Internet applications become closer to the enhancement of experience and the direction of economy development. As the most popular communication platform, the number of Tencent QQ users simultaneously online exceeded 200 million at April, 11th, 2014. Over 70 % of net citizens use the instant Messager, like QQ, Ali Want, but with the development of this kind way of communication, there are more and more cases in which the criminals take advantage of those communication tools to commit crimes.

G. Pu (✉) · Y. Mai · J. Liu · L. Shuang
Hubei University of Police, Wuhan, People's Republic of China
e-mail: 985532010@qq.com

© Springer Science+Business Media Singapore 2016   517
J.J. (Jong Hyuk) Park et al. (eds.), *Advanced Multimedia and Ubiquitous Engineering*, Lecture Notes in Electrical Engineering 393,
DOI 10.1007/978-981-10-1536-6_67

2   Research on the Forensic of Social Network

Social network become a very important part in people's daily life, it also has an immeasurable influence in the information acquisition, thinking and life. As a new network tool, social networking softwares dealing the things about exchanging information and establishing interpersonal relationship. It aims to discover the way to acquire, fix, analyse and demonstrate users' information and communication records file, in order to get the directive, effective and objective evidence of the third party.

In China, social networking software has a large number of users, This also becomes a powerful tool for criminals to conduct criminal activities. There is a great danger behind all kinds of social softwares, so the problem of social networking software forensics is becoming an important research direction of computer forensics.

3   Social Network Software Data Analysis

With the rapid development of the Internet, a wide variety of social softwares are also developed. For example, microblogging, appearance social software, sports social software, game social software, Sharing social software and so on. Forensic research in the storage environment, data file attributes, file structure and data recovery is an important application. Social networking software has a variety of existing forms, like PC, mobilephone terminal and webpage. The following will be analyzed from these three different forms.

3.1   The Data Analysis for PC Forensics

Most of the communication information in the social network software is transmitted through the server. Its accounts, groups, contacts, and so on are preserved in the local, but the local information is likely to take encryption mechanism to protect the data. The storage environment, data file attributes, file structure have similarities. Take Tencent Inc's QQ and Microsoft Corp's Skype as examples to analyse their PC data.

(1) Tencent QQ, called "QQ" for short, is an instant messaging software based on the Internet developed by Tencent. QQ supports functions as online chat, video call, point to point file transmission, file sharing, network hard disk, custom panel, QQ email etc., it can also be connected with different communication terminals. In QQ, all the local user data, chat notes and system preferences are stored in the data files whose suffix are "db", and the file size is not set [1].

QQ data file access in Windows 7:
C:\Users\Administrator\Documents\Tencent Files\QQ
QQ data file access in Mac:
~/Library/Containers/com.tencent.qq/Data/Library/Application Support/QQ/

There are kinds of default "db" data format files, like Msg3.0db (QQ chat record database file), Info.db (Database file for storing QQ numbers), *Infocenter.db (QQ message center database record file), etc. . In the process of data forensics, The files in the QQ folder can become important clues and evidence.

(2) Skype is characterized by language communication, it uses P2P network communication mode, can have video, voice and text chat with friends. XP:

C:\Documents and Setting\[USERNAME]\Application Date\Skype
Vista:
C:\Users\[USERNAME]\AppData\Roaming\Skype

In its data directory, Share.xml files save last login IP, the last login time and other information. In each of Skype's sub directories, there are user settings, user friends and communication logs and other information. Account information, voice recording, contact group and message record are included in the main.db files.

3.2 Data Analysis of Mobile Phone Terminal Forensics(Android)

According to foreign media reports, Deloitte Consulting Company conducted a questionnaire survey, with the continuous increase in communication software, more than 20 % of smart phone users do not use the phone call function. In the year of 2015, nearly 22 % of the respondents did not use the calling function of smart phone. As can be seen, with the development of network technology, the applications of instant messaging software are more and more widely used this requires forensic personnels with higher skills. Take Tencent's WeChat as a example, there are two kinds of storage location in WeChat: phone memory and SD card, pictures, voice and chat records and other information relate to some cases can be read from the phone's memory.

Resource Catalogue:

1. Image path:/storage/emulated/tencent/MicroMsg, and then find the Weixin folder, pictures are kept inside.
2. Voice path:/sdcard/Tencent/MicroMsg/. Open the corresponding backup folder, the files in it usually named by a stack of numbers and letters, then find the "voice" folder, the "arm" format documents are chat voice recording.

Data Catalogue:
Data catalogue saves all the text chat, the sending and receiving time of all the voice messages in the folder named as data/data/com.tencent.mm/MicroMsg.

3.3 Analysis of Social Web Forensics Data

In order to improve the speed of accessing web pages, Internet Explorer will use the cumulative acceleration method, store the contents of the pages you have visited in your computer. We call this storage space IE cache.

The IE cache is installed in the system area. choose "Internet" under the "tools" in IE, then you will see the "Internet temporary file" in the general tab.

Default path:

X:\Documents and Settings\Administrator\Local Settings\Temporary Internet Files Windows 7: X:\Users\Administrator\AppData\Local\Microsoft\Windows \Temporary Internet Files

Through the IE cache and registry queries, data collection can be accessed from the web site of social software.

4   Data Recovery

Recovery of instant messaging data is similar to that of other applications. As long as the data is not covered, there is the possibility of recovery. Some social software's chat records are closed or encrypted, the conventional method cannot carry out data analysis, the chat record information may in the memory, exchange files, hibernation files, so we can recover data through those files.

5   Difficulties in Social Software Forensics

Due to the large number of users, and the high use frequency, so the number of times of social software in a variety of cases is also very high. In the process of data forensics, it is inevitable to encounter various problems. for example, the difficulties in data recovery, crack data encryption mechanism, software update speed and so on. In the field of electronic data forensics, the forensic work of social software is becoming more and more important, and the requirement of the technical personnel is higher and higher.

Reference

1. Liu H, Li J, Liu X (2015) Digit Forensics 10:1

The Effects of Heuristic GUI Principles on the Accessibility of Information in the Context of Mobile Application

Wonjin Jung

Abstract Recently, user-centered user interface design principles for PCs have been presented, such as design consistency or design simplicity. However, those principles are generally based on design specialists' experiences, and thus there are relatively few studies that have explored the design principles based on a theoretical foundation. Therefore, the need for empirical studies on the heuristic GUI design principles has been gradually increasing. This study was designed to identify the effects of the heuristic GUI design principles presented in the environment of PCs on the system users' convenience, i.e., particularly on information access in the current mobile computing environment. The aims of this study are to verify the influence of design consistency and simplicity employed for GUIs of mobile applications on the users' understandability of GUIs; and furthermore, to identify the effects of GUI understandability on the accessibility to information via mobile applications of users. Data were collected through a survey and Structural Equation Modeling (SEM) was employed to analyze the data. The results found that in the environment of mobile application, there was a verification of: the influence of design consistency and design simplicity on the users' GUI understandability of mobile applications; and furthermore, the resulting effects of that GUI understandability on the accessibility to information of users.

Keywords Smartphone · Application · Interface · Principles · Accessibility

1 Introduction

As one of constituent components of a system, an interface denotes the place of interaction between the hardware and software or between two or more systems, and users of systems also interact with those systems via interfaces [1]. Interfaces

W. Jung (✉)
The School of Business and Economics, Dankook University, 152 Jook-Jun-Ro,
Soo-Ji-Goo, Young-In, Kyung-Ki-Do, 448-701 Yonkin, South Korea
e-mail: jungw@dankook.ac.kr; thkim@dankook.ac.kr

© Springer Science+Business Media Singapore 2016
J.J. (Jong Hyuk) Park et al. (eds.), *Advanced Multimedia and Ubiquitous Engineering*, Lecture Notes in Electrical Engineering 393,
DOI 10.1007/978-981-10-1536-6_68

designed by taking the users' convenience into account thus help users to search or access the information in systems or to figure out the structures of the systems [2]. In addition, those interfaces designed by considering the users' convenience also enable effective and efficient use and operation of systems through the reduced possibility of the users' confusion in interactions with systems, and consequently can positively influence the degree of satisfaction or preference to those systems by the users [3].

A lot of previous studies, which delved into the subject of interface in the discipline of human-computer interaction, have been continued so far to take into account the users' convenience. However, most of such studies have focused on the Graphic User Interface (GUI) for PCs [4–6]. Recently, user-centered design principles have been presented, such as design consistency or design simplicity. However, those principles are generally based on design specialists' experiences, and thus there are relatively few studies that have explored the design principles based on a theoretical foundation. Therefore, the need for empirical studies on heuristic GUI design principles has been gradually increasing.

This study was designed to identify the effects of heuristic GUI design principles presented in the environment of PCs on the system users' convenience, i.e., particularly on information access in the current mobile computing environment. Since the release of Apple's iPhone to the market, the individual computing paradigm has shifted rapidly from PCs to mobile appliances. Thus, the effectiveness of heuristic GUI design principles, which was validated for PCs, needs to be identified as to whether or not they are still effective in the mobile computing environment that consists of mostly smartphones.

This study intends to verify the influence of design consistency and simplicity employed for GUIs of mobile applications on the users understandability of GUIs; and furthermore, to identify the effects of GUI understandability on the accessibility to information via mobile applications of users through the following hypotheses.

H1: The GUI consistency of mobile applications positively influences GUI understandability

H2: The GUI simplicity of mobile applications positively influences GUI understandability

H3: The users' GUI understandability of mobile applications positively influences the users' accessibility to information

2 Research Methodology, Data Analysis, and Results

This study aims to examine the effects of heuristic GUI design principles, including consistency and simplicity, on the understandability of GUI, as well as the effect of the understandability of GUI on the accessibility of information in the context of mobile applications. Data were gathered by a survey. A total of 236 college students and practitioners participated in the survey. The gender ratio of the participants was 49.6 % female and 50.4 % male. Most of the participants were in their twenties.

College students made up 66.9 % of the participants and were majoring in various academic programs, including economics, business, computer science, and humanities at three universities in South Korea. Practitioners, on the other hand, made up 33.1 % of the participants and were working in a variety of industries. The kinds of mobile applications that the participants had just used before answering the survey questions were mostly (61.9 %) social networking and communications-related.

This study used Structural Equation Modeling (SEM) to analyze the data and the proposed research model. AMOS (ver. 18) was the statistical software used for the analysis. As a first step of analysis, this study examined the reliability of all observable variables for the purpose of testing the measurement model. The loadings of all observable variables on their respective latent variables should be above 0.6 to meet the reliability requirements [7, 8]. The results of this study showed that all of the loadings were 0.7 or higher, thereby indicating that the reliability is adequate (see Table 1).

Next, this study tested the convergent validity of the measurement model. To do so, the composite reliability (CR) and the average variance extracted (AVE) of each latent variable were examined. Two formulas, suggested by Fornall and Larcker [9] and Hair et al. [10], were used to calculate the values of CR and AVE. The results showed that all latent variables had values for CR higher than the recommended cutoff of 0.7 (see Table 1). Furthermore, the values of AVE for all latent variables were of 0.6 or higher, which was well above the recommended tolerance of 0.5 (see Table 1). Therefore, the convergent validity of the measurement model was confirmed.

Table 1 Standardized regression weights of observable variables, composite reliability (CR), and average variance extracted (AVE)

Latent variables	Estimates	Variance C.R.	Composite reliability	AVE
Consistency	0.835	7.574	0.917	0.704
	0.865	6.664		
	0.817	8.018		
Simplicity	0.781	9.299	0.930	0.749
	0.899	6.247		
	0.911	5.638		
Understandability	0.915	5.197	0.916	0.716
	0.870	7.148		
	0.744	9.521		
Accessibility	0.702	9.563	0.915	0.682
	0.938	2.804		
	0.820	7.437		

$$CR = \left(\sum \text{Standardized Regression Weights}\right)^2 / \left(\left(\sum \text{Standardized Regression Weights}\right)^2 + \left(\sum \text{Variance}\right)\right) \quad (1)$$

$$AVE = \left(\sum \text{Standardized Regression Weights}\right)^2 / N \quad (2)$$

This study also checked the discriminant validity of the measurement model. One commonly used way is to compare the square root of the AVE with the correlations among the variables in the model. To satisfy the requirements, the square root of the AVEs for all variables should be higher than the correlations with other variables in the model [8]. The results of the analysis showed that this is the case (see Table 2). Therefore, the proposed measurement model demonstrated satisfactory discriminant validity as well.

Then, the structural model was test by examining the goodness of fit. The indices, which are usually examined for the structural model, include x^2/df, GFI, AGFI, NFI, TLI, CFI, and RMSEA. The results of the examination for the structural model of this study were as follows: x^2/df = 2.894, GFI = 0.910, AGFI = 0.859, NFI = 0.927, TLI = 0.935, CFI = 0.951, and RMSEA = 0.090. Therefore, the overall fit statistics suggested that the structural model has a pretty good fit.

Lastly, the structural model was tested by examining the significance of the relationships between the variables in the model. As expected, consistency and simplicity had a significant influence on understandability ($\beta = 0.410$, p = 0.001), ($\beta = 0.311$, p = 0.001), respectively. In addition, understandability also had a positive impact on accessibility ($\beta = 0.576$, p = 0.001). Therefore, all hypotheses were supported. The results of the test in detail are shown in Table 3. Figure 1 also presents the results, with R^2 values representing the amount of variance.

Table 2 Correlation coefficient value between constructs and AVE

Constructs	AVE	$\varnothing^2$	$\varnothing^2$	$\varnothing^2$	$\varnothing^2$
Consistency	0.704	0.216	0.419	0.416	1.000
Simplicity	0.749	0.221	0.404	1.000	
Understandability	0.716	0.255	1.000		
Accessibility	0.682	1.000			

Table 3 Hypothesis test

	Paths	Coeff.	Stand. coeff.	P	Results
H1	Consistency $\rightarrow$ understandability	0.410	0.409	0.0001	Accept
H2	Simplicity $\rightarrow$ understandability	0.311	0.383	0.0001	Accept
H3	Understandability $\rightarrow$ accessibility	0.576	0.523	0.0001	Accept

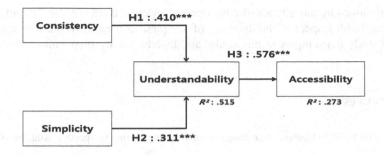

Chi-square=144.681 (df=50) p=.000

Fig. 1 Structural model results

3 Discussion and Conclusion

In this study, the three hypotheses (H1–H3, Sect. 1) were confirmed. That is, in the environment of mobile application, there was a verification of: the influence of design consistency and design simplicity (H1; H2) on the users' GUI understandability of mobile applications; and furthermore, the resulting effects of that GUI understandability on the accessibility to information of users (H3).

The results obtained from statistical analysis conducted in the study showed positive influences of design consistency and simplicity on users' GUI understandability, and furthermore, the users' accessibility to information was identified so that it also improved with the degree of users' understandability on GUIs.

In short, a consistent and simple design of GUIs of mobile applications seemed to improve the level of users' understanding of the corresponding mobile applications, and thus can facilitate the use of mobile applications more conveniently. Furthermore, a higher level of users' understanding of mobile applications also encouraged the users' accessibility to information.

The significance of this study is the identification of the consistent effectiveness of heuristic GUI design principles, developed in the environment of PCs, which, so far, has also been commonly applicable to PCs and mobile applications. Current mobile appliances, including smartphones, support almost all functions available through PCs. This means the functions available through PCs can also be available through mobile appliances. As a result, the functions of mobile applications have been diversified. However, this trend of diversification can engender a complexity of applications that consequently prevents users from convenient and fluent use of those applications. The results obtained from this study suggest that those issues can be alleviated through the use of design principles of GUIs.

The developers of mobile applications are thus encouraged to check the consistency and simplicity of the design of GUIs of mobile applications and in this context, questions included in the questionnaire used in this study can be well-employed by those kinds of developers. However, there are also limitations to this study with respect of the diversity of samples. Consequently, further research should study those topics in this study, and thereby rectify their limitations.

References

1. Lauesen S (2005) User interface design: a software engineering perspective. Addison Wesley, Reading
2. Pullman C (2002) Some things change. http://www.aigany.org/ideas/features/pullman.html. Accessed Dec 2002
3. Shneiderman B, Plaisant C (2005) Designing the user interface. Addison Wesley, UK
4. Stroulia E, El-Ramly M, Iglinski P, Sorenson P (2003) User interface reverse engineering in support of interface migration to the web. Autom Softw Eng J 10(3):271–301
5. Stroulia E, El-Ramly M, Iglinski P, Sorenson P (2004) From legacy to web through interaction modeling. In: Proceedings of 18th international conference for software maintenance, pp 320–329
6. Tucker K, Stirewalt K (1999) Model based user interface reengineering. In: Proceedings of 6th working conference for reverse engineering, pp 56–65
7. Barclay D, Higgins C, Thompson R (1995) The partial least squares (PLS) approach to causal modeling: personal computer adoption and use as an illustration. Technol Stud 2:285–324
8. Chin WW (1998) The partial least squares approach for structural equation modeling. In: Marcoulides GA (ed) Modern methods for business research. Lawrence Erlbaum, Mahwah, pp 295–336
9. Fornell C, Larcker DF (1981) Evaluating structural equation models with unobservable variables and measurement error. J Mark Res 18:39–50
10. Hair JF, Black B, Babin B, Andersong RE, Tatham RL (2006) Multivariate data analysis, 6th edn. Pearson Prentice Hall, Upper Saddle River

Development for Agri-Food Service Platform Using 3D Contents Techniques

Geum-Young Min and Hyoung-Seop Shim

Abstract Recent development in information technology has changed the distribution system for agri-food products. Along with the development in agri-food products, it became necessary to develop an e-commerce system that allows customers to search information about and purchase agri-food products. For the purpose, this study developed a virtual store where customers can purchase agri-food products using smartphones and mobile devices. To development of mobile based virtual store with agri-food ICT convergence—integration (1) implement of agri-food products display, (2) construction of code interface for devices and connected products, (3) development of Service Platform and (4) implementation of 3D content creation system.

Keywords Agri-Food · ICT convergence · Integration platform · Virtual store

1 Introduction

Distribution costs for agri-food products account 40–45 % of the consumer prices and the high distribution costs are caused by lack of competition between distribution channels, and inefficiency in each distribution stage [1]. Therefore, it is necessary to improve distribution system for agri-food products.

Specifically, applying ICT (Information and Communications Technologies) in the agri-food products field can improve product quality and productivity, and, as a result, improve competitive power. However, the budget for information business accounts only 0.29 % of the Ministry of Agriculture, Food and Rural Affairs' whole

G.-Y. Min
Dongguk University, Seoul, South Korea
e-mail: william1540@naver.com

H.-S. Shim (✉)
Kisti, Deajeon, South Korea
e-mail: hsshim@kisti.re.kr

© Springer Science+Business Media Singapore 2016
J.J. (Jong Hyuk) Park et al. (eds.), *Advanced Multimedia and Ubiquitous Engineering*, Lecture Notes in Electrical Engineering 393,
DOI 10.1007/978-981-10-1536-6_69

budget. The percentage is insignificant compare to the budget for information business of other fields that account 2–3 % of the whole budget [2].

To solve the issue, the government developed agri-food ICT integration model by integrating information and communications technology into the agri-food value chain, such as production, distribution, consumption, and etc. [3].

This study developed a virtual agri-food mobile store based on the agri-food ICT integration model to make a new distribution channel; and an open market type mobile service integration platform that comprehensively connecting the agricultural products shopping malls and relevant sites operated by farmers and the local governments.

2 Agri-Food Service Platform

Service platform conducts integrated products display and advertisements by interconnecting mobile devices as shown in the Fig. 1. Product information is arranged and distributed through the management system.

2.1 V-Store Display

The major role of V-Store display is to support consumers' purchase by providing the information consumers want to obtain. V-Store displays the information about

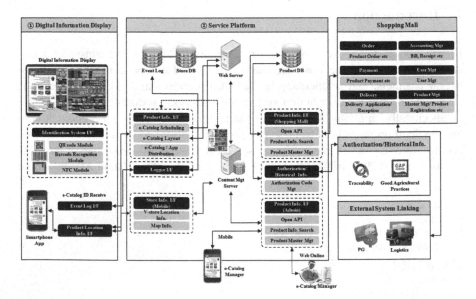

Fig. 1 Agri-food service platform architecture

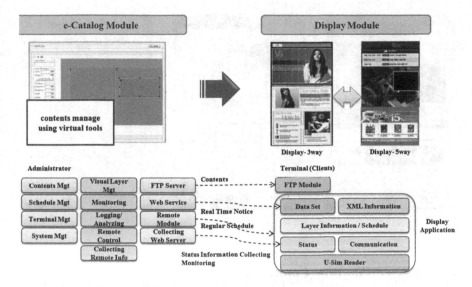

Fig. 2 V-Store display module system

the specific agri-food that consumers want to obtain, after receiving the product information from service platform. It also conducts the process to provide additional information or support consumers' purchase according to consumer behavior henceforward.

Prior to consumers' purchase request, V-Store plays the role to induce consumers to require information by providing the information about various event/promotion/festival relevant to agri-food in addition to providing agri-food products information.

This study designed a display module in DID (Digital Information Display; Digital Signage) to introduce agri-food products as shown in the Fig. 2.

2.2 Code System

We establish the tag/code system that the methodologies and the software Application Program Interfaces (APIs) associated with these technologies for their using Barcode, QR (Quick Response) Code and NFC (Near Field Communication) in smartphone to link agri-food information.

As selecting a product, (1) a detailed product information, (2) certification/ production information provided by Barcode, QR code and NFC as shown in the Fig. 3.

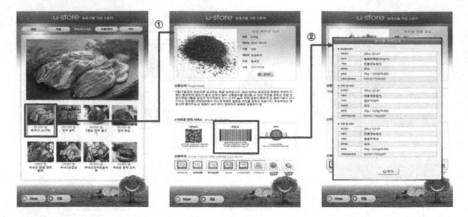

Fig. 3 Information display capture

2.3 Service Platform Connection

Service Platform supports for integrated product display and advertisement by interconnecting DID and Smartphones. The platform is developed to make efficient display management by making arrangement and distribution of the product (contents) information through the management system as shown in the Fig. 4.

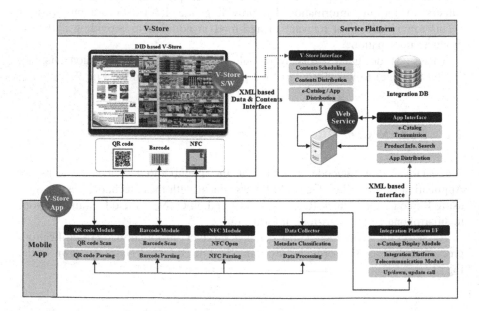

Fig. 4 V-Store and service platform connection

2.4 3D Content Creation Systems

(1) Multi-Camera Digital Acquisition System

To generate 3D content, we first need to acquire 2D information. For that purpose we have built an acquisition space surrounded by a multi-camera system. This system will focus on the technical characteristics needed to obtain an image stream from multiple cameras and to transform it into suitable information for the 3D-modeling [4].

As shown in the Fig. 5, this system generated the 3D contents with 360° rotation function by combining 2D images taken by six cameras.

(2) 3D contents creation

We have Constructed a 3D contents using Multi-Camera Digital Acquisition System. The open-source program CloudCompare is used to perform this 3D contents analysis. This program was used in order to get the best accuracy for the deviation results [5] (Fig. 6).

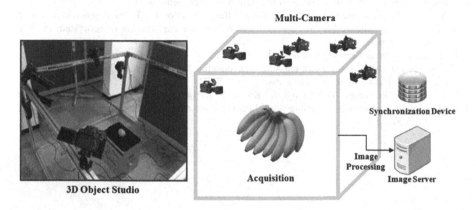

Fig. 5 3D contents acquisition with multi-camera

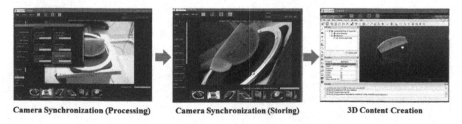

Fig. 6 3D contents creation using cloudcompare

3 Conclusion

This study developed the service platform based on the agri-food ICT convergence as described below.

First, developed the interface to enable consumers to obtain detailed information about products. Second, service platform supports for integrated product display and advertisement by interconnecting DID and Smartphones. Third, conducted the 3D conversion process using 3D camera filming and a program to produce 3D contents, and used the outcome for display.

Future studies will aim to build a Rural Village. The Rural Village will provide information display during the rural theme tour. The information display can be used for information gathering and product purchase.

References

1. Prime Minister's Office (2013) Civil economic agri-food cultural marketing structure improvement and income increase of the farm-fishing households
2. Ministry of Agriculture (2010) Food & Rural Affairs, direction of IT convergence in agri-food
3. Ministry of Agriculture (2013) Food & Rural Affairs, the construction of ecosystem for ICT convergence in agri-food
4. Benjamin P, Jean-Denis L, Clément M, Jérémie A, Jean-Sébastien F, Bruno R, Edmond B, François F (2010) Multicamera real-time 3D modeling for telepresence and remote collaboration. Int J Digit Multimedia Broadcast
5. Thoeni K, Giacomini A, Murtagh R, Kniest E (2014) A comparison of multi-view 3D reconstruction of a rock wall using several cameras and a laser scanner. Remote Sens Spat Inf Sci XL-5:573–580

Exploitation of Clustering Techniques in Disease Distribution of Community Residents

Jinhong Li, Xingxing Xie and Wei Song

Abstract This paper analyzes different disease forms among various administrative areas. It is able to help healthcare authorities make quick and exact decisions in the allocation of medical resources and health services. To solve this problem, we exploit four different clustering algorithms including Hierarchical Agglomerative Clustering (HAC), K-Means, Density-Based Clustering (DBSCAN), Gaussian Mixed Model (GMM). Furthermore, we performed an experimental evaluation of the accuracy and interpretability of four algorithms using disease data. The results of our experiments demonstrate that HAC is significantly more effective in discovering clusters of regional disease.

Keywords Clustering techniques · Data mining · Disease distribution · Public health

1 Introduction

In 2010, the Beijing Municipal Government started "healthy hut" project in 16 counties covering total 343 community health service center. It has now completed blood pressure, blood glucose, body composition and dozens of related data collection and testing. Therefore, the analysis of massive data has become an important challenge. Data mining [1] and visualization techniques have been widely applied to public health-care services in recent years.

This study proposed an approach to cluster administrative regions of similar disease groups using different clustering technique on a real healthcare dataset. In terms of accuracy and interpretability, HAC (hierarchical agglomerative clustering) in regional disease classification is better than other algorithms. Therefore, the

J. Li (✉) · X. Xie · W. Song
North China University of Technology, Beijing, China
e-mail: ljh@ncut.edu.cn

X. Xie
e-mail: xie_star@163.com

© Springer Science+Business Media Singapore 2016
J.J. (Jong Hyuk) Park et al. (eds.), *Advanced Multimedia and Ubiquitous Engineering*, Lecture Notes in Electrical Engineering 393,
DOI 10.1007/978-981-10-1536-6_70

results of HAC could be used to help relevant health authorities understand the disease forms in the various administrative areas of Beijing County, and to further make appropriate decisions on healthcare planning.

The paper is organized as follows: Sect. 2 presents the related work of the disease distribution of community residents; Sect. 3 includes the proposed methods; Sect. 4 illustrates the experimental work and discusses the results; finally, the conclusion of this research work is presented in Sect. 5.

2 Related Work

This section reviews related works to investigating disease forms in various administrative areas, where we emphasize some diversity and the similarities between some of the related works and the suggested work.

For example, Mahoto [2] evaluated the effectiveness of three different clustering algorithms: DBSCAN (Density-Based Clustering), agglomerative hierarchical and k-means in real transactional healthcare data of diabetic patients using internal quality indexes. As a result, DBSCAN performed better than other clustering algorithms (i.e. K-means and Hierarchical) for a dense and disperse healthcare dataset. Lavrač [3] proposed a novel approach concerning using data mining and visualization techniques for decision support in public health-care planning in Slovenia. Furthermore, the authors also create the model of the availability and accessibility of health services to identify the atypical areas. The results are directly useful for decision making by health-care authorities. Nuaimi [4] proposed four models where data mining techniques was used to predict the demand for healthcare services in Abu Dhabi Emirate. The purpose of using different models is to ensure optimal performance of health service balance in Abu Dhabi Emirate. Wei [5] used data mining techniques to analyze the screening disease data of community residents of Taipei County in Taiwan. It was found that the major disease forms and the clustering effects in various administrative areas. As a result, the authors draw up a disease distribution map for different age distributions in each administrative area.

3 Method

3.1 Data Source and Dataset

The data set is retrieved from Statistics 2014 of Healthy hut covering all of administrative districts in Beijing. After preprocessing step, it consists of 1960 instances and 9 attributes as described in Table 1.

Table 1 Screened dataset attribute

Criteria	Sub-criteria	Type
ID	Identify patient	Char
Gender	{'F', 'M'}	Char
Age	{14 < age < 120}	Numeric
Hypertension	{1, 0}	Binary
Hyperglycemia	{1, 0}	Binary
Hyperlipidemia	{1, 0}	Binary
Obesity	{1, 0}	Binary
Region	{'A1' ... 'D5'}	Char
Date	{'2014/2/25'}	Char

3.2 Data Mining Tool

There are many current tools for data mining and knowledge discovery, such as WEKA, R, Orange, RapidMiner, etc. However, R is the most popular overall tool among data miners and data scientists. Because R is free software and has many algorithms that can strong it.

3.3 Clustering Algorithms

Four different clustering algorithms are presented: Hierarchical Agglomerative Clustering (HAC), K-Means, Density-Based Clustering (DBSCAN), and Gaussian Mixture Model (GMM).

HAC [6] which uses a join rule data through a hierarchical architecture approach repeatedly polymerizes the data to form a hierarchical sequence of solutions. Hierarchical aggregation algorithm computational complexity is $O(n^2)$, and suitable for classification of small data sets.

K-Means [7] is the simplest and most commonly used algorithm employing a squared error criterion. The core idea of the algorithm is to find out the K cluster centers ($C_1, C_2 ... C_K$) so that the deviation between each data point x_i and its nearest clustering center C_V is minimized. The k-Means is popular because it is easy to implement, and its time complexity is $O(n)$, where n is the number of patterns.

DBSCAN [8] is a clustering algorithm which relies on a density-based notion of clusters. It can discover the clusters of arbitrary shape while handle noise or outliers effectively. The key idea in DBSCAN is that for each object of a cluster, the neighborhood of a given radius (Eps) has to contain at least a minimum number (MinPts) of objects. In addition, DBSCAN algorithm is efficient for large spatial databases.

GMM [9] is one of the most popular data clustering methods which can be view as a weighted sum of Gaussian component densities. The key idea in GMM is that different cluster is assigned to different Gaussian components through estimating each cluster's own parameters. Because of the more data the more accurate algorithm to estimate the model, GMM is suitable for large data.

4 Experimental Works and Results

In this section, we evaluate the performance of different clustering algorithms, including HAC, K-Means, DBSCAN and GMM.

4.1 Experiment Work

Because the K-Means needs to determine the value of K, we first applied HAC to data analysis. This experiment exploited the widely used Euclidean Distance to measure the degree of affinity between data items. And ward's method was used to calculate the distance between groups of data items. Then the clustering count of HAC can be referenced by other algorithms. Therefore, the value of K in K-Means was equal to 4. Next, DBSCAN starts with an arbitrary object p in D and retrieves all objects in D density-reachable from p with respect to Eps (neighborhood of a point) and MinPts (a minimum number of points). Eps = 22, MinPts = 1. Finally, GMM parameters are estimated from training data using the iterative Expectation-Maximization (EM) algorithm estimation from a well-trained prior model. The clustering results of four algorithms are shown in Fig. 1 and Table 3.

4.2 Results

There are many factors that measure the clustering results, including accuracy and interpretability. In order to evaluate the accuracy of four clustering outcomes, a decision tree learning algorithm (J48 WEKA) was applied to distinguish the clustering results. It is found that HAC algorithm produces best accuracy results.

In terms of interpretability, the major factor is functional localization of administrative region which is highly correlated with disease distribution. From

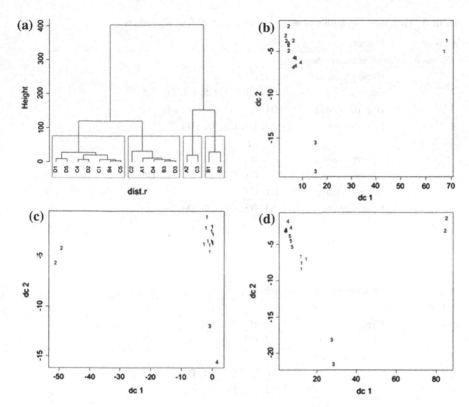

Fig. 1 a HAC. **b** K-Means. **c** DBSCAN. **d** GMM

Table 2 Functional zone for administrative district

Core zone of the capital	Functional development zone	Urban development zone	Ecological conservation zone
A1-Dong Cheng	B1-Chao Yang	C1-Tong Zhou	D1-Men Tou Gou
A2-Xi Cheng	B2-Hai Dian	C2-Shun Yi	D2-Ping Gu
	B3-Feng Tai	C3-Da Xing	D3-Huai Rou
	B4-Shi Jing Shan	C4-Chang Ping	D4-Mi Yun
		C5-Fang Shan	D5-Yan Qing

Tables 2 and 3, it is obtained that cluster 3 (B1, B2) of HAC is more proper than cluster 3 (B1, C3) of K-Means. Consequently, HAC gives better clustering results than others. Table 4 shows the accuracy of four clustering results.

Table 3 The clustering results of disease distribution of four algorithms

Cluster	Disease	Region
Hierarchical agglomerative clustering		
1	Hyperglycemia	A2, C3
2	Obesity	B4, C1, C4, C5, D1, D2, D5
3	Hyperlipidemia	B1, B2
4	Hypertension	A1, B3, C2, D3, D4
K-Means		
1	Hyperglycemia	A2, B2
2	Obesity	B4, C1, C2, C5, D1, D2, D5
3	Hyperlipidemia	B1, C3
4	Hypertension	A1, B3, C4, D3, D4
DBSCAN		
1	Hyperglycemia	A1, B3, B4, C1, C2, C4, C5, D1, D2, D3, D4, D5
2	Hyperglycemia	A2, C3
3	Hyperlipidemia	B1
4	Hyperlipidemia	B2
GMM		
1	Hypertension	A1, B3, D3, D4
2	Hyperglycemia	A2, C3
3	Hyperlipidemia	B1, B2
4	Obesity	B4, C1, C5, D1, D5
5	Obesity	C2, C4, D2

Table 4 Comparison of accuracy

Algorithm	HAC	K-Means	DBSCAN	GMM
Accuracy	83.62 %	62.50 %	56.25 %	62.50 %

5 Conclusion

In this paper, we presented different data mining techniques in order to find the best cluster for disease distribution of community residents. The experiments have shown that HAC divides disease areas into four clusters with the highest accuracy of 83.62 %.

Future research will have to extend this analysis to more historic data so as to predict the trend of distribution of regional disease.

Acknowledgment This research was supported by the National Natural Science Foundation of China (61503005).

References

1. Han J, Kamber M (2011) Data mining: concepts and techniques, 3rd edn. Elsevier, Boston
2. Mahoto NA, Shaikh FK, Ansari AQ (2014) Exploitation of clustering techniques in transactional healthcare data. Mehran Univ Res J Eng Technol 33(1):77–92
3. Lavrac N, Bohanec M, Pur A, Cestnik B, Debeljak M, Kobler A (2007) Data mining and visualization for decision support and modeling of public health-care resources. J Biomed Inform 40:438–447
4. AI Nuaimi N (2014) Data mining approaches for predicting demand for healthcare services in Abu Dhabi. In: Proceedings of 10th international conference on innovations in information technology, IEEE Press, Al Ain, pp 42–47
5. Wei CK, Su S, Yang MC (2012) Application of data mining on the development of a disease distribution map of screened community residents of Taipei County in Taiwan. J Med Syst 36:2021–2027
6. Rokach L, Maimon O (2005) Clustering methods. In: Data mining and knowledge discovery handbook. Springer, Berlin, pp 321–352
7. MacQueen J (1967) Some methods for classification and analysis of multivariate observations. In: Proceedings of fifth Berkeley symposium on mathematical statistics and probability pp 281–297
8. Yue SH et al (2005) A statistical information-based clustering approach in distance space. J Zhejiang Univ 6(1):71–78 (Volume A English version)
9. Tomasi C (2004) Estimating gaussian mixture densities with EM: a tutorial. Duke University, Tech.rep.

Collaborative Ontology Generation Method Using an Ant Colony Optimization Model

Hansaem Park, Jeungmin Lee, Kyunglag Kwon, Jongsoo Sohn, Yunwan Jeon, Sungwoo Jung and In-Jeong Chung

Abstract Ontology has been regarded as the core technology of the semantic web. However, non-experts still have difficulties in participating in ontology generation. So, the growing need for public participation in ontology generation has arisen. We propose a method in which the public may participate in ontology generation by adopting the ACO (Ant Colony Optimization) algorithm. We demonstrate that the ontology generated by the proposed method is satisfactory to justify our method: precision and recall of the ontology are about 94.44 and 99.6 % respectively. The suggested method enables the construction of the semantic web environment with non-experts in the field of ontology engineering.

Keywords Ontology · Semantic web · Ant colony optimization (ACO)

J. Sohn
Service Strategy Team, Visual Display, Samsung Electronics, Suwon
Republic of Korea
e-mail: Jongsoo.sohn@samsung.com

H. Park · J. Lee · K. Kwon · Y. Jeon · S. Jung · I.-J. Chung (✉)
Department of Computer and Information Science, Korea University, Seoul
Republic of Korea
e-mail: chung@korea.ac.kr

H. Park
e-mail: park11232000@korea.ac.kr

J. Lee
e-mail: wjdals543@korea.ac.kr

K. Kwon
e-mail: helpnara@korea.ac.kr

Y. Jeon
e-mail: juw123@korea.ac.kr

S. Jung
e-mail: sigran@korea.ac.kr

© Springer Science+Business Media Singapore 2016
J.J. (Jong Hyuk) Park et al. (eds.), *Advanced Multimedia and Ubiquitous Engineering*, Lecture Notes in Electrical Engineering 393,
DOI 10.1007/978-981-10-1536-6_71

1 Introduction

The semantic web enabled computers to understand the meaning of information on the World Wide Web, making it possible for computers and people to cooperate [1]. The core technology of the semantic web is ontology, which is a structural framework for organizing information for intelligent information systems. As the success of the semantic web strongly depends on the ontologies, the generation of ontologies plays crucial role in an intelligent system. Although There have been many researches, it remains a tedious and cumbersome task on generating ontology for non-expert users.

Web 2.0 environment enables users to create high quality contents by using collective intelligence [2]. We thus suggest a collaborative ontology generation method. The method based on the collective intelligence of non-expert users uses Ant Colony Optimization (ACO), one of the collective intelligence-based optimization algorithms. In this paper, we create ontology through procedures of three ontology generation methods: (a) primitive ontology, (b) mediation ontology, and (c) popular ontology. In the primitive ontology creation, users establish relations between tags entered in the various web applications, and transmit the generated ontologies to the server. We then combine primitive ontologies without filtering, and create mediation ontology in the stored form. Finally, we compute pheromone values for each triple, consisting of subject, predicate, and object, and filter the most widely used triple to create the popular ontology. The proposed method is designed to overcome the flaws of expert-based ontology generation methods. Using this method, non-expert users can collaboratively generate and share ontology with minimal effort. Therefore, we can construct a collection of publicly available ontologies. Through the proposed method, many users can participate in ontology generation, and can create general, lightweight ontologies, not expert-generated or rule-based ontologies.

Compared to vertical ontology generation method, the horizontal approach-based method [3] in this paper utilizes an ontology evolution mechanism. The ontology evolution mechanism can reflect the changes of users' thoughts after generation of the ontology. In addition, we expect to improve the efficiency of retrieval for increasing Internet resources when we apply the semantic relationships obtained from the proposed method in the field of information retrieval. Moreover, by sharing generated ontologies, we can construct semantic web-based intelligence systems in more diverse fields. For the verification of the suggested methodology, we then conduct experiments with a well-known ontology, Pizza Ontology [4] by measuring precision and recall.

2 Related Work

2.1 Ant Colony Optimization (ACO)

ACO, introduced in the early 1990s, is an approximate algorithm to solve the NP-hard problem with a reasonable amount of computation time [5]. In the ACO, each ant is a simple computational agent with the following characteristics [5]. For each iteration of the ACO algorithm, an ant selects the next position (node). Let τ_{ij} be the trail density (density of pheromone) on the edge (i, j). Then, for each iteration of the ACO algorithm, the trail density is updated by Eq. (1):

$$\tau_{ij} = (1 - \rho) \cdot \tau_{ij} + \sum_{k=1}^{m} \Delta \tau_{ij}^{k}$$

$$\Delta \iota_{ij}^{k} = \begin{cases} \frac{Q}{L_k}, & k \text{ th ant arrives the node } (i, j) \\ 0, & \text{other cases} \end{cases} \tag{1}$$

In the above Eq. (1), ρ is the evaporation rate, m is the total number of ants, Q is some constant, and L_k is the tour length of the k-th ant. The proposed method computes pheromones by using model of ACO and Eq. (1).

2.2 Ontology Generation Methods

Studies have been conducted to automate the process of ontology generation using various methodologies [6, 7]. However, the task of generating ontology is still time-consuming, tedious, and difficult. Much work on ontology generation still depends on humans for the manual creation of ontology. Protégé [6] is representative ontology generation tools. This tool provides environment for generating and visualizing ontologies. However, these methods or tools for ontology generation still involve some limitations. In many cases, users still prepare ontologies manually, thus making it difficult to mass-produce diverse fields of lightweight ontologies. In addition, with the rapid increase in user-created contents, many attempts have been made to collaboratively create ontology [3]. A typical ontology development tool is a Collaborative Protégé [8]. In [8], many people can collaboratively create and modify ontology as an extension of Protégé. In Collaborative Protégé, users can search ontology records that other users have changed. This can prevent problems in the process of collaboratively generating ontology. However, Collaborative Protégé has a user interface that is hardly accessible to non-experts. Moreover, we have to rely on the subjective view of the users for the verification of the completed ontology.

3 Definitions

Ontology is a formal, explicit specification of a shared conceptualization in a distributed computing environment [9]. In this paper, we focus on the fundamental RDF ontology generation [10], which is widely used in academic and practical areas. RDF ontology could be extended or included to other expressive ontology languages since OWL shares a lot of characteristics (properties) with RDF [10]. In general, RDF-based ontology consists of triples of concepts, attributes, and semantic relations [9]. Hence, we can represent ontology as triples of (s, r, o), where s, r, and o denote the subject, relationship, and object, respectively. For the cooperative generation of ontology, we define the following four ontologies.

Definition 1 (*Primitive Ontology*) Primitive Ontology (*PO*) is an initial ontology generated by users. Users generate n RDF triples, such as $\{(s_1, r_1, o_1), (s_2, r_2, o_2), \ldots, (s_i, r_i, o_i), \ldots, (s_n, r_n, o_n)$. *PO* is a set of these n RDF triples. Here, s_i, r_i, and o_i denote subject, predicate, and object, respectively. Thus, we can define *PO* in Eq. (2):

$$PO = \{(s_1, r_1, o_1), (s_2, r_2, o_2), \ldots, (s_i, r_i, o_i), \ldots, (s_n, r_n, o_n)\} \tag{2}$$

where $(1 \leq i \leq n)$.

In this method, we can use a variety of relations such as the converse of *is-a*, *is-a-subtype-of*, and user-defined relations.

Definition 2 (*Mediation Ontology*) Mediation Ontology (*MO*) is a collection of all the members of primitive ontologies PO_1, PO_2, ..., PO_m, generated by the m users defined in Eq. (3). Note that there might be duplicate members in *MO*:

$$MO = \bigcup_{i=1}^{m} {}^{*}PO_i \tag{3}$$

In the above Eq. (3), PO_i is a primitive ontology generated by the i-th user, and $\cup^{*}$ is an extension of the union operation of sets that allows duplicate members. For example, if $PO_1 = \{(s_1, r_1, o_1), (s_2, r_2, o_2), (s_3, r_3, o_3)\}$ and $PO_2 = \{(s_4, r_4, o_4), (s_3, r_3, o_3)\}$, then $MO = \{(s_1, r_1, o_1), (s_2, r_2, o_2), (s_3, r_3, o_3), (s_4, r_4, o_4), (s_3, r_3, o_3)\}$. Now, we define the following two sets $A_{s,o}$ and $B_{s,r,o}$, as follows. $A_{s,o}$ is a proper subset of *MO*, where every member in $A_{s,o}$ has identical s and o, as defined in Eq. (4).

$$A_{s,o} = \{(s, r_1, o), (s, r_2, o), \ldots, (s, r_i, o), \ldots, (s, r_l, o)\} \tag{4}$$

where $1 \leq |MO|$, and every element in $A_{s,o}$ has identical s and o.

$B_{s,r,o}$ is a proper subset of $A_{s,o}$, where every member of $B_{s,r,o}$ has the identical s, r, and o, as defined in Eq. (5).

$$B_{s,r,o} = \left\{ (s_1, r_1, o_1), (s_2, r_2, o_2), \ldots, (s_i, r_j, o_i), \ldots, (s_u, r_u, o_u) \right\}$$

where $(1 \leq u \leq |A|)$,

$$(s_1 = s_2 = \cdots = s_u), (r_1 = r_2 = \cdots = r_u), (o_1 = o_2 = \cdots = o_u) \qquad (5)$$

Definition 3 (*Popularity Pheromone*) Popularity pheromone τ represents the popularity index of a relation r that users submit for some subject s and object o. We compute the popularity pheromone τ using the ACO algorithm. We reflect the above Eq. (1), as follows: The pheromone change in Eq. (1) corresponds to the term $\left(\rho \times |B_{s,r,o}| / |A_{s,o}| \right)$ in Eq. (6). This pheromone change denotes the ratio change of distinct predicate r for the identical s and o. Let k be the number of users who submit PO, and ρ be the evaporation rate. Then the popularity pheromone τ can be computed by Eq. (6) for each triple (s, r, o), where $(0 \leq \rho \leq 1)$.

$$\tau(0) - \text{Initial pheromone value } (0 \leq \rho \leq 1)$$
$$\tau(k+1) = (1 - \rho) \cdot \tau(k) + \rho \cdot \left(|B_{s,r,o}| / |A_{s,o}| \right) \qquad (6)$$

Due to intrinsic characteristics of collaborative ontology generation method which many users participate and generate new knowledge, we assume that any new knowledge (i.e. relations r between s and o) generated by most users is always correct.

Definition 4 (*Popular Ontology*) Popular Ontology (LO) is the proper subset of *MO*, where every triple element (s, r, o) in *LO* satisfies the following three conditions. First, the pheromone value τ of (s, r, o) should exceed the threshold value ε since an imprecise, incorrect ontology may be selected as a popular ontology when the threshold value is too small. This indicates that the higher the threshold value ε, the more precise the ontology is generated. The threshold value is decided heuristically. Second, we only select the triple with the largest pheromone value τ, where $0.1 < \varepsilon \leq 1$ if there are some triples in *MO* with identical s and o. Finally, if the value of τ exceeds ε, and the triple element (s, r, o) has the highest value of τ, we regard it as being popular. If there exist more than or equal to two relations for the triple with identical s and o, the method does not select it as being popular. In this paper, we set the threshold value ε larger than 0.5 to prevent the highest pheromone values from being identical. Consequently, it does not allow user to generate two identical ontologies with the highest pheromone values, which are larger than the threshold value ε.

Table 1 shows the proposed ontology generation algorithm using ACO, which demonstrates sequential procedures of *LO* generation. User accounts and their social interactions are used as each input and output in the CollectUserInteractions method of Table 1. The method collects user activity data, such as user information and relations of the data, from the social web, and then filters abnormally generated data, which are not needed for ontology generation.

Table 1 Algorithm for ACO based ontology generation

	Input: [user accounts]	// Step 0 – Loading
	Output: Popular Ontology	// and initializing
		// raw data
	// Step 1 – Generation of *PO*	
1	*socialInterations* ← **CollectUserInteractions**([*user accounts*])	// Initialize the
2	*i* ← 0	// number of *PO*
3	**while** (*number of user accounts*)	
4	**Divide** each user's *socialInteractions* to (*s, r, o*)	
5	*PO_i* ← *socialInteractions_i*	
6	*i* ← *i* + 1	
7	**end while**	
	// Step 2 – Generation of *MO*	
8	*MO* ← $\cup_{i=1}^{m}$ * *PO_i*	
9	**Generate** set $A_{s, o}$ and $B_{s, r, o}$	
	// Step 3 – Calculation of Pheromone value	
10	*j* ← *number of sub sets of MO*	
11	**while**(*j*)	// Calculate
12	**Calculate** *pheromone*	// pheromone
13	**end while**	// by Equation 6
	// Step 4 – Generation *LO*	
14	**while**(*j*)	
15	**if** ($MO_{(max(pheromone\ \tau)\ or\ (pheromone\ \tau\ \geq\ \varepsilon))}$)	
16	**Add** MO_j to *LO*	// Generate *LO*
17	**end if**	
18	**end while**	
19	*PopularOntology* ← **Convert**(*LO* to *RDF triple*)	
20	**return** *PopularOntology*	

4 The Proposed System Architecture and Its Implements

Figure 1 shows the system architecture and its components. The system is constructed using the plug-in programs of the WordPress blog tool, thus allowing users to generate primitive ontology easily. The left hand side of Fig. 1 shows the end user system that is used to generate the primitive ontology. The format manager of the end user system gets the primitive ontology from the users, and saves it to the ontology repository. Knowledge Viewer shows the users' primitive ontologies and popular ontologies. The right hand side of Fig. 1 shows the server system that receives the primitive ontologies from the users, and generates the *MO*. The server system consists of three modules: (1) PO collector, (2) MO generator, and (3) LO generator.

PO collector receives the primitive ontologies from the users, and deposits it to the server. *MO* generator keeps the semantic relation in the database. It computes the two sets *A* and *B* as defined in Eqs. (4) and (5). *LO* generator computes the pheromone values, and then generates the *MO*. Note that the *MO* generated by the *LO* generator is kept in the mediation ontology repository. When there is a request from the end user system, the *MO* repository sends the kept mediation ontology to the end user system.

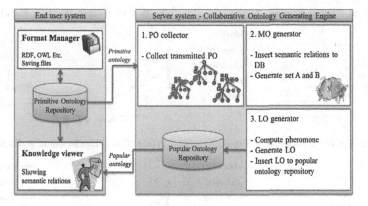

Fig. 1 System architecture

5 Performance Study

For justification of the suggested method, we give keywords for pizza and its toppings to 100 non-expert users without orders, and generate a primitive ontology for the pizza and its toppings. Hence, there are 100 primitive ontologies in this implementation example. We generate mediation ontologies, which have 209 connecting relations, from these 100 primitive ontologies. We heuristically set $\rho = 0.1$, pheromone value $\tau = 0.3$, for the initial values to construct the popular ontology.

Figure 2a, b shows the pheromone value changes for the scenario in Sect. 5.1. As the number of users who input two triples (*Pizza*, *isToppingOf*, *Pizza*) and (*SpicyPizza*, *isA*, *Pizza*) increases, the corresponding pheromone value also gradually increases. The pheromone value gradually decreases from the initial value 0.3, due to the relatively small number of users who input different relations. As shown in Fig. 2a, b, the popularity pheromone value τ of a triple (s, r, o) that users recognize increases from the initial value, and approaches to 1. Otherwise, in the case of relation r that users do not recognize, the pheromone value decreases, and thus comes close to 0. Figure 2c shows another example of pheromone value changes. The figure shows that the changes of pheromone values do not come close to 1 when users are confused on the relation of the same subject s and object o. In this case, the proposed method does not select the generated knowledge as a popular ontology since the pheromone values cannot be higher than the threshold value ε. Figure 2d demonstrates how generated ontology can be evolved. Our proposed method is able to reflect the users' change of thoughts, by computing pheromone values. In this figure, the users have thought '*PizzaTopping* has a relation *isToppingOf* with *Pizza*' from timeslot 1–56, but their thoughts have been changed as '*PizzaTopping* has a relation *hasTopping* with *Pizza*' as time goes by after timeslot 57. At time 96, two pheromone values approach to the same value, and will be changed reversely, depending on changes of the users' thoughts. In this

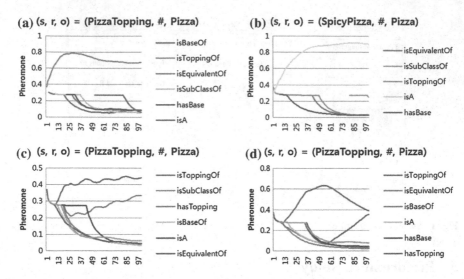

Fig. 2 Pheromone updates about various views in proposed method

case, the suggested method does not select this knowledge as a popular ontology, while the method selects the previous knowledge as a popular ontology. The reason is that the pheromone value should be higher than the threshold value ε with the highest pheromone value. From the Fig. 2d, we are intuitively aware of the pheromone values cannot be higher than 0.5 when there exist two different relations on the same subject s and object o.

To verity the proposed method, we apply the method to the Pizza Ontology, and then compare the generated ontology and the original Pizza Ontology with respect to recall and precision ratio. Precision ratio is the value dividing number of popular ontologies into number of correct relations with comparison to relations in the ground truth ontology, indicating the rate of the correctly determined relations by users. Recall ratio is the value dividing number of relations in popular ontologies into number of relations in the ground truth ontology. Figure 3 shows the results of precision and recall between the ontology generated by our method, and the Pizza Ontology, with respect to a parameter such as the initial popularity pheromone value τ. As shown in Fig. 3, the ontology generated by the suggested method in this paper is satisfactory, i.e. the precision and recall of the ontology are 94.44 and 99.6 %, respectively, with a range of popularity pheromone from 0.3 to 0.6.

Fig. 3 Precision and recall with respect to the popularity pheromone value τ

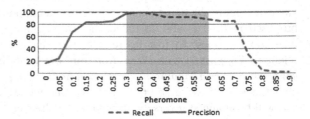

6   Conclusion

In this paper, we propose a method by which many users can partake in generating ontology using ACO algorithms. We use primitive, mediation, and popular ontologies mentioned in Sect. 3 in order to construct collaborative ontology generation method. For the verification of our method, we asked 100 non-experts to make primitive ontologies on pizza and pizza toppings using our systems. We then compared the generated ontologies to that of Pizza Ontologies. The results show 94 and 99 % of precision and recall, respectively. We can now demonstrate that non-experts can also partake in ontology creation. The strength of our method is that through the participation of many users, we can efficiently generate relatively accurate ontologies since the more users are participated in ontology generation, the more precise computations of each pheromone are. Moreover, our method can be widely used, compared to other ontologies that are confined to specific domains, which may be used in limited domains. By using our method in this paper, we can use ontologies needed for the introduction of semantic web-based applications, without much time and cost. Our method also enables users to create and share knowledge via the standard pattern of knowledge representation. This makes a foundation for developing various semantic web-based applications in future.

References

1. Berners-Lee T, Hendler J, Lassila O (2001) The semantic web. A new form of web content that is meaningful to computers will unleash a revolution of new possibilities. Sci Am 284:1–5
2. O'reilly T (2007) What is Web 2.0: design patterns and business models for the next generation of software. Commun Strat 65:17
3. Siorpaes K, Hepp M (2007) myOntology: the marriage of ontology engineering and collective intelligence. Bridg Gep Semant Web Web 2:127–138
4. Drummond N, Horridge M, Stevens R, Wroe C, Sampaio S (2007) Pizza ontology. The University of Manchester
5. Dorigo M, Blum C (2005) Ant colony optimization theory: a survey. Theoret Comput Sci 344:243–278
6. Gennari JH, Musen MA, Fergerson RW, Grosso WE, Crubézy M, Eriksson H et al (2003) The evolution of Protégé: an environment for knowledge-based systems development. Int J Hum Comput Stud 58:89–123
7. Maedche A (2002) Ontology learning for the semantic web. Springer Science & Business Media
8. Tudorache T, Noy NF, Musen MA (2008) Collaborative protege: enabling community-based authoring of ontologies. In: International semantic web conference (Posters & Demos)
9. Fensel D (2000) Ontologies: a silver bullet for knowledge management and electronic-commerce. Berlin: Spring-Verlag
10. Horrocks I, Patel-Schneider PF, Van Harmelen F (2003) From SHIQ and RDF to OWL: the making of a web ontology language. Web Semant Sci Serv Agents World Wide Web 1:7–26

An Approach for User Interests Extraction Using Decision Tree and Social Network Analysis

Jeungmin Lee, Hansaem Park, Kyunglag Kwon, Yunwan Jeon,
Sungwoo Jung and In-Jeong Chung

Abstract In this paper, we propose an effective extraction method for acquiring the interests of users from Social Network Services (SNSs). In the proposed approach, a domain ontology generated by a decision tree is first used to classify domain webpages and each user. A Social Network Analysis (SNA) method is then used to analyze the tags from the Friend-Of-A-Friend (FOAF) profiles of each user; after which, we obtained the interests of the users. The results of an experiment conducted to obtain the interests of 2012 USA presidential candidates indicate that the precision and accuracy of our approach are 91.5 and 93.1 % in classifying the users, respectively.

Keywords Social network service (SNS) · Social network analysis (SNA) · Friend-Of-A-Friend (FOAF) · Interests extraction

J. Lee · H. Park · K. Kwon · Y. Jeon · S. Jung · I.-J. Chung (✉)
Korea University, Seoul, Republic of Korea
e-mail: chung@korea.ac.kr

J. Lee
e-mail: wjdals543@korea.ac.kr

H. Park
e-mail: park11232000@korea.ac.kr

K. Kwon
e-mail: helpnara@korea.ac.kr

Y. Jeon
e-mail: juw123@korea.ac.kr

S. Jung
e-mail: sigran0@korea.ac.kr

© Springer Science+Business Media Singapore 2016   551
J.J. (Jong Hyuk) Park et al. (eds.), *Advanced Multimedia and Ubiquitous Engineering*, Lecture Notes in Electrical Engineering 393,
DOI 10.1007/978-981-10-1536-6_72

1 Introduction

The birth of Social Network Services (SNSs) signaled that the development of networks is entering a new era [1]. The SNSs are a virtual cornucopia of useful information, such as the interests of users. A report in 2013 showed that approximately 83 % of people between the ages of 18 and 29 years, and 77 % of people between the ages of 30 and 49 years, use online social networks [2]. The interests of users play an important role in a variety of areas such as politics. The interests of users in a specific domain are different from those of individual or general users. Users in the same domain have common interests, the same universality, since the users are in the same domain, and a different personality than users from a different domain. Therefore, the value of the interests of users in a specific domain is greater than that of individual or general users in other fields. However, before the interests of specified users can be acquired, the following two difficulties must first be overcome: (a) how to define the domain for users, and (b) how to classify the users from different domain. These difficulties exist because a computer does not have the ability to understand the underlying semantics, thus making it hard to define a domain for users and to classify the users from different domains. Consequently, to deal with these two problems, we propose an effective method for the extraction of users' interests from SNSs.

In our proposed approach, a domain ontology generated by a decision tree is used to classify domain webpages and users. Then, with the aid of Social Network Analysis (SNA) method, we analyze the tags from Friend-Of-A-Friend (FOAF) profiles of the users and their interests, and show feasibility of the proposed method, considering social and politics issues from the analyzed data [3, 4]. To verify the efficacy of our proposed method, we conducted experiments in which we obtained the interests of users in the domain of 2012 USA presidential candidates. The results show that the precision and accuracy are 91.5 and 93.1 % in classifying the users, respectively—which confirm that the interests of users in the specific domain obtained are reliable.

2 The Proposed System

Figure 1 shows the overall architecture of the system. The system consists of four parts: (a) generation of decision tree and domain ontology, (b) classification of domain webpages and users, and (c) acquisition of interests of users using SNA.

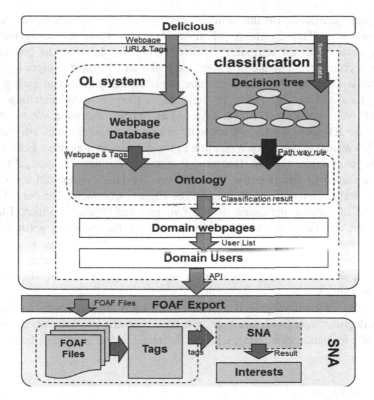

Fig. 1 Architecture of our proposed system

2.1 Generation of Decision Tree and Domain Ontology

Computers are unable to classify the different users using traditional classification schemes due to an inability to understand the meaning of the data. We therefore propose a classification method based on a decision tree to generate the domain ontology and to classify the domain webpages. A decision tree is a popular classifier whose samples are subjected to a sequence of decision rules before they are assigned to a unique class [5]. As the keywords in the tree are used to paraphrase the domain, we use the keywords to describe the webpage in this paper. In addition, a one-to-one correspondence can be established between the attributes in the tree and the keywords. Furthermore, every pathway of the decision tree can be written in a tag rule using Web Ontology Language-Description Logic (OWL-DL); thus, the sub-tree can be translated into the domain ontology without loss, to achieve classification based on semantics. Hence, we obtain a number of training datasets from the Delicious website and generate a domain decision tree that we use to generate the domain ontology.

For the generation of the domain decision tree, we utilize the Iterative Dichotomiser 3 (ID3) algorithm [6]. It builds the decision tree using the given training datasets to test attributes. The following are the steps to generate the domain decision tree. For the first step, we make an ID3 table comprising all the keywords and classes. We then determine the relationships between each piece of training data and the keywords. In the data, if there is a tag matching with a keyword, we record the cell of the keyword as "YES"; otherwise, we record it as "NO" in the ID3 table. Lastly, we compute information gain for each attribute (i.e., tags or keywords) to determine a position in the domain decision tree. For example, seven keywords (e.g. Obama, Romney, Bachmann, Politics, Election, 2012, and Class) are used to describe the kinds of domains such as candidates Obama, Romney, and Bachmann. The webpage "The Choice: Comment: The New Yorker" is a piece of training data, and its top five tags are Obama, Politics, Election, Newyorker, and Endorsement. Next, by comparing the seven keywords with the five tags, we find that Obama, politics, and election match with three keywords. In the ID3 table, we thus record the cell of Obama, politics, and election as "YES," and others as "NO". Finally, all training data are recorded in the ID3 table, as shown in Table 1.

After the information gain is calculated for each attribute, we can draw the domain decision tree. Every attribute will have a position in accordance with the results of information gain. Next, with the domain decision tree created, we make a

Table 1 The ID3 table

Obama	Romney	Bachmann	Politics	Election	2012	Class
NO	NO	YES	YES	NO	YES	Bachmann
NO	NO	YES	YES	NO	NO	Other
NO	NO	NO	NO	NO	NO	Other
NO	YES	YES	NO	NO	NO	Other
NO	NO	YES	NO	NO	NO	Other
YES	NO	YES	NO	NO	NO	Other
NO	NO	YES	YES	YES	NO	Bachmann
NO	NO	YES	NO	NO	NO	Other
NO	NO	YES	YES	NO	NO	Other
NO	NO	YES	YES	NO	YES	Bachmann
NO	NO	YES	YES	NO	YES	Bachmann
NO	NO	YES	YES	YES	YES	Bachmann
NO	NO	YES	NO	NO	NO	Other
NO	NO	YES	NO	NO	NO	Other
NO	NO	YES	NO	YES	NO	Other
NO	NO	YES	NO	NO	NO	Other
YES	NO	YES	YES	NO	YES	Other
NO	NO	YES	NO	YES	YES	Bachmann

domain ontology. In the domain decision tree, there are several pathways to go to different classes via different sub-trees, which means that the same class might have several different pathways. Each pathway consists of several keywords, and it can be expressed as a tag rule using OWL DL. According to the computation results of information gain, the keywords, Obama, election, and Romney, play an important role as attributes in a pathway of the domain decision tree. We thus utilize OWL DL to represent a tag rule for the pathway determined in the domain decision tree as follows: Obama Π election $\Pi\neg$ Romney. In the same manner, with the selected top five tags, each tag rule can be generated for each webpage from the Delicious website. Each tag rule is stored in the webpage database of the Ontology Learning (OL) system. Consequently, for all the pathways in the decision tree, we express each tag rule using OWL DL to represent each class in the domain ontology.

3.3 Classification of Domain Webpages and Users

For inference and classification of the webpage, the data is used to train the domain ontology. Additionally, an Ontology Learning (OL) system is added for ontology learning and classification. The OL system is composed of data storage, learning, and inference sections. We first store a large amount of webpage data, which consists of the URLs of webpages and tags, in the database. We represent each tag rule for each webpage, to infer the class of the webpage, based on the top 5 tags of the webpage using OWL DL. For example, if there is a webpage which consists of URL and tag rule, it goes to the class "Delicious Webpage" of ontology. If the tag rule of the webpage exists in the class "Delicious Webpage," we create a new instance to store the URL, and the instance belongs to the subclass $Condition_n$ that has the same tag rule. If the tag rule of the webpage does not exist in the class "Delicious Webpage," we create a new subclass $Condition_{n+1}$, and store the tag rule as a property in $Condition_{n+1}$. We then create a new instance to store the URL and the instance that belongs to subclass $Condition_{n+1}$. Next, let the tag go to the class "WebpageTag" of ontology. For the same class "Delicious Webpage," if the tag exists in the class, we create a new instance to store the tag and the instance that belongs to subclass Tag_n in the same class. For instance, USA and America belong to the same subclass USA. If the tag does not exist in the class "WebpageTag," we create a new subclass Tag_{n+1}, and then create a new instance to store the tag and the instance that belongs to subclass Tag_{n+1}. When we classify the domain webpage from the Delicious website by domain ontology, the user is easily obtained because we can get a user list of each webpage from the Delicious website. This indicates that a user will be listed in the user list when he or she collects the webpage on the Delicious website. Thus, when the domain webpage is acquired, the lists of users are also obtained.

2.3   *Extraction of Interests of Users Using SNA*

In this step, we get the FOAF profile of each user from the Delicious website using FOAF Export provided by the website. On the Delicious website, users can collect the webpages they like and then mark the webpages using tags. Thus, the users' tags can describe the trend of users' interests if we analyze them. In the proposed system, we use SNA to analyze the tags that come from the FOAF profiles of users, thus enabling us to obtain the interests of users. Next, we extract the top five tags from the collected FOAF profiles of users. The top five most often-used tags represent the contents that are of most concern to users. If the tags of users are considered the interests of users, then the top five tags are the interests that match the preference of users.

We build a social network that consists of users and the top five tags of each user. Using SNA, we then analyze the relationship between users and tags, and obtain the domain interests. To be specific, we use degree centrality analysis, which indicates the importance of each node. First, we calculate degree centrality to find the interests of users because degree centrality measures the activity of the network for each node by using the concept of degrees [7]. We find the nodes that connect the most number of users. This means that most of the users have some similar interests in the same domain. Next, we utilize Freeman's Approach [8]. An interest is a kind of tag that is mentioned and used by the users. From the social network, it is likely to be some interests that are popular with users if each tag of users is regarded as the interests of users. We thus extract interests from the users' tags by calculating degree centrality.

3   Performance Study

3.1   *Data Description*

To make the decision tree for domains, we randomly collect a dataset consisting of the top five tags and webpage links from the Delicious website, and then store them in the form of a table. In the experiment, we chose 2012 U.S. presidential candidates to be validated for domains. The candidates chosen were Barack Obama from the Democratic Party, and Mitt Romney and Michele Bachmann from the Republican Party. In the collected dataset, there were 497,849 webpages about Obama, 12,271 webpages about Romney, and 4570 webpages about Bachmann on the website, respectively. One hundred of the webpages for each candidate were randomly collected for the experiments. We then took 60 Obama, Romney, and Bachmann webpages from the Delicious website as a training dataset to make the ID3 table for the decision tree.

3.2 Results

We calculated the information gain according to the ID3 algorithm and determined all attributes of the decision tree. With Obama, Romney, and Bachmann as candidates, three domains were contained in the same tree, as shown in Fig. 2. The sub-trees expressed the class of candidates Obama, Bachmann, and Romney, respectively.

In a decision tree, every pathway is described by OWL DL-based rules. Based on all rules from the tree, we made ontology to classify the experimental data, and separated it into three different classes, as shown in Fig. 3.

The webpages in the three classes (100 webpages per class) were then classified by ontology. First, 21 webpages and the available 91 links for candidate Obama were extracted from 100 webpages. Next, 24 webpages and the available 88 links for candidate Romney were extracted from 100 webpages. Finally, 26 webpages and the available 99 links for candidate Bachmann were extracted from 100 webpages. After obtaining the webpages for the three candidates, the users were also extracted from the Delicious website. Using the FOAF Export tool, we extracted the top five most frequently used tags from the collected FOAF profiles of users in the domain webpages. Next, we built three social networks, with each social network comprising users and their own tags. We then analyzed the three social networks with measurement of the degree centrality for each tag, and acquired the interests of the users from the three different social networks of the domains.

From the results in Table 2, we can see that the users in the different domains have different interests. For instance, users in the domains of the three candidates are focused on politics, the economy, and other areas—in that order. In the domains of the different candidates, there is only minor difference in the interests of users. In addition to the politics domain, we conduct experiments for the other domains such as guns and daily life. Users in the domain of guns clearly prefer arms, while the

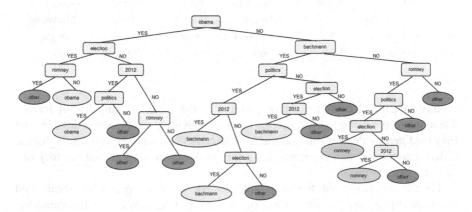

Fig. 2 The decision tree generated for the three domains

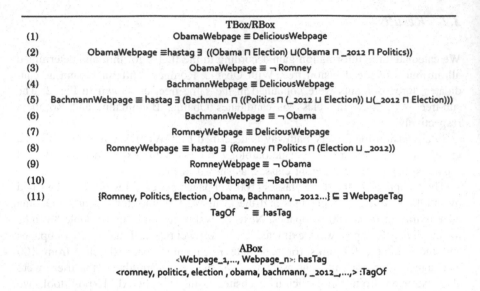

Fig. 3 An example of the generated domain ontology

Table 2 Comparison with different users' interests

No	Obama	Romney	Bachmann	Rifle	Pistol	Normal
1	Politics	Politics	Politics	Gun	Gun	Blog
2	Design	Election	Health	Firearm	Software	Business
3	Obama	Obama	Education	Howto	Blog	Advertising
4	Blog	Iraq	Economy	Software	Shopping	Book
5	Education	Religion	Science	Rifle	Firearms	Art
6	Video	Economics	Reference	Shopping	Howto	Video
7	Tools	Romney	Writing	Blog	Web	Money
8	Photography	News	Funny	AR-15	Glock	Marketing
9	Reference	2008	Religion	Politics	Pistols	Google
10	Inspiration	Books	Food	Survival	Survival	Free

domain of general users pay more attention to the areas of daily life of leisure. These interests belong to most users as well as individuals in the same domain, and they hold great value for different fields. The classified and analyzed results for the different users and their interests using the proposed method are satisfactory and reliable.

For the evaluation of the proposed method, we used precision, recall, and accuracy [9]. Figure 4 shows a set of the results with respect to the candidate Obama, Romney, Bachmann classes, respectively. Each figure shows that the

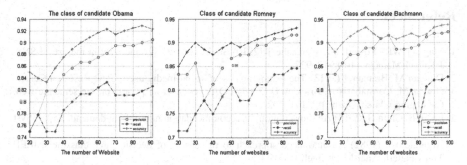

Fig. 4 Precision, recall, and accuracy curves for the domains of three candidates

curves for precision, recall, and accuracy as the number of classified webpages increases. In Fig. 4, we omitted the section of the curves corresponding to the number of webpages being less than 20. In the graph of the domain of candidate Obama, all webpages were classified, and the precision and accuracy were found to be 90.5 and 92.3 %, respectively. We computed precision and accuracy for the other two domains in the same manner. Precision for the Romney and Bachmann domains was 91.5 and 92.3 %, and accuracy was 93.1 and 93.9 %, respectively. Thus, the average values for precision and accuracy in the three domains were 91.5 and 93.1 %, respectively.

Although the details are different, the trends shown by the curves in all three domains are almost similar. Moreover, precision and accuracy increase as the number of webpages that are classified increases. In accordance with the development trends of the curves, we can conclude that when the number of classified webpages increases steadily, the precision and accuracy of the classification of our proposed approach are not less than 91.5 and 93.1 %, respectively.

4 Conclusion

In this paper, we proposed an effective user interests extraction method that utilizes semantic web technology such as OWL DL to describe tag rules and FOAF to define the domain of users for classification of the different users. In our proposed method, the domain ontology, generated by a domain decision tree, then classifies the domain webpages and their users, after which SNA is used to analyze the tags that come from the FOAF profiles of users, and to obtain the interests of the users. To verify the efficacy of our proposed method, we conducted an experiment in which we collated the interests of users who voted for USA presidential candidates. The results obtained in the experiment indicate that our proposed method has a high level of precision and accuracy in classifying users, and the obtained interests of users grow more reliable as more webpages are added to the classification.

References

1. Magnier WR, Yoshida M, Watanabe T (2010) Social network productivity in the use of SNS. J Knowl Manage 14(6):910–927
2. Duggan M, Brenner J (2013) The demographics of social media users. Pew Research Center
3. Graves M, Constabaris A, Brickley D (2007) FOAF: connecting people on the semantic web. Cataloging Classif Quart, pp. 191–202
4. Leem B, Chun H (2013) An impact of online recommendation network on demand. Expert Syst Appl
5. Argentiero P (1982) An automated approach to the design of decision tree classifiers. IEEE Trans Pattern Anal Mach Intell PAMI-4(1)
6. López Mántaras R (1991) A distance-based attribute selection measure for decision tree induction. Mach Learn 6(1):81–92. doi:10.1007/BF00153761
7. Buchwald D, Dick RW (2011) Weaving the native web: using social network analysis to demonstrate the value of a minority career development program. Acad Med 86(6):778–786
8. Elouaer S (2006) Boardroom networks among French companies, 1996 and 2005. Mimeo
9. van Rijsbergen CJ (1979) Information retrieval

Real-Time Line Marker Detection for Night-Time Blind Spot Monitoring System in Suburb Area

Kang Yi, Daewoo Kim and Kyeong-Hoon Jung

Abstract This paper presents a road line marker detection method in order to support night-time Blind Spot Monitor (BSM). In our BSM system, to detect vehicles in blind spot in a real-time manner, line mark detection method is necessary for the determination of exact detection window location and size. We developed a fast line marker detection method which is robust in the night-time suburb environment. Our method depends on the dividing windows and adopting local thresholds of line marker intensity for each window adaptively. We demonstrate a reliable detection performance in a real road environment and our method is light to achieve real-time operation in embedded ADAS devices.

1 Introduction

According to the Statistics from the National Highway Traffic Safety Administration of United States, about 840,000 blind-spot accident occurs in each year resulting in 300 fatalities [1]. Thus, the Blind Spot Monitor (BSM) is necessary as a core function of Advanced Driver Assistance System (ADAS) for safe driving maneuver. Line marker detection is required for our real-time BSM system presented in [2]. In this paper, we present a line mark detection to support the operation of BSM which relies on the line markers information of rear side. Our focus is detecting line markers at night time in rural area which is quite challenging problem due to wild illumination condition.

K. Yi (✉) · D. Kim
School of CSEE, Handong Global University, Pohang, Republic of Korea
e-mail: yk@handong.edu

D. Kim
e-mail: w00606@hotmail.com

K.-H. Jung
School of EE, Kookmin University, Seoul, Republic of Korea
e-mail: khjung@kookmin.ac.kr

© Springer Science+Business Media Singapore 2016   561
J.J. (Jong Hyuk) Park et al. (eds.), *Advanced Multimedia and Ubiquitous Engineering*, Lecture Notes in Electrical Engineering 393,
DOI 10.1007/978-981-10-1536-6_73

There are many efforts on the lane detection and line marker detection. Some works including [3] are based on simple technique of edge detection followed by Hough transform. In order to overcome the proper threshold selection problem for the edge detection, a layered approach for night-time lane detection was presented in [4] by means of temporal frame averaging. Another approach performs inverse perspective transform before performing any edge and line detection [5]. Likelihood of Image Shape LOIS in [6] used Likelihood function of image shape into line marker detection system. Algorithm in [7] depends on the frequency domain features of the lane markings. The lane detection and tracking research area is a mature area as surveyed by [8].

But, most of the existing studies have interest in line marker detection problem in the front side of ego vehicle while our interest in lane detection is on the line markers in the rear side which has very low illumination at night time. The purpose of existing line marker detection works is mainly to generate control signals for moving direction or to generate forward collision warning. On the other hand, our purpose of line marker detection is to support our BSM system which monitors the rear side of ego vehicle. Therefore, the approach and constraints of our problem are different from those of conventional line marker detection. Note that the night time detection of lanes in front view is not so challenging problem because the constant well lighting condition is guaranteed by the front headlamp light of ego vehicle. One of the challenging points in our rear-side line marker detection problem for night time is to determine the proper threshold values for the line markers under the low illumination conditions and the varying lighting condition due to the lights from the head lamp of vehicles approaching in rear side of next lanes.

Our key approach is two folds: The first key is to divide the detection windows into several sub windows and to find local threshold based on the analysis on the sub detection window intensity distribution. The second key is to change the *changing weight* (α) of the current line that is used for moving average computation of line information. The weight, α, for the current detection is computed based on the *prediction trust index* of detection results.

2 Our Problem of Line Mark Detection for BSM

The BSM presented in [2] uses a single rear-view camera which may be a second channel of car black-box camera or a back-up camera used for rear-side monitor. Our idea is to use the existing rear-view camera to monitor the blind spot area that the side mirrors cannot cover.

As shown in Fig. 1, the blind spots uncovered by the side mirrors exists in the next lane area but, by using wide angle rear-view camera, the dead zone can be almost monitored. In order to achieve a real-time performance of detecting the vehicles approaching to the blind spots at rear side, we need to select a detection window based on the road line marker information. If we have the line marker

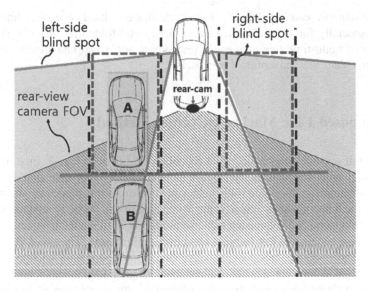

Fig. 1 The blind spot in the rear side can be monitored by the rear-view camera

information, the detection can be localized by means of vanishing point and line markers intersection coordinates.

But, in the nigh time it is a very challenging problem to detect the line markers constantly and reliably as shown in Fig. 2. We have three main hurdles to detect line markers at night time. (1) The illumination of rear side of ego vehicle is very low, especially, in the rural area. Sometimes any line cannot be seen because of total absence of lights. In that extreme case the line detection algorithm should be careful not to incorrectly find lines. (2) The bright lights from approaching vehicle results in wide variances of illumination in terms of space and time in each local area. This problem inhibits finding proper threshold values for the line marker colors because the global mean value of intensity in the ROI becomes too high due to the headlight lights. (3) Different light colors of headlights, streetlamp, and even

Fig. 2 Sample frames from rear view camera for night-time BSM

the rear window coating film of ego vehicle make it hard to extract lines using color, especially for yellow color. Due to these three folded hurdles, the detection problem of night-time line markers in rear side is not trivial and should be solved differently than the conventional approaches.

3   Proposed Line Marker Detection Method

The overall our line marker detection algorithm is shown in Fig. 3. First, the algorithm starts with determining the Region of Interest (ROI) for detection in an input frame to minimize the computing load and maximize the detection accuracy by limiting the detection area. Usually, the lower area of the frame is selected to detect line markers to exclude confusing background lights from the ROI. The input image is very noisy because of low lighting condition at night time. Therefore, it should be preprocessed to reduce noise by median filter. Then, the converted into grayscale image is used to for the next steps. The intensity of grayscale image is used to detect white and yellow lines since the color filter accuracy is not reliable in night time images. But, the finding the proper threshold value for white and yellow color of line

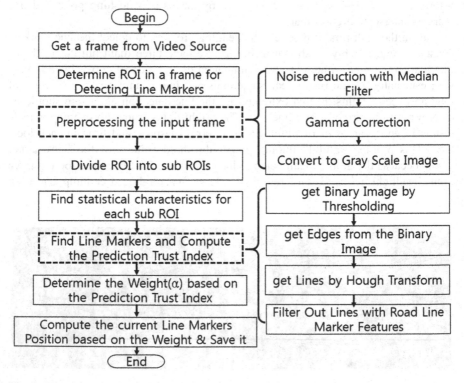

Fig. 3 The proposed algorithm flowchart

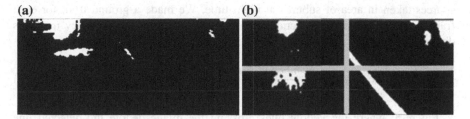

Fig. 4 The results of binarization of ROI for line detection. **a** By using single threshold, **b** By using multiple thresholds

marker is very challenging problem. The problem is caused from the non-uniformity of road color and intensity because of various different surrounding light sources such as approaching vehicle headlight and streetlights. The background intensity in an ROI of a frame varies from one corner to another. This problem makes the single threshold of intensity useless as shown in Fig. 4a. To overcome this problem we divided the ROI into several sub ROIs and compute the statistical characteristics of each ROI as shown in Fig. 4b. Based on the mean and variance values of each sub ROI, the binary image of ROI is computed by the threshold operation. With the binary image, edge detection and line detection is performed by Canny and Hough transform, respectively. Next step is screening line candidates by means of road line marker-specific features including the angles of slopes and width of lane.

It is unavoidable totally to exclude noise information in the detection results. For example, some lines are detected incorrectly and some frames has no visible lines due to the absence of nearby light sources. Because of this limitation, current detection results are not directly considered as the answer for the current line marker information. And, the line marker information is updated by use of moving average of current and of previously accumulated information by the degree of α as shown in (1). We compute the weight of current information, α, based on the Prediction Trust Index which is computed as a function of the amount of noise, ROI lighting condition, and line detection results. For example, if the trust index is very low the value of α is 0 which means we use the prediction of the previous frame as current frame prediction. And, if the trust index is very high we set α as 1.0 to immediately change the prediction of line marker information.

$$\text{LineInfo}_{\text{accum}}{}^{i} = \alpha \cdot \text{LineInfo}_{\text{current}}{}^{i} + (1 - \alpha) \cdot \text{LineInfo}_{\text{accum}}{}^{i-1} \tag{1}$$

4 Experimental Results

We have implemented the proposed line marker detection algorithm with OpenCV 2.4.10 library and C++. To demonstrate the performance of our approach, we measured the run time and detection accuracy of our algorithm with real video sources taken in area of suburbs at night time. We made a ground truth for each frame and compared the detection with the ground truth. The accuracy metric is defined in (2).

$$Accuracy = \frac{Number\ of\ Successfully\ Detected\ Frames}{Total\ Number\ of\ Frames}. \tag{2}$$

Figure 5, where the yellow lines crossing the image denote the detected line markers, shows several detection results by the proposed method. It can be found that the line markers are well detected at night-time even in rural or suburbs area where the lighting conditions are quite poor and timely and spatially varying.

Table 1 shows the accuracies of the proposed method according to three criteria. For the accuracy evaluation, we use three different criteria in terms of pixel position and line slope error tolerance as follows; Criterion 1: ±16 pixels and ±0.15 slope, Criterion 2: ±24 pixels and ±0.15 slope, and Criterion 3: ±32 pixels and ±0.20 slope. The 16 pixel corresponds to the line marker width in our case. As expected, the accuracies of using criterion 3 are the highest because criterion 3 allows the largest margin among the three criteria. Generally, theses accuracies are sufficiently high to be used for night-time BSM. Also, the proposed method can be successfully implemented in real time since every run times are less than 1/30 s.

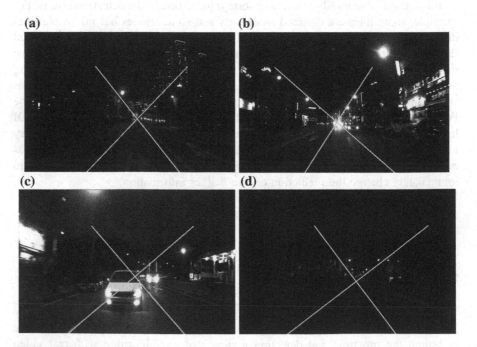

Fig. 5 The detection results of line markers (color figure online)

Table 1 Accuracy and run time of the proposed method

	Number of frames	Accuracy			Run time (ms/frame)
		Criterion 1 (%)	Criterion 2 (%)	Criterion 3 (%)	
Video1	511	99.22	99.61	100	24.37
Video2	382	87.17	94.24	96.34	23.29
Video3	291	81.10	84.54	86.60	24.56
Video4	386	92.50	95.34	97.93	23.58
Video5	184	94.02	99.46	100	23.95
Total	1754	91.56	94.98	96.52	23.95

5   Conclusions

In this paper, we present a road line marker detection algorithm which can be applied for blind spot monitoring using a rear-view camera. Especially, our system targets the night-time suburbs streets environment where the illumination condition is very poor and the non-uniformity of light source is the main hurdle. By dividing the window into several sub-regions and adopting adaptive multiple thresholds, a real-time robust line marker detection method was developed. The detection accuracy and computational complexity feasibility were shown by the experimental results. The proposed method can be combined with night-time vehicle detection [8] for more accurate detection.

Acknowledgments This work was supported by the Center for Integrated Smart Sensors funded by the Ministry of Science, ICT and Future Planning as "Global Frontier Project" (CISS-2011-0031863).

References

1. Blind Spot Accidents (2013) http://www.fortheinjured.com/blind-spot-accident.html
2. Jung K, Yi K (2015) Determination of moving direction by the pose transition of vehicle in blind spot area. In: IEEE international symposium on consumer electronics (ISCE-2015), Madrid, pp. 1–2
3. McDonald J (2001) Detecting and tracking road markings using the Hough transform. In: Irish machine vision and image processing conference
4. Borkar A et al (2009) layered approach to robust lane detection at night, In: IEEE computer intelligence in vehicles and vehicular systems (CIVVS), pp. 51–57
5. Parajuli A, Celenk M, Riley HB (2013) Robust Lane detection in shadows and low illumination conditions using local gradient features, Open J Appl Sci, pp. 68–74

6. Lakshmanan S, Kluge K (1996) LOIS: a real-time lane detection algorithm. In: 30th Annual conference of information science systems, pp. 1007–1012
7. Kreucher C, Lakshmanan S (1999) LANA: a lane extraction algorithm that uses frequency domain features. IEEE Trans Robot Autom 15(2):343–350
8. Zhang Z, Hui C et al (2015) Nighttime vehicle detection for heavy trucks. Internet Veh Safe Intell Mob LNCS 9502:164–175

Research and Application of Ocean Environment Data Visualization Technology Based on MATLAB

Jin Hong Li, Qiu Qi Yang and Wei Song

Abstract Data visualization is a science and technology research on visual representation of the data, it puts the data into a form of visual information and knowledge, and makes full use of people natural ability of quickly identify visual patterns to understand the data. Through data visualization technology, data can be performed intuitively and clearly in various ways, and it is also convenient for data analysis researchers to find the useful information. This paper introduces the basic characteristics and the MATLAB platform graphics advantage, based on the principles of cloud image visualization, built on the MATLAB platform in the data mapping method and the visualization methods, and gives the specific Marine environment data visualization method based on MATLAB implementation, thus making the Sea Surface Temperature and Sea Surface Height and Chlorophyll Concentration these three visual products.

Keywords Data visualization · MATLAB · Cloud picture · Marine data

1 Introduction

With the continuous development of science and technology, network and various electronic communication equipment have been widely used, the amount of data generated by humans is experiencing rapidly growth. Numbers of rich and effective information are hidden behind these huge amounts of data, such as demographic data, meteorological data, financial data, personnel data, etc. However, due to the lack of effective analysis methods and the limitations of human cognitive ability, information cognitive activities are facing unprecedented complexity, it is difficult for people to obtain the hidden information and rules of interest [1–3]. People urgently need new technology to help understand these huge complex data,

J.H. Li (✉) · Q.Q. Yang · W. Song
School of Computer Science and Technology, North China University of Technology,
Beijing, China
e-mail: ljh@ncut.edu.cn

© Springer Science+Business Media Singapore 2016
J.J. (Jong Hyuk) Park et al. (eds.), *Advanced Multimedia and Ubiquitous Engineering*, Lecture Notes in Electrical Engineering 393,
DOI 10.1007/978-981-10-1536-6_74

scientific computing visualization thus came into being. The basic meaning of visualization in scientific computing is to convert the large-scale data produced by scientific and Engineering Computing into intuitive forms such as graphics and images, using the principles and methods of computer graphics or general graphics. It involved in computer graphics, image processing, computer vision, computer aided design and graphical user interface, and other fields, which has become an important direction of current computer graphics research [4]. Powerful computing capability and graphical visualization with computer image processing ability help large set of data records can be converted into static or dynamic graphics, appearing in front of the user, which presents implicit invisible rules and patterns in the data. It provides a means of force for people to analyze and understand the data and look for patterns to make decisions [5]. Marine environment data visualization has many benefits for analysts to analysis extreme weather, design ocean ship routes and forecast the number of fishing sites. So the application of data visualization technology in ocean data research has become a top priority.

In this paper, with the example of Sea Surface Temperature, Chlorophyll Concentration, Sea Surface Height these three kinds of data, using MATLAB platform for development tools, calling the MATLAB function library to draw graphics, I designed and implemented the marine environment data visualization applications based on MATLAB. At the same time, these three products will be made into an executable file reserved call output interface to facilitate the application call directly.

2   Implementation of Visualization Method

2.1   Visualization Principle of Cloud Chart with Color

The visualization method is to use a computer image model with continuous color change to simulate the results of scientific calculation, and the distribution of the data is shown in the color chart with light and shade. The basic concept of drawing cloud images: reading unit fixed point coordinate physical value, then find the maximum and minimum physical value and give different colors to interval divisions in between, so that each point by the size of the physical value had the color coordinate, when using the grid to construct the model with color, the cloud image will be drawn out [6–8]. Generally take unit interior color to fill, unit internal is using Lagrange linear interpolation, which can be used to display the distribution of data in the data field.

2.2 Data Reading and Preprocessing

Using powerful file data reading method hdfread () which provided by MATLAB, the data file can be read and convenient to serialize, assignments, and other operations. First by zeros and matrix variable initialization data, using the fopen () open the file hdfread () to read a file, then to read prepared 2 d matrix which is convenient to figure out the finally land information, making the world's land area into gray. As a result of the read data source exists error or inaccurate data, we need to make the data as accurate as possible through data preprocessing. The method adopted in this paper is to take the data source of multi-source and different satellites, to get a corresponding accurate data through, and then to visualize the data through weighting average of the obtained corresponding accurate data. Data preprocessing methods formula (1) are shown in:

$$\bar{x} = \frac{r_1 f_1 \mid x_i f_i \mid \qquad \mid x_k f_k}{n} \qquad (1)$$

$\bar{x}$ Said for the final physical value, $x_1 x_2 ... x_k$ is the source of data values, $f_1 + f_2 + \cdots + f_k = n$.

2.3 Data Mapping Method

In the satellite cloud map, how to choose the color model mapping from physical quantities to approach, and the color value of the interpolation method are very important, the stander of color mapping directly affects the quality of the image generation, which is also impact the continuous change of physical quantity information. The data format used in this paper is HDF, NC, RT and so on. The useful data is extracted from the data set of central latitude, center latitude, data date, data time and a two-dimensional array. Data mapping processing method is shown in the formula (2):

$$M(m, n) \rightarrow M'(Lon, Lat, value) \rightarrow M'(x, y, color) \qquad (2)$$

Initial M is a m * n two-dimensional matrix, first, the ranks of the matrix change into the latitude and longitude, and then according to the size of the map, transfer the longitude latitude to the image horizontal and vertical coordinates, and the value of the matrix will be converted to the corresponding color.

The purpose of establishing the corresponding relationship between the scalar field and the color table is to use color to express the physical quantity, thus to represent the distribution of physical quantity in the visual color distribution. Due to this article uses satellite ocean data, in order to uniform standard, we will establish a

Fig. 1 Physical
quantity $\longrightarrow$ color mapping
method

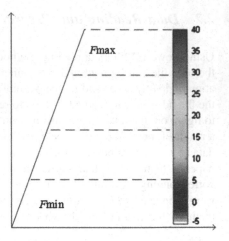

corresponding relationship between unified color and physical value. In Sea Surface
Temperature, for example the minimum $-5\,°C$ corresponds to white, $40\,°C$ red
method corresponds to the maximum, the specific color mapping method as shown
in Fig. 1.

2.4 Implement Process

Cloud image visualization principle applied in matlab, The first step is to create a
color lookup table based on the linear change, establish a linear one to one correspondence relation between color and quantity, which means to establish a colormap parameter file, this paper divided color into 25 interval according to the
numbers, which making the regional color more delicate and precise. The second
step, establish a land mask two-dimensional array of documents, make the ranks of
the information in the file consistent with the data file, and then set all the land area
into maximum color value 255, record the land information of the world map. It is
convenient to set these areas to gray when visualizing the data. Specific visualization process is shown in Fig. 2.

Overall process is divided into six parts: the first step is to read operation
parameters file, and land_mask colormap files. The running parameter file is called
the txt parameter file, which records the data center latitude and longitude, data date
time, all quantity data address of data source, output file path and resolution and so
on. Colormap and land_mask documents are two mat parameter files that prepared
in advance, recorded the color lookup table information and global land area
parameter information. The second step, using hdfread () circulation method reads
all the data from the data source, and determine whether the source is available,
abandon the unavailable data, weight after calculate the average, and fusion all the
data, figure out the eventually data information for the need of visualization. The

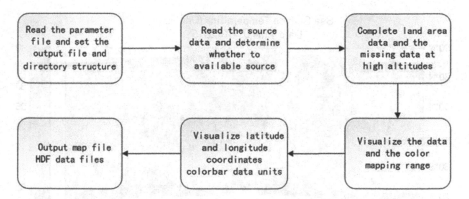

Fig. 2 The proposed ocean environment data visualization process

third step: the land information assigned to the data mainly in the land_mask file, and completes the missing data according to demand. For example, Sea Surface Temperature data of high altitude data is empty, if the direct visualization will not be able to distinguish the land and countless region, so take the high latitudes of the land area fill the missing data at the lowest Temperature of 5 °C, which making the visual effect better. The fourth step, using the imagesc () method visualize data, and using the caxis() regulate the scope of color map. Fifth, figure out and visualize the latitude and longitude coordinates, and also the colorbar unit information and data. To global Sea Surface Temperature data, for example: The global Sea Surface Temperature data is the two-dimensional matrix data of 2048 * 4096, according to the longitudinal coordinate global latitude 90° to 90° south latitude, longitude 180° west to the horizontal axis by 180°, converse coordinate scale visualization. Step 6, in accordance with the required data range and file path in TXT generate product figure and HDF data file.

3 Examples of Application

Figure 3 is the product figure of the global Sea Surface Temperature data, the data comes from Chinese national satellite ocean application center.

Figure 4 is part product figure of the local ocean Chlorophyll Concentration data, the data comes from Chinese national satellite ocean application center. The display Chlorophyll Concentration in red result performed not great, so we change the picture into a general mainly in green color mapping scheme, the specific order is black-green-blue-purple-white.

Figure 5 is the local Sea Surface Height data, the data comes from Chinese national satellite ocean application center.

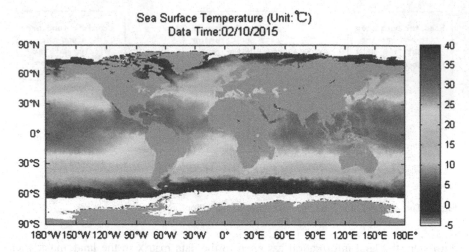

Fig. 3 Product figure of the global sea surface temperature data

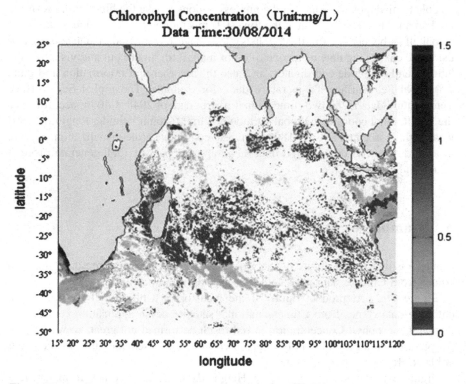

Fig. 4 Product figure of the local ocean chlorophyll concentration data

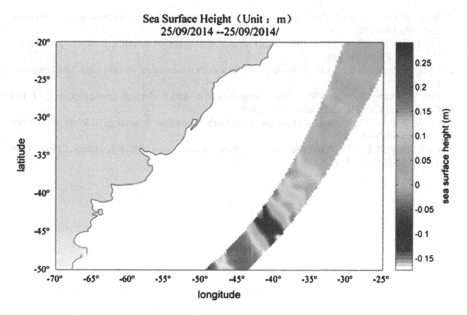

Fig. 5 Product figure of the local sea surface height data

4 Conclusion

This paper provides a visualize method based on color cloud picture visualization theory on the MATLAB platform, and intend to regulate specified color mapping interval according to rang of the actual physical quantities number, so that can reflect the distribution of physical quantity of data field more really. MATLAB platform has the characteristics of convenient development, strong processing ability, comprehensive graphics processing capabilities, and can be extended and so on. Through these 3 application examples, Sea Surface Temperature and Sea Surface Height, Chlorophyll Concentration, which developed base on the MATLAB platform, show that this method can response the characteristics of the data in a better way, and it is convenient for analysis to observe data.

Acknowledgment This research was supported by the National Natural Science Foundation of China (61503005).

References

1. Chen C (2005) Top 10 unsolved information visualization problems. IEEE Comput Graph Appl 12–16
2. Liu K, Zhou X, Zhou D (2002) Research and development of data visualization. Comput Eng 28(8):1–2

3. Zhang H, Guo C (2012) Trend and classification of data visualization technology. Softw Guide 2012(05):169–172
4. Liu J, Yan B, Ji J, Chen Z (2014) MATLAB visualization of scientific computing. Zhejiang University Press, Zhejiang
5. Chen W, Zhang S, Lu A (2013) Basic principle and method of data visualization. Science press, Beijing
6. Luo T, Zhang Y, Chen W (2000) Using OpenGL finite element post-processing. J Ind Commercial Coll Hubei Province 15(4):7–9
7. Du X, Wang C (2013) A new cloud image algorithm based on contour data. J Northeast Univ Nat Sci 05:624–627
8. Lv Z, Jiang M, Lou M (2007) Method for realizing visualization of flow field data. China Water Transp 2007(04):145–147

The Application and Improvement of ID3 Algorithm in WEB Log Data Mining

Weihua Feng and Xingquan Cai

Abstract Data mining comes into being as a new area of research, WEB data mining technology is known as one of the major information processing technology in the future. ID3 algorithm is a often used classical algorithm in data mining technology, which is mainly applied to the implementation of data mining. It always creates the smallest tree structure and is proved that the system design has good effect to transaction analysis of log files by proofing instances, this system is effective in the log files analysis and improvement of ID3 algorithm.

Keywords Data mining · Log mining · ID3 algorithm · Web log analysis tools · XML language

1 Introduction

With the mature and development of information technology and computer network technology, although database technology has been increasingly mature and widely used, database technology has become more mature and although widely used, but it's just the basic way of information storage and management, A large number of valuable data is hidden in the data and can not be used by us [1]. Data mining as a new area of research emerged [2], WEB data mining technology is known as one of the major information-processing technology in the future [3].

A large number of data has been a full time to enrich our lives and work, but also the data that human beings can have also increased dramatically [4], it is no exaggeration to present the world as a metaphor for the data. Looking back on the progress of human science and technology, we find that with the continuous

W. Feng
Henan Judicial Police Vocational College, Zhengzhou, China
e-mail: asktom@126.com

X. Cai (✉)
North China University of Technology, Beijing, China
e-mail: xingquancai@126.com

© Springer Science+Business Media Singapore 2016   577
J.J. (Jong Hyuk) Park et al. (eds.), *Advanced Multimedia and Ubiquitous Engineering*, Lecture Notes in Electrical Engineering 393,
DOI 10.1007/978-981-10-1536-6_75

development of technology, corresponding to the data processing technology has also changed accordingly.

Database technology is mature and widely used [5], but it is the basic way of information storage and management, database system just can be used in simple access and operation data, therefore, the data obtained is also limited, it is not be used in the system analysis of data, as a new research field, data mining emerges as the times require [6]. Data mining technique is known as one of the main technologies of the future information processing, it through a new way to deal with the data, changed the way people used to data processing.

Data mining is the basis of the data sources, the world's largest data source is the World Wide Web [7]. We take Google as an example of how large the amount of data on the World Wide Web is. In 1998 [8], when, Google's web page index quantity is just 26 million, just after two years, in 2000, Google released data show that its index amount 1 billion, recently, when Google announced its web page index, the number has more than 1,000 billion, every day, a new increase of Google in the web page index is more than ten billion, this is very huge. Web Mining is the largest Mining of the largest source of information-the World Wide Web, so as long as it is on the World Wide Web resources can be the source of data mining [9].

The main task of Web log mining is to analyze the web log, but Web log is not structured [10], and there is a large number of redundant information, how to effectively structure the unstructured data into Web logs structured data structure, eliminating redundant information in log data is a problem to be processed in Web log mining. Due to the choice of Web log mining algorithm and the way of data preprocessing, the result of Web log mining is not the same, which is the problem of accuracy. How to improve the accuracy of Web log mining is also a problem in Web log mining.

In this paper, the algorithm of Web log mining is deeply studied, the related issues of XML technology are introduced, and the important relationship between XML technology and Web log mining is discussed in detail.

2 Web Log Mining

For Web log mining, set of things that are formed when the raw data is pre processed, according to different needs with different data mining algorithms, algorithm in Web log mining is the most frequently used include: clustering, classification, association rules and so on.

Classification algorithm belongs to supervised learning, the classification of the data mainly through the two steps to achieve:

Learning steps. Classification algorithms need to learn classification rules, which need to be analyzed or constructed from the training of the classifier. In the database, the data is composed of tuples, each tuple can be viewed as an n-dimensional vector space, corresponding to an object for each tuple and reality, classifier based on features of the object attributes of different objects to learn, to judge the object's properties, when the learning of the classifier is mature, we can analyze the other objects.

Supervised learning. The so-called supervised learning is to learn a classifier in the defendant know each training tuples that belong to which class is a precondition of, to plan the tuple in advance.

Prior to the classification algorithm, the original data need to be pre processed, the original data preprocessing is to improve the effectiveness and accuracy of classification. In the original data, the possible existence of is may exist strong correlations between different attributes in a tuple, the so-called strong correlation is refers to the attribute between mutual association reached a certain threshold, which can make two attributes can be mutual dependence or derivation, when two properties with a strong correlation after a property may become redundant data, so of original data of classification need tuple attribute relevance judgments, namely the tuple correlation analysis was carried out. In the data preprocessing stage, the original data is also needed for data mining. Data preprocessing methods are often used for data conversion, reduction, and the raw data cleaning.

Commonly used classification and prediction algorithms are: the decision tree induction classification, Bayes classification, rule-based taxonomy, the backward propagation classification, etc.

3 ID3 Decision Tree Algorithm and Improve

3.1 ID3 Decision Tree Algorithm

The classification algorithm for data mainly includes decision tree induction classification, rule-based classification method, Byes, artificial neural network, K-nearest neighbor, support vector machine and association rule classification. On these data classification methods, the classification process can be summed up as: the first is the classification rule learning, namely rule learning stage is to construct the classifier stage; the second stage is stage of test data, the treatment of classified data using a classifier analyze, and treats the data classification to classify.

The most frequent use of the classification algorithm is the decision tree algorithm, the decision tree is a kind of hierarchy of objects to judge, and according to the object of the object to find the best classification of the object. Decision tree induction algorithm was proposed by Ross Quinlan in the early 80s of last century. Its abbreviation for ID3, ID3 on the path of the search model is based on the greedy algorithm, is non-backtracking. The main algorithm of ID3 algorithm is expressed as:

ID3 algorithm,the input is class label and training tuple of the set M, the candidate attribute set Attrset, search for the branch function Selectmethod () and Output is Decision Tree, following method.

First Create R node, if the M in the tuple is the same class C; then Node M is a leaf node, which is denoted as C and Judgment, Attrset==Null if that candidate attribute set is empty; then Use a majority vote, the majority of the tag M in the class, to return to the M as a node R; Second Call function selectmethod (Attrset, M), looking for the branch attribute, using split_attr to label the branch, To judge, to find the Attrset attribute Attrset Case is a discrete value and can have multiple branches; then Attrset=Attrset-split_attr, For each output of the branch attribute Mj split_attr For cycle so Mj is a subset of M; Third If Mj is empty, then To Mj in the class of the majority vote, to return the majority of Mj in the class tag, the increase of a node R to return the tag If Mj! =Null, recursive call ID3 algorithm End for and Return decision tree.

Algorithm contains three parameters, the parameter M is a collection of records of, is generally a training set of records, the parameter Attrset is collection of columns in the class attribute, which is referred to as the candidate attribute column, the column is used to generate branch node of a decision tree. Selectmethod is selection of the optimal effect properties function and used is a heuristic procedure. In the Selectmethod method, we need to choose the attributes of the candidate attributes, and the selection criterion is the mathematical measure of attributes. In the splitting criterion "Selectmethod". The selected attribute is called the splitting attribute, according to the splitting attribute branch operations to be performed on the node, on the nodes of the branch has three kinds of situations, the splitting criterion is divided into three kinds of cases. Set V is the split attribute selected by Selectmethod; there are V {v1, v2, ..., vn} values.

When the split attribute V for discrete values, the V of each known value to create a branch, and the use of V in the Mj value for the class VI tag, tag the tuple.

When the value of V is continuous, the splitting point usually takes the focus of two adjacent points of V, which may not be the actual value in the training data.

When the V is a discrete value and must be generated when the two fork tree, whether the value of A can be used to determine whether the value of the training value is to be judged to produce different judgment conditions. For the decision tree algorithm, a recursive partitioning step for the training set M is given, when one of the following conditions is satisfied, the algorithm terminates.

The advantage of ID3 algorithm is clear and easy to implement. It has a very good effect on the processing of non numeric data. However, the ID3 algorithm also has its own disadvantages. Due to the ID3 algorithm only considering properties of single set of single attribute effect on the splitting rule, so ID3 algorithm tendency in choosing attribute value relatively more tuples, and more tuples is not optimal, therefore easy to make decision tree produced repeated decision rules and production branch path overlapping problems. Secondly because the ID3 algorithm of data noise and outliers processing, so easy to produce unreliable branch. Finally, due to the ID3 algorithm can only deal with the discrete attributes, for the continuous type of attributes, in front of the classification need the discrete process.

3.2 Improved ID3 Algorithm

For the shortcomings of the ID3 algorithm mentioned in the last section, the improvement of the ID3 algorithm is mainly reflected in the following aspects:

The pruning of decision tree. As the tuples from the influence of noise and outliers, the generated decision tree will produce many of the training data set of abnormal, pruning is mainly processing algorithm to over fitting of the data problems. The pruning methods are mainly pre pruning and post pruning. Pre pruning is mainly through the split the subset in setting a threshold S, the threshold is used to describe the statistical characteristics of the sub set of tuples can also be such as Gini, gain rate standard. Sub set of tuples through to threshold s judgment to decide whether to branch, when given a set of tuples with threshold requirements of the branch, or branching algorithm end. After pruning is first generated decision tree, by removing the branches of the decision tree and the leaf node instead of to form a new decision tree, cart algorithm costs complexity to achieve pruning. The computational complexity of the cost of the internal nodes of the decision tree pruning and expected after the new the node cost complexity. The comparison between the two, replacing price complex degree is small, for the selection of structure. And C4.5 using pessimistic pruning method, which uses statistics for the training set error rate, increases a threshold to achieve the training set accuracy of correct.

The use of information gain rate *GainR*. In order to overcome the shortcoming that the information gain *Gain* has the attribute of choosing a large number of values, to overcome this shortcoming, C4.5 uses the information gain rate to determine the split attribute. The calculation of the information gain rate is as follows:

(a) Calculate the classification information *SplitInfA(M)*, the calculation formula is as follows Eq. (1):

$$SplitInf(M) = -\sum_{i=1}^{n} \frac{|Mi|}{|M|} \times \log\left(\frac{|Mi|}{|M|}\right) \tag{1}$$

where $|Mi|$ is the number of attributes that are included, the number of M is a tuple set.

(b) Calculate the information gain *Gain(M)*.
(c) Calculation the information gain rate *GainR(M)*, the calculation formula is as follows Eq. (2):

$$GainR(M) = \frac{Gain(M)}{SplitInf(M)} \tag{2}$$

Gini uses the attribute tuple of the non purity to be divided, and its definition, such as follows Eqs. (3) and (4):

$$Gini(M) = 1 - \sum_{j=1}^{n} pi \times pi \qquad (3)$$

$$Gini(M) = \frac{|M1|}{|M|} Gini(M1) + \frac{M2}{M} Gini(M2) \qquad (4)$$

Gini algorithm is only for the division of the two fork tree, if the partition of the T can be divided into the *M* group *M*1, *M*2 for a given partition *Gini*:

For attributes, the need to consider every possible division, for example, attribute grade has three optional value set {research, research 2, research 3}, binary division of the property {research, research 2, research 3}, { }, {research, research 2}, {1 research, research 3}, {2 research, research 3} for the different division, its complement is not listed, in the division and space division need to be deleted, because the Division has no practical significance.

The above analysis of the decision tree splitting rule of three metrics: information gain and gain ratio and the *Gini*, and decision tree improvement strategies showdown, information gain bias in multi valued attributes, information gain ratio of the adjustment, but the more likely to unbalanced division and *Gini* tend to divide and purity of equal size.

4 Conclusion

This paper introduces the algorithm used in log mining, and focuses on the implementation process of the decision tree algorithm ID3. The ID3 algorithm is verified by an example, and the advantages and disadvantages of the algorithm are pointed out. At the same time, aiming at the shortcomings of ID3 algorithm, the improved ID3 algorithm is proposed, and the gain information rate and Gini are introduced, which are the improved method of decision rules for ID3 using information gain.

References

1. Han J, Kamber M (2000) Data mining concepts and techniques. Morgan Kaufmann Publishers, Burlington, pp 3–10
2. Kantardzic M (2002) Data mining concepts, models, and algorithms. IEEE Press, China, pp 101–102
3. Dunham MH (2003) Data mining introductory and advanced topics. Pcarson Education Press, New York, p 179
4. Li JL (2009) Pretreatment of the log and data mining technology. Comput Knowl Technol 5 (14):3602–3605
5. Berry MW (2006) Lecuture notes in data mining. World Scientific Press, Singapore, p 178

6. Roiger RJ, Geatz MW (2003) Data mining: a tutorial-based primer. Pearson Education Press, New York, pp 154–160
7. Pyle D (2006) Business modeling and data mining. Elsevier Science, New York, pp 120–132
8. Berry MW (2012) Lecture notes in data mining. Wiley, New York, pp 180–184
9. Soares C, Peng Y, Meng J, Washio T, Zhou Z-H (2008) Application of data mining in e-business and finance. IOS Press, Amsterdam (2008)
10. Guo Y, Robert G (2000) High performance data mining: scaling algorithms, applications and systems. Kluwer Academic Publishers, Dordrecht, pp 69–75

The Research of Dentition Defect Expert System Based on the AND/OR Tree with Positive and Negative Constraints

Danyang Cao, Yan Shi and Peijun Lv

Abstract The purpose of this research is to solve multiple combination and inefficient of complex dentition defect diagnosis and treatment, we put forward the thought of building data structure of AND/OR tree and set the problem node as "AND tree" and the treatments rules as "OR tree", through introducing the positive and negative constraints to prioritization the complex rules of oral treatment and generating a diagnostic report with treatments order for medical staff make a diagnosis quickly and efficient. Results show that it is feasible to use AND/OR tree with the positive and negative constraints for reasoning data of dentition defect. Ensuring the accuracy of diagnosis in practical application and improving the efficiency of the diagnosis.

Keywords Dentition defects · Expert system · AND/OR tree · Positive constraints · Negative constraints · Reasoning and sorting

D. Cao (✉) · Y. Shi
College of Computer Science and Technology,
North China University of Technology, Beijing, China
e-mail: ufocdy@163.com

P. Lv
Center of Digital Dentistry, Peking University School
and Hospital of Stomatology, Beijing, China

P. Lv
Department of Prosthodontics, Peking University School
and Hospital of Stomatology, Beijing, China

P. Lv
National Engineering Laboratory for Digital and Material Technology
of Stomatology, Research Center of Engineering and Technology
for Digital Dentistry, Ministry of Health, Beijing, China

© Springer Science+Business Media Singapore 2016
J.J. (Jong Hyuk) Park et al. (eds.), *Advanced Multimedia and Ubiquitous Engineering*, Lecture Notes in Electrical Engineering 393,
DOI 10.1007/978-981-10-1536-6_76

585

1 Introduction

Dentition defects is incomplete of permanent dentition caused by the part of the tooth loss, because the different parts and the number of missing teeth and the extent of its impact is different, incomplete permanent dentition will directly lead to the body unhealthy situation, Such as the effects of chewing, pronunciation and dental aesthetics, and even a threat to the health of stomatognathic system. Today, domestic for clinical diagnosis and treatment of complex defective dentition, the way of diagnosis and treatment still stay in artificial diagnosis relying on medical experts who has many years of experience and extensive expertise in a career in medicine. Not only inefficient but also the richness of the experience will directly affect the success rate of treatment. Moreover, so rich and valuable expertise how to save and make effective use by artificial way, it is oral medicine have been discussed and the research topic.

Domestic and foreign scholars in expert system have done a lot of research work, and achieved remarkable results. The first expert system for the diagnosis of oral diseases is Leonard and his colleagues developed the system for craniofacial pain diagnosis and treatment in 1973, through data analysis of clinical cases, assigning a weight parameters for inference machine. The first oral expert system in China is temporomandibular joint disorder syndrome diagnosis expert system established in 1990 by Qin et al. [1]. Through access to relevant data, there is not a large expert system in the complex dentition defect and clinical diagnosis decision-making. There are two reasons, first, this expert system not only involves aspects of computer-related knowledge, but also need to have a basic knowledge of medical aspects of dentition defect and reasoning knowledge. Second, the lack of reasoning mechanism. Dentition defect of repair design has always been regarded as a complex problem of oral medicine, a combination of the type of edentulous only maxilla(or jaw) may have 65, 534 kinds [2]. We can not design all combinations for each treatment rules, therefore, We need to establish a complete system with expert reasoning mechanism to deal with various combinatorial problems.

After analysis of the complex dentition defect problem, we converted reasoning which is the most difficult part of dentition defect problem into a special data structure which is "and or" tree to come complete treatment programs. Due to the special nature of dentition defect problem, the traditional "and or" tree with weights can not solve the problem perfectly. So, we introduced the innovative concept of positive and negative constraints in nodes of "and or" tree, it can be said to achieve the expert system is based on this AND/OR tree with positive and negative constraints. Moreover, System treatment rules, diagnostic rules and constraints have excellent maintainability.

2 Basic Definition

Before making diagnostic decisions, system requires the user to enter the relevant inspection information. After the data were classified and analyzed, it will be defined as type 3, inspection category, inspection item and inspection result. Moreover, system for reasoning tasks into two categories, diagnostic of reasoning and treatment of reasoning. Diagnostic reasoning is to infer the appropriate diagnostic results based on the data entered, treatment of reasoning is based on the input data through positive and negative constraint condition selection and reasoning out the corresponding treatment options, both need the corresponding medical knowledge as a basis to reasoning, so the system also must have a corresponding inference rules——Diagnosis and treatment of rules.

- **Definition 1 Fill In The Inspection Item**: It is to fill information of inspection into the system when doctor examining the patient, information of inspection is divided into three items, category, inspection items and inspection results, hierarchical relationships with tree structure.

  Category: Category examination belongs, such as routine oral examination, edentulous area examining and residual roots and crowns inspection etc.

  Inspection items: It is subordinate of category, such as missing teeth (belonging to oral routine examination item), mesial and distal space (belonging to the edentulous area item), etc.

  Inspection results: It is subordinate of inspection items, mainly the contents of the specific results, such as missing/not missing (belonging to missing teeth item), mesial and distal space was normal/large/small (belonging to the mesial and distal space item).

- **Definition 2 Diagnostic Rules**: Known there is a random inspection results R, it is only the corresponding diagnosis of I, we call the form $\{\exists R$ and have unique corresponding I = True, (R, I)$\}$ of rules as diagnostic rules.

  Diagnostic rules is actually a two-dimensional relational table which is test results and diagnosis results corresponding to each other, but both are not one-to-one correspondence, a inspection result or a combination of the multiple inspection results are only corresponding for one diagnosis, whereas a diagnosis result may correspond to multiple inspection results.

- **Definition 3 Treatment Rules**: Known there is a random inspection results R, it is the corresponding treatment method of C, we call the form $\{\exists R$ and have corresponding C = True, (R, C)$\}$ of rules as treatment rules.

  Unlike diagnosis rules, in the same inspection result of treatment rules may correspond to multiple treatment methods, the same treatment method may correspond to multiple inspection results, so the nature of the treatment rule is a many-to-many two dimensional table.

3 AND/OR Tree and Positive and Negative Constraint Conditions

3.1 The Definition of AND/OR Tree

AND/OR tree is one of the most basic representation problem method of artificial intelligence, it is also a kind of the mining algorithm based on figure [3]. Smith puts forward the concept of structure of decision problem, he believes that the structure of the decision problem is a measure of the adequacy of knowledge [4]. When a question is complex, it is always difficult to solve if directly to solve this problem. The main task of protocol of complex problem is by appropriate methods for complex problem to decompose and transform [5] put it in a series of simple sub-problems after the change for substitution. Finally, achieving the original problem solving by solving these sub-problem.

- **Definition 4 Problem Decomposition**: Suppose the original problem P can be decomposed into a number of sub-problems of P1, P2, P3, ... Pn, when all the sub-problems Pi (i = 1, 2, 3, ... n) have been resolved, the original problem P can be resolved, then we called all the sub-questions sequence [Pi] is equivalent to the original problem of P. This decomposition of the original problem can be represented by an "AND tree" as shown in Fig. 1.
- **Definition 5 Problems Conversion**: Suppose the original problem P can be transformed into a number of sub-problems of P1, P2, P3, ... Pn, when any one of sub-problem Pi (i = 1, 2, 3, ... n) have been resolved, the original problem P can be resolved, then we called the sub-question sequence of any one element [Pi] is equivalent to the original problem P. This transformation can be represented by an "or tree" as shown in Fig. 2.

Ge and Li [6] who applied the principles of Bayesian in diagnostic reasoning module of oral periodontal disease diagnosis expert system, in contrast, clinical diagnosis and treatment of dentition defect Decision Expert System does not involve probability, it uses "AND/OR tree" to implement the reasoning process. The data of tooth defect problem can be roughly divided into two parts of information and treatment methods. In the process of diagnosis, tooth may appear several subproblems including P1, P2, P3, ... Pn, for each child Pi (i = 1, 2, 3, ... n)

Fig. 1 The "AND tree"

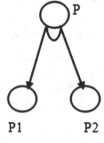

Fig. 2 The "OR tree"

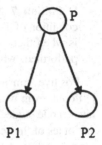

P

P1   P2

Fig. 3 The structure of
AND/OR tree

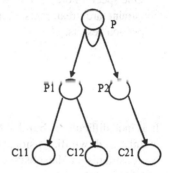

P

P1   P2

C11   C12   C21

is corresponding several treatment methods of Cij (i = 1, 2, 3, ... n; j = 1, 2, 3, ... m). When all the problem of P to be solved, teeth problem is solved, that the relationship between Pi is "and". And for each Pi, in theory any treatment method Cij can be used to solve corresponding problems of Pi, that the relationship of Cij (i = 1, 2, 3, ... n; j = 1, 2, 3, ... m) is "or". From this perspective, the diagnosis problem of tooth defect can be converted to a data of special "AND/OR tree" structure to solve problem. The structure of AND/OR tree as shown in Fig. 3.

3.2 Positive and Negative Constraintss of AND/OR Tree

Determining the feasibility of treatment method that is to determine the current oral environment whether there is any restrictions on the treatment method. We call this restrictive conditions of treatment method as constraint conditions and constraints can be divided into two types-positive and negative constraints.

- **Definition 6 Positive constraint**: Treatment method of C has a constraint condition of T, the relation between the both defined as $\{\exists\, T, P\,(C, T) = 1\}$, that is when there is a constraint condition of T, treatment method of C can be performed, whereas can't.

- **Definition 7 Negative constraint**: Treatment method of C has a constraint condition of T, the relation between the both defined as $\{\exists\, T, P\,(C, T) = 0\}$, that is when there is a constraint condition of T, treatment method of C can not be performed, whereas can't.

Positive constraints marked as "pos", negative constraints marked as "neg". Different from weighted value of AND/OR tree, in the treatment method of the third layer node added constraints (for short cc) after removing weighted value of attributes of the second problem nodes. When system sorting sequence, it can judge the feasibility of treatment methods directly.

One special note, in fact whether it is positive or negative constraint, objects of constraint are treatments method, and the content of the constraint is actually inspection results.

4 Building Algorithm of AND/OR Tree

It is not difficult to build AND/OR tree with positive and negative constraints, mainly need two-dimensional relational tables of treatments method and child table of constraints of the positive and the negative, building process can be roughly divided into the following several steps:

- **Step1 Getting dataset of examination result**: This step is to get all of inspection results and corresponding satellite information, thereby generating second layer problem nodes of AND/OR trees;
- **Step2 Accessing to treatments method by treatment rules**: For each inspection results of nodes to matching by "and" treatment rules, getting possible treatments method for each inspection results, thereby generating the third layer of treatment node;
- **Step3 Adding positive and negative constraints for AND/OR tree**: For each treatments method to match constraints through the child table of "and" treatment rules, thereby resulting in complete AND/OR tree with positive and negative constraints;
- **Step4 Reasoning treatments plan**: This process is using the positive and negative constraints to judge each treatments method is feasible or not, then choosing available treatments method and simulation of the complete treatment process.

5 Reasoning Process with Positive and Negative Constraints

According to the process of the forward reasoning machine and knowledge-base of the expert system's update frequency is extremely low, thereby creating a new structure of reasoning tree [7]. The process of reasoning is arranging the treatment order of pi according to the positive and negative constraints and solve this problem one by one. System reasoning process roughly as follows:

- **Step1**: The system extracts the patient case that is all the problems nodes of Pn;
- **Step2**: To Treatment problem of Pi (i = 1, 2, 3 ... n) and to search treatments method of cij (j = 1, 2, 3 ... n);
- **Step3**: Checking whether there is a constraint condition of the treatments method of c11, if does not, it is available to use c11 to solve problem of p1, repeating step2, continue to solve the problem of p2; if there has constraints, then checking the positive and negative constraints of c11 whether existing in the nodes of pi, if not, it is available to use c11 to solve problem of p1, repeating step2, continue to solve the problem of p2; if existing constraint condition of pk ∈ pi, then priority to solve problem of pk, repeating step2;
- **Step4**: If treatments method of ckj for problem of pk has not positive constraints or treatment rules, then j plus 1 that choosing the next treatments method;
- **Step5**: Solving all problems of pn and finally presenting problem of pi and treatments method of cij according to the order to solve the problem.

6 Experimental Description

Question P: the patient medical records has been given and test results including p1, p2, p3, p4, it needs given appropriate treatment plan by reasoning inspection items as shown in Table 1.

According to inference rules of AND/OR tree with the positive and negative constraints, firstly to arrange inspection items one by one, further to check constraint nodes whether included in the records, according to information of records in above table, the first treatments method of c11 for p1 requires p0, due to inspection

Table 1 Instances of patient medical records

Inspection item	Treatments method	Positive constraint condition	Negative constraint condition
p1	c11	p0	–
p1	c12	–	p2
p2	c21	–	p3
p3	c31	–	–
p4	c41	–	p10

item does not contain p0 thus abandons treatments method of c11, then to judgment method of c12. Using method of c12 needs prioritized resolve p2 to resolve p1 because p2 contained in the medical records. c21 treatment p2 p3 problem should first solve the problem. c21 treatment p2 p3 problem should first solve the problem. Treatments method of c21 for p2 needs prioritized resolve p3 to resolve p2 because p3 contained in the medical records. Treatments method of c31 for p3 has not constraint condition, therefore the order to resolve the problem is p3 → p2 → p1. The problem of p4 can be directly adopt c41 methods to solve because there has not p10 in case. So treatment plan is c31 → c21 → c12 → c41.

7 Conclusion

The system proposed thought of building data structure of AND/OR tree for multiple combination and inefficient of complex dentition defect diagnosis and treatment to set the problem node as "AND trees", set the rules as "OR tree". The complex rules of oral treatment for prioritization through introducing the positive and negative constraints in order to solve all oral problems and ultimately to give a diagnostic report with treatment order to quick and efficient diagnosis. Experimental results show that it is feasible to use AND/OR tree with the positive and negative constraints for reasoning data of dentition defect. This method is scalability and suitable for situations that nodes of priority dynamically changing. Through AND/OR tree to divide data into multiple layers greatly reduces the coupling of data, thus improves the maintainability of expert system.

Acknowledgments This work is supported by Beijing Municipal Science and Technology Project (Z131100006813021), supported by training project for outstanding young teachers of North China University of Technology.

References

1. Qin Z, Chai Z, Feng X (2005) Expert system research and application in the field of oral medicine in China. Oral Med Res 21(1):103–104
2. Li L (2000) Advances expert system of removable partial denture design. Int J Oral Med 1:28–31
3. Yen SJ, Chen ALP (2001) A graph-based approach for discovering various types of association rules. IEEE Trans Knowl Data Eng 13(5):839–845
4. Smith GF (1988) Towars a heuristic theory of problem structuring. Manage Sci 14(12):1489–1506
5. Wang H, Feng Y (2007) Based on the cloud with AND/OR tree regulations complex decision problem research. J Harbin Inst Technol Univ 39(7):1131–1134
6. Ge X, Li B, Chai H et al (2006) The initial realization expert system of oral periodontal disease diagnosis. Chin J Oral Med 4(2):105–107
7. Huang W (2007) A kind of new reasoning tree structure based on production rule. Microelectron Comput 24:76–78

Identification of Influential Weather Factors on Traffic Safety Using K-means Clustering and Random Forest

Oh Hoon Kwon and Shin Hyoung Park

Abstract This study proposes a novel methodology to forecast traffic safety level based on weather factors by administrative district in South Korea. These administrative districts are grouped by their characteristics, such as population, number of vehicles, and length of railways, with the use of k-means clustering. To identify major weather factors that affect traffic safety level for the clustered district groups, the random forest technique was applied. The performance of such random forest models combined with k-means clustering is evaluated using a test dataset. With the results obtained from the analysis, this study highlights that its proposed models outperform a simple random forest model without clustering.

Keywords Traffic safety forecasting · Weather factor · K-means clustering · Random forest

1 Introduction

For effective control of traffic accidents, it is crucial to identify the factors that come into play in such incidents. In general, weather factors which fall under environmental factors are considered as direct causes of traffic accidents. However, despite their reputation as one of the direct causes of traffic accidents, weather conditions remain uncontrollable risk sources. Nevertheless, if the relationship between weather factors and accident occurrence can be identified, measures can be taken to lower risk levels under certain dangerous weather conditions. In addition, by forecasting traffic safety levels across different weather conditions, drivers can be provided applicable traffic safety information.

O.H. Kwon · S.H. Park (✉)
Department of Transportation Engineering, College of Engineering, Keimyung University,
1095 Dalgubeol-daero, Dalseo-gu, Daegu 42601, Republic of Korea
e-mail: shpark@kmu.ac.kr

O.H. Kwon
e-mail: ohoonkwon@kmu.ac.kr

© Springer Science+Business Media Singapore 2016   593
J.J. (Jong Hyuk) Park et al. (eds.), *Advanced Multimedia and Ubiquitous Engineering*, Lecture Notes in Electrical Engineering 393,
DOI 10.1007/978-981-10-1536-6_77

In studies on traffic accident forecasting, Zhou et al. [1] used fuzzy generalized neural networks to deal with subjective factors in traffic accident prediction and improve the computations of the predetermination model for traffic safety. The results of the study showed that the improved model was effective to forecast traffic accidents. Paz et al. [2], on the other hand, used time series analysis to forecast the number of fatalities and serious injuries in Nevada over a five-year horizon. They applied deterministic and stochastic models and found a stochastic model that provided the best forecasting measures. For a different approach, Jin et al. [3] used a Gaussian mixture model (GMM) and a Kalman filter for online forecasting of traffic safety on expressways. The precision and robustness of the prediction model were demonstrated in their study. Lee [4] used the decision tree model to analyze the factors that cause traffic accidents, categorizing traffic accidents by severity level: into accidents that result in serious injuries and accidents that result in death. Through this analysis, Lee identified the key factors that affect the severity levels of traffic accidents across different districts.

For efforts on weather conditions, the Korea Transportation Safety Authority (KOTSA) [5] recently launched the local traffic safety forecasting service in charge of disseminating daily weather information including the weather forecast. This service assesses the injury severities and the risk levels of traffic accidents using data on past accidents and weather data to forecast the risk levels under different weather conditions.

This study utilizes the same injury severity index used by KOTSA in its traffic safety forecasting service to assess risk levels. The index is categorized into five levels based on the distribution to evaluate traffic safety levels, and the key weather factors that affect traffic safety levels are analyzed with the use of the random forest method. To account for the influence of local characteristics, this study uses the k-means clustering method to group the districts and enhance the prediction capability of the model. Traffic accident data, weather data, and local characteristics data are used for the analysis and the accuracy of the proposed prediction model is evaluated using a test dataset.

2 Data Description and Methodology

2.1 Data Description

The districts analyzed in this study are classified based on the administrative districts of the Republic of Korea. Included in this scope are *Gus* of metropolitan cities, local cities, and *Guns*. The data representing the local characteristics of each administrative districts include the variables on *population, aging population over 80, number of households, number of businesses, number of employees, number of vehicle registrations, length of roadways,* and *area of roadways*.

Table 1 Categorization criteria of traffic safety levels

Traffic safety level	Range of ECLO	Distribution of accident data
Very high-risk	ECLO > 35	46,619 (19.4 %)
High-risk	22 < ECLO ≤ 35	45,659 (19.0 %)
Normal-risk	13 < ECLO ≤ 22	51,618 (21.5 %)
Low-risk	8 < ECLO ≤ 13	37,066 (15.4 %)
Very low-risk	ECLO ≤ 8	59,544 (24.7 %)

The traffic accident data for each district include information on daily fatalities, serious injuries, slight injuries, and injuries for five years from 2007 to 2011. KOTSA [5] provides the definitions of *fatality, serious injury, slight injury,* and *injury* caused by traffic accidents, which are listed in order of injury severity. To represent the severity levels of traffic accidents using a single index, this study used the Equivalent Casualty Loss Only (ECLO) index ——an injury severity index used to calculate risks of traffic accidents for the traffic safety forecasting service of KOTSA [5]. The figures are calculated using Eq. (1), and the values are the *number of fatalities, serious injuries,* and *slight injuries* compiled into the number of *injuries.* In the present study, ECLO is categorized into five traffic safety levels for the class variable of the random forest model. Table 1 shows the criteria for categorizing traffic safety levels based on the ECLO distribution.

$$ECLO = (1 \times injuries) + (3 \times slight\,injuries) + (5 \times serious\,injuries) + (10 \times fatalities).$$
$$(1)$$

The weather data used in this study contain the variables on the *average temperature* (°C), *maximum temperature* (°C), *minimum temperature* (°C), *rainfall* (mm), *snowfall* (cm), *average wind speed* (m/s), *average humidity* (%), *cloud amount* (1/10), and *sunshine duration* (hour) of specific days in a district. As for various types of weather, this study uses binary variables that each represent *very cloudy sky, slightly covered sky, clear, shower, fog, hail, drizzle, sleet, thunder and lightning, dust, cloudy, snow,* or *rain.*

The number of data ultimately used in this study is 240,506, excluding the missing values. A total of 168,354 of the data, which accounts for 70 % the total data used, were used as a training dataset to learn the model, and the other 30 %, or 72,152 of the data, were used as a test dataset to evaluate the performance of the model.

2.2 Methodology

Factors that cause traffic accidents may vary depending on local characteristics. For example, a district with a high population density and a large number of registered vehicles may demonstrate a high risk level because of the large number of accidents resulting therefrom, and certain weather factors may affect the traffic safety level in the region. To consider such local characteristics, this study used k-means clustering to group the districts that carry similar characteristics, and the random forest method on each group to generate a forecasting model of traffic safety level. The key weather factors are identified using the generated models and, afterward, are compared with the key weather factors identified by the simple random forest model without clustering. In addition, the prediction performances of the two models are compared to verify performance enhancement. For the analysis, this study used R which is a statistics tool.

K-means Clustering. This is a popular clustering method that aims to partition observations into k clusters in which each observation belongs to the cluster with the nearest mean [6]. In the present study, the districts were clustered using *normalized population, aging population over 80, number of households, number of businesses, number of employees, number of vehicle registrations, length of roadways*, and *area of roadways* as variables.

Random Forest. This is an advanced classification technique that avoids overfitting to the respective training dataset by constructing a multitude of decision trees [7]. A decision tree classifier identifies feature variables (explanatory variables) in order of influence on class variable (dependent variable) in consideration of dependency among the feature variables. However, overfitting to the training dataset by growing tree deeply diminishes the prediction accuracy of the tree model. To remedy the weakness of the decision tree, random forest constructs a multitude of decision trees by randomly selecting subsets of feature variables and observations. In the present study, random forest models are constructed by cluster of districts using weather factors and traffic safety level as feature variables and class variable respectively.

3   Results

Table 2 shows the results of k-means clustering for districts. The appropriate number of clusters was determined as three by examining the within-groups sum of squares according to the number of clusters. Group 1 is a group of larger districts with high variable values across all local characteristics, and Group 3 consists of smaller districts with low variable values. On the other hand, Group 2 is a group of medium-sized districts.

3.1   Identification of Influential Weather Factors

Figure 1 shows the significance of the impact of each weather factor on traffic safety levels using the Mean Decrease Gini index. A higher Mean Decrease Gini

Table 2 Results of k-means clustering for districts

Mean of normalized variables	Group 1	Group 2	Group 3
Population	2.13	0.39	−0.77
Aging population	2.12	0.33	−0.72
Household	2.13	0.40	−0.78
Business	2.06	0.35	−0.72
Employee	1.91	0.26	−0.62
Vehicle registration	2.29	0.29	−0.71
Length of roadways	1.76	−0.01	−0.34
Area of roadways	1.82	−0.01	−0.35

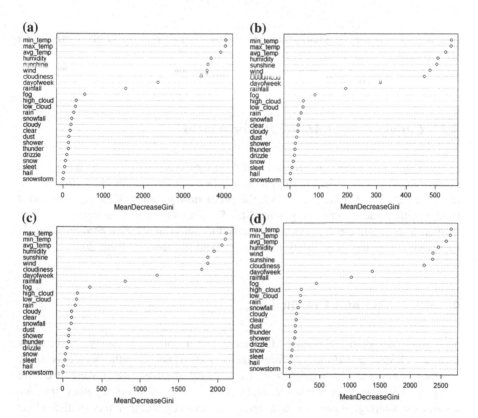

Fig. 1 Importance of influential weather factors on traffic safety level for **a** overall districts without clustering, **b** districts of Group 1, **c** districts of Group 2, and **d** districts of Group 3

index represents a more significant impact on traffic safety levels. This study found *temperature*, *humidity*, *average wind speed*, *sunshine duration*, and *cloud amount* across both models as the factors with significant impact. In addition, *day of the week*, *rainfall*, and *fog* had moderately significant impact compared with the remaining weather factors. As for the sizes of the districts, *minimum temperature*

Table 3 Confusion matrixes of random forest models for a test dataset

Reference	Prediction by model without clustering					Prediction by model with clustering				
	Very low	Low	Normal	High	Very high	Very low	Low	Normal	High	Very high
Very low	**9614**	784	2858	1530	2959	**11521**	1027	2656	1606	935
Low	5551	**534**	2033	1073	1971	6055	**642**	2022	1473	970
Normal	7164	587	**3006**	1766	3000	6474	727	**3403**	2675	2244
High	6045	526	2666	**1607**	2877	4070	524	3031	**2821**	3275
Very high	5780	444	2385	1633	**3759**	2087	324	2250	2631	**6709**
Sum	34,154	2875	12,948	7609	14,566	30,207	3244	13,362	11,206	14,133

was a more significant factor than *maximum temperature* in larger districts. In smaller districts, however, *average wind speed* had more impact on traffic safety levels compared with *sunshine duration*.

3.2   Comparison of Model Performances

Table 3 shows confusion matrixes of random forest models for a test dataset. The prediction accuracy of the simple random forest model without clustering of districts was 25.7 %. On the other hand, the prediction accuracy of the random forest model with k-means clustering was 34.8 %, showing a 9 % increase over the former. In addition, the findings of the study that show an accurate prediction vastly increased across all traffic safety levels (see bold numbers in Table 3).

4   Discussion and Conclusions

This study analyzed the impact of weather factors on traffic safety levels using k-means clustering and random forest techniques. Data on traffic accidents, daily weather, and local characteristics in each administrative district were used for analysis. Districts with similar characteristics were grouped together through k-means clustering. Based on such grouping, the key weather factors that affect traffic safety levels were identified for each group with the use of random forest models in consideration of the dependency among weather factors. The analysis showed that the most significant factors that determine traffic safety levels are *temperature, humidity, wind speed, sunshine duration*, and *cloud amount*, followed by *day of the week, rainfall*, and *fog*. While most of the factors did not greatly vary depending on district sizes, *minimum temperature* was the most significant factor in larger districts, and *average wind speed* exerted more impact than *sunshine duration* in smaller districts.

To evaluate the performance of the proposed random forest models, a single random forest model was generated for overall districts without clustering, and its prediction accuracy was compared with that of the random forest model with k-means clustering. The result showed that the performance of the model with clustering for the districts was vastly higher. The random forest models with k-means clustering represents a model far more advanced than the conventional traffic safety forecasting based on simple statistics without considering district characteristics. The findings contribute to enhancing the prediction accuracy of the model. With this, the model developed in this study can be used to provide drivers with more accurate and useful traffic safety information, and provide assistance for the preparation of plans aimed at promoting traffic safety based on the identified key weather factors.

Acknowledgements This research was supported by the Keimyung University Research Grant of 2015.

References

1. Zhou S, Jiang G, Huang Y (2010) Forecast of traffic safety based on fuzzy generalized neural network. In: Proceedings of the 10th international conference of Chinese transportation professionals, pp 805–815
2. Paz A, Veeramisti N, de La Fuente-Mella H (2015) Forecasting performance measures for traffic safety using deterministic and stochastic models. In: 18th international IEEE conference on intelligent transportation systems (ITSC 2015), pp 2965–2970
3. Jin S, Wang DH, Xu C, Ma DF (2013) Short-term traffic safety forecasting using Gaussian mixture model and Kalman filter. J Zhejiang Univ Sci A 14(4):231–243
4. Lee MY (2013) Analysis of traffic accident factor using decision tree model. PhD thesis, Myongji University, Seoul
5. Korea Transportation Safety Authority, Traffic Safety Forecasting, http://www.ts2020.kr/nsi/ssi/InqDetCRSTransSafFore.do
6. Hartigan JA, Wong MA (1979) Algorithm AS 136: a K-means clustering algorithm. J R Stat Soc Ser C 28(1):100–108
7. Ho TK (1995) Random decision forests. In: Proceedings of the 3rd international conference on document analysis and recognition, Montreal, QC, vol 1, pp 278–282

Efficient Skeleton Extraction Method Based on Depth Data in Infrared Self-help Camera System

Xingquan Cai, Shiyu Li, Lijian Zhao, Zishu Liu and Qianru Ye

Abstract In order to resolve the problem of unclear identification of human body region, incorrect extraction of skeleton and location of joint position, this paper mainly provides the skeleton extraction method based on depth data in self-help camera system. Firstly, we use the method of structure light to acquire the image and then use the binary way to process it to divide target from background. Then, we combine the algorithm of corrosion and expansion with the threshold method to get a skeletal structure. Finally, we get the relative position of human body, then find out the most likely bend points and locate the joint position according to the largest triangle method. The experiments results show that the skeleton extraction method based on depth data can extract skeletal structure better, and this method segments the background without unnecessary noisy point and blank to extract skeleton in an accurate way. We also design the human–computer interaction of taking photos using this method, and the system is feasible and effective.

Keywords Depth data · Skeleton extraction · Thinning method · Joint location

1 Introduction

With the development of science and technology, virtual reality and augmented reality interaction gradually get into people's vision. Currently, the virtual reality of human–computer interaction has been used in medical, gaming, health care [1] and many other fields. The computer can identify the body region, and communicate with people based on a series of parameters of people's action according to certain algorithms. The most important point is to extract the human skeleton accurately.

X. Cai (✉) · S. Li · L. Zhao · Z. Liu · Q. Ye
School of Computer Science and Technology, North China University of Technology,
Beijing, China
e-mail: xingquancai@126.com

© Springer Science+Business Media Singapore 2016
J.J. (Jong Hyuk) Park et al. (eds.), *Advanced Multimedia and Ubiquitous Engineering*, Lecture Notes in Electrical Engineering 393,
DOI 10.1007/978-981-10-1536-6_78

601

The traditional extraction techniques typically extract skeleton from the geometric model of skeleton, such methods are not only for humans but also for four-legged animals, so it is not an effective way for human skeleton. In addition, traditional skeleton extract method is more limited in extracting skeleton from different postures. Therefore, it is necessary to study a particular extraction way for human skeleton.

2 Related Work

First, the traditional skeleton extraction methods in acquiring a body area there will be some errors. There are two ways of static and dynamic detection of the body area and there are three main categories of dynamic human detection algorithm, namely optical flow method [2], the frame difference method [3] as well as background subtraction method. The optical flow method has the problem of calculation complicated, more time-consuming. These three measures do not resolve the shadows as a problem part of the human body.

Secondly, after the success of extracting human body from the background segmentation and human skeleton structure generally have the following approaches. Allen [4] proposed a template-based method for extracting the joint center. Zhuang [5] and Ding [6] provided a method based on geodesic distance to get the body topology. Cai [7] and Jin [8] performed bone joints positioned by the further study through that method.

3 Skeleton Extraction Method Based on Depth Data in Infrared Self-help Camera System

In order to extract the human skeleton information more accurately, we need to divide human from the background on the image we have captured, and then extract skeleton structure from what we get. In order to ensure the accuracy of the detected body area and extraction of skeleton, this paper studies the human skeleton extraction algorithm based on depth data.

The specific procedure of the skeleton extraction based on depth data are as follows: (1) Obtain depth data. Measure three-dimensional data of the image obtained by structured light, and concert it into depth image. After that, use the method of nonlinear median filtering algorithm to process data. (2) Extract the human skeleton. Use the method of edge detection based on the background image segmentation first to segment regions, and use the method of morphological to improve the extracting effect. (3) Extract the bone joints. Fix the bone joints according to the human body structure combined with the largest triangle.

3.1　Obtaining the Depth Data

Structured light measurement technology has the advantages of real-time, more accurate and fast measurement speed and so on. Using an infrared laser light source is projected structured light pattern, while using infrared camera after receiving structured light projected onto the object returned image. Depth data can be obtained by the distance between camera and laser projector.

$$D = \frac{L * H * f}{H * p + L * f} \tag{1}$$

In Formula (1), D is the depth of the corresponding position, H is the distance from the reference plane laser photographic apparatus or camera plane, f is the focal length of the camera, p is the offset of the imaging camera Patterns.

In this paper, our method is based on nonlinear median filter algorithm to sort the statistical theory of depth images for further processing. Filtering operation before proceeding to determine the mid-point of the window, if found to be noise filtering operation is performed, or not performed. Median filtering formulas used in this paper is as follows.

$$g(x, y) = med\{f(x - m, y - n)\} \quad (m, n \in W) \tag{2}$$

In Formula (2), W is a two-dimensional filtering template, m is the length of the template, n is the width of the template, g(x, y) is the depth of the image after the filtering process, f(x, y) of the original image.

3.2　Extracting the Human Skeleton

Regional depth image segmentation region segmentation generic image compared to the more complex it is, because the pixel gray roommate depth information maps each point from the edge gradient of each region is not obvious. So we use the threshold method for image object extraction, extraction formula below.

$$f(x, y) = \begin{cases} 0, & d(x, y) > \theta \\ 1, & d(x, y) < \theta \end{cases} \tag{3}$$

In Formula (3), f(x, y) for the picture logical value (x, y) at, d(x, y) is the depth of the image coordinates (x, y) at a depth value, θ is the threshold depth image.

After the morphological transformation of the depth of the images, this paper is expanded, corrosion of image processing operations. Expansion can effectively resolve the blank appearing in the image. The main purpose is to increase the expansion of the target volume, so you can point contact with the object as the target object to the background is divided into remove the voids. Corrosion can shrink inward to remove some invalid point boundary pixels. Dilation formula and formula respectively etching operation is as follows.

$$U = X \otimes Y = \cup \{x + y | x \in X, y \in Y\} \qquad (4)$$

$$Z = X \Theta Y = \cap \{z \in \Omega Y^z \subseteq X\} \qquad (5)$$

In Formulae (4) and (5), U is the result set X by Y set after expansion, Z is the result set X by Y etched set.

The proposed segmentation method based on background depth image more complete removal of body parts, be able to retain full effective regional body. Compared with the frame difference wears, this method effectively overcome on a stationary object extraction problems extracting effect is more superior.

3.3   Locating Joint Positions of Human

Winter [6] studies have shown that, although there are some differences in individual terms, but relative to the length of each part of the body height is very close. So, we first determine the approximate joint position based on the data provided by NASA human proportions. Then, use the largest triangular method to identify the most likely about turning points, finally get the coordinates of the body's major joints.

The maximum triangle, as shown below arc is extracted human skeleton arm bones diagram chart, connecting point A and point B can constitute a triangle with a point on the arc, to find the location of the point can be constructed where the largest triangle. In point of multiple possibilities, choose the largest possible to form a triangle point, as determined D point of the elbow joint bones position, just as Fig. 1 shows.

Fig. 1 Largest triangular method

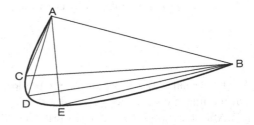

4 Results

In order to verify the feasibility and effectiveness of method based on depth data, this paper designs and implements this method which has been used in camera system in reality. The hardware environment is as follows: CPU with Intel Core i5 3.2 GHz, memory with 4 GB, graphics card with NVIDIA GeForce315. The software environment is as follows: Windows7, VS2010, OpenCV and so on.

4.1 The Experiment of Extracting Skeleton Structure

Measure three-dimensional data of the image obtained by structured light, and concert it into depth image, then use the method of nonlinear median filtering algorithm to process data. Figure 2a is the original image, Fig. 2b is the depth of the image by the structured light measurement technology acquired, Fig. 2c is the non-linearly in the value of the extracted image filtering algorithms.

4.2 Contrast Experiment with the Traditional Skeleton Extract

Skeleton extraction is good or bad judgment standard, it can be divided into three areas: accuracy, connectivity, and a single pixel. Figure 3a, d showed the skeleton graph obtained by the research of Ding [6] and Cai [7]. Figure 3b, c, e, f were obtained through the proposed method of treatment of human skeletal structure. Can be found, based on the depth image skeleton extraction method can be better achieved extraction of the human skeleton and significantly better than traditional methods. Through experimental results can be seen, this design method can accurately extract the human skeletal structure and human joints for accurate positioning.

(a) **(b)** **(c)**

Fig. 2 Obtain depth image

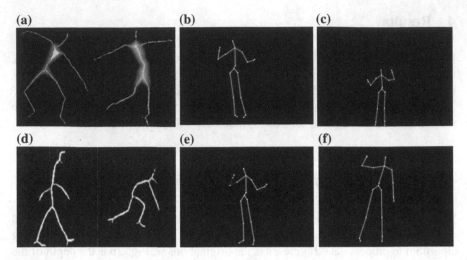

Fig. 3 Contrast images with traditional skeleton extraction method

4.3 The Human–Computer Interaction of Taking Photos

This article is designed an interactive camera system based on infrared. People can interact with their movement computer through an infrared camera. When people enter the camera range, the use of this method on human region detection, identification and division, based on the acquired images of the human skeleton was

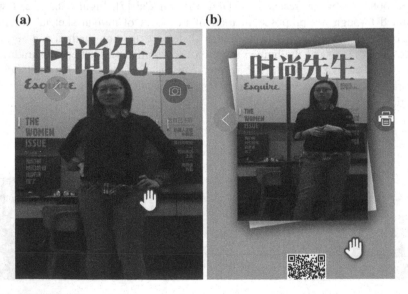

Fig. 4 Interactive camera system

extracted, and then determine the body's joint position, determine human hand joints to determine the operator operation needed to complete the interaction between man and computer.

In this paper, the corresponding operation of the system and collected a series of operating results, to achieve a good man–machine interactive experience taking pictures, a good application of the methods described herein. Figure 4a, b are effect diagram.

5 Conclusions and Future Work

This article is designed and implemented a human skeleton extraction method based on depth data. Using the structured light measurement technology and binary processing to obtain depth data; segmented the target area from image according to the threshold method, the use of corrosion, expansion and opening and closing operation gradually refined finally get the body skeleton; the use of the relative position of the body between the joint acquisition of key points, and then find out the maximum bending triangle method most likely point to determine the key joints of the human skeleton. Experiments show that the extraction method based on depth data is better in extracting skeleton of human body; performed when the background region and the body region segmentation, removes unnecessary noise and voids, the body area to be better identified extraction of bone, significantly better than traditional methods; Method This design, design and implementation of interactive camera system, the system is stable and reliable.

Future work including improving the applicability of our method to solve the problem of human self-occlusion, deeply using Euclidean distance transform algorithm to optimize our human skeleton extraction method.

Acknowledgments This research was supported by Project of National Science and Technology Support Plan (2012BAF84F02).

References

1. Meng M, Yang F, Luo Z (2015) Human joint location and gait analysis based on depth image. Huazhong Univ Sci Tech (Nat Sci Ed) S1:359–362
2. Horn BKP, Schunck BG (1981) Determining optical flow. Artif Intell 17:185–203
3. Stauffer C, Grimson W (2000) Learning patterns of activity using real-time tracking. IEEE Trans Pattern Anal Mach Intell 747–757
4. Allen B, Curless B, Popovic Z (2003) The space of all bodyshapes: reconstruction and parameterization from rangescans. In: Proceedings of ACM SIGGRAPH
5. Zhuang Y, Liu X, Pan Y, Yang J (2000) 3D human skeleton reconstruction from motion image sequence. J Comput Aided Des Comput Graph 245–250

6. Ding J, Wang Y, Yu L (2010) Extraction of human body skeleton based on Silhouette images. IEEE Ed Technol Comput Sci (ETCS) 1:71–74
7. Cai J, Kong L, Li H (2012) Calibration based on Euclidean distance transformation of human 2D joints. Comput Simul 29(7):243–246
8. Jin P, Bouman CA, Sauer KD (2015) A model-based image reconstruction algorithm with simultaneous beam hardening correction for X-ray CT. IEEE Trans Comput Imaging 1(3): 200–216

Optimal Location of Regional Emergency Trauma Centers Using Geocoded Crash Data

Shin Hyoung Park and Oh Hoon Kwon

Abstract Crashes on highways tend to be more serious on account of the high-speed driving of the vehicles involved. Therefore, a delay in handling a crash or transporting a patient may mean additional personal injury. To prevent such injury, quick emergency response is required. The purpose of this study is to analyze the optimal locations of regional emergency trauma centers, which allow for the effective handling of emergency trauma patients, and to determine the priority of each candidate hospital in terms of establishing trauma centers. Under such purpose, this study geocoded highway crash records to create a basis for spatial analysis and determined the priority of each candidate hospital by calculating the number of crashes handled based on the traffic volume and the severity of crashes using the maximum covering location problem model. The significance of this study is that it provides a basis for prioritizing the government's financial supports for the candidate hospitals.

Keywords Maximum covering location problem · Geocoding · Regional emergency trauma center · Equivalent property damage only · Spatial analysis

1 Introduction

The number of persons killed or injured by crashes on highways between 2012 and 2014 is 286 and 1452, respectively. Crashes on highways tend to be more serious because of the high-speed driving of the vehicles involved. Therefore, a delay in handling a crash or transporting a patient may mean additional personal injury. To prevent such injury, quick emergency response is required. For this reason, many

S.H. Park · O.H. Kwon (✉)
Department of Transportation, Engineering College of Engineering, Keimyung University,
1095 Dalgubeol-daero Dalseo-gu, Daegu 42601, Republic of Korea
e-mail: ohoonkwon@kmu.ac.kr

S.H. Park
e-mail: shpark@kmu.ac.kr

© Springer Science+Business Media Singapore 2016   609
J.J. (Jong Hyuk) Park et al. (eds.), *Advanced Multimedia and Ubiquitous Engineering*, Lecture Notes in Electrical Engineering 393,
DOI 10.1007/978-981-10-1536-6_79

commentators have pointed out the need for trauma centers complete with facilities, equipment, and workforce to treat patients with multiple fractures or bleeding (severely injured) patients, who require treatment outside the capabilities of typical emergency rooms as soon as they arrive at the hospital. To address such need, the Korean Ministry of Health and Welfare established a plan to establish 17 regional emergency trauma centers evenly distributed across the nation by 2017 so that severely injured patients may receive treatment within an hour anywhere in Korea.

The regional emergency trauma centers need to be located close to locations where crashes occur at a higher frequency to ensure quick treatment of severely injured patients and, therefore, to improve their survivability. To be more precise, the efficacy of a regional emergency trauma center can be improved by locating it closer to places where a higher number of serious crashes occur. Therefore, this study seeks to identify the optimal locations for regional emergency trauma centers to ensure the quick transportation of patients injured by crashes on highways and, therefore, to lower the fatalities caused by such crashes. To identify such locations, this study first collected crash records on highways and geocoded these records using the Geographic Information System (GIS) application to draw up a digital crash map. Then, each crash was given a severity weight based on the number of fatalities and the number of injuries to convert it into the index "number of crashes handled." Lastly, hospitals satisfying the requirements and criteria for regional emergency trauma center establishment were selected as primary candidate hospitals and were set the priority for establishment based on the number of crashes handled.

2   Literature Review

2.1   Geocoding

Geocoding of crashes means assigning geographical location information, such as the lateral/longitudinal coordinates to individual crash data [1]. Geocoded crash records can be mapped on a digital map for visualization or can provide useful information through spatial analysis. The method to geocode crash data using the postmiles of highways was proposed by Bigham et al. [1], who used the records of crashes on highways in California, and Park et al. [2], who used highway crash records in Korea. The two studies applied the linear referencing method to map crash data with postmile information on road networks. Another study identified hazardous sections of highways by performing spatial analyses on geocoded crash records using GIS [3].

This study applied the geocoding method proposed by Park et al. [2] to geocode the crash records on highways in Korea and used the coded data to analyze the locations of regional emergency trauma centers.

2.2 Analysis on Optimal Locations

"Maximum covering location problem" refers to the problem of maximizing the serviceable volume within a certain scope through a given number of locations. This model, first proposed by Church et al. [4], is one of the most widely used location model to determine the location of fire stations, emergency centers, and police stations [5]. In Korea, the model was used by Kim et al. [5] to determine the optimal locations for highway patrol.

This study developed the "number of crashes handled" index and applied the maximum covering problem model to set priorities for trauma center establishments to candidate hospitals capable of maximizing the number of crashes handled.

3 Methodology

3.1 Data Description

The expressway network and collision data were provided by the Korea Expressway Corporation. The 2015 street network included information on main sections of each expressway line, individual line segment lengths, and locations of reference points such as interchanges (ICs) and Junctions (JCs). A total of 29,960 collision records were obtained from 2012 to 2014, an annual average of approximately 9987 records.

3.2 Crash Geocoding

Geocoding is completed through a process consisting of the following steps: "creating routes", "adding postmile markers", "calibrating routes" and "geocoding collisions using linear referencing". For the details, please refer to Park et al. [2].

3.3 Equivalent Property Damage Only (EPDO)

This study used the Equivalent Property Damage Only (EPDO) method to convert the weight of each individual crash into an index that reflects its severity. The EPDO is a weighted sum of the number of crashes where a property damage only crash counts as a single accident, a crash with any fatality counts as 12 crashes, a crash with any serious injury counts as 6 crashes, and a crash with any slight injury counts as 3 crashes. By converting the number of individual crashes into EPDO, the number of crashes included in the coverage of a candidate hospital for regional emergency trauma center establishment is calculated using the sum of EPDO rather than the simple total number of crashes. This allows for assigning higher priorities on candidate hospitals capable of handling higher numbers of serious crashes.

3.4 Calculation Model for Accident Handling Volume

This study built a model equation to calculate the "number of crashes handled" index to compare the priorities of the candidate hospitals for the trauma center.

The unit segment used for index calculation was the segment between two adjacent ICs, or between an IC and a JC. In general, the number of crashes is proportional to the traffic volume. The segments between two ICs or an IC and a JC are suitable to be used as unit segments for analysis because vehicles enter or exit highways only through ICs and JCs, which means that the traffic volumes at such segments are conserved. For the reasons above, the unit segments for calculating the number of crashes handled were defined as the segments between adjacent entry/exit facilities.

The model equation was established as shown in Eq. (1) below.

$$X_k = \frac{\sum_i^n \frac{A_{ij} \times B_{ij}}{L_j}}{D_{kj}} \tag{1}$$

where
k Regional emergency trauma center candidate hospital (hospital),
i Years (i = 2012, 2013, and 2014),
A_{ij} Annual Average Daily Traffic (AADT) of section j in year i,
B_{ij} EPDO of section j in year i, L_j: Length of section j,
D_{kj} Distance from hospital k to section j ($D_{kj} \leq 50$ km), and
X_k Volume of accidents handled by hospital k.

The segments considered by the equation are limited to those within a 50 km radius from a candidate hospital. 50 km radius is the range where an ambulance can make a round trip to a crash position within an hour at an average driving speed of 100 km/h. A patient who sustained a very serious injury is transported using an emergency helicopter. Assuming that the speed of such helicopter is 250 km/h, the 50 km radius represents the distance where a helicopter can arrive at a crash point within 15 min.

By multiplying the traffic volume of each segment with its EPDO, then dividing the result by the length of the segment, the number of crashes handled can be given a weight based on the traffic volume and the severity of the crashes per unit length (1 km). The resulting value is divided by the distance from the hospital to the segment to consider the weight based on the movement distance. In other words, the equation considers the fact that it is more effective to position a severe-trauma center closer to a highway segment where a higher traffic volume leads to a higher likelihood of accidents and where serious accidents occur at a higher frequency. Using the number of crashes handled (X_k) calculated from the model equation, the priority of each severe-trauma center location can be determined.

When the coverage is set at 50 km, there may be overlapping segments between hospitals. For such segments, the overlapping number of crashes handled was divided by the number of hospitals and were assigned to each hospital.

4 Result

A total of 14 hospitals were analyzed, including 6 hospitals with existing trauma centers and 8 candidate hospitals for regional emergency trauma center establishment. The list and the IDs of the hospitals are shown in Table 1.

To determine the priority for additional establishment, this study calculated the number of crashes handled by a candidate hospital when the candidate hospital is added to the existing six hospitals operating trauma centers, as shown in Table 2.

The analysis shows that Ajou University Hospital holds the 1st priority, followed by Kyungpook National University Hospital. Ajou University Hospital is located in the Seoul Metropolitan Area, where 40 % of the entire South Korean population live. Considering the ratio of the population, a trauma center needs to be established at Ajou University Hospital. In addition, the high priority of

Table 1 List of hospitals analyzed

ID	Hospital name	Note	ID	Hospital name	Note
1	Gachon University Gil Medical Center	Trauma center in operation	8	National Medical Center	To be established
2	Dankook University Hospital	Trauma center in operation	9	Busan University Hospital	To be established
3	Mokpo Hankook Hospital	Trauma center in operation	10	Uijeongbu St. Mary's Hospital	To be established
4	Ulsan University Hospital	Trauma center in operation	11	Ajou University Hospital	To be established
5	Wonju Severance Christian Hospital	Trauma center in operation	12	Andong Hospital	To be established
6	Chonnam National University Hospital	Trauma center in operation	13	Eulji University Hospital	To be established
7	Kyungpook National University Hospital	to be established	14	Chungbuk National University Hospital	To be established

Table 2 Candidate Priority Calculation

Rank	ID	No. of crashes handled	Rank	ID	No. of crashes handled
1	11	2,669,164	5	9	548,963
2	7	2,358,661	6	13	429,291
3	10	2,302,840	7	14	326,846
4	8	2,218,704	8	12	81,371

Kyungpook National University Hospital can be attributed to its location in Daegu Metropolitan City, a city with a population of 2.5 million, and the fact that there is currently no severe-trauma center covering the southeastern part of the country.

5 Conclusion

This study determined the priorities of candidate hospitals for severe-trauma centers by geocoding crash data and performing a space analysis. When a severe collision occurs on a highway where vehicles drive at a high speed, it is imperative to quickly transport injured patients to a severe-trauma center for emergency treatment to improve their survivability. For this reason, this study estimated the number of crashes handled by each candidate hospital for regional emergency trauma center establishment using EPDO, which represents the number of crashes weighted with the traffic volume and the seriousness of the accidents. The result was used to determine the priorities for establishing regional emergency trauma centers.

The facilities, equipment, and workforce required for the operation of a regional emergency trauma center is financed by the government, which requires a large amount of financial resources to set up and operate. Therefore, it would be more cost-effective to begin establishing trauma centers, starting from high-priority candidate hospitals with locations that allow them to treat higher numbers of injured patients. Then, the significance of this study is that it provides a basis for prioritizing the government's financial supports for the candidate sites.

Future researches are required to develop methods that consider policy-related aspects, such as a balanced development across different regions, as well as quantitative indexes, such as the number of crashes handled. In addition, a possibly useful research theme would be analyzing the minimum number of regional emergency trauma centers and their locations, which maximizes the number of crashes handled by the entire system, without limiting the number of trauma centers. As for the methodology, a method needs to be developed, which applies the p-center problem model to minimize the distance to the most distant point from a center, as a replacement for the maximum covering location problem model, which limits the range of coverage.

Acknowledgements This research was supported by the Bisa Research Grant of Keimyung University in 2014

References

1. Bigham JM, Rice TM, Pande S, Lee J, Park SH, Gutierrez NB, Ragland DR (2009) Geocoding police collision report data from California: a comprehensive approach. Int J Health Geogr 8:72
2. Park SH, Bigham JM, Kho SY, Kang S, Kim DK (2011) Geocoding vehicle collisions on Korean expressways based on postmile referencing. KSCE J Civ Eng 15(8):1435–1441
3. Park SH, Jang K, Kim DK, Kho SY, Kang S (2015) Spatial analysis methods for identifying hazardous locations on expressways in Korea. Sci Iran Trans B Mech Eng 22(4):1594–1603
4. Church R, Velle CR (1974) The maximal covering location problem. Pap Reg Sci 32(1): 101–118
5. Kim M, Kim HS, Kim DK, Lee C (2013) Optimal location of expressway patrol vehicle stations using maximum covering and weighted p-center problems. J Korea Inst Intell Transp Syst 12 (1):43–50

Design and Android Application for Monitoring System Using PLC for ICT-Integrated Fish Farm

Jun-Ho Huh

Abstract There have been many cases of mass mortality of fish due to the power interruptions caused by natural disasters, human errors or acts of sabotage by the employees hired by rival companies, discouraging the small and medium-sized fish farmers. Thus, in this paper, a system that can monitor the power status of fish farms to cope with such situations is being proposed. The system utilizes both PLC and ICT technologies to respond to crisis. Electric power is a critical parameter for both the land-based and the water recycling fish farms. The mass mortality of fish due to natural disasters was the highest risk in the aquaculture industry. The proposed system allows immediate response for the power interruptions and consistent power monitoring by the employees. To compensate the signal transmission loss often caused by the noise power typical in the PLC-utilized models, RUDP is proposed for the transmission layer. Also, for the Android application, a graphic user interface was designed to manage overall fish farm activities, photoperiod, seawater control, Smart Aquafarm, access control, location check, withdrawal period, and secondary battery check.

Keywords Energy harvesting · PLC · Smart aquafarm · Fish farm · Application

1 Introduction

To achieve a "Creative Economy" in the Republic of Korea (ROK), economic democratization must be realized first. People will be able to put their best efforts with hopes only when a fair market order is established. It is a very important goal for the government to implement a development policy for the small and

J.-H. Huh (✉)
Department of Computer Engineering, Pukyong National University,
Busan, Republic of Korea
e-mail: 72networks@pukyong.ac.kr

J.-H. Huh
SUNCOM Co, Busan, Republic of Korea

© Springer Science+Business Media Singapore 2016
J.J. (Jong Hyuk) Park et al. (eds.), *Advanced Multimedia and Ubiquitous Engineering*, Lecture Notes in Electrical Engineering 393,
DOI 10.1007/978-981-10-1536-6_80

medium-sized companies to let them succeed in their business and to coexist with larger firms. For this, the Korean government is trying to eradicate unfair trading practices of the past and the present so that company workers and owners in every industry can demonstrate their best ability. Contrary to such efforts, in the aquaculture industry, there are still many troubling cases and the power interruption is one of major problems. Power interruptions usually result from natural disasters but human-related incidents cannot be ignored. Thus, this paper proposes a crisis-response system and an Android application for the small and medium-sized fish farms, using the PLC and ICT technologies. The power management is a major parameter for the land-based and water recirculating fish farms [1, 2]. The mass mortality caused by the natural disasters (e.g., typhoons, abnormal temperatures or red tides, etc.) are the major problems and the power interruption at the farming site has been considered to be the worst situation. The proposed system has been designed to cope with power interruptions. For the system model, the use of RUDP on a transport layer which is one of the seven OSI layers, is proposed to compensate transmission losses caused by noise powers typical in the PLC models.

2   Related Research

2.1   Power Line Communication (PLC)

The current PLC can speed up to 1Mbps to 1Gbps and has reached commercialization for the home and the multimedia networks [1–5]. Its biggest problem is data loss due to the noises generated by the power lines but they can be compensated by using transformers [6–13]. This technology has been applied to light and home appliance control or telephone networks and is now receiving the spotlight as a core technology for IoT system construction. The major advantage of using PLC for IoT construction process is that no additional communication network construction is necessary to exchange information between devices or equipments since communications can be established with power line(s) only, without any other communication circuits. For instance, in the ROK, Logistics, Energy Korea Co., Ltd. (KOSDAK listed company) developed the attachable PLC modems and the external PLC modems, both for watt-hour meters. Other instance is that the Korea Electrotechnology Research Institute has succeeded in developing the PLC-based broadcast circuit for the first time in the ROK. It's being expected that use of the PLC technology will be increased in other application fields but there always has been a problem of reliability in communication process. Thus, using RUDP for the transport layer to compensate losses by the noises is proposed.

2.2   Reliable User Datagram Protocol (RUDP)

To compensate transmission or data loss often caused by the noises typical in the PLC-based models, RUDP [6, 7] was selected for the use for the transport layer. A reliable transfer protocol is required to send signals on a network. Such protocol should be able to support various architectures of used applications. To check RUDP's reliability, a simulation has been carried in the preceding research [8, 11] in addition to its performance evaluation. The results of the performance evaluation for the simulation are as follows.

$$\sum_{t=0}^{n} \frac{\partial P_{TCP}}{\partial T} = 0.99 \tag{1}$$

Sum of the time-derivatives against received packet volume when TCP is used.

$$\sum_{t=0}^{n} \frac{\partial P_{UDP}}{\partial T} = 0.97 \tag{2}$$

Sum of the time-derivatives against received packet volume when UDP is used.

$$\sum_{t=0}^{n} \frac{\partial P_{RUDP}}{\partial T} = 0.98 \tag{3}$$

Sum of the time-derivatives against received packet volume when RUDP is used.

Although TCP has the best speed but UDP is used often instead as TCP has some vulnerability in security. RUDP has been improved in speed factor so that RUDP is proposed to compensate noise-oriented transmission losses.

3   System Design for ICT-Integrated Fish Farm Monitoring and Its Android Application

Figure 1 shows overall description of the system in discussion. When operating a fish farm, human resource management is deeply associated with monetary aspects. Financial losses can resulted from accidents or wrong-doings by the employees when they exhibit some problems due to their situations and behaviors. Such losses are the risk factors for the small business companies but they can be efficiently reduced with the ICT technology.

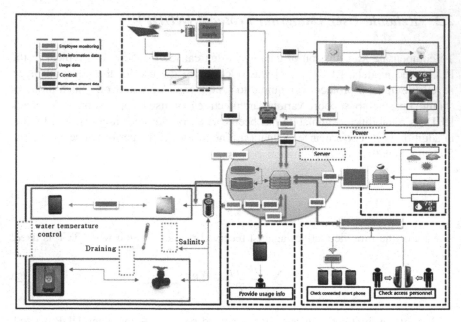

Fig. 1 A system design for ICT-integrated fish farm monitoring and its android application

3.1 Employee Monitoring

By using the fish farm theft-prevention tags, the management can monitor working situations of employees. The farm owner can have the advantage of easily and precisely checking individual employee's location, working situation and monthly attendance. This will not only prevent financial losses but also can secure employees' safety by informing the dangers to them when accidents or problems should occur. On the other hand, employees do not have to rely on the time cards to check their attendance records, which are the basis of their wages, to avoid unnecessary dispute.

The technology being described was designed based on a method that was used for a door-lock system using wireless AP, and RUDP was selected to improve communication efficiency and reliability. The system application has been programmed with C and C ++ languages followed by the implementation with Java Android. This system has the merit of not requiring any additional circuits to establish communications between devices or equipments as existing power line(s) will be used. Since electric power is available for most of fish farms despite of their remote locations in the agriculture and fishing villages, farmers will be able to establish a PLC network with low costs using the existing facilities provided by the Korean Electric Power Corporation (KEPCO). The core algorithm of the employee monitoring system is described in Fig. 2.

A_p : Address accessed in the past

A_n: Current address being accessed

$f(x) = (\sum Number(A_p) - \sum Number(A_n))$

//Comparison of the numbers of the past and current addresses approached

if $f(x) = 0$ //If the numbers are identical

    if $\sum Time(A_n) \geq 1Hour$ //If the current approach time exceeds 1 hour

    Then Warning Message transmission to the User's phone

    Not $Return(f(x))$ //Return to f(x) comparison

Not $(= f(x) \neq 0)$ // If the numbers are not identical

    if $\sum Number(A_n) \geq 2(= g(x))$//Assume that the number of current

                               //approaching address is 2 or more

    Then $Return(g(x))$ //Return to g(x) comparison

    Not

    if $\sum Time(A_n) \geq 0.5Hour$

//If the current approach time exceeds 0,5 hour

    Then Visitation request message transmission to the User's phone

    Not $Return(f(x))$ //Return to f(x) comparison

Fig. 2 The core algorithm of the employee monitoring system

By using the employee monitoring algorithm in addition to positioning service, it is possible to prevent employee's negligence of duties and thefts of value fishes. Moreover, the system can save employees in times of emergencies in an early stage by checking the whereabouts of them periodically and informing them of fore-coming dangers. Figure 3 show the method of employee monitoring.

Most of fish farms hire people living close by the fishing villages so that the major portion of the employees is comprised of older generations as many younger ones are leaving the area. Such situation brings about dangerous situations (e.g., exhaustion fainting by heat waves, etc.) especially in summer for these employees but with the system equipped with the proposed algorithm and design, their lives

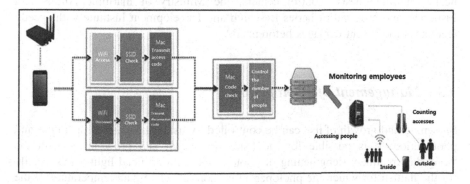

Fig. 3 A method of monitoring employees

can be saved by checking their movements. The system will recognize the danger when a employee does not move for long hours.

Fish farms ship out fishes and shells when their growth have reached the scheduled levels so that the seasonal, not continuous, transactions will be carried out. The theft or the accidents in such periods will bring a devastating damage.

The theft prevention systems used at the existing fish farms require much investment and more expenses are needed for the installment by the professional companies. Compare to this, the PLC-based system will require a moderate expenses in an early stage of installment and can be operated continuously efficiently. After designating the people who can access the farm, tags will be attached to them to check their access times, access statuses and periods. The access by one without the tag will be notified to the owner or the management through the application embedded in the smart phones, preventing thefts.

3.2 Farming Environment Monitoring

Various factors must be balanced within an appropriate environment when culturing marine products. For the ocean cage-fishing farms, seawater temperatures, weathers, currents and tides should be considered and for the land-based farms, water temperatures, pH and salinity are the important factors. Especially the latter is often influenced by the temperature changes caused by the nearby factories who use seawater as a coolant or by the changes in salinity within the tanks resulting from salty substances carried from the seaside, leading to mass mortality of fishes and shells. Since these changes cannot be visually recognized, it is difficult for the small and medium-sized fish farms. Even a little changes could present much damage and if they accumulate, a greater damage can be expected. However, it is possible to check these changes with the proposed application immediately and by setting the checking categories to issue an alarm, farmers will be able to prevent damages and reduce manpower waste. Meanwhile, by creating a database for the fish-oriented diseases and intelligently operating the system, relevant information can be sent to nearby marine disease control centers, the Ministry of maritime Affairs and Fisheries, and National Fisheries Research and Development Institute with speedy feedbacks to prevent damages beforehand.

3.3 Management of Photoperiod

Spawning and growth of fish can be controlled by using the water temperature and photoperiod. It is possible for the fishes to spawn and grow faster with the "long-day treatment (lengthening of photoperiod with artificial lights)", especially for the flatfish for which the photoperiod is more effective than temperature. If the photoperiod can be controlled with automatic light adjustments through the application, the number of fishes will be multiplied much faster.

3.4 Aspects of Energy and Environmental Conservation

3.4.1 Auxiliary Batteries and Sollar Cells

Currently, typhoons during the summer are the major concern of fish farmers as the power interruptions by them can be fatal to their farms. Even a short interruption can result in entire mortality within the farm so that they prepare for the emergency situations when typhoon alerts are issued. To deal with such situations, the auxiliary batteries, which can be charged at dawn and used in the daytime during which the same batteries can be re charged through solar pipes, can be considered. In this way, farmers can save the power within the batteries 24 h a day to get ready for unexpected or notified power interruptions, reducing damages.

3.4.2 Controlling Withdrawal Period

Use of antibiotics are inescapable when growing the fishes and shells. Since antibiotics often remain in the body of marine organisms for a certain period of time, fishes and shells must be shipped out after going through withdrawal time. However, for the reason that there are so many kinds of antibiotics and they are being used frequently, the management and workers do not know their exact quantities for use and recommended/required withdrawal times. Thus, the application includes a Guide to Medicines for Marine Products (Korea National Fisheries Research and Development Institute 2014) in their database to notify the ending day of withdrawal period by alarm once the kind and quantity of antibiotic being used are entered into the system. This function will provide a greater safety image for the marine products.

The two most important elements for aquaculture, dissolved oxygen and temperature, need to be continuously observed and managed but in many cases, employees at the site were unable to cope with emergency situations. Figure 4 shows design of Android application. The application is comprised of five menus: Fish Farm Management, Access Control, Positioning, Withdrawal Period Checking and Auxiliary Battery. Under the Fish Farm Management menu includes photoperiod and seawater managements. In addition to photoperiod, DO (Dissolved Oxygen), pH and temperature of seawater can be check here for each block. Access Control manages the access personnel for theft-prevention purpose and should an unauthorized person enters the farm, alarm will sound through Smart phone(s). Positioning menu locates whereabouts of employees in real time and lets them to be ready for the emergency situations. Withdrawal Period Checking will notify the user the last day of the period by alarm. Auxiliary Battery menu indicates the level

Fig. 4 Design of fish farm android application

of remaining power and lets the user to be prepared for the emergencies such as power interruptions.

4 Conclusion and Future Work

The electrical power is a critical parameter for both the land-based and the water recycling fish farms. Especially, the power interruptions caused by typhoons present a grave consequences to the farms leading to a mass mortality. The proposed algorithm and application will assist the farmers to deal with such situations and allow an efficient and continuous monitoring.

In this paper, the use of RUDP has been proposed for the transport layer to compensate the transmission loss usually caused by the typical noises of the PLC-based communication models. Also, for the Android application a graphic user interface has been developed to manage fish farm activities, photoperiod, and to control seawater condition, Smart aquafarm, access, as well as checking the location of employees, withdrawal period and secondary batteries. This research will be disclosed on a journal after registering and applying the technology for a patent. Author expects that the small and medium-sized fish farms will easily find this system acceptable as it can reduce a small portion of repetitive damages every year. Furthermore, since the application will control the use of antibiotics, which is the major concern of our public, the fear will be allayed and trust of marine products will be increased.

References

1. Akinnikawe A, Butler-Purry KL (2009) Investigation of broadband over power line channel capacity of shipboard power system cables for ship communication networks. IEEE Power Energy Society General Meeting, Calgary, pp 1–9
2. Barmada S, Bellanti L, Raugi M, Tucci M (2010) Analysis of power-line communication channels in ships. IEEE Trans Veh Technol 59(7):3161–3170
3. Antoniali M, Tonello AM, Lenardon M, Qualizza A (2011) Measurements and analysis of PLC channels in a cruise ship, IEEE international symposium on power line communications and its applications, Udine, pp 102–107
4. Ding QM, Li D, Zhao D, Linlin L (2010) Design and implementation of a sensors node oriented water quality monitoring in aquaculture, Home/Sens Lett 8(1)
5. Yang YM, Fang-Tsou C-T (2014) Aquaculture cloud management system, J Inf Technol Appl 8(2): pp 1–3
6. Bova, T., Krivoruchka, T.: Reliable UDP Protocol. IETF Internet-Draft (1999)
7. Thammadi A (2011) Reliable user datagram protocol (RUDP). Kansas State University Master's Thesis, pp 2–13
8. Huh J-H, Seo K (2015) RUDP design and implementation using LNEE, vol 330. LNEE. Springer, Heidelberg, pp 913–919
9. Huh J-H, Lee D-G, Seo K (2015) Design and implementation of the basic technology for realtime smart metering system using power line communication for smart grid. In: Advances in computer science and ubiquitous computing, vol 373. LNEE. Springer, Singapore, pp 663–669 (2015)
10. Huh J-H, Seo K (2015) Hybrid advanced metering infrastructure design for micro grid using the game theory model. Int J Softw Eng Appl 9(9):257–268
11. Huh J-H, Je S-M, Seo K (2016) Communications-based technology for smart grid test bed using OPNET simulations, vol 376. In: ICISA 2016. LNEE. Springer, Singapore, pp 227–233
12. Huh J-H, Koh T, Seo K (2016) Design of NMEA2000 can bus integrated network system and its test bed: setting up the PLC system in between bridge–bow room section on a container ship as a backbone system. In: Microelectronics, electromagnetics and telecommunications, vol 372. LNEE. Springer, India, pp 191–204
13. Huh J-H, Otgonchimeg S, Seo K (2016) Advanced metering infrastructure design and test bed experiment using intelligent agents: focusing on the PLC network base technology for smart grid system. J Supercomput 72(5):1862–1877

Modified Wavelet Domain Hidden Tree Model for Texture Segmentation

Yulong Qiao and Ganchao Zhao

Abstract The wavelet-domain hidden Markov tree (HMT) model provides a powerful approach for image modeling and processing because it captures the key features of the wavelet coefficients of real-world data. However, it is usually assumed that the subbands at the same level are independent in the traditional HMT model. This paper proposes a modified HMT model, SHMT-S, in which a vector constructed from the coefficients at the same location of the subbands of the same level, is controlled by a hidden state. Meanwhile we also use the vector Laplace mixture distributions to fit the wavelet coefficients vector, which is peakier in the center and has heavier tails compared with Gaussian distribution. By using the HMT segmentation framework, we develop SHMT-S based segmentation methods for image textures and dynamic textures. The experimental results demonstrate the effectiveness of the proposed method.

Keywords Wavelet-domain hidden Markov tree · Laplace distribution · Texture segmentation · Dynamic texture

1 Introduction

Texture is an important component of natural images. It's generally recognized that the image texture is defined as a function of the spatial variation in pixel gray values. Dynamic textures or temporal textures are the textures which are in motion, which can be described as visual processes of complex dynamical objects such as smoke, sea waves [1]. They provide important visual cues for various image (video)

Y. Qiao · G. Zhao (✉)
College of Information and Communication Engineering,
Harbin Engineering University, Harbin, China
e-mail: zhaogc929@163.com

Y. Qiao
e-mail: qiaoyulong@hrbeu.edu.cn

© Springer Science+Business Media Singapore 2016   627
J.J. (Jong Hyuk) Park et al. (eds.), *Advanced Multimedia and Ubiquitous Engineering*, Lecture Notes in Electrical Engineering 393,
DOI 10.1007/978-981-10-1536-6_81

processing problems. Therefore, texture analysis is an important and interesting research field.

Multi-scale Bayesian approaches for texture segmentation have been proven efficient to integrate both features and the contextual information into the estimation of class labels. Crouse [2] proposed the wavelet-domain HMT model to achieve the statistical characterization of signals by capturing inter-scale dependencies of wavelet coefficients across scales. The wavelet-domain HMT-3S developed by Fan [3] integrates the three DWT subbands into one tree structure with the help of graphical grouping technique, has been proved an effective method for presenting the statistical dependencies across DWT subbands. However, the feature size of HMT-3S is larger than the original HMT, and this model is difficult to apply to dynamic texture analysis. The segmentation method derived in [4, 5], HMTseg, has been proved as a very useful solution by combining the parametric wavelet-domain statistical modeling, direct likelihood calculation, and multi-scale Bayesian decision fusion [6].

In this paper, we propose a modified wavelet-domain modeling method by integrating the three DWT subbands into one tree structure, whose interscale dependencies are captured by the Markov chain based on the scalar hidden states across scale. Specifically, the hidden state is scalar, and the wavelet coefficients of different subbands at the same level are stacked into a vector, on which the modified HMT model SHMT-S is based. Thus the model can capture the intrascale relationship of the wavelet coefficients. In addition, because the Laplacian distribution is peakier in the center and has heavier tails compared with Gaussian distribution [7], we also refine the model by using Laplace mixture model (LMM) for the wavelet coefficient vector. Then the segmentation method with the modified model is introduced.

The rest of this paper is organized as follows. In Sect. 2, we briefly review the basic concepts of HMT models, and introduce the SHMT-S model structure. In Sect. 3, we propose the Laplace distributions based SHMT-S model and its parameter estimation. In Sect. 4, we introduce SHMT-S model based image texture segmentation and dynamic texture segmentation. Experimental results are shown and analyzed in the fifth section, and then the conclusion is given in Sect. 6.

2   Wavelet Domain SHMT-S Model

2.1   Wavelet Domain HMT Model

The wavelet domain HMT model has been successfully applied in many signal processing fields. To capture the mutual dependencies between wavelet coefficients across scales, the HMT uses a probabilistic tree to model Markovian dependencies between the hidden states. In the traditional wavelet domain HMT model, the marginal distribution $f(w_i)$ of each coefficient node w_i is assumed to be a Gaussian mixture distribution. In generally, the random variables are treated as independent given the hidden states due to the parameter estimation of HMT. As shown in Fig. 1a, in the pyramid quad-tree structure of the wavelet transform, four children

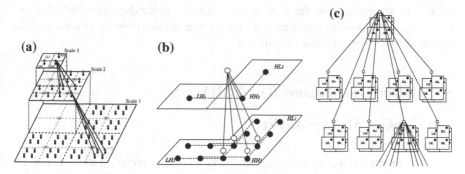

Fig. 1 Different HMT models. **a** The original wavelet domain HMT model, **b** the modified 2D SHMT-S model and **c** spatial-temporal wavelet domain SHMT-S model

wavelet coefficients divide the spatial localization of the parent coefficients. An HMT model is specified in terms of the probability of a state at the root node in the coarsest scale, state transition matrices and the parameters of the pdf given the state, which can be estimated with the tree-structure Expectation-Maximization (EM) algorithm [8].

2.2 Wavelet Domain SHMT-S Model

For natural textures, in particular for structural textures, the regular or periodic spatial structures or patterns result in certain statistical dependencies across DWT subbands, and it is possible to improve the accuracy of texture characterization by capturing dependencies across DWT subbands. Therefore, we introduce the modified wavelet domain HMT model, SHMT-S. As shown in Fig. 1b, the wavelet coefficients of different subbands at the same level are stacked into a vector, which is controlled by the scalar hidden state. That is to say, wavelet coefficients from the subbands at the same level share a common hidden state variable.

In the SHMT-S model, a coefficient vector $\vec{w}_i = \left[w_i^{LH}, w_i^{HL}, w_i^{HH}\right]$ contains three wavelet coefficients. Thus we model it as a multivariate Gaussian mixture density with a hidden state. Given the hidden state $S_i = m$, the coefficient vector $\vec{w}_i$ is multivariate Gaussian with mean $\vec{\mu}_{i,m}$ and covariance $\Sigma_{i,m}$.

$$f\left(\vec{w}_i \middle| S_i = m, \vec{\mu}_{i,m}, \Sigma_{i,m}\right) = \frac{1}{(2\pi)^{3/2} |\Sigma_{i,m}|^{1/2}} \exp\left\{-\frac{1}{2}\left(\vec{w}_i - \vec{\mu}_{i,m}\right)^T \Sigma^{-1}\left(\vec{w}_i - \vec{\mu}_{i,m}\right)\right\}$$

(1)

For the SHMT-S model of a texture, it is parameterized by a parameter vector θ^{3S}. It means that there is just one parameter set in SHMT-S compared with three parameter sets in HMT. Besides capturing the joint DWT statistics as HMT, the

SHMT-S can also exploit the dependencies across subbands. Since SHMT-S and HMT share the same tree structure, they have the similar training process and the similar computation of model likelihood.

3 Laplace Distributions Based SHMT-S

3.1 Laplace Mixture Model

In order to match the compression property of the wavelet transform that the majority of coefficients have small values and the minority of coefficients have large values, the marginal distribution $f_W(w_i)$ of each coefficient node w_i of the traditional HMT model is modeled as Gaussian mixture model (GMM). In many applications, the 2-component GMM has been proved to be effective. However, for some image textures and dynamic textures, such as texture "mosaic" shown in Fig. 2, a Laplace mixture model (LMM) provides a better fitness to the histogram than the Gaussian mixture model, because the histogram is peakier in the center and has heavier tails. That is to say, LMM can describe the marginal distribution of $f_W(w_i)$ better. Therefore, we introduce Laplace mixture distributions based SHMT-S models to describe the textures, which is also named as LMM based SHMT-S for short. We will use the multivariate Laplace distribution with probability density function (pdf),

$$l(x; \mu, \Sigma) = \mathbb{C}|\Sigma|^{-1/2}\exp\left\{-\frac{1}{2}\left[(x-\mu)^T\Sigma^{-1}(x-\mu)\right]^{1/2}\right\}$$
$$= \mathbb{C}|\Sigma|^{-1/2}\exp\left\{-\frac{|x-\mu|}{2\Sigma^{1/2}}\right\} \qquad (2)$$

where $\mathbb{C} = \frac{d\Gamma(d/2)}{\pi^{d/2}\Gamma(1+d)2^{1+d}}$, Γ is Gamma Function, and d is the vector dimension.

(a)

(b)

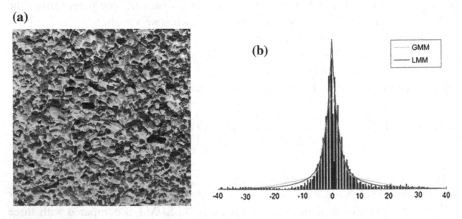

Fig. 2 a "Floor" texture and **b** its wavelet coefficient histogram fitted with two-state, zero mean GMM and LMM

3.2 Parameter Estimation

In the LMM based SHMT-S model, the Laplace probability density functions of each coefficient vector $\vec{w}_i$ in state S_i can be expressed as

$$f(\vec{w}_i|S_i = m) = l(\vec{w}_i; 0, \Sigma_{i,m}) = \mathbb{C}|\Sigma_{i,m}|^{-1/2}\exp\left(-\frac{|\vec{w}_i|}{2(\Sigma_{i,m})^{1/2}}\right) \quad (3)$$

Therefore, as the traditional wavelet domain HMT model, an LMM based SHMT-S model is specified in terms of the following parameters: (1) The probability of the state m at the root node i in the coarsest scale $p_{S_i}(m)$; (2) The state transition probability is $\varepsilon_{i,\rho(i)}^{m,n} = p_{S_i|S_{\rho(i)}}(S_i = m|S_{\rho(i)} = n)$. It is the conditional probability that S_i is in state m given parent state $S_{\rho(i)} = n$. And the covariance matrix $\Sigma_{i,m}$, given $S_i = m$.

The LMM-SHMT-S model of a texture that belongs to class c is parameterized by parameter vector θ_c^{SHMT-S} as the GMM-HMT model. We can make use of tree-structure Expectation-Maximization (EM) algorithm to re-estimate the parameters with K wavelet trees as follows

$$p_{S_i}(m) = \frac{1}{K}\sum_{k=1}^{K}p\left(S_i^k = m \middle| \overrightarrow{w_i^k}, \theta_i\right) \quad (4)$$

$$\varepsilon_{i,\rho(i)}^{m,n} = \frac{\sum_{k=1}^{K}p\left(S_i^k = m, S_{\rho(i)}^k = n \middle| \overrightarrow{w_i^k}, \theta_i\right)}{Kp_{S_{\rho(i)}}(n)},$$

$$\Sigma_{i,m} = \frac{\sum_{k=1}^{K}\left|\overrightarrow{w_i^k}\right|p(S_i^k = m|\overrightarrow{w_i^k}, \theta_i)}{Kp_{S_i}(m)} \quad (5)$$

4 SHMT-S Based Texture Segmentation

The HMT model based Bayesian segmentation method, called HMTseg, has been proposed in [4, 5]. The SHMT-S model based texture segmentation is similar with HMTseg. The segmentation method consists of three steps, raw maximum likelihood segmentation, context-based multi-scale fusion, and pixel-level segmentation, which is summarized in Fig. 3.

632   Y. Qiao and G. Zhao

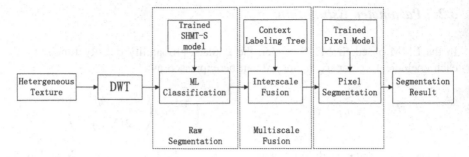

Fig. 3 The flow diagram of texture segmentation based on SHMT-S model. It consists of the raw segmentation, the multi-scale fusion and the pixel-level segmentation

The introduced dynamic texture segmentation is based on spatial-temporal wavelet domain SHMT-S. For the spatial-temporal wavelet transform, each level transform results in one approximate subband and seven detail subbands as shown in Fig. 1c, from which the octree structure is formed. Each parent node is connected to its eight child wavelet coefficients. Therefore, there are seven parallel octree structures. Then we tie the seven octree structure together, and treat them as a vector that owns a hidden state variable. Finally the spatial-temporal wavelet domain SHMT-S is built as shown In Fig. 1c.

5 Experimental Results

In order to evaluate the segmentation method based on SHMT-S model and the Laplace distributions based SHMT-S model, we conduct the experiments on image texture and dynamic texture segmentation, and quantify the segmentation performance with the accuracy rate $accuracy = \frac{N_{correct}}{N} \times 100\%$, where $N_{correct}$ is the number of correctly segmented pixels, and N is the total number of pixels.

For image texture segmentation, the experimental texture images IT1 and IT2 synthesized with the Brodatz textures [9] and the experimental results are shown in Fig. 4. The segmentation accuracy rates are listed in Table 1. It is demonstrated that the proposed LMM based SHMT-S method is better than the original HMT model and SHMT-S model with the Gaussian distribution based methods.

For dynamic texture segmentation, the experiments are conducting on the synthesized videos that are constructed with the dynamic textures of the DynTex dataset [10]. All videos consist of 64 frames, and the size of each frame is 176 * 168. in In Fig. 5, we show three adjacent frames selected from the experimental synthesized video and the corresponding segmentation results with different models.

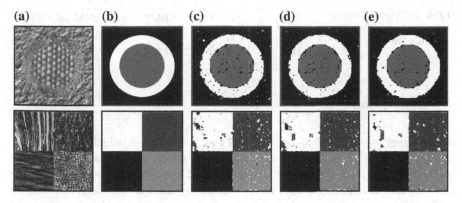

Fig. 4 Image texture segmentation results. **a** Experimental texture images; **b** ground truth; **c** segmentation results with original HMT; **d** segmentation results with SHMT-S; **e** segmentation results using the LMM based SHMT-S

Table 1 Image texture segmentation results (accuracy rate %)

Texture	HMT	SHMT-S	LMM-SHMT-S
IT1	94.32	94.79	95.25
IT2	96.01	96.45	96.71

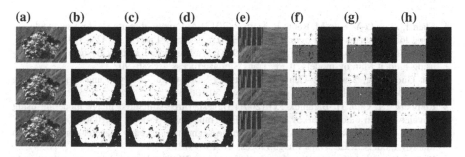

Fig. 5 Dynamic texture segmentation results. **a, e** Experimental dynamic textures; **b, f** segmentation results with the original HMT; **c, g** segmentation results with SHMT-S; **d, h** segmentation results using the LMM based SHMT-S

We can see these new methods produce better visual effect than the orignal HMT model method. There are few misclassified pixels and more smooth texture boundaries. The segmentation accuracy rates are listed in Table 2, in which we show the average accuracy rate of the whole 64 frames. It is demonstrated from the results that SHMT-S model can improve the description performance.

Table 2 Dynamic texture segmentation results (accuracy rate %)

Texture	HMT	SHMT-S	LMM-SHMT-S
DT1	95.23	96.16	96.21
DT2	97.19	97.71	98.62

6 Conclusion

In this paper, we introduce a modified HMT model SHMT-S, which can exploit the cross-correlation across DWT subbands, from which the texture segmentation methods are derived. Meanwhile we make use of Laplace mixture distributions to describe the wavelet coefficients vector. For the dynamic texture segmentation, we utilize the spatial-temporal wavelet transform to construct the 3-dimensional SHMT-S model. The segmentation experiments are conducted on the image textures and dynamic textures, from which the performance of the proposed method is verified.

Acknowledgments This work is partially supported by National Natural Science Foundation of China 61371175 and Fundamental Research Funds for the Central Universities HEUCFQ20150812.

References

1. Chen J, Zhao G-Y, Salo M, Rahtu E, Matti P (2013) Automatic dynamic texture segmentation using local descriptors and optical flow. IEEE Trans Image Process 22:326–339
2. Crouse MS, Nowak RD, Baraniuk RG (1998) Wavelet-based statistical signal processing using hidden Markov models. IEEE Trans Signal Process 46:886–902
3. Fan Guo-Liang, Xia Xiang-Gen (2003) Wavelet-based texture analysis and synthesis using hidden Markov models. IEEE Trans Circ Syst 50:106–120
4. Romberg JK, Choi H, Baraniuk RG (2001) Bayesian tree-structured image modeling using wavelet-domain hidden Markov models. IEEE Trans Image Process 10:1056–1068
5. Choi H, Baraniuk RG (2001) Multiscale image segmentation using wavelet-domain hidden Markov models. IEEE Trans Image Process 10:1309–1321
6. Durand J-B (2004) Computational methods for hidden Markov tree models—an application to wavelet trees. IEEE Trans Signal Process 52:2551–2560
7. Rasheed HA, Nadia JA (2014) Some Bayes' estimators for Laplace distribution under different loss functions. J Babylon Univ 22:975–983
8. Jordan M, Kleinberg J, Bernhard S (2006) Pattern recognition and machine learning, pp 424–429
9. Brodatz P (1966) Textures: a photographic album for artists & designers, dover (1966)
10. Péteri R, Fazekas S, Huiskes MJ (2010) DynTex: a comprehensive database of dynamic textures. Pattern Recogn Lett 31:1627–1632

Enhanced User Interface for a Sexual Violence Prevention Education App

Donguk Kim, Jeonghoon Kwak, Yunsick Sung, Hyung Jin Park
and Kyung Min Park

Abstract Recently there has been various forms of sexual assault against elementary school children at various locations. In order to prevent such incidents, various educational applications for sexual violence prevention are being developed. As mobile devices are becoming more prevalent, the prevention education applications developed are optimized for the mobile devices. However, a more precise user interface design is required to enhance the efficacy of the education. This research suggests a method to enhance the user interface of an already existing sexual violence prevention application for elementary school students. It also explains a case in which the suggested user interface design method was implemented on an application according to the configuration of the proposed user interface. The results showed the learning experience was effective with the enhancements made on the user interface.

Keywords User interface · Sexual violence prevention · Education app

D. Kim · Y. Sung
Faculty of Computer Engineering, Keimyung University,
Daegu, South Korea
e-mail: donguk@kmu.ac.kr

Y. Sung
e-mail: yunsick@kmu.ac.kr

J. Kwak
Department of Computer Engineering, Graduate School,
Keimyung University, Daegu, South Korea
e-mail: jeonghoon@kmu.ac.kr

H.J. Park
Faculty of Art and Media, Keimyung University, Daegu, South Korea
e-mail: phj@kmu.ac.kr

K.M. Park (✉)
Department of Nursing, Keimyung University, Daegu, South Korea
e-mail: kmp@kmu.ac.kr

© Springer Science+Business Media Singapore 2016
J.J. (Jong Hyuk) Park et al. (eds.), *Advanced Multimedia and Ubiquitous Engineering*, Lecture Notes in Electrical Engineering 393,
DOI 10.1007/978-981-10-1536-6_82

1 Introduction

Methods of sexual violence prevention are urgently required as sexual abuse has become more frequent recently. As one such method, a sexual violence prevention application for elementary school children was suggested [1, 2]. To maximize the learning experience for the children, the user interface (UI) needs to be enhanced based on the Bayesian probability. However, the UI of the existing application has difficulties transferring information to users because it blocks many parts of an episode scene. Furthermore, although the target users are elementary school students, the statements are too long for the children at that level.

This research suggests a way to enhance the learning efficacy by enhancing the UI of an existing sexual violence prevention application. This paper is organized as follows: Sect. 2 proposes an enhanced user interfaces for a sexual violence prevention education app. Finally, Sect. 3 concludes this paper.

2 Improved Sexual Violence Prevention Education App

This chapter entails the methods used to improve the existing sexual violence prevention application. Firstly, the narration UI is improved. The previous narration UI prevented the users from viewing the episode in progress during the sexual prevention education. This will be improved by modifying the transparency and the size of the narration UI so that the users can view the surrounding environment. The UI is improved as in Fig. 1. such that users can identify the surrounding environment while the sexual abuse situation is being explained.

Secondly, the script in the speech bubble was modified. Previous speech bubble showed all of the script at once. However, this is too much information for elementary school students' literacy level. In order to improve this issue, the script was written to show only important points of the episode as in Fig. 2.

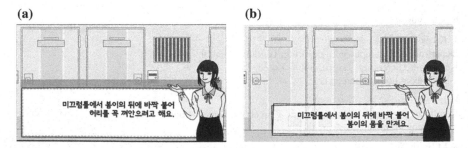

(a)   **(b)**

Fig. 1 This is the result of modification of the narration UI **a** is the previous narration UI which blocks the background scene of the episode while the situation is being explained, **b** is the improved narration UI which lets the background scene to be more visible to the users

(a)   **(b)**

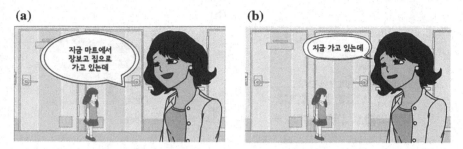

Fig. 2 This is the result of shortening the script **a** shows the script before the improvement: the script was too long for elementary students to understand, **b** shows the script after the improvement: only the important points of the episode are shown

(a)   **(b)**

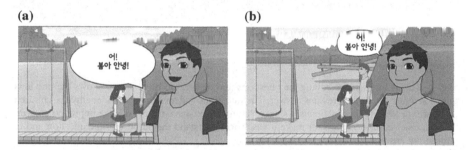

Fig. 3 This is the result of modifying the speech bubble UI **a** shows the previous speech bubble UI, which blocks a lot of the background and has unnecessary empty space, **b** is the improved speech bubble UI with a smaller size, which allows the users to recognize the background and located differently so it does not cover the character

Thirdly, the size of the speech bubble was improved. The size of the bubble was too big for the size of the screen. The speech bubble UI blocked the episode screen, which was a distraction. In order to improve this issue, the speech bubble was made smaller and it was moved to another location to minimize the distraction as seen in Fig. 3.

Fourthly, the UI for binary questions and the answers were summarized. The script of the question and the answer about the situation during the episode is lengthy. It is difficult for elementary school level students to understand the question and to identify the key points for their answers. In order to improve this issue, the questions and the answers were edited to contain only the key points, to make it easier for children to understand, as shown in Fig. 4.

Fifthly, the episode scenes were improved. Some of the episodes show the characters' action in an awkward manner or it is difficult to identify the action. This issue was improved by zooming into the actions of the characters as described by the script to emphasize the sexual harassment occurring in the episode. In order to let students have a better understanding of the situation, the following improvement is suggested as seen in Fig. 5.

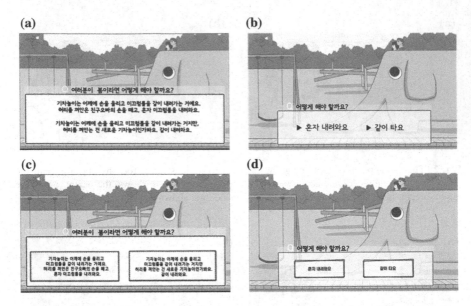

Fig. 4 This is the result of editing the questions and answers to be concise **a** shows the previous question and **c** shows the previous answer. The questions and answers are too lengthy for children to answer or identify the key points **b** shows the improved question and **d** is the improved answer. The concise question and answer make it easier to understand the purpose of the question and to choose the answer

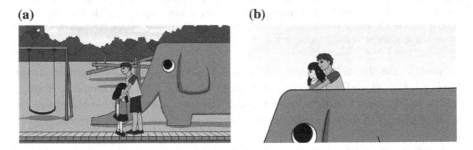

Fig. 5 This is the result of improving the actions of the characters within the episode **a** is the previous episode scene which shows a man hugging a child. It is difficult to identify his action **b** is the improved episode scene which is zoomed into the man who's trying to go down the slide while hugging the child

3 Conclusions

This article suggests an improved UI for sexual prevention education application. With the purpose of enhancing the learning experience of the children, the structure of the episode scene, the location and size of the UI, and the shape of the UI have been modified. In order to let students to identify the purpose of the lesson, the script, questions and answers shown in the UI were edited to be concise. These improvements allowed the students to easily understand the episode and identify a sexual violence situation.

Acknowledgments This research was supported by Basic Science Research Program through the National Research Foundation of Korea (NRF) funded by the Ministry of Education (NRF-2015009659).

References

1. Sung Y, Kim D, Park HJ, Park KM (2015) Bayesian probability-based UI control framework of sexual violence prevention education apps. Adv Sci Technol Lett 106:65–68
2. Kim D, Kwak J, Sung Y, Park HJ, Park KM (2015) Implementation of sexual violence prevention education app. In: Korea information processing society fall conference, Jeju Korea, vol 22(2), pp 1322–1323, 31 Oct 2015

On the Benefits of Information Retrieval and Information Extraction Techniques Applied to Digital Forensics

David Lillis and Mark Scanlon

Abstract Many jurisdictions suffer from lengthy evidence processing backlogs in digital forensics investigations. This has negative consequences for the timely incorporation of digital evidence into criminal investigations, while also affecting the timelines required to bring a case to court. Modern technological advances, in particular the move towards cloud computing, have great potential in expediting the automated processing of digital evidence, thus reducing the manual workload for investigators. It also promises to provide a platform upon which more sophisticated automated techniques may be employed to improve the process further. This paper identifies some research strains from the areas of Information Retrieval and Information Extraction that have the potential to greatly help with the efficiency and effectiveness of digital forensics investigations.

Keywords Digital forensics · Information retrieval · Information extraction

1 Introduction

Digital forensic investigations remain a labour-intensive manual task. A long backlog has emerged in many jurisdictions whereby investigations may take months or years to yield useful results. This has consequences for the timeline of prosecutions reaching the courtroom, but also has the effect that the timeline involved in a digital forensic investigation is at odds with the normal timeline of investigation, with the digital evidence often being unavailable during the crucial initial stages of a criminal investigation. Clearly, expedited investigations are desirable, and the digital forensics community have been working towards this end.

D. Lillis (✉)
Beijing-Dublin International College, Dublin, Ireland
e-mail: david.lillis@ucd.ie

D. Lillis · M. Scanlon
School of Computer Science, University College Dublin, Dublin, Ireland
e-mail: mark.scanlon@ucd.ie

© Springer Science+Business Media Singapore 2016
J.J. (Jong Hyuk) Park et al. (eds.), *Advanced Multimedia and Ubiquitous Engineering*, Lecture Notes in Electrical Engineering 393,
DOI 10.1007/978-981-10-1536-6_83

The primary goal is increased levels of automation so as to reduce the amount of manual work required to conduct an investigation. This can be achieved by improving the speed of evidence processing so as to reduce the time spent waiting for results. If this can be done, there is then scope for more sophisticated automated techniques to be applied to the problem.

Researchers in the areas of Information Retrieval (IR) and Information Extraction (IE) have been developing techniques for decades that help people to sift through large quantities of information as quickly and efficiently as possible. To date, few of these techniques have made the cross-over to the day-to-day lives of digital forensic investigators. This paper seeks to examine the context within which these may be applied to investigations, and the advantages they may bring to this area.

2 A Platform for More Efficient Processing

Traditional digital forensics generally involve the examination of a seized hard drive, using specialist digital forensic software installed on a workstation. Examination of evidence is a lengthy, manual process, which has led to long backlogs in evidence processing for police forces throughout the world.

However, more recent developments in digital forensics technologies, though not yet widely deployed, promise a future forensic investigation platform upon which more sophisticated technologies may be deployed.

The growth of cloud computing in recent years has caused its own challenges for the digital forensics community, as evidence becomes more widely spread across jurisdictional boundaries. However, it also offers great benefits in terms of evidence processing. This type of cloud-based evidence processing has become known as Digital Forensics as a Service (DFaaS) [1] and it has already been deployed with success in the European Cybercrime Centre (EC3), based in the Netherlands [2].

Moving the processing of evidence to the cloud allows for the application of greater computing resources through the use of parallelisation and distribution. Additionally, it allows the introduction of high performance computing techniques, including the application of specialist hardware to particular tasks. It also allows prioritisation of certain investigations as operational requirements demand.

A further advantage of a cloud-based system is that investigations no longer occur in isolation. Many seized hard disks contain large quantities of data in common (e.g. operating system and application files), all of which must be processed anew for each investigation. DFaaS offers a platform for deduplication techniques to be applied [3]. This involves the identification of identical files on different seized hard disks through the use of hashing, which has numerous advantages. Firstly, files that have previously been analysed in an earlier investigation do not require re-examination. This can be used either to eliminate files from consideration or to identify files that have been considered pertinent to a previous investigation (e.g. a shared collection of child pornographic images). An additional speed advantage is that duplicate files do not need to be transferred to the system again, which reduces the time required to capture all available evidence. This is of particular concern when using remote acquisition techniques that transfer evidence through an internet connection while in the field [4]. Reducing the quantity of data to be transferred and analysed is a key step in expediting the investigation process.

3 The Applicability of Information Retrieval

With the development of a high-capacity, cloud-based digital forensic investigation platform comes the opportunity to add more sophisticated automated techniques to the traditional digital forensic process. This has the potential to reduce the time spent by investigators in carrying out their existing tasks, while also potentially empowering them to take a more active role in other aspects of the investigation. One source of such techniques is the field of IR, which is concerned with identifying documents (traditionally text documents, though multimedia IR is also an active research area) that satisfies a user's "information need". Applied in the context of digital forensics investigations, the information need is for anything that is pertinent to the investigation being conducted.

Traditionally, IR effectiveness is evaluated using the oft-conflicting measures of precision and recall. A system with high precision avoids returning documents that are not relevant, whereas a high-recall system aims to ensure that all available relevant documents are returned to the user. While a high level of both is desirable in any situation, different application areas would tend to favour one over the other if this cannot be achieved. Indeed, it is frequently the case whereby improving on one measure involves sacrificing effectiveness according to the other. The classic example of a use case where precision is key is the area of web search. Since potentially millions of relevant documents exist, users do not require access to all of them, and have a strong aversion to spending time on non-relevant documents. In contrast, legal search is frequently proposed as a scenario where recall is of paramount importance. In a situation where a single piece of missing evidence may be crucial to a case, a user will be more tolerant of non-relevant documents if full recall can be provided.

Digital forensics is typically seen as the latter situation (e.g. in [5, 6]). Whereas high recall inevitably leads to a higher rate of false positives, this is tolerated due to the requirement to find all available evidence. Certainly for a case to be presented in court, all available evidence must be identified, which requires recall to be maximised. Absent evidence clearly has the potential to undermine both criminal and civil cases. The principal advantage of using IR techniques is that it helps to achieve this. Once the initial processing stage has been completed, queries can be run extremely quickly. Indeed, achieving high recall likely requires many queries to be run. As noted in [7], there is a large degree of variation in the vocabulary that searchers use to describe their information needs. Less than 20 % of users use the same keywords for topics they are interested in. The use of standard IR techniques such as synonym matching and query expansion can aid with the process of improving recall, without requiring investigators to enter every possible query manually.

One example of this is [8], where query expansion and query reduction techniques were applied to the popular Enron email dataset to improve retrieval performance. WordNet was used for domain-independent query expansion, with a Latent Semantic Indexing approach to query reduction being applied afterwards.

However, this focus on recall arguably has negative consequences at earlier stages in the investigation. As noted in [2], because the results of digital forensics investigation are not typically available within the first few days of an investigation, they are rarely taken into account during the crucial initial stages where hypotheses are being formed and leads being investigated. This leads to the observation that while high recall is necessary for court, the manual work it requires is too time-consuming for the early stages of the investigation.

Figure 1 offers a simple illustration of the timeline of an investigation. At the end of the investigation, evidence is required to be complete and court-admissible in order to prove a case on court. This requires high recall as in classic legal search scenarios. However, towards the initial stage of an investigation, precision is of far greater importance. Investigators will require relevant documents quickly. This allows the most relevant evidence to be used during the early stages of the investigation process as quickly as possible. Additionally, in cases where large numbers of devices have been seized (e.g. from an office or data centre), a triage stage is required to identify hard disks that may contain pertinent information. Achieving high precision at early stages has the potential to very quickly identify those machines that merit further investigation.

As the investigation progresses, there is a growing requirement for higher recall, leading to the classic legal search by the end. However, it is clear that investigative requirements shift during the process of an investigation, and a configurable approach to IR is likely to very advantageous in both increasing the quality and the efficiency of the process.

Additional features of IR research that have been applied to digital forensics include visualisation approaches such as ranking [9] and clustering [10]. While these have become commonplace in many search implementations, they have not yet reached ubiquity in popular forensic software. Innovations such as these have the potential to reduce the manual burden on investigators, even when the late recall-oriented stage of the investigation is reached.

Fig. 1 Investigation timeline

4 The Applicability of Information Extraction

In addition to IR, which seeks only to identify documents containing relevant information, IE further attempts to extract meaningful structured information from unstructured files. This also has the potential to improve the efficiency of investigations by automatically discovering and extracting evidence on an investigator's behalf.

Initial efforts have already begun in applying IE to forensics investigations. For example, [11] uses two-phase IE for forensic investigation (evaluated using the Enron dataset). The two phases employed were named entity recognition and association rule mining. The initial phase sought to identify entities in emails (people, places, organisations, etc.) with the second attempting to identify how entities are related. This type of system has great potential in aiding investigators. This work also had a strong emphasis on the visualisation aspects of the system, whereby named entities were highlighted in text, named entities were displayed in word clouds and the nature of named entity relationships were presented also. Another application in the context of email can be found in [12], while named entity extraction has also previously been applied to police reports [13]. All of these approaches help to lower the cognitive load placed on an investigator while examining large quantities of digital evidence.

One other long-standing aspect of IE that has potential for digital forensics is text summarisation [14]. This is most commonly seen in news reports and web search results where relevant snippets of a document are presented to a user to help decide whether a document is relevant without requiring the entire document to be read. By showing the context in which key words are displayed, time can be saved in identifying relevant documents. While this has not yet reached mainstream forensic investigation interfaces, it has the potential to expedite the process if incorporated in the future.

A further consideration is that event timeline reconstruction is extremely important in criminal investigations [15]. Investigators desire to construct a chain of events in temporal order. Existing automated approaches to this task are typically done at a low level (e.g. filesystem and logging events) [16], with events such as connecting a USB stick being considered as "high-level" in that context.

Related to this, efforts have been ongoing to extract temporal information from unstructured text [17]. While the tasks are not identical, both the Text REtrieval Conference (TREC)[1] and the Text Analysis Conference (TAC)[2] feature a temporal track. In the TAC Event Track, participants are asked to extract information about events so that a knowledge base can be populated. This is then used to identify when mentions of events in text related to the same event, as well as to link mentions in terms of the role they play in an event and their timing within it. The TREC Temporal Summarization Track has the goal of developing systems that

---

[1]http://trec.nist.gov.
[2]http://www.nist.gov/tac.

can efficiently monitor event details over time. These are research areas with the potential to be of great benefit to digital forensics investigators.

5   Conclusions

Research from the text retrieval and analysis communities have great potential for reducing the manual workload on digital forensics investigators. This in turn has the potential to help clear the evidence backlog, and so allow for digital evidence to be meaningfully included at an earlier stage in investigations. The traditional focus on recall for IR in forensics is not necessarily appropriate for all stages of an investigation, with precision being arguably more appropriate at earlier stages. A movement of forensics towards cloud computing and related technologies will provide a platform upon which cutting-edge techniques such as named entity extraction, association rule mining, temporal information extraction and others to be incorporated into the investigation process in the future.

References

1. Lee J, Un S (2012) Digital forensics as a service: a case study of forensic indexed search. In: International conference on ICT convergence (ICTC), pp 499–503
2. Van Baar RB, van Beek HMA, van Eijk EJ (2014) Digital forensics as a service: a game changer. Digital Investig 11:S54–S62
3. Watkins K, McWhorte M, Long J, Hill B (2009) Teleporter: an analytically and forensically sound duplicate transfer system. Digital Investig 6(suppl):43–47
4. Scanlon M, Kechadi MT (2010) Online acquisition of digital forensic evidence. In: Goel S (ed) Digital forensics and cyber crime: first international ICST conference, ICDF2C 2009, Albany, NY, USA, 30 Sept–2 Oct 2009, revised selected papers. Springer, Berlin, pp 122–131
5. Beebe NL, Clark JG (2007) Digital forensic text string searching: improving information retrieval effectiveness by thematically clustering search results. Digital Investig 4(suppl): 49–54
6. Beebe N (2009) Digital forensic research: the good, the bad and the unaddressed. In: Advances in digital forensics V. Springer, Berlin, pp 17–36
7. Furnas GW, Deerwester S, Dumais ST, Landauer TK, Harshman RA, Streeter LA, Lochbaum KE (1988) Information retrieval using a singular value decomposition model of latent semantic structure. In: SIGIR '88: proceedings of the 11th annual international ACM SIGIR conference on Research and development in information retrieval, New York, NY, USA, pp 465–480
8. Du L, Jin H, de Vel O, Liu N (2008) A latent semantic indexing and WordNet based information retrieval model for digital forensics. In: 2008 IEEE international conference on intelligence and security informatics, IEEE, pp 70–75
9. Beebe NL, Liu L (2014) Ranking algorithms for digital forensic string search hits. Digital Investig 11(suppl. 2):314–322
10. Beebe NL, Clark JG, Dietrich GB, Ko MS, Ko D (2011) Post-retrieval search hit clustering to improve information retrieval effectiveness: two digital forensics case studies. Decis Support Syst 51(4):732–744

11. Yang M, Chow KP (2015) An information extraction framework for digital forensic investigations. In: Advances in digital forensics XI. Springer, Berlin, pp 61–76
12. De Vel O, Anderson A, Corney M, Mohay G (2001) Mining e-mail content for author identification forensics. ACM Sigmod Record 30(4):55–64
13. Chau M, Xu JJ, Chen H (2002) Extracting meaningful entities from police narrative reports. In: Proceedings of the 2002 annual national conference on Digital government research, Digital Government Society of North America, pp 1–5
14. Salton G, Singhal A, Mitra M, Buckley C (1997) Automatic text structuring and summarization. Inf Process Manage 33(2):193–207
15. Chabot Y, Bertaux A, Kechadi MT, Nicolle C (2014) Event reconstruction: a state of the art. In: Handbook of research on digital crime, cyberspace security and information assurance. IGI Global, pp 231–245
16. Hargreaves C, Patterson J (2012) An automated timeline reconstruction approach for digital forensic investigations. Digital Investig 9:S69–S79
17. Campos R, Dias G, Jorge AM, Jatowt A (2014) Survey of temporal information retrieval and related applications. ACM Comput Surv 47(2):1–41

Leadership of Information Security Managers on the Effectiveness of Information Systems Security Through Mediate of Organizational Culture

Myeonggil Choi and Jeongsuk Song

Abstract The effectiveness of information security in an organization much depends on the leadership of information security manager. The leadership of information security is somewhat influenced by culture of an organization. This paper tries to explain the process how leadership of information security manager could influence the effectiveness of information security through organization culture

Keywords Information security manager · Security effectiveness · Culture

1 Introduction

Rapidly increasing attacks to number of databases and interconnected networks is causing alertness of Information Systems Security (ISS). The vulnerabilities of ISS are becoming the general situation rather than the exceptional case. A computer security magazine finds that organizations suffer over 100 successful cyber-attacks per week in U.S.. While advanced technological investment for ISS are constantly conducted to combat trials of cyber-attacks, the efforts to fight threats to ISS often turn out to be useless without organizational commitment and compliance by employees.

Information security manager is a centric role in directing organizational efforts for ISS and drawing efforts of employees for compliance with ISS. While information security manager could not directly order all of employees through ISS

M. Choi (✉)
Dept.of Business Administration, Chung-Ang University,
84 Hugsuk-Dong, Seoul, Korea
e-mail: mgchoi@cau.ac.kr

J. Song
Dept.of Economics, Chung-Ang University,
84 Hugsuk-Dong, Seoul, Korea
e-mail: jssong@cau.ac.kr

© Springer Science+Business Media Singapore 2016   649
J.J. (Jong Hyuk) Park et al. (eds.), *Advanced Multimedia and Ubiquitous Engineering*, Lecture Notes in Electrical Engineering 393,
DOI 10.1007/978-981-10-1536-6_84

policy, they have to constantly direct, care, and warn all of organizational members. Even they have to persuade top manager to invest resources for ISS. The leadership of information security manager could influence the compliance of employees with ISS and alertness of top manager, resulting in elevating ISS effectiveness.

The leadership of information security managers could influence ISS effectiveness through mediates of organizational culture. Culture is the single most important factor influencing success or failure of an organization [3]. Organization culture is the media between organizational behavior and management. Since, the organizational culture certainly could impact day-to-day operations of an organization, organizational culture should be regarded as an important factor for improving ISS effectiveness [7]. Including leadership of information security managers, the certification, job year and education duration of them also influence ISS effectiveness.

This study is designed to explore and expose how the leadership of information security managers shape and motivate employees to comply with ISS policies and may lead to ISS effectiveness through organizational culture.

2 Literature Review and Hypothesis

2.1 Leadership of Information Security Managers and Organizational Culture

The relationship between information security mangers and other employees could be considered relationship between leaders and followers. To keep employees within an organization comply with ISS, information security managers try to persuade, inspire, and motivate them. While information security managers do not have any direct rights to order, monitor, and punish other employees, information security managers should activate leadership.

The need to shift from transactional leadership to transformational leadership was suggested. Transformational leadership has vitalized higher-order values and has elevated followers' aspirations so that followers identify their mission/vision, are better about their work, and work to perform well their part beyond base expectations and mere transactions. The transformational leadership appeals the moral values of followers in an attempt to raise their consciousness about ethical issues and to mobilize their energy and resources to reform institutions. The transformational leadership has positively relation with leadership effectiveness and organizational outcomes across different types of organizations, situations, and cultures. The effects of transformational leadership are realized in regard to performance outcomes [1].

Researchers suggested that the behavior of transformational leadership is composed of four characteristics: inspirational motivation, idealized influence, individualized consideration, and intellectual stimulation. Inspirational motivation means the presentation and creation of symbols and emotional argument, the demonstration of optimism and enthusiasm, and an attractive vision. Idealized influence includes behaviors such as demonstration of ethical standards, self-sacrifice for the group, and set of a personal model. Individualized consideration provides followers with coaching, encouragement, and supports. Intellectual stimulation contains behavior that gives a challenge to followers to consider problems with a new perspective. Previous researches suggest that transformational leadership has been positively related with high performance of employee and leadership effectiveness.

The concept of organizational culture was differently defined by many scholars. Organization culture was direct products of the continuing interactions about meanings, values, and proprieties among the members of an organization. Based on two classifying axes such as the internal/external axis orientation and the flexibility/control orientation, a model identifies and classifies organizational culture into four types: group culture, developmental culture, hierarchical culture, and rational culture [3], Denison et al. categorized organizational culture into four types in terms of cultural traits; mission, consistency, adaptability and involvement [4]. Based on Quinn and Spreitzer's model, Boggs classified organizational culture into four types; clan culture, hierarchy culture, adhocracy culture, and market culture [2].

Directing a way how members of organization think and act, culture is like the fundamental systems of the organization. The paradigm of culture conclusively is closely related with existing roles and practices in an organization. Thus, we establish the following hypothesis;

(H-1a) Inspirational motivation of transformational leadership is positively related with the culture of consistency.
(H-1b) Inspirational motivation of transformational leadership is positively related with the culture of effectiveness.
(H-2a) Idealized influence of transformational leadership is positively related with the culture of consistency.
(H-2b) Idealized influence of transformational leadership is positively related with the culture of effectiveness.
(H-3a) Individualized consideration of transformational leadership is positively related with the culture of consistency.
(H-3b) Individualized consideration of transformational leadership is positively related with the culture of effectiveness.
(H-4a) Intellectual stimulation of transformational leadership is positively related with the culture of consistency.
(H-4b) Intellectual stimulation of transformational leadership is positively related with the culture of effectiveness.

Based on previous studies about organizational culture, we utilized the two categorizing dimensions, such as the internal/external orientation culture and the flexibility/control culture. Our study focuses on the security of public and government sector. Since public and government sector follows laws and regulation, the culture of that falls in control culture. We classify the culture into two types; internal and control, and external and control. The culture of internal and control orientation, which can be called the culture of consistency, focuses on order, rules and regulations, uniformity, and efficiency. These characteristics are regarded typically important in a formalized and regular organization. The culture of external and control orientations, which can be called the culture of effectiveness, focuses on competitiveness, goal achievement, production, effectiveness, and benefit-oriented measures. Emphasizing these characteristics is conducted in a result-oriented and benefit-oriented organization. Thus, we establish the following hypothesis;

(H-5) The culture of consistency is positively related with the effectiveness of ISS.
(H-6) The culture of effectiveness is positively related with the effectiveness of ISS.

2.2 The Effectiveness of Information Systems Security

The effectiveness of ISS can be defined how much the objectives and goals of an ISS program are achieved, an information program is securely operated and information is operated, securely. ISS effectiveness is influenced how detail security contents are addressed in a security policy and how content is implemented and conveyed users. The security items, organizational factors, and security measures specified in security policy can enhance ISS effectiveness.

3 Research Model

3.1 Measurement of Construct

This study adopts the research model presented in Fig. 1. We measure the variables through previously validated items and then further modified as needed. The measurement of all variables adopts a five-point Likert scale, in which 1 denotes "strongly disagree" and 5 denotes "strongly agree."

To measure idealized influence, three items are drawn from Viator [8] and Podsakoff et al. [6]. Three items measuring intellectual stimulation are taken from Ke and Wei [5] and Podsakoff et al. [6]. Three items measuring individualized consideration are based on Viator [8] and Ke and Wei [5]. Three items for measuring inspirational motivation came from Viator and Ke and Wei [5, 8].

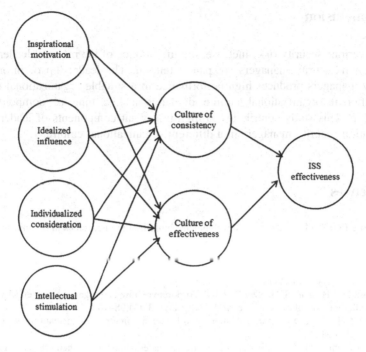

Fig. 1 Research model

3.2 Data Collection

We plan to collect data from public and government sector. A reason to collect data from public and government sector is that information security is regard highly important in these organizations. Data collected from the sector could effectively show relationship between the variables. We will send paper based questionnaire to about 150 institutions and twenty paper-based questionnaires to each questionnaire.

3.3 Data Analysis

We plan to analyze collected data utilizing SPSS and smart PLS software package. To decide the relations between variables, we will conduct path analysis and make a conclusion of accepting hypothesis.

4 Conclusion

As the various security risks increase, the importance of the role and leadership of information security managers are paid attention. The leadership of information security managers produces high performance in a suitable organizational culture. The different organizational culture demands a fine tune of components of leadership. This study contributes to highlight what components of leadership of information security managers in a different organizational culture.

References

1. Avolio BJ (1999) Full leadership development: building the vital forces in organization. Sage, Thousand Oaks, p 234
2. Boggs WB (2004) TQM and organizational culture: a case study. Qual Manage J 11(2):42–52
3. Deal T, Kennedy A (1982) Corporate culture: the rites and rituals of corporate life. Addison-Wesley, New York
4. Denison DR, Haaland S, Goelzer P (2004) Corporate culture and organizational effectiveness: is Asia different from the rest of the world? Org Dyn 33(1):98–109
5. Ke and Wei (2008) Organizational culture and leadership in erp implementation. Decis Support Syst 45:208–218
6. Podsakoff Philip M et al (1990) Transformational leader behavior and their effects on followers' trust in leader, satisfaction, and organizational citizenship behaviors. Leadersh Quart 1(2): 107–142
7. Chang SE, Lin C-S (2007) Exploring organizational culture for information security management. Ind Manage Data Syst 107(3):438–458
8. Viator RE (2001) The relevance of transformational leadership to nontraditional accounting services: information systems assurance and business consulting. J Inf Syst 15(2):99–125

Coping with Uncertainty
in Sensor Networks

Hoon-Kyu Kim and Kyung-Chang Kim

Abstract Context aware computing is a computing paradigm in smart space that provides quality service by being aware of users and its neighboring contexts. Uncertainty in context aware systems affects the complexity of context processing and context collection mechanism. If uncertainty exists in a context aware application, user satisfaction in the application drops sharply making it obsolete. Environment monitoring with sensor network is a good example of context aware computing. In a sensor network system, since human intervention is not possible, the level of effort to eliminate the uncertainty greatly affects the reliability of the system. In this paper, we propose a technique to cope with uncertainty in environment monitoring with sensor network. We propose strategies to identify the source of uncertainty for contexts, to represent uncertain context information and methods to process such contexts. Experiments performed on an environment monitoring system shows stable monitoring performance of the proposed technique.

Keywords Context · Context aware computing · Uncertainty · Experiments · Sensor network · Environment monitoring

1 Introduction

Compared to the well-defined and static traditional computing environment, ubiquitous computing environment has dynamic and open characteristics. Smart space, like intelligent home, smart office and smart car, is an implementation of ubiquitous computing technology and is getting a lot of attention these days [1]. In practice,

H.-K. Kim
Agency for Defense Development, Seoul, Korea
e-mail: hunk@add.re.kr

K.-C. Kim (✉)
Department of Computer Engineering,
Hongik University, Seoul, Korea
e-mail: kckim@hongik.ac.kr

© Springer Science+Business Media Singapore 2016   655
J.J. (Jong Hyuk) Park et al. (eds.), *Advanced Multimedia and Ubiquitous Engineering*, Lecture Notes in Electrical Engineering 393,
DOI 10.1007/978-981-10-1536-6_85

many of the devices in smart space communicate with each other using wireless sensor network.

In context aware computing, uncertainty occurs from uncertain, ambiguous or incorrect context information. Uncertainty can be the source of the problems in application functionality making the application not stable and not useful to users [2]. To have a more stable and reliable application that tolerate failure, it is necessary to include uncertainty management techniques during application development.

Environment monitoring with sensor network is a good example of context aware computing [3]. In this paper, we propose a technique to manage uncertainty in context aware computing and expand it to cope with uncertainty in environment monitoring with sensor network. We propose strategies to identify the source of uncertainty for contexts, to represent uncertain context information and methods to process such contexts in a sensor network environment. In comparison with other techniques, our technique is easy to implement and minimizes human intervention.

The rest of the paper is organized as follows. We discuss related works in Sect. 2. In Sect. 3, we present a technique to manage uncertainty in context aware computing and expand it to environment monitoring with sensor network. Experiments are performed on an environment monitoring system that implements our technique in Sect. 4. The conclusion is given in Sect. 5.

2 Related Works

Several approaches were proposed to deal with uncertainty of contexts in context aware computing environment. A concept was proposed to deal with the quality of context in [4], as shown in Fig. 1. In this concept, precision of context information was defined to show the degree of real world phenomenon represented. In addition, accuracy was defined as the probability of how accurate the real world phenomenon is represented matching some context instance. In [5], a method was proposed to measure the quality of context based on accuracy and completeness.

In [6], they focus on modeling and computing of aware context information with uncertainty for making dynamic decision during seamless mobility. Their insight is to combine dynamic context-aware computing with improved Random Set Theory (RST) and extended D-S Evidence Theory (EDS).

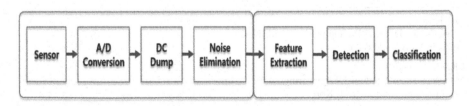

Fig. 1 Processing uncertainty in sensor node

In [7], the Bayesian network and ontology was also used but they focused on reusing the definition of context ontology. In order to produce ontology suitable for each application domain, an expert's help is not only needed but a lot of work and effort must be carried out by the application developer. In addition, converting from ontology to Bayesian network is a difficult task since it is not automated.

3   Management of Uncertainty

In this Section, we propose a technique to manage uncertainty in an environment monitoring system connected by a sensor network.

Since the context information gathered in the sensor node can contain uncertainty, the collected context information must be merged in the server to produce the final context information. Hence, the monitoring system provides a stable service and increased performance and reliability only when the uncertain contexts are appropriately managed and processed to produce reliable contexts.

The real-time environment monitoring system is vulnerable to internal and external effects like sensor node defect, wireless communication failure, sensor node location change, environmental change among others and the sensor data may easily include defects or errors. The sensor is affected by sunlight, wind, climate and humidity and the electromagnetic noise generated in the circuit board lowers signal noise ratio (SNR) causing problems in the sensing algorithm that differentiate signal and noise. In addition, the change in surrounding temperature causes change in sensor signal producing thermal drift effect and interference in magnetic sensing circuit generating data error. These diverse problems can be regarded as uncertainty in environment monitoring with sensor network.

There is a two-step procedure in processing uncertainty just like the procedure steps in determining intrusion detection; sensor node level and sensor field level. In sensor node level, the original and derived uncertainty that exists within the node is processed to raise the reliability of context information. In sensor field level, the context information generated in a node and the context information generated in neighboring nodes are merged to process derived uncertainty. As a result, accurate context information is generated and appropriate service can be provided to users. The three step procedure to manage uncertainty in environment monitoring with sensor network is as follows.

Step 1: Identify Uncertainty

Sensor type to be used: Since a sensor used in sensor node can generate errors, select stable sensors with high performance through experiment and analysis. In environment monitoring system, vibration, sound, magnetic, PIR sensors are used among others.

Context element type to be used in application: Use context type that is detected from sensors like physical context, time context, computing context among others.

Step 2: Determine Uncertainty

Sensor node level: The sensed value and critical value are compared to determine if the sensed value is intrusion context. Since each sensor has different monitoring range, time continuity and detection range criteria is used and based on rules that are compliant with intruder direction and pattern of movement, the detection context by sensor is merged to eliminate uncertainty and decide intrusion detection context in sensor node level.

Sensor field level: The detected results from neighboring sensor nodes are merged to increase the reliability of detected context information. When the intruder enters and moves in the sensor field range, rules are applied to the context information of sensor nodes that are placed in the path of movement to decide on the success or failure of detection. The rules can be defined heuristically based on simple modelling or diverse scenarios.

Step 3: Process Uncertainty

In real-time environment monitoring system, the whole procedure of uncertainty processing is carried out automatically without human intervention. For the context elements identified in Step 1, diverse rules defined in Step 2 are applied to eliminate various uncertainty and accurate results are produced.

From the viewpoint of context aware application, the uncertainty processing is carried out at two levels: sensor node level and sensor field level. The uncertainty processing procedure in a sensor node is shown in Fig. 1. The signal input from a sensor goes through A/D converter. The DC offset and noise is then eliminated. The characteristic features are extracted, uncertainty is detected and classified.

The proposed processing procedure eliminates uncertain elements in intrusion situations and the sensor node uses detection result of intruders to produce detection context.

To produce a more accurate intrusion detection context by eliminating uncertainty in the detected context identified in a sensor node, the intrusion detection context is decided through a process of merging context information in sensor field level. Figure 2 shows information merging procedure to process uncertainty in a sensor field. The procedure includes alignment, estimation, gating and association.

In alignment, the target detection information is sorted by unit, space, time and dimension. In estimation, target location for the sorted target is optimally estimated using Kalman filter. In gating, based on the estimated location of target, the best size and shape estimate is produced using Circular algorithm. In association, by comparing the estimated location of target and location of sensor detection, the best association is found using the Nearest Neighbor algorithm.

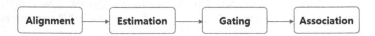

Fig. 2 Processing uncertainty in sensor field

4 Experiments

In this Section, the performance of proposed uncertainty processing is verified by conducting experiments with a real-time environment monitoring system. In our experiment, 32 sensor nodes loaded with sound, magnetic, vibration and PIR sensors is used. The network used is Star topology, the sensor field area is 200 m by 80 m, node interval is 20–30 m arranged in grid pattern and wired communication is used between sensor field and server.

The objective of the experiment is to detect intruders at a specific area. The procedure used in the experiment is to collect signals, test false alarm rate and then test target detection and identification. To test false alarm rate, determine occurrence of event in condition when no actual event occurs and analyze the number of such event occurrence per hour. To test for target detection and identification, deploy target in the sensor field, determine ability to detect intrusion and identify target and analyze rate of detection/identification for deployed target.

Initially, the environmental noise for sensor node is measured to set critical value to judge or determine intrusion detection in input signal. In our experiment, false alarm rate and detection rate is measured. False alarm rate measures the occurrence of false detection for the case of no actual intrusion event during 1 h period and is denoted as number of false alarm produced in 1 h. The detection rate represents success rate of detection for the total detection event generated in the system. If the uncertainty information embedded in the context information is not well controlled, the false alarm rate increases and detection rate drops.

Figure 3 shows the result of measurement of false alarm in vibration sensor. The experiment result shows that detected signal from a sensor node is more stable against noise and false alarm when uncertainty processing technique is applied. In addition, when the technique is applied, the sensor node generates more stable detection information.

In our experiment, a standard performance requirement recommended for a military weapon system is used to measure the performance of an environment

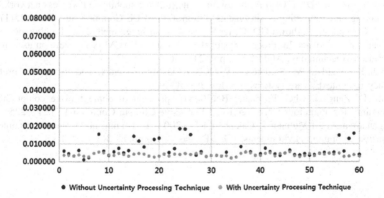

Fig. 3 Comparison of false alarm in vibration sensor

monitoring system applying our proposed technique. The recommended requirement is above 90 % for detection rate, above 80 % for identification rate, false alarm rate is 1 within 1 h and accuracy of target location on average is within 10 m. Using our technique, the performance test result is above 90 % for detection rate, above 90 % for identification rate, false alarm rate is 1 within 1 h and accuracy of target location on average is within 8 m. The performance of our proposed technique easily met the recommended standard performance requirement.

5   Conclusion

In this paper, we defined, classified and explained uncertainty in context that must be dealt with in context aware computing to increase the understanding of uncertainty. The fact that false information can cause uncertainty in context aware application is also described. A mechanism is proposed to identify, decide and process uncertainty in context aware computing. We expanded our technique and applied it to manage uncertainty in environment monitoring with sensor network.

Experiments were performed applying our technique in an environment monitoring system using a sensor network. Experimental results showed that our proposed technique helped increase the stability and reliability of the system by managing uncertainty.

Acknowledgments This work was supported by 2015 Hongik University Research Fund.

References

1. Broens T, Halteren AV, Sinderen MV, Wac K (2007) Towards an application framework for context-aware m-health application. Int J Internet Protoc Technol 2(2):109–116
2. Satyanarayanan M (2003) Coping with uncertainty. IEEE Pervasive Comput 2(3)
3. Makris P, Skoutas DN (2013) A survey on context-aware mobile and wireless networking: on networking and computing environments' integration. IEEE Commun Surv Tutor 15(1)
4. Dey AK, Mankoff J, Abowd GD, Carter S (2002) Distributed mediation of ambiguous context in aware environments. In: Proceedings of the 15th annual ACM symposium on user interface software and technology, ACM Press, pp 121–130
5. Sheikh K, Wegdam M, Sinderen MV (2008) Quality-of-context and its use for protecting privacy in context aware systems. J Softw 3(3):83–93
6. Zhang D, Zeng G, Chen E, Zhang B (2005) Approach of context-aware computing with uncertainty for ubiquitous active service. J Pervasive Comput Commun 1(3):217–225
7. Ranganathan A, Al-Muhtadi J, Campbell RH (2004) Reasoning about uncertain contexts in pervasive computing environments. IEEE Pervasive Comput J 3(2):62–70

Encryption Method of Compressed Images with JPEG Compliance by Shuffling Information Both in Spatial and Frequency Domains

Kang Yi and Kyungmi Kim

Abstract Efficient compressed image data encryption is crucial issue for privacy protection because most of the images are stored in the standard compressed form. In this paper, we propose a fast and robust JPEG image encryption method. Our approach achieves efficient and robust image encryption by shuffling both spatial information and frequency domain information. Our method performs encryption in a hierarchical manner from global to local part of images. We shuffle the data while keeping the format compliance with JPEG standard because we want to apply our method on encrypting a part of the whole JPEG image. The partial image encryption is required with images having privacy-sensitive data such as the pedestrian faces or the license plates. Our proposed method uses a single 1024 bits encryption key, from which all the information shuffling and masking data are generated and applied for image encryption. The proposed method is secure against any cryptographic attack as well as perceptual information cracking. Besides, ours is faster than any of the standard data encryption method.

Keywords Image encryption · JPEG compliant encryption · Multimedia security · Fast encryption · Perceptual security · DCT coefficients shuffling · AC coefficient shuffling

1 Introduction

The demands for Image encryption is constantly increasing in recent years for the privacy protection issue. One of the naive approach is to use standard data encryption method such as AES or RSA. But, such conventional methods require long computing time and, what it makes worse, it produces a file that could not be

K. Yi (✉)
School of CSEE, Handong Global University, Pohang, Republic of Korea
e-mail: yk@handong.edu

K. Kim
School of GLS, Handong Global University, Pohang, Republic of Korea
e-mail: kmkim@handong.edu

© Springer Science+Business Media Singapore 2016   661
J.J. (Jong Hyuk) Park et al. (eds.), *Advanced Multimedia and Ubiquitous Engineering*, Lecture Notes in Electrical Engineering 393,
DOI 10.1007/978-981-10-1536-6_86

handled by the standard JPEG decoder. Such a format-incompatibility inhibits the partial encryption of images and cannot support controllability of security level. Suppose a case that we want to hide only human faces or license plates in a picture and the hidden information might be retrieved later by someone authorized such as policemen or national prosecutors for criminal investigation. In this case, partial encryption for ROI (region of interest) should be very useful. Suppose another case that we want to hide details of image information while we want reveal the overall rough contents of pictures to the public for commercial reason or public purpose. This case motivates the encryption level controllability.

A number of researches have proposed to encrypt JPEG file preserving format compliance. These include techniques such as zig zag permutation which significantly increases the file size [1] and the use of permuted Huffman tables [2]. And DC bit plane scrambling as proposed in [3] also increases the file size. A length-preserving approaches are proposed in [4] by randomly toggling DCT (Discrete Cosine Transform) DC and/or AC coefficient signs. However, this approach is known to be vulnerable to the cryptographic attacks. Some works rely on standard encryption methods. In [5], selective encryption for JPEG images based on AES cipher is proposed. The encryption is performed in the Huffman coding stage of the JPEG using the AES encryption algorithm in the CFB mode. Unterweger and Uhl [6] proposed swapping code words of equal length between blocks for AC value histogram spreading. But, this has high computational complexity.

In this paper, we present a new JPEG format-compliant encryption method which provides a spectrum of security levels (against attacks) and encryption overheads (such as time and file size) by selective encryption options. In our method, we apply different combinations of encryption options to the various stages of standard JPEG. Some of our options preserve the file size while other options try to minimizes the file size overhead that provide high security level.

2 Proposed JPEG Encryption Approach

Our proposed algorithm consists of the five options as shown in Table 1, each of which contributes in different scope and encrypt information of different domain. Our main idea is that we can achieve desired security level of encryption and computing complexity by combining these five different encryption options.

Table 1 Five encryption options of our method

Encryption option	Operation data domain	Scope of effects
MCU (minimum coding unit) shuffle	Spatial	Global
DCT block shuffle	Spatial	in a Macro block
AC coefficient shuffle	Frequency	In a DCT block
AC value change	Frequency	In a DCT block
DC value change	Frequency	In a DCT block

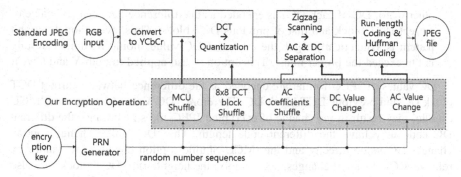

Fig. 1 The functional blocks for JPEG encoding and related encryption options

Figure 1 shows the standard JPEG encoding functional blocks together with the related image encryption options mentioned in Table 1. We also represent the random number generator which uses a single 1024 bit secret key. Random number generator produces a pseudo random sequences that are used as permutation maps for MCU Shuffle, DCT Block Shuffle, and AC Shuffle operation. Also, the random sequences are used as a mask for bitwise-XOR operation for AC and DC coefficient changes. The input picture frame is divided into MCUs and each MCU consists of DCT blocks.

Each of the above encryption option is described as follows:

1. MCU Shuffle: Based on the random number sequence, the MCU shuffle map is constructed. The global-level information hiding effect is achieved through the MCU block shuffle.
2. DCT Block Shuffle: Each MCU consists of one or more DCT blocks. In the 4:2:0 subsampling, DCT block shuffle can be applied to only Y MCU. But, no shuffling is possible with Cb and Cr DCT block with the 4:2:0 subsampling.
3. AC Coefficient Shuffle: After DCT and quantization stages, one DC coefficient and 63 AC coefficients are obtained in each DCT block. Most of AC coefficients become zero by quantization. The encoded non-zero AC coefficients can be shuffled within each DCT block. We perform this encryption by VLC Huffman-coded symbol shuffling within DCT code block. This option is applied to both luminance (Y) and chrominance (Cb and Cr) DCTs.
4. AC Value Change: The VLC Huffman-coded symbol for AC values can be changed by bitwise-XOR operation with random bitmask. The random mask is obtained from a bit slice of the random number sequences generated by the PRNG (Pseudo Random Number Generator). The AC coefficients are encoded as a pair of 'number of bits for code' + 'code value', and the 'code value' can be replaced without breaking format compliance by any value while the length of 'code value' is preserved. This option is also applied to both Y and Cb/Cr.
5. DC Value Change: The VLC Huffman-coded symbol for DC values can be changed by any other value while the value range is in a legal range. Note that the DC value is encoded by DPCM (Differential Pulse Coded Modulation), in

other word, DC of each DCT is encoded as the difference between DC value of current DCT block and that of previous DCT block. Thus, even though any bit pattern is syntactically legal, the choice of DC value should be done carefully not to exceed the proper range. This option is also applied to both Y and Cb/Cr.

DC values of JPEG format are encoded as the difference between current DCT block DC and previous DCT block DC. Therefore, 'DC Value Change' and 'MCU Shuffle' may result in the change of encrypted JPEG file size because the different DC code may have the different code length. The 'DC Value change' option changes DC value directly and the 'MCU Shuffle' option changes DC values by relative MCU location changes, accordingly, the neighboring DCT blocks are also influenced. The MCU shuffle method slightly increases file size (2.5 % on average) while DC value change method results in significant file size increase (10.6 % on average).

3 Experimental Results

We implemented the proposed JPEG encryption approach by modifying the existing JPEG encoder source code in C. Figure 2 shows encryption results with different combinations of encryption options.

In Fig. 2, we only present eight combinations of encryption options among all the 31 possible combinations of five basic encryption options because most of the other combinations show the similar perceptual security level with one of the eight presented encryption results. Figure 2a is the original JPEG image and Fig. 2b–f are the results encrypted with one of the basic five encryption options. In Fig. 2b–d, g have relatively low security level, while Fig. 2e–f and Fig. 2h–i have relatively high security level. Note the 'DC Value Change' and 'MCU Shuffle' methods result in strong information hiding effects. However, 'DC Value Change' method alone leaks a silhouette of original image as shown in Fig. 2e. Figure 2d is the result by the method of existing work [6].

We illustrate the performance and cost for each encryption option as shown in Fig. 3. The size of circle area denotes the execution time ratio that is the overhead of each encryption operation.

We conclude that the combination of 'MCU shuffle' and 'AC value change' is most efficient in terms of file size increase and perceptual security level. We compare our best method and the published existing work [6] which is the same approach as 'AC shuffle' and 'DCT shuffle'. Figure 4 illustrates the encryption results by ours and [6].

In Table 2, we summarized the comparison results in terms of security level, file size increase, and the execution time quantitatively. Ours outperforms the existing works [6] except file size increase but which is not significant overhead.

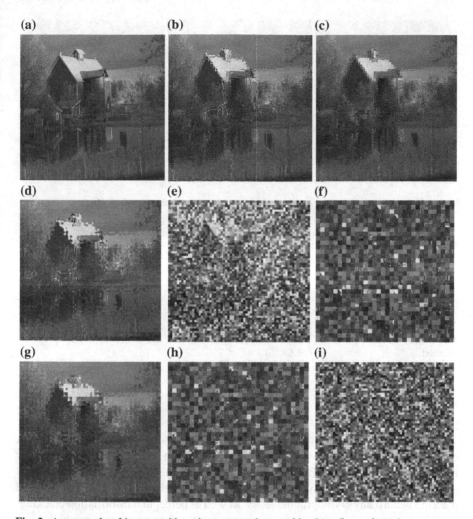

Fig. 2 An example of images with various encryption combinations (house image)

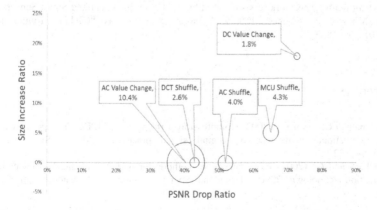

Fig. 3 File size increase, PSNR-drop, and execution time ratio of encryption methods

| Original | Encrypted by [6] | Encrypted by ours |

Fig. 4 Encryption performance comparison between ours and existing work [6]

Table 2 Comparison between ours and existing work

	JPEG format compliance	PSRN drop ratio	Encryption time overhead	File size increase ratio	Security level scalability
Existing work [6]	Yes	15.76 (51.64 %)	10.4 %	0.0 %	No
Our method	Yes	11.07 (66.68 %)	4.3 %	2.5 %	Yes

4 Conclusion

This paper aims to propose a robust JPEG encryption method that has JPEG-format compliance. We developed an encryption method that balances between security level and overheads. Our JPEG encryption method shuffles image information both in spatial domain and frequency domain resulting in the high security level. Our method is secure against any cryptographic attack as well as perceptual information cracking. In addition, ours is faster than conventional complex data encryption methods.

Acknowledgments This work was supported by the Center for Integrated Smart Sensors funded by the Ministry of Science, ICT and Future Planning as "Global Frontier Project" (CISS-2011-0031863).

References

1. Kailasanathan C, Naini RS (2002) Compression performance of JPEG encryption scheme. In: 14th international conference on digital signal processing 2002, DSP 2002. IEEE, pp 1329–1332
2. Wu CP, Kuo CCJ (2001) Fast encryption methods for audiovisual data confidentiality. In: Information technologies 2000. International Society for Optics and Photonics, pp 284–295

3. Khan MI, Jeoti V, Khan MA (2010) Perceptual encryption of JPEG compressed images using DCT coefficients and splitting of DC coefficients into bitplanes. In: International conference on intelligent and advanced systems (ICIAS). IEEE, pp 1–6
4. Potdar U, Talele KT, Gandhe ST (2009) Comparison of MPEG video encryption algorithms. In: Proceedings of the international conference on advances in computing, communication and control. ACM, pp 289–294
5. Puech, W, Rodrigues JM, Bors AG: analysis and cryptanalysis of a selective encryption method for JPEG images. In: WIAMIS'07 8th international workshop on image analysis for multimedia interactive services, 2007. IEEE, pp 77-80
6. Unterweger A, Uhl A (2012) Length-preserving Bit-stream-based JPEG Encryption. In: Proceedings of the on multimedia and security. ACM, pp 85–90

Multiple Regression Analysis of Climatic Factors in Greenhouse Using Data Partitioning

Yu Fu, Aziz Nasridinov, Minghao Piao and Keun Ho Ryu

Abstract One of the most important works of planting crops in greenhouse is climatic factors control. In this paper, we propose to predict air temperature, relative humidity and carbon dioxide concentration in greenhouse using multiple regression models. We also propose to improve the accuracy of prediction using clustering technique. In other words, we first perform the cluster analysis and then build models for the data in each cluster. The results of predictions were compared with raw experimental data for evaluating quality of these models. The experiment results demonstrate that the proposed method outperforms the existing method. The aim of this study is to provide a feasible climatic factors control method to automatic environmental monitoring systems.

Keywords Climatic factors prediction · Data clustering · Greenhouse

Y. Fu · K.H. Ryu (✉)
Database/Bioinformatics Laboratory, School of Electrical and Computer Engineering,
Chungbuk National University, Cheongju, South Korea
e-mail: khryu@dblab.chungbuk.ac.kr

Y. Fu
e-mail: fuyu@dblab.chungbuk.ac.kr

A. Nasridinov
Department of Computer Science, Chungbuk National University,
Cheongju, South Korea
e-mail: aziz@chungbuk.ac.kr

M. Piao
Department of Computer Engineering, Dongguk University Gyeongju Campus,
Gyeongsangbuk, South Korea
e-mail: myunghopark@gmail.com

© Springer Science+Business Media Singapore 2016   669
J.J. (Jong Hyuk) Park et al. (eds.), *Advanced Multimedia and Ubiquitous Engineering*, Lecture Notes in Electrical Engineering 393,
DOI 10.1007/978-981-10-1536-6_87

1 Introduction

Greenhouse is a special environment for separating plants from the natural environment. It is a place where various conditions such as heat, moisture and light can be controlled that enables to grow plants that are difficult to grow in natural environment. However, it takes a long period of time to adjust climatic factors in a large space such as greenhouse. Thus, it can be beneficial to control climatic factors in advance according to the predicted results.

In modern greenhouses, automatic environmental monitoring systems are used to control climatic factors based on data measured in greenhouse. There have been several research efforts to analyze this data. For example, Ferreira et al. [1] applied radial basis function neural networks to predict air temperature in greenhouse. Caponetto et al. [2] proposed a framework for the development of soft computing-based climate controllers in modern greenhouses. Teodosiu et al. [3] used a numerical model to predict indoor air humidity and its effect on indoor environment. Fu et al. [4] proposed to predict temperature, relative humidity and carbon dioxide concentration in greenhouse using statistical measurement.

In this paper, we propose a multiple regression analysis to predict various climatic factors. We also propose improve the quality of prediction by data pre-processing. More specifically, we make the following contribution in this paper:

- We propose to use multiple regression analysis technique to predict climatic factors in greenhouse. Multiple regression models were generated to predict climatic factors after 5 min. Then these models were repeatedly applied to predict longer time by using predicted data as input.
- We propose to partition the greenhouse climate data into groups. We used k-means clustering algorithm to divide climate data into different weather patterns. This enables to achieve higher prediction accuracy.
- We demonstrate that the proposed method outperforms the existing method using experiments.

The rest of the paper proceeds as follows. Section 2 discusses the related study. Section 3 explains the proposed method and shows experiment results. Section 5 describes conclusions.

2 Related Study

Radial basis function neural networks (RBFNNs) were applied to model the inside air temperature of a hydroponic greenhouse as a function of the outside air temperature, solar radiation and the inside relative humidity in a research [1]. Based on a Levenberg-Marquardt method, the authors presented a new algorithm that explicitly exploits the linear-non-linear structure of RBFNNs. Compared with some other methods, this new algorithm showed better results in terms of error performance and parameter convergence, and with smaller computational costs. However, a neural network algorithm requires a lot of computation and the process could not be understood easily.

Proportional-integral (PI) control is a conventional control technique which controls variables by calculating error continuously. Pseudo-Derivative-Feedback (PDF) control was compared with PI control through simulation using an approximated dynamic system thermal model of the greenhouse [5]. PDF control was better than PI with advantage of time delay. The algorithm showed satisfactory results when it was tested to control a greenhouse section. A problem of this kind of control methods is that they always work after error has appeared.

Artificial intelligence (AI) techniques were also applied to model and control climate factors in greenhouse [2]. The authors proposed a framework for developing soft computing-based controllers in modern greenhouses. Fuzzy logic and distributed proportional-integral-derivative were applied in the controllers. Although it showed good results, this method still has some problems such as universality and complicated model. A numerical model was built to predict indoor air humidity and its effect on indoor environment [3]. Based on the computational fluid dynamics technique, the approach was developed using turbulence models. Obviously, airflow is not a conventional input factor which can be measured easily and the models were complex and thus calculations are massive.

3 Proposed Method

The proposed method consists of the following three steps: data collection, k-means clustering and prediction with regression analysis. Section 3.1 introduces data collection strategy. Section 3.2 describes clustering result with k-mean clustering algorithm. Section 3.3 shows prediction process using regression analysis.

3.1 Data Collection

Raw data were collected in a greenhouse which is located in Cheongju, Chungbuk, South Korea using data collection device from local greenhouse. The area of the greenhouse is 2500 m^2. For avoiding human influence, control module of the automatic environmental monitoring system was not enabled during the period when climatic factors were monitored so that the climatic factors only affected by natural factors.

An automatic monitoring system was used for measuring air temperature inside the greenhouse (Tin, Celsius), air temperature outside the greenhouse (Tout, Celsius), relative humidity inside the greenhouse (RH, %), solar radiation (SR, W/m^{-2}), cumulative solar radiation (CSR, J/m^{-2}) and atmospheric carbon dioxide concentration inside the greenhouse (CO_2, ppm). This system contains a computer

Table 1 Format of raw data obtained from the greenhouse

Time	Tin (°C)	Tout (°C)	RH (%)	CO_2 (ppm)	SR (W/m^{-2})	CSR (J/m^{-2})
2013-04-05 11:05 am	25.4	19.3	64.5	397	845	25
2013-04-05 11:10 am	26	19.4	65.1	396	868	26
2013-04-05 11:15 am	26.9	19.8	62.7	403	931	28

and several sensors. One temperature sensor was placed at the outside of the wall of greenhouse to measure temperature outside greenhouse. One temperature sensor, one carbon dioxide concentration sensor and an illuminometer were placed at a platform in the center of the greenhouse to measure climatic factors in the greenhouse. All these sensors and meter were connected to the computer. Table 1 shows format of raw data obtained from the greenhouse.

Once data is collected, we encountered several challenges in terms of abnormal data that are caused by wrong measurement and recording mistakes. Thus, we have detected and reduced the influences of these mistakes in prediction. In obtained data, we discovered values that are too large or too tiny than adjacent values caused by equipment failures or electricity interruption. The influence of this problem would cause a generation of wrong models although the abnormal data were very rare. Thus, in order to solve this problem, we have normalized abnormal values to the nearest data. This is possible due to the fact that data obtained from greenhouse does not change rapidly and this enables the smoothing of the dataset.

3.2 Clustering

Clustering is a task of grouping a set of objects in such a way that objects in the same cluster are more similar to each other than to those in other clusters. The reason of this cluster analysis is that we consider that climatic factors may change differently in different weather patterns. We assume that building models of climatic factors for each pattern can improve result of predictions. Our experiment proved this opinion in Sect. 4 By comparing errors of prediction results, clustering process improved the results for about 5 %.

The climatic factors outside greenhouse, temperature and solar radiation, were used to generate clusters. At first, the data of these two factors are normalized because they have different scales. Each data was mapped to [0, 1] by comparing with all data which were measured at the same time in each day. The smallest value was mapped to 0 and largest value was mapped to 1. We used k-means algorithm to cluster the data. In first step of k-means, the number of clusters k should be determined. By observing collected data, we conclude that all measured values and mapped values of solar radiation are 0 at nighttime, so these data can become a cluster. It is hard to identify many different weather types because only solar

Fig. 1 Result of k-means clustering

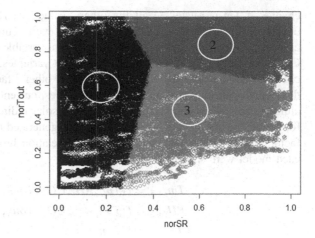

radiation and temperature were measured. Thus, we decided to identify two patterns at daytime and one at nighttime. Thus, k was set to 3.

Figure 1 shows the result of clustering. In the figure, norSR is normalized solar radiation and norTout is normalized temperature outside greenhouse. According to distribution of data points, cluster 1 contains all the small values of solar radiation so cluster 1 is the nighttime group. Cluster 2 and cluster 3 are daytime groups. Compared with cluster 3, mapped values of temperature in cluster 2 are higher, that means the weathers in this group are good, such as sunny. And the weathers in cluster 3 make lower temperature. After clustering, we got centroid of each cluster. When new data are obtained from greenhouse, we can assign them to closest centroid to get their cluster label.

3.3 Prediction

Regression analysis is a statistical process for estimating the relationships among variables. There are a lot of regression analysis techniques that can be used for modeling and analyzing climate factors. The main idea of regression analysis is to identify a similarity between a dependent variable and one or more independent variables. The advantage of regression models is that these models can perform well with only several inputs as independent variables. Relationships between dependent variable and independent variables can be express ed well by the parameters of items in regression models. Calculation of multiple regression analysis is also small relatively. Because of these advantages, multiple regression models were applied to predict climatic factors in our research.

Multiple regression models were developed with clustered data. Before generating the models, independent variables of each model should be determined according to relationships among the climatic factors. In these five climatic factors, change of Tin is related to all the others, same as RH and CO_2. So model was developed to predict data of Tin after 5 min while current measured data of five climatic factors were considered as independent variables. In the same way, RH and CO_2 were modeled with the same independent variables. Tout and CSR are outside climatic factors so that they are not affected by other 3 factors. So their models were developed with only two independent variables, current measured data of temperature outside the greenhouse and cumulative solar radiation. We generated models for inside climatic factors in each cluster and generated models for outside climatic factors in whole data set. According to these relationships, independent variables of each model were shown as below.

$$Tin_{t+5} = f(Tin_t, RH_t, CO_{2t}, Tout_t, CSR_t)$$
$$RH_{t+5} = f(Tin_t, RH_t, CO_{2t}, Tout_t, CSR_t)$$
$$CO_{2t+5} = f(Tin_t, RH_t, CO_{2t}, Tout_t, CSR_t)$$
$$Tout_{t+5} = f(Tout_t, CSR_t)$$
$$CSR_{t+5} = f(Tout_t, CSR_t)$$

We have considered quadratic interactive multiple regression models for analyzing five climatic factors, so each model contains all combinations of the independent variables. Table 2 shows multiple regression models of the climatic factors. It also shows model generated indices, which underwent evaluation using adjusted R^2 (R^2 adj.) and residual standard error (RSE). Adjusted R^2 is a number ranges from 0 to 1 which indicates how well data fit a statistical model, the more it is the better the model represented the dependent variable. All the adjusted R^2s shown here are close to 1, so these models can predict the climatic factors after 5 min.

More predicted data were generated by iteration with these models. Table 3 shows comparisons between raw data and predicted data using average error rate (AER) and standard error (SE). Average error rate can be used to measure accuracy of prediction. Average error rate is average of error rate between predicted data and corresponding original data. Obviously, the value of average error rate ranges from 0 to 1, and the closer this coefficient is to zero, the better the prediction.

As seen in Table 3, average error rate of predicting air temperature, relative humidity and atmospheric carbon dioxide concentration in greenhouse for at most 90 min. All these values are less than 0.06, much closer to 0 than to 1, so that we can consider that these models can predict well in 90 min.

4 Experiment Results

As the format of data in Table 1, the experiment data set contains 6 attributes. The monitoring system recorded data of climatic factors per 5 min. Climatic factors were monitored from April 1 to June 26, 2013, so the data set contains about 30,000 tuples. R environment was used in our research for analyzing and predicting.

Table 2 Models obtained from multiple regressions to predict the climatic factors

Model		R^2 adj.	RSE
$\mathbf{Tout_{t+5}} = 1.005 \times Tout_t + 0.0502 \times CSR_t + 0.00007988 \times Tout_t \times CSR_t - 0.005626 \times CSR_t^2 - 0.0003461 \times Tout_t^2 - 0.02763$		0.9988	0.2556
$\mathbf{CSR_{t+5}} = 1.0016 \times CSR_t - 0.0002321 \times Tout_t - 0.0004324 \times Tout_t \times CSR_t - 0.00281 \times CSR_t^2 + 0.00006105 \times Tout_t^2 + 0.01833$		0.9548	0.4753
Cluster 1	$\mathbf{Tin_{t+5}} = 1.02 \times Tin_t + 0.004654 \times RH_t \times CSR_t + 0.0004955 \times Tout_t + 0.00001764 \times Tout_t \times CO_{2t} + 0.0006062 \times Tin_t \times Tout_t - 0.02199 \times Tin_t \times CSR_t - 0.000137 \times Tout_t \times RH_t - 1.212$	0.995	0.2254
	$\mathbf{RH_{t+5}} = 0.9834 \times RH_t + 0.00001158 \times RH_t \times CO_{2t} - 0.0007669 \times CSR_t^2 + 0.00003981 \times CO_{2t} \times CSR_t + 1.113$	0.977	1.567
	$\mathbf{CO_{2t+5}} = 0.9879 \times CO_{2t} - 0.000005022 \times CO_{2t}^2 + 0.09036 \times CSR_t^2 + 0.08342 \times RH_t \times CSR_t + 0.1148 \times Tout_t \times CSR_t - 0.008011 \times CO_{2t} \times CSR_t - 1.893$	0.9927	4.574
Cluster 2	$\mathbf{Tin_{t+5}} = 1.023 \times Tin_t + 0.002469 \times RH_t \times CSR_t - 0.2962 \times Tout_t - 0.00004827 \times Tout_t \times CO_{2t} - 0.01296 \times Tin_t \times Tout_t + 0.003157 \times Tin_t \times CSR_t + 0.002995 \times Tout_t \times RH_t - 1.301$	0.9911	0.4611
	$\mathbf{RH_{t+5}} = 0.9905 \times RH_t + 0.0005442 \times RH_t \times CO_{2t} - 0.0236 \times CSR_t^2 + 0.0001688 \times CO_{2t} \times CSR_t + 1.735$	0.968	2.134
	$\mathbf{CO_{2t+5}} = 0.9614 \times CO_{2t} + 0.000149 \times CO_{2t}^2 + 0.006538 \times CSR_t^2 + 0.01011 \times RH_t \times CSR_t + 0.003933 \times Tout_t \times CSR_t - 0.0104 \times CO_{2t} \times CSR_t + 7.77$	0.9895	7.395
Cluster 3	$\mathbf{Tin_{t+5}} = 0.9757 \times Tin_t + 0.0008419 \times RH_t \times CSR_t + 0.07595 \times Tout_t + 0.00004477 \times Tout_t \times CO_{2t} - 0.0006125 \times Tin_t \times Tout_t - 0.002637 \times Tin_t \times CSR_t - 0.0007287 \times Tout_t \times RH_t + 0.3678$	0.992	0.3752
	$\mathbf{RH_{t+5}} = 0.9936 \times RH_t - 0.0001703 \times RH_t \times CO_{2t} - 0.0181 \times CSR_t^2 + 0.003041 \times CO_{2t} \times CSR_t + 1.386$	0.973	1.772
	$\mathbf{CO_{2t+5}} = 0.9646 \times CO_{2t} + 0.0002426 \times CO_{2t}^2 - 0.04435 \times CSR_t^2 - 0.02122 \times RH_t \times CSR_t + 0.09292 \times Tout_t \times CSR_t - 0.001618 \times CO_{2t} \times CSR_t + 6.377$	0.9912	6.021

Subscript of the variables describe the moment when the variables were measured or predicted. Compared with t, $t + 5$ is 5 min later

Figure 2 shows comparisons of average error rate of temperature, relative humidity and carbon dioxide concentration between clustered and non-clustered predictions for 90 min. The figures present predictions of temperature and carbon dioxide concentration were improved by clustering, but prediction of relative humidity was not. This is a because relative humidity is the most stable climatic

Table 3 Comparisons between raw data and predicted data

Climatic factor		Prediction time					
		15 min	30 min	45 min	60 min	75 min	90 min
Tin	AER	0.0156	0.0232	0.0314	0.03378	0.0448	0.0520
	SE	1.33793	2.31628	3.19463	4.07298	4.95133	5.82968
RH	AER	0.0152	0.0199	0.0256	0.0304	0.0356	0.0403
	SE	1.39266	1.80158	2.2105	2.61942	3.02834	3.43726
CO_2	AER	0.0159	0.0241	0.0313	0.0382	0.0455	0.0535
	SE	9.55641	14.9010	20.04559	25.29018	30.43477	35.47936

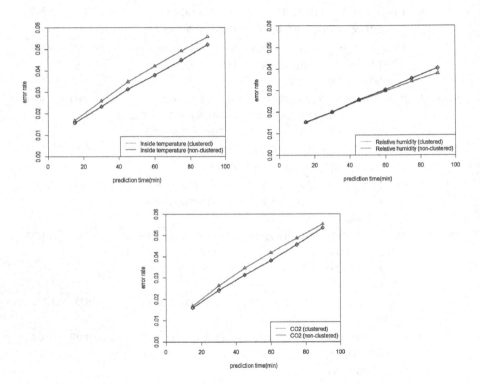

Fig. 2 Average error rate of inside climatic factors predictions between clustered and non-clustered data

factor in greenhouse. In this enclosed environment, relative humidity changes periodically and is not sensitive to weather. Totally, the clustering process improved prediction results for about 5 %.

# 5	Conclusions

In this paper, we proposed a method to predict climatic factors in greenhouse. The method consists of 3 steps: anomaly detection, k-means clustering and prediction with regression models. Anomaly detection is used to avoid influences of measure or recording mistakes. Then climatic data are divided to several clusters as weather pattern. Regression models are generated to predict climatic factors in greenhouse after five minutes at first for each cluster, climatic factors after longer time were predicted by iteration with these models. According to comparisons between raw data and predicted data, these models can predict climatic factors in the greenhouse in at least 90 min. The clustering process was proved useful by comparing with result of predictions without clustering. The result of experiment shows that this method can be used for controlling climatic factors in greenhouse smoothly.

There are also some limitations of this method. As the experimental data were all obtained from April to June, performance of this method was not proved in the other period of year. So more data measured in other months are required to improve the models. And data of more climatic factors outside greenhouse will be helpful to increase number of clusters which is number of weather pattern.

Acknowledgments This research was supported by Basic Science Research Program through the National Research Foundation of Korea (NRF) funded by the Ministry of Science, ICT & Future Planning (No.2013R1A2A2A01068923).

References

1. Ferreira PM, Faria EA, Ruano AE (2002) Neural network models in greenhouse air temperature prediction. Neurocomputing 43(1):51–75
2. Caponetto R, Fortuna L, Nunnari G, Occhipinti L, Xibilia MG (2000) Soft computing for greenhouse climate control. IEEE Trans Fuzzy Syst 8(6):753–760
3. Teodosiu C, Hohota R, Rusaouën G, Woloszyn M (2003) Numerical prediction of indoor air humidity and its effect on indoor environment. Build Environ 38(5):655–664
4. Fu Y, Piao M, Kim KA, Ryu KH (2015) Prediction of temperature, relative humidity and carbon dioxide concentration in greenhouse using multiple regression models
5. Setiawan A, Albright LD, Phelan RM (2000) Application of pseudo-derivative-feedback algorithm in greenhouse air temperature control. Comput Electron Agric 26(3):283–302

A Statistical Correlation Analysis on Road Accidents in South Korea

Aziz Nasridinov, Kwan-Hee Yoo and Tae-Kyung Lee

Abstract Road safety is main concern of South Korean government, as in 2010–2015, car accidents took around 25,000 people lives. It is important to understand the reasons behind these accidents in order to prevent them from happening. In this short paper, we propose to statistically measure the factors that influence on road accidents in South Korea. Specifically, we perform correlation analysis between car accident occurrences and various factors. The analysis that influences each of the presented correlation result enables government to focus their strength in the most problematic areas.

Keywords Correlation analysis · Car accident · Influential factors

1 Introduction

In recent decades, South Korea has become a country with one of the leading economies in the world. The better economic conditions allow people to effort various properties, and among these properties, a car plays an important role as it significantly improves quality of many individuals. According to statistics, people, who received a car driving license in South Korea, have increased up to 11 % in recent 5 years [1]. However, driving car also comes with car accidents that annually take millions of lives worldwide. Although, South Korea has a better road conditions and advanced car safety measurements, in 2014, car accidents took 4762

A. Nasridinov · K.-H. Yoo
Department of Computer Science, Chungbuk National University, Cheongju, Korea
e-mail: aziz@chungbuk.ac.kr

K.-H. Yoo
e-mail: khyoo@chungbuk.ac.kr

T.-K. Lee (✉)
Department of Computer Engineering, Dongguk University at Gyeongju, Gyeongju, Korea
e-mail: tklee@dongguk.ac.kr

© Springer Science+Business Media Singapore 2016   679
J.J. (Jong Hyuk) Park et al. (eds.), *Advanced Multimedia and Ubiquitous Engineering*, Lecture Notes in Electrical Engineering 393,
DOI 10.1007/978-981-10-1536-6_88

people lives [1]. It is important to understand the reasons behind these accidents in order to prevent them from happening.

There have been several papers that propose method to analyze the reasons behind the car accidents. For example, Park et al. [2] studied factors that influence the severity of vehicle crashes in South Korea. The result of analysis demonstrates that dozing off, increase of speed and road violations by pedestrians were the major factors of car accidents. Choi et al. [3] proposed a study to statistically analyze factors for jaywalking that leads to pedestrian accidents. The study have found that increase of speed were major factors that influence on pedestrian accidents, where elderly were the most vulnerable.

In this short paper, we propose a statistical correlation analysis on road accidents in South Korea. We measured the correlations between car accident occurrences and various factors that can influence on road incidents. These factors include alcohol consumption, average speed of a car, age and gender of a driver, model of a car and urbanization. We provide an analysis that influences on each of the presented correlation result in Sect. 2 and provide discussions in Sect. 3.

2 Correlation Analysis on Road Accidents

In this section, we explain the correlation analysis performed in order to determine the most influential factors to the car accident. All correlations were carried out in a statistical tool, called R. For correlation analysis, we used a statistical measurement, called, Pearson product-moment correlation that defines the strength of linear relationship between two attributes in region of -1 and 1. Figure 1 demonstrates the result of correlation analysis.

Correlation of car accidents and alcohol consumption. South Korea is a special alcohol drinking culture. However, this has a lot of negative effect as well. For example, according to statistics, there have been nearly one million car accidents due to drunk driving, which took more than five thousands lives [1]. This is confirmed by Fig. 1a that reveals that drunk driving is one of the most influential factors to the car accidents. There is a strong correlation ($r = 0.974$) between car accidents and alcohol consumption. This indicates that the more drunk driving, the more car accidents are likely to occur.

Correlation of car accidents and urbanization. In recent decades, South Korea has gained a significant economic growth that resulted in urbanization to reach all of its regions. We may infer that urbanization has a negative effect on car accidents as it is statistically confirmed that most of the car accidents occur in highways. However, in cities with a lot pedestrian, traffic congestions and traffic lights, drivers tend to drive slowly and thus cause less car accidents. Figure 1b confirms our observation meaning that there a slight correlation between car accidents and urbanization ($r = 0.095$). We can explain a slight correlation as follows. The capital of South Korea, Seoul, has the highest number of car accidents (3,435,816 accidents) and has the highest urbanization (100 %). On the other hand, Gwangju city

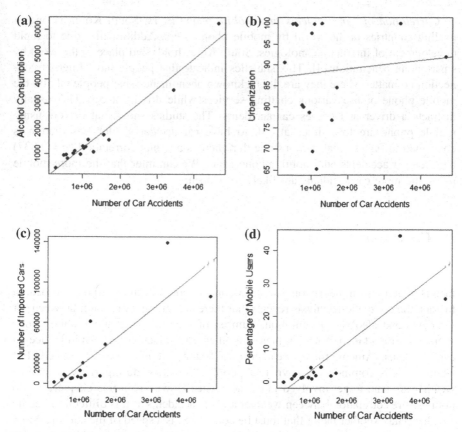

Fig. 1 Correlation analysis between car accident and other attributes

has smallest number of car accidents (569,642), but its urbanization reaches similar level as Seoul (100 %). This explains a slight correlation between car accidents and urbanization in South Korea.

Correlation of car accidents and imported cars. In recent years, car industry of South Korea has made a huge step forward in terms of in terms of safety and price. Most of the people prefer to buy domestic brands that have a good quality. However, even though their expensive cars, some people prefer to buy luxury imported cars. According to the statistics, approximately 10 % of cars registered every year are imported cars. One may argue that driving imported cars may cause more car accidents. Figure 1c shows that our assumption is correct as there is a strong correlation ($r = 0.839$) between car accidents and number of imported cars. This can be explained as follows. Most of these imported cars possess a speed that is several times faster than domestic cars in South Korea. As increased speed is a main cause of all most of the car accidents, we can infer that driving an imported car can be one of the leading factors that influence car accidents.

Correlation of car accidents and mobile phone users. South Korea is one of leading countries in the world by mobile phone users. Additionally, due to rapid development of Internet technologies, South Korea holds 2nd place in the word by smartphone penetration [4]. This statistics indicate that people have Internet connection no matter where they are. It is a known phenomenon that people talk on the mobile phone or use various chatting services while driving a car. This usually distracts a driver and causes car accidents. The studies show that drivers using mobile phone are four times at risk to have car accidents. Our observation is confirmed in Fig. 1d that demonstrate that there is a strong correlation ($r = 0.837$) between car accidents and mobile phone users. We can infer that the more mobile users, the more car accidents are likely to happen.

3   Conclusion

In this short paper, we studied the correlation between car accidents and several factors that may influence on car accidents in South Korea. Among measured factors, the correlation analysis reveals that there is a strong correlation between car accidents and alcohol consumption, number of imported cars and mobile phone users. It is important to note that there are other critical factors that can influence on car accidents. Among them, weather is a factor that must be considered. For example, it is commonly known that people who drive during rainy or snowy weather are tend to get involved in car accidents. However, in this chapter, we do not measure correlation between weather and car accidents as it is difficult to get the weather data. Another factor that must be considered is a speed of the car. Increased speed is a cause of most car accidents. However, similar to weather data, average speed information is not available in South Korea. Thus, we do not perform correlation analysis using average speed.

References

1. Traffic Accident Analysis System in South Korea. Available at: http://taas.koroad.or.kr/
2. Park S, Jang K, Park SH, Kim DK, Chon KS (2012) Analysis of injury severity in traffic crashes: a case study of Korean expressways. KSCE J Civil Eng 16(7):1280–1288
3. Choi J, Kim S, Kim S, Hong H, Baik S (2013) Pedestrian crashes during jaywalking, can we afford to overlook? In: Proceeding of the 16th Road Safety on Four Continents Conference. Beijing, China, pp 1–16
4. Public Data Portal in South Korea. Available at: https://www.data.go.kr

An Accident Prediction in Military Barracks Using Data Mining

HyunSoon Shin, Kwan-Hee Yoo and Aziz Nasridinov

Abstract Recently, several accidents have occurred in South Korean military barracks that caused a social concern. In this paper, we argue that these accidents can be prevented. Specifically, we describe an ongoing project that applies well-known data mining techniques to predict accidents in military barracks in South Korea. For this, we first collect various soldiers' data, such as social media, personal history and medical data, and then, use ranking, clustering, classification and text mining techniques to analyze this data.

Keywords Data mining · Military barracks · Accident prediction

1 Introduction

Recently, various accidents have occurred in South Korean military barracks. Specifically, the accidents like suicide and murder of fellow soldiers triggered a concern of the both ordinary citizens and government. In this paper, we argue that we can prevent these situations from happening using data mining techniques. More specifically, we propose to collect various soldiers' data, such as social media, personal history and medical data and apply data mining techniques to analyze these data.

However, there are several difficulties in application of data mining techniques. First of all, the data from military barracks is highly confidential and is not publicly

K.-H. Yoo · A. Nasridinov (✉)
Department of Computer Science, Chungbuk National University,
Cheongju, South Korea
e-mail: aziz@chungbuk.ac.kr

K.-H. Yoo
e-mail: khyoo@chungbuk.ac.kr

H. Shin
Things and Emotion Convergence Research Team, ETRI, Daejeon, South Korea
e-mail: hsshin@etri.re.kr

© Springer Science+Business Media Singapore 2016
J.J. (Jong Hyuk) Park et al. (eds.), *Advanced Multimedia and Ubiquitous
Engineering*, Lecture Notes in Electrical Engineering 393,
DOI 10.1007/978-981-10-1536-6_89

available. Since the accuracy of data mining techniques is dependent on data size, there is a need for a data collection technique. Further, most of the state-of-the art data mining techniques suffer from a poor performance when these are presented with a huge amount of data. Thus, there a need for improving data mining techniques so that these can handle potentially large amount of data. Lastly, timely analysis of the accidents is vital as this enables to save the life of soldiers. Similarly, accuracy of the data mining technique must be high as well. Thus, there is a need to perform extensive experiments that verifies the performance of the data mining technique in various cases.

In this paper, we describe the ongoing project that applies data mining technique to analyze military data. More specifically, project contains the following tasks:

- We collect and store various soldiers' data, such as social media, personal history and medical data.
- We apply data mining techniques that are modified and improved to handle a huge amount of military data.
- We evaluate the performance of each data mining technique to verify its applicability in particular case.

The rest of the paper is organized as follows. Section 2 describes the main differences of the proposed project and other similar projects. Section 3 explains the project and its modules in details. Section 4 concludes the paper and highlights the future work.

2 Related Work

Recently, data mining and machine learning techniques have been used in military applications. In this section, we briefly describe these applications.

A large body of research was conducted outside of South Korea to analyze military data. Military Health Data Mining Algorithms Library (M-HDML) [1] is a project initiated by US Department of Defense (DoD) that applies data mining technologies and techniques to the storage and retrieval of patient data, helping doctors in the DoD's vast medical health system (MHS) to more accurately diagnose their patients. Durkheim Project [2] uses data mining techniques to analyze data from soldier and veteran and predict if these may commit the suicide. The project contains three phases. In the first phase, the medical records of soldiers were collected and analyzed. In the second phase, social media postings and social media and mobile content were analyzed. In the third phase, a new method is proposed to prevent serious suicide risk. The main advantage of the proposed project is that it provides a real-time predictive analytics for negative events, such as suicide or violent action. The experiment results were performed that demonstrate 70 % of accuracy in its peak and 67 % of accuracy on average. Researchers at Harvard University [3] used the data mining to analyze near one million US soldiers those who are most prone to commit violent crimes in army. Investigators combined these data along with other administrative records such as military career and demographic information along with crime and medical records to predict violent offenders. Specifically, the authors used machine learning techniques, such as cross-validated stepwise regression, random forests, penalized regressions, to constructing models for crimes that occur in military and then validated in an independent 2011–2013 sample. As data mining techniques to analyze military data in South Korea, Woo and Park [4] proposed to compare well-known data mining algorithms to predict soldier's depression. Specifically, the authors collected data from 544 soldiers and applied multiple regression and Classification and Regression Tree (CART) to analyze this data. The experiment results discover several interesting facts. First of all, around 23.6 of participants had mild depression. Also, both algorithms in experiments output the identical result, where anxiety is the major factor for soldier's depression.

3 Proposed Method

In this section, we describe the proposed method in details. Figure 1 demonstrates the overall architecture of the proposed method. The proposed method contains three main phases, such as data collection, data mining analysis and performance evaluation.

In data collection phase, data related to the soldier's social network, personal history in military barrack and medical data are collected. The reason we collected social network postings is that it may reveal potential risk to suicide. We collect the data of soldier from well-known social media platforms, such as Facebook and Twitter using open APIs. On the other hand, personal history in military barrack may reveal soldiers who are more likely to commit violent crimes. Medical data can help to reveal soldiers who are likely to commit crimes based on their mental state. The combination of this data is stored in database that is later used for data mining analysis.

Analyzing accidents manually takes a huge amount of time as the accident data is usually large and has many attributes. On the other hand, we can use data mining techniques to ease this task. However, each data mining technique performs different task. For example, data mining classification techniques can be applied to labeled soldier data to classify if a particular case is accident or not. On the other hand, we can use skyline method to choose only representative accidents from the accident dataset. Thus, there is a need to select specific data mining technique according to the specific accident case. For this, the second phase of the proposed method is so called data miner that consists of data preprocessing and data mining analysis process. Once data is collected, we can perform data mining analysis. However, the raw data that is stored in database may contain noise and outliers. For example, the social media posting may contain a considerable amount of false data or noise not related to the suicide analysis, such as video, advertisement or friend's

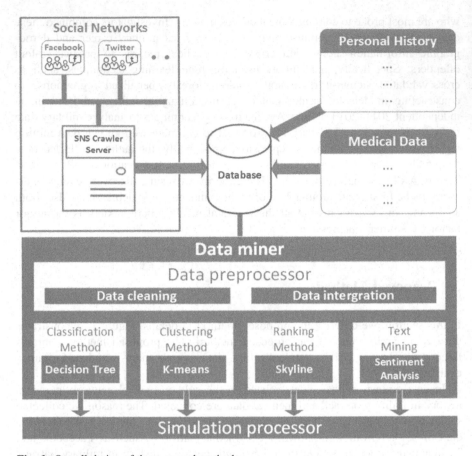

Fig. 1 Overall design of the proposed method

tags. Thus, before performing data mining analysis, we first perform data cleaning and data integration procedures.

The cleaned data can be used to perform data mining analysis. Here, we use ranking, clustering, classification and text mining techniques. For clustering, we use well-known k-means algorithm that groups data according to specific criteria. This algorithm can be useful to analyzing personal history. For example, we can easily group soldiers who more likely to commit crime and soldiers who not likely. For classification, we use the well-known ID3 decision tree algorithm. This algorithm is used to classify accidents according to the types and predict them. For example, we can use decision tree algorithm to analyze the medical data, where nodes of decision tree represent medical data attributes such as age, disease history, mental state, etc., and leaves represent decisions, such as dangerous or not. For ranking, we use skyline [5, 6] method that is based on domination criteria determines a set of representative data records. This algorithm may help to rank the most dangerous cases in order and determine which cases need a special attention by military management. For text mining, we used sentimental analysis algorithm. This algorithm can be used to analyze the social media postings of soldiers and detect if there is a risk to commit a suicide. For example, it is commonly known that most of the soldiers use social networking for posting their feelings. A frustrated or sad soldier makes a post regarding his bad feeling. If analyzed, we can prevent potential case of suicides.

The third phase of proposed method is simulation processor. Recall from Sect. 1 that timely analysis of the accident is important for prediction as this enables to save the life of soldiers. However, only timely analysis of soldier dataset is not sufficient as these algorithms should operate well in terms of accuracy and memory usage. For example, accuracy of the data mining algorithm can predict more accidents, and thus, save many of lives. On the other hand, many military agencies are still on old fashioned computers, and thus, timeliness and memory usage of data mining algorithms should be appropriate. Thus, in order to verify the performance of the data mining technique in various cases, we perform experiments using the data collected in first phase. This is important to note that most of the state-of-the art data mining techniques suffer from a poor performance when these are presented with a huge amount of data. Thus, in order to make these algorithms to handle a large amount of data, we implemented in parallel style using GPU processing.

4 Conclusion

In this paper, we described ongoing project to prevent accidents from happening in military barracks. Our method use modified and improved data mining techniques to predict accidents. For this, we described three main phases of the proposed method, such as data collection, data mining analysis and performance evaluation. The main advantage of the proposed method is that it can make predictions in timely manner and is accurate and memory efficient. On the other hand, it is unified framework that can perform various analysis and thus, can prevent from more cases of crimes. In the future, we are planning to present more detailed overview of the each modified and improved algorithm and demonstrate the result of experiments.

Acknowledgments This work was supported by the IT R&D program of MSIP. (Development of Military Life Management System based on Emotion Recognition.)

References

1. Agarwal R, Carnahan D, Crowley P, Bonnema A, Calvo A, Eisen S, Sanderson IC (2012) Leveraging the air force health services data warehouse for transformational healthcare research: an action agenda for the health informatics research initiative. In: American Medical Informatics Association annual symposium (AMIA 2012)
2. Thompson P, Bryan C, Poulin C (2014) Predicting military and veteran suicide risk: cultural aspects. In: Proceedings of the workshop on computational linguistics and clinical psychology, pp 1–6

3. Rosellini AJ, Monahan J, Street AE, Heeringa SG, Hill ED, Petukhova M, Reis BY, Sampson NA, Bliese P, Schoenbaum M, Stein MB, Ursano RJ, Kessler RC (2015) Predicting non-familial major physical violent crime perpetration in the US Army from administrative data. Psychol Med 46(2):303–316
4. Woo CH, Park JY (2014) A study on comparison of classification and regression tree and multiple regression for predicting of soldiers' depression. J Psychiatr Ment Health Nurs 23 (4):268–277
5. Stephan B, Donald K, Konrad S (2001) The skyline operator. ICDE 2001:421–430
6. Chomicki J, Godfrey P, Gryz J, Liang D (2005) Skyline with presorting: theory and optimizations, In: Intelligent information processing and web mining. Springer, Berlin, pp 595–604

An Ontology-Based Approach for Searching Crime Big Data

Eun-Suk Choi, Aziz Nasridinov and Kwan-Hee Yoo

Abstract The growing availability of information technologies has enabled law enforcement agencies to collect detailed data about various crimes. However, the volume of crime has made the process of searching and finding the useful information from the crime data difficult. In this paper, we propose an ontology-based approach for searching the knowledge in crime big data. That is, we propose to diversify the search result using ontology-based rules. In order to achieve the goal, we developed crime domain ontology and then performed the search in well-known social media such as Naver and Daum by using developed ontology.

Keywords Big data · Crime · Ontology · Search

1 Introduction

The rapid development of computer and Internet technologies has enabled police agencies to collect a massive amount of information that often comes from criminal data and crime history. Criminologists often use this data to find useful information related to the particular case. However, the volume of crime data has made the process of searching difficult as it takes much time to get the valuable result after the query is issued [1]. Therefore, there is a requirement for a technique to assist in searching the crime data.

There have been several approaches that tried to facilitate the searching of the crime data. For example, in [4], the authors proposed a STT (spatio-temporal-textual)

E.-S. Choi · A. Nasridinov · K.-H. Yoo (✉)
Department of Computer Science, Chungbuk National University, Chungdae-ro 1ga,
Seowon-gu, Cheongju, Chungbuk 28644, Korea
e-mail: khyoo@chungbuk.ac.kr

E.-S. Choi
e-mail: chl1439@chungbuk.ac.kr

A. Nasridinov
e-mail: aziz@chungbuk.ac.kr

© Springer Science+Business Media Singapore 2016   689
J.J. (Jong Hyuk) Park et al. (eds.), *Advanced Multimedia and Ubiquitous
Engineering*, Lecture Notes in Electrical Engineering 393,
DOI 10.1007/978-981-10-1536-6_90

search engine for performing a set of actions, such as extracting, indexing, querying and visualizing crime information. The authors in [6] further improved SST by proposing a data mining framework to the search engine. The framework provides predictions, hotspots, correlations analysis, and topic exploration to facilitate the identification of spatial trends and patterns. The authors in [2] proposed to use well-known data mining techniques such as entity extraction and association rule mining that help to discover various patterns in the crime. However, the purpose of the most of the aforementioned approaches is to find various correlations and patterns in crime data. In this paper, we focus on finding more relevant information by expanding the search result.

More precisely, in this paper, we propose an ontology-based approach for searching crime big data. The main idea of the proposed method is to diversify the search result using ontology-based rules. For this, we developed a domain ontology that consists of the main concepts and terminologies in the field of crime. By using the developed ontology, we perform the search of data in the well-known social media such as Naver and Daum. The experiment results demonstrate that the proposed method can improve the search result by several times comparing to the traditional method.

2 Related Study

There have been numerous research efforts on analyzing the crime data. In this section, we briefly describe these approaches.

Numerous methods were proposed that use data mining techniques to analyze the crime data. For example, Liu et al. [4] proposed a STT (spatio-temporal-textual) search engine for extracting, indexing, querying and visualizing crime information. The authors give scores to each of the data factors (spatial, temporal, and textual) and use these scores to rank the crime data. This tool helps crime detection by identifying crime trend and patterns that are useful for investigators, decision makers and researchers, and security of city life for citizens. Wang et al. [6] proposed an integrated framework for spatio-temporal-textual search and mining. The proposed framework contains an efficient search engine with multiple indexing, ranking and scoring schemes, spatio-temporal-textual pattern mining and topic modeling. Thus, the framework provides predictions, hotspots and correlations analysis, and topic exploration to facilitate the identification of spatial trends and patterns. Similar method was proposed by Chen et al. [2], where the authors use entity extraction and association rule mining to discovery frequent patterns in large collection of crime data.

Various methods were proposed to simplify crime investigation. For example, Furtado et al. [3] proposed WikiCrimes system. The main idea of the proposed system is to use collaborative intelligence where each individual creates useful information for everyone. Specifically, WikiCrimes offers a common interaction environment for the ordinary citizens, so that they can share criminal occurrences and monitor locations where they occur. Onnoom et al. [5] proposed to use ontology for recommendation in crime scene investigation. That is, the authors developed an ontology that is able to automatically fill-in words and sentences in crime report. The experiments show that proposed method is accurate enough to perform the task of recommendation and thus, helps to reduce long delays in police centers.

3 Searching Crime Big Data

This section describes the proposed method. In this paper, we propose an ontology-based approach that can improve the search result in crime big data. For this, we first describe the overall design of the proposed method. We then describe the crime ontology that was used to improve the search result.

3.1 Overview

Figure 1 shows the overall design of the proposed method. Here, it is important to note that the proposed method performs as a middleware between user and social media. That is, the user first defines an input keyword for searching crime related terminologies in well-known social media. The input keyword is then transferred to the inference engine, where using ontology, the proposed method infers other keywords related to the crime terminology. For example, suppose a user is looking for a "crime" keyword. Using the ontology that will be described in next subsection, we can infer several other keywords, such as murder, robbery, rape, etc. These inferred keywords, including the original keyword, are passed to the recursive gathering engine, where the search is conducted in Naver and Daum. For accessing to these social media platforms, we used the open API provided. Once the searching process is finished, the result is parsed using XML and JSON techniques, and shown to the end user by classifying results according to the inferred keywords.

The algorithm that reflects the construction process of the proposed algorithm is shown in Fig. 2.

3.2 Crime Ontology

Ontology is a formal explicit specification of shared conceptualization and one of the main components of the proposed method [2]. Within the proposed method, all terms and concepts used by other elements are defined in ontology. As the first step of the development of proposed prototype, ontology using concepts and attributes of crime details is developed. This ontology represents a common vocabulary used

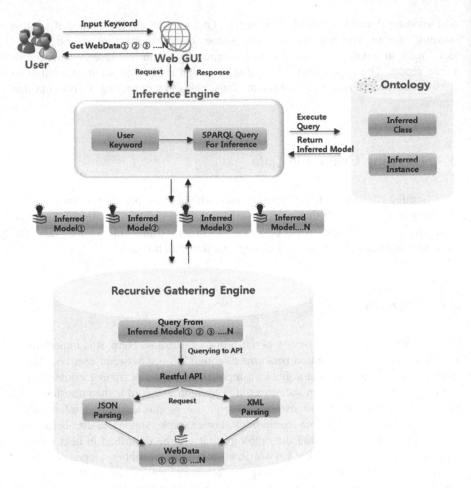

Fig. 1 General overview of the proposed system

in criminology and by the criminalist to describe the crime details. This subsection presents details of this ontology development.

Figure 3 shows a partial visualization of the crime ontology developed in Protégé environment. The proposed ontology has main two classes, such as crime and crime types. In crime class, we define the instances of the popular crime types, such as robbery, murder, rape, violence, etc. In crime types, we define instances of the crimes according to their types. For example, the robbery crime can be subdivided into theft, sneak thieving, pickpocket, steal, extortion, etc. The relationship between ontology classes are defines as well. For example, we define a property called similar Type for the crimes that are similar in nature like steal and theft. In order to make inference, we used Jena API that is Java based framework and provides a set of functions to access the ontology. We have also used SPARQL queries that provide a set of instructions to query the ontology. The resulting

Algorithm Constructing

Input :
      (1) Q: SPARQL query set
      (2) K: Ontology inference
      (3) L: Maximum length of Open API response
Output :
      (1) R: Result set of the each keywords
Algorithm :
1. Initialize the Gathering engine GetContents(K)
2. Set Query Q=QueryFactory.create(queryString)
3.   Query result K=Q.executeQuery( )
4. **IF** HttpConnection = TRUE
5. **FOR** i=0 **TO** L.length **DO**
6.   Find Contents GetContents(K)
7. **WHILE** GetContents ≠ NULL **DO**
8.   Repetition removal Remover(GetContents(K))
9.   **END WHILE**
10. **END FOR**
11. **RETURN :** R[1,2,3...L.length]

Fig. 2 The algorithm for constructing the proposed method

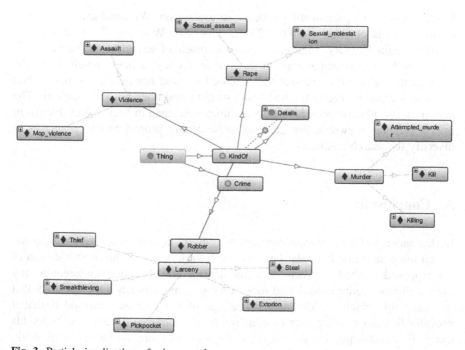

Fig. 3 Partial visualization of crime ontology

Fig. 4 The result of
experiment with different
keywords

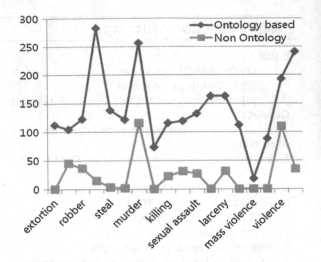

ontology contains more than 70 crime related terminologies and can be utilized as
domain ontology for the purpose of reusability in other fields.

4 Performance Evaluation

In this section, we present the performance evaluation. We conducted all experiments on an Intel Core i5-4460 3.2 GHz processor Windows 7 32 bit PC with
8 GB of main memory. Figure 4 shows the result of experiments. Here, x axis
shows the keywords and y axis shows their frequency in query result. From the
experiment, we can observe that the proposed method has nearly 10 times better
performance comparing to the traditional method that does not use ontology. The
reason for this phenomenon is that the ontology described in Sect. 3.2 enables us to
infer additional keywords that are used in searching procedure and enable us to
diversify the search result.

5 Conclusion

In this paper, we have proposed an ontology-based approach for diversifying the
search result in crime big data. For this, we have introduced the overall design of
the proposed method that acts as a middleware and thus does not require any
pre-installation from the back-end user. Also, we have described the ontology that
was used for searching. The main advantage of the proposed method is that it
provides flexibility to the user by enabling him to observe diverse results for his
query. This also improves the accuracy of the search engine. As for the future work,

we are working on the ontology that expand the crime ontology and can be used to provide flexibility in any fields of big data search. We are also working on extensive experiment results that demonstrate the advantage of the proposed method from different perspective.

Acknowledgments This work was supported by the MSIP (Ministry of Science, ICT and Future Planning), Korea, under the ITRC (Information Technology Research Center) support program (IITP-2016-H8501-16-1013) supervised by the IITP(Institute for Information and communication Technology Promotion).

References

1. Baumgartner K, Ferrari S, Palermo G (2008) Constructing Bayesian networks for criminal profiling from limited data. Knowl Based Syst 21(7):563–572
2. Chen H, Chung W, Xu JJ, Wang G, Qin Y, Chau M (2004) Crime data mining: a general framework and some examples. Comput 37(4):50–56
3. Furtado V, Ayres L, Oliveira M, Vasconcelos E, Caminha C, D'Orleans J, Belchior M (2010) Collective intelligence in law enforcement—the WikiCrimes system. Inf Sci 180:4–17
4. Liu X, Jian C, Lu CT (2010) A spatio-temporal-texture crime search engine. in: Proceeding of the 18th SIGSPATIAL international conference on advances in geographical information systems, pp 528–529
5. Onnoom B, Chiewchanwattana S, Sunat K, Wichiennit N (2014) An ontology framework for recommendation about a crime scene investigation. In: Proceeding of the international symposium on communications and information technologies, pp 176–180
6. Wang B, Dong H, Boedihardjo AP, Lu CT, Yu H, Chen IR, Dai J (2012) An integrated framework for spatio-temporal-textual search and mining. In: Proceeding of the 20th international conference on advances in geographic information systems, pp 570–573

Detecting Network Community by Propagating Labels Based on Contact-Specific Constraint

Xiaolan Wu and Chengzhi Zhang

Abstract As a famous community detection algorithm with near linear time complexity, Label Propagation Algorithm (LPA) has been an active research direction. However, that LPA regards that all the neighbor have the same importance to target node in target node's label update process make it get stuck in poor stability. From the view of structural holes in sociology, people who fill structural holes bring social order to the network, so we improve LPA based on contact-specific constraint measuring structural holes. Experiments show that our improvement successfully detects communities with the highest stability in several commonly used real-world and synthetic networks.

Keywords Label propagation algorithm · Community detection · Network constraint · Structural holes · Social network

1 Introduction

Since the amount of social network data has proliferated in recent years, such as blog or Social Network Service datasets, detecting communities in large social networks has been an active field for years, many authors use community detection

X. Wu · C. Zhang
Department of Information Management,
Nanjing University of Science and Technology,
Nanjing 210094, Jiangsu Province, China
e-mail: wuxiaolananhui@163.com

X. Wu
School of Management Science and Engineering,
Anhui University of Finance and Economics,
Bengbu 233030, Anhui Province, China

C. Zhang (✉)
Key Laboratory of Data Services and Knowledge Engineering,
Nanjing 210093, Jiangsu Province, China
e-mail: zhangcz@njust.edu.cn

© Springer Science+Business Media Singapore 2016   697
J.J. (Jong Hyuk) Park et al. (eds.), *Advanced Multimedia and Ubiquitous Engineering*, Lecture Notes in Electrical Engineering 393,
DOI 10.1007/978-981-10-1536-6_91

to understand the evolution of social networks, such as epidemic spreading [1], opinion formation [2], etc. However, for large networks, the speed of algorithms is very important. There have been some algorithms that can detect communities in large networks efficiently [3–5], one of the fastest algorithms is the label propagation algorithm (LPA) proposed by Raghavan et al. [5]. In fact, LPA offers a number of other desirable qualities, including conceptual simplicity, ease of implementation. However, LPA is prone to get stuck in poor stability, it may result in totally different network partitions and even get unreasonable community structures. To detect communities with high stability, we improve LPA with Burt Constraint in structural holes [6] and devise a new algorithm called LPA-CC in this paper. Experiments show that LPA-CC successfully detects communities with the highest stability in several commonly used real-world and synthetic networks.

The structure of the paper is as follows: Sect. 2 introduces some related works, Sect. 3 gives a description about Burt Constraint and provides some intuitive justifications on our improved algorithm, Sect. 4 shows the experiment on benchmarks, Conclusion and future works appear in Sect. 5.

2 The Label Propagation Algorithm

The main procedure of LPA is as follows: (1) To initialize, all nodes are assigned with a unique label, which is used to show the node belongs to the community. (2) Repeatedly, each node updates its label by the label shared by the maximum number of its neighbor in each iteration. (3) When there is no label change, communities are the groups of nodes having the same label.

The label propagation technology has been an active research direction, many research articles have been published in recent years, such as [1, 7–9]. Leung et al. [1] proposed a label hop attenuation technique to stop the label from spreading too far from its origin. Subelj and Bajec [7] used node balancers to counteract for randomness. Zhao et al. [8] improved the robustness of label propagation algorithm by controlling node update in entropic order from small to large. He et al. [9] used PageRank on the whole network to obtain the core nodes and detected communities by extending the label of the core nodes outward layer by layer.

Summarize the above methods, we found that recent works improved the stability of LPA by controlling the update order or node preference in each iteration. In other words, they ignored the effects of edges between nodes. From ego-network of $v2$ in the tiny network [7] (as shown in Fig. 1b), the edge between node $v1$ and node $v3$ makes $v1$, $v3$, $v2$ become a clique (a Sociology term [10]). If $v2$ adopts label of $v1$ or $v3$ at each iteration, LPA will steadily detect the correct communities, while according to the random strategy in LPA, $v2$ may adopt the label of $v4$ in its iteration and then all the nodes are misclassified to B community. Apparently, the effects of edges between nodes is important, so we focus on these influence of edges between each neighbor and propose a new method based on Contact-specific Constraint to eliminate randomness of LPA in this paper.

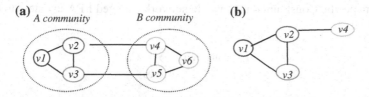

Fig. 1 A tiny sample network. **a** Whole network. **b** The ego-network of v2

3 Label Propagation Algorithm Based on Contact-Specific Constraint

Contact-specific Constraint is a metric in Burt's Network Constraint Index, which observes the lack of Structural Holes within a network [11]. Structural Holes was defined as empty spaces between groups in the social network by Burt [12]. People who fill these structural holes bring social order to the network because they control information flow and are rewarded with power and wealth, and four metrics were proposed by Burt to measure Structural Hole: network size, density, hierarchy, and network constraint [12]. According to Burt [6], Burt constraint is a summary function of network size, density, and hierarchy that measures the extent to which relations are directly or indirectly concentrated in a single contact, and calculation of network constraint is applied to contact-specific constraint, the extent to which node i's network is concentrated in the relationship with node j is defined as follows:

$$C_{ij} = \left(p_{ij} + \sum_q p_{iq} q_{qj} \right)^2 \tag{1}$$

where p_{ij} is proportion of i's relations invested in node j on the ego-network, the sum $\sum_q p_{iq} p_{qj}$ is the portion of i's relations invested in nodes q who are in turn invested in node j. From Formula 1, three Contact-specific Constraints of $v2$ in Fig. 1b are calculated as follows: $C_{v2,v1} = (1/3 + 1/3 * 1/2)^2 = 0.25$, $C_{v2,v4} = (1/3)^2 = 0.11$, $C_{v2,v3} = (1/3 + 1/3 * 1/2)^2 = 0.25$. If we use contact-specific constraint to distinguish neighbors, $v2$ must adopt the label of node $v1$ or $v3$ instead of node $v4$, as a result, the tiny network in Fig. 1a must be divided into two communities correctly.

Just based on the above observation, we improve LPA by contact-specific constraint on ego-network and do many experiments, the experiment result shows that this method indeed improve the stability of the LPA, but extracting the ego-network is very time consuming. In order to reduce time consumption, we redefine Contact-specific Constraint function on the whole network as follows: $C_{v2,v1} = (1/3 + 1/3 * 1/3)^2 = 0.1975$, $C_{v2,v4} = (1/3)^2 = 0.11$, $C_{v2,v3} = (1/3 + 1/3 * 1/2)^2 = 0.25$. Then $v2$ still prefers to choose label of node $v3$, the tiny network is still divided into two communities correctly, so we use

Contact-specific Constraint on the whole network changed LPA updates strategy in Formula 2.

$$L_v = \arg \max_l \sum_{u \in N^l(v)} C_{vu} \tag{2}$$

where, $N^l(v)$ is the set of neighbors for node v that share the label l, C_{vu} is contact-specific constraint u poses for node v on the whole network.

After that, we do a lot of experiments to achieve the best results and avoid oscillations in the network. Experiments show that using both asynchronous strategy [5] and comparative strategy [9] can get the best results, so the final improved algorithm based on contact-specific constraint on the whole network (named LPA-CC) is in Table 1.

For a graph with n nodes and m edges, the time complexity calculation of LPA-CC is as follows: (1) Time is spent on finding simple paths with path length is 2 between two nodes. For each vertex x, it iterates through $O\ (m/n)$ neighbors, and for each neighbor y, it iterates through all neighbors (average number of neighbors is m/n) to find simple paths. There are n vertices in the whole network, so time for this phase is $O\ (m/n \cdot m/n \cdot n) = O\ (m2/n)$. (2) Initializing each node with unique label requires $O\ (n)$ time. (3) Arranging n nodes randomly needs $O\ (n)$. (4) Grouping neighbors of node v according to their labels requires $O\ (d_v)$ (d_v is the degree of node v), then picking groups with the largest sum of constraint and assign its label to v requiring a worst-case time of $O\ (d_v)$, this process is repeated at all

Table 1 Label propagation algorithm based on contact-specific constraint

Description	
Input:	Graph $G = (V, E)$
Output:	Communities C
Step 1	Calculating the contact-specific constraint for each pair of nodes on the whole network
Step 2	For a given node v, $Cv(0) = v$, where $Cv(0)$ is the initial label of node v; $l_v^{old}(0) = 0$, where $l_v^{old}(0)$ is the initial value of node v obtaining the initial label
Step 3	Set $t = 1$ (t represents the number of iterations)
Step 4	Arrange all the nodes in random and store the sorting results in S
Step 5	According with sequence S, for each $v \in S$, let $(C_v(t), l_v^{new}(t)) = f(C_{vi1}(t), \ldots, C_{vim}(t), C_{vi(m+1)}(t-1), \ldots, C_{vik}(t-1))$, f here returns the label coming from the group whose constraint were added together up to form the maximum sum, where $v_{i1}, \ldots, v_{im}$ are neighbors of node v that have already been updated at the tth iteration, while $v_{i(m+1)}, \ldots, v_{ik}$ are neighbors that had been updated at $t - 1$th iteration. If $l_v^{new}(t) > l_v^{old}(t-1)$, use $C_v(t)$ to update node and $l_v^{old}(t) \leftarrow l_v^{new}(t-1)$, else node v doesn't change its label
Step 6	When each node is labelled by the group with the largest sum of constraint, the algorithm terminates. Otherwise, set $t = t + 1$ and return to step 4

nodes. Total time is $O(n \cdot d_v) \approx O(m)$. Phases 3–4 are repeated, the time that LPA-CC algorithm performs k iteration is $O(k \cdot (n + m))$, so total time complexity of our algorithm is therefore $O(m2/n + n)$ plus $O(k \cdot (n + m))$, approximate to $O(n)$ on sparse graph.

4 Experimental Results and Discussion

4.1 Test Networks

At first, we do experiments on four real-world networks with known community structures, whose basic information are shown in Table 2.

Then we further test LPA-CC on six LFR synthetic networks [17] with various mixing parameter μ ranging from 0.1 to 0.6, abd the other standard configuration of LFR synthetic network used in this experiment is: $n = 1000$, $\tau 1 = 1$, $\tau 2 = 2$, $k = 15$, $maxk = 50$, $minc = 20$, $maxc = 50$.

4.2 Test Metrics

To measure communities detection, modularity was be proposed by Newman and Girvan [18]. The formulation of modularity is computed as Formula 3.

$$Q = \frac{1}{2m} \sum_{ij} (A_{ij} - P_{ij}) \cdot \delta(C_i, C_j) \tag{3}$$

where, A_{ij} is adjacency matrix of graph, m is total number of edges in graph, P_{ij} represents expected number of edges between vertices i and j in the null model. $\delta(C_i, C_j) = 1$ if vertices i and j belong the same community, zero otherwise.

Normalized mutual information (NMI) [19] is another standard measure in the networks with known communities, its calculation is as Formula 4.

Table 2 General information of the real-world networks

Networks	Description	Node	Edge
Karate	Zachary's karate club [13]	34	78
Books	Books about US politics [14]	105	441
Football	American College football union [15]	115	616
Blogs	Blogs on US politics [16]	1490	16,715

$$NMI(\pi^a, \pi^b) = \frac{\sum_{h=1}^{k(a)} \sum_{l=1}^{k(b)} n_{h,l} \log\left(\frac{n \cdot n_{h,l}}{n_h^{(a)} \cdot n_l^{(b)}}\right)}{\sqrt{\left(\sum_{h=1}^{k(a)} n_h^{(a)} \log \frac{n_h^a}{n}\right)} \cdot \sqrt{\left(\sum_{l=1}^{k(b)} n_h^{(b)} \log \frac{n_l^b}{n}\right)}} \tag{4}$$

where, π^a and π^b represent the two network partitions, n_h^a denote number of nodes in community h belongs to π^a partition, n_l^b denote number of nodes in community l belongs to π^b partition, $n_{h,l}$ denote the number of nodes belongs to both community h and community l. NMI(A,B) reaches 1 if the found partition are identical to the real partition, and NMI(A,B) is 0 if found partition are totally independent of real partition.

The standard deviation of NMI (σ_{NMI}) [8] is used to reflect robustness of algorithm, it can be computed by Formula 5.

$$\sigma_{NMI} = \sqrt{\frac{1}{n-1} \sum_{i=1}^{n} \left(NMI_i - \overline{NMI}\right)^2} \tag{5}$$

where, n is size of the sample, $\overline{NMI}$ is mean value of NMI. The smaller σ_{NMI} is, the closer it gets to the average value of NMI, $\sigma_{NMI} = 0$ if all NMI are completely identical with each other.

Jaccard's index [10] is another metric in measuring community detection. If a denotes pairs of nodes that are classified in the same community in both partitions, b for pairs of nodes that are in the same community in the first partition and different in the second and c vice versa, then Jaccard's index is calculated as Formula 6.

$$J(\pi_a, \pi_b) = \frac{a}{(a+b+c)} \tag{6}$$

Jaccard's index takes values between 0 and 1, higher values indicate stronger similarity between two partitions.

4.3 Test Results and Discussion

To show performance, we test four propagation algorithms, such as LPA, LPA-E, LPAp, and LPA-CC. LPA-E was proposed by Zhao [8], LPAp was proposed by He et al. [9]. In our test, we run each algorithm 100 times on each network, the result are respectively shown in Figs. 2 and 3.

From the experimental results in Fig. 2, we can see: (1) LPA-CC performs better than original LPA on most networks except Books, because NMI and Jaccard'Index of LPA-CC are larger than those of original LPA, especially, results on Karate

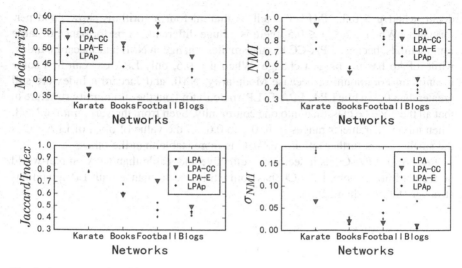

Fig. 2 Average results of four algorithms on real-world networks

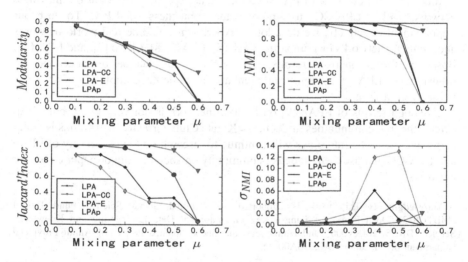

Fig. 3 Average results of four algorithms on LFR networks

network and Football network show its high performance. (2) LPA-CC also performs better than LPA-E on most networks except Books in terms of NMI and Jaccard'Index. (3) Comparing results of LPA-CC and LPAp, LPA-CC performs better than LPAp on Football and Blogs, but performs more badly than LPAp on Karate and Books. (4) According to σ_{NMI}, LPA-CC and LPAp are very stable, LPA and LPA-E have poor stability.

As Fig. 3 shows: when communities are more and more fuzzy ($\mu \rightarrow 0.6$), it is more and more difficult to use four algorithms to detect the community structure. In detail, when $\mu \leq 0.3$, NMI > 0.8 tell us that all four algorithms show good performance; When $0.4 \leq \mu \leq 0.5$, there is a huge difference in performance of these four methods, because LPA-CC has the smallest change in NMI and Jaccard's Index, while LPAp has the biggest change; When $\mu = 0.6$, only LPA-CC can find some meaningful communities, because Modularity, NMI, and Jaccard's Index are still greater than 0.3, while LPA, LPA-E, LPAp don't find out the community structure in that all the node be classified into one community. Seen from the variogram of NMI, when mixing parameter ranges from 0.1 to 0.6, all the value of σ_{NMI} of LPA-CC is the smallest, this further tell us LPA-CC is more stable than the others.

In a word, LPA-CC is indeed more effective and stable than LPA on real-world networks. Furthermore, LPA-CC has competitive performance with LPAp and has stronger stability than LPAp.

5 Conclusion and Future Works

In this paper, we propose a LPA based on contact-specific constraint on the whole network, called LPA-CC, to improve the robustness of LPA. To test our improvement effectively, we do a lot of experiment on some real-world networks and synthetic networks by comparing LPA [5], LPA-E [8], LPAp [9], and LPA-CC. Based on the comparison results, we conclude that: the performance and the robustness of LPA-CC is significantly enhanced, while the complexity of LPA-CC is increased a little.

Although results of LPAp [9] on football network is not very good, but LPAp detects the true communities in Zacharys Karate Club correctly in 100 runs is really surprising, so in the future, we will continue to research on the peculiarity of LPAp and LPA-CC and use them to detect community on social media or paper co-author networks.

Acknowledgments This work is supported by National Social Science Fund Project (14BTQ033), Open Project of Jiangsu Key Laboratory of Data Engineering and Knowledge Service (DEKS2014KT006), and Humanities and Social Science Project of Anhui Provincial Department of Education (SK2016A0025).

References

1. Leung IX, Hui P, Lio P, Crowcroft J (2009) Towards real-time community detection in large networks. Phys Rev E 79:066107-1–066107-10
2. Iñiguez G, Kertész J, Kaski KK, Barrio RA (2009) Opinion and community formation in coevolving networks. Phys Rev E 80:066119-1–066119-9
3. Rosvall M, Bergstrom CT (2008) Maps of random walks on complex networks reveal community structure. In: Proceedings of the National Academy of Sciences of the United States of America. PNAS Press, Washington, pp 1118–1123

4. Blondel VD, Guillaume J-L, Lambiotte R, Lefebvre E (2008) Fast unfolding of communities in large networks. J Stat Mech Theory Exp 10
5. Raghavan UN, Albert R, Kumara S (2007) Near linear time algorithm to detect community structures in large-scale networks. Phys Rev E 76 036106-1–036106-11
6. Burt R (1992) Structural holes: the social structure of competition. Harvard University Press, Cambridge
7. Šubelj L, Bajec M (2011) Robust network community detection using balanced propagation. Eur Phys J B Condens Matter Complex Syst 81:353–362
8. Zhao Y, Li S, Chen X (eds) (2012) Community detection using label propagation in entropic order. In: IEEE 12th international conference on computer and information technology (CIT). IEEE Press, New York, pp 18–24
9. He M, Leng M, Li F, Yao Y, Chen X (2014) A Node importance based label propagation approach for community detection. Knowledge engineering and management. Springer, Berlin, pp 249–257
10. Fortunato S (2010) Community detection in graphs. Phys Rep 486:75–174
11. Burt RS (2005) Brokerage and closure: an introduction to social capital. OUP Oxford, Oxford
12. Burt RS (2004) Structural holes and good ideas1. Am J Sociol 110:349–399
13. Zachary WW (1977) An information flow model for conflict and fission in small groups. J Anthropol Res 33:452–473
14. Itubs WA (2008) Network of co-purchased books about U.S politics. http://www.orgnet.com/
15. Girvan M, Newman ME (2002) Community structure in social and biological networks. In: Proceedings of the national academy of sciences of the United States of America. PNAS Press, Washington, DC, pp 7821–7826
16. Adamic LA, Glance N (eds) (2005) The political blogosphere and the 2004 US election: divided they blog. In: Proceedings of the 3rd international workshop on Link discovery. ACM Press, New York, pp. 36–43
17. Lancichinetti A, Fortunato S, Radicchi F (2008) Benchmark graphs for testing community detection algorithms. Phys Rev E 78:046110-1–046110-5
18. Newman ME, Girvan M (2004) Finding and evaluating community structure in networks. Phys Rev E 69:026113-1–026113-15
19. Tang L, Liu H (2010) Community detection and mining in social media. In: Synthesis lectures on data mining and knowledge discovery, vol 2, pp 1–137

Effects of Question Style in User's Emotion Survey: Using the Case of FWA's Best Award Winning Website

Sangmin Lee, Joo Hyun Park, Dongho Kim and Han Young Ryoo

Abstract An emotional design that measures human emotion for new product has been emerging in several fields. The most pervasive method of measuring the human emotion is evaluating the users' emotions with the questionnaire including the most common emotional vocabularies. The objective of this study is evaluating the level of user's emotion with three different questionnaires in sentence length and expression styles. In order to achieve the study objective, the main page of best award winning website from the FWA (Favourite Website Awards), an industry recognized internet award program, was selected for evaluating the human emotion. This study found that different question style has no significant effect on human emotion evaluation. The findings from this study are a lot different from the research reported in the literature outside the Korea. This implies that additional research might be necessary by adopting different target participants or investigating the characteristics of the survey respondents.

Keywords Question style · User's emotion · User's sensibility

1 Introduction

Recently, an emotional design research and development which is targeting to measure and analyze the human emotion and to make application of it for the development of a brand new product have been made in several fields. These trends

S. Lee · D. Kim
Soongsil University, Seoul, Republic of Korea
e-mail: sangmin_lee@ssu.ac.kr

D. Kim
e-mail: dkim@ssu.ac.kr

J.H. Park · H.Y. Ryoo (✉)
Ewha Womans University, Seoul, Republic of Korea
e-mail: hyryoo@ewha.ac.kr

J.H. Park
e-mail: joohpark@ewha.ac.kr

© Springer Science+Business Media Singapore 2016   707
J.J. (Jong Hyuk) Park et al. (eds.), *Advanced Multimedia and Ubiquitous Engineering*, Lecture Notes in Electrical Engineering 393,
DOI 10.1007/978-981-10-1536-6_92

are totally different from the functional design which was focused on the most optimized physical functions and economic feasibility. The most pervasive method of measuring the human emotions in emotional design research and development (R&D) is to evaluate the users' emotions with the questionnaire including the most common emotional vocabularies [1]. Therefore, the measurement of human emotion with the emotional vocabulary test is the basic and crucial research method. However, the question styles of the questionnaire for the research are various. In other words, some researches present only emotional words in some questions [2, 3], and others presents more detailed situation or specified sentences including emotional words [4, 5].

The precedent researches of the development of the evaluation questions show the question styles can make effects on the results of evaluations, and recommend that the words of questions should be simple and clear in meaning for the understanding of participants [6]. And also, some study shows that the method of asking questions, the number of questions, the length of pages, and layout of questionnaire as well as question styles can affect the result of evaluations. However, it is hard to find an emotional design research considering those factors in Korea. The purpose of this study is to investigate the effects of question styles on measuring the user's emotion, and to present a proper way of evaluating questions with emotional words.

2   Emotion Measurement by Survey Question Style

2.1   Overview

This study was performed in following steps; the questionnaires which are various in question lengths and expression styles were used to evaluate the users' emotions. For this step, the main page of best award winning website from the FWA (Favourite Website Awards), a worldwide industry recognized internet award program, was selected for the evaluation of the human emotion. Then, emotional words were selected from the literature of website, and web questionnaire system was built with the most common question styles in emotional design researches.

2.2   Selection of Emotional Vocabulary and Survey Question Style

Form the precedent study of Hong et al. [7], 23 emotional words selected and these are represented in Table 1.

The evaluation questions were classified according to the sentence expression styles that are basic methods in emotional design research. Table 2 shows that the emotional word 'intense' was used in three question sentences.

Table 1 Emotional vocabulary that is being used for emotion measurement

Intense	Refreshing	Funny
Luxurious	New	Young
Cute	Refined	Calm
Unique	Cool	Classical
Stylish	Mysterious	Comfortable
Futuristic	Leisurely	Gorgeous
Cheerful	Unfamiliar	Unordinary
Neat	Free	

Table 2 Survey questions by style

Style	Survey question
1	Intense
2	The design of this website is intense
3	I feel that the design of this website is intense

2.3 Development of Web Based Survey System

The main page of best design award winning site from FWA (Favourite Website Awards) was selected for the testing. Then, the web-based questionnaire system was constructed using the 23 emotional words and the evaluation questions in three sentence styles. The participants of questionnaire were recommended to answer the questions constituted with 23 emotional words after looking at the image of the selected website. The scales of answering the questions were seven ranging from strongly disagree to strongly agree. The web-based questionnaire system was constructed in each three different sentence styles and a participant should answer only one questionnaire style. This web-based questionnaire system was modified using small pilot survey with 9 participants.

2.4 The Result of Emotion Measurement by Different Types of Survey Questions

The participants of questionnaire were Korean college students. 50 students participated for each questionnaire style, so 150 students participated in total. The results of emotional evaluation are represented in Fig. 1, and it shows the average value of 23 question items in three styles.

The difference of average value can be found in some questions, however, the overall big difference is not found. Also the result of Analysis of Variance (ANOVA), which finds statistical significance of the test, shows that there were no differences among three question styles with 23 questions in the level of significance 0.05. The result of ANOVA is represented in Table 3.

Fig. 1 Average comparison
by question style

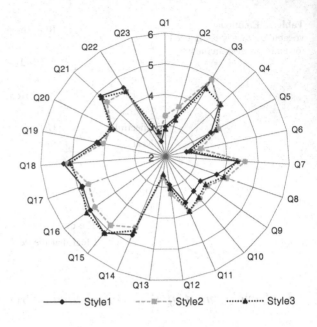

Table 3 ANOVA result of
emotion evaluation

Question	Sum of square	Mean of square	F ratio	p-value
Q1	5.493	2.747	2.267	.107
Q2	5.320	2.660	1.821	.165
Q3	4.093	2.047	1.352	.262
Q4	.093	.047	.032	.969
Q5	2.013	1.007	.658	.519
Q6	5.560	2.780	1.928	.149
Q7	1.960	.980	.482	.618
Q8	3.053	1.527	1.013	.366
Q9	2.080	1.040	.760	.470
Q10	2.893	1.447	.917	.402
Q11	3.000	1.500	.971	.381
Q12	2.280	1.140	.805	.449
Q13	.253	.217	.103	.902
Q14	1.693	.847	.471	.625
Q15	3.413	1.707	1.457	.236
Q16	2.573	1.287	1.180	.310
Q17	1.653	.827	.534	.587
Q18	1.053	.527	.380	.685
Q19	1.053	.527	.307	.736
Q20	.280	.140	.064	.938
Q21	2.173	1.087	.814	.445
Q22	.653	.327	.228	.797
Q23	2.893	1.447	1.037	.357

3   Conclusion

This study performed the emotional evaluation of users to investigate the effects of questions styles on human emotion. For this purpose, the main page of FWA's best award winning website was selected for testing and three different questionnaires in sentence length and expression styles were used to evaluate the level of user's emotion and compare the results. The findings of the test show that the results of human emotion measurement were not different in spite of the different question styles. This result in Korea was significantly different from many other research results in other countries. It leads us to study for the future by focusing on human factors of users or on other targets for testing. The literature reported the importance of survey questionnaire items to conduct a survey successfully. Even statistical validation is required for the survey questionnaire items. However, the research regarding this issue in Korea is hardly found. Thus, the objective of this study is to find an effect of the different survey question styles on emotion evaluation. In order to achieve this objective, this study measured the emotion level of the website users by applying different question items with different sentence lengths and expression styles for the same website. This study found that different question style has no significant effect on human emotion evaluation. The findings from this study are a lot different from the research reported in the literature outside the Korea. This implies that additional research might be necessary by adopting different target participants or investigating the characteristics of the survey respondents.

Acknowledgments This work was supported by Design Innovation Capability Development Program (No. 10054099), funded by the Ministry of Trade, Industry and Energy (MOTIE).

References

1. Plutchik R (2003) Emotions and Life: perspectives from psychology, biology, and evolution. American Psychological Association, Washington, DC
2. Sun JH, Cho KJ, Han KH (2003) A Study on sensibility of web page. Korean J Sci Emot Sensibility 6(4):34–40
3. Yoo HW, Cho KJ, Hong JY, Park SE (2004) WebSES: web site sensibility evaluation system based on color combination. Korean J Sci Emot Sensibility 7(1):51–64
4. Jeong SH (2007) Development a self-report questionnaire-type scale for measuring user's emotions while using a product. Korean J Sci Emot Sensibility 10(3):403–410
5. Park JH, Ryoo HY (2008) Emotion of people with visual disability for enhancing web accessibility. Korean J Sci Emot Sensibility 11(4):589–598
6. Dillman DA (2007) Mail and internet surveys: the tailored design method. Wiley, Hoboken
7. Hong SY, Lee HJ, Jin KN (2009) A study on the image scale through the classification of emotion in web site. Korean J Sci Emot Sensibility 12(1):1–10

Design and Implementation of MapReduce-Based Book Recommendation System by Analysis of Large-Scale Book-Rental Data

Joon-Min Gil, JongBum Lim and Dong-Mahn Seo

Abstract We design and implement a book recommendation system that can extract and suggest the books preferred by users through keyword-matching based on the information of frequently checked out books. The MapReduce programming model on the Hadoop platform is used to extract frequently rented books by using keyword-mapping with a target book. The MapReduce operations designed and implemented in this paper are performed to analyze the actual book-rental log data accumulated in university library, which has the characteristics of big data. An illustrative example shows that our book recommendation system can provide users with the information of the recommended books by keyword-mapping in the next book rent.

Keywords Book-rental · Recommendation · MapReduce · Hadoop · Big data

1 Introduction

Recently, big data processing and analysis have been actively achieved in various fields [1]. Since big data is unstructured and large-scale data, it is inadequate to be analyzed and processed by traditional computing systems and tools [1, 2]. The log data on rental books recorded in the electronic library of universities, one form of big data, includes various information on book-rental, such as users' major and

J.-M. Gil (✉) · D.-M. Seo
School of Information Technology Engineering,
Catholic University of Daegu, Gyeongbuk, South Korea
e-mail: jmgil@cu.ac.kr

D.-M. Seo
e-mail: sarum@cu.ac.kr

J. Lim
IT Convergence Education Center, Dongguk University,
Seoul, South Korea
e-mail: jblim@dongguk.edu

© Springer Science+Business Media Singapore 2016   713
J.J. (Jong Hyuk) Park et al. (eds.), *Advanced Multimedia and Ubiquitous Engineering*, Lecture Notes in Electrical Engineering 393,
DOI 10.1007/978-981-10-1536-6_93

interest, rental date, return date, keywords, etc. Such data are not only large-scale but also unstructured, making it difficult for them to be searched, managed, and stored via traditional relational databases and file systems. Moreover, the analysis and processing of book-rental data by traditional computing systems and tools are even more difficult.

In general, it has a possibility that the frequently rented books have similar or the same keywords as the books that have previously rented. Based on this property, these books can be classified according to keywords; such the classification can be utilized to offer useful information for the next book rent. However, it is time-consuming and requires much effort to extract the meaningful patterns of rental books by matching the keywords of the books that have previously rented by users, due to a large volume of book-rental log data and its unstructured form.

Therefore, we apply MapReduce programming model to analyze and process book keywords in book-rental big data and to classify highly related books with the information of frequently rented books by a user. To this end, we design and implement a book recommendation system that can extract and classify relevant books by keyword-matching. Eventually, the system provides users with book recommendation information by keyword-mapping in their next book rent.

The rest of this paper is organized as follows. In Sect. 2, we provide an overview of Hadoop platform and MapReduce programming model used as fundamental system models in our book recommendation system. Section 3 presents the detailed design and implementation of the book recommendation system, focusing on keyword-mapping by MapReduce programming model. In Sect. 4, system environment and implementation results are presented. The illustrative example applied to actual book-rental log data accumulated in an electronic library of university is also provided in this section. Finally, Sect. 5 concludes the paper.

2   Hadoop Platform and MapReduce Programming Model

With the increase in the size of datasets for processing over the Internet, the MapReduce programming model has been widely adopted for data-intensive distributed computing in various fields of areas, such as webpage indexing and search, data mining, machine learning, social computing, bioinformatics, etc. [1]. Hadoop is an open-source software framework of MapReduce written in Java for distributed storage and processing of big data on computing clusters [2].

The MapReduce programming model was developed by Google in 2004 with the purpose of the parallel and distributed processing of big data in the cloud computing environment [3]. Basically, it consists of two kinds of fundamental functions: Map and Reduce. The input for this programming model is a list of ($key1$, $value1$) pairs. The map function is applied to each pair to compute intermediate key-value pairs, ($key2$, $value2$). The intermediate key-value pairs are then grouped together on the key-equality basis, i.e. ($key2$, list ($value2$)). For each $key2$, the reduce function works on the list of all values, then produces zero or more aggregated results [4].

Consequently, the map function divides the large-scale data on the Hadoop file system for distributed processing and executes the programming codes defined inside it. The reduce function combines the results of the map function for final processing [3]. When the MapReduce programming model is used for big data processing, users should specify the programming codes in the map and reduce functions according to the parallel applications to be applied. We will define the map and reduce functions for the keyword-matching of book-rental information, which play a pivotal role in our book recommendation system, in the next section.

3 Design and Implementation of Book Recommendation System

3.1 System Architecture

The overall system architecture of our book recommendation system is shown in Fig. 1. The system presented in the figure consists of two subsystems.

- Keyword-matching analysis subsystem: It is a system to extract the degree of keyword-matching of each book from book-rental log data. The MapReduce programming model is utilized to extract the degree of keyword-matching which is periodically saved and updated into the keyword-matching database.
- Keyword-search subsystem: It provides users with the keyword-based book recommendation information for each book using the keyword-matching database built by the keyword-matching analysis subsystem.

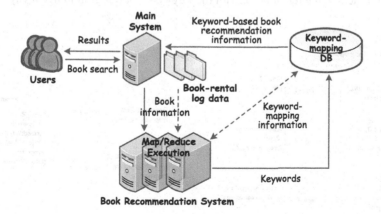

Fig. 1 System architecture of book recommendation system

The dotted line in Fig. 1 shows the flow of the keyword-search subsystem, and the solid line shows the flow of the keyword-matching analysis subsystem. We focus on designing and implementing the keyword-matching analysis subsystem based on MapReduce programming model on Hadoop platform that plays a crucial role in our book recommendation system.

3.2 Keyword-Matching by MapReduce Programming Model

The book-rental log data, which is used as basic data for keyword-matching, includes the book- rental information of users. Each line of the log data consists of user information, book information, book-rental date, book-return date, etc. Based on such the log data, we apply MapReduce programming model to extract the recommended books by matching the keywords of frequently rented books with that of a target book. Figure 2 shows the overall process, by which the keyword-matching analysis is performed.

The operation process in Fig. 2 is largely divided into two operations: map and reduce. In the map operation, the book-rental log data are first divided into 'n' parts, which are then allocated to 'n' map functions. Each map function calculates the degree of correspondence of the keyword of a target book to that of rental book on the log data. Once one or more keywords of the target book are matched with that of the rental book, the number of corresponding keywords increases by one as the frequency of book-rental; initially, the number is zero. For instance, the keywords of a target book in Fig. 2 are [Java, programming], and the degree of correspondence is calculated for the first book with a keyword of [Java] on the first map function (map #1 in Fig. 2). Based on keyword-matching, the number of corresponding keywords of the first book is set to '1,' because one of the keywords of the target book ('Java') appears as a keyword of the first book. Meanwhile, in the map #n function, the rental book with the keywords of [programming, Java] exactly

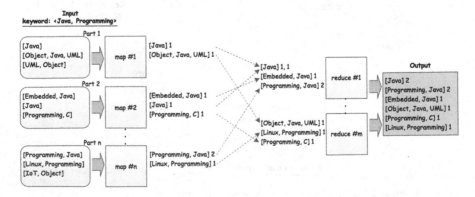

Fig. 2 MapReduce process for keyword-mapping

corresponds with those of the target book, despite the difference in the order. Thus, the number of corresponding keyword becomes 2. The output of each map function is labelled ([keyword], frequency). The frequencies with an identical [keyword] for all pairs are combined into a single list and then sent to reduce functions together with the [keyword].

The reduce function receives the pairs of keyword and frequency list as input values. In each reduce function, a frequency for rental books with the identical keywords is printed out as an output value. Let us consider one of the inputs of reduce #1 function, ([Java], 1, 1), in Fig. 2. In the input ([Java], 1, 1), [Java] means a keyword and 1, 1 means a list of the number of corresponding keywords. Such inputs are distributed to each reduce function, and then all values of the list for inputs with identical keywords are added. Because the list for the keyword of [Java] is 1, 1, the output of reduce function becomes 2.

In the same method shown in Fig. 2, MapReduce operations are performed for each target book. Each of books is ordered according to the number of frequency of keywords, and then saved in the keyword-matching DB. Since the rental books occur in real time, the keyword-matching DB should be renewed to provide users with an up-to-date recommendation information for book-rental. This is done by the periodic execution of MapReduce operations.

4 System Environment and Implementation Results

To demonstrate the effectiveness of our book recommendation system, we make a system environment based on actual university library. The book-rental log data provided by Central Library in Catholic University of Daegu is used and analyzed. To avoid the complexity caused by the vast amount of the log data, we limit the whole books to a total of 1377 books in the field of information technology, and a total of 10,018 rentals for these books are used as rental counts without any restrictions on users' major.

The detailed system configurations used for the extraction of book-rental information by keyword-matching is as follows: Apache Hadoop (version 2.6.0) is used for the distributed file system and MapReduce programming model on a desktop PC with Ubuntu linux (14.04 LTS). We carry out MapReduce operations in a standalone mode on one PC equipped with an Intel Core i5 CPU and 4G memory. The map and reduce functions are implemented in the same way as shown in Fig. 2, and Apache Maven version 3.0.5 is used for compiling.

MapReduce-based keyword-matching was carried out for a total of 1377 books. As for English keywords, there was no distinction between uppercase and lower-case letters. Table 1 lists the top 20 recommended books obtained from our book recommendation system for the keyword of [Java]. The results of Table 1 show that rental books with the keyword of [Java] has top ranking in the list. Although some books had the identical keyword with [Java], they were ranked differently according to the number of rentals.

Table 1 List of recommended books by keyword-matching

Ranking	Book title	Keywords	Frequency
1	Essential JavaFX	Java, Application, Software	10
2	Java Script Definitive Guide: Supplement	Java, Script, Definitive, Guide	9
2	Java Programming	Java, Programming	9
2	High-Level Java Programming (for IT Convergence Technology)	Java, Programming	9
5	Fun Java Puzzler	Java	8
5	Leaning Data Structure with Java	Java, Data structure	8
7	Fiction-like Java	Java	7
7	Java Script Definitive Guide	Java, Script, Definitive, Guide	7
7	Eclipse bible (for Java Developer)	Java, Eclipse, Bible	7
7	Eclipse (Covering World of Java)	Java, Eclipse	7
7	Animation & Graphics using Java	Java, Desktop, Application, Animation, Graphics	7
7	Java Network Programming	Java, Network, Programming	7
7	Maven (Leading Java World Build)	Java, Javascript, Maven	7
14	(Definitive) Java Programming	Java	6
14	(Java) Data Structure Theory	Java, Data structure	6
16	Java how to program	Java	5
16	Programming closer: Java	Java, Programming	5
18	(Perfect foundation) Java Programming	Java	4
18	Coding Habit and Tuning Story that Determines Java Performance	Java, Coding, Java tuning, Programming	4
18	(Passionate Lecture) Java Programming	Java, Programming	4

5 Conclusion and Future Works

We presented the design and implementation of a book recommendation system capable of processing keyword-matching computations for frequently rented books using MapReduce programming model on the Hadoop platform. The system extracts frequently rented books from the actual book-rental log data, which has the characteristics of big data, by keyword-mapping. The extracted information makes it convenient for users to rent books according to their preference and similarity between books.

The system implemented in this paper extracted book recommendation information using MapReduce operations on the Hadoop platform configured to a standalone mode. In a near future, it is expected that the extension of a standalone mode to a fully distributed one will speed up the processing of MapReduce operations. More importantly, in this paper, we considered the degree of keyword-mapping with only one target book. Further research is needed to consider keyword-mapping for one or more books with associativity and to apply this into the extraction of a more refined book recommendation information.

Acknowledgments This research was supported by Basic Science Research Program through the National Research Foundation of Korea (NRF) funded by the Ministry of Education (NRF-2014R1A1A2055463).

References

1. Chen CLP, Zhang C-Y (2014) Data-intensive applications, challenges, techniques and technologies: a survey on big data, information. Science 275:314–347
2. White T (2015) Hadoop: the definitive guide, 4th edn. O'Reilly Media, Sebastopol
3. Dean J, Ghemawat S (2004) MapReduce: simplified data processing on large clusters. In: Proceedings of the 6th conference on symposium on operating systems design & implementation, p 10
4. Lee KH, Lee YJ, Choi H, Chung YD, Moon B (2011) Parallel data processing with MapReduce: a survey. SIGMOD Rec 40:11–20

Modeling a Big Medical Data Cognitive System with *N*-Ary Formal Concept Analysis

Fei Hao, Doo-Soon Park, Se Dong Min and Sewon Park

Abstract The dramatic explosion of huge number of heterogeneous medical data in smart healthcare, is leading to many difficulties on both obtaining the intelligence, cognition and natural interactions between doctors and patients. Toward to this end, this paper proposed a big medical data cognitive system with the proposed methodology that is n-ary formal concept analysis. The unique features of this cognitive system include efficient big data representation, high-quality data associations, and natural semantics interpretation among dimensions.

Keywords Medical data · Tensor · Formal concept analysis · Cognitive system

1 Introduction

Nowadays, the aging of world's population is speeding up the sharp increase of diseases of the elder people [1]. The emerging novel technologies, such as pervasive networks, Internet of Things, and Cloud Computing may enhance the treatment interactions between doctors and patients by providing ubiquitous medical moni-

F. Hao · D.-S. Park (✉)
Department of Computer Software Engineering,
Soonchunhyang University, Asan, Korea
e-mail: parkds@sch.ac.kr

F. Hao
e-mail: fhao@sch.ac.kr

S.D. Min
Department of Medical IT Engineering,
Soonchunhyang University, Asan, Korea
e-mail: medi1223@gmail.com

S. Park
School of Biological Sciences, College of Natural Science,
Seoul National University, Seoul, Korea
e-mail: sewon14@gmail.com

© Springer Science+Business Media Singapore 2016   721
J.J. (Jong Hyuk) Park et al. (eds.), *Advanced Multimedia and Ubiquitous Engineering*, Lecture Notes in Electrical Engineering 393,
DOI 10.1007/978-981-10-1536-6_94

toring [2, 3], medical data access, and emergency communication. In particular, smart healthcare cognitive system is investigated broadly by researchers from the communities of computer science as well as medical science [4]. For example, IBM Watson for Oncology, trained by Memorial Sloan Kettering Cancer Center, helps oncologists treat cancer patients with individualized evidence-based treatment options by analyzing patient data against the huge number of historical cases.[1] In another words, the big medical data cognitive system can greatly help doctors to narrow down the options and pick the best treatments for their patients. In addition, it also can make the process of data sensing faster and more accurate.

As a matter of fact, there lack many communication channels for bridging the doctors/patients to the medical equipment. Aiming to dredge these channels, this paper mainly presents a big medical data cognitive system based on the proposed n-ary formal concept analysis methodology. Its advantages for this cognitive system lie in efficient big data representation, high-quality data associations, and rich semantics interpretation among dimensions. Then, the proposed system can enable people and machines to interact more naturally to expand the human intelligence and cognition.

The remainder of this paper is constructed as follows. Section 2 presents the proposed n-ary formal concept analysis methodology. Based on our methodology, a big medical data cognitive system is modeled in Sect. 3. Finally, Sect. 4 concludes this paper.

2 N-Ary Formal Concept Analysis

Since the big data usually owns the high dimension, and heterogeneous features, this section first introduces a new methodology, n-ary Formal Concept Analysis (NFCA) which can characterize the big data uniformly. Then, the definition of n-ary context is formally provided. Further, the n-ary concept-forming operators are introduced for inducing the n-ary concept.

2.1 N-Ary Formal Context

Similar with the formal context in conventional formal concept analysis [5], an n-ary formal context is regarded as a generalized version of formal context, it is formally represented as a $(n + 1)$-tuple $\langle O, A_1, A_2, \ldots, A_{n-2}, T, I \rangle$ where $O, A_1, A_2, \ldots, A_{n-2}, T$ and I are non-empty sets, and I is an n-ary relation between $O, A_1, A_2, \ldots, A_{n-2}$ and T, i.e., $I \subseteq O \times A_1 \times A_2 \times \ldots A_{n-2} \times T$. Here, O indicates the set of objects, $A_1, A_2, \ldots, A_{n-2}$ denote the multiple sets of attributes; T is the

---

[1]http://www.research.ibm.com/cognitive-computing.

Fig. 1 Tensorization of n-ary formal context

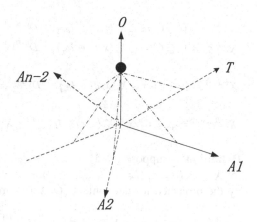

time condition; I is interpreted as the incidence relation. Therefore, $\langle o, a_1, a_2, \ldots, a_{n-2}, t \rangle \subseteq I$ can be interpreted as: object o has attributes $a_1, a_2, \ldots, a_{n-2}$ under the condition time t. In this case, we say that $o, a_1, a_2, \ldots, a_{n-2}, t$ are related by I.

Note that the n-ary formal context can be represented with a "0" and "1" n-order tensor [6] as shown in Fig. 1.

2.2 Concept-Forming Operators

To induce the n-ary formal concept, a given n-ary formal context can be projected into C_n^2 2-dimensional space which corresponds to C_n^2 formal contexts. The following concept-forming operators (CFOs) are presented, respectively.

Definition 1 Suppose $\langle O, A_1, A_2, \ldots, A_{n-2}, T, I \rangle$ be an n-ary formal context, $X \subseteq O$, for $B_1 \subseteq A_1, B_2 \subseteq A_2, \ldots, B_{n-2} \subseteq A_{n-2}, D \subseteq T$, $(2n - 4)$ concept-forming operators induced by the projected formal context $(A_1, A_2, \ldots, A_{n-2}, T, I_X)$ are formally defined as follows,

$$B_1^{(X,\cdot,\cdot)} = \{t \subseteq T | \forall a \in B_1, (a, c) \in I_X\}, \quad B_2^{(X,\cdot,\cdot)} = \{t \subseteq T | \forall a \in B_2, (a, c) \in I_X\}$$

$$\ldots$$

$$B_i^{(X,\cdot,\cdot)} = \{t \subseteq T | \forall a \in B_i, (a, c) \in I_X\} \ldots B_{(n-2)}^{(X,\cdot,\cdot)} = \{t \subseteq T | \forall a \in B_{(n-2)}, (a, c) \in I_X\}$$

$$D^{(X,B_1,\cdot)} = \{a \subseteq A_1 | \forall c \in D, (a, c) \in I_X\}, \quad D^{(X,B_2,\cdot)} = \{a \subseteq A_2 | \forall c \in D, (a, c) \in I_X\}$$

$$\ldots$$

$$D^{(X,B_i,\cdot)} = \{a \subseteq A_i | \forall c \in D, (a, c) \in I_X\} \ldots D^{(X,B_{n-2},\cdot)} = \{a \subseteq A_{(n-2)} | \forall c \in D, (a, c) \in I_X\}$$

Definition 2 Suppose $\langle O, A_1, A_2, \ldots, A_{n-2}, T, I \rangle$ be an n-ary formal context, $B_i \subseteq A_i$ $(i = 1, 2, \ldots, n - 2)$, for $X \subseteq O, D \subseteq T$, $(2n - 4)$ concept-forming operators induced by the projected context (O, T, I_B) are formally defined as follows,

$$X^{(\cdot,B_1,\cdot)} = \{c \subseteq C | \forall x \in X, (x,c) \in I_{B_1}\}, \quad D^{(\cdot,B_1,\cdot)} = \{x \subseteq O | \forall c \in D, (x,c) \in I_{B_1}\}$$
$$X^{(\cdot,B_2,\cdot)} = \{c \subseteq C | \forall x \in X, (x,c) \in I_{B_2}\}, \quad D^{(\cdot,B_2,\cdot)} = \{x \subseteq O | \forall c \in D, (x,c) \in I_{B_2}\}$$
$$\cdots$$
$$X^{(\cdot,B_i,\cdot)} = \{c \subseteq C | \forall x \in X, (x,c) \in I_{B_i}\}, \quad D^{(\cdot,B_i,\cdot)} = \{x \subseteq O | \forall c \in D, (x,c) \in I_{B_i}\}$$
$$\cdots$$
$$X^{(\cdot,B_{(n-2)},\cdot)} = \{c \subseteq C | \forall x \in X, (x,c) \in I_{B_{(n-2)}}\}, \quad X^{(\cdot,B_{(n-2)},\cdot)} = \{c \subseteq C | \forall x \in X, (x,c) \in I_{B_{(n-2)}}\}$$

Definition 3 Suppose $\langle O, A_1, A_2, \ldots, A_{n-2}, T, I \rangle$ be an n-ary formal context, $D \subseteq C$, for $X \subseteq O, B_i \subseteq A_i$ ($i = 1, 2, \ldots n - 2$), $(2n - 4)$ concept-forming operators induced by the projected formal context (O, A, I_D) are formally defined as follows,

$$X^{(\cdot,B_1,D)} = \{a \subseteq A_1 | \forall x \in X, (x,a) \in I_D\}, \quad B_1^{(\cdot,\cdot,D)} = \{x \subseteq O | \forall a \in B_1, (x,a) \in I_D\}$$
$$X^{(\cdot,B_2,D)} = \{a \subseteq A_2 | \forall x \in X, (x,a) \in I_D\}, \quad B_2^{(\cdot,\cdot,D)} = \{x \subseteq O | \forall a \in B_2, (x,a) \in I_D\}$$
$$\cdots$$
$$X^{(\cdot,B_i,D)} = \{a \subseteq A_i | \forall x \in X, (x,a) \in I_D\}, \quad B_i^{(\cdot,\cdot,D)} = \{x \subseteq O | \forall a \in B_i, (x,a) \in I_D\}$$
$$\cdots$$
$$X^{(\cdot,B_{(n-2)},D)} = \{a \subseteq A_{(n-2)} | \forall x \in X, (x,a) \in I_D\}, \quad B_{(n-2)}^{(\cdot,\cdot,D)} = \{x \subseteq O | \forall a \in B_{(n-2)}, (x,a) \in I_D\}$$

2.3 N-Ary Formal Concept

After the introduction of concept-forming operators under C_n^2 projected formal contexts, an n-ary formal concept is defined as follows,

Definition 4 (*n-ary concept*) Suppose $\langle O, A_1, A_2, \ldots, A_{n-2}, T, I \rangle$ be an n-ary formal context, for $X \subseteq O, B_i \subseteq A_i$ ($i = 1, 2, \ldots n - 2$), $D \subseteq T$, if $B_i = D_i^{(X,\cdots)}$, $D = B_i^{(X,B_i,\cdot)}$, $X = B_i^{(\cdot,\cdot,D)}$, $B_i = X^{(\cdot,B_i,D)}$, then an n-tuple $(X, B_1, B_2, \ldots, B_{n-2}, D)$ is called as an n-ary concept of the n-ary formal context $\langle O, A_1, A_2, \ldots, A_{n-2}, T, I \rangle$, where X, B_i ($i = 1, 2, \ldots, n - 2$) and D refer to the "*extent*", "i_{th} *intent*", and "*condition*", respectively.

3 Modeling Big Medical Data Cognitive System with N-Ary Formal Concept Analysis

The construction of big medical data cognitive system can help doctors and patients to understand the hidden semantics among objects, and reveal the correlation between concepts. Therefore, this section firstly provides an overall framework of the proposed big medical data cognitive system. With this framework, tensor-based representation for big data is elaborated. Then, the modeling process of a big data cognitive system is mathematically provided.

Figure 2 shows a framework of big medical data cognitive system based on n-ary formal concept analysis. Clearly, the bottom layer is data collection about various types of medical data. After collecting the data, those data will be tensorized with a unified tensor. Further, an extended formal concept analysis-NFCA is adopted for revealing the associations among different dimensions. Based on the extracted associations, the upper layer will apply advanced analytics and cognitive computing for transforming insights. Then, the outcomes will be driven in engagement layer. The top layer includes the various concrete smart medical applications, such as wellness, diagnosis, and treatment planning [7].

Definition 5 (*Tensor-based Big Data Representation*) Based on our previous work [6] on unified tensor-based representation model of big data, this model is defined as a 6-order tensor which is a multidimensional matrix,

$$\Lambda \in \Re^{I_t \times I_x \times I_y \times I_z \times I_c \times I_u}$$

where $\Re$ is defined on the real number domain; $I_t, I_x, I_y, I_z, I_c, I_u$ refer to the time, space coordinates (I_x, I_y, I_z), cyber resources and users. $I_t \times I_x \times I_y \times I_z \times I_c \times I_u$ denotes the Cartesian product operation of $I_t, I_x, I_y, I_z, I_c, I_u$. The value of each element a_{ijklmn}, $i \in I_t, j \in I_x, k \in I_y, l \in I_z, m \in I_c, n \in I_u$ in the 6-order is obtained from various cyber resources. Each element a_{ijklmn} measures the big data information m of a user n in a certain physical space (i, j, k) at time i.

From the n-ary formal concept analysis point of view, the above tensorized big data can be converted into a 6-ary formal context $\langle U, I_x, I_y, I_z, I_c, I_t, R \rangle$. Based on the

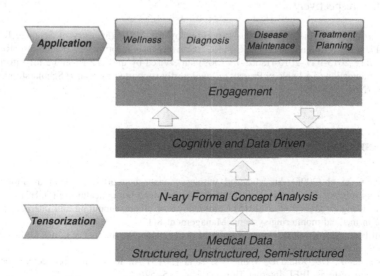

Fig. 2 Framework of the proposed big medical data cognitive system

constructed 6-ary formal context for big data, the following big data cognitive system is presented.

Definition 6 (*Big Data Cognitive System*) For a tensorized big data, i.e., 6-ary formal context $\langle U, I_x, I_y, I_z, I_c, I_t, R \rangle$, for $X \subseteq U, B_1 \subseteq I_x, B_2 \subseteq I_y, B_3 \subseteq I_z, B_4 \subseteq I_c, D \subseteq I_t$, we can induce the following operations according to Definition 3.

$$X^{(.,B_1,D)} = \{a \subseteq I_x | \forall x \in X, (x,a) \in I_D\}, \quad B_1^{(.,.,D)} = \{x \subseteq U | \forall a \in B_1, (x,a) \in I_D\}$$

$$X^{(.,B_2,D)} = \{a \subseteq I_y | \forall x \in X, (x,a) \in I_D\}, \quad B_2^{(.,.,D)} = \{x \subseteq U | \forall a \in B_2, (x,a) \in I_D\}$$

$$X^{(.,B_3,D)} = \{a \subseteq I_z | \forall x \in X, (x,a) \in I_D\}, \quad B_3^{(.,.,D)} = \{x \subseteq U | \forall a \in B_3, (x,a) \in I_D\}$$

$$X^{(.,B_4,D)} = \{a \subseteq I_c | \forall x \in X, (x,a) \in I_D\}, \quad B_4^{(.,.,D)} = \{x \subseteq U | \forall a \in B_4, (x,a) \in I_D\}$$

If $X^{(.,B_i,D)(.,B_i,D)} \supseteq X$, $B_i^{(.,.,D)(.,.,D)} \supseteq B_i$, then $(U, I_x, I_y, I_z, I_c, I_t,^{(.,B_i,D)(.,.,D)})$ is called as a big data cognitive system.

4 Conclusions

To enable human-machines interactions more naturally and to expand the human intelligence and cognition, this paper proposed a novel big medical data cognitive system based on n-ary formal concept analysis. First, we extended the conventional formal concept analysis from 2-dimension space to n-dimensional space for better mastering the associations among different dimensions. Based on this extension, a framework and mathematical modeling of the big medical data cognitive system are presented, respectively.

Acknowledgments This research was supported by the MSIP (Ministry of Science, ICT and Future Planning), Korea, under the C-ITRC (Convergence Information Technology Research Center) (IITP-2015-IITP-2015-H8601-15-1009) supervised by the IITP (Institute for Information and communications Technology Promotion) and partly supported by Shanxi Scholarship Council of China (No. 2015-068).

References

1. Virone G et al (2006) An advanced wireless sensor network for health monitoring. In: Transdisciplinary conference on distributed diagnosis and home healthcare (D2H2)
2. Liu Y, Dong B, Guo B et al (2015) Combination of cloud computing and internet of things (IOT) in medical monitoring systems. Management 8(12)
3. Riazul Islam SM, Kwak D, Humaun Kabir M et al (2015) The internet of things for health care: a comprehensive survey. IEEE Access, 3:678–708
4. Catarinucci L, De Donno D, Mainetti L et al (2015) An IoT-aware architecture for smart healthcare systems. IEEE Internet Things J 2(6):515–526

5. Hao F, Min G, Pei Z, Park DS, Yang LT (2015) K-clique community detection in social networks based on formal concept analysis. IEEE Syst J. doi:10.1109/JSYST.2015.2433294
6. Kuang L, Hao F, Yang LT, Lin M, Luo C, Min G (2014) A tensor-based approach for big data representation and dimensionality reduction. IEEE Trans Emerg Top Comput 2(3):280–291
7. Hao F, Park DS, Woo SY (2015) Green treatment plan selection based on three dimensional fuzzy evaluation model. In: Advances in computer science and ubiquitous computing. Springer Singapore, pp 417–423

Study of Multi-source Data Fusion in Topic Discovery

Hai Yun Xu, Chao Wang, Li Jie Ru, Zeng Hui Yue, Ling Wei
and Shu Fang

Abstract This review provides an introduction to MSDF in topic discovery, and discusses the status quo of the methods and applications of MSDF. This review has investigated the main thoughts of MSDF and proposed that MSDF could be divided into the fusion of data types and fusion of data relations. Furthermore, the fusion of data relations could be divided into the cross integration of multi-mode data and matrix fusion of multi-relational data. This paper studied the methods and technological process of MSDF applicable to information analysis, especially in the competitive intelligence of scientific and technological area.

Keywords Data fusion · Relations fusion · Multi-mode analysis · Multi-source data

1 Introduction

Multi-source data fusion (MSDF) refers to comprehensively analyzing different types of information sources or relational data by a specific method, and utilizing information together to reveal characteristics of the research object for obtaining

H.Y. Xu · C. Wang · L.J. Ru · L. Wei · S. Fang
Chengdu Library of Chinese Academy of Sciences,
Chengdu, Sichuan 610041, People's Republic of China

H.Y. Xu
Institute of Scientific and Technical Information of China,
Beijing 100038, People's Republic of China

C. Wang (✉) · L.J. Ru · L. Wei
University of Chinese Academy of Science, Beijing 100190,
People's Republic of China
e-mail: wngchao2015@mail.las.ac.cn

Z.H. Yue
Information Engineering, Faculty of Jining Medical University,
Rizhao, Shandong 276826, People's Republic of China

© Springer Science+Business Media Singapore 2016   729
J.J. (Jong Hyuk) Park et al. (eds.), *Advanced Multimedia and Ubiquitous Engineering*, Lecture Notes in Electrical Engineering 393,
DOI 10.1007/978-981-10-1536-6_95

more comprehensive and objective measurement results. The MSDF study, which has been mostly concentrated in the sensor field, has also become a key subject of bioinformatics, artificial intelligence, face recognition and other disciplines. In recent years, with the development of data science and complex network, clustering researches on the fusion of different networks have received more attention.

This paper systematically investigates current research and application on MSDF, then pertinently analyzes research progress of MSDF in areas such as sensor and automation. Subsequently, considering the features of topic discovery, we learn from the methods of MSDF in sensors or some other fields, and innovate these methods to be suitable for topic discovery. In order to make up for the deficiencies of the function of single-type relationship, a function that can reveal correlation between associated entities is proposed and it can facilitate expansion of topic discovery analysis methods.

2 Overview of MSDF in Topic Discovery

2.1 Basic Types of Relation

We propose that multi-source data fusion can be divided into two kinds: fusion of data types and fusion of data relations.

The fusion of data types is to merge different data types into the same analysis object. Currently, data types mainly include journal articles, conference information, dissertations, patent information, project information, book information and so on. Hua [1] divided multi-source data into homogeneous information with heterologous source, heterogeneous information and multilingual information. And he indicated that fusion of data types was a basic work involving field mapping, field splitting, filtering repeated data, weighting heterogeneous data, which was inevitable step of data processing in future topic discovery analysis. This article focuses on the fusion of data relations, so there are few descriptions on the method of data types fusion here.

The fusion of data relations is to merge different data relations into a new one to characterize the relationship among entities. Based on citation relationship, Shibata et al. [2] conducted a comparative research on three networks, co-citation network, bibliographic coupling network and citation network. And results showed that citation network could find new topics earlier and was the most effective way of identifying research fronts. By contrast, co-citation network was the worst. In addition, the content clustering based on the citation network had both the highest similarity and the least risk of omitting a new research field. Klavans [3] discovered the clustering network built by direct citation, comparing with co-citation, it had more similar content.

2.2 Fusion of Data Relations

According to the different ways of fusion, the fusion of multi-source data relations can be divided into the cross-integration of multi-mode data and matrix fusion of multi-relational data.

Cross-integration of multi-mode data shows associations among different types of entities taking advantage of cross co-occurrence technique, but ignoring the same types of entities.

Matrix fusion of multi-relational data merges similar matrixes or distance matrixes of multi-source data into a new matrix that seeks to present all relations, and then performs multivariate statistical analysis, such as cluster analysis, factor analysis, etc.

Both the cross- integration of multi-mode data and matrix fusion of multi-relational data eventually form a comprehensive matrix. For cross- integration of multi-mode data, the dimension of the newly formed matrix is the sum of dimensions of all the original matrixes. But for matrix fusion of multi-relational data, the dimension of the new matrix dose not change.

2.2.1 Cross-Integration of Multi-Mode Data

In social network analysis, mode refers to the collection of actors, specifically, the number of the types of these collections. The network of relationships between two collections is called a 2-mode crossing network. Similarly, the network of relationships among three collections is called a 3-mode crossing network, and multi-mode network corresponds to more than three collections. Cross-integration of multi-mode data can be defined as the process of combining multi-source data to form a multi-mode matrix, where connections only exist among different types of nodes.

Some researchers combined bibliography and words to discover research topics. We find out there are two approaches for the combination: one is to use the bibliography as a qualification of the relationship between the words, and the other is to use citation to build the relationship between bibliography and words. When using indexing terms in the study of domain description, we may encounter some inherent problems because of linguistic phenomenons, such as polysemy. However, bibliography provides a specific context for indexing terms which, to a certain extent, can avoid the above problems.

2.2.2 Matrix Fusion of Multi-Relational Data

Braam et al. [4] combined co-citation cluster analysis with content words analysis to identify research topics. Based on co-citation clusters, they counted the frequency of words contained in references to test whether the cluster could gather literatures possessing similar terms into a class. Calero-Medina et al. [5] analyzed the knowledge creation and flow process between scientific publications by combining word co-occurrence and citation network analysis. They used word co-occurrence to find related terms and theories, and used citation network analysis to discover the key literatures in this field. Zhang [6] indicated that co-word clustering and strategic coordinates analysis were powerful tools to research discipline hotspots, and the combination of co-words and cited frequency could lead to better results. The rest of this section discusses two main types of relation fusion: the fusion between two types of relations and the fusion among the triple relations.

1. Fusion between two types of relations

In the field of information retrieval, Weiss et al. [7] developed a prototype system of hierarchical network search engine—HyPursuit system, which was used for retrieval and browsing by detecting the content-link clustering of hypertext documents. The clustering algorithm of content-link was based on a literature similarity function which considered the similarity of the terms and hyperlinks similarity factor. The result of the function was the maximum value of similarities. Using the approaches based on reference links and co-words, Small [8] identified the direct and indirect connection relationship between literatures. Janssens et al. [9] learnt from the method of combining web content and hyperlink, and merged the relationship based on words and the relationship based on bibliographic coupling together. They used Fisher's inverse chi-square method for constructing new relational data sets, and conducted an empirical study, the result of which showed that the method was applicable to find the structure of research field on bioinformatics and information science.

2. Fusion in the triple relations

Wang and Kitsuregawa [10] proposed a clustering algorithm based on content-link coupling to retrieve web pages. They integrated outbound links, inbound links and terms to improve retrieval performance. He et al. [11] proposed a web text clustering method merging the structure of text-based hyperlink, co-citation and text content. They used the structure of text-based hyperlink to calculate similarities, whose intensity was moderated by the text similarities, and then integrated both the hyperlink structure similarity and text similarity with co-citation by linear weighting to build a weighted adjacency matrix.

3. Evaluation of relational fusion results

Compared with multi relationship, the evaluations of single-relationship clustering results differ in researches. The experiment conducted by Calado [12] showed that web page retrieval based on link relations was superior to text classification, but some other experiments showed that the similarity clustering based on words was superior to the similarity clustering based on citations. To sum up, all the experiments indicated the clustering results after the fusion was better than the one based on single-type relationships.

In the field of topic discovery, linear fusion is the mainly used algorithm in the relational fusion research. However, MSDF is complex, and the three main types of data relationships are often not independent but are correlated with each other, which is why a simple linear operation is not enough to solve the problem of data fusion. Still, we can learn the methods of MSDF from other research fields, such as sensor, automation and so on, to improve and enrich the MSDF methods in topic discovery analysis

3 Research and Application on Relational Fusion

The cross-integration of multi-mode data is usually used to visualize the association among different data, which has no difficulties with visualization techniques. Currently, the module identification of multi-mode data is a research hotspot in complex network researches. In the case of 2-mode network, community detecting methods can be roughly divided into two types: the non-mapping method and mapping method. The mapping method is to convert 2-mode networks into 1-mode networks, which will lead to information loss and cannot reflect the nature of all original network. Latapy [13] summed up three drawbacks of mapping method: leading to information loss, increasing the number of edges of entire network and increasing unnecessary new information that does not exist in the original network.

To ensure the accuracy of the analysis process, the non-mapping method is more reliable, which identifies the module directly on the original 2-mode network. Guimerà et al. [14] defined the modularity based on 2-mode network, and proposed the corresponding algorithm of community discovery. Both algorithms aim to maximize the modularity, but what's different is the way that they maximize. These have enriched the theory of community detecting based on 2-mode networks.

4 Future Method of MSDF in Topic Discovery

This paper assumes a future research model of MSDF in topic discovery. The method can realize the fusion among different kinds of information, data relations and clustering results.

Firstly, collect a variety of data sources, such as journal articles, conference information, dissertations, patent information, project information, book information, and even industrial and economic data should be included in the scope of topic discovery analysis.

Secondly, obtain various data relations and fuse them effectively. Whether cross-integration of multi-mode data or matrix fusion of multi-relational data has its corresponding fusion methods, which complement each other, based on the data features.

There are basically two modes for multi-source data fusion, one is to obtain a variety of associated data types respectively, and fuse relation matrixes of different data types by mapping; the other is to directly identify the community topics of multi-mode data. Both methods can enhance the data relationship strength by acquiring complementary information.

Cross-integration of multi-mode data identifies modules by learning from non-mapping identification methods of complex heterogeneous networks, and considers the relationships among different dimensions in specific problems of topic discovery analysis. However, the visualization of cross co-ocurrence of multi-mode data still has much room for improvement, for example, visualizing information and association of more dimensions, which is important for knowledge discovery.

Matrix fusion of multi-relational data can bring in existing fusion methods from the field of sensor, automation and so on. According to the objects and characteristics of topic discovery, we can improve these methods and eventually formed fusion methods applied to topic discovery. The matrix fusion has different ways of fusion, which derive from different rationales, strengths and weaknesses, so they can complement each other to enhance the effectiveness of matrix fusions.

5 Conclusion

By investigating the main thoughts of MSDF, this review proposes that MSDF can be divided into the fusion of data type and fusion of data relation in topic discovery. The fusion of data type can be subdivided into the cross-integration of multi-mode data and matrix fusion of multi-relational data. The clustering results of relation matrix can be optimized by the clustering ensemble. In addition, we assume that the improvement of MSDF methods requires a strong mathematical foundation, and breakthrough of MSDF in future may come from advanced fields in data fusion research and their applications, such as sensors, the automation, etc. Topic Discovery should draw on the experience of these advanced fields and build its own analytic methodology of MSDF in the future.

Acknowledgments This work was supported by National Social Science Fund of China (Grant No. 14CTQ033), West Light Fund of Chinese Academy of Science (Grant No: Y4C0091001), and Youth Innovation Fund of Promotion Association, CAS.

References

1. Hua BL (2013) Research on the methods of multi-source fusion. Inf Stud Theory Appl 36 (11):16–19
2. Shibata N, Kajikawa Y, Takeda Y, Matsushima K (2009) Comparative study on methods of detecting research fronts using different types of citation. J Am Soc Inf Sci Technol 60(3):571–580

3. Klavans R, Boyack KW (2006) Quantitative evaluation of large maps of science. Scientometrics 68(3):475–499
4. Braam RR, Moed HF, Van Raan AF (1991) Mapping of science by combined co-citation and word analysis. I Struct Aspects JASIS 42(4):233–251
5. Calero-Medina C, Noyons EC (2008) Combining mapping and citation network analysis for a better understanding of the scientific development: the case of the absorptive capacity field. J Informetrics 2(4):272–279
6. Zhang H, Wang XY, Cui L (2007) Trend: Co—word analysis method combined with literature CI research thematic areas. Inf Stud Theory Appl 30(3):378–380
7. Weiss R, Vélez B, Sheldon MA (1996) HyPursuit: a hierarchical network search engine that exploits content-link hypertext clustering. In: 7th ACM conference on hypertext, pp 180–193
8. Small H (1998) A general framework for creating large-scale maps of science in two or three dimensions: the SciViz system. Scientometrics 41(1–2):125–133
9. Janssens F, Glänzel W, De Moor B (2008) A hybrid mapping of information science. Scientometrics 75(3):607–631
10. Wang Y, Kitsuregawa M (2002) Evaluating contents-link coupled web page clustering for web search results. In: 11th international conference on Information and knowledge management, pp 499–506
11. He X, Zha H, Ding CH, Simon HD (2002) Web document clustering using hyperlink structures. Comput Stat Data Anal 41(1):19–45
12. Calado P et al (2006) Link-based similarity measures for the classification of Web documents. J Am Soc Inf Sci Technol 57(2):208–221
13. Latapy M, Magnien C, Del Vecchio N (2008) Basic notions for the analysis of large two-mode networks. Soc Netw 30(1):31–48
14. Guimerà R, Sales-Pardo M, Amaral LAN (2007) Module identification in bipartite and directed networks. Phys Rev E 76(3):036102

Novel Mobile Motion Prediction Algorithm for Predicting Pedestrian's Next Location

Yan Zhuang, Simon Fong and Meng Yuan

Abstract This paper describes a novel mobile motion prediction algorithm to meet the need of today's mobile system and application which is based on Markov model. As in different time period, the things people always do usually are different, so does the route they have taken. It provides a way to constrain the path sample with time interval to enhance the prediction. In the end, the prediction accuracy is experimented up to 92 %.

Keywords Location prediction · Trajectory mining · GPS trajectory analysis

1 Introduction

In daily life, most people always have regular routes. Student usually follow the same route to go to school and back home. Adult also take the same trips when they go to a place where they usually go. As the development of mobile phone, Smart phones with GPS become more and more popular. Also the position technique is evolving with a rapid speed. Today, users carrying wirelessly connected mobile device are able to request and obtain geographic information services as they travel through the geographic space [1]. The ability of predicting a person's location is needed more and more for today's mobile system and application. Nissan showed that if the route of vehicle is known in advance, it's possible to improve hybrid fuel economy by up to 7.8 % [2]. Tate and Boyd also explore the optimal control

Y. Zhuang · S. Fong (✉) · M. Yuan
Department of Computer and Information Science, University of Macau,
Macau Sar, People's Republic of China
e-mail: ccfong@umac.mo

Y. Zhuang
e-mail: syz@umac.mo

M. Yuan
e-mail: 250625774@qq.com

© Springer Science+Business Media Singapore 2016   737
J.J. (Jong Hyuk) Park et al. (eds.), *Advanced Multimedia and Ubiquitous Engineering*, Lecture Notes in Electrical Engineering 393,
DOI 10.1007/978-981-10-1536-6_96

scheme for a hybrid assuming the route is already known [3]. To support the growing need, we have designed a novel algorithm based on Markov model [4].

1.1 Probability Interference Path

In the algorithm of Jeung et al [5], let Du be a set of (historical) network trajectories (of the user u). Given two adjacent edges $e_i \succ e_j$, we define the support $\tau(Du, e_i \succ e_j)$ as the number of trajectories in Du that contain $e_i \succ e_j$.

Given two edges e_i and e_j incident to the vertex v, we define the transition probability from e_i to e_j as:

$$M(v)[e_i, e_j] = \frac{\tau(Du, e_i \succ e_j)}{\sum_{e_k} \tau(Du, e_i \succ e_k)} \tag{1}$$

According to above equation, movement paths can be inferred as Fig. 1.

In Fig. 1 assuming the green and red line indicates the history path which belong to a single pedestrian. The direction of paths shown in red line is from V12 to v1. This pedestrian is walking from V8 to V5. $\tau(Du, e_4 \succ e_2) = 30$. $\tau(Du, e_4 \succ e_1) = 400$. $\tau(Du, e_4 \succ e_3) = 60$.

At here, we assuming $\tau r(Du, e_4 \succ e_1)$ as the number of trajectories in Du that contain $e_4 \succ e_1$ shown in red line, $\tau g(Du, e_4 \succ e_1)$ as the number of trajectories in Du that contain $e_4 \succ e_1$ shown in green line. So, here $\tau(Du, e_4 \succ e_1) = \tau r(Du, e_4 \succ e_1) + \tau g(Du, e_4 \succ e_1)$. And, suppose, $\tau r(Du, e_4 \succ e_1)$ equals 350, and $\tau r(Du, e_4 \succ e_1)$ equals 50.

According to Formula 1, the probability of taking e_1 is:

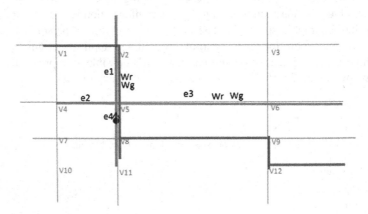

Fig. 1 Illustration of pedestrian paths

$$M(v)[e_4, e_1] = \frac{\tau(Du, e_4 \succ e_1)}{\tau(Du, e_4 \succ e_1) + \tau(Du, e_4 \succ e_2) + \tau(Du, e_4 \succ e_3)} = \frac{400}{400 + 30 + 60} = \frac{40}{49}$$

$$M(v)[e_4, e_2] = \frac{3}{49}$$

$$M(v)[e_4, e_3] = \frac{6}{49}$$

The most likelihood probability path is e_1. But, if the intersection path of the path shown in red line and the path shown in green is only on the path segment from V8 to V2 which number is 50, the red line path may not contribute to calculate the actual most likelihood probability. In fact the result with red line path removed, may could more exactly reflects truth. Results with red line path removed:

$$M'(v)[e_4, e_1] = \frac{\tau g(Du, e_4 \succ e_1)}{\tau g(Du, e_4 \succ e_1) + \tau(Du, e_4 \succ e_2) + \tau(Du, e_4 \succ e_3)} = \frac{50}{50 + 30 + 60} = \frac{5}{14}$$

$$M'(v)[e_4, e_2] = \frac{3}{14}$$

$$M'(v)[e_4, e_3] = \frac{6}{14}$$

Now, the most likelihood probability path has changed to e_3. So, there are some interference factor to the real result in the circumstance like above.

In our algorithm, all the history path would not be mapped with pedestrian, even if two different path taken by one pedestrian, they will be identified by two different path ID. In the prediction every history paths which is the same as current path will be extracted to precise the prediction by matching current path ID in first middle and last junction separately with the corresponding junctions of the history path. So, the result is hardly to be affected by useless path.

2 Prediction Algorithm

2.1 Predictor

The algorithm depends on Markov model. Assuming each junction is represented by J. Let H be the set of all history path, $|H|$ be the number of history path in set H. Let hj be any of the history path in H ($hj \in H$, $1 \leq j \leq |H|$). $|hj|$ be the number of junctions which is contained in hj. Any junction in hj is represented to $hjJi$ ($1 \leq i \leq |hj|$). Here, we make the person's current position to be $C = CJi, CJi + 1 \ldots CJi + m - 1$. The next state is depended on C. Assuming one of the next possible position is assumed to be $CJi + m$. The probability from $CJi + m - 1$ to $CJi + m$ is represented as following.

$$P(Xi+m = CJi+m|Xi = C) = \frac{Num(h(i, i+m))}{Num(h(i, i+m-1))} \qquad (2)$$

where $h(x, y)$ denotes the history path from Jx to Jy. $Num(h(x, y))$ denotes the total number of history path from Jx to Jy.

2.2 Time Based Predictor

At one junction, the probabilities of taking each route maybe have not too much difference. Different time duration may filtrate some history path which cannot contribute to the prediction. For example, the total history path from Ji to Jk contains the history path of going to restaurant at noon, but the current path prediction took place in the afternoon. Obviously the history path generated at noon of going to restaurant contributes nothing to the prediction. So, time duration based on prediction is proposed.

$$P(Xi+m = CJi+m|Xi = C) = \frac{Num(h(i, i+m, t))}{Num(h(i, i+m-1, t))} \qquad (3)$$

where $h(x, y, t)$ denotes the history path from Jx to Jy with in the same time duration of one day.

2.3 Prediction Process

Let each two near junction to be a node, which is represented by $Ji \rightarrow Ji + 1$. Giving every path a ID and also the node. The data structure could be represented as following.

Node is defined as the two junctions, which are contained in any history path and between the two junctions there is no other junction. Node ID is the ID of the node. PID denotes the history path IDs, which passed through this node. T denotes the time when the traveler went through the corresponding node.

Each two near junctions which are contained in the same history path will be represented as the data structure shown in Fig. 2. Given a current path which should be considered to be C, the probability of going to the next junction could be estimated as following. Get the first, middle and last node from C, CJi $CJi + 1$, $CJ(i + m - 1)/2$ $CJ(i + m - 1)/2 + 1$, $CJi + m - 2$ $CJi + m - 1$. Fined them

Fig. 2 Data structure

Node ID	P		...	PI	
Data	ID_1	1		D_i	i	structure

separately from the nodes of history path and get each PID set from each node. Finally PID sets set1, set2 and set3 could be obtained. PID set illustrates the path ids which has passed through the corresponding node. Calculate the intersection of the three set. The element number of the intersection is $\text{Num}(h(i, i+m-1))$. $\text{Num}(h(i, i+m-1, t))$ could be obtained by filtrating $\text{Num}(h(i, i+m-1))$ by time. Assuming the next junction is $Ji + m$ and there is no junction between $CJi + m - 1$ and $Ji + m$. Find this node $(CJi + m - 1 \ Ji + m)$ from node set of history path. Let PIDs in this node as set4. The element number of intersection which is calculated by intersecting set1, set2, set3 and set4 is $\text{Num}(h(i, i+m))$. $\text{Num}(h(i, i+m, t))$ is also can be got by filtrating $\text{Num}(h(i, i+m))$ by time.

3 Simulation

3.1 Simulation with Real Map

First of all, mark each junction with a circle in real map. Give each circle a coordinate. The value is X and Y value which is projected into X and Y axis as shown in Fig. 3. Each junction will get a unique coordinate. For example, $(X1, Y0) = (0.9, 3.1)$; $(X2, Y1) = (1.2, 3.3)$; $(X4, Y3) = (2.7, 3.6)$; $(X6, Y1) = (3.4, 5.5)$; $(X7, Y2) = (4.2, 6.6)$; $(X5, Y0) = (2.8, 7.0)$; $(X4, Y4) = (2.7, 7.5)$; $(X4, Y5) = (2.6, 8.2)$.

In Fig. 3, red line denotes current path. The blue shows history paths which have same route with current path. Green one is the history path which have partial common route with current path. $\{(Xi, Ym) \rightarrow (Xj, Yn)\}$ denotes the set of history path which went from junction (Xi, Ym) to (Xj, Yn). So, $\{(X2, Y1) \rightarrow (X6, Y2)\}$, $\{(X3, Y0) \rightarrow (X4, Y6)\}$ and $\{(X6, Y0) \rightarrow (X1, Y1)\}$ are sets of blue path. $\{(X7, Y3) \rightarrow (X11, Y2)\}$, $\{(X1, Y0) \rightarrow (X1, Y1)\}$ and $\{(X1, Y1) \rightarrow (X6, Y2)\}$ are green ones'. Bpath and Gpath mean one of the blue path or green path. Path IDs which belonged to blue path set and green path set are represented as following.

$\forall$ Bpath, Bpath $\in \{(X2, Y1) \rightarrow (X6, Y2)\}$; $\exists$ Path ID $= c \ (c \in N, 1 \leq c \leq 50)$.
$\forall$ Bpath, Bpath $\in \{(X3, Y0) \rightarrow (X4, Y6)\}$; $\exists$ Path ID $= c \ (c \in N, 51 \leq c \leq 140)$.
$\forall$ Bpath, Bpath $\in \{(X6, Y0) \rightarrow (X1, Y1)\}$; $\exists$ Path ID $= c \ (c \in N, 141 \leq c \leq 150)$.
$\forall$ Gpath, Gpath $\in \{(X6, Y0) \rightarrow (X1, Y1)\}$; $\exists$ Path ID $= c \ (c \in N, 151 \leq c \leq 225)$.
$\forall$ Gpath, Gpath $\in \{(X11, Y2) \rightarrow (X7, Y3)\}$; $\exists$ Path ID $= c \ (c \in N, 226 \leq c \leq 336)$.
$\forall$ Gpath, Gpath $\in \{(X1, Y1) \rightarrow (X6, Y2)\}$; $\exists$ Path ID $= c \ (c \in N, 337 \leq c \leq 357)$.

The node which represents two near junctions contains all the path IDs and time of the paths which passed through the node. We denote $|(Xi, Ym) \rightarrow (Xj, Yn)|$ to be the number of paths which went from (Xi, Ym) to (Xj, Yn). So the number of path which went through the node are indicated as following.

$|(X2, Y1) \rightarrow (X4, Y3)| = 500$
$|(X1, Y0) \rightarrow (X4, Y3)| = 750$
$|(X3, Y0) \rightarrow (X4, Y3)| = 900$

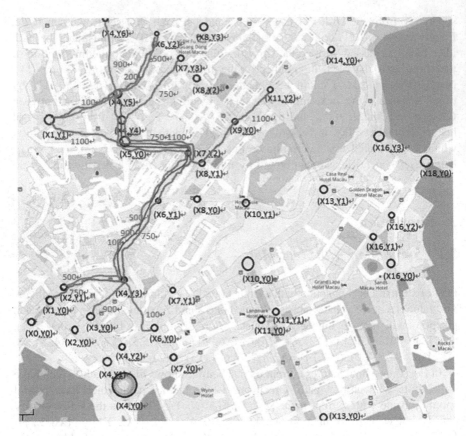

Fig. 3 Illustration of junctions as circles

$$|(X6, Y0) \rightarrow (X4, Y3)| = 100$$
$$|(X4, Y3) \rightarrow (X6, Y1)| = 100 + 500 + 900 + 750 = 2250$$
$$|(X6, Y1) \rightarrow (X7, Y2)| = 100 + 500 + 900 + 750 = 2250$$
$$|(X7, Y2) \rightarrow (X5, Y0)| = 100 + 500 + 900 + 750 + 1100 = 3350$$
$$|(X5, Y0) \rightarrow (X4, Y4)| = 100 + 500 + 900 + 750 = 3350$$
$$|(X4, Y4) \rightarrow (X4, Y5)| = 100 + 500 + 900 = 1500$$
$$|(X4, Y5) \rightarrow (X1, Y1)| = 100$$
$$|(X4, Y5) \rightarrow (X4, Y6)| = 900$$
$$|(X4, Y5) \rightarrow (X6, Y2)| = 500 + 200 = 700$$

According to the algorithm, get first, middle and last node of current node. Here they are $(X4, Y3) \rightarrow (X6, Y1)$, $(X7, Y2) \rightarrow (X5, Y0)$ and $(X4, Y4) \rightarrow (X4, Y5)$. Fined them in history path which is shown by blue and green path. Figure out the number of common path ids. The result is the number of blue path that's $100 + 900 + 500 = 1500$.

$$\text{Num}(h(i-m+1,i)) = 1500$$

Find the next possible junctions, here, they are $(X1, Y1)$, $(X4, Y6)$ and $(X6, Y2)$. From current position $(X4, Y5)$ to each junction, there could be three nodes. They are $(X4, Y5) \rightarrow (X1, Y1)$, $(X4, Y5) \rightarrow (X4, Y6)$ and $(X4, Y5) \rightarrow (X6, Y2)$ called possible nodes. Compare each possible node with nodes of current path, get the same path IDs then figure out the number of the path IDs. In this situation, the numbers separately are 100, 900 and 500. Choose the biggest one which is the most possible path. There would be $\text{Num}(h(i-m+1,i+1)) = 900$. The most possible node is $(X4, Y5) \rightarrow (X4, Y6)$. The most possible next position could be $(X4, Y6)$. The probability is illustrated as following.

$$P(Xi+1 = Nci+1|Xi = C) = \frac{\text{Num}(h(i-m+1,i+1))}{\text{Num}(h(i-m+1,i))} = \frac{900}{1500} = 60\ \%$$

Usually, in a specific time period, people always do the same thing. Like in the morning, people usually go to work or school. At noon, go for lunch from workplace. At nightfall, they go back home. Drivers often take the same route they familiar with. Postman and deliveryman often deliver in the same route at a same time. To a certain extent, they always have a regular activity in a single day.

Give a time attribute to the node. It's the time when history path went through the node. Assuming current path occurs at 6:00 PM. Filter the history path which has the same path with current one with time. The history path around 6:00 PM is shown as Fig. 4.

$|(X4, Y3) \rightarrow (X6, Y1)| = 20 + 225 + 100 + 75 = 420$
$|(X6, Y1) \rightarrow (X7, Y2)| = 20 + 225 + 100 + 75 = 420$
$|(X7, Y2) \rightarrow (X5, Y0)| = 20 + 225 + 100 + 75 + 110 = 530$
$|(X5, Y0) \rightarrow (X4, Y4)| = 20 + 225 + 100 + 75 = 420$
$|(X4, Y4) \rightarrow (X4, Y5)| = 20 + 225 + 100 = 345$
$|(X4, Y5) \rightarrow (X1, Y1)| = 20$
$|(X4, Y5) \rightarrow (X4, Y6)| = 225$
$|(X4, Y5) \rightarrow (X6, Y2)| = 100 + 20 = 120$

With the same method, comparing nodes of current path, find the same path ID and figure out the number of the same path. The result is the number of blue path that's 20 + 225 + 100 = 345.

$$\text{Num}(h(i-m+1,i,t)) = 345$$

Compare each possible node with nodes of current path, get the same path ID then figure out the number of the same path. At here, the numbers separately are 20, 225 and 100. Choose the largest one. There would be $\text{Num}(h(i-m+1,i+1,t)) = 225$. The most possible node is $(X4, Y5) \rightarrow (X4, Y6)$. The most possible next position could be $(X4, Y6)$. The probability is illustrated as following.

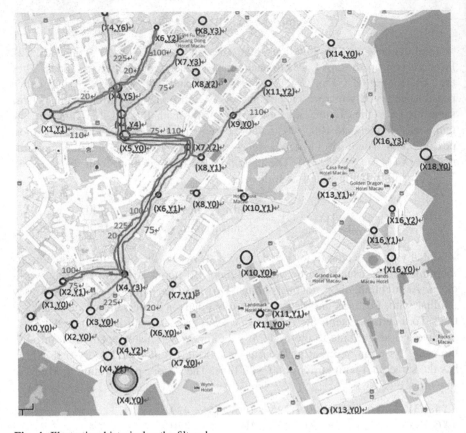

Fig. 4 Illustrating historical paths filtered

$$P(Xi+1 = Nci+1 | Xi = C) = \frac{\text{Num}(h(i-m+1, i+1, t))}{\text{Num}(h(i-m+1, i, t))} = \frac{225}{345} = 65.2\ \%$$

4 Experiment

The algorithm is tested by 3500 paths with GPS equipment carriers. In the experiment, first of all, each single path should be split into segments by two near junctions on it, which also could be called nodes. So there is a node set which is composed by all nodes. Mining the node set, finally each node gets a path ID set that is all the IDs of paths which passed though the corresponding node. Each path ID will be labeled by time interval.

Testing method extracted ten groups path from history path. Here, path number of each group is shown on X-axis of Fig. 5. Then randomly extract a route from the

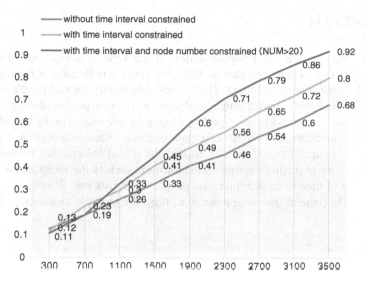

Fig. 5 Experiment results; X-axis: path number of each sample; Y-axis: accuracy

each path group to be current path. Evaluate each path set with corresponding current path. Result is shown in Fig. 5. There are three ways of testing. They are without time interval constrained test, time interval constrained and with time and node number constrained test.

In Fig. 5, blue line shows prediction without time interval constrained. Yellow shows time interval constrained and green one shows both time interval and node number which is contained in any of history path sample constrained. The node length which are shown in blue and yellow lines are less than 20 nodes. The green one is more than 20 nodes.

According to the figure shown, when the number of sample path is less than 700 the worst accuracy is the green one. After 1100, the best is green and the worst is blue. Yellow line always performs better than the blue. There is the conclusion. In the beginning, there is not enough sample for time interval and node number constrained test, it performed the worst. As the number of extracted path increase, the advantage of this algorithm come out. The gap between the other two lines become more and more large. When the number of sample path come up to 3500, method of time interval and node number constrained performed the best. The accuracy could get to 92 %. In fact, if the test path could be supplied as much as needed, the slope of the three line will get smaller and smaller even to zero respectively. The objective laws of each test pattern will be reflected. And the blue one will come first, the second is the yellow. The green line would be the last which is just the most accuracy one.

5 Conclusion

In recent years, as the rapid popularization of the vehicle navigation equipment, intelligent mobile phone and other portable devices, the collection of the trajectory data has become more convenient. The historical trajectory data of people contains important information, and through analyzing it we can predict the user's next location, which can provide more perfect service for the user. The factors affecting the location prediction are varied. Like path distance, weather condition, landform analysis. This paper focused on how to find the useful information from the historical trajectory to predict the user's next location, such as the location that people took up a lot of time to do activities, and people travel patterns. We can also further research in the route of user after a period of time, the multiple locations rather than a location.

Acknowledgments The authors of this paper are thankful to the financial supports of the grant offered with code: MYRG2015-00024, called "Building Sustainable Knowledge Networks through Online Communities", by RDAO, University of Macau.

References

1. Hui L, Lei Y (2009) Mobile geographic information services. IGI Global, pp 944–945
2. Deguchi Y, Kuroda K, Shouji M, Kawabe T (2004) HEV charge/discharge control system based on navigation information. In: Convergence international congress & exposition on transportation electronics. pp 21–28
3. Tate E, Boyd S (2000) Finding ultimate limits of performance for hybrid electric vehicles. In: Proceedings of Society of Automotive Engineers 2000 future transportation technology conference. pp. 1–12
4. Yu XG, Liu YH, Wei D, Ting M (2006) Hybrid Markov model used for path prediction. In: Proceedings. 15th international conference on computer communications and network. ICCCN 2006, pp 374–379
5. Jeung H, Yiu ML, Zhou X (2010) Path prediction and predictive range querying in road network databases. VLDB J 585–602

Mining Foursquare User Check-in Habit Based on Historical Check-in Records

Yan Zhuang, Simon Fong and Meng Yuan

Abstract Location prediction is the latest development direction in these year. This paper proposes a new method which does not need each individual history path and ID to match his/her history path with prediction path database to predict the user's next location. In this experiment, we used two pair of coordinates to give a prediction. It's based on the foursquare dataset. And through changing the factors that affect the location prediction, like length and time, in the general experiment, the accuracy of the prediction will be enhanced.

Keywords Data mining · Next location prediction · Foursqure

1 Introduction

Foursquare is a local search [1] and discovery service [2] mobile app which provides search results for its users. Foursquare featured a social networking layer that enabled a user to share their location with friends, via the 'check in'—a user would manually tell the application when they were at a particular location using a mobile website, text messaging, or a device-specific application by selecting from a list of venues the application locates nearby. Check-in points [3] are the stay points that are the locations where people speed a period of time to do something important.

Y. Zhuang · S. Fong (✉) · M. Yuan
Department of Computer and Information Science, University of Macau,
Taipa, Macau SAR
e-mail: ccfong@umac.mo

Y. Zhuang
e-mail: syz@umac.mo

M. Yuan
e-mail: 250625774@qq.com

© Springer Science+Business Media Singapore 2016   747
J.J. (Jong Hyuk) Park et al. (eds.), *Advanced Multimedia and Ubiquitous Engineering*, Lecture Notes in Electrical Engineering 393,
DOI 10.1007/978-981-10-1536-6_97

2 Difference Between Foursquare and Continuous Trajectory

In the case of Foursquare, it's somewhat different from the prediction of continuous trajectory [4]. As the next coordinate of Foursquare may could be lots of points, not like the continuous trajectory prediction, its next coordinate is near the Decision point, also the number is from 2 to 3.

Figure 1 is one of the Foursquare case, one person has checked-in at S1 then S2. S2 is decision point. D1, D2, D3, D4 and D5 are the next probable check-in coordinates. In the graph, the probable check-in coordinates distributed unregularly, some are near the decision point, some are far from it. Also the direction is not regular. But in Fig. 2, which is the continuous trajectory prediction case, from S1 to S2 is the continuously path who has walked from S1 to S2. S2 is the decision point. The probable next coordinate may could be D1, D2 or D3. D1, D2 and D3 distributed regularly around the decision point. It's constrained by road network [5].

3 Proposed Algorithm

We consider the entire map as $m = \langle V, E \rangle$. The beginning known check-in points is represented by Ps. The last known check-in points is represented by Pe. The check-in points from Ps to Pe, are input data of the algorithm. Any next probable check-in point could be denoted as Dn.

The probability of a person checked-in from Ps to Pe at last checked-in at Dn could be represented as following.

$$Pro(Ps, Pe, Dn) = Pro(Dn|Ps, Pe) \tag{1}$$

In check-in historical data set, checked-in history from Ps to Pe could be represented as $His(Ps, Pe)$. Checked-in history from Ps to Pe then checked-in at Dn could be represented as $His(Ps, Pe, Dn)$. The path number of all people who has checked-in from Ps to Pe in historical data set is denoted as $|His(Ps, Pe)|$. So, $His(Ps, Pe, Dn)|$ also represents the path number of all people who has checked-in from Ps to Pe then Dn in historical data set. So, the equation could be changed like following.

$$Pro(Ps, Pe, Dn) = Pro(Dn|Ps, Pe) = \frac{|His(Ps, Pe, Dn)|}{|His(Ps, Pe)|} \tag{2}$$

Fig. 1 Foursquare

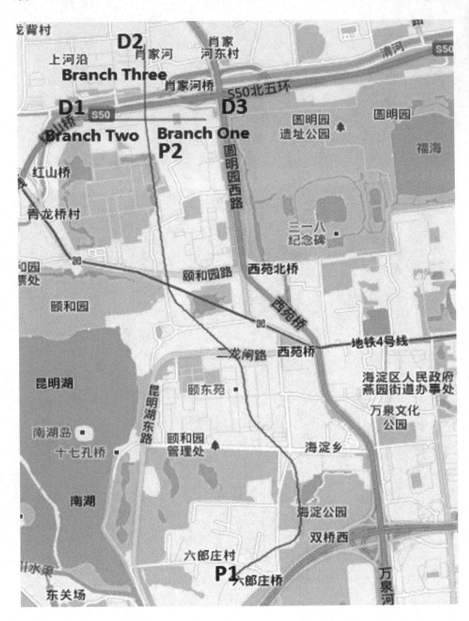

Fig. 2 Continuous trajectory

4 Simulation

In Fig. 3, a person has checked-in from $S1$ to $S2$, the next probable check-in point may be various. In the graph, they are $D1$, $D2$, $D3$, $D4$ and $D5$. Also, they all could be represented by $Dn1$, $Dn2$, $Dn3$, $Dn4$ and $Dn5$. The experiment is to get the

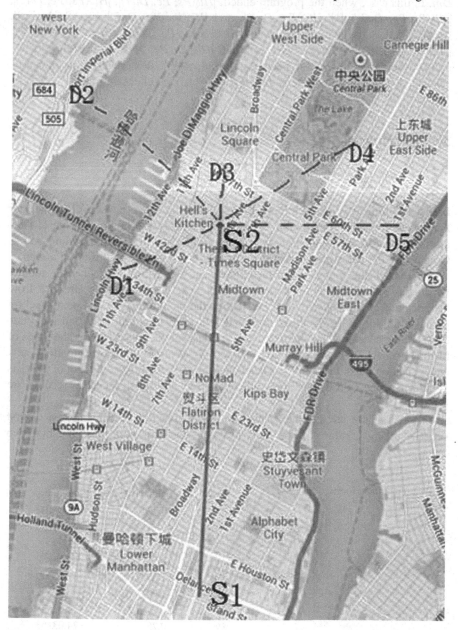

Fig. 3 Simulation graph

number of all people who has checked-in from $S1$, $S2$ then Dni. (Dni could be represent any next possible point. In Fig. 3, they are $Dn1$, $Dn2$, $Dn3$, $Dn4$ and $Dn5$).

First, input the known coordinates $S1$ and $S2$ into program. The program will mine the number of paths which the person has checked-in from $S1$ to $S2$ at last ended at Dni. In this case, when the program ended, $|His(Ps, Pe, Dn1)|$, $|His(Ps, Pe, Dn2)|$, $|His(Ps, Pe, Dn3)|$, $|His(Ps, Pe, Dn4)|$, and $|His(Ps, Pe, Dn5)|$ are all obtained. $|His(Ps, Pe)|$ is the summarized value of $|His(Ps, Pe, Dn1)|$, $|His(Ps, Pe, Dn2)|$, $|His(Ps, Pe, Dn3)|$, $|His(Ps, Pe, Dn4)|$, and $|His(Ps, Pe, Dn5)|$. According to formula 1, the probability of the person get each possible next check-in point can be calculated. The maximum one is the most possible next check-in point.

5 Experiment

5.1 General Experiment

In the experiment, we used four cases for testing our proposed algorithm for Foursquare movement prediction. The data of the cases are shown in Table 1. They are input data to the simulation system with different starting and ending points. Graphically the paths are shown in Figs. 4, 5, 6 and 7 superimposed on a map.

For each of the four cases in the experiment, we data mine each path number which has passed Ps, Pe and then to each next check-in point after Pe from historical check-in data set. At last, calculate the probability of each next check-in point. In the following Tables 2, 3, 4 and 5 of results, latitude (lat) and longitude (lng) are the coordinate of the next check-in data for each test. Num is the times of historical check-in data which has passed Ps, Pe and the corresponding next check-in coordinate. Probability is calculated by formula 1. Result detail of the tests is shown in the following Tables where the top five most accuracy records are listed.

In test 1, there are 115 next check-in points, but only the Num area of first sixteen are bigger than 1. The most probable check-in points are the first two

Table 1 Input data format and values			Latitude	Longitude
	Test 1	Ps	40.7743	−73.87192
		Pe	40.77128	−73.98193
	Test 2	Ps	40.71769	−73.9906
		Pe	40.76261	−73.98752
	Test 3	Ps	41.90311	−87.62949
		Pe	41.90363	−87.62672
	Test 4	Ps	40.7451	−74.03828
		Pe	40.751	−74.03163

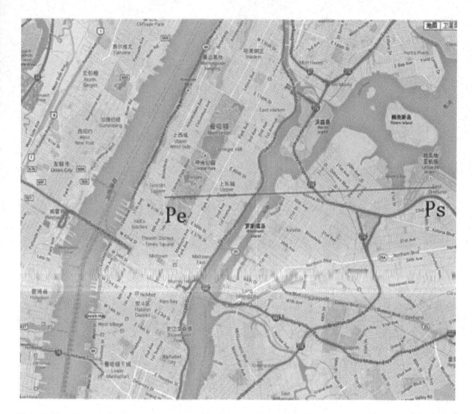

Fig. 4 Test 1

coordinates. They are (40.7713, −73.9821) and (40.7678, −73.9823). The probabilities are 8.955 and 6.965 % respectively.

In test 2, there are 129 next check-in points, the Num area of first fifty-three are bigger than 1. The most probable check-in point are the first two coordinates. They are (40.7608, −73.9879) and (40.76437, −73.9869). Probabilities are 7.306 and 4.566 %.

In test 3, there are 6 next check-in points. Num area of first and the second are bigger than 1. The most probable check-in points are the first two coordinates. They are (41.90273, −87.6319) and (41.91062, −87.6532). The probabilities are 40 and 20 % respectively.

In test 4, there are 16 next check-in points. Num area of first six are bigger than 1. The most probable check-in points are the first two coordinates. They are (40.7451, −74.0383) and (40.751, −74.0316). The probabilities are 32.895 and 28.947 % respectively.

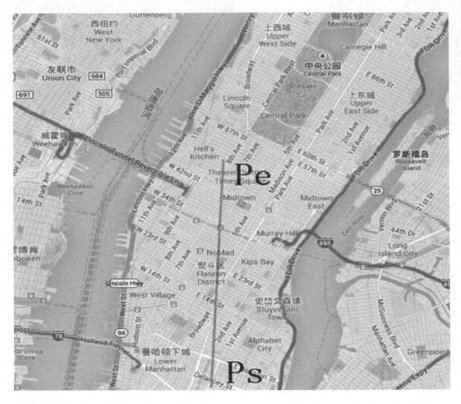

Fig. 5 Test 2

5.2 Experiment on Various Lengths and Accuracies

If a person checked-in at location A, then location B. If the distance between A and B were farther, the prediction accuracy may become smaller. There are seven test paths listed in the following to be used in the experiment.

In Table 6, the distance is from Ps to Pe. For each path, we choose the top three highest accuracy. They are $acc1$, $acc2$ and $acc3$. Relationships between path length and accuracy are shown in Fig. 8.

$AccSum$ is the sum of values of $acc1$, $acc2$ and $acc3$. Form the graph, we could obtain the conclusion that prediction accuracy is concerned with the path length which is from Ps to Pe. As path length increased, the accuracy decreased.

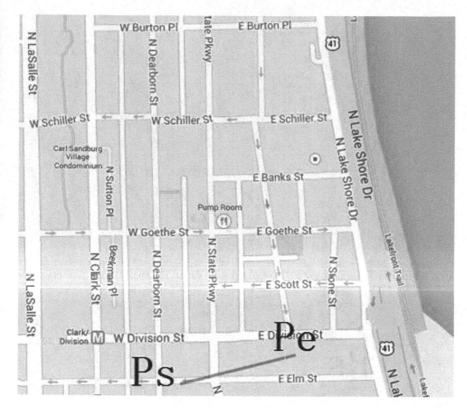

Fig. 6 Test 3

5.3 Time Filter: Accuracy on Each Test Path

For different times, people may do different kinds of things. In this case we give the prediction to the paths of general experiment constrained by time [6] to enhance the prediction accuracy. In the four tests, all check-ins are created from 17:00 to 22:30. In big cities like New York and Chicago, it may be the most bustling period. Compared with General Experiment, result is shown in the following Figs. 9, 10, 11, 12. From the Figures, we could know whether the time filter enhanced the prediction accuracy.

6 Conclusion

With the rapid development of mobile Internet, location-based services are becoming more and more intelligent, which puts forward higher requirements for location prediction technology. This paper mainly uses the Foursquare database and

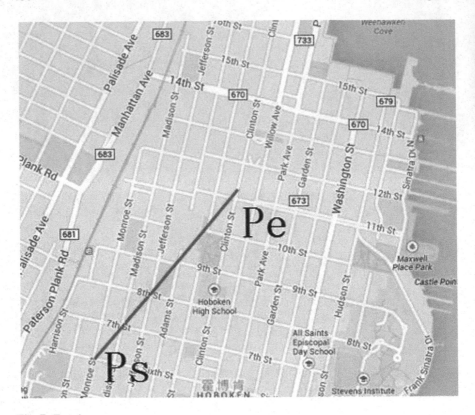

Fig. 7 Test 4

Table 2 Results of Test 1

Test 1 result

lat	lng	Num	Probability (%)
40.7713	−73.9821	18	8.955
40.7678	−73.9823	14	6.965
40.76225	−73.9861	8	3.980
40.7747	−73.9818	5	2.488
40.77255	−73.9843	4	1.990
Total Num		201	

Table 3 Results of Test 2

Test 2 result

lat	lng	Num	Probability (%)
40.7608	−73.9879	16	7.306
40.76437	−73.9869	10	4.566
40.7597	−73.9859	6	2.740
40.76315	−73.9841	6	2.740
40.76169	−73.9911	4	1.826
Total Num		219	

Table 4 Results of Test 3

Test 1 result			
lat	lng	Num	Probability (%)
41.90196	−87.62853	22	9.13
41.90396	−87.63008	22	9.13
41.90273	−87.6319	11	4.56
41.9039	−87.629	9	3.73
41.89373	−87.63565	7	2.9
Total Num		241	

Table 5 Results of Test 4

Test 1 result			
lat	lng	Num	Probability (%)
40.7451	−74.0383	25	32.895
40.751	−74.0316	22	28.947
40.74863	−74.0316	10	13.158
40.74606	−74.0279	3	3.947
40.73689	−74.0311	3	3.947
Total Num		76	

Table 6 Results of various lengths and accuracies

	Distance (m)		Latitude	Longitude
Path 1	320	Ps	40.72921	−73.99197
		Pe	40.75756	−74.00024
Path 2	400	Ps	40.7256	−73.9992
		Pe	40.72235	−73.99663
Path 3	600	Ps	40.76012	−73.98468
		Pe	40.76105	−73.97742
Path 4	1200	Ps	40.7653	−73.97567
		Pe	40.75763	−73.98576
Path 5	1700	Ps	40.69548	−73.96719
		Pe	40.711	−73.96487
Path 6	2200	Ps	40.76457	−73.99599
		Pe	40.75478	−73.97332
Path 7	3500	Ps	40.76308	−73.97981
		Pe	40.73603	−74.00173

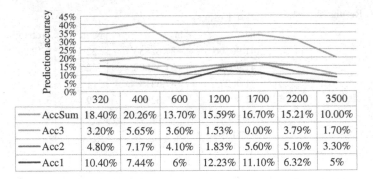

	320	400	600	1200	1700	2200	3500
AccSum	18.40%	20.26%	13.70%	15.59%	16.70%	15.21%	10.00%
Acc3	3.20%	5.65%	3.60%	1.53%	0.00%	3.79%	1.70%
Acc2	4.80%	7.17%	4.10%	1.83%	5.60%	5.10%	3.30%
Acc1	10.40%	7.44%	6%	12.23%	11.10%	6.32%	5%

Fig. 8 Results of various lengths and accuracies

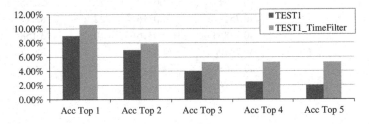

Fig. 9 Test 1 comparison

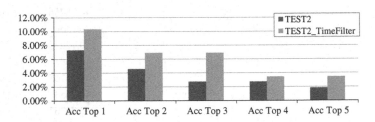

Fig. 10 Test 2 comparison

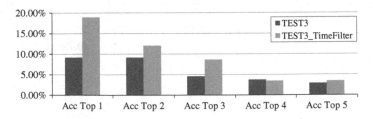

Fig. 11 Test 3 comparison

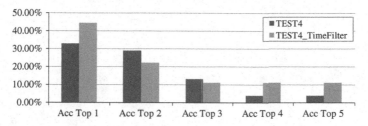

Fig. 12 Test 4 comparison

new algorithm to predict the use's next location. We report a set of experiments with different factors on the new method and we find that when the time factor is considered in the prediction, the results will be more accurate.

Acknowledgments The authors of this paper are thankful to the financial supports of the grant offered with code: MYRG2015-00024, called "Building Sustainable Knowledge Networks through Online Communities" by RDAO, University of Macau.

References

1. Chong W-H, Dai B-T, Lim E-P (2015) Prediction of venues in foursquare using flipped topic models. Advances in information retrieval, volume 9022 of the series lecture notes in computer science, pp 623–634
2. He W, Liu X, Ren M (2011) Location cheating: a security challenge to location-based social network services. In: ICDCS'11 proceedings of the 2011 31st international conference on distributed computing systems, Washington DC, USA, pp 740–749
3. Cramer H, Rost M, Holmquist LE (2011) Performing a check-in: emerging practices, norms and 'conflicts' in location-sharing using foursquare. In: Proceedings of the 13th international conference on human computer interaction with mobile devices and services, ACM New York, NY, USA, pp 57–66
4. Calliess J-P, Osborne M, Roberts SJ (2014) Conservative collision prediction and avoidance for stochastic trajectories in continuous time and space. In: Proceedings of the 2014 international conference on autonomous agents and multi-agent systems, pp 1109–1116
5. Piórkowski M, Grossglauser M (2006) Constrained tracking on a road network. Wireless sensor networks, volume 3868 of the series lecture notes in computer science, pp 148–163
6. Guarino Lo Bianco C, Wahl FM (2011) A novel second order filter for the real-time trajectory scaling. In: 2011 IEEE international conference on robotics and automation (ICRA), 9–13 May 2011, pp 5813–5818

Dependence Analysis for Web Services Data Mutation Testing

Bo Yang

Abstract Testing web services is more challenging compared to traditional systems due to the absence of source code and the complexity of web services. In this paper, a dependency analysis approach is presented in web services data mutation testing. The approach at first analyzes the OWL-S (and related OWL specifications) to extract the ontology definitions associated with I/O parameters of SUT (System Under Test). Then it derives the input data syntax dependency, and semantic constraints on class, property, and parameter dependency from such ontology definitions and TCN-3 functional test suite. Base on the analysis of these dependency information, generates invalid inputs according to the dependency analysis. At last automates the test execution by using the interaction scenarios defined in TTCN-3 functional test cases to achieve invalid input injection and test verdict determination. We conducted a case study on web services use this approach. In the case study, our proposal is supported by three experiments in which web services have been tested. The preliminary results show that our approach is feasible and effective.

Keywords Dependency analysis · Web services testing · Data mutation · TTCN-3 · OWL-S

1 Introduction

A web service is a software system designed to support interoperable machine-to-machine interaction over a network [1]. The aim of web services is to provide a general technical platform across hereditary infrastructures independent of operating platform or programming language. Applications deployed on different platforms could be interconnected and integrated based on this common technol-

B. Yang (✉)
College of Computer Sciences, North China University
of Technology, Beijing 100144, China
e-mail: yangbo090313@163.com

© Springer Science+Business Media Singapore 2016
J.J. (Jong Hyuk) Park et al. (eds.), *Advanced Multimedia and Ubiquitous Engineering*, Lecture Notes in Electrical Engineering 393,
DOI 10.1007/978-981-10-1536-6_98

ogy. With the growing number of web service software systems, if its quality could not be guaranteed, the consequences would be disastrous. The testing is an important means to ensure software quality. Web service testing is accepted to be more complex to the traditional systems testing. It brings new challenges to software testing [2–4]. Mutation testing is a very effective testing technique for testing web services. This technique had been proposed by Richard DeMillo and his colleagues as a testing technique in 1978 [5]. It has been empirically found to be the most effective in detecting faults [6].

Data Mutation is one of the approaches of mutation testing, But like the other mutation testing techniques, data mutation testing also face similar difficulties, which are hampered by many testers. Therefore, it is an approach which needs to use data mutation testing for testing web services efficiently whether web service still meets the users' requirements in both functional and non-functional aspects. A strategy must be chosen to find an effective data mutation for web services testing, because injecting in all of input data would be a great effort. The strategy proposed is an adaptation of chaining based on dependencies analysis [7], to reduce the portions of a data mutation operators and data mutation test cases.

Several approaches have been proposed for testing web services using mutation techniques [8–10]. While our work shares much in common with these approaches. In this paper we apply dependency analysis approach in data mutation testing, and present an experiment in which web services have been analyzed to evaluate the effectiveness of this approach. Which provide some evidence to suggest dependency analysis for web service data mutation testing that could be used to inform the on-going testing process.

The rest of the paper is organized as follows. We start by discussing the generation of dependency graph is described. Next presents dependence analysis approach for web service data mutation. In Sect. 3, a case study is discussed. Finally, in Sect. 4, we present the conclusion and discuss future work.

2 Dependence Analysis for Web Services Data Mutation Testing

2.1 Generate Dependency Graph

This section highlights the features of the dependence graph generate framework as developed within in this work. The framework describes an information process with four distinct stages i.e. initialization OWL-S and WSDL files, getting interface information, getting semantic information, and generating dependency information —which includes input data syntax dependency, and semantic constraints on class, property, and parameter dependency from such ontology definitions. Two major changes compared to other dependency analyses practices are proposed, i.e. (i) many kinds of dependency relationship, which is the base of data mutation cost reduction; (ii) by adding the ontology knowledge to dependency analysis, in order to get accurate information about dependency.

During the initial step of the dependency analysis, the SUT specifications including WSDL, OWL-S should be identified, and organized with respect to the later information. Interface of web services should include input data, output data, preconditions, and fault hander of servers that should be extracted from SUT specifications. According to the mapping between "operation" in WSDL and "AtomicProcess" in OWL-S, we could find the ontology definitions of input and output, along with precondition and fault hander, which are associated with the semantic information. Taking as inputs the ontology definitions of IOPE, as well as the related domain ontology, the test generation process extracts a set of semantic constraints from them. Such constraints could be divided into Class Constraint, Property Constraint, Property Cardinality Constraint, and Parameter Dependency Constraint. Based on the extracted semantic information, the dependency relationships are generated by applying a dependency analysis approach. Finally, we could get dependence graphs from dependency information. The service generation process will be presented in the next section.

2.2 Dependency Analysis for Testing

Test cases can be classified into two categories in this study, according to their dependence information. One needs to mutate, the other one needs not to mutate. Chain based scoring is used to identify test cases. This approach calculates affected-by chains and affects chains for every server.

Definition 1 (CHAIN-SCORE) Given a test case T, the chain-score is based on the following formula (1):

$$CS = \frac{AB + AC}{TC}. \tag{1}$$

Where AB is the number of affected-by chains, AC is the number of affect chains, and TC is the number of total chains. A high CS indicates that the observation on the test case is important.

Reducing the cost of mutation testing techniques are divided into two categories. One is reduction of the generated mutants; the other is reduction of the execution cost. In general, however, data mutation cost is spent mostly in choosing test suit size. A set of initial test cases must be prepared as the seed for the generation of more test cases before data mutation [15]. As such, the test suit size for mutation is smaller; the cost for mutation is lower. In addition, another key factor that needs to be incorporated into the above discussion of costs is the mutation operators for mutation operators which play an import role in mutation testing.

For data mutation, the improvement of mutation efficiency includes reducing reasonable both the costs of choosing test suit and the size of the mutation operators. In order to know dependence relationships by dependence analysis, we conduct a study in which a part of test cases are selected in terms of these relationships, as they relate to web service interfaces or operations. The objective of this study is to identify those test cases that are more clearly mutated.

The selecting mutation test suite process comprises a sequence of the following activities. The static service dependency graph is generated by applying a dependency analysis approach. The next step of the process is to generate dynamic service dependency graph by executing functional test suite. This static graph is limited to rank functional test suite because the guidance on which dependency information is based indicates that in static way should not be used to draw definitive conclusions about the relationship between test case and server. The dynamic graphs are also limited to because of there are a lot of test cases with mutation flow that many service interfaces are invoked abnormally, and the ranking test case should be confusing if have no static dependency graph.

And then, ranking test cases and consider two sets separately, one is the mutation test cases, which ranking value is greater than threshold; the other is the test cases which cannot be mutated and ranking value is less than threshold. The process of selecting mutation test cases is iterative, if mutation test suite could not comply with evaluation criterion after executing. The threshold should be modified until the result is satisfactory.

The data mutation testing on procedure requires a more automatically approach to how invalid input data is achieved, and how this data is mutated. The two problems should not only be judged by special computer language, but also by special approaches. A number of mutation operations and rules based on TTCN-3 are proposed for obtaining invalid input data and mutating data.

A mutation operator is defined as a function MO which could mutate the input data of test cases. The MO's output is the invalid data MTD = MO (TS, FLD, P). Where TS is a test case, FLD is a particular field of the test case, and P is a parameter which to modify a FLD in the seed data of TS.

The mutation operators work on test data model (TDM) which based on TTCN-3 types. For all 14 TTCN-3 metatypes, 48 mutation operators are designed in this paper.

2.3 Selective Mutation

Mutation operators generate different number of mutants, and some of there mutants turn out to be redundant [17]. In addition to reduce the data mutation costs of performing a given seed test cases selective technology, the study also seeks to find a small set of mutation operators that generate a subset of all possible mutants without significant loss of test effectiveness.

The first steps of mutation selective approach takes input data of a test case as input. The approach then proceeds to example what is known about constrains of type for each individual input data, including value constrains, length constrains, optional constrains, and sequence constrains. These constrains are based on TTCN-3 and can obtain from data dependency graph which contains semantic constraints on class, property, and parameter dependency.

For each input data several parameters can be selected by constrains. For example, if a parameter has value constrains, the inside and outside of value is selected; if the value is a range, the boundary values and their adjacent values are also used; if a parameter has a length constrains, the upper and lower boundary of value length is selected. In addition, the parameter which can be selected is not only the data type, but also data encoding format, such as delimiters and string format. These selected parameters can produce invalid data aimed at delimiter parsing bugs and format string vulnerabilities. In order to mutate a given test data, mutation operations need to work beside selected parameters. For the type of each field of the selected parameters, suitable mutation operators can pick out by user defined selection strategy which including round robin selection, random selection, weighted random selection (for example, the risk-aware selection strategy and feedback-directed selection (modify the selection adaptively according to previous test results). The approach iterates the above process until the number of mutation rules reaches a user defined threshold. The output of the approach is a set of mutation rules.

3 Case Study

In this section, the effectiveness of the approach is evaluated and compare it with random selection strategies first proposed by Budd [19]. Five open-source web services programs that are publicly available on the Internet [20], namely MediCare Supplier, FedACH, Fedwire, GeoIPService, StockQuote. The five web services are frequently used in the Internet without source code, and each of them applies the one or more operations separately.

The aim of approach in this study is to reduce the cost-consuming of data mutation for web services testing. Hence, this approach needs to be examined by metrics that related to data mutation, and applied to real application by providing means to measure these criterions. In the following, metrics of approach in this study is presented.

The live mutant score is selected in this study, which is defined in formula (2), Where LM is the number of live mutants, TM is the total number of mutants, and EM is the number of equivalent mutants.

$$LMS = \frac{LM - EM}{TM - EM}.$$

(2)

Accepted rate is defined in formula (3), indicates that the mutation test cases accepted by SUT.

$$ACR = \frac{A}{A+R}.$$ (3)

Where ACR is the accepted rate, A is the number of test cases that accepted by SUT, D is the number of test cases that rejected by SUT. A low ACR indicates that the observation on the tolerance of SUT is insufficient.

Exception handling coverage rate is defined in formula (4), indicates that the mutation test cases enter into the exception handling of a software system.

$$EHC = \frac{C}{C+U}.$$ (4)

Where EHC is the exception handling coverage rate, C is the number of test cases that enter into the exception handling of the system, U is the number of test cases that does not enter. A low EHC indicates that the observation on the mutation test suite is insufficient.

In order to get such invalid inputs, we used the weight based selection strategy combined with feedback direction. The weight for each kind of mutation operator represented the probability of attack by the invalid inputs generated by such operator. Because a large number of string fields are defined in the web service message has proved prone to string, we assigned a high weight to the mutation operators associated with string type. During test process, the weight could be dynamically adjusted according to how many problems have been revealed by the invalid inputs. Once the type needs to mutate is generated, the number of mutation operations generated by the DMT tool, and number of mutation rules obtained by the given strategy. The results are summarized in Table 1.

The affected chains of the server or operation can be as monitors. These monitors should be observed to detect the outgoing data and raised exceptions that will be seen by the users. The test verdict will be obtained by analysis these monitors. The number of equivalent mutants, number of umber of live mutants, and number of live mutants with a specific type of mutation operators generated. In order to obtain

Table 1 Mutation information

Server	Dependency analysis			Random selection		
	Seed test cases	MO	MR	Seed test cases MO		MR
MediCare supplier	5	2	37	5	3	48
FedACH	8	3	52	11	5	60
Fedwire	3	2	26	5	2	33
GeoIPService	2	2	21	2	3	29

Table 2 The metric information of experiment 2

Server	Dependency analysis			Random selection		
	LMS	ACR	EHC	LMS	ACR	EHC
MediCare supplier	0.55	0.351	0.243	0.607	0.562	0.125
FedACH	0.475	0.423	0.173	0.489	0.516	0.116
Fedwire	0.60	0.346	0.192	0.773	0.394	0.09
GeoIPService	0.375	0.476	0.238	0.455	0.517	0.138

the exception handling coverage rate, runtime information should be collected by monitor tool. The results are summarized in Table 2.

From Tables 1 and 2, it is seen that the number of seed test cases, MO and MR with dependency analysis approach is smaller than random selection approach. At the same time, The LMS value with dependency analysis is lower than random selection. The ACR and the EHC value with dependency analysis is higher than random selection.

4 Conclusion

In this article we have tried to show that the dependency analysis provides a useful conceptual approach for dealing with the web service data mutation testing. The dependency analysis incorporates some of the central concepts in the mutation testing, and it defines these concepts in a way that permits reduction and effectiveness of particular process in data mutation testing. Attitudes toward the seed test cases selective, mutation selective, and mutation operations based on TTCN-3 data types with respect to the effective of data mutation, especially absence of source code like web services, is shown a significant preference. The general conclusion is that there are need functional test suite based on TTCN-3 which test adequacy is satisfactory, if not met, can lead to a result unexpected. Future work will focus on these directions. Moreover, another direction is analysis of mutation equivalence with dependency information.

Acknowledgments This work supported by National Natural Science Foundation of China (No.61502011), Scientific Research Project of Beijing Educational Committee (No. KM201610009007), The plan project of Beijing college students' scientific deep research (No. XN003-16).

References

1. Dong W (2009) Testing wsdl-based web service automatically 3:521–525
2. Ladan MI (2010) Web services testing approaches: a survey and a classification. In: Networked digital technologies 2, volume 88 of communications in computer and information science. Springer-Verlag, Berlin, pp 70–79

3. Bai X, Dong W, Tsai WT, Chen Y (2005) Wsdl-based automatic test case generation for web services testing. 2005:215–220
4. Tsai WT, Bai XY, Chen YN, Zhou XY (2005) Web service group testing with windowing mechanisms. In Celballos S (ed) SOSE 2005: IEEE international workshop on service-oriented system engineering, 2005. Beijing, pp 213–218, 20–21 Oct 2005
5. DeMillo RA, Lipton RJ, Sayward FG (1978) Hints on test data selection: help for the practicing programmer. Computer 11(4):34–41
6. Mathur AP, Wong WE (1995) Reducing the cost of mutation testing: an empirical study. J Syst Softw 31:185–196
7. Stafford JA, Richardson DJ, Wolf AL (1997) Chaining: a software architecture dependence analysis technique. Citeseer
8. Hanna S, Munro M (2008) Fault-based web services testing. In: Fifth international conference on information technology: new generations, 2008. ITNG 2008, pp 471 476
9. Xu W, Offutt J, Luo J (2005) Testing web services by xml perturbation. In: 16th IEEE international symposium on software reliability engineering, 2005. ISSRE 2005, pp 10, pp -266
10. da Silva Solino AL, Vergilio SR (2009) Mutation based testing of web services. In: 10th Latin American test workshop, 2009. LATW '09, pp 1–6

Does the Speed of Problems Comment Affect GitHub Open Source Software Development Process?

Bo Yang, Gang Meng, Wei Zhang and Runze Du

Abstract There are more than 12 million open source software in GitHub so far. Many studies analyzed the impact factors in development process of GitHub open source software. However, there is a lack of correlation analysis between impact factors. In this paper we propose an approach to analysis the correlation of between the speed of problem comment and the speed of problem solving. It's proving the existence of certain factors among some relevance after experiments.

Keywords GitHub · Impact factors · Correlation analysis · Problem solving · Data mining

1 Introduction

Open source software is a software form based on open source listed within the OSI protocol which allows the user to use, modify the source code and even allows to combine the source code with other software code for use [1]. The rise of open source software has promoted the advancement of software and related technology vigorously. Open source software development has been a great success, all the successes have been verified from WEB server to the mobile operating system and database development and other related technologies [2]. The social development

B. Yang (✉) · W. Zhang · R. Du
College of Computer Sciences, North China University of Technology,
Beijing 100144, China
e-mail: yangbo090313@163.com

W. Zhang
e-mail: 15510625552@163.com

R. Du
e-mail: 137061915@qq.com

G. Meng
Beijing Institute of Remote Sensing Information, Beijing 100192, China
e-mail: menggangmark@126.com

© Springer Science+Business Media Singapore 2016
J.J. (Jong Hyuk) Park et al. (eds.), *Advanced Multimedia and Ubiquitous Engineering*, Lecture Notes in Electrical Engineering 393,
DOI 10.1007/978-981-10-1536-6_99

platform named GitHub is one of the open source software communities, It not only allows individuals and organizations to found and browse code base, but also severs community-based software development capabilities, such as allowing users to follow other users, organizations, dynamic and tracking of bases, changes of the code, Bug and reviews. GitHub also provides Wiki for bases use and co-development project with GitHub [3]. It has more than 12 million open source project on GitHub so far, and the number keeps increasing [4]. The impact factors correlation analysis in GitHub open source software development procession reveal the level and quality progress of GitHub open source software development to a certain degree.

There are many factors affecting the GitHub development process, such as the level of the software developers, the number of software developers, large software companies supporting, commercial enterprises sponsoring, the speed of open source software's problems solving and participated users' encouragement, etc.

This article started from the perspective of analyzing data generated from open source software development process, analyzed the speed of problem comment in GitHub open source software development process, generated problem-solving speed, and analyzed the correlation about these impact factors.

At first we introduced some researches focused on GitHub open source software, and then made a detailed description the method to analyze the correlation of the impact factors in GitHub open source software development process. Section 4 utilized the methods to do some experiment and made a detailed analysis about the results of the experiment. At last, summarize the whole paper, and prospects for the future work.

2   Related Work

The advent of distributed version control system gave the birth of the open-source software and to promote its development [4]. Open source software and traditional software differ in many respects [5, 6]. Many scholars studied focus on a variety of characteristics of open source software. Mockus et al. [7] made a research of how the developers interact with each other in large software development process. Krishanmurthy [8] analyzed the before 100 open source soft-ware in Sourceforge. net, and obtained composition of open source software developers and managers.

Hars and Ou [9] made a research of the motivation that the open source software could keep develop, and obtained the inner motivation is altruism, he sense of identity in open source community, the external motivation is the contributor being optimistic about the future development of open source software as well as personal needs. von Krogh et al. [10] made a research of the encouragement the contributor needed, and pointed that kind of encouragement came from the demand for software improvement and fun incentive to participate in discussions in source software development process. Sohn and Mok [11] used the traditional software quality evaluation system named ISO/IEC9126, and made a research for the effect of the quality factors in open source software for users application, the result evidenced that the quality factors including functionality, effectiveness and sharing etc. have a significant direct impact on users application, and the other quality factors such as software portability, reliability and serviceability have the in-direct impact for users. Subramaniam et al. [12] made a research of the success factors of open source software, pointed there are 2 kinds of factors: time-invariant variables and time-varying variable, time-invariant variables include the programming language used, license type used, time-varying variables include the development process of the software project and the number of users on the previous period etc. Crowston et al. [13] made a research about the reasons for the ultimate failure of some open source software, pointed that the communication quality of users participated between the inter-core contributors of open source software is the key to success. Because the GitHub character is pull-request, which made the character of research in development process of open source software appeared. Dabbish et al. [14] found the transparency of GitHub made contributors can manage the development process of the project better. Pham et al. [15] found that there is much similarity between open source software and traditional software development process, however, the difference is that the open source software development process is faster in modify and refresh. Gousios et al. [16] made a research of software development model based on push, pointed there are many advantages to base on this kind of model (such as GitHub), for example, they could make communication between contributors more frequently.

From all the researches listed, we can know that many researchers are focused on the impact factors in open source software development process, however, they ignored the correlation between these factors. The analysis of the correlation between the factors can certainly help contributors do better in development and maintenance process, and may improve the efficiency and quality of the open source software development job.

In this paper we focus on the speed of problem comment and the speed of problem solving. We want to find the correlation of them. Therefore, this paper proposes the following special research questions:

RQ1. What are the speed of problem comment and the speed of problem solving in open source software development process?
RQ2. Are there any correlations between these impact actors? If yes, what correlations do they have?

In response to these research questions, this paper will make a detailed analysis.

3   The Speed of Problem Comment and the Speed of Problem Solving

3.1   *GitHub Open Source Software Development Process*

In GitHub open source software development process a large amount of data will be generated, these data can reflect the impact factors in the development process. To obtain these data and Mining, we need to analyze the development process of GitHub open source software. Generally, there are many work process to develop a GitHub open source software, the Fig. 1 is a typically GitHub work process, there are 5 steps included—**discuss, specify, carry out, check out** and **iterate** after problem-solving. The developers need to discuss to make sure what function they need to change or add; After the discussion, they need to specify an issue about the function; Then they need to carry out to make the change; After they finished, the function need to be checked out; Finally, they would merge the function into the master. After analyzed the work processes, we could found the factors impact the development process of GitHub open source software. Then the formal definition GitHub workflow was given.

Def1: GitHub workflow (GHW)

GitHub workflow can be presented as GHW = {S, P, M, N}, S presented submit, can be presented by S = {s_num, comment_s, author}, and s_num means the number submitted, comment_s is the comment about submit, author means the person who submit the job.

P is the problem discussed, be presented as P = {des, comment_p, sta}, des means the description of the problem, comment_p means the comment of the problem, sta means the status of the problem.

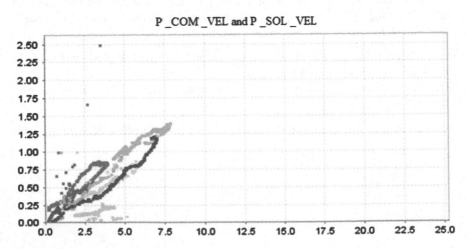

Fig. 1   The relationship of the speed of problems comment and problems solving

M means request to merge, can be presented as M = {add_m, del_m, comment_m,m_id}, add_m means the number of lines increasing in merge process, del_s means the number of lines descending in merge process, comment_m means the comments of the merge process, m_id means the id number of the merge request.

N means the number of developers. From the analysis of S, P, M and N, the content in GitHub workflow can be specify, then the formal definition of S, P, M and N will be given.

3.2 The Speed of Problem Comment and the Speed of Problem Solving

Def2: The speed of problems commented (P_COM_VEL)

P_COM_VEL means in a part of time (recorded as d) the average number of the problem commented. P_COM_VEL can be calculated as:

$$P\_COM\_VEL = \frac{comment\_p\_all}{d} \tag{1}$$

comment_p_all the amount of the comment in d, d means the number of days in this part of time.

Def3: The speed of problem solving (P_SOL_VEL)

P_SOL_VEL means in a part of time (recorded as d) the average number of the problems solved. P_SOL_VEL can be calculated as:

$$P\_SOL\_VEL = \frac{p\_sol\_all}{d} \tag{2}$$

p_sol_all means the amount of problems solved, d means the number of days in this part of time.

The speed of problem commends P_COM_VEL and the speed of problem solving P_SOL_VEL After analyzed the correlation between P_COM_VEL and P_SOL_VEL, we can know that following with the increasing of problem commend, the speed of problem solving will get faster. During analyze the correlation between P_COM_VEL and P_SOL_VEL, we made the P_COM_VEL as X-axis and P_SOL_VEL as Y-axis. Then we map the chart as the data we grabbed, in that way we could know if there are correlation between these two factors.

4 Case Study

In order to facilitate experiments, we made a tool which can grab and analyze the data from GitHub open source software development process named Ghda. Our experiment chose 8 GitHub open source software including AFNetworking, bottle, GPUImage, pop, Mantle, paramiko, ActionBarSherlock and cancan. The size of these software from 2000 to 640,138 KB. The interval of these data open source software from 1 year to nearly 6 years, the specific information in the following Table 1. There are 8 rows in the chart, in the first row is the names of these software. Introduction refers to a description of the main functions of the open-source software. Size refers to the size of open source software, In KB. Refers to the number of collection was commended on GitHub. Concern refers on GitHub to be concerned about (watch) times. Copy indicates the number of copies on the GitHub fork. Creation date showing on GitHub repository creation date. Updated on GitHub repository represents the most recent update dates

The results shown in Fig. 1, all eight warehouses exist the phenomenon that problem comments faster, and their problems solving faster.

Table 1 List of open source software

Name	Summary	Size	Attention	Watch	Copy	Created time	Updated time
AFNetuorking	A delightful networking framework for iOS	640,138	17,913	1407	5299	2011-06-01	2015-06-10
Bottle	Authentication module for the bottle and flask web frameworks	9373	2962	219	598	2009-07-01	2013-05-27
GPUImage	An open source iOS framework for GPU-based image and video processing	52,907	8858	362	2154	2012-02-13	2015-05-27
Pop	An extensible iOS and OS X animation library	2836	11,455	872	1617	2014-03-31	2015-06-10
Mantle	Model framework for Cocoa and Cocoa Touch	64,338	6762	350	795	2012-09-05	2015-05-27
Paramiko	Native python SSHv2 protocol library	8445	1796	166	525	2009-02-12	2015-05-27
ActionBarSherlock	Action bar implementation	18,403	6869	845	3989	2011-03-08	2014-12-20
Cancan	Authorization gem for ruby on rails	8361	5838	182	809	2009-11-17	2013-09-06

5 Conclusion

We analyzed the impact factors in GitHub open source software development process, proposed the speed of problem comment and the speed of problem solving. By the experiment about the typical GitHub open source software, we got some positive conclusions of GitHub open source software development process. Since GitHub open source software development process is very complex, this article certainly there are still some where for improvement. In the follow up study, we will think about more about the impact factors and their correlation.

Acknowledgments This work supported by National Natural Science Foundation of China (No. 61502011), Scientific Research Project of Beijing Educational Committee (No. KM201610009007). The plan project of Beijing college students' scientific deep research (No. XN003-16).

References

1. Berglund E, Priestley M (2001) Open-source documentation: in search of user-driven, just-in-time writing. In: SIGDOC
2. Sen R, Singh SS, Borle S (2012) Open source software success: measures and analysis. Decis Support Syst 52:364–372
3. Heller B, Marschner E, Rosenfeld E, Heer J (2011) Visualizing collaboration and influence in the open-source software community. In: MSR
4. Bird C, Rigby PC, Barr ET, Hamilton DJ, Germran DM, Devanbu PT (2009) The promises and perils of mining git. In: MSR
5. Zhou M (2012) Looking for micro-process in large-scale data. In: The 2nd international workshop on evidential assessment of software technologies
6. Kalliamvakou E, Gousios G, Blincoe K, Singer L, Germran DM, Damian D (2014) The promises and perils of mining GitHub. In: MSR
7. Mockus A, Fielding RT, Herbsleb JD (2002) Two case studies of open source software development: Apache and mozilla. ACM Trans Softw Eng Methodol 11:309–346
8. Krishnamurthy S (2002) Cave or community? An empirical examination of 100 mature open source projects. First Monday, 7, 2002
9. Hars A, Ou S (2001) Working for free? Motivations of participating in open source projects. In: HICSS
10. von Krogh G, Haeiger S, Spaeth S, Wallin MW (2012) Carrots and rainbows: motivation and social practice in open source software development. MIS Q 36:649–676
11. Sohn SY, Mok MS (2008) A strategic analysis for successful open source software utilization based on a structural equation model. J Syst Softw 81:1014–1024
12. Subramaniam C, Sen R, Nelson ML (2009) Determinants of open source software project success: a longitudinal study. Decis Support Syst 46:576–585
13. Crowston K, Wei K, Howison J, Wiggins A (2012) Free/libre open-source software development: what we know and what we do not know. ACM Comput Surv 44:7
14. Dabbish L, Stuart HC, Tsay J, Herbsleb JD (2013) Leveraging transparency. IEEE Softw 30:37–43
15. Pham R, Singer L, Liskin O, Figueira Filho FM, Schneider K (2013) Creating a shared understanding of testing culture on a social coding site. In: ICSE
16. Gousios G, Pinzger M, Deursen A (2014) An exploratory study of the pull-based software development model. In: ICSE

Analysis of RNA Pseudoknots with a Context-Sensitive Grammar

Keum-Young Sung

Abstract In this study, a context-sensitive grammar is suggested to analyze some patterns and configurations of RNA secondary structures. The use of context-sensitive grammar to analyze pseudoknots allows us to represent RNA structures more naturally comparing with a conventional approach of using Stochastic context-free grammar to model pseudoknots. The suggested technique directly reflects the characteristic appearance of several forms of RNA secondary structure, i.e., hairpins, internal loops, double helixes, and bulge loops.

Keywords Context free grammar · Context-sensitive grammar · Pseudoknots · RNA sequence

1 Introduction

1.1 DNA and RNA

The DNA consists of sugar phosphate backbone on the outside of the helix and four nitrogenous bases on the inside of the double strand [1]. The ladder part, rung, is composed of two base pairs, adenosine (A)-thymine (T) pair and cytosine (C)-guanine (G) pair. When the DNA is replicated into RNA, the helix is separated and matched into RNA as in Fig. 1.

The process of making protein, which is called protein synthesis, consists of three stages, i.e., transcription, splicing, and translation. In the transcription phase, one DNA sequence is replicated to a complementary RNA which is called pre mRNA. In the splicing phase, the introns (the non-coding region) of the pre mRNA are removed, and the remaining exons (coding region) are connected together, which becomes mRNA. Today, the introns are believed to play some role to express

K.-Y. Sung (✉)
Handong Global University, Pohang, South Korea
e-mail: kysung@handong.edu

© Springer Science+Business Media Singapore 2016
J.J. (Jong Hyuk) Park et al. (eds.), *Advanced Multimedia and Ubiquitous Engineering*, Lecture Notes in Electrical Engineering 393,
DOI 10.1007/978-981-10-1536-6_100

Fig. 1 Double stranded
DNA sequences and RNA

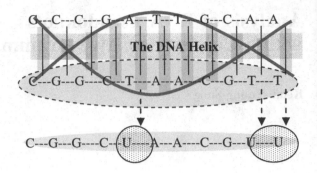

genes, which was regarded as junk in the early days [2]. The protein is synthesized
in the translation phase by joining together amino acid encoded in the mRNA.

1.2 Pseudoknots and Context-Free Grammar

The recognition and prediction of RNA secondary structure, especially RNA
pseudoknots, plays an important role in protein synthesis, e.g., ribosomal
frameshifting, an infectious or tumor virus, a mutation of HIV, RNA-protein
interaction, etc. [3]. Various forms of context-free grammars have been used to
recognize and model RNA sequence [4]. Pseudoknots are tertiary RNA sequence
consisting of base pairing between a secondary loop structure and complimentary
bases outside the loop. Conventionally context-free grammars have been used to
identify the secondary structure of RNA molecules from the given nucleotide
sequence when we consider an RNA sequence as a string (or a valid sentence) of a
programming language. There are typical types of pseudoknots, i.e., an interior
loop, a bulge loop, a hairpin loop, and a helix.

The context-free grammar has been used to define the syntactic definition of a
programming language. The grammar is a major tool for a parser to build a parse
tree to check if the given string is a valid sentence [5]. The whole leaves of a parse
tree constitute a sentence of the language defined by the grammar. It consists of a
starting non-terminal, production rules, a set of non-terminals, and a set of terminals. Left hand side (LHS) and right hand side (RHS) comprise a production rule as
shown below.

LHS_Nonterminal → a Sequence of Grammar Symbols

Following is a context-free grammar for an RNA language, in which S_A is
related to A-U pair, and S_G is related to A-U pair and C-G pair.

$S \rightarrow S_A \mid S_G$
$S_A \rightarrow A\ S_A\ U \mid U\ S_A\ A \mid A\ S_G\ U \mid U\ S_G\ A \mid S_I\ S_H \mid S_H\ S_I \mid PIN$
$S_G \rightarrow G\ S_G\ C \mid C\ S_G\ G \mid G\ S_A\ C \mid C\ S_A\ G \mid G\ S_H\ S_I\ C \mid C\ S_H\ S_I\ G \mid PIN$
$S_H \rightarrow A\ S_H\ U \mid U\ S_H\ A \mid A\ S_A\ U \mid U\ S_A\ A \mid S_I \mid PIN$

$S_I \rightarrow G\ S_I\ C\ |\ C\ S_I\ G|\ C\ S_G\ G\ |\ G\ S_G\ C\ |\ S_H\ |\ PIN$
$PIN \rightarrow LEFT\_SKEW\ |\ RIGHT\_SKEW$
$LEFT\_SKEW \rightarrow S_I\ A\ |\ S_I\ U\ |\ S_I\ G\ |\ S_I\ C\ |\ PIN\ |\ TERMINAL$
$RIGHT\_SKEW \rightarrow A\ S_H\ |\ U\ S_H\ |\ G\ S_H\ |\ C\ S_H\ |\ PIN\ |\ TERMINAL$
$TERMINAL \rightarrow A\ |\ U\ |\ G\ |\ C$

The above grammar formulates the paring of nucleotides, A-U and C-G which constitute base parings, and unpaired nucleotides which forms pseudoknots represented by the PIN non-terminal. The parse tree in Fig. 2 generated with a given grammar shows base pairing regions and unpaired hairpin regions. As the name, context-free grammar, implies, the non-terminals on the left-hand side of a production rule does not consider the context in which it is situated. Figure 3 shows the derivation of the hairpin using a simplified parse tree based on the given grammar.

In Fig. 5, the part surrounded by dashed circle-line comprises non-paired nucleotides and the one surrounded by solid circle represents paired region of RNA.

Fig. 2 A parse tree construction of a pseudoknot

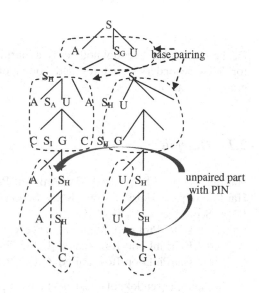

Fig. 3 The secondary structure derived from the parse tree

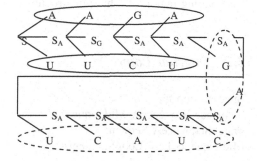

1.3 Stochastic Context Free Grammar and Hidden Markov Model

The hidden Markov model (HMM) and Stochastic context free grammar (SCFG) have been used to predict and analyze RNA sequence. The HMM is an extension of regular language with probabilistic approach and the SCFG is an extension of context free grammar with probability assigned to each alternative right-hand side of production rule [6, 7]. For both approaches, there needs a dataset for determining probability factors for a deterministic finite automaton for HMM and the right hand side of a production rule for SCFG. The SCFG has more power to predict gene sequence than HMM because context-free grammar allows recursion while regular language does not allow recursion.

2 A Context-Sensitive Grammar for the Structure of Pseudoknots

Of the four typical pseudoknots, only a hairpin and an internal loop are illustrated for RNA secondary structures and corresponding context-sensitive sequence of grammar symbols.

2.1 Hairpin

Hairpin_Loop ::= SequenceA HairPinLoop PairedSequenceA
HairPinLoop ::= HairPinLoop | RNA_Sequence
RNA_Sequence := A | U | G | C
SequenceA HairPinLoop PairedSequenceA ::=
A_Paired HairPinLoop Rev_Paired_U | U_Paired HairPinLoop Rev_Paired_A |
G_Paired HairPinLoop Rev_Paired_C | C_Paired HairPinLoop Rev_Paired_G

The hairpin pseudoknot consists of a base-pairing region and a non-paired region (Fig. 4). The nonterminals, SequenceA and PairedSequenceA comprise the base-pairing region of a hairpin structure.

2.2 Internal Loop

InternalLoop ::=
Sequence SequenceA MidSequence1
PairedSequenceA Sequence
MidSequence1 ::= LoopSegmentA

Fig. 4 Hairpin

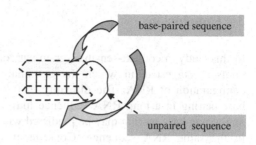

SequenceB Sequence
PairedSequenceB LoopSegmentB
LoopSegmentA ::= LoopSegmentA | RNA_Sequence
RNA_Sequence := A | U | G | C
LoopSegmentB ::= LoopSegmentB | RNA_Sequence
RNA_Sequence := A | U | G | C
SequenceA MidSequence1 PairedSequenceA ::=
A_Paired MidSequence1 Rev_Paired_U |
U_Paired MidSequence1 Rev_Paired_A |
G_Paired MidSequence1 Rev_Paired_C |
C_Paired MidSequence1 Rev_Paired_G |
SequenceB PairedSequenceB ::=
A_Paired Rev_Paired_U |
U_Paired Rev_Paired_A |
G_Paired Rev_Paired_C |
C_Paired Rev_Paired_G |

In Fig. 5, there are two base-pairing regions, i.e., one with SequenceA and PairedSequenceA, and another with SequenceB and PairedSequenceB. The two separate non-paired sequences, LoopSegmentA and LoopSegmentB, make an internal loop.

Fig. 5 Internal loop

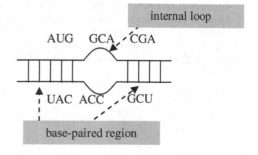

3 Conclusions

In this study, a context-sensitive grammar for analyzing several forms of pseudo-knots is suggested, in which the grammar is to be expanded for more varied configuration of RNA. The difficulty in this study is that the searching time of base-pairing in a long RNA sequence may become prohibitively prolonged, and that wrong base-pairing may be predicted when a variety of pseudoknots are mixed in the same RNA sequence. Consequently, more study for solving indicated problems includes the following:

- The reduction time to arrange base-pairing for a long RNA sequence;
- Accurate matching of a loop in a mixed chain of paired and non-paired nucleotides; and
- Augmentation of the suggested context-sensitive grammar for more various configuration of an RNA pseudoknots.

Even with all the difficulties related to context-sensitivity approach to recognize specific Pseudoknot from a given RNA sequence, the suggested technique introduces more natural way to specify typical configurations of RNA pseudoknots comparing with using a stochastic context-free grammar. With the suggested technique, the pattern of target RNA sequence may be directly described based on context-sensitivity of RNA pseudoknots without the need of determining probabilities that are applied to SCFG and HMM.

References

1. Campbell NA, Mitchell LG, Reece JB (1997) Biology concepts and connections, 2nd edn. Addison Wesley, Boston
2. Fredholm L (2003) The discovery of the molecular structure of DNA—the double helix. http://www.nobelprize.org/
3. Wang C et al (1995) An RNA pseudoknot, an essential structure of the ribosome entry site located within the C virus 5' noncoding region. RNA 1:526–537
4. Kobayashi S, Yokomore T (1994) Modeling RNA secondary structure using tree grammars. In: Proceedings of genome informatics workshop V. University Academy Press, pp 29–38
5. Sipser M (2006) Introduction to the theory of computation, 2nd edn. Thompson, Toronto
6. Durbin R, Eddy S, Krogh A, Mitchinson G (1998) Biological sequence analysis: probabilistic models of proteins and nucleic acids. Cambridge: Cambridge University Press
7. Koski T (2001) Hidden Markov model for bioinformatics. Springer, Berlin

Simplified Way of Learning White-Box Testing with JUnit

Keum-Young Sung

Abstract In this study, a way of using Eclipse JUnit to perform an independent path testing and composite component testing is suggested. The suggested technique simplifies the complex arrangement of variable value setting of independent path testing so that JUnit facility of Eclipse may be conveniently used to perform a white box testing. A way of using JUnit to perform a Java component consisting of several classes with inheritance relationships is also suggested. To make a use of JUnit for the independent path testing several variables included for a testing purpose may be traced to have the similar effect of the independent path testing. Constructor arguments may be used to check right inheritance declarations to test a composite component with layered inheritance relationships. Using the suggested technique, the process to perform independent path testing and composite component testing may be simplified using Eclipse JUnit facility.

Keywords Independent path testing · Eclipse JUnit · White box testing · Black box testing

1 Introduction

1.1 Black Box Testing with JUnit

White box testing and black box testing are fundamental testing methods in software testing, which may be carried out with the Eclipse JUnit facility. White box testing or transparent box testing is to test internal workings of the target software while black box testing does not consider internal program logic [1, 2].

With black box testing internal implementation is not considered, but an interface to the target component is used [3]. JUnit is a Java object for a unit testing

K.-Y. Sung (✉)
Handong Global University, Pohang, South Korea
e-mail: kysung@handong.edu

© Springer Science+Business Media Singapore 2016   783
J.J. (Jong Hyuk) Park et al. (eds.), *Advanced Multimedia and Ubiquitous Engineering*, Lecture Notes in Electrical Engineering 393,
DOI 10.1007/978-981-10-1536-6_101

framework used with Java programming language [4]. The following code for a binary tree searching [5] is a good example to show a test case for a black box testing.

```
public class binTree {
 public static void search ( int key, int [] elemArray, Result r )
  {int bottom = 0 ;
   int top = elemArray.length - 1 ;
   int mid ; r.found = false ;
   r.index = -1 ;
   while ( bottom <= top )
   {  mid = (top + bottom) / 2 ;
    if (elemArray [mid] == key)
   {   r.index = mid ;  r.found = true ;
     return ;  } // if part
    else {  if (elemArray [mid] < key)
       bottom = mid + 1 ; else top = mid - 1 ;  }
   } //while loop
  } // search  }
```

The following is the Result class which is one of the passed parameter to the binary tree class. The Result class is used for recording the result of a searching with the binary tree.

```
public class Result {
 int index; boolean found;
 Result(){ index = 0;found = false;}
 Result(int i, boolean b) {index = i; found = b;};
 }
```

An example black box test case with the Eclipse JUnit is as follows, in which the input data using a target array and a key to be searched is given, and the expected output is given with an assertion:

```
import org.junit.Test;
public class testCaseOutOfRange {
  @Test
  public void test() {
  int[] eleArray = {1,2,3,4,5};
  int key = 6;
  Result r = new Result(0, false);
  binTree.search(key, eleArray, r);
  assertSame("Same key Value",r.found, false  );
  }
 }
```

In the above JUnit code, because a key value which is not in the given array is given to the search tree, the JUnit predicate, "assertSame," asserts that the Boolean variable, found, should be false.

Fig. 1 Independent basis paths

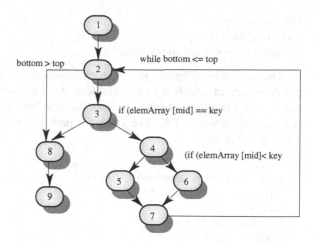

1.2 White Box Testing with JUnit

The flow graph of the given example binary tree in Fig. 1 is well illustrated in [5]:

Based on the cyclomatic complexity [6], the number of paths is the number of decision plus 1, the independent paths of the above flow graph are [5]:

1, 2, 3, 8, 9: path 1
1, 2, 3, 4, 6, 7, 2: path 2
1, 2, 3, 4, 5, 7, 2: path 3
1, 2, 3, 4, 6, 7, 2, 8, 9: path 4

For white box testing based on independent path testing, each path can be tested by adjusting the values of variables that are in the target path. For example, to test path 2 the setting of the variables are as follows:

bottom <= top
elmArray[mid] != key
eleArray[mid] < key'
expected output: control back to node 2

The essence of independent path testing is to minimize the number of paths for testing while all the statements should be tested at least once.

2 Independent Path Testing with JUnit

2.1 Testing a Single Component with JUnit

The suggested technique with JUnit for testing a single component is to make the same condition as the one shown in the original basis path condition. The condition for the path 1 is as given below:

bottom <= top
elmArray[mid] = key
expected output: true, index value

The suggested technique in this study makes use of a loop count variable and a result object, in which a loop variable is for tracking how the program control flows, and a resulting object expresses the searching result with a Boolean value. The running session of Eclipse JUnit for path 1 is given in Fig. 2, and the JUnit code is as below:

```
@Test
public void IndependentPathTesting () {
int[] eleArray = {1,2,3,4,5};
int key = 3;
Result r = new Result(0, false);
binTree.search(key, eleArray, r);
assertSame("Same key Value",r.found, true  );
}
```

The output window of the above figure shows the mid-value of the array index, status of key matching, and the number of loop repetition as follows:

mid value: 2
key value is matched
loop count: 1

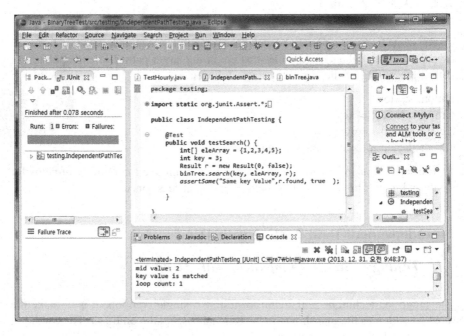

Fig. 2 A white box testing for searching a mid-index key

The output of JUnit reflects exactly the condition of the independent path testing for path 1, which was given as below:

bottom <= top
elmArray[mid] = key
expected output: true, index value

The testing for paths 2 and 3 is prepared with the same procedure, which also makes use of a loop variable to track program control flow, and uses the object of Result class. The JUnit code for testing paths 2 and 3 is as below, and the running session is in Fig. 3.

```
@Test
  public void testSearch() {
  int[] eleArray = {1,2,3,4,5,6,7,8,9};
  int key = 3;
  Result r = new Result(0, false);
  binTree.search(key, eleArray, r);
  assertSame("Same key Value", r.found, true );
  }
```

The output shows the progressive change of array mid value and the number of loop repetition count as below:

mid value: 4
loop count: 1

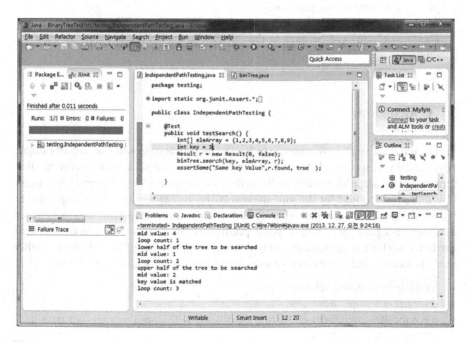

Fig. 3 A white box testing for paths 2 and 3

lower half of the tree to be searched
mid value: 1
loop count: 2
upper half of the tree to be searched
mid value: 2
key value is matched
loop count: 3

The above running result reflects the testing condition of paths 2 and 3 which is as follows:

bottom <= top
elmArray[mid] != key
eleArray[mid] < key or eleArray[mid] > key
expected output: control back to while condition statement

2.2   Composite Component Testing

When we test a composite component consisting of many sub-components, the interface testing is generally used. With the help of the design tool, StartUML [7], inheritance hierarchy can be visualized. Using the visualized inheritance, we can set up assertions to test if an inherited attribute from the superclass has been used properly by a subclass as given below:

assertSame("test SuperClass, StaffMember-attribute", staffObj.name, "John");

The "name" attribute belongs to the "StaffMember" class, is being used by the subclass.

3   Conclusions

In this study, a way of performing an independent path testing with the help of Eclipse JUnit facility is suggested. Instead of the complex value settings for variables that form specific independent path, additional variables for tracking the program control flow and a result object for showing the result of computation have been suggested to reflect independent basis path testing. For a composite component testing with an example Java package, a use of JUnit predicates that tests a legal use of inherited attributes has been suggested. In addition to the suggested use of JUnit facility, further study is recommended for more various forms of testing including the following:

- multiple inheritance relationships;
- concurrent computation; and
- a composite component consisting of objects with complex message passing.

Consequently, a proper use of auxiliary variables to trace program control flows along with JUnit predicates has been suggested to help prepare a white box test case for a single component and a composite component.

References

1. Pressman R (2009) Software engineering: a practitioner's approach, 7th edn. MaGraw-Hill
2. Ghezzi C (2002) Fundamentals of software engineering, 2nd edn. Pearson
3. Khan ME (2011) Different approaches to white box testing technique for finding errors. Int J Softw Eng Appl 5(3)
4. Tahchiev P (2010) JUnit in action. Manning Publications
5. Sommerville I (2007) Software engineering, 8th edn. Addison Wesley
6. McCabe TJ (1976) A complexity measure. IEEE Trans Softw Eng SE-2(4):308–320
7. StarUML available at http://en.wikipedia.org/wiki/StarUML

Printed in the United States
By Bookmasters